American Experiences

American Experiences

READINGS IN AMERICAN HISTORY

★ ★ ★

Volume II   From 1877

Sixth Edition

★

Randy Roberts
Purdue University

★

James S. Olson
Sam Houston State University

New York   San Francisco   Boston
London   Toronto   Sydney   Tokyo   Singapore   Madrid
Mexico City   Munich   Paris   Cape Town   Hong Kong   Montreal

Vice President and Publisher: Priscilla McGeehon
Executive Marketing Manager: Sue Westmoreland
Production Manager: Denise Phillip
Project Coordination, Text Design, and Electronic Page Makeup: Shepherd Incorporated
Cover Design Manager: John Callahan
Cover Designer: John Callahan
Cover Image: Michael Staats
Photo Researcher: Photosearch, Inc.
Senior Manufacturing Buyer: Alfred C. Dorsey
Printer and Binder: Hamilton Printing
Cover Printer: Phoenix Color Corporation

For permission to use copyrighted material, grateful acknowledgment is made to the copyright holders on p.353, which are hereby made part of this copyright page

Library of Congress Cataloging-in-Publication Data

Constructing the American past : a source book of a people's history / [edited by] Elliott J.
    Gorn, Randy Roberts, Terry D. Bilhartz.—5th ed.
      p. cm.
    Includes bibliographical references and indexes.
    ISBN 0-321-21642-3 (v. 1)—ISBN 0-321-21641-5 (v. 2)
    1. United States—History—Sources. I. Gorn, Elliott J., 1951– II. Roberts, Randy, 1951–
III. Bilhartz, Terry D.

E173.C69 2004
973—dc22   2004052998

Please visit our website at http://www.ablongman.com

ISBN 0-321-21643-1

1 2 3 4 5 6 7 8 9 10—HT—07 06 05 04

To Our Families

Contents

★ ★ ★

Preface

★ ★ ★

American History instructors enjoy talking about the grand sweep of the American past. Many note the development of unique traditions such as the American political tradition and the American diplomatic tradition. They employ the article *the* so often that they depict history as a seamless garment and Americans as all cut from the same fabric. Nothing could be further from the truth. America is a diverse country, and its population is the most ethnically varied in the world—white and black, Indian and Chicano, rich and poor, male and female. No single tradition can encompass this variety. *American Experiences* shows the complexity and richness of the nation's past by focusing on the people—how they coped with, adjusted to, or rebelled against America. The readings examine Americans as they worked and played, fought and made love, lived and died.

We designed *American Experiences* as a supplement to the standard textbooks used in college survey classes in American history. Unlike other readers, it covers ground not usually found in textbooks. For example, instead of a discussion of the political impact of the Populist movement, we explore *The Wizard of Oz* as a Populist parable. In short, *American Experiences* presents different slants on standard and not-so-standard topics.

We have tested each essay in classrooms so that *American Experiences* reflects not only our interest in social history but also student interests in American history in general. We have selected essays that are readable, interesting, and help illuminate important aspects of America's past. For example, to show the nature of the class system in the South and to introduce the topic of southern values, we selected one essay on gambling and horse racing in the Old South and another on gouging matches in the southern backcountry. As an introduction to the conventional and medical view of women in the late nineteenth century, we selected an essay about Lizzie Borden. Each essay, then, serves at least two purposes: to tell a particular story well and to help illustrate the social or political landscape of America.

This reader presents a balanced picture of the experiences of Americans. The characters in these volumes are not exclusively white males from the Northeast, whose eyes are continually focused on Boston, New York, and Washington. Although their stories are certainly important, so too are the stories of blacks adjusting with dignity to a barbarous labor system, Chicanos coming to terms with Anglo society, and women striving for increased opportunities in a gender-restricted society. We have looked at all of these stories and, in doing so, we have assumed that Americans express themselves in a variety of ways: through work, sex, and games, as well as politics and diplomacy.

Changes to the New Edition

During the past three years, we have solicited a variety of opinions from colleagues and students about the selections for Volume II of *American Experiences*. Based on that feedback, we have made a number of changes in the sixth edition, always with the intent of selecting articles that undergraduate students will find interesting and informative. The new articles for the second volume of this edition follow:

- Allen W. Trelease, "Knights of the Rising Sun"
- Robert A. Caro, "The Sad Irons"
- David Welky, "Superman in Depression and War"
- E. B. Sledge, "Okinawa: Of Mud and Maggots"
- Regina Markell Morantz, "The Scientist as Sex Crusader: Alfred C. Kinsey and American Culture"
- Susan J. Douglas, "Why the Shirelles Mattered"
- Randy Roberts and David Welky, "Oliver Stone and Vietnam"
- Peter Braunstein, "Ms. America: Jane Fonda"

American Experiences is divided into standard chronological and topical parts. Each part is introduced by a brief discussion of the major themes of the period or topic. In turn, each selection is preceded by a short discussion of how it fits into the part's general theme. We employed this method to give students some guidance through the complexity of the American experience. At the conclusion of each selection is a series of study questions and a brief bibliographic essay. These are intended to further the usefulness of *American Experiences* for students as well as teachers.

We would like to acknowledge the help of our reviewers and thank them for their efforts: Anna Bates, Aquinas College; Paul E. Doutrich, York College of Pennsylvania; Steve Goodson, State University of West Georgia; Cheryl T. Kalny, St. Norbert College; Dennis Lythgoe, University of Utah; Timothy R. Mahoney, University of Nebraska; Marc Maltby, Owensboro Community and Technical College; Constance M. McGovern, Frostburg State University; Johnny S. Moore, Radford University; Susan E. Myers-Shirk, Middle Tennessee State University; Richard Pate, Danville Area Community College.

Randy Roberts
James S. Olson

American Experiences

★ ★ ★

Reconstruction and the West

Although the Civil War did not begin as a crusade against slavery, it ended that way. The Emancipation Proclamation and Thirteenth Amendment to the Constitution made human bondage in the United States illegal, and during Reconstruction Republicans worked diligently to extend full civil rights to southern blacks. Despite the concerted opposition of President Andrew Johnson, the Radical Republicans in Congress pushed through a strong legislative program. The Civil Rights Act of 1866 and the Fourteenth and Fifteenth Amendments to the Constitution were all basically designed to bring the emancipated slaves into the political arena and build a respectable Republican party in the South. Both of these goals were stillborn, however, when Congress removed the troops from the last southern states. In 1877, the old planter elite resumed its control of southern politics. They disfranchised and relegated blacks to second-class citizenship, and the South became solidly Democratic. The South had indeed been brought back into the Union, but the grandiose hopes for a true reconstruction of southern life would not be realized for more than a century.

Genuine change in the southern social structure required more than most Northerners could accept. Confiscation and redistribution of the plantations among poor whites and former slaves was too brazen an assault on property rights; northern businessmen feared that someday their own workers might demand similar treatment. Nor were Northerners prepared for real social change. Advocating political rights for blacks was one thing; true social equality was quite another. Prejudice ran deep in the American psyche, too deep in the 1870s to allow for massive social change. Finally, most Americans were growing tired of the debate over civil rights and becoming preoccupied with business, money, and economic growth. Heavy industry in the East and vacant land in the West were absorbing their energies.

Just as Reconstruction was coming to an end, out west, ambitious farmers were rapidly settling the frontier, anxious to convert the land into an agricultural empire. Civilization was forever replacing a wilderness mentality with familiar political, economic, and social institutions. Already the "Old West" was becoming the stuff of which nostalgia is made. Normal, if somewhat eccentric, people were being transformed into larger-than-life heroes as American society tried to maintain its rural, individualistic roots. Back East, cities and factories were announcing a future of bureaucracies, interest groups, crowds, and enormous industrial production. America would never be the same again. The cult of Western heroes helped people forget the misery of the Civil War and vicariously preserve a disappearing way of life.

READING 1

★ ★ ★

Knights of the Rising Sun

Allen W. Trelease

Periodically, even today, Klu Klux Klansmen rally in America, burning crosses on the lawns of new black neighbors, painting swastikas on the walls of a Jewish synagogue, or marching on Martin Luther King, Jr.'s birthday somewhere in small-town, southern America. They remain a dark legacy of the Civil War, which killed more than 600,000 Americans, and the institution of slavery. When the war ended, the South lay in ruins. For the next twelve years, northern Republicans tried to "reconstruct" the South in a chaotic crusade that mixed retribution, corruption, and genuine idealism. Intent on punishing white Southerners for their disloyalty while enfranchising millions of former slaves, the northern Republicans, especially the "Radicals," tried to extend full civil rights via the Fourteenth and Fifteenth Amendments, but for a variety of reasons the attempt failed. By 1877, political power in the South had reverted to the white elite.

A major factor in the failure of Radical Republicans to "reconstruct" the South was the rise of the Ku Klux Klan. Enraged at the very thought of black political power, Klansmen resorted to intimidation and violence, punishing southern blacks even suspected of sympathizing with Radical goals for the South. In "Knights of the Rising Sun," historian Allen Trelease describes Klan activities in Texas during the late 1860s. Isolated from the main theaters of the Civil War, much of Texas remained unreconstructed, and the old white elite, along with their Klan allies, succeeded in destroying every vestige of black political activity and in eliminating the Republican party from the state's political life.

Large parts of Texas remained close to anarchy through 1868. Much of this was politically inspired despite the fact that the state was not yet reconstructed and took no part in the national election. In theory the Army was freer to take a direct hand in maintaining order than was true in the states which had been readmitted, but the shortage of troops available for this duty considerably lessened that advantage. At least twenty counties were involved in the Ku Klux terror, from Houston north to the Red River. In Houston itself Klan activity was limited to the holding of monthly meetings in a gymnasium and posting notices on lampposts, but in other places there was considerable violence.

By mid-September disguised bands had committed several murders in Trinity County, where two lawyers and both justices of the peace in the town of Sumter were well known as Klansmen. Not only did the crimes go unpunished, but Conservatives used them to force a majority of the Negroes to swear allegiance to the Democratic party; in return they received the familiar protection papers supposedly guaranteeing them against further outrage. "Any one in this community opposed to the Grand Cyclops and his imps is in danger of his life," wrote a local Republican in November. In Washington County the Klan sent warning notices to Republicans and committed at least one murder. As late as January 1869 masked parties were active around Palestine, shaving heads, whipping, and shooting among the black population, as well as burning down their houses. The military arrested five or six men for these offenses, but the Klan continued to make the rounds of Negroes' and Union men's houses, confiscating both guns and money. Early in November General J. J. Reynolds, military commander in the state, declared in a widely quoted report that "civil law east of the Trinity river is almost a dead letter" by virtue of the activities of Ku Klux Klans and similar organizations. Republicans had been publicly slated for assassination and forced to flee their homes, while the murder of Negroes was too common to keep track of. These lawless bands, he said, were "evidently countenanced, or at least not discouraged, by a majority of the white people in the counties where [they] are most numerous. They could not otherwise exist." These statements did not endear the general to Conservative Texans, but they were substantially true.

The worst region of all, as to both Klan activity and general banditry, remained northeast Texas. A correspondent of the Cincinnati *Commercial* wrote from Sulphur Springs early in January 1869:

Armed bands of banditti, thieves, cut-throats and assassins infest the country; they prowl around houses, they call men out and shoot or hang them, they attack travellers upon the road, they seem almost everywhere present, and are ever intent upon mischief. You cannot pick up a paper without reading of murders, assassinations and robbery. . . . And yet not the fourth part of the truth has been told; not one act in ten is reported. Go where you will, and you will hear of fresh murders and violence. . . . The civil authority is powerless—the military insufficient in number, while hell has transferred its capital from pandemonium to Jefferson, and the devil is holding high carnival in Gilmer, Tyler, Canton, Quitman, Boston, Marshall and other places in Texas.

Judge Hardin Hart wrote Governor Pease in September to say that on account of "a regularly organized band which has overrun the country" he could not hold court in Grayson, Fannin, and Hunt counties without a military escort.

Much of this difficulty was attributable to outlaw gangs like those of Ben Bickerstaff and Cullen Baker, but even their activities were often racially and politically inspired, with Negroes and Union men the chief sufferers. Army officers and soldiers reported that most of the population at Sulphur Springs was organized into Ku Klux clubs affiliated with the Democratic party and some of

---

"Texas: The Knights of the Rising Sun" from *White Terror: The Ku Klux Klan Conspiracy and Southern Reconstruction* by Allen W. Trelease. Copyright © 1971 by Allen W. Trelease. Reprinted by permission of the author.

the outlaws called themselves Ku Klux Rangers. At Clarksville a band of young men calling themselves Ku Klux broke up a Negro school and forced the teacher to flee the state.

White Conservatives around Paris at first took advantage of Klan depredations among Negroes by issuing protection papers to those who agreed to join the Democratic part. But the marauding reached such proportions that many freedmen fled their homes and jobs, leaving the crops untended. When a body of Klansmen came into town early in September, apparently to disarm more blacks, some of the leading citizens warned them to stop. The freedmen were not misbehaving, they said, and if they needed disarming at a later time the local people would take care of it themselves. Still the raiding continued, and after a sheriff's posse failed to catch the culprits the farmers in one neighborhood banded together to oppose them by force. (Since the Klan had become sacred among Democrats, these men claimed that the raiding was done by an unauthorized group using its name. They carefully denied any idea of opposing the Klan itself.) Even this tactic was ineffective so far as the county as a whole was concerned, and the terror continued at least into November. The Freedmen's Bureau agent, Colonel DeWitt C. Brown, was driven away from his own farm thirty miles from Paris and took refuge in town. There he was subjected to constant threats of assassination by Klansmen or their sympathizers. From where he stood the Klan seemed to be in almost total command.

The Bureau agent at Marshall (like his predecessor in the summer) suspected that the planters themselves were implicated in much of the terrorism. By driving Negroes from their homes just before harvest time the Klan enabled many landowners to collect the crop without having to pay the laborers' share.

Jefferson and Marion County remained the center of Ku Klux terrorism, as the Cincinnati reporter pointed out. A garrison of twenty-six men under Major James Curtis did little to deter violence. Bands of hooded men continued to make nocturnal depredations on Negroes in the sur-

rounding countryside during September and October as they had for weeks past. "Whipping the freedmen, robbing them of their arms, driving them off plantations, and murdering whole families are of daily, and nightly occurrence," wrote the local Bureau agent at the end of October, "all done by disguised parties whom no one can testify to. The civil authorities never budge an inch to try and discover these midnight marauders and apparently a perfect apathy exists throughout the whole community regarding the general state of society. Nothing but martial law can save this section as it is at present. . . . " Inside town, Republicans hardly dared go outdoors at night, and for several weeks the county judge, who was afraid to go home even in the daytime, slept at the Army post. The local Democratic newspapers, including the *Ultra Ku Klux,* encouraged the terror by vying with one another in the ferocity of their denunciations of Republicans.

Major Curtis confirmed this state of affairs in a report to General Reynolds:

Since my arrival at the Post. . . . [in mid-September] I have carefully observed the temper of the people and studied their intentions. I am constrained to say that neither are pacific. The amount of unblushing fraud and outrage perpetrated upon the negroes is hardly to be believed unless witnessed. Citizens who are esteemed respectable do not hesitate to take every unfair advantage. My office is daily visited by large numbers of unfortunates who have had money owing them, which they have been unable to obtain. The moral sense of the community appears blunted and gray headed apologists for such men as Baker and Bickerstaff can be met on all the street corners. . . . The right of franchise in this section is a farce. Numbers of negroes have been killed for daring to be Radicals, and their houses have so often been broken into by their Ku Klux neighbors in search of arms that they are now pretty well defenceless. The civil officers cannot and will not punish these outrages. Calvary armed with double barrelled shotguns would soon scour the country and these desperadoes be met on their own ground. They do not fear the arms that the troops now have, for they shoot from behind hedges and fences or at night and then run. No more notice is taken here of the death of a Radical negro than of a mad dog. A democratic negro however, who was shot the other day by another of his stripe, was followed to his grave through the streets of this city by a long procession in carriages, on horseback, and on foot. I saw some of the most aristocratic and respectable white men in this city in the procession.

On the same night that Curtis wrote, the new Grand Officers of the Knights of the Rising Sun were installed in the presence of a crowd of 1,200 or 1,500 persons. "The town was beautifully illuminated," a newspaper reported, "and the Seymour Knights and the Lone Star Club turned out in full uniform, with transparencies and burners, in honor of the occasion." Sworn in as Grand Commander for the ensuing twelve months was Colonel William P. Saufley, who doubled as chairman of the Marion County Democratic executive committee. Following the installation "able and patriotic speeches" were delivered by several notables, including a Democratic Negro.

As usual, the most hated Republican was the one who had the greatest Negro following. This was Captain George W. Smith, a young Union army veteran from New York who had settled in Jefferson as a merchant at the end of the war. His business failed, but the advent of Radical Reconstruction opened the prospect of a successful political career; at the age of twenty-four Smith was elected to the state constitutional convention by the suffrage of the Negro majority around Jefferson. At the convention, according to a perhaps overflattering posthumous account, he was recognized as one of the abler members. "In his daily life he was correct, almost austere. He never drank, smoked, chewed, nor used profane language." However, "he was odious as a negro leader, as a radical, as a man who could not be cowed, nor scared away." Smith may also have

alienated his fellow townspeople by the strenuous efforts he made to collect debts they owed him. Even a few native Republicans like Judge Charles Caldwell, who was scarcely more popular with Conservatives, refused to speak from the same platform with him. As his admirer pointed out, Smith "was ostracized and his life often threatened. But he refused to be scared. He sued some of his debtors and went to live with colored people." One day, as he returned from a session of the convention, his carpetbag—perhaps symbolically—was stolen, its contents rifled, and a list of them published in a local newspaper.

The beginning of the end for Smith came on the night of October 3, after he and Anderson Wright, a Negro, had spoken at a Republican meeting. As he opened the door of a Negro cabin to enter, Smith was fired upon by four men outside including Colonel Richard P. Crump, one of Jefferson's leading gentry. Smith drew his revolver and returned the fire, wounding two of the assailants and driving them away. He then went to Major Curtis at the Army post. Here Crump, with the chief of police and others, soon arrived bearing a warrant for his arrest on a charge of assault. The attackers' original intention to kill Smith now assumed greater urgency because he and several Negroes present had recognized their assailants. Smith objected strenuously to their efforts to get custody of him, protesting that it was equivalent to signing his death warrant. Nevertheless Curtis turned him over to the civil authorities on their assurance of his safety. Smith was taken off to jail and a small civilian guard was posted around it. The major was uneasy, however, and requested reinforcements from his superior, but they were refused.

The next day there were signs in Jefferson of an assembling of the Knights of the Rising Sun. Hoping to head off a lynching, Curtis dispatched sixteen soldiers (the greater part of his command) to help guard the jail. At 9 p.m., finally, a signal was sounded—a series—of strokes on a bell at the place where the Knights held their meetings. About seventy members now mobilized under the command of Colonel Saufley and proceeded to march in formation toward the jail; they were in disguise and many carried torches. The jail building lay in an enclosed yard where at that time four black men were confined for a variety of petty offenses. One of the prisoners was Anderson Wright, and apparently the real reason for their being there was that they had witnessed the previous night's attempt to murder Smith; they may even have been fellow targets at that time. When the Knights reached this enclosure they burst through it with a shout and overpowered the guard, commanded by a young Army lieutenant. The invaders then turned to the Negro prisoners and dragged them into some adjoining woods. Wright and a second man, Cornelius Turner, managed to escape from them, although Wright was wounded; the other two prisoners were shot nearly to pieces. As soon as Major Curtis heard the shooting and firing he came running with his remaining soldiers; but they too were quickly overpowered. Repeatedly the major himself tried to prevent the mob from entering the jail building in which Smith was confined, only to be dragged away from the door each time. They had no trouble unlocking the door, for city marshall Silas Nance, who possessed the key, was one of the conspirators.

At first Smith tried to hold the door shut against their entry. Eventually failing at this, he caught the foremost man, pulled him into the room, and somehow killed him. "It is common talk in Jefferson now," wrote a former Bureau agent some months later, "that Capt. Smith killed the first man who entered—that the Knights of the Rising Sun afterward buried him secretly with their funeral rites, and it was hushed up, he being a man from a distance. It is an established fact that one Gray, a strong man, who ventured into the open door, was so beaten by Capt. Smith that he cried, 'Pull me out! He's killing me!' and he was dragged out backward by the leg." All this took place in such darkness that the Knights could not see their victim. Some of them now went outside and held torches up to the small barred window of Smith's cell. By this light they were able to shoot him four times. "The door was burst open

By 1868 the Ku Klux Klan had become a full fledged terrorist organization involving community members of all classes and ranks, many of whom were veterans of the Confederate army.

and the crowd surged in upon him as he fell, and then, man after man, as they filed around fired into the dying body. This refinement of barbarity was continued while he writhed and after his limbs had ceased to quiver, that each one might participate in the triumph."

Once the mob had finished its work at the jail it broke up into squads which began patrolling the town and searching for other Republican leaders. County Judge Campbell had anticipated trouble earlier in the evening and taken refuge as usual at Major Curtis' headquarters. Judge Caldwell was hated second only to Smith after his well-publicized report as chairman of the constitutional convention's committee on lawlessness. Hearing the shooting around the jail, he fled from his home into the woods. In a few moments twenty-five or thirty Knights appeared at the house, looking for him. Some of the party were for killing him, and they spent two hours vainly trying to learn his whereabouts from his fifteen-year-old son, who refused to tell. Another band went to the house of G. H. Slaughter, also a member of the convention, but he too escaped.

The next day the few remaining white Republicans in town were warned by friends of a widely expressed desire to make a "clean sweep" of them. Most of them stayed at the Haywood House hotel the following night under a military guard. Meanwhile the KRS scoured the city looking for dangerous Negroes, including those who knew too much about the preceding events for anyone's safety. When Major Curtis confessed that the only protection he could give the white Republicans was a military escort out of town, most of them decided to leave. At this point some civic leaders, alarmed at the probable effects to the town and themselves of such an exodus under these circumstances, urged them to stay and offered their protection. But the Republicans recalled the pledge to Smith and departed as quickly as they could, some openly and others furtively to avoid ambush.

White Conservatives saw these events—or at least their background and causes—in another light. They regarded Smith as "a dangerous, unprincipled carpet-bagger" who "lived almost entirely with negroes, on terms of perfect equality." Whether there was evidence for it or not, they found it easy to believe further that this "cohabitation" was accompanied by "the most unbridled and groveling licentiousness"; according to one account he walked the streets with Negroes in a state of near-nudity. For at least eighteen months he had thus "outraged the moral sentiment of the city of Jefferson," defying the whites to do anything about it and threatening a race war if they tried. This might have been overlooked if he had not tried repeatedly to precipitate such a colli-

sion. As head of the Union League he delivered inflammatory speeches and organized the blacks into armed mobs who committed assaults and robberies and threatened to burn the town. When part of the city did go up in flames earlier in the year Smith was held responsible. Overlooking the well-attested white terrorism which had prevailed in the city and county for months, a Democratic newspaper claimed that all had been peace and quiet during Smith's absence at the constitutional convention. But on his return he resumed his incendiary course and made it necessary for the whites to arm in self-defense.

According to Conservatives the initial shooting affray on the night of October 3 was precipitated by a group of armed Negroes with Smith at their head. They opened fire on Crump and his friends while the latter were on their way to protect a white man whom Smith had threatened to attack. Democrats did not dwell over-long on the ensuing lynching, nor did they bother to explain the killing of the Negro prisoners. In fact the affair was made deliberately mysterious and a bit romantic in their telling. According to the Jefferson *Times,* both the soldiers and the civilians on guard at the jail characterized the lynch party as "entirely sober and apparently well disciplined." (One of the party later testified in court that at least some of them had put on their disguises while drinking at a local saloon.) "After the accomplishment of their object," the *Times* continued, "they all retired as quietly and mysteriously as they came—none knowing who they were or from whence they came." (This assertion, it turned out, was more hopeful than factual.)

The *Times* deplored such proceedings in general, it assured its readers, but in this case lynching "had become . . . an unavoidable necessity. The sanctity of home, the peace and safety of society, the prosperity of the country, and the security of life itself demanded the removal of so base a villain." A month later it declared: "Every community in the South will do well to relieve themselves [*sic*] of their surplus Geo. Smiths, and others of like ilk, as Jefferson rid herself of hers. This is not a healthy locality for such incendiaries, and no town in the South should be." Democratic papers made much of Judge Caldwell's refusal to appear publicly with Smith—which was probably inspired by his Negro associations. They claimed that Smith's fellow Republicans were also glad to have him out of the way, and noted that the local citizens had assured them of protection. But there was no mention of the riotous search and the threats upon their lives which produced that offer, nor of their flight from the city anyway.

The Smith affair raises problems of fact and interpretation which appeared in almost every Ku Klux raid across the South. Most were not so fully examined or reported as this, but even here it is impossible to know certainly where the truth lay. Republican and Democratic accounts differed diametrically on almost every particular, and both were colored by considerations of political and personal interest. But enough detailed and impartial evidence survives to sustain the Republican case on most counts. Negro and Republican testimony concerning the actual events in October is confirmed by members of the KRS who turned state's evidence when they were later brought to trial. Smith's prior activities and his personal character are less clear. Republicans all agreed later that he was almost puritanical in his moral code and that he was hated because of his unquestioned social associations and political influence with the blacks. He never counseled violence or issued threats to burn the town, they insisted; on the contrary, the only time he ever headed a Negro crowd was when he brought a number of them to help extinguish the fire which he was falsely accused of starting.

As elsewhere in the South, the logic of some of the charges against Smith is not convincing. Whites had a majority in the city and blacks in the county. Theoretically each could gain by racial violence, offsetting its minority status. But Conservatives always had the advantage in such confrontations. They were repeatedly guilty of intimidating the freedmen, and in case of an open collision everyone (including Republicans) knew they could win hands down. Democrats were certainly sincere in their personal and political detestation of Smith; almost as certainly they were sincere in their fears of his political activity and what it might lead to. From their viewpoint an open consorter with and leader of Negroes was capable of anything. It was easy therefore to believe the worst and attribute the basest motives without clear evidence. If some Negroes did threaten to burn the town—often this was a threat to retaliate for preceding white terrorism—it was easy to overlook the real cause and attribute the idea to Smith. The next step, involving hypocrisy and deliberate falsehood in some cases, was to charge him with specific expressions and activities which no other source substantiates and which the logic of the situation makes improbable. Men who practiced or condoned terrorism and murder in what they conceived to be a just cause would not shrink from character assassination in the same cause.

Interestingly enough, most of the character assassination—in Smith's case and generally—followed rather than preceded Ku Klux attacks. This did not arise primarily from a feeling of greater freedom or safety once the victim was no longer around to defend himself; some victims, unlike Smith, lived to speak out in their own behalf. Accusations after the fact were intended rather to rationalize and win public approval of the attack once it had occurred; since these raids were the product of at least semisecret conspiracy there was less need to win public approval beforehand. Sometimes such accusations were partially true, no doubt, and it was never easy for persons at a distance to judge them; often it is no easier now. Democrats tended to believe and Republicans to reject them as a matter of course. The *Daily Austin Republican* was typical of Radical papers in its reaction to Democratic newspaper slurs against Smith after his death: "We have read your lying sheets for the last *eighteen* months, and this is the first time you have made any such charges. . . . " It was surely justified in charging the Democratic editors of Texas with being accessories after the fact in Smith's murder.

The military authorities had done almost nothing to stop KRS terrorism among the Negroes before Smith's murder, and this violence continued for at least two months afterward. Similar conditions prevailed widely, and there were too few troops—especially cavalry—to patrol every lawless county. But the murder of a white man, particularly one of Smith's prominence and in such a fashion, aroused officials to unwonted activity. The Army recalled Major Curtis and sent Colonel H. G. Malloy to Jefferson as provisional mayor with orders to discover and bring to justice the murderers of Smith and the two freedmen killed with him. More troops were also sent, amounting ultimately to nine companies of infantry and four of cavalry. With their help Malloy arrested four of Jefferson's leading men on December 5. Colonel W. P. Saufley, whom witnesses identified as the organizer of the lynching, would have been a fifth, but he left town the day before on business, a Democratic newspaper explained, apparently unaware that he was wanted. (This business was to take him into the Cherokee Indian Nation and perhaps as far as New York, detaining him so long that the authorities never succeeded in apprehending him.) That night the KRS held an emergency meeting and about twenty men left town for parts unknown while others prepared to follow.

General George P. Buell arrived soon afterward as commandant, and under his direction the arrests continued for months, reaching thirty-seven by early April. They included by common repute some of the best as well as the worst citizens of Jefferson. Detectives were sent as far as New York to round up suspects who had scattered in all directions. One of the last to leave was General H. P. Mabry, a former judge and a KRS leader who was serving as one of the counsel for the defense. When a soldier revealed that one of the prisoners had turned state's evidence and identified Mabry as a leader in the lynching, he abruptly fled to Canada.

The authorities took great pains to recover Anderson Wright and Cornelius Turner, the Negro survivors of the lynching, whose testimony would be vital in the forthcoming trials. After locating Wright, General Buell sent him with an Army officer to find Turner, who had escaped to New Orleans. They traveled part of the way by steamboat and at one point, when the officer was momentarily occupied elsewhere, Wright was set upon by four men. He saved himself by jumping overboard and made his way to a nearby Army post, whence he was brought back to Jefferson. Buell then sent a detective after Turner, who eventually was located, and both men later testified at the trial.

The intention of the authorities was to try the suspects before a military commission, as they were virtually sure of acquittal in the civil courts. Defense counsel (who consisted ultimately of eleven lawyers—nearly the whole Jefferson bar) made every effort to have the case transferred; two of them even went to Washington to appeal personally to Secretary of War Schofield, but he refused to interfere. R. W. Loughery, the editor of both the Jefferson *Times* and the *Texas Republican* in Marshall, appealed to the court of public opinion. His editorials screamed indignation at the "terrible and revolting ordeal through which a refined, hospitable, and intelligent people are passing, under radical rule," continually subject to the indignity and danger of midnight arrest. He also sent requests to Washington and to Northern newspapers for intercession against Jefferson's military despotism. The prisoners, he said, were subject to brutal and inhuman treatment. Loughery's *ex parte* statement of the facts created a momentary ripple but no reversal of policy. In reality the prisoners were treated quite adequately and were confined in two buildings enclosed by a stockade. Buell released a few of them on bond, but refused to do so in most cases for the obvious reason that they would have followed their brothers in flight. Although they seem to have been denied visitors at first, this rule was lifted and friends regularly brought them extra food and delicacies. The number of visitors had to be limited, however, because most of the white community regarded them as martyrs and crowded to the prison to show their support.

After many delays the members of the military commission arrived in May and the trial got under way; it continued into September. Although it proved somewhat more effective than the civil courts in punishing Ku Klux criminals, this tribunal was a far cry from the military despotism depicted by its hysterical opponents. The defense counsel presented their case fully and freely. Before long it was obvious that they would produce witnesses to swear alibis for most or all of the defendants. Given a general public conspiracy of this magnitude, and the oaths of KRS members to protect each other, this was easy to do; and given the dependence of the prosecution by contrast on Negro witnesses whose credibility white men (including Army officers) were accustomed to discounting, the tactic was all too effective. The results were mixed. At least fourteen persons arrested at one time or another never went to trial, either for lack of evidence or because they turned state's evidence. Seventeen others were tried and acquitted, apparently in most cases because of sworn statements by friends that they were not present at the time of the lynching. Only six were convicted. Three of these were sentenced to life terms, and three to a term of four years each in the Huntsville penitentiary. General Reynolds refused to accept the acquittal of Colonel Crump and three others, but they were released from custody anyway, and the matter was not raised again. Witnesses who had risked their lives by testifying against the terrorists were given help in leaving the state, while most of the defendants returned to their homes and occupations. The arrests and trials did bring peace to Jefferson, however. The Knights of the Rising Sun rode no more, and the new freedom for Radicals was symbolized in August by the appearance of a Republican newspaper.

Relative tranquillity came to northeast Texas generally during the early part of 1869. Some Republicans attributed this to the election of General Grant, but that event brought no such result to other parts of the South. Both Ben Bickerstaff and Cullen Baker were killed and their gangs dispersed, which certainly helped. The example of military action in Jefferson likely played a part; it was accompanied by an increase of military activity throughout the region as troops were shifted here from the frontier and other portions of the state. Immediately after the Smith lynching in October, General Reynolds ordered all civil and military officials to "arrest, on the spot any person wearing a mask or otherwise disguised." Arrests did increase, but it was probably owing less to this order than to the more efficient concentration of troops. In December the Bureau agent in Jefferson had cavalry (for a change) to send out after men accused of Ku Klux outrages in Upshur County. Between October 1868 and September 1869 fifty-nine cases were tried before military commissions in Texas, chiefly involving murder or aggravated assault; they resulted in twenty-nine convictions. This record was almost breathtaking by comparison with that of the civil courts.

The Texas crime rate remained high after 1868. Organized Ku Klux activity declined markedly, but it continued in sporadic fashion around the state for several years. A new state government was elected in November 1869 and organized early the next year under Republican Governor E. J. Davis. In his first annual message, in April 1870, Davis called attention to the depredations of disguised bands. To cope with them he asked the legislature to create both a state police and a militia, and to invest him with the power of martial law. In June and July the legislature responded affirmatively on each count. The state police consisted of a mounted force of fewer than 200 men under the state adjutant general; in addition, all county sheriffs and their deputies and all local marshals and constables were considered to be part of the state police and subject to its orders. In November 1871 a law against armed and disguised persons followed. Between July 1870 and December 1871 the state police arrested 4,580 persons, 829 of them for murder or attempted murder. Hundreds of other criminals probably fled the state to evade arrest. This activity, coupled with occasional use of the governor's martial law powers in troubled localities, seems to have diminished lawlessness by early 1872. There still remained the usual problems of prosecuting or convicting Ku Klux offenders, however, and very few seem to have been punished legally.

Study Questions

1. Why was Klan terrorism so rampant in Texas? Did the federal government possess the means of preventing it?

2. What was the relationship between the Ku Klux Klan in Texas and the Democratic party?

3. How did well-to-do white planters respond to the Ku Klux Klan?

4. What were the objectives of the Ku Klux Klan in Texas?

5. Who were the white conservatives? How did they interpret Klan activities?

6. Why did the state government try to curtail Klan activities in the early 1870s? Did state officials succeed?

Bibliography

The book that created two generations of stereotypes by vindicating the South and indicting the North is William A. Dunning's *Reconstruction, Political and Economic* (1907). The first major dissent came from W. E. B. DuBois's classic *Black Reconstruction in America, 1860-1880* (1935). It was not until the civil rights movement of the 1960s that historians engaged in a fresh look at Reconstruction. John Hope Franklin's *Reconstruction After the Civil War* (1961) took Dunning to task, as did Kenneth Stampp in *The Era of Reconstruction* (1965). For a look at political corruption during the era of Reconstruction, see Mark W. Summers, *The Era of Good Stealings* (1993). Since its inception in the 1870s, the Ku Klux Klan rose and fell, then rose and fell again, and then resurrected again, waxing and waning in rhythm with American debates over race, immigration, and ethnicity. Allan Trelease's *White Terrorism: The Ku Klux Klan Conspiracy and Southern Reconstruction* (1971) is a good place to begin a study of the early Klan. Also see Stanley F. Horn, *Invisible Empire: The Story of the Ku Klux Klan, 1866-1871* (1969). For general histories of the Klan, see Wyn Craig Wade, *Fiery Cross: The KKK in America* (1986) and Mark David Chalmers, *Hooded Americanism: The History of the Ku Klux Klan* (1981). For the recent history of the Klan, see Mark David Chalmers, *Backfire: How the KKK Helped the Civil Rights Movement* (2003).

READING 2

★ ★ ★

A Road They Did Not Know

Larry McMurtry

The battle remains even today, over 125 years later, shrouded in mystery and a pop culture fog. The great Sioux warrior chiefs—Crazy Horse and Sitting Bull—took on one of the United States Army's most flamboyant officers, and when the dust settled, all of the white soldiers, including Lt. Col. George Armstrong Custer, were dead, killed in a tactical blunder of epic proportions. The death of Custer and the troops in his 7th Cavalry captured the American imagination in the 1870s; and since then, it has continued to inspire curiosity, awe, and inquiry. It has spawned a scholarly literature and a mythology unequaled in United States history. In the following article, one of America's most gifted novelists—Larry McMurtry—deciphers exactly what happened on June 25-26, 1876, at the Battle of the Little Big Horn, why it happened, and what it has meant to Americans.

By the summer of 1875 a crisis over the Black Hills of South Dakota could no longer be postponed. Lt. Col. George Armstrong Custer had made a grand announcement that there was gold in the hills, and it caught the nation's attention. After that miners could not be held back. The government was obviously going to find a way to take back the Black Hills, but just as obviously, it was not going to be able to do so without difficulty and without criticism. The whites in the peace party were vocal; they and others of various parties thought the government ought to at least *try* to honor its agreements, particularly those made as solemnly and as publicly as the one from 1868 giving the Sioux the Black Hills and other lands. So there ensued a period of wiggling and squirming, on the part of the government and the part of the Sioux, many of whom had become agency Indians by this time. The free life of the hunting Sioux was still just possible, but only in certain areas: the Powder River, parts of Montana, and present-day South Dakota west of the Missouri River, where the buffalo still existed in some numbers.

By this time most of the major Indian leaders had made a realistic assessment of the situation and drawn the obvious conclusion, which was that their old way of life was rapidly coming to an end. One way or another they were going to have to walk the white man's road—or else fight until they were all killed. The greatest Sioux warriors, Crazy Horse and Sitting Bull, were among the most determined of the hostiles; two others, Red Cloud and Spotted Tail, rivals at this point, both had settled constituencies. They were administrators essentially, struggling to get more food and better goods out of their respective agents. As more and more Indians came in and enrollment lists swelled, this became a full-time job, and a vexing and frustrating one at that.

There were of course many Indians who tried to walk a middle road, unwilling to give up the old ways completely but recognizing that the presence of whites in what had once been their country was now a fact of life. Young Man Afraid of His Horses, son of the revered Old Man Afraid of His Horses, was one of the middle-of-the-roaders.

The whites at first tried pomp and circumstance, bringing the usual suspects yet again to Washington, hoping to tempt them—Red Cloud, Spotted Tail, anyone—to sell the Black Hills. They would have liked to have had Sitting Bull and Crazy Horse at this grand parley, or even a moderate, such as Young Man Afraid of His Horses, but none of these men or any of the principal hostiles wanted anything to do with this mini-summit. Red Cloud and Spotted Tail had no authority to sell the Black Hills, or to do anything about them at all, a fact the white authorities should have realized by this time. There were still thousands of Sioux on the northern plains who had not given their consent to anything. The mini-summit fizzled.

Many Indians by this time had taken to wintering in the agencies and then drifting off again once the weather improved. Thousands came in, but when spring came, many of them went out again.

Crazy Horse, who was about thirty-five years old, enjoyed in 1875–76 what was to be his last more or less unharassed winter as a free Indian. How well or how clearly he realized that his time was ending, we don't know. Perhaps he still thought that if the people fought fiercely and didn't relent, they could beat back the whites, not all the way to the Platte perhaps, but at least out of the Powder River country. We don't really know what he was thinking and should be cautious about making him more geopolitically attuned than he may have been. At this juncture nobody had really agreed to anything, but as the spring of 1876 approached, the Army directed a number of its major players toward the northern plains. To the south, on the plains of Texas, the so-called Red River War was over. The holdouts among the Comanches and the Kiowas had been defeated and their horse herd destroyed. Ranald S. Mackenzie and Nelson A. Miles both distinguished themselves in the Red River War and were soon sent north to help subdue the Cheyennes and the northern Sioux. Gen. George Crook was already in the field, and Col. John

Larry McMurtry, "A Road They Did Not Know," *American Heritage,* 50 (February–March 1999), 52–65.

Sitting Bull

Lt. Col. George Armstrong Custer

Gibbon, Gen. Alfred Terry, and, of course, George Armstrong Custer were soon on their way.

By March of 1876 a great many indians were moving north, toward Sitting Bull and the Hunkpapa band of Sioux, ready for a big hunt and possibly for a big fight with the whites, if the whites insisted on it, as in fact they did. The Little Bighorn in eastern Montana was the place chosen for this great gathering of native peoples, which swelled with more and more Indians as warmer weather came.

General Crook—also known as Three Stars, or the Grey Fox—struck first. He located what the scout Frank Grouard assured him was Crazy Horse's village, made a dawn attack, captured the village, destroyed the ample provender it contained (some of which his own hungry men could happily have eaten), but killed few Indians. Where Crazy Horse actually was at this time is a matter much debated, but the camp Crook destroyed seems not to have been his. For Crook the encounter was more vexation than triumph. The Sioux regrouped that night and got back most of their horses, and the fight drove these peace-seeking Indians back north toward Sitting Bull. Crook continued to suppose that he had destroyed Crazy Horse's village; no doubt some of

the Indian's friends were there, but the man himself was elsewhere.

A vast amount had been written about the great gathering of Indians who assembled in Montana in the early summer of 1876. It was to be the last mighty grouping of native peoples on the Great Plains of America. For the older people it evoked memories of earlier summer gatherings—reunions of a sort—such as had once been held at Bear Butte, near Crazy Horse's birthplace. Many of these Indians probably knew that what was occurring was in the nature of a last fling; there might be no opportunity for such a grand occasion again. Most of the Indians who gathered knew that the soldiers were coming, but they didn't care; their numbers were so great that they considered themselves invincible. Many Indians, from many tribes, remembered it as a last great meeting and mingling, a last good time. Historically, from this point on, there is a swelling body of reminiscence about the events of the spring and summer of 1876. Indeed, from the time the armies went into the field in 1876 to the end of the conflict, there is a voluminous memoir literature to be sifted through—most of it military memoirs written by whites. Much of this found its way into the small-town newspapers that by then dotted the plains. These memoirs are still emerging. In 1996 four letters written by the wife of a captain who was at Fort Robinson when Crazy Horse was killed were discovered and published. The woman's name was Angie Johnson. It had taken more than a century for this literature to trickle out of the attics and scrapbooks of America, and it is still trickling. Of course it didn't take that long for the stately memoirs of Generals Sheridan and Sherman and Miles and the rest to be published.

Though the bulk of this memoir literature is by white soldiers, quite a few of the Sioux and the Cheyennes who fought at the Little Bighorn managed to get themselves interviewed here and there. It is part of the wonder of the book *Son of the Morning Star* that Evan S. Connell has patiently located many of these obscurely published reminiscences from both sides of the fight and placed them in his narrative in such a way as to create a kind of mosaic of firsthand comment. These memoirs don't answer all the questions, or even very many of them, but it is still nice to know what the participants *thought* happened, even if what we're left with is a kind of mesquite thicket of opinion, dense with guessing, theory, and speculation. Any great military conflict— Waterloo, Gettysburg, et cetera—leaves behind a similar confusion, a museum of memories but an extremely untidy one. Did the general say that or do this? Was Chief Gall behind Custer or in front of him or nowhere near him? The mind that is troubled by unanswered and possibly unanswerable questions should perhaps avoid military history entirely. Battles are messy things. Military historians often have to resort to such statements as "it would at this juncture probably be safe to assume. . . ." Stephen E. Ambrose is precisely right (and uncommonly frank) when he says plainly that much of the fun of studying the Battle of the Little Bighorn is the free rein it offers to the imagination. Once pointed toward this battle, the historical imagination tends to bolt; certainly the field of battle that the Indians called the Greasy Grass has caused many imaginations to bolt.

What we know for sure is that when June rolled around in 1876, there were a great many Indians, of several tribes, camped in southern Montana,

with a fair number of soldiers moving west and north to fight them. Early June of that year may have been a last moment of confidence for the Plains Indians: They were many, they had meat, and they were in *their* place. Let the soldiers come.

This buildup of confidence was capped by what was probably the best-reported dream vision in Native American history—namely, Sitting Bull's vision of soldiers falling upside down into camp. This important vision did not come to the great Hunkpapa spontaneously; instead it was elaborately prepared for. Sitting Bull allowed a friend to cut one hundred small pieces of flesh from his arms, after which he danced, staring at the sun until he fainted. When he came out of his swoon, he heard a voice and had a vision of soldiers as numerous as grasshoppers falling upside down into camp. There were some who were skeptical of Sitting Bull—he could be a difficult sort—but this vision, coming as it did at the end of a great Sun Dance, convinced most of his people that if the soldiers did come, they would fall. (It is worth mentioning that Sitting Bull had mixed luck with visions. Not long before his death a meadowlark, speaking in Sioux, told him that his own people would kill him—which is what occurred.)

Shortly after this great vision of soldiers falling had been reported and considered, some Cheyenne scouts arrived with the news that General Crook was coming from the south with a lot of soldiers and a considerable body of Crow and Shoshone scouts. This was a sign that Sitting Bull had not danced in vain, although Crook never got very close to the great encampment, because Crazy Horse, Sitting Bull, and a large force immediately went south to challenge him on the Rosebud Creek, where the first of the two famous battles fought that summer was joined.

When the Indians attacked, Crook's thousand-man force was very strung out, with soldiers on both sides of the river, in terrain that was broken and difficult. Crow scouts were the first to spot the great party from the north; by common agreement the Crows and Shoshones fought their hearts out that day, probably saving Crook from the embarrassment of an absolute rout. But Crazy Horse, Black Twin, Bad Heart Bull, and many others were just as determined. Once or twice Crook almost succeeded in forming an effective battle line, but Crazy Horse and the others kept dashing right into it, fragmenting Crook's force and preventing a serious counterattack. There was much close-quarter, hand-to-hand fighting. In a rare anticipation of women in combat, a Cheyenne woman rushed in at some point and saved her brother, who was surrounded. (The Cheyennes afterward referred to the Battle of the Rosebud as the Battle Where the Girl Saved Her Brother.) Crook struggled all day, trying to mount a strong offensive, but the attackers were so persistent that they thwarted him. Finally the day waned, and shadows began to fall across the Rosebud. The Indians, having enjoyed a glorious day of battle, went home. They had turned Three Stars back, allowing him nowhere near the great gathering on the Little Bighorn.

Because the Indians left the field when the day was over, Crook claimed a victory, but nobody believed him, including, probably, himself. The Battle of the Rosebud was one of his most frustrating memories. It was indeed a remarkable battle between forces almost equally matched; in some ways it was more interesting than the fight at the Little Bighorn eight days later. Neither side could mount a fully decisive offensive, and both sides suffered unusually high casualties but kept fighting. The whites had no choice, of course; their adversaries in this case fought with extreme determination. The body count for the two sides varies with the commentator. Among historians who have written about the battle, George Hyde puts Crook's loss as high as fifty-seven men, a number that presumably includes many Crows and Shoshones who fell that day. Stephen Ambrose says it was twenty-eight men; Stanley Vestal says it was ten; and Robert Utley and Evan Connell claim it was nine. The attacking Sioux and Cheyennes may themselves have lost more than thirty men, an enormous casualty rate for a native force. Accustomed as we are to the wholesale slaughter of the two world wars, or even of the Civil War, it is hard to keep in mind that when Indian fought Indian, a death count of more than three or four was unusual.

At the end of the day, General Crook at last accepted the advice his scouts had offered him earlier, which was that there were too many Indians up ahead for him to fight.

Had the full extent of Crook's difficulties on the Rosebud been known to the forces moving west into Montana, the sensible officers—that is, Gibbon and Terry—would have then proceeded with extreme caution, but it is unlikely that any trouble of Crook's would have slowed Custer one whit. Even if he had known that the Indians had sent Crook packing, it is hard to imagine that he would have proceeded differently. He had plenty of explicit—and, at the last, desperate—warnings from his own scouts, but he brushed these aside as he hurried the 7th Cavalry on to its doom. He plainly did not want to give his pessimistic scouts the time of day. He refused the offer of extra troops and also refused a Gatling gun, for fear that it might slow him down and allow the Indians to get away. It was only in the last minutes of his life that Custer finally realized that the Indians were fighting, not running. Custer was convinced that he could whip whatever body of Indians he could persuade to face him. He meant to win, he meant to win alone, and he meant to win rapidly, before any other officers arrived to dilute his glory.

Custer, that erratic egotist, has been studied more than enough; he has even been the subject of one of the best books written about the West, Evan Connell's *Son of the Morning Star.* Historians have speculated endlessly about why he did what he did at the Little Bighorn on the twenty-fifth of June, 1876; and yet what he did was perfectly in keeping with his nature. He did what he had always done: push ahead, disregard orders, start a fight, win it unassisted if possible, then start another fight. He had seldom done otherwise, and there was no reason at all to expect him to do otherwise in Montana that summer.

It may be true, as several writers have suggested, that he was covertly running for President that summer. The Democratic National Convention was just convening; a flashy victory and a timely telegram might have put him in contention for the nomination. Maybe, as Connell suggests, he thought he could mop up on the Sioux, race down to the Yellowstone River, hop on the steamer *Far West,* and make it to the big opening of the Philadelphia Centennial Exposition on July 4. So he marched his men most of the night and flung them into battle when—as a number of Indians noted—they were so tired their legs shook as they dismounted. As usual, he did only minimal reconnaissance, and convinced himself on no evidence whatever that the Indians must be running away from him, not toward him. The highly experienced scouts who were with him—the half-breed Mitch Bouyer and the Arikara Bloody Knife and the Crow Half Yellow Face—all told Custer that they would die if they descended into the valley where the Indians were. None of them, in all their many years on the plains had ever seen anything to match this great encampment. All the scouts knew that the valley ahead was for them the valley of death. Half Yellow Face, poetically, told Custer that they would all go home that day by a road they did not know. The fatalism of these scouts is a story in itself. Bouyer, who knew exactly what was coming, sent the young scout Curly away but then himself rode on with Custer, to his death.

Whatever they said, what wisdom they offered, Custer ignored. It may be that he *was* running for President, but it is hard to believe that he would have done anything differently even if it had been an off year politically. Maj. Marcus Reno and Capt. Frederick Benteen, whom he had forced to split off, both testified much later that they didn't believe Custer had any plan when he pressed his attack. He was—and long had been—the most aggressive general in the American army. It didn't matter to him how many Indians there were. When he saw an enemy, he attacked, and would likely have done so even if he had had no political prospects.

In the week between the fight on the Rosebud and the one at the Little Bighorn, Crazy Horse went back to the big party. The great General Crook had been whipped; the Indians felt invincible again. Everyone knew that more soldiers were coming, but no one was particularly concerned. These soldiers could be whipped in turn.

Some commentators have suggested that a sense of doom and foreboding hung over the northern plains during this fatal week; Indian and soldier alike were said to feel it. Something dark and terrible was about to happen—and yet it was high summer in one of the most beautiful places in Montana, the one time when that vast plain is usually free of rain clouds or snow clouds. But this summer, Death was coming to a feast, and many felt his approach. On the morning of the battle, when most of the Sioux and Cheyennes were happily and securely going about their domestic business, never supposing that any soldiers would be foolish enough to attack them, Crazy Horse, it is said, marked a bloody hand in red pigment on both of his horse's hips and drew an arrow and a bloody scalp on both sides of his horse's neck. Oglala scouts had been keeping watch on Custer, following his movements closely. Crazy Horse either knew or sensed that the fatal day had come.

The Battle of the Little Bighorn, June 25 and 26, 1876, is one of the most famous battles in world history. I doubt that any other American battle—not the Alamo, not Gettysburg—has spawned a more extensive or more diverse literature. There are books, journals, newsletters, one or another of which has by now printed every scrap of reminiscence that has been dredged up. Historians, both professional and amateur, have poured forth voluminous speculations, wondering what would have happened if somebody—usually the unfortunate Major Reno—had done something differently, or if Custer hadn't foolishly split his command, or if and if and if. Though the battle took place more than 120 years ago, debate has not much slackened. In fact the sudden rise in Native American studies has resulted in increased reprinting of Indian as opposed to white reminiscences; now the Sioux and the Cheyennes are pressing the debate.

A number of white historians have argued that one or another Indian leader made the decisive moves that doomed Custer and the 7th; for these historians the battle was decided by strategy and generalship, not numbers. Both Stephen Ambrose and Mari Sandoz have written many pages about the brilliance of Crazy Horse in flanking Custer and seizing the high ground—today called Custer Hill—thus ending Custer's last hope of establishing a defensive position that might have held until reinforcements arrived. Others argue for their favorite chief, whether Gall, Two Moon, or another. Evan Connell, in his lengthy account of the battle, scarcely mentions Crazy Horse's part in it. All these arguments, of course, depend on Indian memory, plus study of the battleground itself. To me they seem to be permanently ambiguous, potent rather than conclusive. It is indeed an area of study where historians can give free rein to their imaginations; what Stephen Ambrose doesn't mention is that the Sioux and the Cheyennes, in remembering this battle, might be giving *their* imaginations a little running room as well. A world in which all whites are poets and all Indians sober reporters is not the world as most of us know it.

We are likely never to know for sure who killed Custer. He had his famous hair short for this campaign; had it still been long, many Indians might have recognized him. It is as well to keep in mind that as many as two thousand horses may have been in motion during this battle; between the dust they raised and the gun smoke, the scene would have become phantasmagorical; it would have been difficult for anyone to see well, or far. It is thus little wonder that no one recognized Custer. At some sharp moment Custer must have realized that his reasoning had been flawed. The Indians he had assumed were running away were actually coming to kill him, and there were a lot of them. Whether he much regretted his error is doubtful. Fighting was what Custer did, battle thrilled him, and now he was right in the dead thick of the biggest Indian fight of all. He may have enjoyed himself right up to the moment he fell.

For his men, of course, it was a different story. They had been marching since the middle of the night; a lot of them were so tired they could barely lift their guns. For them it was dust, weariness, terror, and death.

No one knows for certain how many Indians fought in this battle, but two thousand is a fair es-

timate, give or take a few hundred. Besides their overpowering numbers they were also highly psyched by the great Sun Dance and their recent victory over Crook. When Major Reno and his men appeared at the south end of the great four-mile village, the Indians were primed. Reno might have charged them and produced, at least, disarray, but he didn't; the Indians soon chased him back across the Little Bighorn and up a bluff, where he survived, just barely. A lucky shot hit Bloody Knife, the Arikara scout, square in the head; Major Reno, standing near, was splattered with his brain matter. Some think this gory accident undid Major Reno, but we will never know the state of his undoneness, if any. Gall, the Hunkpap warrior, who, by common agreement, was a major factor in this battle, soon had fifteen hundred warriors mounted and ready to fight. If Reno *had* charged the south end of the village, he might have been massacred as thoroughly as Custer.

Exactly when Crazy Horse entered the battle is a matter of debate. Some say he rode out and skirmished a little with Reno's men; others believe he was still in his lodge when Reno arrived and that he was interested only in the larger fight with Custer. Most students of the battle think that when it dawned on Custer that he was in a fight for survival, not glory, he turned north, toward the high ground, hoping to establish a defensive redoubt on the hill, or rise, that is now named for him. But Crazy Horse, perhaps at the head of as many as a thousand warriors himself, flanked him and seized that high ground, sealing Custer's doom while, incidentally, making an excellent movie role for Errol Flynn and a number of other leading men.

So Crazy Horse may have done it, but it was Gall and *his* thousand or so warriors who turned back Reno and then harried Custer so hard that the 7th Cavalry—the soldiers who fell into camp, as in Sitting Bull's vision—could never really establish *any* position. If Crazy Horse did flank Custer, it was of course good quarter-backing, but it hardly seems possible now to insist that any one move was decisive. Gall and his men might have finished Custer without much help from anyone;

Gall had lost two of his wives and three of his children early in the battle and was fighting out his anger and his grief.

From this distance of years the historians can argue until their teeth rot that one man or another was decisive in this battle, but all these arguments are unprovable now. What's certain is that George Armstrong Custer was very foolish, a glory hound who ignored orders, skipped or disregarded his reconnaissance, and charged, all but blindly, into a situation in which, whatever the quality of Indian generalship, he was quickly overwhelmed by numbers.

What I think of when I walk that battleground is dust. Once or twice in my life I rode out with as many as thirty cowboys; I remember the dust that small, unhurried group made. The dust of two thousand milling, charging horses would have been something else altogether; the battleground would soon have been a hell of dust, smoke, shooting, hacking; once the two groups of fighting men closed with each other, visibility could not have been good. Custer received a wound in the breast and one in the temple, either of which would have been fatal. His corpse was neither scalped nor mutilated. Bad Soup, a Hunkpapa, is said to have pointed out Custer's corpse to White Bull. "There he lies," he said. "He thought he was going to be the greatest man in the world. But there he is."

Most of the poetic remarks that come to us from this battle are the work of writers who interviewed Indians, or those who knew Indians, who thought they remembered Bad Soup saying something, or Half Yellow Face making (probably in sign) the remark about the road we do not know, or Bloody Knife staring long at the sun that morning, knowing that he would not be alive to see it go down behind the hills that evening. All we can conclude now is that Bloody Knife and Bad Soup and Half Yellow Face were right, even if they didn't say the words that have been attributed to them.

Hundreds of commentators, from survivors who fought in the battle to historians who would not be born until long years after the dust had set-

tled in the valley of the Little Bighorn, have developed opinions about scores of issues that remain, in the end, completely opaque. Possibly Crazy Horse fought as brilliantly as some think—we will never really know—but he and Sitting Bull and Two Moon survived the battle and Custer didn't. General Grant, no sentimentalist, put the blame for the defeat squarely on Custer, and said so bluntly. The Indians made no serious attempt to root out and destroy Reno, though they could have. Victory over Long Hair was enough; Custer's famous 1868 dawn attack on the Cheyenne chief Black Kettle was well avenged.

The next day, to Major Reno's vast relief, the great gathering broke up, the Indians melting away into the sheltering vastness of the plains.

What did the Sioux and Cheyenne leaders think at this point? What did they feel? Several commentators have suggested that once the jubilation of victory subsided, a mood of foreboding returned. Perhaps the tribes recognized that they were likely never to be so unified again, and they were not. Perhaps the leaders knew that they were likely never to have such a one-sided military victory again either—a victory that was thrown them because of the vainglory of one white officer.

Or perhaps they didn't think in these terms at all—not yet. With the great rally over, the great battle won, they broke up and got on with their hunting. Perhaps a few did reckon that something was over now, but it is doubtful that many experienced the sense of climax and decline as poetically as Old Lodge Skins in Thomas Berger's novel *Little Big Man:* "Yes, my son," he says, "it is finished now, because what more can you do to an enemy than beat him? Were we fighting red men against red men—the way we used to, because that is a man's profession, and besides it is enjoyable—it would now be the turn of the other side to whip us. We would fight as hard as ever and perhaps win again, but they would definitely start with an advantage, because that is the *right* way. There is no permanent winning or losing when things move, as they should, in a circle. . . .

"But white men, who live in straight lines and squares, do not believe as I do. With them it is everything or nothing: Washita or Greasy Grass. . . . Winning is all they care about, and if they can do that by scratching a pen across a paper or saying something into the wind, they are much happier. . . . "

Old Lodge Skins was right about the Army's wanting to win. Crook's defeat at the Rosebud had embarrassed the Army, and the debacle at the Little Bighorn shamed it. The nation, of course, was outraged. By August of 1876 Crook and Terry were lumbering around with a reassuring force of some four thousand soldiers. Naturally they found few Indians. Crazy Horse was somewhere near Bear Butte, harrying the miners in the Black Hills pretty much as the mood struck him. There was a minor engagement or two, of little note. The Indians were not suicidal; they left the massive force alone. Crook and Terry were such respecters now that they were bogged down by their own might.

In the fall of that year, the whites, having failed to buy the Black Hills, simply took them, with a travesty of a treaty council at which the Indians lost not only the Black Hills but the Powder River, the Yellowstone, the Bighorns. By the end of what was in some ways a year of glory, 1876, Crazy Horse had to face the fact that his people had come to a desperate pass. It was a terrible winter, with subzero temperatures day after day. The Indians were ragged and hungry; the soldiers who opposed them were warmly clothed and well equipped. The victories of the previous summer were, to the Sioux and the Cheyennes, now just memories. They had little ammunition and were hard pressed to find game enough to feed themselves.

During this hard period, with the soldiers just waiting for spring to begin another series of attacks, Sitting Bull decided to take himself and his people to Canada. Crazy Horse perhaps considered this option and then rejected it because in Canada the weather was even colder, or maybe he just didn't want to leave home. But in early May of 1877, he had eleven hundred people with him, and more than two thousand horses, when he came into Red Cloud agency at Fort Robinson in northwestern Nebraska. Probably neither the generals nor Crazy Horse himself ever quite believed that a true surrender had taken place, but this august event, the surrender of "Chief" Crazy Horse, was reported in *The New York Times* on May 8, 1877.

Study Questions

1. What happened to Native Americans on the Great Plains in the nineteenth century, and why did so many Indian leaders feel that they had no choice but to "either walk the white man's road" or die fighting?

2. Describe Crazy Horse and Sitting Bull.

3. What role did General George Crook play in the events leading up to Little Big Horn?

4. Why, in early June 1876, did the Indians consider themselves invincible in the face of the invading white army?

5. Describe the personality of Lieutenant Colonel George Armstrong Custer.

6. When Custer's troops went into battle, what disadvantages did they face? How did Custer's personality contribute to their problems? What miscalculations did Custer make just prior to the battle?

7. What happened to the Sioux and to the Black Hills after the battle?

Bibliography

For general surveys of the "conquest" of the American West, see Patricia Nelson Limerick, *The Legacy of Conquest: The Unbroken Past of the American West* (1987), *"It's Your Misfortune and None of My Own": A History of the American West* (1991); and Robert Hine and John Mack Faragher, *The American West: A New Interpretive History* (2000). Excellent studies of the Plains Indians include Morris W. Foster, *Being Comanche: A Social History of an American Indian Community* (1991) and Catherine Price, *The Oglala People, 1841–1879* (1996). For biographies of the major figures involved in the Battle of the Little Big Horn, see John G. Neihardt, *Black Elk Speaks: Being the Life Story of a Holy Man of the Oglala Sioux (1961); Mari Sandoz, Crazy Horse: The Strange Man of the Oglalas* (1961); Stephen Ambrose, *Crazy Horse and Custer: The Parallel Lives of Two American Warriors* (1996); Robert M. Utley, *Cavalier in Buckskin: George Armstrong Custer and the Western Military Frontier* (1988); and *The Lance and the Shield: The Life and Times of Sitting Bull* (1993).

PART

The Gilded Age

★ ★ ★

Change dominated the American scene during the last quarter of the nineteenth century. Noted throughout most of the century for its agricultural output, America suddenly became an industrial giant, and by 1900 it led the world in industrial production. Unfettered by governmental codes and regulations, industrialists created sprawling empires. In 1872, Scottish immigrant Andrew Carnegie built his first steel mill, and his holdings steadily expanded until, almost 30 years later, he sold his steel empire to J. Pierpont Morgan for close to a half billion dollars. In oil, meat packing, and other industries the pattern was the same—a handful of ruthless, efficient, and farsighted men dominated and directed America's industrial growth.

Just as important as the ambitious industrialists were the millions of men and women who provided the muscle that built the industries and ran the machines. Some came from the country's farmlands, victims of dropping agricultural prices or of the loneliness and boredom of farm life. Others were immigrants who came to the United States to escape poverty and political oppression. Crowded into booming cities, the workers—native and immigrant alike—labored long and hard for meager rewards.

The changes wrought by industrial growth and urban expansion created an atmosphere characterized by excitement and confusion. Some people, like Andrew Carnegie and John D. Rockefeller, moved from relatively humble origins to fabulous wealth and impressive social standing. Each symbolized the possibility of rising from rags to riches. New opportunities created new wealth, and the important older American families were forced to make room for the new. As a result, wealthy Americans went to extraordinary lengths to display their status. J. P. Morgan bought yachts and works of art, while other industrialists built mansions along the rocky shore of Newport, Rhode Island. Both the boats and houses marked the owners as men who had "arrived." The clubs, restaurants, and resorts of the late nineteenth century were part of an attempt to define the new American aristocracy.

Other people suffered during this time of change. For example, the social and economic positions of farmers declined during the late nineteenth century. Once considered the "salt of the earth" and "the backbone of America," they were instead viewed as ignorant rubes and country bumpkins. Outmatched by unpredictable weather, expanding railroads, and declining prices produced by overexpansion, they consistently tried to overcome their problems by working harder, organizing cooperatives, and forming political parties. They labored heroically, but most of their efforts and organizations ended in failure.

Minority and ethnic Americans similarly faced difficult battles. Most of them were locked out of the opportunities available to educated white male Americans. It was also difficult for women to improve their social and economic positions. They experienced the excitement of the period from a distance, but they knew the pain and frustration firsthand.

READING 3

★ ★ ★

American Assassin: Charles J. Guiteau

James W. Clarke

Abraham Lincoln, James Garfield, William McKinley, Huey Long, John Kennedy, Robert Kennedy, Martin Luther King, Jr.—our history has been too often altered by an assassin's bullet. Some of America's political assassins were clearly insane, others were motivated by political beliefs or dark personal desires. Normally it is difficult to determine where political partisanship ends and insanity begins. In "American Assassin," James W. Clarke recounts the case of Charles J. Guiteau, a tireless self-promoter who shot President James A. Garfield on July 2, 1881. Guiteau was certainly unusual; part con-man, part religious fanatic, he believed he was destined for some sort of greatness. But was he insane? And if so, was his insanity a legal defense for his actions? These and other questions had to be answered by the jurors who sat in judgment of Guiteau. In an age before Sigmund Freud's work, when individuals were held responsible for their own actions, these questions were difficult, if not impossible, to fully answer.

With the single exception of Richard Lawrence, there has been no American assassin more obviously deranged than Charles Guiteau. Unlike Lawrence [who attempted to assassinate Andrew Jackson], however, who could be described as a paranoid schizophrenic, Guiteau was not paranoid. Indeed, he possessed a rather benign view of the world until shortly before he was hanged. On the gallows, he did lash out at the injustice of his persecutors, but even then his anger was tempered by a sense of martyrdom, glories anticipated in the next world, and a dying man's belief that in the future a contrite nation would erect monuments in his honor.

That Lawrence was confined in mental hospitals for the remainder of his life and Guiteau hanged can be attributed primarily to two facts: Jackson survived; Garfield did not. For certainly the symptoms of severe mental disturbance in Guiteau's case, although of a different sort, were as striking as in Lawrence's. As we will see, the convenient label and implied motive—"disappointed office-seeker"—that has been attached to Guiteau by writers and historians confuses symptoms with causes.

Religion, Law, and Politics

Charles Julius Guiteau was born on September 8, 1841, in Freeport, Illinois. His mother, a quiet, frail woman, died seven years later of complications stemming from a mind-altering "brain fever" she had initially contracted during her pregnancy with Charles. In addition to Charles, she was survived by her husband, Luther, an intensely religious man and Charles' older brother and sister, John and Frances.

From the beginning, people noticed that little Julius, as he was called (until he dropped the name in his late teens because "there was too much of the Negro about it"), was different. Luther Guiteau

soon became exasperated with his inability to discipline his unruly and annoying youngest son and, as a result, Julius was largely raised by his older sister and her husband, George Scoville. Years later, in 1881, Scoville would be called to represent the accused assassin at his trial.

Although plagued by a speech impediment, for which he was whipped by his stern father, Guiteau was, in his fashion, a rather precocious youngster who learned to read quickly and write well. An annoying aversion to physical labor was observed early and remained with him the rest of his life. At the age of eighteen, Charles became interested in furthering his education and, against his father's will, used a small inheritance he had received from his grandfather to enter the University of Michigan.

His father, who was scornful of secular education, had urged his son to seek a scripture-based education at the utopian Oneida Community in New York. The curriculum there focused on study of the Bible. The elder Guiteau had hopes that his errant son might also acquire some self-discipline in a more authoritarian God-fearing environment.

After a couple of semesters at Ann Arbor, Charles, as he was now called, decided to heed his father's advice and transfer to Oneida where, in addition to religious instruction, he had recently learned that they practiced free love. With sex and the Lord on his mind, he enthusiastically entered the New York commune in June 1860. Like his father, Charles now believed that Oneida was the first stage in establishing the Kingdom of God on Earth.

Not long after his arrival, Charles came to believe that he had been divinely ordained to lead the community because, as he announced with a typical lack of humility, he alone possessed the ability. Since no one else had received this revelation, Charles soon found himself at odds with the community leadership. Moreover, the Oneida leaders believed that Charles' vigorously protested need of increasing periods for contemplative pursuits was merely evidence of the slothfulness his father had hoped they would correct.

Other tensions also began to build. Young Charles was becoming increasingly frustrated because the young women of the community were not responding to his amorous overtures. Convinced of his personal charm, this nervous, squirrel-like little man was annoyed because these objects of his intended affection were so unresponsive. Adding insult to injury they soon laughingly referred to him as Charles "Gitout."

As his position within the community continued to deteriorate, Charles became more isolated and alienated until, in April 1865, he left for New York City. He wrote to his father to explain his decision after arriving in Hoboken:

Dear Father:

I have left the community. The cause of my leaving was because I could not conscientiously and heartily accept their views on the labor question. They wanted to make a hard-working businessman of me, but I could not consent to that, and therefore deemed it expedient to quietly withdraw, which I did last Monday. . . .

I came to New York in obedience to what I believed to be the call of God for the purpose of pursuing an independent course of theological and historical investigation. With the Bible for my textbook and the Holy Ghost for my schoolmaster, I can pursue my studies without interference from human dictation. In the country [Oneida] my time was appropriated, but now it is at my own disposal, a very favorable change. I have procured a small room, well furnished, in Hoboken, opposite the city, and intend to fruitfully pursue my studies during the next three years.

Then he announced a new scheme:

And here it is proper to state that the energies of my life are now, and have been for months, pledged to God, to do all that within me lies to extend the sovereignty of Jesus Christ by placing at his disposal a powerful daily paper. I am persuaded that theocratic presses are destined, in due time, to supersede to a great extent pul-

pit oratory. There are hundreds of thousands of ministers in the world but not a single daily theocratic press. It appears to me that there is a splendid chance for some one to do a big thing for God, for humanity and for himself.

With a new suit of clothes, a few books, and a hundred dollars in his pocket, he planned to publish his own religious newspaper that would, he was convinced, spearhead a national spiritual awakening.

In another lengthy letter to his father, Charles continued to detail his plans for the "Theocratic Daily" that would "entirely discard all muddy theology, brain philosophy and religious cant, and seek to turn the heart of men toward the living God." Buoyed with an ill-founded sense of well-being and enthusiasm, Charles went on euphorically: "I claim that I am in the employ of Jesus Christ and Co., the very ablest and strongest firm in the universe, and that what I can do is limited only by their power and purpose." And knowing full well that *he* would edit the paper, he announced confidently:

Whoever edits such a paper as I intend to establish will doubtless occupy the position of Target General to the Press, Pulpit, and Bench of the civilized world; and if God intends me for that place, I fear not, for I know that He will be "a wall of fire round me," and keep me from all harm.

Confidently expecting to promote the Kingdom of God without the restrictions of the Oneida Community and, not incidentally, also enjoy wealth and fame in the process, Guiteau sought financial backing for the paper in New York City. In a flurry of optimistic salesmanship, he scurried about presenting his proposal to prospective subscribers and advertisers; they, as it turned out, were not impressed with this odd little entrepreneur and his religious views. Soon finding himself short of money, somewhat discouraged, and tiring of a diet of dried beef, crackers, and lemonade that he ate in his dingy Hoboken room, Charles returned to Oneida after only three months in the big city.

But his return only confirmed his original reservations about the place, and he soon left again—this time more embittered by his experiences there than ever before. Again without money, Charles wrote to the Community requesting a $9,000 reimbursement—$1,500 a year for the six years he had spent there. When the community refused to pay, Charles sued, threatening to make public the alleged sexual, as well as financial, exploitation employed by the Oneida leadership—especially its founder, John Humphrey Noyes.

Undoubtedly bitter about the rejection he had endured in this sexually permissive environment, Charles lashed out in an unintentionally amusing attack on both Noyes and the Oneida women. Charging that Noyes lusted after little girls, Guiteau angrily told a reporter: "All the girls that were born in the Community were forced to cohabit with Noyes at such an early period it dwarfed them. The result was that most of the Oneida women were small and thin and homely."

Obviously stung by such criticism, Noyes threatened to bring extortion charges against Guiteau. In a letter to Charles' father, who was mortified by his son's behavior, he advised that Charles had admitted to, among other sins, stealing money, frequenting brothels, and being treated for a venereal ailment. Noyes added that Charles also had apparently thrown in the towel, so to speak, in an uninspired battle with masturbation. Such appraisals confirmed his father's sad suspicion that Charles' real purpose in going to Oneida was "the free exercise of his unbridled lust." Charles' "most shameful and wicked attack" and subsequent episodes convinced Luther Guiteau that his prodigal son was "absolutely insane." In despair, he wrote to his oldest son John that, unless something stopped him, Charles would become "a fit subject for the lunatic asylum."

Having thus incurred his father's anger and facing the prospects of a countersuit for extortion, Charles abandoned his legal claim and left New York for Chicago. There, given the standards of the day, he began to practice law, after a fashion.

In 1869, he married a young woman he had met at the Y.M.C.A., a Miss Annie Bunn. After only one memorably incoherent attempt to argue a case, his practice of law was reduced to collecting delinquent bills for clients. By 1874, the law practice and marriage had both failed, the latter as a result of his adultery with a "high toned" prostitute and the occasional beatings he used to discipline his beleaguered wife.

When his marriage ended, Charles wandered back to New York. Continually borrowing small sums of money that he never repaid voluntarily, Guiteau soon found himself, as usual, in trouble with creditors. Resentful of such unseemly harassment, he wrote an indignant letter to his brother John addressing him as "Dear Sir." This and other letters reveal the unfounded arrogance and unintentional humor of a man with only the most tenuous grasp of the reality of his position:

Your letter from Eaton . . . dated Nov. 8, '72, received. I got the $75 on my supposed responsibility as a Chicago lawyer. I was introduced to Eaton by a gentleman I met at the Young Men's Christian Association, and it was only incidentally that your name was mentioned.

I wrote to Eaton several times while at Chicago, and he ought to have been satisfied, but he had the impertinence to write you and charge me with fraud, when he knew he let me have the money entirely upon my own name and position. Had he acted like a "white" man, I should have tried to pay it long ago. I hope you will drop him.

Yours truly,
CHARLES J. GUITEAU.

A few days after this letter was written, Charles' exasperated brother himself became the target of an angry response when he requested a repayment of a small loan:

J. W. GUITEAU: NEW YORK, March 13th, 1873
Find $7 enclosed. Stick it up your bung-hole and wipe your nose on it, and that will remind you of the estimation in which you are held by
CHARLES J. GUITEAU

Sign and return the enclosed receipt and I will send you $7, but not before, and that, I hope, will end our acquaintance.

Disdainful of the pettiness of such small lenders, Charles confidently launched another major venture in the publishing business: he wanted to purchase the Chicago *Inter-Ocean* newspaper. But businessmen and bankers, from whom he sought financial backing, were unimpressed and not a little skeptical about this seedy little man with a confidential manner. Frustrated but ever the undaunted optimist, Charles turned again to religion.

Impressed with the bountiful collection plates at the Chicago revival meetings of Dwight Moody where he served as an usher in the evening services, Charles decided to prepare himself for the ministry. After a short period of voracious reading in Chicago libraries, he soon had himself convinced that he alone had ascertained the "truth" on a number of pressing theological questions. With familiar enthusiasm, he launched his new career with pamphlets and newspaper advertisements. Adorned with sandwich board posters, Charles walked the streets inviting all who would listen to attend his sermons on the physical existence of hell, the Second-Coming, and so forth. The self-promotion campaign was repeated in one town after another as he roamed between Milwaukee, Chicago, New York, and Boston.

In handbills, Charles proclaimed himself "the Eloquent Chicago Lawyer." His performances, in fact, followed a quite different pattern: a bombastic introduction that soon deteriorated into a series of incoherent nonsequiturs, whereupon he would end inconclusively and abruptly dash from the building amid the jeers and laughter of his audiences—the whole episode lasting perhaps ten to fifteen minutes. With his dubious reputation as an evangelist growing, Charles darted from one town to another leaving in his path a growing accumulation of indignant audiences and unpaid bills. Often arrested, he was periodically jailed for short periods between 1877 and 1880 when he again turned his attention to politics.

The Garfield Connection

Describing himself as a "lawyer, theologian, and politician," Guiteau threw himself into the Stalwart faction's fight for the 1880 Republican presidential nomination in New York. When a third term was denied the Stalwart's choice, Ulysses S. Grant, the nomination went to a darkhorse, James A. Garfield. Guiteau quickly jumped on the Garfield bandwagon. In New York, he began to hang around the party headquarters and, as he was to remind people later, he did work on the "canvass" for the candidate. In his view, his most noteworthy contribution to the campaign and Garfield's subsequent election, however, was an obscure speech he wrote (and may have delivered once in Troy, New York) entitled, "Garfield vs. Hancock." A few weeks before, the same speech had been entitled "Grant vs. Hancock." Undeterred by the change in candidates, the speech, Guiteau later claimed, originated and developed the issue that won the election for Garfield. That issue, in brief, was the claim that if the Democrats gained the presidency it would mean a resumption of the Civil War because the Democrats had only sectional, rather than national, loyalties. In a personal note, dated March 11, 1881, to the newly appointed secretary of state, James G. Blaine, Guiteau explained his claim:

I think I have a right to claim your help on the strength of this speech. It was sent to our leading editors and orators in August. It was the first shot in the rebel war claim idea, and it was their idea that elected Garfield. . . . I will talk with you about this as soon as I can get a chance. There is nothing against me. I claim to be a gentlemen and a Christian.

Indeed, from the moment the election results were in, Guiteau had begun to press his claims in letters to Garfield and Blaine. He also became a familiar figure at the Republican party headquarters in New York, confident that he would be rewarded for his efforts with a consulship appointment; the only question remaining, he believed, was the location. Would it be Paris, Vienna, or some other post of prominence? With this in mind, he moved from New York to Washington on March 5, 1881, where he began to badger not only the President's staff but Blaine and the President himself in the corridors of the White House. Striking a posture of gallingly unwarranted familiarity with those he encountered, he also let loose a barrage of "personal" notes written in the same annoying style. Typical is the following:

[Private]
GEN'L GARFIELD
From your looks yesterday I judge you did not quite understand what I meant by saying "I have not called for two or three weeks." I intended to express my sympathy for you on account of the pressure that has been on you since you came into office.
I think Mr. Blaine intends giving me the Paris consulship with your and Gen. Logan's approbation, and I am waiting for the break in the Senate.
I have practiced law in New York and Chicago, and presume I am well qualified for it.
I have been here since March 5, and expect to remain some little time, or until I get my commission.

Very respectfully,
CHARLES GUITEAU.
AP'L 8.

Shortly before he had written to the secretary of state to inquire whether President Hayes' appointments to foreign missions would expire in March 1881, as he expected. Learning that they would, Guiteau became more persistent in pressing his claims for an appointment to the missions of either Vienna, Paris, or possibly Liverpool. Earlier he had written again to Garfield, whom he had never met, to advise him of his plans to wed a wealthy and cultured woman (whose acquaintance, also, he had not at that time, or ever, made). Such unknowingly ludicrous acts were intended, in the bizarre judgment of Charles J. Gui-

teau, to enhance his already eminent qualifications for a foreign ministry.

In the meantime, the newspapers were filled with the controversy that had developed between the new President and the boss-dominated Stalwart faction of the Republican party over patronage appointments in New York. Finally, on May 13, 1881, the two most powerful of the Stalwart bosses, Roscoe Conkling and Tom "Me Too" Platt of New York, resigned their Senate seats in protest over the President's failure to follow their preferences in his patronage appointments. In so doing, they discounted the fact that Garfield had accepted their man, "Chet" Arthur, as his running mate and vice-president. Angrily condemning the beleaguered Garfield's disloyalty and traitorous tactics, the resignations triggered numerous editorial attacks and denunciations of the President and his mentor Blaine, which were to continue until July 2, 1881.

On the same day the resignations were announced, Guiteau once again approached Blaine with his by now familiar blandishments, only to have the exasperated secretary roar, "Never bother me again about the Paris consulship as long as you live!" But Guiteau persisted. A week later, he wrote again to the President:

[Private]
General GARFIELD:
I have been trying to be your friend; I don't know whether you appreciate it or not, but I am moved to call your attention to the remarkable letter from Mr. Blaine which I have just noticed.
According to Mr. Farwell, of Chicago, Blaine is "a vindictive politician" and "an evil genius," and you will "have no peace till you get rid of him."
This letter shows Mr. Blaine is a wicked man, and you ought to demand his immediate resignation; otherwise you and the Republican party will come to grief. I will see you in the morning, if I can, and talk with you.

Very respectfully
CHARLES GUITEAU.
May 23.

If past behavior is any clue to the future, at this point Guiteau would have begun to consider yet another occupational change, returning again perhaps with his typical enthusiastic optimism to theology or law. Previously, Guiteau had accepted failure with remarkable equanimity, sustained always by the exalted opinion he had of himself. As one scheme after another collapsed—his leadership aspirations at Oneida, his journalistic ventures, the law practice, and the evangelistic crusade—his bitterness and disappointment were short-lived as he moved on to other careers. His confidence in his own ability and the Horatio Alger-like opportunities that abounded in nineteenth-century America remained unshaken. Even his angry exchanges with the Oneida establishment possessed the tone of someone who enjoyed the battle as well as the spoils; certainly these exchanges reflected none of the desperation of the all-time loser that he, in fact, was. In Guiteau's delusional world, these frustrations were merely temporary setbacks in a career that was, he remained convinced, destined for wealth and fame.

Now, for the first time in his oddly chaotic life, Guiteau found himself sharing his outsider status with men he admired: Conkling and Platt and the other Stalwarts. And it was in this realization—not the denial of the various appointments he had sought—that his assassination scheme germinated. Indeed, a month later, on June 16, he wrote in his "Address to the American People":

I conceived of the idea of removing the President four weeks ago. Not a soul knew of my purpose. I conceived the idea myself. I read the newspapers carefully, for and against the administration, and gradually the conviction settled on me that the President's removal was a political necessity, because he proved a traitor to the men who made him, and thereby imperiled the life of the Republic. At the late Presidential election, the Republican party carried every Northern State. Today, owing to the misconduct of the President and his Secretary of State, they could hardly carry ten Northern States.

They certainly could not carry New York, and that is the pivotal State.

Ingratitude is the basest of crimes. That the President, under the manipulation of his Secretary of State, has been guilty of the basest ingratitude to the Stalwarts admits of no denial. . . . In the President's madness he has wrecked the once grand old Republican party; and for this he dies. . . .

I had no ill-will to the President.

This is not murder. It is a political necessity. It will make my friend Arthur President, and save the Republic. I have sacrificed only one. I shot the President as I would a rebel, if I saw him pulling down the American flag. I leave my justification to God and the American people.

I expect President Arthur and Senator Conkling will give the nation the finest administration it has ever had. They are honest and have plenty of brains and experience.

[signed] Charles Guiteau

Later, on June 20, he added this even more bizarre postscript:

The President's nomination was an act of God. The President's election was an act of God. The President's removal is an act of God. I am clear in my purpose to remove the President. Two objects will be accomplished: It will unite the Republican party and save the Republic, and it will create a great demand for my book, "The Truth." This book was written to save souls and not for money, and the Lord wants to save souls by circulating the book.

Charles Guiteau

It is unlikely that Guiteau would have chosen the course of action he did without the sense that he was in good company—"a Stalwart of the Stalwarts," as he liked to describe himself. In his distorted mind, to "remove" the President, as he euphemistically described it, would provide the same status and recognition he had sought in a consulship appointment, and, more importantly, in every hare-brained scheme he had botched since the

Charles J. Guiteau, assassin of President James Garfield (1881). Much of the public viewed his insanity plea as a dodge, arguing that Guiteau's methodical planning and self-seeking motives could not be the product of a disturbed mind.

time he first entered the Oneida Community to establish the Kingdom of God on Earth. In this last grandly deluded plan, his aspirations in theology, law, and politics were to culminate in a divinely inspired and just act "to unite the Republican party and save the Republic" and, not incidentally, launch a new career for Charles Guiteau not only as a lawyer, theologian, and politician, but as a national hero with presidential aspirations.

With this in mind, on June 8, Guiteau borrowed fifteen dollars and purchased a silver-mounted English revolver. He planned to have it, along with his papers, displayed after the assassination at the Library of the State Department or the Army Medical Museum. To prepare for the big event, he began target practice on the banks of the Potomac. After stalking the President for several weeks and bypassing at least two opportunities to shoot him, Guiteau rose early on Saturday, July 2, 1881. He had rented a room a few days before at the Riggs House and, on this morning,

began preparations to meet the President at the Baltimore and Potomac Railroad Station. The President was scheduled to leave that morning for a vacation trip. Downing a hearty breakfast, which he charged to his room, he pocketed the last of a series of bizarre explanations:

July 2, 1881

To the White House:
The President's tragic death was a sad necessity, but it will unite the Republican party and save the Republic. Life is a fleeting dream, and it matters little when one goes. A human life is of small value. During the war thousands of brave boys went down without a tear. I presume the President was a Christian, and that he will be happier in Paradise than here.
It will be no worse for Mrs. Garfield, dear soul, to part with her husband this way than by natural death. He is liable to go at any time anyway.
I had no ill-will towards the President. His death was a political necessity. I am a lawyer, a theologian, a politician. I am a Stalwart of the Stalwarts. I was with General Grant and the rest of our men in New York during the canvass. I have some papers for the press, which I shall leave with Byron Andrews and his co-journalists at 1440 N.Y. Ave., where all the reporters can see them.
I am going to jail.

[signed] Charles Guiteau

Guiteau then walked to the banks of the Potomac where after taking a few final practice shots he proceeded to the railroad station to await the President's arrival. Once at the station, he used the men's room, had his shoes shined, and, after estimating that his assignment would be completed shortly before the President's train was scheduled to leave, he reserved a hackman for an anticipated 9:30 arrest and departure to the District Prison. He had already checked the prison's security, lest in the emotion of the moment he might be attacked by crowds who had not had time to realize what a great patriotic service he had just rendered. He was convinced that after his explanation was published the wisdom and justice of his act would be appreciated. Until such time, however, he had taken a further precaution of drafting a letter requesting that General Sherman see to his safekeeping in jail. The letter, which fell from his pocket during the scuffle that followed the shooting, read as follows:

TO GENERAL SHERMAN:

I have just shot the President. I shot him several times, as I wished him to go as easily as possible. His death was a political necessity. I am a lawyer, theologian and politician. I am a Stalwart of the Stalwarts. I was with General Grant and the rest of our men in New York during the canvass. I am going to jail. Please order out your troops and take possession of the jail at once.

Very respectfully,
[signed] Charles Guiteau

So it was with this completely distorted view of reality that Charles Guiteau fired two shots into the President's back as he walked arm-in-arm with Secretary Blaine toward the waiting train. The President, failing to respond to treatment, lingered two and a half months before dying on September 19, 1881.

The Trial

Throughout his lengthy seventy-two-day trial, Guiteau's delusional state was apparent to anyone inclined to acknowledge it. His brother-in-law, George Scoville, represented him at the trial and entered a plea of insanity. In Scoville's opening statement for the defense, he described in some detail the history of mental illness in the Guiteau family: at least two uncles, one aunt, and two cousins, not to mention his mother who died of "brain fever" but was probably insane. He went on to mention the highly eccentric behavior of his father that, at least

one physician thought, properly qualified him for this category. It should also be noted that Guiteau's sister, Frances, the wife of George Scoville, behaved so strangely during her brother's trial that her probable insanity was noted by one participating physician who had occasion to observe her closely. And indeed, her husband later had her declared insane and institutionalized in October 1882, after her brother's execution.

This seemingly overwhelming evidence of a hereditary affliction was ignored or discounted by expert witnesses and finally the jury. Also discounted were the defendant's own delusional symptoms evident in the past schemes, bizarre letters to prominent persons he had never met, and his distorted conception of reality, which was apparent in his remarks throughout the trial and to the day he was executed. Scoville's line of defense was rejected by the defendant himself and greatly resented by John W. Guiteau, Charles' older bother. In a letter to Scoville, dated October 20, 1881, shortly after the trial began, John denied the history of family insanity described by the defense. Rather than heredity, he argued indignantly, most of the cases Scoville cited could be explained by self-induced factors such as insobriety and "mesmerism"; the others, specifically his parents' symptoms, he categorically denied. Falling into line with previous diagnoses of the causes of Charles' problems, most notably that of leaders of the Oneida Community, John Guiteau wrote: "I have no doubt that masturbation and self-abuse is at the bottom of his [Charles'] mental imbecility."

As for Charles himself, thoroughly contemptuous of his brother-in-law's legal abilities, he drafted his own plea, which read as follows:

I plead not guilty to the indictment and my defense is threefold:

1. Insanity, in that it was God's act and not mine. The Divine pressure on me to remove the President was so enormous that it destroyed my free agency, and therefore I am not legally responsible for my act.

Throughout his trial, Guiteau would acknowledge only this interpretation of insanity; that is, he was insane only in the sense that he did something that was not his will but God's. He did not accept the idea that he was in any way mentally deficient. Typical of his remarks on this issue made throughout the trial is the following:

. . . the Lord interjected the idea [of the President's removal] into my brain and then let me work it out my own way. That is the way the Lord does. He doesn't employ fools to do his work; I am sure of that; he gets the best brains he can find.

His plea continued describing two rather novel circumstances that, he claimed, were the Lord's will just as the assassination:

2. The President died from malpractice. About three weeks after he was shot his physicians, after careful examination, decided he would recover. Two months after this official announcement he died. Therefore, I say he was not fatally shot. If he had been well treated he would have recovered.

The third circumstance had to do with the court's jurisdiction:

3. The President died in New Jersey and, therefore, beyond the jurisdiction of this Court. This malpractice and the President's death in New Jersey are special providences, and I am bound to avail myself of them in my trial in justice to the Lord and myself.

He went on to elaborate:

I undertake to say that the Lord is managing my case with eminent ability, and that he had a special object in allowing the President to die in New Jersey. His management of this case is worthy of Him as the Deity, and I have entire confidence in His disposition to protect me, and to send me forth to the world a free and innocent man.

The jury's guilty verdict notwithstanding, it was clear that Guiteau had no grasp of the reality of his situation. Almost to the last, he believed he would be acquitted, at which point, he planned to begin a lecture tour in Europe and later return to the United States in time to re-enter politics as a presidential contender in 1884. He was confident that the jury, like the great majority of Americans, would recognize that Garfield's "removal" was divinely ordained and that the Almighty himself was responsible. He was convinced they would recognize that he was only an instrument in the Master's hands.

Contrary to some assessments, there was no evidence of paranoia in his behavior. Buoyed by a delusion-based optimism, he mistook the crowds of curious on-lookers at the jail as evidence of respect and admiration: bogus checks for incredible sums of money and ludicrous marriage proposals that were sent to him by cranks were sincerely and gratefully acknowledged; and promotional schemes evolved in his distorted mind to market his ridiculous books and pamphlets—all this while anticipating a run for the presidency in 1884! Meanwhile, in high spirits, the poor wretch ate heartily and slept well in a small cell located both literally and figuratively in the shadow of the gallows.

The Execution

When at the very last he realized that there was no hope for survival, his anger was, considering the circumstances, tempered much as it had been during his dispute with the Oneida Community. There were warnings of divine retribution for the ungrateful new president, Chester Arthur, the unfair prosecuting attorneys, and the jury, but again his anger lacked the intensity and desperation of someone facing death. As the execution date approached, Charles, realizing failure once again, simply set his sights elsewhere as he had on many previous occasions. Eschewing politics, the presidency, the Stalwarts, and the law that had failed him, the lawyer and politician once again became the theologian. Anticipating an other-worldly position at the side of the Almighty, Charles walked serenely to the gallows. Earlier he had given the letter below to the chaplain who stood by him at the last:

> *Washington, D.C.*
> *June 29, 1882*
>
> TO THE REV. WILLIAM W. HICKS:
>
> *I, Charles Guiteau, of the City of Washington, in the District of Columbia, now under sentence of death, which is to be carried into effect between the hours of twelve and two o'clock on the 30th day of June, a.d., 1882, in the United States jail in the said District, do hereby give and grant to you my body after such execution; provided, however, it shall not be used for any mercenary purposes.*
>
> *And I hereby, for good and sufficient considerations, give, deliver and transfer to said Hicks my book entitled "The Truth and Removal" and copyright thereof to be used by him in writing a truthful history of my life and execution.*
>
> *And I direct that such history be entitled "The Life and Work of Charles Guiteau"; and I hereby solemnly proclaim and announce to all the world that no person or persons shall ever in any manner use my body for any mercenary purpose whatsoever.*
>
> *And if at any time hereafter any person or persons shall desire to honor my remains, they can do it by erecting a monument whereon shall be inscribed these words: "Here lies the body of Charles Guiteau, Patriot and Christian. His soul is in glory."*
>
> *[signed] Charles Guiteau*
> *Witnesses: Charles H. Reed*
> *James Woodward*

Before the noose was placed around his neck, he was given permission to read his "last dying prayer" to the crowd of faces gazing up at him from the prison yard below. Comparing his situa-

tion to that of Christ at Calvary, Guiteau condemned President Arthur's ingratitude "to the man that made him and saved his party and land" and warned of divine retribution.

After completing his prayer, he again looked thoughtfully out over the crowd before announcing in a loud clear voice:

I am now going to read some verses which are intended to indicate my feelings at the moment of leaving this world. If set to music they may be rendered effective. The idea is that of a child babbling to his mamma and his papa. I wrote it this morning about 10 o'clock.

Then with childlike mournfulness, Guiteau read:

> *I am going to the Lordy. I am so glad.*
> *I am going to the Lordy. I am so glad.*
> *I am going to the Lordy. Glory,*
>   *hallelujah; glory hallelujah.*
> *I am going to the Lordy;*
> *I love the Lordy with all my soul;*
>   *glory, hallelujah.*
> *And that is the reason I am going to*
>   *the Lord.*
> *Glory, hallelujah; glory, hallelujah. I*
>   *am going to the Lord.*
> *I saved my party and my land; glory,*
>   *hallelujah.*
> *But they have murdered me for it, and*
>   *that is the reason*
> *I am going to the Lordy.*
> *Glory, hallelujah; glory, hallelujah. I*
>   *am going to the Lordy.*
> *I wonder what I will do when I get to*
>   *the Lordy;*
> *I guess that I will weep no more when*
>   *I get to the Lordy.*
> *Glory, hallelujah!*
> *I wonder what I will see when I get to*
>   *the Lordy,*
> *I expect to see most splendid things, be-*
>   *yond all earthly conception.*

As he neared completion, he raised his voice to a very high pitch and concluded with

> *When I am with the Lordy, glory, hallelujah!*
> *Glory, hallelujah! I am with the Lord.*

Whereupon attendants strapped his legs, adjusted the noose, and placed a black hood over his head as Rev. Hicks prayed, "God the Father be with thee and give thee peace evermore." Guiteau, according to his own request, signaled the hangman by dropping a slip of paper from his fingers. As the trap sprung, Charles Guiteau slipped confidently into eternity with "Glory, Glory, Glory" on his lips.

Conclusions

Although the debate on the true state of Guiteau's mental condition was to continue among physicians for some years afterward, a brief article in the *Medical News* a day after the execution seems to have been representative of the prevailing view of the medical profession. While conceding that the neurologists who testified to the assassin's obvious insanity may have been correct, society would still be better, the editors reasoned, for having rid itself of such persons. As a further practical matter, it is unlikely that in 1881 any jury in the country would have acquitted the President's assassin whatever his mental condition.

Study Questions

1. Was Guiteau's life before the assassination consistent with his plea of insanity?

2. What were the political motivations for Guiteau's actions?

3. What were the problems with evaluating the evidence presented by the experts on insanity? Did Guiteau, according to the author, actually suffer from paranoia?

4. How would you describe Guiteau's religious beliefs? In your opinion, did those values inhibit his ability to interpret reality?

5. Was the verdict of the jury just? Could any other verdict have been reasonably justified?

Bibliography

The most thoughtful and thought-provoking exploration of the Guiteau episode is Charles E. Rosenberg, *The Trial of the Assassin Guiteau* (1968). Also see Kenneth D. Ackerman, *The Dark House: The Surprise Election and Political Murder of President James A. Garfield* (2003). However, some contemporary articles also make interesting reading. John P. Gray, a leading late-nineteenth-century American expert on insanity and an important witness in the Guiteau trial, presented his conclusions in "The United States vs. Charles J. Guiteau," *American Journal of Insanity* 38 (1882). Edward C. Spitzka, the other major expert in the case, offered his opinion in "A Contribution to the Question on the Mental Status of Guiteau and the History of His Trial," *Alienist and Neurologist* 4 (1883). The most recent work on American political assassinations is James W. Clarke, *American Assassins: The Darker Side of Politics* (1982). Clarke provides a good general bibliography on the subject. For the politics of the period, see H. Wayne Morgan, *From Hayes to McKinley: National Party Politics, 1877–1896* (1969) and John M. Taylor, *Garfield of Ohio: The Available Man* (1970).

★ ★ ★

The Wizard of Oz: Parable on Populism

Henry M. Littlefield

The late nineteenth century was not a period known for its social justice. Angry and exploited workers found little sympathy in the halls of government. During strikes, federal authorities consistently intervened on the side of management rather than labor, even though strikes were usually responses to wage cuts. In the 1894 Pullman strike, for example, President Grover Cleveland sided with the rights of property over the rights of labor and crushed the strike. Thus, the newly formed unions won few concessions for their members. At the end of the century, the work week for the "average" industrial worker was almost 60 hours. The average skilled worker earned 20 cents an hour, twice as much as the average unskilled worker.

Life on the farms in the Midwest and South was probably even worse than life in the northern industries. Technological innovations and scientific farming techniques led to increased production, which in turn sent prices spiraling downward. Discriminatory railroad rates and the government's tight money policies further weakened the economic positions of farmers. As a result, farmers faced an economic depression that cost many their farms. Returning to his midwestern home in 1889, writer Hamlin Garland noted, "Nature was as bountiful as ever . . . but no splendor of cloud, no grace of sunset could conceal the poverty of these people; on the contrary, they brought out, with a more intolerable poignancy, the gracelessness of these homes, and the sordid quality of the mechanical routine of these lives." In the following essay, Henry M. Littlefield takes a fascinating look at Lyman Frank Baum's *The Wonderful Wizard of Oz* and the light it shed on the workers' and farmers' plight in the late nineteenth century.

On the deserts in North Africa in 1941 two tough Australian brigades went to battle singing,

Have you heard of the wonderful
  wizard,
The wonderful Wizard of Oz,
And he is a wonderful wizard,
If ever a wizard there was.

It was a song they had brought with them from Australia and would soon spread to England. Forever afterward it reminded Winston Churchill of those "buoyant days." Churchill's nostalgia is only one symptom of the worldwide delight found in an American fairy-tale about a little girl and her odyssey in the strange land of Oz. The song he reflects upon came from a classic 1939 Hollywood production of the story, which introduced millions of people not only to the land of Oz, but to a talented young lady named Judy Garland as well.

Ever since its publication in 1900 Lyman Frank Baum's *The Wonderful Wizard of Oz* has been immensely popular, providing the basis for a profitable musical comedy, three movies and a number of plays. It is an indigenous creation, curiously warm and touching, although no one really knows why. For despite wholehearted acceptance by generations of readers, Baum's tale has been accorded neither critical acclaim, nor extended critical examination. Interested scholars, such as Russell B. Nye and Martin Gardiner, look upon *The Wizard of Oz* as the first in a long and delightful series of Oz stories, and understandably base their appreciation of Baum's talent on the totality of his works.

The Wizard of Oz is an entity unto itself, however, and was not originally written with a sequel in mind. Baum informed his readers in 1904 that he had produced *The Marvelous Land of Oz* reluctantly and only in answer to well over a thousand letters demanding that he create another Oz tale. His original effort remains unique and to some degree separate from the books which follow. But its uniqueness does not rest alone on its peculiar and transcendent popularity.

Professor Nye finds a "strain of moralism" in the Oz books, as well as "a well-developed sense of satire," and Baum stories often include searching parodies on the contradictions in human nature. The second book in the series, *The Marvelous Land of Oz,* is a blatant satire on feminism and the suffragette movement. In it Baum attempted to duplicate the format used so successfully in *The Wizard,* yet no one has noted a similar play on contemporary movements in the latter work. Nevertheless, one does exist, and it reflects to an astonishing degree the world of political reality which surrounded Baum in 1900. In order to understand the relationship of *The Wizard* to turn-of-the-century America, it is necessary first to know something of Baum's background.

Born near Syracuse in 1856, Baum was brought up in a wealthy home and early became interested in the theater. He wrote some plays which enjoyed brief success and then, with his wife and two sons, journeyed to Aberdeen, South Dakota, in 1887. Aberdeen was a little prairie town and there Baum edited the local weekly until it failed in 1891.

For many years Western farmers had been in a state of loud, though unsuccessful, revolt. While Baum was living in South Dakota not only was the frontier a thing of the past, but the Romantic view of benign nature had disappeared as well. The stark reality of the dry, open plains and the acceptance of man's Darwinian subservience to his environment served to crush Romantic idealism.

Hamlin Garland's visit to Iowa and South Dakota coincided with Baum's arrival. Henry Nash Smith observes,

Garland's success as a portrayer of hardship and suffering on Northwestern farms was due in part to the fact that his personal experience happened to parallel the shock which the entire West received in the later 1880s from the combined ef-

From Henry M. Littlefield, "The Wizard of Oz: Parable on Populism" in *American Quarterly,* Vol. 16 (Spring 1964). © The Johns Hopkins University Press. Reprinted by permission.

fects of low prices, . . . grasshoppers, drought,
the terrible blizzards of the winter of 1886–1887,
and the juggling of freight rates. . . .

As we shall see, Baum's prairie experience was no less deeply etched, although he did not employ naturalism to express it.

Baum's stay in South Dakota also covered the period of the formation of the Populist party, which Professor Nye likens to a fanatic "crusade." Western farmers had for a long time sought governmental aid in the form of economic panaceas, but to no avail. The Populist movement symbolized a desperate attempt to use the power of the ballot. In 1891 Baum moved to Chicago where he was surrounded by those dynamic elements of reform which made the city so notable during the 1890s.

In Chicago Baum certainly saw the results of the frightful depression which had closed down upon the nation in 1893. Moreover, he took part in the pivotal election of 1896, marching in "torch-light parades for William Jennings Bryan." Martin Gardiner notes besides, that he "consistently voted as a Democrat . . . and his sympathies seem always to have been on the side of the laboring classes." No one who marched in even a few such parades could have been unaffected by Bryan's campaign. Putting all the farmers' hopes in a basket labeled "free coinage of silver," Bryan's platform rested mainly on the issue of adding silver to the nation's gold standard. Though he lost, he did at least bring the plight of the little man into national focus.

Between 1896 and 1900, while Baum worked and wrote in Chicago, the Great Depression faded away and the war with Spain thrust the United States into world prominence. Bryan maintained Midwestern control over the Democratic party, and often spoke out against American policies toward Cuba and the Philippines. By 1900 it was evident that Bryan would run again, although now imperialism and not silver seemed the issue of primary concern. In order to promote greater enthusiasm, however, Bryan felt compelled once more to sound the silver leitmo-

tif in his campaign. Bryan's second futile attempt at the presidency culminated in November 1900. The previous winter Baum had attempted unsuccessfully to sell a rather original volume of children's fantasy, but that April, George M. Hill, a small Chicago publisher, finally agreed to print *The Wonderful Wizard of Oz.*

Baum's allegiance to the cause of Democratic Populism must be balanced against the fact that he was not a political activist. Martin Gardiner finds through all of his writings "a theme of tolerance, with many episodes that poke fun at narrow nationalism and ethnocentrism." Nevertheless, Professor Nye quotes Baum as having a desire to write stories that would "bear the stamp of our times and depict the progressive fairies of today."

The Wizard of Oz has neither the mature religious appeal of a *Pilgrim's Progress,* nor the philosophic depth of a *Candide.* Baum's most thoughtful devotees see in it only a warm, cleverly written fairy tale. Yet the original Oz book conceals an unsuspected depth, and it is the purpose of this study to demonstrate that Baum's immortal American fantasy encompasses more than heretofore believed. For Baum created a children's story with a symbolic allegory implicit within its story line and characterizations. The allegory always remains in a minor key, subordinated to the major theme and readily abandoned whenever it threatens to distort the appeal of the fantasy. But through it, in the form of a subtle parable, Baum delineated a Mid-westerner's vibrant and ironic portrait of this country as it entered the twentieth century.

We are introduced to both Dorothy and Kansas at the same time:

Dorothy lived in the midst of the great Kansas prairies, with Uncle Henry, who was a farmer, and Aunt Em, who was the farmer's wife. Their house was small, for the lumber to build it had to be carried by wagon many miles. There were four walls, a floor and a roof, which made one room; and this room contained a rusty-looking cooking stove, a cupboard for the dishes, a table, three or four chairs, and the beds.

When Dorothy stood in the doorway and looked around, she could see nothing but the great gray prairie on every side. Not a tree nor a house broke the broad sweep of flat country that reached to the edge of the sky in all directions. The sun had baked the plowed land into a gray mass, with little cracks running through it. Even the grass was not green, for the sun had burned the tops of the long blades until they were the same gray color to be seen everywhere. Once the house had been painted, but the sun blistered the paint and the rains washed it away, and now the house was as dull and gray as everything else.

When Aunt Em came there to live she was a young, pretty wife. The sun and wind had changed her, too. They had taken the sparkle from her eyes and left them a sober gray; they had taken the red from her cheeks and lips, and they were gray also. She was thin and gaunt, and never smiled now. When Dorothy, who was an orphan, first came to her, Aunt Em had been so startled by the child's laughter that she would scream and press her hand upon her heart whenever Dorothy's merry voice reached her ears; and she still looked at the little girl with wonder that she could find anything to laugh at.

Uncle Henry never laughed. He worked hard from morning till night and did not know what joy was. He was gray also, from his long beard to his rough boots, and he looked stern and solemn, and rarely spoke.

It was Toto that made Dorothy laugh, and saved her from growing as gray as her other surroundings. Toto was not gray; he was a little black dog, with long silky hair and small black eyes that twinkle merrily on either side of his funny, wee nose. Toto played all day long, and Dorothy played with him, and loved him dearly.

Hector St. John de Crèvecoeur would not have recognized Uncle Henry's farm; it is straight out of Hamlin Garland. On it a deadly environment dominates everyone and everything except Dorothy and her pet. The setting is Old Testa-

Dorothy and her friends prepare to "follow the yellow brick road." The spectacularly successful 1939 film based on The Wizard of Oz came out during another Great Depression and prefigured happiness in "Somewhere Over the Rainbow."

ment and nature seems grayly impersonal and even angry. Yet it is a fearsome cyclone that lifts Dorothy and Toto in their house and deposits them "very gently—for a cyclone—in the midst of a country of marvelous beauty." We immediately sense the contrast between Oz and Kansas. Here there are "stately trees bearing rich and luscious fruits . . . gorgeous flowers . . . and birds with . . . brilliant plumage" sing in the trees. In Oz "a small brook rushing and sparkling along" murmurs "in a voice very grateful to a little girl who had lived so long on the dry, gray prairies."

Trouble intrudes. Dorothy's house has come down on the wicked Witch of the East, killing her. Nature, by sheer accident, can provide benefits, for indirectly the cyclone has disposed of one of the two truly bad influences in the Land of Oz. Notice that evil ruled in both the East and the West; after Dorothy's coming it rules only in the West.

The wicked Witch of the East had kept the little Munchkin people "in bondage for many years, making them slave for her night and day." Just what this slavery entailed is not immediately clear, but Baum later gives us a specific example. The Tin Woodman, whom Dorothy meets on her way to the Emerald City, had been put under a spell by the Witch of the East. Once an independent and hardworking human being, the Woodman found that each time he swung his axe it chopped off a different part of his body. Knowing no other trade he "worked harder than ever," for luckily in Oz tinsmiths can repair such things. Soon the Woodman was all tin. In this way Eastern witchcraft dehumanized a simple laborer so that the faster and better he worked the more quickly he became a kind of machine. Here is a Populist view of evil Eastern influences on honest labor which could hardly be more pointed.

There is one thing seriously wrong with being made of tin; when it rains rust sets in. Tin Woodman had been standing in the same position for a year without moving before Dorothy came along and oiled his joints. The Tin Woodman's situation has an obvious parallel in the condition of many Eastern workers after the depression of 1893. While Tin Woodman is standing still, rusted solid, he deludes himself into thinking he is no longer capable of that most human of sentiments, love. Hate does not fill the void, a constant lesson in the Oz books, and Tin Woodman feels that only a heart will make him sensitive again. So he accompanies Dorothy to see if the Wizard will give him one.

Oz itself is a magic oasis surrounded by impassable deserts, and the country is divided in a very orderly fashion. In the North and South the people are ruled by good witches, who are not quite as powerful as the wicked ones of the East and West. In the center of the land rises the magnificent Emerald City ruled by the Wizard of Oz, a successful humbug whom even the witches mistakenly feel "is more powerful than all the rest of us together." Despite these forces, the mark of

goodness, placed on Dorothy's forehead by the Witch of the North, serves as protection for Dorothy throughout her travels. Goodness and innocence prevail even over the powers of evil and delusion in Oz. Perhaps it is this basic and beautiful optimism that makes Baum's tale so characteristically American—and Midwestern.

Dorothy is Baum's Miss Everyman. She is one of us, levelheaded and human, and she has a real problem. Young readers can understand her quandary as readily as can adults. She is good, not precious, and she thinks quite naturally about others. For all of the attractions of Oz Dorothy desires only to return to the gray plains and Aunt Em and Uncle Henry. She is directed toward the Emerald City by the good Witch of the North, since the Wizard will surely be able to solve the problem of the impassable deserts. Dorothy sets out on the Yellow Brick Road wearing the Witch of the East's magic Silver Shoes. Silver shoes walking on a golden road; henceforth Dorothy becomes the innocent agent of Baum's ironic view of the Silver issue. Remember, neither Dorothy, nor the good Witch of the North, nor the Munchkins understand the power of these shoes. The allegory is abundantly clear. On the next to last page of the book Baum has Glinda, Witch of the South, tell Dorothy, "Your Silver Shoes will carry you over the desert. . . . If you had known their power you could have gone back to your Aunt Em the very first day you came to this country." Glinda explains, "All you have to do is to knock the heels together three times and command the shoes to carry you wherever you wish to go." William Jennings Bryan never outlined the advantages of the silver standard any more effectively.

Not understanding the magic of the Silver Shoes, Dorothy walks the mundane—and dangerous—Yellow Brick Road. The first person she meets is a Scarecrow. After escaping from his wooden perch, the Scarecrow displays a terrible sense of inferiority and self doubt, for he has determined that he needs real brains to replace the common straw in his head. William Allen White wrote an article in 1896 entitled "What's the Matter with Kansas?" In it he accused Kansas farmers of ignorance, irrationality and general muddle-headedness. What's wrong with Kansas are the people, said Mr. White. Baum's character seems to have read White's angry characterization. But Baum never takes White seriously and so the Scarecrow soon emerges as innately a very shrewd and very capable individual.

The Scarecrow and the Tin Woodman accompany Dorothy along the Yellow Brick Road, one seeking brains, the other a heart. They meet next the Cowardly Lion. As King of Beasts he explains, "I learned that if I roared very loudly every living thing was frightened and got out of my way." Born a coward, he sobs, "Whenever there is danger my heart begins to beat fast." "Perhaps you have heart disease," suggests Tin Woodman, who always worries about hearts. But the Lion desires only courage and so he joins the party to ask help from the Wizard.

The Lion represents Bryan himself. In the election of 1896 Bryan lost the vote of Eastern labor, though he tried hard to gain their support. In Baum's story the Lion, on meeting the little group, "struck at the Tin Woodman with his sharp claws." But, to his surprise, "he could make no impression on the tin, although the Woodman fell over in the road and lay still." Baum here refers to the fact that in 1896 workers were often pressured into voting for McKinley and gold by their employers. Amazed, the Lion says, "he nearly blunted my claws," and he adds even more appropriately, "When they scratched against the tin it made a cold shiver run down my back." The King of Beasts is not after all very cowardly, and Bryan, although a pacifist and an anti-imperialist in a time of national expansion, is not either. The magic Silver Shoes belong to Dorothy, however. Silver's potent charm, which had come to mean so much to so many in the Midwest, could not be entrusted to a political symbol. Baum delivers Dorothy from the world of adventure and fantasy to the real world of heartbreak and desolation through the power of Silver. It represents a real force in a land of illusion, and neither the Cowardly Lion nor Bryan truly needs or understands its use.

All together now the small party moves toward the Emerald City. Coxey's Army of tramps and in-digents, marching to ask President Cleveland for work in 1894, appears no more naively innocent than this group of four characters going to see a humbug Wizard, to request favors that only the little girl among them deserves.

Those who enter the Emerald City must wear green glasses. Dorothy later discovers that the greenness of dresses and ribbons disappears on leaving, and everything becomes a bland white. Perhaps the magic of any city is thus self-imposed. But the Wizard dwells here and so the Emerald City represents the national Capital. The Wizard, a little bumbling old man, hiding behind a facade of papier mâché and noise, might be any President from Grant to McKinley. He comes straight from the fairgrounds in Omaha, Nebraska, and he symbolizes the American criterion for leadership—he is able to be everything to everybody.

As each of our heroes enters the throne room to ask a favor the Wizard assumes different shapes, representing different views toward national leadership. To Dorothy, he appears as an enormous head, "bigger than the head of the biggest giant." An apt image for a naive and innocent little citizen. To the Scarecrow he appears to be a lovely, gossamer fairy, a most appropriate form for an idealistic Kansas farmer. The Woodman sees a horrible beast, as would any exploited Eastern laborer after the trouble of the 1890s. But the Cowardly Lion, like W. J. Bryan, sees a "Ball of Fire, so fierce and glowing he could scarcely bear to gaze upon it." Baum then provides an additional analogy, for when the Lion "tried to go nearer he singed his whiskers and he crept back tremblingly to a spot nearer the door."

The Wizard has asked them all to kill the Witch of the West. The golden road does not go in that direction and so they must follow the sun, as have many pioneers in the past. The land they now pass through is "rougher and hillier, for there were no farms nor houses in the country of the West and the ground was untilled." The Witch of the West uses natural forces to achieve her ends; she is Baum's version of sentient and malign nature.

Finding Dorothy and her friends in the West, the Witch sends forty wolves against them, then forty vicious crows and finally a great swarm of black bees. But it is through the power of a magic golden cap that she summons the flying monkeys. They capture the little girl and dispose of her companions. Baum makes these Winged Monkeys into an Oz substitute for the plains Indians. Their leader says, "Once . . . we were a free people, living happily in the great forest, flying from tree to tree, eating nuts and fruit, and doing just as we pleased without calling anybody master." "This," he explains, "was many years ago, long before Oz came out of the clouds to rule over this land." But like many Indian tribes Baum's monkeys are not inherently bad; their actions depend wholly upon the bidding of others. Under the control of an evil influence, they do evil. Under the control of goodness and innocence, as personified by Dorothy, the monkeys are helpful and kind, although unable to take her to Kansas. Says the Monkey King, "We belong to this country alone, and cannot leave it." The same could be said with equal truth of the first Americans.

Dorothy presents a special problem to the Witch. Seeing the mark on Dorothy's forehead and the Silver Shoes on her feet, the Witch begins "to tremble with fear, for she knew what a powerful charm belonged to them." Then "she happened to look into the child's eyes and saw how simple the soul behind them was, and that the little girl did not know of the wonderful power the Silver Shoes gave her." Here Baum again uses the Silver allegory to state the blunt homily that while goodness affords a people ultimate protection against evil, ignorance of their capabilities allows evil to impose itself upon them. The Witch assumes the proportions of a kind of western Mark Hanna or Banker Boss, who, through natural malevolence, manipulates the people and holds them prisoner by cynically taking advantage of their innate innocence.

Enslaved in the West, "Dorothy went to work meekly, with her mind made up to work as hard as she could; for she was glad the Wicked Witch had decided not to kill her." Many Western farmers have held these same grim thoughts in less mystical terms. If the Witch of the West is a dia-

bolical force of Darwinian or Spencerian nature, then another contravening force may be counted upon to dispose of her. Dorothy destroys the evil Witch by angrily dousing her with a bucket of water. Water, that precious commodity which the drought-ridden farmers on the Great Plains needed so badly, and which if correctly used could create an agricultural paradise, or at least dissolve a wicked witch. Plain water brings an end to malign nature in the West.

When Dorothy and her companions return to the Emerald City they soon discover that the Wizard is really nothing more than "a little man, with a bald head and a wrinkled face." Can this be the ruler of the land?

Our friends looked at him in surprise and dismay.

"I thought Oz was a great Head," said Dorothy. . . . "And I thought Oz was a terrible Beast," said the Tin Woodman. "And I thought Oz was a Ball of Fire," exclaimed the Lion. "No; you are all wrong," said the little man meekly. "I have been making believe."

Dorothy asks if he is truly a great Wizard. He confides, "Not a bit of it, my dear; I'm just a common man." Scarecrow adds, "You're more than that . . . you're a humbug."

The Wizard's deception is of long standing in Oz and even the Witches were taken in. How was it accomplished? "It was a great mistake my ever letting you into the Throne Room," the Wizard complains. "Usually I will not see even my subjects, and so they believe I am something terrible." What a wonderful lesson for youngsters of the decade when Benjamin Harrison, Grover Cleveland and William McKinley were hiding in the White House. Formerly the Wizard was a mimic, a ventriloquist and a circus balloonist. The latter trade involved going "up in a balloon on circus day, so as to draw a crowd of people together and get them to pay to see the circus." Such skills are as admirably adapted to success in late-nineteenth-century politics as they are to the humbug wizardry of Baum's story. A pointed comment on

Midwestern political ideals is the fact that our little Wizard comes from Omaha, Nebraska, a center of Populist agitation. "Why that isn't very far from Kansas," cries Dorothy. Nor, indeed, are any of the characters in the wonderful land of Oz.

The Wizard, of course, can provide the objects of self-delusion desired by Tin Woodman, Scarecrow and Lion. But Dorothy's hope of going home fades when the Wizard's balloon leaves too soon. Understand this: Dorothy wishes to leave a green and fabulous land, from which all evil has disappeared, to go back to the gray desolation of the Kansas prairies. Dorothy is an orphan, Aunt Em and Uncle Henry are her only family. Reality is never far from Dorothy's consciousness and in the most heartrending terms she explains her reasoning to the Good Witch Glinda,

Aunt Em will surely think something dreadful has happened to me, and that will make her put on mourning; and unless the crops are better this year than they were last I am sure Uncle Henry cannot afford it.

The Silver Shoes furnish Dorothy with a magic means of travel. But when she arrives back in Kansas she finds, "The Silver Shoes had fallen off in her flight through the air, and were lost forever in the desert." Were the "her" to refer to America in 1900, Baum's statement could hardly be contradicted.

Current historiography tends to criticize the Populist movement for its "delusions, myths and foibles," Professor C. Vann Woodward observed recently. Yet *The Wonderful Wizard of Oz* has provided unknowing generations with a gentle and friendly Midwestern critique of the Populist rationale on these very same grounds. Led by naive innocence and protected by good will, the farmer, the laborer and the politician approach the mystic holder of national power to ask for personal fulfillment. Their desires, as well as the Wizard's cleverness in answering them, are all self-delusion. Each of these characters carries within him the solution to his own problem, were he only to view himself objectively. The fearsome

Wizard turns out to be nothing more than a common man, capable of shrewd but mundane answers to these self-induced needs. Like any good politician he gives the people what they want. Throughout the story Baum poses a central thought; the American desire for symbols of fulfillment in illusory. Real needs lie elsewhere.

Thus the Wizard cannot help Dorothy, for of all the characters only she has a wish that is selfless, and only she has a direct connection to honest, hopeless human beings. Dorothy supplies real fulfillment when she returns to her aunt and uncle, using the Silver Shoes, and cures some of their misery and heartache. In this way Baum tells us that the Silver crusade at least brought back Dorothy's lovely spirit to the disconsolate plains farmer. Her laughter, love and good will are no small addition to that gray land, although the magic of Silver has been lost forever as a result.

Noteworthy too is Baum's prophetic placement of leadership in Oz after Dorothy's departure. The Scarecrow reigns over the Emerald City, the Tin Woodman rules in the West and the Lion protects smaller beasts in "a grand old forest." Thereby farm interests achieve national importance, industrialism moves West and Bryan commands only a forest full of lesser politicians.

Baum's fantasy succeeds in bridging the gap between what children want and what they should have. It is an admirable example of the way in which an imaginative writer can teach goodness and morality without producing the almost inevitable side effect of nausea. Today's children's books are either saccharine and empty, or boring and pedantic. Baum's first Oz tale—and those which succeed it—are immortal not so much because the "heart-aches and nightmares are left out" as that "the wonderment and joy" are retained.

Baum declares, "The story of 'the Wonderful Wizard of Oz' was written solely to pleasure children of today." In 1963 there are very few children who have never heard of the Scarecrow, the Tin Woodman or the cowardly Lion, and whether they know W. W. Denslow's original illustrations of Dorothy, or Judy Garland's whimsical characterization, is immaterial. *The Wizard* has become a genuine piece of American folklore because, knowing his audience, Baum never allowed the consistency of the allegory to take precedence over the theme of youthful entertainment. Yet once discovered, the author's allegorical intent seems clear, and it gives depth and lasting interest even to children who only sense something else beneath the surface of the story. Consider the fun in picturing turn-of-the-century America, a difficult era at best, using these ready-made symbols provided by Baum. The relationships and analogies outlined above are admittedly theoretical, but they are far too consistent to be coincidental, and they furnish a teaching mechanism which is guaranteed to reach any level of student.

The Wizard of Oz says so much about so many things that it is hard not to imagine a satisfied and mischievous gleam in Lyman Frank Baum's eye as he had Dorothy say, "And oh, Aunt Em! I'm so glad to be at home again!"

Study Questions

1. Why was Lyman Frank Baum in a good position to understand the problems of workers in the late nineteenth century?

2. What sort of picture does *The Wonderful Wizard of Oz* paint of farm life? What was the effect of agrarian labor on the farmers themselves?

3. How does the story detail the complexities of the silver issue? Does Baum seem to feel that the gold standard was the major problem facing the farmers?

4. How does the Tin Woodman dramatize the plight of the northern industrial worker? How does the Scarecrow symbolize the plight of the farmers?

5. In what ways is the Cowardly Lion similar to William Jennings Bryan?

6. What roles do the good and bad witches play in the story?

7. Is *The Wonderful Wizard of Oz* an effective parable?

Bibliography

Martin Gardiner and Russell B. Nye, *The Wizard of Oz and Who He Was* (1957), examine Baum and his works. The best studies of the Populist movement are John D. Hicks, *The Populist Revolt* (1931); C. Vann Woodward, *Tom Watson: Agrarian Rebel* (1938); Lawrence Goodwyn, *Democratic Promise: The Populist Movement in America* (1976); Robert C. McMath, Jr., *Populist Vanguard: A History of the Southern Farmers' Alliance* (1975); and Stanley B. Parsons, *The Populist Context: Rural Versus Urban Power on a Great Plains Frontier* (1973). Paul W. Glad, *McKinley, Bryan, and the People* (1964) and Robert F. Durden, *The Climax of Populism: The Election of 1896* (1965) examine the crucial election of 1896. For industrial working conditions in the late nineteenth century, see Herbert G. Gutman, *Work, Class, and Society in Industrializing America* (1976); David Brody, *Steelworkers in America: The Nonunion Era* (1960); Albert Rees, *Real Wages in Manufacturing, 1890-1914* (1961) and Paul Krause, *The Battle for Homestead: Politics, Culture, and Steel, 1880-1892* (1992). Also see Steven Hahn, *The Roots of Southern Populism* (1983).

READING 5

★ ★ ★

She Couldn't Have Done It, Even If She Did

Kathryn Allamong Jacob

There is something infinitely compelling and fascinating about an unsolved murder. England has Jack the Ripper, and although it has been more than 100 years since the last Ripper murder was committed, historians of the crimes still speculate on the identity of the murderer. The American equivalent to Jack the Ripper is Lizzie Borden, who very likely killed her father and stepmother on August 2, 1892. Although she was judged innocent of the murders, strong circumstantial evidence points toward her guilt. However, in a larger sense the jury was more concerned with the physical and psychological nature of upper-class womanhood than with the actual crimes. As Kathryn Allamong Jacob writes, during the summer of 1893 "the entire Victorian conception of womanhood was on trial for its life." The question most commonly asked that summer was to the point: How could a well-bred woman, who by her very nature was innocent, childlike, and moral, commit such a horrible crime? The answer of most well-bred men, and of all 12 of the prosperous, Yankee jurors, was that she could not. An examination of the case thus illuminates an entire cultural landscape, casting light especially on American attitudes toward women. Were women, as a writer for *Scribner's* believed, "merely large babies . . . shortsighted, frivolous, and [occupying] an intermediate stage between children and men . . . "? Or was there something more to the issue?

During the summer of 1893, Americans riveted their attention on the town of New Bedford, Massachusetts, where Lizzie Andrew Borden was being tried for the gruesome ax murder of her father and stepmother. All other news paled in comparison, for here, in south-eastern Massachusetts, not only a particular woman, but the entire Victorian conception of womanhood, was on trial for its life.

The drama began in August of 1892 at Number 92 Second Street in Fall River, Massachusetts, the home of Andrew Jackson Borden, whose family coat of arms prophetically bore a lion holding a battle-ax. The household consisted of Andrew, seventy; Abby Gray Borden, sixty-five, his wife; his two daughters, Lizzie Andrew and Emma Lenora, aged thirty-two and forty-two; and Bridget Sullivan, twenty-six, an Irish servant who had been with the family for nearly three years.

Andrew Borden began his business career as an undertaker. It was rumored that he had cut the feet off corpses to make them fit into undersized coffins, but however ill-gotten his initial profits, Borden invested them wisely. By 1892 he was worth nearly half a million dollars, served as a director of several banks and as a board member of three woolen mills, and had built the imposing A. J. Borden Building on Main Street as a testimony to his business acumen. To keep his fortunes increasing, Borden foreclosed, undercut, overcharged, and hoarded without flinching.

Borden's first wife, Sarah, had died in 1862 after bearing him three daughters, only two of whom survived past infancy. Two years later, he married Abby Gray, a thirty-eight-year-old spinster. Nothing suggests that Abby was anything but kind to the two little girls whose stepmother she became, but they never returned her affection. After her marriage, Abby became a compulsive eater. Only a little over five feet tall, by 1892 she weighed more than two hundred pounds.

"She Couldn't Have Done It, Even If She Did" by Kathryn Allamong Jacob, from *American Heritage* 29 (February/March, 1978) pp. 42–53. Reprinted by permission.

Emma, the older daughter, still lived at home at age forty-two. By all accounts, she was dowdy and narrow-minded. Lizzie Borden, ten years younger, also lived at home. Otherwise tightfisted, Andrew Borden doted on his younger daughter: over the years he lavished on Lizzie expensive gifts—a diamond ring, a sealskin cape, even a Grand Tour of Europe. Lizzie worshiped her father in return, and even gave him her high school ring to wear as a token of her affection.

Like her sister, Lizzie had evidently given up hope of marriage, but she led a more active life, centered around good works and the Central Congregational Church, where she taught a Sunday-school class of Chinese children, the sons and daughters of Fall River laundrymen. Though she loathed doing housework, she enthusiastically helped cook the church's annual Christmas dinner for local newsboys. In addition to being secretary-treasurer of the Christian Endeavor, Lizzie was active in the Ladies' Fruit and Flower Mission, the Women's Christian Temperance Union, and the Good Samaritan Charity Hospital.

Lizzie's Christian charity did not extend to her own home. The Borden family was not happy. While Emma tolerated her stepmother, Lizzie openly disliked her. Ill feelings increased in 1887, when Andrew gave Abby a house for the use of her sister. Seeking peace, Andrew gave his daughters a house of greater value to rent out, but they were not placated. A dressmaker later remembered making the mistake of referring to Abby as Lizzie's "mother," causing Lizzie to snap, "Don't call her that to me. She is a mean thing and we hate her."

Even the house Lizzie lived in vexed her. Its Grant-era furnishings contrasted sharply with her stylish clothes. There was no bath and no electricity, though such conveniences were common elsewhere in town. Beside the water closet in the basement stood a pile of old newspapers for sanitary purposes. No interior space was wasted on hallways. Rooms simply opened into one another, making it difficult for anyone to pass through unnoticed. Lizzie longed to live "on the hill," Fall River's most elegant neighborhood and the symbol of the social prominence she craved. While her father's wealth entitled her to live there, Andrew insisted on living on déclassé Second Street.

On Tuesday, August 2, 1892, strange things began to happen in the Borden house. Mr. and Mrs. Borden and Bridget suffered severe vomiting; Lizzie later claimed she felt queasy the next day. Emma, on vacation in Fairhaven, was spared. Over Andrew's objections, Abby waddled across the street to Dr. Bowen's to tell him she feared they had been poisoned. When he learned that the previous night's dinner had been warmed-over fish, the doctor laughingly sent her home.

The next day, Uncle John Morse, brother of the first Mrs. Borden, arrived unexpectedly on business. Like Andrew, Morse was single-minded in his pursuit of wealth, and the two men had remained friends. That evening, Lizzie visited Miss Alice Russell, a friend of Emma's. Miss Russell later testified that their conversation had been unsettling. Lizzie had spoken of burglary attempts on the Borden home, of threats against her father from unknown enemies. "I feel as if something was hanging over me that I cannot throw off . . . ," she said. "Father has so much trouble. . . . " Though Miss Russell tried to reassure her, Lizzie left on an ominous, but prescient, note: "I am afraid somebody will do something."

On Thursday morning, August 4, Bridget rose about six and lit the breakfast fire. Around seven, the elder Bordens and their guest sat down to eat in the dining room. Lizzie did not appear downstairs till nine. By then, Mrs. Borden had begun dusting the downstairs and Morse had left the house to visit relatives across town. Lizzie told Bridget she did not feel well enough to eat breakfast, but sat in the kitchen sipping coffee. About twenty after nine, Andrew, too, left the house, setting off downtown to oversee his investments. Perhaps ten minutes later, Abby Borden went upstairs to tidy the guest room, and Bridget went outside to begin washing the downstairs windows. Only Lizzie and Abby remained in the house; Abby was never seen alive again.

Perhaps because of the oppressive heat, Andrew broke his long-established routine by coming home for lunch at a quarter of eleven, an hour and a half early. Bridget later testified that she had just begun scrubbing the inside of the windows when she heard him struggling with the front-door lock and let him in. Lizzie, by her own admission, was coming down the stairs from the second floor where Abby's body lay. (At the Borden trial the following year, the prosecution would produce witnesses who testified that Abby's body, lying on the guest-room floor, was clearly visible from the staircase, while the defense claimed it was almost completely obscured by a bed). Andrew asked Lizzie about Abby's whereabouts, according to Bridget, and Lizzie told him that Abby had received a note asking her to attend a sick friend.

Bridget finished her windows and climbed the back stairs to her attic room to rest at about eleven. Andrew lay down on the parlor sofa to nap. On the guest-room floor above him lay Abby's bleeding corpse. The house was hot and silent. Within minutes, Bridget recalled, she was awakened by Lizzie calling, "Come down quick; father's dead; somebody came in and killed him."

Little was left of Andrew's face. Half an eye hung from its socket. Doctors testified that a single ax blow had killed him; nine others had been gratuitous. Shortly after the police arrived, Bridget and a neighbor ventured upstairs for a sheet to cover the hideous sight, and there they found Abby. Her plump body lay face down in a pool of blood, her head and neck a bloody mass. Those first on the scene noted that Lizzie remained remarkably calm throughout the ordeal. While one woman claimed that there were tears in her eyes, several others testified that Lizzie's eyes were dry and her hands steady.

News traveled fast from neighbor to neighbor and even before the evening presses rolled, everyone in Fall River seemed to know of the horrifying incident. A local reporter recalled that "The cry of murder swept through the city like a typhoon . . . murder committed under the very glare of the midday sun within three minutes walk of the City Hall. . . . " By the next day, the story was front-page news throughout the country and when, after two days, no crazed ax-wielder was produced, newspapers which had praised the police began to question their competence. Trial transcripts suggest that the police did err on the side of caution. If the victims had not been so prominent, matters would have been simpler. The *New York Times* appreciated this fact, and on August 6 noted that "The police are acting slowly and carefully in the affair giving way, no doubt, to feelings of sentiment because of the high social standing of the parties involved." No systematic search of the Borden house was conducted until thirty-two hours after the murders. Out of deference to the bereaved daughters, neither Lizzie nor Emma, who had been summoned home from her vacation, was closely questioned for nearly three days.

Yet, by Saturday, the day of the funerals, the police felt that they had little choice but to arrest Lizzie. She alone, they felt, had had the opportunity to commit the murders. They found it hard to believe that anyone could have passed through the house unseen by Lizzie, who claimed to have been on the first floor while Abby was being murdered above. It also strained credibility to assert, as Lizzie did, that Abby's 210-pound body had crashed to the floor without a sound. Furthermore, despite a reward offered by the Borden sisters, no sender of the note that Lizzie claimed had called Abby to town could be found.

Lizzie's own contradictory answers to the first questions put to her by police were highly damaging. When asked her whereabouts when her father was killed, she gave different answers to different interrogators: "In the back yard"; ". . . in the loft getting a piece of iron for sinkers"; ". . . up in the loft eating pears." The closed barn loft would have been so insufferably hot that day that few would have visited it voluntarily, much less lingered to eat pears. Furthermore, an officer who claimed to have been the first to examine the loft after the crimes testified that the dust on the floor was undisturbed by footprints or trailing skirts.

In Lizzie's favor was the fact that she had been neat and clean when first seen after the murders. The police were certain that the murderer would have been covered with blood. (Medical experts would later examine the trajectories of the spurting blood and argue otherwise, but belief in a blood-drenched killer persisted.)

Though puzzled by Lizzie's cleanliness, police were certain that they had found the murder weapon. Lying in a box of dusty tools, stored high on a chimney jog in the basement, was a hatchet head. It was neither rusty nor old, though it had been freshly rubbed in ashes, perhaps to make it appear so. Moreover, its wooden handle, from which blood would have been difficult to remove, had been broken off near the head.

When the news broke that Lizzie was under suspicion, newspaper readers were horrified—not over the possibility that Lizzie might have murdered her parents, but that the police would harbor such horrid thoughts. The Boston *Globe* expressed its readers' indignation: "The only person that the government can catch is one whose innocence placed her in its power; the poor, defenseless child, who ought to have claimed by very helplessness their protection."

Angry letters denouncing the police flooded newspaper offices from New York to Chicago. Editorials appeared castigating the brutish officers who would suspect a grieving daughter of such a crime. Americans were certain that well-brought-up daughters could not commit murder with a hatchet on sunny summer mornings. And their reaction was not entirely without rationale.

Throughout the 1890s nearly every issue of *Forum, Arena, Scribner's, North American Review, Popular Science Monthly,* and *Harper's* (one of Lizzie's favorites) carried at least one article attesting to the gentleness, physical frailty, and docility of the well-bred American woman. Many of these articles were written in response to the growing number of women who were demanding equal rights, and were written with the intention of proving women hopelessly unable to handle the sacred privileges of men. After having read many such articles written by "learned gentlemen"—and antifeminist women—by the summer of 1892, men and women, regardless of how they stood on women's rights, felt certain that Lizzie Borden could not have hacked her parents to death. Physical and psychological frailties simply made it impossible.

Popular theories about women's physiological and psychological make-up took on new importance to followers of the Borden case. After detailed anatomical analysis, scientists confidently declared that the women of their era differed little from their prehistoric sisters. They spoke with assurance of women's arrested evolution. The fault, they agreed, lay in her reproductive capacity, which sapped vital powers that in men contributed to ever-improving physique and intellect.

The defects of the female anatomy included sloping shoulders, broad hips, underdeveloped muscles, short arms and legs, and poor coordination. To those who believed Lizzie innocent, evidence was abundant that no short-armed, uncoordinated, weakling of a woman could swing an ax with enough force to crash through hair and bone almost two dozen times.

But there was more to it than that. Having already noted woman's smaller frame, anatomists should hardly have been surprised to find her skull proportionately smaller than man's, yet they held up this revelation, too, as further proof of her inferiority. Rather than follow intellectual pursuits, for which they were woefully ill-equipped, women were advised to accept their intended roles as wives and mothers. After all, they were reminded, "Woman is only womanly when she sets herself to man 'like perfect music unto noble works.'"

Spinsters like Lizzie were, as one author charitably put it, "deplorable accidents," but they were not wholly useless. The nation's old maids were urged to devote themselves to Christian charities and to teaching—a "reproductive calling." Lizzie's devotion to good works and the church followed this prescription precisely. Compelling indeed was the image of this pious daughter serving steaming bowls of soup to indigent newsboys and diligently trying to bring the gospel to the heathen Chinese of Fall River.

While anatomists studied the size of woman's skull, psychologists examined its contents. Among the qualities found to be essentially female were spiritual sensitivity, a good memory for minutiae, and a great capacity for "ennobling love." These positive attributes, however, could not obscure the psychologists' basic premise; women were illogical, inconsistent, and incapable of independent thought.

It is not accident that these traits bore striking resemblance to those attributed to children. As one psychologist pointed out in *Scribner's:* "Women are merely large babies. They are short-sighted, frivolous and occupy an intermediate stage between children and men. . . . "

Several authors manfully chuckled over woman's inability to plan and think things through. Clearly the murderer of the Bordens had planned things quite well. Not only had "he" managed to murder two people and elude the police, but "he" had shown remarkable tenacity by hiding for more than an hour after murdering Abby in order to do the same to Andrew.

Woman was considered man's superior in one area only: the moral sphere. She was thought to possess more "natural refinement," "diviner instincts," and stronger "spiritual sensibility" than man. She was inherently gentle, and abhorred cruelty—hardly the virtues of an ax murderer. Woman was also truthful, though some authors attributed her inability to lie to a lack of intelligence rather than to innate goodness. When reporters interviewed Lizzie's friends, the young women repeatedly mentioned her honesty.

Lizzie benefited greatly from the prevailing stereotypes of feminine delicacy and docility: her cause was also served by the widely accepted stereotype of the female criminal. Ironically, the same periodicals which carried articles about women's gentle nature also carried enough sordid stories of crimes committed by them to cast considerable doubt on their moral superiority. But writers did not find the situation paradoxical. To them, there were clearly two types of women: the genteel ladies of their own class and those women beneath them. Gentlemen authors believed that the womanly instincts of gentleness and love were the monopoly of upper-class women.

Scientists could hardly charge women of their own class with propensities toward violence without casting doubt on their own good breeding. For lower-class women with whom they had no intimate ties (at least none to which they would admit), the situation was quite different. These writers made it very clear that no woman servant, housekeeper, prostitute, nurse, washerwoman, barmaid, or factory girl could be above suspicion.

Several authors even believed that the female criminal had to look the part. In an article in *North American Review,* August, 1895, one criminologist thoughtfully provided the following description: "[She] has coarse black hair and a good deal of it. . . . She has often a long face, a receding forehead, overjutting brows, prominent cheek-bones, an exaggerated frontal angle as seen in monkeys and savage races, and nearly always square jaws."

She could also be marked by deep wrinkles, a tendency toward baldness, and numerous moles. Other authors noted her long middle fingers, projecting ears, and overlapping teeth. While Lizzie had a massive jaw, her hair was red, her teeth were straight, and her ears flat. Perhaps fortunately for Bridget, a member of the suspect servant class, she was mole-free and brown-haired, and she did not have protruding middle fingers.

Criminal women supposedly exhibited neither the aversion to evil nor the love of mankind which ennobled their upper-class sisters. Among their vices were said to be great cruelty, passionate temper, a craving for revenge, cunning greed, rapacity, contempt for truth, and vulgarity. Such women were thought to be "erotic," but incapable of devoted love. Certainly the Bordens' murderer had been exceedingly cruel. But, while Lizzie was admittedly fond of money and volunteered her dislike of her stepmother, few would have called her rapacious or vengeful, and erotic was hardly an adjective one would have applied to the chaste treasurer of the Fruit and Flower Mission.

The ferocity of the criminal woman fascinated many authors. A favorite murderess was Catherine Hayes, who, in 1890, stabbed her husband to death, cut off his head with a penknife, and boiled it. But then, Mrs. Hayes was a mill worker. One writer did admit that murders might be committed by well-bred women; their weapon would be poison, however, rather than a penknife or an ax, because its passivity appealed to their nature.

Lizzie's attorneys skillfully exploited these two stereotypes—the genteel young woman and the wart-ridden murderess—to their client's advantage throughout the Borden trial. Even before the case reached court, the press had firmly implanted in the public mind a clear picture of Lizzie as bereaved daughter. The image-making began with the very first—and entirely false— story about Lizzie printed in the Boston *Globe* on the day after the murders; "The young woman, with her customary cheery disposition, evidenced her feelings in the tuneful melody from *Il Trovatore,* her favorite opera, which she was singing as she returned to the house. . . . One glance into the living room changed her from a buoyant-spirited young woman into a nervous wreck, every fiber of her being palpitating with the fearful effects of that look. . . . "

In the dozens of articles that followed, Lizzie became the embodiment of genteel young womanhood. A reporter who interviewed her friends found "not one unmaidenly nor a single deliberately unkind act." Voicing the belief of many, he concluded, "Miss Borden, without a word from herself in her own defense, is a strong argument in her own favor."

The attributes of womanliness which vindicated Lizzie did not apply to Bridget. A servant, semiliterate, nearly friendless, Catholic and Irish, Bridget was the perfect target for suspicion. To the dismay of many, no evidence or motive ever could be found to implicate her in the deaths of her employers. Nevertheless, the police received dozens of letters urging her arrest. One man wrote demanding that Bridget and "her Confessor"—that is, her priest—be thrown into prison until she admitted her guilt.

The inquest began in Fall River on August 9. Two pharmacists from Smith's Drug Store testified that Lizzie had been shopping for poison on the afternoon before the murders. She had not asked for arsenic, which was sold over the counter, they said, but for the more lethal prussic acid, claiming she needed it to clean her sealskin cape. On the stand, Lizzie steadfastly denied the pharmacists' story, even denied knowing where Smith's Drug Store was, though it had been there for fourteen years on a street not five minutes from the house in which she had lived since childhood.

Lizzie's own testimony was full of contradictions. Discrepancies in her story might have been explained by hysteria or grief, but she had displayed neither. On August 5, a reporter at the murder scene for the Providence *Journal* noted: "She wasn't the least bit scared or worried. Most women would faint at seeing their father dead, for I never saw a more horrible sight. . . . She is a woman of remarkable nerve and self-control."

Such self-control seemed unnatural in an age when women were expected to swoon, and many people were alarmed by it. The reverend Mr. Buck, Lizzie's minister, reassured her champions that "her calmness is the calmness of innocence." Her lawyer, Mr. Jennings, sought to explain away her inconsistent answers by noting that "she was having her monthly illness" on the day of the murders, thereby evoking embarrassed nods of understanding.

Public sentiment on Lizzie's behalf rose to extraordinary heights. In full agreement with their pastor, her church declared her innocent. Ecclesiastical supporters were joined by several noted feminists. Mary Livermore, Susan Fessenden (president of the Women's Christian Temperance Union), and Lucy Stone took up the cudgels on Lizzie's behalf. Livermore declared her arrest to be another outrage perpetrated by "the tyrant man." Lizzie became the sacrificial lamb, the simple, warmhearted girl offered up by corrupt police to the altar of a power-hungry district attorney.

Nonetheless, the judge ordered her arrest at the inquest's end.

Reporters found Lizzie disappointingly composed after the indictment. With no tears to report, they concentrated on her cherry trimmed hat and the two ministers on whose arms she

leaned as she went off to jail in Taunton, the county seat. The horrible cell that awaited her was described in detail. In fact, Lizzie was not confined to a cell, but spent much of her time in the matron's room. Little mention was made of the flowers that graced the prison's window sill, or the lace-edged pillow slips brought by Emma, or of the meals which Lizzie had sent over from Taunton's best hotel.

When the preliminary hearing before Judge Blaisdell began in late November, reporters from more than forty out-of-town newspapers attended. Police held back huge crowds while ladies and gentlemen from Fall River's elite filed into the courtroom to claim the best seats.

A new piece of evidence, damaging to Lizzie's cause, was introduced. She had turned over to the police a spotlessly clean, fancy, blue bengaline dress that she swore she had worn on the day of the murders. Women in New England were surprised. No one wore party dresses of bengaline, a partly woolen fabric, around the house in the August heat. While witnesses swore that Lizzie was indeed wearing blue that day, none could swear that this dress was the one they had seen. To confound the problem, Alice Russell reluctantly admitted that she had seen Lizzie burn a blue cotton dress in the kitchen stove three days after the murders. The dress was soiled, she said Lizzie had told her, with brown paint—a color, noted the prosecutor, not unlike that of dried blood.

Except for rubbing her shoe buttons together, Lizzie sat quietly and displayed little interest. On the very last day, however, she broke into sobs as she heard her lawyer declare that no "person could have committed that crime unless his heart was black as hell." Delighted newspaper artists sketched a tearful Lizzie listening to Mr. Jennings as he asked: "Would it be the stranger, or would it be the one bound to the murdered man by ties of love? . . . what does it mean when we say the youngest daughter? The last one whose baby fingers have been lovingly entwined about her father's brow? Is there nothing in the ties of love and affection?"

Judge Blaisdell listened to all the evidence. It was no stranger who sat before him, but the daughter of a family he knew well. Jennings' image of the twining baby fingers was compelling, but so was the evidence prosecutor Hosea Knowlton produced. The judge finally began to speak: "Suppose for a single moment that *a man* was standing there. He was found close by that guestchamber which to Mrs. Borden was a chamber of death. Suppose that *a man* had been found in the vicinity of Mr. Borden and the only account he could give of himself was the unreasonable one that he was out in the barn looking for sinkers, that he was in the yard. . . . Would there be any question in the minds of men what should be done with such a man?" The judge's voice broke, but he continued: " . . . the judgment of the court is that you are probably guilty and you are ordered to wait the action of the Superior Court."

The trial began in New Bedford, Massachusetts, on June 5, 1893. Reporters from all over the East Coast converged on the town. Every hotel room within miles was reserved. Fences had to be erected around the courthouse to control the crowds.

Lizzie's newly inherited fortune of several hundred thousand dollars bought her excellent counsel. George Robinson, former governor of the state, was a masterful orator with a politician's shrewd sense of public opinion: at his suggestion, Lizzie went into mourning for the first time since the murders. Laboring against him were District Attorneys Hosea Knowlton and William Moody (a future U.S. Supreme Court justice), as able as Robinson, but with a distaste for flamboyance. Among the three judges who would hear Lizzie's case was Justice Justin Dewey, whom Robinson had elevated to the bench while governor.

One hundred and forty-eight men awaited jury selection. It was assumed that all had formed opinions; they were asked only if their minds were still open enough to judge the evidence fairly. The first man called claimed he could never convict a woman of a capital offense and was dismissed. Of the final twelve, the foreman was a real estate broker and sometime politician, two were manufacturers, three were mechanics, and

Lizzie Borden, accused of the ax murders of her father and stepmother in Fall River, Massachusetts (August 1892), was acquitted by an all-male jury that refused to believe that a well-bred woman could be capable of such an act.

six were farmers with considerable acreage. Not one foreign-sounding name was among them. Nearly all were over fifty: all were good Yankees.

The first blow to the prosecution came when Judge Dewey ruled Lizzie's damaging inquest testimony inadmissible and barred evidence regarding the alleged attempt to buy poison. While these rulings made Knowlton's task more difficult, his biggest worry was that jury men believed, as did the Boston *Globe,* in the "moral improbability that a woman of refinement and gentle training . . . could have conceived and executed so bloody a butchery." As he repeatedly reminded the jury, "We must face this case as men, not gallants."

Knowlton produced medical experts from Harvard who testified that any average-sized woman could have swung an ax with force enough to commit the murders, and that the trajectory of blood would have been away from the assailant: Lizzie's tidy appearance minutes after the crimes had no bearing on her guilt or innocence. Robinson blithely discounted their testimony by asking the jurymen whether they put more store in Harvard scientists than in their own New England common sense.

Though Lizzie later professed to be shocked at his bill of $25,000, Robinson was worth every penny. As she sat before the jury, a Sunday-school teacher and loving youngest daughter, the jurymen, nearly all of whom were fathers themselves, heard Robinson conclude: "If the little sparrow does not fall unnoticed, then indeed in God's great providence, this woman has not been alone in this court room."

The jury was sent off to deliberate with what one reporter called Judge Dewey's "plea for the innocent." The other two judges were said to have been stunned by his lack of objectivity. Though Dewey was indeed grateful to Robinson for his judgeship, a more compelling reason for his unswerving belief in Lizzie's innocence may have been the three daughters he had at home, the eldest of whom was Lizzie's age.

The jurors who filed out with Dewey's plea ringing in their ears were bewhiskered, respectable, family men. If they could believe that a gentlewoman could pick up a hatchet such as surely lay in their own basements, and by murdering her parents become an heiress, what could they think next time they looked into their own girls' eyes?

They returned in one hour. The *New York Times* reported that Lizzie's "face became livid, her lips were compressed as she tottered to her feet to hear the verdict!" Before the clerk could finish asking for it, the foreman cried, "Not guilty!" Lizzie dropped to her seat as an enormous cheer went up from the spectators who climbed onto the benches, waving hats and handkerchiefs and weeping.

It would have been difficult for any jury to convict "beyond all reasonable doubt" on the circumstantial evidence presented. However, in the nearby bar to which the jurors dashed, a reporter learned that there had been no debate at all among the twelve. All exhibits were ignored. Their vote had been immediate and unanimous. It was only to avoid the impression that their minds had been made up in advance that they sat and chatted for an hour before returning with their verdict.

The following morning, Americans found reflected in the headlines their own joy that the jury had been so wise. Lizzie and Emma returned to Second Street.

Fall River society, which had defended her throughout her ordeal, fell away thereafter, and Lizzie was left pretty much alone. Undaunted, she determined to have all the things she had missed in her youth. With what some considered indiscreet haste, she bought a large house on the hill and named it Maplecroft. She also asked to be called Lisbeth and stopped going to the church whose parishioners had defended her so energetically. Matters were not improved when townspeople learned that she had bought and destroyed every available copy of local reporter Edwin Porter's *The Fall River Tragedy,* which had included portions of her inquest testimony.

Lizzie sealed her isolation in 1904 by striking up a friendship with Nance O'Neil, a Boston actress. The following year, to her neighbors' horror, Lizzie gave a party—complete with caterers and potted palms—for Miss O'Neil and her troupe. That night, Emma quietly moved out and never spoke to or saw Lizzie again.

Lizzie continued to live at Maplecroft in increasing isolation. Undoubtedly, she heard the nasty rhyme children began to sing to the tune of "Ta-Ra-Ra Boom-De-Ay!":

Lizzie Borden took an ax
And gave her mother forty whacks;
When she saw what she had done,
She gave her father forty-one!

Lizzie Borden died on June 1, 1927, at the age of sixty-six in Fall River. Emma died ten days later in New Hampshire. Few gravestones conceal a puzzle more intricate than that sealed away by the imposing Borden monument in Oak Grove Cemetery. The truth about the events on Second Street lies buried there along with Andrew, Abby, Emma, and Lizzie, but back then, in the summer of 1893, most Americans knew in their hearts that no young lady like Lizzie could have murdered her parents with an ax. Reputable authors in respectable magazines assured them their intuition was correct. They did not even want to think that it could be otherwise.

Study Questions

1. How did Lizzie Borden's class and social standing influence the way she was treated by legal authorities?

2. What were the physical, psychological, intellectual, and moral characteristics that popular magazines in the late nineteenth century attributed to well-bred women? How closely did Lizzie conform to these expectations?

3. What did late-nineteenth-century writers mean by such concepts as "arrested evolution" and "deplorable accidents"? How do these concepts indicate a sexually biased society?

4. In what area were women considered superior to men? Why was this so?

5. How did popular attitudes toward upper-class and lower-class women differ? Why were many people more inclined to suspect Bridget Sullivan than Lizzie Borden of the crime?

6. How was Lizzie's behavior during the entire episode interpreted?

7. Why was the trial politically and symbolically significant?

Bibliography

The Borden murder case has been examined and reexamined. Victoria Lincoln, *Lizzie Borden, a Private Disgrace* (1967) and Robert Sullivan, *Goodbye Lizzie Borden* (1974) argue that she was indeed guilty of the crimes. Edward D. Radin, *Lizzie Borden: The Untold Story* (1961) views the case from a different perspective. Recent historical scholarship has only begun to explore the complexities of American attitudes toward women. Lois W. Banner, *Women in Modern America: A Brief History* (1974, second edition 1984) presents a fine introduction to the topic and a good bibliography. Other useful studies on women in the late nineteenth century include John S. Haller, Jr., and Robin M. Haller, *The Physician and Sexuality in Victorian America* (1974); G. J. Barker-Benfield, *The Horrors of the Half-Known Life: Male Attitudes Toward Women and Sexuality in Nineteenth-Century America* (1976); Linda Gordon, *Woman's Body, Woman's Right: A Social History of Birth Control in America* (1976); and Lois Banner, *American Beauty* (1983). Two other books present different views of the role of women in America. Kate Chopin, *The Awakening* (1980) is a wonderful novel written with depth and sensitivity. Questions of isolation and alienation in a small American town are touched upon in Michael Lesy, *Wisconsin Death Trip* (1973).

★ ★ ★

The First Chapter of Children's Rights

Peter Stevens and Marian Eide

Today it is sadly common, a story whose ending is so often tragic. It is a story set in some of America's worst slums, and in some of the country's wealthiest neighborhoods. In the late 1980s the case of Joel Steinberg and Hedda Nussbaum focused the public consciousness on the issue of child abuse. In the mid-1980s, Steinberg, a New York criminal lawyer, and Nussbaum, a former editor and writer of children's books, illegally "adopted" two children. Soon a cycle of physical and mental abuse began. In the early morning of November 2, 1987, Nussbaum's 911 call brought paramedics to their apartment. On the floor the paramedics found six-year-old Lisa, naked, bruised, emaciated, and unable to breathe. She was in a coma. Tied to a "playpen" they discovered 16-month-old Mitchell, whose body also displayed clear signs of physical abuse.

Lisa never recovered, dying less than a week later. Examinations of her body told a tale of violent and prolonged abuse. The horror of her short life became evident during the sensational trial of Steinberg (all charges against Nussbaum were dropped in return for her testimony). In the end, Steinberg was found guilty and sentenced to serve 8 1/2 to 25 years in prison, and the state of New York passed new legislation—the "Lisa Law"—to end some of the loopholes in private adoptions. But perhaps even more importantly, it reminded Americans that child abuse knew no economic or social boundaries.

In "The First Chapter of Children's Rights," Peter Stevens and Marian Eide show that child abuse is not the product of the twentieth century. The issue of a child's rights versus the rights of parents to raise a child was as pressing in the 1870s as in the 1990s. It is important to keep in mind that in the decade before the Mary Ellen McCormack case, Congress abolished slavery in the United States and passed the Fourteenth Amendment, making it unlawful to deprive any American "of life, liberty, or property, without due process of law; nor deny to any person . . . the equal protection of the laws."

I n the quiet New York courtroom, the little girl began to speak. "My name is Mary Ellen McCormack. I don't know how old I am. . . . I have never had but one pair of shoes, but can't recollect when that was. I have had no shoes or stockings on this winter. . . . I have never had on a particle of flannel. My bed at night is only a piece of carpet, stretched on the floor underneath a window, and I sleep in my little undergarment, with a quilt over me. I am never allowed to play with any children or have any company whatever. Mamma has been in the habit of whipping and beating me almost every day. She used to whip me with a twisted whip, a raw hide. The whip always left black and blue marks on my body. I have now on my head two black and blue marks which were made by mamma with the whip, and a cut on the left side of my forehead which was made by a pair of scissors in mamma's hand. She struck me with the scissors and cut me. I have no recollection of ever having been kissed, and have never been kissed by mamma. I have never been taken on my mamma's lap, or caressed or petted. I never dared to speak to anybody, because if I did I would get whipped. . . . Whenever mamma went out I was locked up in the bedroom. . . . I have no recollection of ever being in the street in my life."

At the beginning of 1874 there were no legal means in the United States to save a child from abuse. Mary Ellen's eloquent testimony changed that, changed our legal system's view of the rights of the child.

Yet more than a century later the concerns that arose from Mary Ellen's case are still being battled over in the courts. The classic dilemmas of just how deeply into the domestic realm the governmental arm can reach and what the obligations of public government are to the private individual take on particular urgency in considering child abuse.

"The First Chapter of Children's Rights" by Peter Stevens and Marian Eide in *American Heritage,* Vol. 41/No. 5, July/August 1990, pp. 84–91. Reprinted by permission of *American Heritage* Magazine, a division of Forbes, Inc. © Forbes, Inc., 1990.

Early in 1989, in the case of *DeShaney* v. *Winnebago County,* the Supreme Court declared that the government is not obligated to protect its citizens against harm inflicted by private individuals. DeShaney brought the case before the court in a suit against county social service agencies that had failed to intervene when her estranged husband abused their son, Joshua, who, as a result of his father's brutality, suffered permanent brain damage. The father was convicted, but his former wife believes that fault also lies with the agencies, whose failure to intercede violated her son's Fourteenth Amendment right not to be deprived of life or liberty without due process of the law. Chief Justice William H. Rehnquist wrote that intervening officials are often charged with "improperly intruding into the parent-child relationship." Justice William J. Brennan, Jr., dissenting, wrote: "Inaction can be every bit as abusive of power as action, [and] oppression can result when a State undertakes a vital duty and then ignores it."

The difficulty in bringing Mary Ellen McCormack into the New York Supreme Court in 1874 grew from similar controversy over the role of government in family matters, and Mary Ellen's sad history is not so different from Joshua DeShaney's.

When Mary Ellen's mother, Frances Connor, immigrated to the United States from England in 1858, she took a job at the St. Nicholas Hotel in New York City as a laundress. There she met an Irishman named Thomas Wilson who worked in the hotel kitchen shucking oysters. They were married in April 1862, shortly after Wilson had been drafted into the 69th New York, a regiment in the famous Irish Brigade. Early in 1864 she gave birth to their daughter, whom she named Mary after her mother and Ellen after her sister.

The birth of her daughter seems to have heralded the beginning of Frances Wilson's own decline. Her husband was killed that same year in the brutal fighting at Cold Harbor, Virginia, and with a diminished income she found it necessary to look for a job. In May 1864, unable to pay someone to watch the baby while she was at work, she gave Mary Ellen over to the care of a woman named Mary Score for two dollars a week, the whole of her widow's pension. Child farming was a common practice at that time, and many women made a living taking in unwanted children just as others took in laundry. Score lived in a tenement in the infamous warrens of Mulberry Bend, where thousands of immigrants crowded into small, airless rooms, and it is likely that providing foster care was her only means of income.

Finally Frances Wilson became unable to pay for the upkeep of her child; three weeks after the payments ceased, Score turned Mary Ellen over to the Department of Charities. The little girl—whose mother was never to see her again—was sent to Blackwells Island in July 1865. Her third home was certainly no more pleasant than Mulberry Bend. Mary Ellen was among a group of sick and hungry foundlings; fully two-thirds of them would die before reaching maturity.

The same slum-bred diseases that ravaged the children on Blackwells Island had also claimed all three children of a couple named Thomas and Mary McCormack. So when Thomas frequently bragged of the three children he had fathered by another woman, his wife was more receptive to the idea of adopting them than she might otherwise have been. Those children, he told her, were still alive, though their mother had turned them over to the care of the city.

On January 2, 1866, the McCormacks went to the Department of Charities to reclaim one of the children Thomas's mistress had abandoned. The child they chose as their own was Mary Ellen Wilson. Because the McCormacks were not asked to provide any proof of relation to the child and gave only the reference of their family doctor, there is no evidence that Thomas was in any way related to the child he brought home that day. More than a month later an indenture was filed for Mary Ellen in which the McCormacks promised to report on her condition each year. There were no other requirements.

Shortly after bringing the child home, Thomas McCormack died, and his widow married a man named Francis Connolly. Little more than that is known of the early childhood of Mary Ellen. She came to her new home in a flannel petticoat, and

when her clothing was removed from Connolly's home as evidence six years later, there was barely enough to fill a tiny suitcase. She was beaten, set to work, deprived of daylight, and locked in closets for days at a time; she was rarely bathed, never kissed, and never addressed with a gentle word. During the six years she lived with Connolly, only two reports on her progress were filed with the Commissioners of Charities and Correction.

Late in 1873 Etta Angell Wheeler, a Methodist caseworker serving in the tenements of New York City, received a disturbing report. It came from Margaret Bingham, a landlord in Hell's Kitchen, and told of a terrible case of child abuse. The child's parents had been tenants of Bingham for about four years, and almost immediately after they moved in, Bingham began to observe how cruelly they treated their child, Mary Ellen. They confined her in close quarters during hot weather, kept her severely underdressed in cold, beat her daily, and left her unattended for hours at a time. On several occasions Bingham tried to intervene; each time the child's mother said she would call upon the fullest resources of the law before she would allow any interference in her home. Finally Bingham resorted to threat: The beatings and ill treatment would have to stop, or the family would be evicted. When her plan backfired and the family left, Bingham, in a last-ditch effort, sent for Etta Wheeler. In order to observe Mary Ellen's predicament, Wheeler went to the Connollys's neighbor, an ailing tubercular woman named Mary Smitt. Enlisting Smitt's aid, she proposed that Mary Ellen be sent over each day to check on the patient. Smitt reluctantly agreed, and on the pretext of inquiring about this sick neighbor, Wheeler knocked on Mary Connolly's door.

Inside she saw a "pale, thin child, bare-foot, in a thin, scanty dress so tattered that I could see she wore but one garment besides.

"It was December and the weather bitterly cold. She was a tiny mite, the size of five years, though, as afterward appeared, she was then nine. From a pan set upon a low stool she stood washing dishes, struggling with a frying pan about as heavy as herself. Across the table lay a brutal whip of twisted leather strands and the child's meager arms and legs bore many marks of its use. But the saddest part of her story was written on her face in its look of suppression and misery, the face of a child unloved, of a child that had seen only the fearsome side of life. . . . I never saw her again until the day of her rescue, three months later. . . . "

Though social workers often witnessed scenes of cruelty, poverty, and grief, Wheeler found Mary Ellen's plight especially horrifying. She went first to the police; they told her she must be able to furnish proof of assault in order for them to act. Charitable institutions she approached offered to care for the child, but first she must be brought to them through legal means. There were none. Every effort Wheeler made proved fruitless. Though there were laws to protect children—laws, in fact, to prevent assault and battery to any person—there were no means available for intervention in a child's home.

Finally Wheeler's niece had an idea. The child, she said, was a member of the animal kingdom; surely Henry Bergh, the founder of the American Society for the Prevention of Cruelty to Animals, who was famous for his dramatic rescue of mistreated horses in the streets of New York, might be willing to intervene. Within the hour Wheeler had arranged a meeting with Bergh. Despite its apparent strangeness, this sort of appeal was not new to Bergh. Once before he had tried to intervene in a case of child abuse and had failed. This time he was more cautious.

"Very definite testimony is needed to warrant interference between a child and those claiming guardianship," Bergh told Wheeler. "Will you not send me a written statement that, at my leisure, I may judge the weight of the evidence and may also have time to consider if this society should interfere? I promise to consider the case carefully."

Wheeler provided a statement immediately, including in it the observations of neighbors to whom she had spoken. Bergh was convinced. "No time is to be lost," he wrote his lawyer, Elbridge T. Gerry. "Instruct me how to proceed."

The next day Wheeler again visited the sick woman in Hell's Kitchen and found in her room a young man who, on hearing Wheeler's name, said, "I was sent to take the census in this house. I have been in every room." Wheeler then knew him to be a detective for Bergh.

On the basis of the detective's observations and the testimony provided by Etta Wheeler, Bergh's lawyers, Gerry and Ambrose Monell, appeared before Judge Abraham R. Lawrence of the New York Supreme Court to present a petition on behalf of Mary Ellen. They showed that Mary Ellen was held illegally by the Connollys, who were neither her natural parents nor her lawful custodians, and went on to describe the physical abuse Mary Ellen endured, the marks and bruises on her body, and the general state of deprivation that characterized her existence. They offered a list of witnesses willing to testify on behalf of the child and concluded by stating that there was ample evidence to indicate that she was in clear danger of being maimed or even killed. The lawyers requested that a warrant be issued, the child removed from her home and placed in protective custody, and her parents brought to trial.

Bergh testified that his efforts on behalf of the child were in no way connected to his work with abused animals and that they did not make use of the special legal provisions set up for that purpose. Because of Bergh's association with animal rescue, to this day the case is often described as having originated in his conviction that the child was a member of the animal kingdom. Bergh, however, insisted that his actions were merely those of any humane citizen and that he intended to prevent cruelties inflicted on children through any legal means available.

Judge Lawrence issued a warrant under Section 65 of the Habeas Corpus Act as requested. This provision read in part: "Whenever it shall appear by satisfactory proof that any one is held in illegal confinement or custody, and that there is good reason to believe that he will . . . suffer some irreparable injury, before he can be relieved by the issuing of a *habeas corpus* or *certiorari,* any court or officer authorized to issue such writs, may issue a warrant . . . [and] bring him before such court or officer, to be dealt with according to law."

Many children, like these girls in the garment industry, grew up in factories. In 1874, Henry Bergh, Elbridge Gerry, and James Wright founded the New York Society for the Prevention of Cruelty to Children and eventually secured passage of a bill that made labor by children under the age of fourteen illegal.

The press of the day hailed Gerry's use of Section 65 of the Habeas Corpus Act as brilliant. The act was rarely invoked, and the legal means for removing a child from its home were nonexistent. In using the little-known law, Gerry created a new method for intervention.

That same day, April 9, 1874, Mary Ellen was taken from her home and brought into Judge Lawrence's court. Having no adequate clothing of her own, the child had been wrapped in a carriage blanket by the policemen who held her in custody. A reporter on the scene described her as "a bright little girl, with features indicating unusual mental capacity, but with a care-worn, stunted, and prematurely old look. . . . No change of custody or condition could be much for the worse."

The reporter Jacob Riis was present in the court. "I saw a child brought in . . . at the sight of which men wept aloud, and I heard the story of little Mary Ellen told . . . that stirred the soul of a

city and roused the conscience of a world that had forgotten, and as I looked, I knew I was where the first chapter of children's rights was being written." Her body and face were terribly bruised; her hands and feet "showed the plain marks of great exposure." And in what almost instantly seemed to condemn Mrs. Connolly before the court, the child's face bore a fresh gash through her eyebrow and across her left cheek that barely missed the eye itself. Mary Ellen was to carry this scar throughout her life.

Interestingly, there is no further mention in the ample reports surrounding Mary Ellen's case of her foster father, Francis Connolly. He was never brought into court, never spoke publicly concerning the child. All her life Mary Ellen exhibited a frightened timidity around men, yet it was against her foster mother that she testified.

On the evening of her detention, Mary Ellen was turned over to the temporary custody of the matron of police headquarters. The next day, April 10, the grand jury read five indictments against Mary Connolly for assault and battery, felonious assault, assault with intent to do bodily harm, assault with intent to kill and assault with intent to maim. Once the stepmother had been brought into the legal system, there were ample means to punish her.

Mary Ellen herself was brought in to testify against the woman she had called her mother. On her second appearance in court she seemed almost wholly altered. She was clothed in a new suit, and her pale face reflected the kindness that surrounded her. She carried with her a new picture book, probably the first she had ever owned. She acted open and uninhibited with strangers, and interestingly, seemed to show no great fear of her mother or any apparent enmity toward her.

The lawyers Gerry and Monell gathered several witnesses against Mary Connolly, among them neighbors, Wheeler, and Mary Ellen herself. Margaret Bingham said she had seen the child locked up in a room and had told other neighbors, but they said there was no point in interfering since the police would do nothing. Bingham had tried to open the window of the child's room to let in some air, but it would not lift more than an inch. As a constant presence and reminder, a cowhide whip was locked in the room with the child. Wheeler recounted her first visit to Mary Ellen, during which the child washed dishes that seemed twice her size and was apparently oblivious of the visitor's presence. The whip lay on the table next to her. The next day, when Wheeler came by again, the child was sewing, and the whip lay on a chair near her.

Then it was the mother's turn to testify. On the witness stand Mary Connolly showed herself to be a woman of some spirit. Despite her treatment of the child, there is something compelling in Connolly's strength and humor. At one point the prosecutor asked if she had an occupation beyond house-keeping. "Well," she said, "I sleep with the boss." As the trial wore on, she became enraged at Gerry's prodding questions; finally she accused him of being "ignorant of the difficulties

of bringing up and governing children." Yet she admitted that contrary to regulations, in the six years she had Mary Ellen in her custody, she had reported on her condition to the Commissioners of Charities and Correction only twice.

Two indictments were brought against Connolly, the first for her assault on the child with scissors on April 7, the second for the continual assault inflicted on the child throughout the years 1873 and 1874. After twenty minutes of deliberation the jury returned a verdict of guilty of assault and battery. Connolly was sentenced to one year of hard labor in the city penitentiary, then known as the Tombs. In handing down this sentence, the judge defined it not only as a punishment to Connolly but also as a statement of precedence in child abuse cases.

Mary Ellen never returned to the Connollys' home. In the ensuing months the publicity that her case received brought in many claims of relation. But on investigating, her guardian, Judge Lawrence, discovered the stories were fictions, and he finally placed the child in the Sheltering Arms, a home for grown girls; soon after, she was moved to the Woman's Aid Society and Home for Friendless Girls. This mirrors another critical problem in the system's treatment of minors. All juveniles were handled by the Department of Charities and Correction, and whether they were orphaned or delinquent, their treatment was the same. And so it was that the ten-year-old Mary Ellen was placed in a home with mostly delinquent adolescents.

Etta Wheeler knew this was wrong for Mary Ellen, and she expressed her hesitations to Judge Lawrence. He, in turn, consulted with Henry Bergh, and eventually they agreed to turn the girl over to Etta Wheeler herself. Unable to imagine giving up her work in the slums of New York City but believing that Mary Ellen deserved a better environment, Wheeler brought the child to her mother in North Chili, New York. Wheeler's mother became ill shortly afterward, and Mary Ellen was raised mostly by Wheeler's sister.

"Here began a new life," Wheeler wrote. "The child was an interesting study, so long shut within four walls and now in a new world. Woods, fields, 'green things growing,' were all strange to her, she had not known them. She had to learn, as a baby does, to walk upon the ground,—she had walked only upon floors, and her eye told her nothing of uneven surfaces. . . . But in this home there were other children and they taught her as children alone can teach each other. They taught her to play, to be unafraid, to know her rights and to claim them. She shared their happy, busy life from the making of mud pies up to charming birthday parties and was fast becoming a normal child."

The happiness of her years in the upstate New York countryside lies in stark contrast to her early childhood. And indeed, as Wheeler wrote, she learned by example the ways of normal childhood. She grew up strong and well, learning how to read and playing with friends and pet kittens. In 1875 Wheeler reported to Gerry that Mary Ellen was growing up as a normal child. "She has some faults that are of the graver sort. She tells fibs and sticks to them bravely, steals lumps of sugar & cookies and only confesses when the crumbs are found in her pocket—in short she is very much like other children, loving—responding to kindness & praise, hating a task unless there be a play, or a reward thereof, and inevitably 'forgetting' what she does not wish to remember—what children do not do some or all of these forbidden things! She is a favorite with nearly all the people who have come to know her."

When she was twenty-four, Mary Ellen married a widower named Louis Schutt and with him had two children, Etta—named after the woman who had rescued her—and Florence. She adopted a third, orphaned child, Eunice. She also raised Louis Schutt's three children from his first wife.

In 1911 Wheeler visited her protégé in her home, "finding her well and happy. . . . The family income is small, but Mary Ellen is a prudent housewife and they are comfortable. The two daughters are promising girls." The eldest daughter, Etta, worked industriously through that summer, finished high school, and became a teacher.

Florence followed her sister's path, teaching first grade for thirty-eight years. When she retired, the elementary school in North Chili was renamed in her honor. Eunice earned a business degree, married, and raised two sons.

Florence remembers her mother as a solemn woman who came alive whenever she listened to Irish jigs and especially to "The Irish Washerwoman." She was unfailingly generous with her time and her affection. Her years in North Chili had saved her from the vicious cycle abused children often suffer of becoming abusers themselves. According to Florence her mother was capable of sternness and certainly willing to punish her daughters, but the terrible experiences of her early childhood never spilled into her own child rearing. As Etta Wheeler wrote, "To her children, two bright, dutiful daughters, it has been her joy to give a happy childhood in sharp contrast to her own."

Etta and Florence often asked their mother about the Connollys, but Mary Ellen was reluctant to speak of her early years. She did show her daughters the scars on her arms where she had been burned with a hot iron, and of course they could see the scissors scar across her face. Florence distinctly recalls that in the few times they spoke of her mother's years in New York City, she never mentioned a woman inflicting her injuries; it was always a man.

In October of 1913 Mary Ellen Schutt attended a meeting of the American Humane Society in Rochester. She was accompanied by Etta Wheeler, who was there to present a paper entitled "The Finding of Mary Ellen." The paper concluded: "If the memory of her earliest years is sad, there is this comfort that the cry of her wrongs awoke the world to the need of organized relief for neglected and abused children."

Mary Ellen died on October 30, 1956, at the age of ninety-two. She was survived by her two daughters, her adopted daughter, three stepchildren, three grandchildren, and five great-grandchildren. More important, she was survived by the beginning of a movement to prevent the repetition of tragedies like her own. On December 15, 1874, Henry Bergh, Elbridge Gerry, and James Wright founded the New York Society for the Prevention of Cruelty to Children (SPCC) with the ample assistance of Cornelius Vanderbilt. It was the first organization of its kind in America. At the outset of their work the founders signed a statement of purpose: "The undersigned, desirous of rescuing the unprotected children of this city and State from the cruelty and demoralization which neglect and abandonment engender, hereby engage to aid, with their sympathy and support, the organization and working of a Children's Protective Society, having in view the realization of so important a purpose."

The SPCC saw its role essentially as a legal one. As an agent or a friend of the court, the society endeavored to intervene on the behalf of children, enforcing the laws that were in existence to prevent cruelty toward them and at the same time introducing new legislation on their behalf.

At the first meeting of the SPCC on December 16, 1874, Gerry stressed the fact that the most crucial role of the society lay in the rescue of children from abusive situations. From there, he pointed out, there were many excellent groups available to care for and shelter children and many state laws to punish abusive parents. He went on to predict that as soon as abusers learned that the law could reach them, there would be few cases like that of Mary Ellen.

Bergh was less optimistic. At the same meeting, he pointed out that neglected and abused children were to become the mothers and fathers of the country and that unless their interests were defended, the interests of society in general would suffer.

In its first year the SPCC investigated more than three hundred cases of child abuse. Many people felt threatened by the intrusion of the government into their private lives; discipline, they believed, was a family issue, and outside influence was not only unwelcome but perhaps even unconstitutional. When, with the aid of a state senator, James W. Booth, Gerry introduced in the New York legislature a law entitled "An Act to Prevent and Punish Wrongs to Children,"

the proposal was immediately and vigorously attacked. The New York *World* wrote that Bergh was to be authorized to "break into the garrets of the poor and carry off their children upon the suspicion of spanking." According to the *World,* the law would give Bergh "power to discipline all the naughty children of New York. . . . We sincerely hope that it may not be finally kicked out of the legislature, as it richly deserves to be, until the public mind shall have had time to get itself thoroughly enlightened as to the state of things in which it has become possible for such a person as Mr. Bergh to bring the Legislature to the point of seriously entertaining such an impudently senseless measure. This bill is a bill to supersede the common law in favor of Mr. Bergh, and the established tribunals of justice in favor of an irresponsible private corporation." The bill was passed in 1876, however, and became the foundation upon which the SPCC performed its work.

From its initial concentration on preventing abuse in the home, the society broadened its franchise to battle neglect, abandonment, and the exploitation of children for economic gain. In 1885, after considerable effort by the SPCC and in the face of yet more opposition, Gerry secured passage of a bill that made labor by children under the age of fourteen illegal.

As the explosive story of the death of Lisa Steinberg in the home of her adoptive parents revealed to the nation in 1987, abuse still haunts American society. There are still legal difficulties in removing a child from an abusive situation. In 1987 the House Select Committee on Children, Youth, and Families reported that the incidence of child abuse, particularly sexual abuse and neglect, is rising; in 1985 alone almost two million children were referred to protective agencies. In part, the committee said, this increase was due to a greater awareness of the issue, and there has also been an increased effort to educate children themselves about situations that constitute abuse or molestation and about ways to get help.

Despite a plethora of programs designed to address abuse, the committee concluded that not enough is being done. The most effective pro-grams were found to be those that worked to prevent the occurrence of abuse at the outset through education in parenting techniques, through intervention in high-risk situations, such as unwanted pregnancies, and through screening for mental and emotional difficulties. However, funding for public welfare programs has fallen far below the demands, and what funding there is must frequently be diverted to intervene in more and more sensational and hopeless cases.

If there is still much hard, sad work ahead, there is also much that has been accomplished. And all of it began when Mary Ellen McCormack spoke and, in speaking, freed herself and thousands of other children from torment.

Study Questions

1. What issues did the case of Mary Ellen McCormack raise? What role should the state and federal governments play in the private lives of citizens?

2. What was the practice of "child farming"?

3. What problems did Etta Angell Wheeler face when she attempted to help Mary Ellen McCormack? Why did she turn to Henry Bergh? What role did Bergh play in the case and in Mary Ellen's life?

4. What can you tell about the life of Mary Connolly from this essay?

5. What happened to Mary Ellen after she was separated from Mary Connolly?

6. How did the case of Mary Ellen McCormack lead to new laws to benefit children? How did the laws change the problem of child abuse and exploitation?

Bibliography

Only recently have historians begun a serious study of the private lives of American families and the connections between private behavior and public policy. An excellent place to start is Steven Mintz and Susan Kellogg, *Domestic Revolutions: A Social History of American Family Life* (1988), as well as Steven Mintz, *A Prison of Expectations: The Family in Victorian Culture* (1983). The career of Henry Bergh is covered in Gerald Carson, "The Great Meddler," *American Heritage* (December, 1967). Social conditions of New York's slums are explored in the writings of Jacob Riis, especially *How the Other Half Lives* (1890). An outstanding study of the problems of social reform in the cities is Paul Boyer, *Urban Masses and Moral Order in America, 1820-1920* (1978).

War and Peace
in a New Century

The period between the assassination of William McKinley in 1901 and America's entry into the Great War in 1917 has been labeled as the Progressive Era. In character and tone the years mirrored the first Progressive president, Theodore Roosevelt. Animated and energetic, T. R. used the presidency as a "bully pulpit," readily giving his opinion on a variety of subjects, ranging from literature and politics to football and divorce. Roosevelt believed that America's greatness was the result of its Anglo-Saxon heritage. Although he hoped to bring a "Square Deal" to all Americans, his reforming impulse was conservative in nature; he maintained that only through moderate reform could America preserve its traditional social, economic, and political structure. He had no sympathy for such "radical fanatics" as socialists or anarchists, nor did he trust the masses of American people who lacked his breeding and education. His answer for any sort of mob action was "taking ten or a dozen of their leaders out, standing . . . them against a wall, and shooting them dead."

Despite their ethnocentricity and self-righteousness, Roosevelt and the next two Progressive presidents—William Howard Taft and Woodrow Wilson—did attempt to curb some of the worst abuses of the urban-industrial society. They saw legislation through Congress that limited the number of hours that women and children could work and enacted the Pure Food and Drug Act (1906) and the Meat Inspection Act (1906). However, other Progressives, often with the support of the president, supported prohibition and antidivorce legislation, thereby seeking to regulate the private lives of millions of Americans.

A major shortcoming of the Progressive movement was the general reluctance to support minority and ethnic groups. Such Progressives as James K. Vardaman and Theodore G. Bilbo, both from Mississippi, supported forward-looking legislation for whites but were violent race-baiters. Progressives rarely attacked the Jim Crow system in the South or introduced antilynching legislation in Congress. Segregation within the federal government expanded under Woodrow Wilson.

In 1901, Theodore Roosevelt said that he believed in the adage, "Speak softly and carry a big stick; you will go far." With this concept behind his foreign policy, he became a powerful arbitrator of many world disputes.

Similarly, vocal and independent labor unions and women's rights organizations seldom found support among influential Progressives. Margaret Sanger's birth control movement met strong opposition from middle-class men and women who saw it as a threat to family and morality. Such radical working-class organizations as the Industrial Workers of the World (the IWW, or "Wobblies") were not embraced by the mainstream of the Progressive movement.

The Progressive movement, however, did not really survive World War I. As a result of the Spanish-American War of 1898, the United States had acquired new territories in the distant Pacific, requiring a two-ocean navy and leaving Americans with global responsibilities. Those responsibilities eventually complicated and compromised the reform spirit. The Great War of 1914–1918 damaged the reform impulses of Progressivism. It inspired skepticism, pessimism, and ultimately cynicism, and in the death-filled trenches of Western Europe, the Progressive movement met its demise.

The following essays deal with different characteristics of the Progressive movement. Confronted by the powerful forces of urbanization and industrialization, Americans attempted—sometimes successfully, often unsuccessfully—to come to terms with their changing society. Amidst that attempt, World War I complicated Progressivist dreams with the reality of horror, stupidity, and mass death.

READING 7

★ ★ ★

Teddy Roosevelt
and the Rough Riders

Robert J. Maddox

Anchored off the coast of Cuba, aboard the *Yucatan,* Theodore Roosevelt received news on the evening of June 21, 1898 that he and his men, a volunteer cavalry regiment dubbed the Rough Riders, should disembark from the safety of the ship and join the fighting ashore. It was a welcomed invitation, celebrated with cheers, war dances, songs, boasts, and toasts. "To the officers—may they get killed, wounded, or promoted," urged one toast that captured the mood aboard ship.

Who were these Rough Riders who seemed so bent on winning glory? As one of them told Roosevelt, "Who would not risk his life for a star?" And who was Theodore Roosevelt, the energetic rich kid who lusted after fame and perhaps had his eyes—albeit nearsighted—focused on the presidency? Robert J. Maddox retells this story of Theodore Roosevelt, the Rough Riders, and America's "splendid little war" with Spain. In the process he tells a great deal about the future president and the nation that made him its hero.

The war against Spain in 1898 was one of the more popular conflicts in American history. Victory came easily, there were relatively few casualties, and the cause seemed just in the minds of most people. From it the United States acquired the Philippine Islands, Puerto Rico, Guam, and a virtual protectorate over Cuba. The nation acquired several heroes as well, Admiral Dewey to name one, but none more colorful than the flamboyant Teddy Roosevelt. His exploits in Cuba, at the head of his Rough Riders, made him a legend in his own lifetime and helped make him President of the United States.

Roosevelt was in the prime of his life when the war broke out. Not yet forty years old, he possessed an imposing if somewhat overweight physique which he kept fit by almost daily exercise. In this regard he was a self-made man. Spindly and a trifle owlish as a youngster, Roosevelt, through what one of his biographers termed the "Cult of Strenuosity," had built up his body by relentless physical activity. Only one of his faculties had failed to respond—his eyesight. Cursed from boyhood with extreme nearsightedness, which grew worse over the years, Roosevelt was very self-conscious about this weakness in an otherwise healthy organism. During the war he was so worried it would betray him in combat that he had at least a half-dozen pairs of spectacles sewn in various parts of his uniform as insurance.

Mentally, Roosevelt was a complex individual. Exceedingly bright, he read voraciously, and penned his own books and articles without the help of a ghostwriter. He was, or would become, friendly with some of the leading intellectuals of the era. One side of him, however, remained boyish until the day he died. "You must always remember," a British diplomat wrote a friend some years later, "that the President [Roosevelt] is about six." Without in any way belittling his patriotism,

An 1889 photo shows Teddy Roosevelt as colonel of the Rough Riders. Teddy's uniforms, which had extra spectacles sewn into them, were tailored by Brooks Brothers to ensure a proper fit.

"Teddy Roosevelt and the Rough Riders" by Robert J. Maddox. This article is reprinted from the November 1977 issue of *American History Illustrated* 12, pp. 8–15, 18–19, with the permission of Cowles History Group, Inc. Copyright *American History Illustrated* magazine.

it seems safe to say that Teddy's enthusiasm for fighting the Spaniards stemmed at least as much from his desire to have a "bully" time doing it.

No one ever accused Roosevelt of being a pacifist. During the 1880s and 1890s the United States had gotten into a number of scrapes with other nations over issues large and small. Almost invariably T. R. had called for the most militant actions in response to these situations, and had denounced those who urged caution. War to him was not a catastrophe to be avoided; it could be a tonic to the nation's bloodstream. A country too long at peace, he believed, tended to grow soft and effeminate, while war encouraged "manliness," a characteristic he prized above all else.

Before 1897 Roosevelt had held no office which dealt directly with military or foreign affairs. He had served in the New York state legislature as federal Civil Service Commissioner, and as a commissioner of the New York City Police Department. Despite having held such prestigious jobs for a man of his years, Roosevelt's political future was clouded by his tendency to alienate some of those who could help him and by the strident views on foreign policy which he never hesitated to voice—often to the great embarrassment of his own party. When, as a reward for his services in the election of 1896, T. R.'s friends began pushing for his appointment as Assistant Secretary of the Navy in the new Republican administration, they encountered stiff opposition. The President-elect himself had reservations about Teddy, but named him anyway. "I hope he has no preconceived plans," McKinley said wistfully, "which he would wish to drive through the moment he got in."

McKinley hoped in vain. Within two months of his appointment, Roosevelt wrote the well-known naval expert, Captain Alfred Thayer Mahan, that:

If I had my way, we would annex those islands [Hawaii] tomorrow. If that is impossible, I would establish a protectorate. . . . I believe we should build the Nicaraguan Canal at once, and should build a dozen new battleships, half of them on the Pacific Coast. I am fully alive to the danger from Japan.

These and similar sentiments clearly demonstrated that T. R. had no intention of vanishing into the bureaucracy. Nor did he. A short time later, when Secretary of the Navy John D. Long went on vacation, one newspaper reported that Roosevelt soon had "the whole Navy bordering on a war footing. It remains only to sand down the decks and pipe to quarters for action." Teddy did not try to conceal his delight in being left to mind the store. "The Secretary is away," he wrote in one letter, "and I am having immense fun running the Navy." One story had it that when asked about his Assistant Secretary, Long dourly responded "Why 'Assistant'?"

Sticking pins in maps and running around on inspection tours must have amused him, but Roosevelt wanted some real action. Spain provided the most likely source. Once the possessor of a world empire, Spain by this time was a minor power clinging grimly to its few remaining territories. One of these, Cuba, lay less than 100 miles from American shores, and for several years had smoldered with insurrection against Spanish domination. Though he refrained from speaking out publicly, Roosevelt, in private talks and correspondence, recommended war against Spain almost from the day he became Assistant Secretary. American honor demanded it, he said, and a brief war would help rekindle martial instincts which had flagged through years of peace. There would be an additional dividend, he wrote on one occasion, that being "the benefit done our military forces by trying both the Army and Navy in actual practice."

Roosevelt did not bring on the war with Spain, of course, however much he tried. Cuban propaganda, sensationalist American newspapers, and jingoes in and outside Congress, combined to keep talk of war before the public. Still, through 1897, President McKinley refused to be stampeded, and the Spanish Government (which very much wished to avoid war) repeatedly gave in to American demands over the treatment of Cuba.

Then, early in 1898, two events occurred which made war virtually inevitable. First, a letter critical of McKinley, written by the Spanish minister in Washington, was stolen from the mails and reprinted in the American press. Trivial in itself, this blunder enraged many Americans. More important, the warship *Maine* blew up in a Cuban harbor with the loss of more than 200 sailors. Though not a shred of evidence has ever emerged to indicate that the Spanish were responsible, most Americans (abetted by much of the press) assumed that they were and demanded revenge. McKinley simply was not strong enough to stand against this pressure. On April 10 he asked Congress for what amounted to a declaration of war.

Well before the war began Roosevelt had told others that if it came he would not be content to remain in Washington. He was true to his word. By March he was beseeching New York state officials to permit him to raise a regiment of volunteers, which unit, he promised, would be "jim-dandy." That he had never served in the military, let alone seen combat, fazed Teddy not at all. He was greatly miffed when his generous offer was spurned.

Roosevelt, as usual, had other irons in the fire. Due to the minuscule size of the Regular Army, Congress had authorized the recruitment of three volunteer cavalry regiments from the Southwest. Because of his political connections, which he used to the utmost, Roosevelt was offered the command of one of these units. Modesty suddenly descended upon him. Estimating that it might take him a month or so to familiarize himself thoroughly with military procedures and tactics, T. R. asked that his friend, Captain Leonard Wood (at that time a military surgeon), be promoted to colonel and given command of the regiment. He would be satisfied with a mere lieutenant-colonelcy and would serve under Wood. Roosevelt's light could not be hidden, however, and from the start the First Volunteer Cavalry was known as "Roosevelt's Rough Riders."

Teddy was eager to get going. Quickly ordering the appropriate uniforms from Brooks Brothers (to ensure a proper fit), he began complaining that the war might be over before he could get into it—"it will be awful if we miss the fun." At last, in early May, he set out for San Antonio, Texas, where the First Volunteers were undergoing preliminary training. He arrived to the welcome of a brass band and "his boys."

And what a group it was. "Mingling among the cowboys and momentarily reformed bad men from the West," Henry Pringle has written, "were polo players and steeplechase riders from the Harvard, Yale, and Princeton clubs of New York City." Though from time to time Roosevelt protested against the carnival atmosphere which pervaded the camp, he enjoyed himself hugely. After one period of mounted drill, for instance, he told his men to "drink all the beer they want, which I will pay for" and had a few himself. Colonel Wood admonished Teddy for this kind of behavior, which the latter admitted was out of

place. "Sir," Roosevelt replied, "I consider myself the damnedest ass within ten miles of this camp."

Two weeks after Teddy arrived in San Antonio, the Rough Riders were ordered to report to the Tampa, Florida staging area for the expedition against Cuba. By this time they had been transformed from an undisciplined group in civilian clothes to an undisciplined group in uniform. Tampa was, if possible, even more chaotic than San Antonio had been. Units of Regulars, National Guard, and volunteers milled about with little over-all direction and inadequate facilities. Some units were without arms, others had arms but no ammunition, still others lacked uniforms, bedding, or tents. It was a mess. "No head," Roosevelt wrote angrily in his diary, "a breakdown of both the railroad and military systems of the country."

With an aroused public clamoring for action, the War Department ordered the expedition to sail despite its obvious lack of preparation. At this point the Rough Riders had what amounted to their first engagement of the war—against other American soldiers. Port Tampa lay about nine miles from Tampa, where the troops were quartered, with only a single track railway connecting them. The orders sent to individual regiments included no scheduling, so it was up to each unit to get to the port as best it could. A mad scramble ensued to commandeer whatever rolling stock was available. The Rough Riders were lucky enough to come upon an engine with some coal cars which they promptly seized. But the excitement was not yet over. Arriving at the port, Roosevelt and Wood found that the ship allotted to them was also designated for two regiments and there was not enough space for all three. As Teddy later recounted the episode:

Accordingly, I ran at full speed to our train; and leaving a strong guard with the baggage I double-quicked the rest of the regiment up to the boat just in time to board her as she came into the quay and then to hold her against the 2d Regulars and the 71st, who had arrived a little too late. . . . There was a good deal of expostulation, but we had possession.

It was a false alarm. On the eve of departure another message arrived from the War Department. "Wait until you get further orders before you sail," it read. "Answer quick." As things turned out the officers and men of the expeditionary force spent almost two weeks sweating and cursing in the tightly packed ships at anchor under the Florida sun. At last, on June 14, thirty-two steamers moved out of Port Tampa heading slowly toward Cuba. The Fifth Army Corps, as it was designated, consisted of two divisions and an independent brigade of infantry, a division of dismounted cavalry, four batteries of field artillery, and some auxiliary troops. The Rough Riders were aboard, of course, but like the other cavalry units they had nothing to ride. Because of the lack of space, the only animals brought along were horses for the officers and mules for carrying supplies.

Eventually the flotilla reached Cuba and landings were made virtually unopposed in several places. The debarkations resembled the disorder which had reigned at Tampa Bay. The men and equipment were brought ashore in helter-skelter fashion by an assortment of launches and other small boats. The animals were even less fortunate: They were driven off the sides of ships and left to fend for themselves. Some reached shore safely, others swam to watery graves. Once again, Teddy was unwilling to trust luck. Recognizing the captain of a small vessel which drew alongside as a man he had known in the Navy Department, Roosevelt directed that the ship be used solely for getting the Rough Riders ashore as quickly as possible. After spending weeks aboard what they referred to as "prison hulks," the men must have appreciated the initiative of their second-in-command.

The course of the Cuban campaign cannot be recounted in detail here. The most charitable single word to describe it is "muddled." The commander of the Fifth Corps was General William R. Shafter, a rather lethargic man who weighed well over 300 pounds. Suffering from the heat since arriving in Florida, Shafter, during the latter part of the fighting, had to be transported reclining on a barn door. His immediate subordinates were three other general officers, who seemed at least as much concerned with outdoing one another as with fighting the Spaniards. One of them, "Fighting Joe" Wheeler, had last seen combat as a Confederate officer during the Civil War. During moments of stress, it was reported, he became confused as to who his opponents were and several times referred to them as "those Yankees." Fortunately for the Americans, the Spanish were in even worse shape. Although some individual Spanish troops and units fought well, they were badly led and defeatism permeated the defending forces.

Once a semblance of order was created on the beach, preparations were made for the expedition's advance against the main target, the harbor city of Santiago, less than twenty miles west along the coastline. The only available overland route, however, swung inland through jungles which provided excellent concealment for defenders. The movement took place in fits and starts and was not without incident—and losses. The Spanish fought a brief rearguard action at a place called Las Guásimas, for instance, during which sixteen Americans were killed and another fifty wounded. The Rough Riders took part in this engagement, as did some regular units, and there is evidence to indicate that Wood and Roosevelt led their men into an ambush. In later years Roosevelt indignantly denied any such thing and claimed that "every one of the officers had full knowledge of where he would find the enemy." In any event, Teddy boasted, ". . . we wanted the first whack at the Spaniards and we got it."

Finally, by the end of June, American forces were within striking distance of Santiago. Their way was blocked by a series of fortifications and trenches located on a chain of hills surrounding the city—the most prominent of which was San Juan Hill. The difficulty in moving supplies and ammunition by pack animal along narrow jungle trails caused the troops to remain before Santiago for several days. The plan of attack was simple. One division would move several miles north to attack a stronghold at El Caney, the rest of the units would march head-on against the San Juan and nearby hills. Both assaults began on the morning of July 1.

From where they had grouped, American troops had to push through several miles of jungle and ford a stream before reaching clear ground in front of the hills. They began taking losses while still in the jungle. There were only two trails they could use and Spanish artillery had these zeroed in. One column had at its head an observation balloon pulled along by men holding guy ropes. It proved to be of little help to the Americans, but showed Spanish artillery-men exactly where the enemy was. Fortunately for the men underneath it, the bag was pierced several times and settled gently to the ground before it could cause even greater damage.

The jungle ended abruptly at a stream which ran along its edge roughly parallel to the Spanish lines on the ridges. Across the stream there were several hundred yards of meadowlands before reaching the slopes. As the troops emerged from the jungle, therefore, they were exposed to withering Spanish rifle fire from above. What little order there was broke down as the advancing columns began clogging up at the jungle's edge. Some units refused to cross the stream, others became disorganized as they tried to move through and get into position. The situation presented a cruel dilemma to American commanders. To attack with insufficient numbers of men would be to risk defeat. To wait until all units were deployed would mean exposing those who crossed the stream first to an extended period under the crippling fire. Finally, a little past noon and before elements in the rear had left the jungle, the assault began.

San Juan Hill was the main objective. Somewhat to the right and much closer to American lines lay Kettle Hill, assigned to the dismounted cavalry. Since Colonel Wood earlier had taken command of a brigade, Roosevelt now led the Rough Riders. This was what he had been waiting for, and he would not be found wanting. Showing complete disdain for enemy bullets, Teddy galloped around on his horse, Little Texas, exhorting his men to form up for attack. They were joined by elements from several other regiments, including black troops from the 10th Cavalry. Roosevelt waved his hat and the men moved for-

ward. "By this time we were all in the spirit of the thing and greatly excited by the charge," he wrote later, "the men cheering and running forward between shots. . . . I . . . galloped toward the hill. . . ."

According to his own account Roosevelt quickly moved ahead of the men, preceded only by his orderly, Henry Bardshar, "who had run ahead very fast in order to get better shots at the Spaniards. . . ." About forty yards from the crest Teddy encountered a wire fence and jumped off Little Texas, letting the horse run free. Almost immediately he saw Bardshar shoot down two Spaniards who emerged from the trenches. Soon Roosevelt and Bardshar were surrounded by the rest of the men as they swarmed over the hill, capturing or killing the few Spanish troops who had not retreated. The charge up Kettle Hill was over.

From their newly won position, Roosevelt and his men had an excellent view of the assault against San Juan Hill. Earlier artillery barrages had failed to cause much damage to the breastworks, and the black powder used in American guns produced smoke which drew Spanish counterfire. Now, however, three Gatling guns opened up with good effect. "They went b-r-r-r, like a lawn mower cutting grass over our trenches," a Spanish officer said later. "We could not stick a finger up when you fired without getting it cut off." Still the Spaniards held their positions as the ragged blue lines moved forward. Despite heavy losses, the Americans pushed doggedly up the hill. At last, just before they reached the top, the Spanish defenders fired a last volley and fled.

Beyond Kettle Hill and to the right of San Juan lay another ridge from which the enemy kept shooting. Rallying his men again, Roosevelt led them down the far side of Kettle, across the intervening valley, and up the slopes. "I was with Henry Bardshar, running up at the double," Teddy later recalled, "and two Spaniards leaped from the trenches and fired at us, not ten yards away. As they turned to run I closed in and fired twice, missing the first and killing the second. My revolver was from the sunken battleship *Maine*." Again the Americans drove the Spanish before them. When they took possession of these crests, "we found ourselves overlooking Santiago."

Although the Americans had won the day, the battle for Santiago was not yet over. The Spanish had about 16,000 men to defend the city, the Americans an equal number to take it. The latter were exhausted from their attacks and lacked reserves, food, and ammunition. By July 3, two days after the initial assaults, the Americans had lost 224 men killed and 1,370 wounded. The result was a stand-off. Spanish units did not attempt to break out of the ring; the Americans were in no shape to move against the city's defenses. "Tell the President for Heaven's sake to send us every regiment and above all every battery possible," Roosevelt wrote a friend. "We have won so far at a heavy cost, but the Spaniards fight very hard and charging these intrenchments against modern rifles is terrible. . . . We *must* have help— thousands of men, batteries, and *food* and ammunition." Fortunately, the Spanish launched no major counter attacks.

While the men dug themselves into the hills, the battle for Santiago was decided by another engagement—at sea. A Spanish fleet had been bottled up in Santiago Harbor for some time: Shafter's expedition was supposed to take the city, thereby forcing the Spanish ships to leave the harbor or surrender. At 9:30 A.M. on July 3, Spanish ships began coming out singly under the guns of the blockaders. It was a courageous but futile effort. Despite some bungling on the part of the U.S. Navy, all the opposing ships were sunk or disabled. After two weeks of negotiation Shafter received the surrender of Santiago, and less than a month after that the Spanish Government sued for peace.

Although the war had ended in complete victory for the United States, it came in for a great deal of criticism in the period following. Charges of incompetence were leveled against the top echelons, there were undignified exchanges between generals and admirals over who deserved credit for which victory, and the condition of the men returning from Cuba caused a public outcry. Many troops died from tropical illnesses, and still others from food poisoning caused by tainted meat.

It was probably for these reasons that Roosevelt's star came to shine so brightly. He had performed heroically, after all, and he was sufficiently subordinate in rank to escape any blame about the war's mismanagement.

Teddy himself was not loath to accept the limelight; indeed, he eagerly sought it. Almost immediately he began campaigning for the governorship of New York state and, lest anyone forget his exploits, kept the Rough Rider bugler at his side during his speeches. Roosevelt had other assets, of course, but being the "Hero of San Juan Hill" (he was not disposed to argue about which hill he had climbed) did him no harm. He had become fixed in the national mind as Colonel Teddy Roosevelt of the Rough Riders.

"I would honestly rather have my position of colonel," Roosevelt had told his men at their mustering-out ceremony, "than any other position on earth." No doubt he meant it at the time. As governor of New York, and later as President of the United States, he looked back fondly on his days in Cuba and the men who had served with him. In both positions he tried to accommodate as many as possible of the former Rough Riders who petitioned him for a job. His loyalty, if not his judgment, could scarcely be questioned. In one case he tried to have appointed as territorial marshal a man who, it was found, was serving time in prison for homicide. Undaunted, Teddy later tried to have the person installed as warden of the very prison in which he had been confined. "When I told this to John Hay," Roosevelt said, "he remarked (with a brutal absence of feeling) that he believed the proverb ran, 'Set a Rough Rider to catch a thief.'"

For once in his life, Teddy was at a loss for a reply.

Study Questions

1. What character traits inclined Roosevelt toward war? What events led the United States to war with Spain?

2. What sorts of men joined the Rough Riders?

3. What problems did the United States have mobilizing for war?

4. What role did the Battles of Kettle Hill and San Juan Hill play in the war in Cuba?

5. How did Roosevelt capitalize on his newly won fame?

Bibliography

The best overview of the Spanish-American War is David Trask, *The War with Spain in 1898* (1981). Shorter, but still useful is Frank Freidel, *The Splendid Little War* (1958). For a provocative study of the intersection between gender studies and military history, see Kristin Hoganson, *Fighting for American Manhood, How Gender Politics Provoked the Spanish-American and Philippine-American Wars* (2000). Theodore Roosevelt's own account of his moments of glory is *The Rough Riders* (1899). Among the more readable biographies of Roosevelt are Edmund Morris, *The Rise of Theodore Roosevelt* (1979) and his more recent *Theodore Rex* (2001), and David McCullough, *Mornings on Horseback* (1981). More scholarly biographies are G. Wallace Chessman, *Theodore Roosevelt and the Politics of Power* (1969) and Howard K. Beals, *Theodore Roosevelt and the Rise of America to World Power* (1956). On the war also see Gerald F. Linderman, *The Mirror of War: American Society and the Spanish-American War* (1974) and H. Wayne Morgan, *America's Road to Empire* (1965). Also see Stuart C. Miller, *"Benevolent Assimilation": The American Conquest of the Philippines, 1899–1903* (1982).

READING 8

★ ★ ★

Living and Dying in Packingtown, Chicago from The Jungle

Upton Sinclair

In the late fall of 1904, Upton Sinclair, a young ambitious novelist imbued with a zealous sense of socialism, traveled to Chicago to gather information about the horrors and abuses of the meatpacking industry. For the next seven weeks, as a cold fall gave way to a brutal winter, Sinclair lived in the workers' ghetto of Packingtown, talked with workers, and studied the meatpacking industry.

On Christmas Day of 1904, he began writing *The Jungle,* the story of Jurgis Rudkus. A Lithuanian immigrant of great strength, Rudkus came to America full of hope—only to be used, abused, and discarded by the unfeeling powers of Packingtown. Sinclair wrote frantically for three months, stopping only occasionally to eat or sleep. He poured all his emotions into Rudkus's story, hoping to show Americans how evil the industry—and by extension, capitalism—had become. He recorded the stench and unhealthy conditions of Packingtown and the dangers of working in the packinghouses. Of the work, one historian wrote, "Each job had its own dangers: the dampness and cold of the packing rooms and hide cellar, the sharp blade of the beef boner's knife, the noxious dust of the wood department and fertilizer plant, the wild charge of a half-crazed steer on the killing floor." The following selection from *The Jungle* describes some of the working and living conditions in Packingtown.

During this time that Jurgis was looking for work occurred the death of little Kristoforas, one of the children of Teta Elzbieta. Both Kristoforas and his brother, Juozapas, were cripples, the latter having lost one leg by having it run over, and Kristoforas having congenital dislocation of the hip, which made it impossible for him ever to walk. He was the last of Teta Elzbieta's children, and perhaps he had been intended by nature to let her know that she had had enough. At any rate he was wretchedly sick and undersized; he had the rickets, and though he was over three years old, he was no bigger than an ordinary child of one. All day long he would crawl around the floor in a filthy little dress, whining and fretting; because the floor was full of draughts he was always catching cold, and snuffling because his nose ran. This made him a nuisance, and a source of endless trouble in the family. For his mother, with unnatural perversity, loved him best of all her children, and made a perpetual fuss over him—would let him do anything undisturbed, and would burst into tears when his fretting drove Jurgis wild.

And now he died. Perhaps it was the smoked sausage he had eaten that morning—which may have been made out of some tubercular pork that was condemned as unfit for export. At any rate, an hour after eating it, the child had begun to cry with pain, and in another hour he was rolling about on the floor in convulsions. Little Kotrina, who was all alone with him, ran out screaming for help, and after a while a doctor came, but not until Kristoforas had howled his last howl. No one was really sorry about this except poor Elzbieta, who was inconsolable. Jurgis announced that so far as he was concerned the child would have to be buried by the city, since they had no money for a funeral; and at this the poor woman almost went out of her senses, wringing her hands and screaming with grief and despair. Her child to be buried in a pauper's grave! And her stepdaughter to stand by and hear it said without protesting! It

Upton Sinclair, "Living and Dying in Packingtown, Chicago." From Upton Sinclair, *The Jungle.* Chicago, 1905.

was enough to make Ona's father rise up out of his grave to rebuke her! If it had come to this, they might as well give up at once, and be buried all of them together! . . . In the end Marija said that she would help with ten dollars; and Jurgis being still obdurate, Elzbieta went in tears and begged the money from the neighbors, and so little Kristoforas had a mass and a hearse with white plumes on it, and a tiny plot in a graveyard with a wooden cross to mark the place. The poor mother was not the same for months after that; the mere sight of the floor where little Kristoforas had crawled about would make her weep. He had never had a fair chance, poor little fellow, she would say. He had been handicapped from birth. If only she had heard about it in time, so that she might have had the great doctor to cure him of his lameness! . . . Some time ago, Elzbieta was told, a Chicago billionaire had paid a fortune to bring a great European surgeon over to cure his little daughter of the same disease from which Kristoforas had suffered. And because this surgeon had to have bodies to demonstrate upon, he announced that he would treat the children of the poor, a piece of magnanimity over which the papers became quite eloquent. Elzbieta, alas, did not read the papers, and no one had told her; but perhaps it was as well, for just then they would not have had the car-fare to spare to go every day to wait upon the surgeon, nor for that matter anybody with the time to take the child.

All this while he was seeking for work, there was a dark shadow hanging over Jurgis; as if a savage beast were lurking somewhere in the pathway of his life, and he knew it, and yet could not help approaching the place. There are all stages of being out of work in Packingtown, and he faced in dread the prospect of reaching the lowest. There is a place that waits for the lowest man—the fertilizer-plant!

The men would talk about it in awe-stricken whispers. Not more than one in ten had ever really tried it; the other nine had contented themselves with hearsay evidence and a peep through the door. There were some things worse than even starving to death. They would ask Jurgis if he had worked there yet, and if he meant to; and Jurgis would debate the matter with himself. As poor as they were and making all the sacrifices that they were, would he dare to refuse any sort of work that was offered to him, be it as horrible as ever it could? Would he dare to go home and eat bread that had been earned by Ona, weak and complaining as she was, knowing that he had been given a chance, and had not had the nerve to take it?—And yet he might argue that way with himself all day, and one glimpse into the fertilizer-works would send him away again shuddering. He was a man, and he would do his duty; he went and made application—but surely he was not also required to hope for success.

The fertilizer-works of Durham's lay away from the rest of the plant. Few visitors ever saw them, and the few who did would come out looking like Dante, of whom the peasants declared that he had been into hell. To this part of the yards came all the "tankage" and waste products of all sorts; here they dried out the bones—and in suffocating cellars where the daylight never came you might see men and women and children bending over whirling machines and sawing bits of bones into all sorts of shapes, breathing their lungs full of the fine dust, and doomed to die, every one of them, within a certain definite time. Here they made the blood into albumen, and made other foul-smelling things into things still more foul-smelling. In the corridors and caverns where it was done you might lose yourself as in the great caves of Kentucky. In the dust and the steam the electric lights would shine like far-off twinkling stars—red and blue, green and purple stars, according to the color of the mist and the brew from which it came. For the odors in these ghastly charnel-houses there may be words in Lithuanian, but there are none in English. The person entering would have to summon his courage as for a cold-water plunge. He would go on like a man swimming under water; he would put his handkerchief over his face, and begin to cough and choke; and then, if he were still obstinate, he would find his head beginning to ring, and the veins in his forehead to throb, until finally he would be assailed by an overpowering blast of ammonia fumes, and would turn and run for his life, and come out half-dazed.

On top of this were the rooms where they dried the "tankage," the mass of brown stringy stuff that was left after the waste portions of the carcasses had had the lard and tallow dried out of them. This dried material they would then grind to a fine powder, and after they had mixed it up well with a mysterious but inoffensive brown rock which they brought in and ground up by the hundreds of carloads for that purpose, the substance was ready to be put into bags and sent out to the world as any one of a hundred different brands of standard bone-phosphate. And then the farmer in Maine or California or Texas would buy this, at say twenty-five dollars a ton, and plant it with his corn; and for several days after the operation the fields would have a strong odor, and the farmer and his wagon and the very horses that had hauled it would all have it too. In Packingtown the fertilizer is pure, instead of being a flavoring, and instead of a ton or so spread on several acres under the open sky, there are hundreds and thousands of tons of it in one building, heaped here and there in haystack piles, covering the floor several inches deep, and filling the air with a choking dust that becomes a blinding sandstorm when the wind stirs.

It was to this building that Jurgis came daily, as if dragged by an unseen hand. The month of May was an exceptionally cool one, and his secret prayers were granted; but early in June there came a record-breaking hot spell, and after that there were men wanted in the fertilizer-mill.

The boss of the grinding room had come to know Jurgis by this time, and had marked him for a likely man; and so when he came to the door about two o'clock this breathless hot day, he felt a sudden spasm of pain shoot through him—the boss beckoned to him! In ten minutes more Jurgis had pulled off his coat and overshirt, and set his teeth together and gone to work. Here was one more difficulty for him to meet and conquer!

His labor took him about one minute to learn. Before him was one of the vents of the mill in which the fertilizer was being ground—rushing forth in a great brown river, with a spray of the finest dust flung forth in clouds. Jurgis was given a shovel, and along with half a dozen others it was his task to shovel this fertilizer into carts. That others were at work he knew by the sound, and by the fact that he sometimes collided with them; otherwise they might as well not have been there, for in the blinding dust-storm a man could not see six feet in front of his face. When he had filled one cart he had to grope around him until another came, and if there was none on hand he continued to grope till one arrived. In five minutes he was, of course, a mass of fertilizer from head to feet; they gave him a sponge to tie over his mouth, so that he could breathe, but the sponge did not prevent his lips and eyelids from caking up with it and his ears from filling solid. He looked like a brown ghost at twilight—from hair to shoes he became the color of the building and of everything in it, and for that matter a hundred yards outside it. The building had to be left open, and when the wind blew Durham and Company lost a great deal of fertilizer.

Working in his shirt-sleeves, and with the thermometer at over a hundred, the phosphates soaked in through every pore of Jurgis's skin, and in five minutes he had a headache, and in fifteen was almost dazed. The blood was pounding his brain like an engine's throbbing; there was a frightful pain in the top of his skull, and he could hardly control his hands. Still, with the memory of his four months' siege behind him, he fought on, in a frenzy of determination; and half an hour later he began to vomit—he vomited until it seemed as if his innards must be torn to shreds. A man could get used to the fertilizer-mill, the boss had said, if he would only make up his mind to it; but Jurgis now began to see that it was a question of making up his stomach.

At the end of that day of horror, he could scarcely stand. He had to catch himself now and then, and lean against a building and get his bearings. Most of the men, when they came out, made straight for a saloon—they seem to place fertilizer and rattlesnake poison in one class. But Jurgis was

too ill to think of drinking—he could only make his way to the street and stagger on to a car. He had a sense of humor, and later on, when he became an old hand, he used to think it fun to board a streetcar and see what happened. Now, however, he was too ill to notice it—how the people in the car began to gasp and sputter, to put their handkerchiefs to their noses, and transfix him with furious glances. Jurgis only knew that a man in front of him immediately got up and gave him a seat; and that half a minute later the two people on each side of him got up; and that in a full minute the crowded car was nearly empty—those passengers who could not get room on the platform having gotten out to walk.

Of course Jurgis had made his home a miniature fertilizer-mill a minute after entering. The stuff was half an inch deep in his skin—his whole system was full of it, and it would have taken a week not merely of scrubbing, but of vigorous exercise, to get it out of him. As it was, he could be compared with nothing known to men, save that newest discovery of the savants, a substance which emits energy for an unlimited time, without being itself in the least diminished in power. He smelt so that he made all food at the table taste, and set the whole family to vomiting; for himself it was three days before he could keep anything upon his stomach—he might wash his hands, and use a knife and fork, but were not his mouth and throat filled with the poison?

And still Jurgis stuck it out! In spite of splitting headaches he would stagger down to the plant and take up his stand once more, and begin to shovel in the blinding clouds of dust. And so at the end of the week he was a fertilizer man for life—he was able to eat again, and though his head never stopped aching, it ceased to be so bad that he could not work.

So there passed another summer. It was a summer of prosperity, all over the country, and the country ate generously of packinghouse products, and there was plenty of work for all the family, in spite of the packers' efforts to keep a superfluity of labor. They were again able to pay their debts and to begin to save a little sum; but

Chicago's meatpacking industry grew up with little or no government control. These sausage makers at Armour & Co. worked in extreme temperatures and without adequate ventilation, causing many to faint or to vomit from the stench.

there were one or two sacrifices they considered too heavy to be made for long—it was too bad that the boys should have to sell papers at their age. It was utterly useless to caution them and plead with them; quite without knowing it, they were taking on the tone of their new environment. They were learning to swear in voluble English; they were learning to pick up cigar-stumps and smoke them, to pass hours of their time gambling with pennies and dice and cigarette-cards; they were learning the location of all the houses of prostitution on the "Levée," and the names of the "madames" who kept them, and the days when they gave their state banquets, which the police captains and the big politicians all attended. If a visiting "country-customer" were to ask them, they could show him which was "Hinkydink's" famous saloon, and could even point out to him by name the different gamblers and thugs and "hold-up men" who made the place their headquarters. And worse yet, the boys were getting out of the habit of coming home at night. What was the use, they would ask, of wasting time and energy and a possible car-fare riding out to the stockyards every night when the weather was pleasant and they could crawl under a truck or into an empty doorway and sleep exactly as well? So long as they brought home a half dollar for each day, what mattered it when they brought it? But Jurgis declared that from this to ceasing to come at all would not be a very long step, and so it was decided that Vilimas and Nikalojus should return to school in the fall, and that instead Elzbieta should go out and get some work, her place at home being taken by her younger daughter.

Little Kotrina was like most children of the poor, prematurely made old; she had to take care of her little brother, who was a cripple, and also of the baby; she had to cook the meals and wash the dishes and clean house, and have supper ready when the workers came home in the evening. She was only thirteen, and small for her age, but she did all this without a murmur; and her mother went out, and after trudging a couple of days about the yards, settled down as a servant of a "sausage-machine."

Elzbieta was used to working, but she found this change a hard one, for the reason that she had to stand motionless upon her feet from seven o'clock in the morning till half-past twelve, and again from one till half-past five. For the first days it seemed to her that she could not stand it—she suffered almost as much as Jurgis had from the fertilizer—and would come out at sundown with her head fairly reeling. Besides this, she was working in one of the dark holes, by the electric light, and the dampness, too, was deadly—there were always puddles of water on the floor, and a sickening odor of moist flesh in the room. The people who worked here followed the ancient custom of nature, whereby the ptarmigan is the color of dead leaves in the fall and of snow in winter, and the chameleon, who is black when he lies upon a stump and turns green when he moves to a leaf. The men and women who worked in this department were precisely the color of the "fresh country sausage" they made.

The sausage-room was an interesting place to visit, for two or three minutes, and provided that you did not look at the people; the machines were perhaps the most wonderful things in the entire plant. Presumably sausages were once chopped and stuffed by hand, and if so it would be interesting to know how many workers had been displaced by these inventions. On one side of the room were the hoppers, into which men shoveled loads of meat and wheelbarrows full of spices; in these great bowls were whirling knifes that made two thousand revolutions a minute, and when the meat was ground fine and adulterated with potato-flour, and well mixed with water, it was forced to the stuffing-machines on the other side of the room. The latter were tended by women; there was a sort of spout, like the nozzle of a hose, and one of the women would take a long string of "casing" and put the end over the nozzle and then work the whole thing on, as one works on the finger of a tight glove. This string would be twenty or thirty feet long, but the woman would have it all on in a jiffy; and when she had several on, she would press a lever, and a stream of sausage-meat would be shot out, taking the casing with it as it came. Thus one might

stand and see appear, miraculously born from the machine, a wriggling snake of sausage of incredible length. In front was a big pan which caught these creatures, and two more women who seized them as fast as they appeared and twisted them into links. This was for the uninitiated the most perplexing work of all; for all that the woman had to give was a single turn of the wrist; and in some way she contrived to give it so that instead of an endless chain of sausages, one after another, there grew under her hands a bunch of strings, all dangling from a single centre. It was quite like the feat of a prestidigitator—for the woman worked so fast that the eye could literally not follow her, and there was only a mist of motion, and tangle after tangle of sausages appearing. In the midst of the mist, however, the visitor would suddenly notice the tense set face, with the two wrinkles graven in the forehead, and the ghastly pallor of the cheeks; and then he would suddenly recollect that it was time he was going on. The woman did not go on; she stayed right there—hour after hour, day after day, year after year, twisting sausage-links and racing with death. It was piece-work, and she was apt to have a family to keep alive; and stern and ruthless economic laws had arranged it that she could only do this by working just as she did, with all her soul upon her work, and with never an instant for a glance at the well-dressed ladies and gentlemen who came to stare at her, as at some wild beast in a menagerie.

With one member trimming beef in a cannery, and another working in a sausage factory, the family had a first-hand knowledge of the great majority of Packingtown swindles. For it was the custom, as they found, whenever meat was so spoiled that it could not be used for anything else, either to can it or else to chop it up into sausage. With what had been told them by Jonas, who had worked in the pickle-rooms, they could now study the whole of the spoiled-meat industry on the inside, and read a new and grim meaning into that old Packingtown jest—that they use everything of the pig except the squeal.

Jonas had told them how the meat that was taken out of pickle would often be found sour, and how they would rub it up with soda to take away the smell, and sell it to be eaten on free-lunch counters; also of all the miracles of chemistry which they performed, giving to any sort of meat, fresh or salted, whole or chopped, any color and any flavor and any odor they chose. In the pickling of hams they had an ingenious apparatus, by which they saved time and increased the capacity of the plant—a machine consisting of a hollow needle attached to a pump; by plunging this needle into the meat and working with his foot, a man could fill a ham with pickle in a few seconds. And yet, in spite of this, there would be hams found spoiled, some of them with an odor so bad that a man could hardly bear to be in the room with them. To pump into these the packers had a second and much stronger pickle which destroyed the odor—a process known to the workers as "giving them thirty percent." Also, after the hams had been smoked, there would be found some that had gone to the bad. Formerly these had been sold as "Number Three Grade," but later on some ingenious person had hit upon a new device, and now they would extract the bone, about which the bad part generally lay, and insert in the hole a white-hot iron. After this invention there was no longer Number One, Two, and Three Grade—there was only Number One Grade. The packers were always originating such schemes—they had what they called "boneless hams," which were all the odds and ends of pork stuffed into casing; and "California hams," which were the shoulders, with big knuckle-joints, and nearly all the meat cut out; and fancy "skinned hams," which were made of the oldest hogs, whose skins were so heavy and coarse that no one would buy them—that is, until they had been cooked and chopped fine and labelled "head cheese"!

It was only when the whole ham was spoiled that it came into the department of Elzbieta. Cut up by the two-thousand-revolutions-a-minute fly-ers, and mixed with half a ton of other meat, no odor that ever was in a ham could make any difference. There was never the least attention paid to what was cut up for sausage; there would

come all the way back from Europe old sausage that had been rejected, and that was mouldy and white—it would be dosed with borax and glycerine, and dumped into the hoppers, and made over again for home consumption. There would be meat that had tumbled out on the floor, in the dirt and sawdust, where the workers had tramped and spit uncounted billions of consumption germs. There would be meat stored in great piles in rooms; and the water from leaky roofs would drip over it, and thousands of rats would race about on it. It was too dark in these storage places to see well, but a man could run his hand over these piles of meat and sweep off handfuls of the dried dung of rats. These rats were nuisances, and the packers would put poisoned bread out for them; they would die, and then rats, bread, and meat would go into the hoppers together. This is no fairy story and no joke; the meat would be shovelled into carts, and the man who did the shovelling would not trouble to lift out a rat even when he saw one—there were things that went into the sausage in comparison with which a poisoned rat was a tidbit. There was no place for the men to wash their hands before they ate their dinner, and so they made a practice of washing them in the water that was to be ladled into the sausage. There were the butt-ends of smoked meat, and the scraps of corned beef, and all the odds and ends of the waste of the plants, that would be dumped into old barrels in the cellar and left there. Under the system of rigid economy which the packers enforced, there were some jobs that it only paid to do once in a long time, and among these was the cleaning out of the waste-barrels. Every spring they did it; and in the barrels would be dirt and rust and old nails and stale water—and cart load after cart load of it would be taken up and dumped into the hoppers with fresh meat, and sent out to the public's breakfast. Some of it they would make into "smoked" sausage—but as the smoking took time, and was therefore expensive, they would call upon their chemistry department, and preserve it with borax and color it with gelatine to make it brown. All of their sausage came out of the same bowl, but when they came to wrap it they would stamp some of it "special," and for this they would charge two cents more a pound.

Such were the new surroundings in which Elzbieta was placed, and such was the work she was compelled to do. It was stupefying, brutalizing work; it left her no time to think, no strength for anything. She was part of the machine she tended, and every faculty that was not needed for the machine was doomed to be crushed out of existence. There was only one mercy about the cruel grind—that it gave her the gift of insensibility. Little by little she sank into a torpor—she fell silent. She would meet Jurgis and Ona in the evening, and the three would walk home together, often without saying a word. Ona, too, was falling into the habit of silence—Ona, who had once gone about singing like a bird. She was sick and miserable, and often she would barely have strength enough to drag herself home. And there they would eat what they had to eat, and afterwards, because there was only their misery to talk of, they would crawl into bed and fall into a stupor and never stir until it was time to get up again, and dress by candlelight, and go back to the machines. They were so numbed that they did not even suffer much from hunger, now; only the children continued to fret when the food ran short.

Yet the soul of Ona was not dead—the souls of none of them were dead, but only sleeping; and now and then they would waken, and these were cruel times. The gates of memory would roll open—old joys would stretch out their arms to them, old hopes and dreams would call to them, and they would stir beneath the burden that lay upon them, and feel its forever immeasurable weight. They could not even cry out beneath it; but anguish would seize them, more dreadful than the agony of death. It was a thing scarcely to be spoken—a thing never spoken by all the world, that will not know its own defeat.

They were beaten; they had lost the game, they were swept aside. It was not less tragic be-cause it was so sordid, because it had to do with wages and grocery bills and rents. They had dreamed of freedom; of a chance to look about them and learn something; to be decent and clean, to see their child grow up to be strong. And now it was all gone—it would never be! They had played the game and they had lost. Six years more of toil they had to face before they could expect the least respite, the cessation of the payments upon the house; and how cruelly certain it was that they could never stand six years of such a life as they were living! They were lost, they were going down—and there was no deliverance for them, no hope; for all the help it gave them the vast city in which they lived might have been an ocean waste, a wilderness, a desert, a tomb. So often this mood would come to Ona, in the night-time, when something wakened her; she would lie, afraid of the beating of her own heart, fronting the blood-red eyes of the old primeval terror of life. Once she cried aloud, and woke Jurgis, who was tired and cross. After that she learned to weep silently—their moods so seldom came together now! It was as if their hopes were buried in separate graves.

Jurgis, being a man, had troubles of his own. There was another spectre following him. He had never spoken of it, nor would he allow any one else to speak of it—he had never acknowledged its existence to himself. Yet the battle with it took all the manhood that he had—and once or twice, alas, a little more. Jurgis had discovered drink.

He was working in the steaming pit of hell; day after day, week after week—until now there was not an organ of his body that did its work without pain, until the sound of ocean breakers echoed in his head day and night, and the buildings swayed and danced before him as he went down the street. And from all the unending horror of this there was a respite, a deliverance—he could drink! He could forget the pain, he could slip off the burden; he would see clearly again, he would be master of his brain, of his thoughts, of his will. His dead self would stir in him, and he would find himself laughing and cracking jokes with his companions—he would be a man again, and master of his life.

It was not an easy thing for Jurgis to take more than two or three drinks. With the first drink he could eat a meal, and he could persuade himself that that was economy; with the second he could eat another meal—but there would come a time when he could eat no more, and then to pay for a drink was an unthinkable extravagance, a defiance of the age-long instincts of his hunger-haunted class. One day, however, he took the plunge, and drank up all that he had in his pockets, and went home half "piped," as the men phrase it. He was happier than he had been in a year; and yet, because he knew that the happiness would not last, he was savage, too—with those who would wreck it, and with the world, and with his life; and then again, beneath this, he was sick with the shame of himself. Afterward, when he saw the despair of his family, and reckoned up the money he had spent, the tears came into his eyes, and he began the long battle with the spectre.

It was a battle that had no end, that never could have one. But Jurgis did not realize that very clearly; he was not given much time for reflection. He simply knew that he was always fighting. Steeped in misery and despair as he was, merely to walk down the street was to be put upon the rack. There was surely a saloon on the corner—perhaps on all four corners, and some in the middle of the block as well; and each one stretched out a hand to him—each one had a personality of its own, allurements unlike any other. Going and coming—before sunrise and after dark—there was warmth and a glow of light, and the steam of hot food, and perhaps music, or a friendly face, and a word of good cheer. Jurgis developed a fondness for having Ona on his arm whenever he went out on the street, and he would hold her tightly, and walk fast. It was pitiful to have Ona know of this—it drove him wild to think of it; the thing was not fair, for Ona had never tasted drink, and so could not understand. Sometimes, in desperate hours, he would find himself wishing that she might learn what it was,

so that he need not be ashamed in her presence. They might drink together, and escape from the horror—escape for a while, come what would.

So there came a time when nearly all the conscious life of Jurgis consisted of a struggle with the craving for liquor. He would have ugly moods, when he hated Ona and the whole family, because they stood in his way. He was a fool to have married; he had tied himself down, and made himself a slave. It was all because he was a married man that he was compelled to stay in the yards; if it had not been for that he might have gone off like Jonas, and to hell with the packers. There were single men in the fertilizer-mill—and those few were working only for a chance to escape. Meantime, too, they had something to think about while they worked—they had the memory of the last time they had been drunk, and the hope of the time when they would be drunk again. As for Jurgis, he expected to bring home every penny; he could not even go with the men at noontime—he was supposed to sit down and eat his dinner on a pile of fertilizer dust.

This was not always his mood, of course; he still loved his family. But just now was a time of trial. Poor little Antanas, for instance—who had never failed to win him with a smile—little Antanas was not smiling just now, being a mass of fiery red pimples. He had had all the diseases that babies are heir to, in quick succession—scarlet fever, mumps, and whooping-cough in the first year, and now he was down with the measles. There was no one to attend him but Kotrina; there was no doctor to help him because they were too poor, and children did not die of the measles—at least not often. Now and then Kotrina would find time to sob over his woes, but for the greater part of the time he had to be left alone, barricaded upon the bed. The floor was full of draughts, and if he caught cold he would die. At night he was tied down, lest he should kick the covers off him, while the family lay in their stupor of exhaustion. He would lie and scream for hours, almost in convulsions; and then when he was worn out, he would lie whimpering and wailing in his torment. He was burning up with fever, and his eyes were running sores; in the daytime he was a thing uncanny and impish to behold, a plaster of pimples and sweat, a great purple lump of misery.

Yet all this was not really cruel as it sounds, for sick as he was, little Antanas was the least unfortunate member of that family. He was quite able to bear his sufferings—it was as if he had all these complaints to show what a prodigy of health he was. He was the child of his parents' youth and joy; he grew up like the conjurer's rose bush, and all the world was his oyster. In general, he toddled around the kitchen all day with a lean and hungry look—the portion of the family's allowance that fell to him was not enough, and he was unrestrainable in his demand for more. Antanas was but little over a year old, and already no one but his father could manage him.

It seemed as if he had taken all of his mother's strength—had left nothing for those that might come after him. Ona was with child again now, and it was a dreadful thing to contemplate; even Jurgis, dumb and despairing as he was, could not but understand that yet other agonies were on the way, and shudder at the thought of them.

For Ona was visibly going to pieces. In the first place she was developing a cough, like the one that had killed old Dede Antanas. She had had a trace of it ever since that fatal morning when the greedy street-car corporation had turned her out into the rain; but now it was beginning to grow serious, and to wake her up at night. Even worse than that was the fearful nervousness from which she suffered; she would have frightful headaches and fits of aimless weeping; and sometimes she would come home at night shuddering and moaning, and would fling herself down upon the bed and burst into tears. Several times she was quite beside herself and hysterical; and then Jurgis would go half mad with fright. Elzbieta would explain to him that it could not be helped, that woman was subject to such things when she was pregnant; but he was hardly to be persuaded, and would beg and plead to know what had happened. She had never been like this before, he would argue—it was monstrous and unthinkable. It was the life she had to live, the accursed work she had to do, that was killing her by inches. She was not fitted for it—no woman was fitted for it, no woman ought to be allowed to do such work; if the world could not keep them alive any other way it ought to kill them at once and be done with it. They ought not to marry, to have children; no working-man ought to marry—if he, Jurgis, had known what a woman was like, he would have had his eyes torn out first. So he would carry on, becoming half hysterical himself, which was an unbearable thing to see in a big man; Ona would pull herself together and fling herself into his arms, begging him to stop, to be still, that she would be better, it would be all right. So she would lie and sob out her grief upon his shoulder, while he gazed at her, as helpless as a wounded animal, the target of unseen enemies.

Study Questions

1. What was health care like for children in Packingtown?

2. What sort of men worked in the fertilizer plants? What were the hazards of the job?

3. How did the constant demand for money affect families?

4. What were the abuses of the "spoiled-meat" industry?

5. What response was Upton Sinclair hoping to achieve with *The Jungle?*

Bibliography

On the life of Upton Sinclair, see Floyd Dell, *Upton Sinclair: A Study in Social Protest* (1927); Jon Yoder, *Upton Sinclair* (1975); Leon Harris, *Upton Sinclair, American Rebel* (1975); and his own *The Autobiography of Upton Sinclair* (1962). Three good books on the literature of the period are Daniel Aaron, *Writers of the Left* (1969); James Burkhart Gilbert, *Writers and Partisans: A History of Literary Radicalism in America* (1968); and Larzer Ziff, *The American 1890s: Life and Times of a Lost Generation* (1966). On the meatpacking industry, Packingtown, and the lives of the workers, consult Louis Carroll Wade, *Chicago's Pride: The Stockyards, Packingtown, and Environs in the Nineteenth Century* (1987) and James R. Barrett, *Work and Community in the Jungle: Chicago's Packinghouse Workers* (1988).

★ ★ ★

Rose Schneiderman and the Triangle Shirtwaist Fire

Bonnie Mitelman

The progress Americans made during the Progressive Era depended on one's perspective. For middle-class Americans, progress was everywhere visible. Real income rose and the government worked to ensure order and efficiency in the industrial world. For their part, most large industrialists cooperated with the government's effort to impose order, which often resulted in the elimination of bothersome competition. For example, leading meatpackers supported the Meat Inspection Act of 1906. The act raised inspection standards, thereby driving out small competitors and guaranteeing the quality of American meat on the competitive world market.

America's working class, however, had reason to question the nature of the "progress" that was being made. The men and women who labored in industrial America often performed uncreative, repetitive tasks at a pace set by machines. Possibly worse than the monotony of industrial life was the danger of it. Machines were blind and uncaring; they showed no sympathy for tired or bored workers who allowed their fingers to move too close to moving cogs. Injuries were common, and far too often industrialists were as unsympathetic as their machines. And for most unskilled workers, labor unions were weak and unrecognized by leading industrialists and manufacturers. In the following essay, Bonnie Mitelman discusses the 1911 Triangle Waist Company fire, a tragedy in which 146 workers died. The fire and its results raise serious questions about the extent and nature of progress during the early twentieth century.

On Saturday afternoon, March 25, 1911, in New York City's Greenwich Village, a small fire broke out in the Triangle Waist Company, just as the 500 shirtwaist employees were quitting for the day. People rushed about, trying to get out, but they found exits blocked and windows to the fire escape rusted shut. They panicked.

As the fire spread and more and more were trapped, some began to jump, their hair and clothing afire, from the eighth and ninth floor windows. Nets that firemen held for them tore apart at the impact of the falling bodies. By the time it was over, 146 workers had died, most of them young Jewish women.

A United Press reporter, William Shepherd, witnessed the tragedy and reported, "I looked upon the heap of dead bodies and I remembered these girls were the shirtwaist makers. I remembered their great strike of last year in which these same girls had demanded more sanitary conditions and more safety precautions in the shops. These dead bodies were the answer."

The horror of that fire touched the entire Lower East Side ghetto community, and there was a profuse outpouring of sympathy. But it was Rose Schneiderman, an immigrant worker with a spirit of social justice and a powerful way with words, who is largely credited with translating the ghetto's emotional reaction into meaningful, widespread action. Six weeks following the tragedy, and after years of solid groundwork, with one brilliant, well-timed speech, she was able to inspire the support of wealthy uptown New Yorkers and to swing public opinion to the side of the labor movement, enabling concerned civic, religious, and labor leaders to mobilize their efforts for desperately needed safety and industrial reforms.

The Triangle fire, and the deaths of so many helpless workers, seemed to trigger in Rose Schneiderman an intense realization that there was absolutely nothing or no one to help working women except a strong union movement.

With fierce determination, and the dedication, influence, and funding of many other people as well, she battled to regulate hours, wages, and safety standards and to abolish the sweatshop system. In so doing, she brought dignity and human rights to all workers.

The dramatic "uprising of the 20,000" of 1909-1910, in which thousands of immigrant girls and women in the shirtwaist industry had endured three long winter months of a general strike to protest deplorable working conditions, had produced some immediate gains for working women. There had been agreements for shorter working hours, increased wages, and even safety reforms, but there had not been formal recognition of their union. At Triangle, for example, the girls had gained a 52-hour-week, a 12-15 percent wage increase, and promises to end the grueling subcontracting system. But they had not gained the only instrument on which they could depend for lasting change: a viable trade union. This was to have disastrous results, for in spite of the few gains that they seemed to have made, the workers won no rights or bargaining power at all. In fact, "The company dealt only with its contractors. It felt no responsibility for the girls."

There were groups as well as individuals who realized the workers' importance, but their attempts to change the situation accomplished little despite long years of hard work. The Women's Trade Union League and the International Ladies' Garment Workers' Union, through the efforts of Mary Dreier, Helen Marot, Leonora O'Reilly, Pauline Newman, and Rose Schneiderman had struggled unsuccessfully for improved conditions: the futility that the union organizers were feeling in late 1910 is reflected in the WTUL minutes of December 5 of that year.

A scant eight months after their historic waist-makers' strike, and three months before the deadly Triangle fire, a Mrs. Malkiel (no doubt Theresa Serber Malkiel, who wrote the legendary account of the strike, *The Diary of a Shirtwaist Striker: A Story of the Shirtwaist Makers' Strike in New York*), is reported to have come before the League to urge action after a devastating fire in Newark, New Jersey killed twenty-five working women. Mrs. Malkiel attributed their loss to the greed and negligence of the owners and the proper authorities. The WTUL subsequently demanded an investigation of all factory buildings and it elected an investigation committee from the League to cooperate with similar committees from other organizations.

The files of the WTUL contain complaint after complaint about unsafe factory conditions; many were filled out by workers afraid to sign their names for fear of being fired had their employers seen the forms. They describe factories with locked doors, no fire escapes, and barred windows. The *New York Times* carried an article which reported that fourteen factories were found to have no fire escapes, twenty-three had locked doors, and seventy-eight had obstructed fire escapes. In all, according to the article, 99 percent of the factories investigated in New York were found to have serious fire hazards.

Yet no action was taken.

It was the Triangle fire that emphasized, spectacularly and tragically, the deplorable safety and sanitary conditions of the garment workers. The tragedy focused attention upon the ghastly factories in which most immigrants worked; there was no longer any question about what the strikers had meant when they talked about safety and sanitary reform, and about social and economic justice.

The grief and frustration of the shirtwaist strikers were expressed by one of them, Rose Safran, after the fire: "If the union had won we would have been safe. Two of our demands were for adequate fire escapes and for open doors from the factories to the street. But the bosses defeated us and we didn't get the open doors or the better fire escapes. So our friends are dead."

The families of the fire victims were heartbroken and hysterical, the ghetto's *Jewish Daily Forward* was understandably melodramatic, and the immigrant community was completely enraged. Their Jewish heritage had taught them an emphasis on individual human life and worth; their shared background in the *shtetl* and common experiences in the ghetto had given them a sense of fellowship.

They were, in a sense, a family—and some of the most helpless among them had died needlessly.

The senseless deaths of so many young Jewish women sparked within these Eastern Europeans a new determination and dedication. The fire had made reform absolutely essential. Workers' rights were no longer just socialist jargon: They were a matter of life and death.

The Triangle Waist Company was located on the three floors of the Asch Building, a 10-story, 135-foot-high structure at the corner of Greene Street and Washington Place in Greenwich Village. One of the largest shirtwaist manufacturers, Triangle employed up to 900 people at times, but on the day of the fire, only about 500 were working.

Leon Stein's brilliant and fascinating account of the fire, entitled simply *The Triangle Fire,* develops and documents the way in which the physical facilities, company procedures, and human behavior interacted to cause this great tragedy. Much of what occurred was ironic, some was cruel, some stupid, some pathetic. It is a dramatic portrayal of the eternal confrontation of the "haves" and the "havenots," told in large part by those who survived.

Fire broke out at the Triangle Company at approximately 4:45 P.M. (because time clocks were reportedly set back to stretch the day, and because other records give differing times of the first fire alarm, it is uncertain exactly what time the fire started), just after pay envelopes had been distributed and employees were leaving their work posts. It was a small fire at first, and there was a calm, controlled effort to extinguish it. But the fire began to spread, jumping from one pile of debris to another, engulfing combustible shirtwaist fabric. It became obvious that the fire could not be snuffed out, and the workers tried to reach the elevators or stairway. Those who reached the one open stairway raced down eight flights of stairs to safety; those who managed to climb onto the available passenger elevators also got out. But not everyone could reach the available exits. Some tried to open the door to a stairway and found it locked. Others were trapped between long working tables or behind the hordes of people trying to get into the elevators or out through the one open door.

Under the work tables, rags were burning; the wooden floors, trim, and window frames were also afire. Frantically, workers fought their way to the elevators, to the fire escape, and to the windows—to any place that might lead to safety.

Fire whistles and bells sounded as the fire department raced to the building. But equipment proved inadequate, as the fire ladders reached only to the seventh floor. And by the time the firemen connected their hoses to douse the flames, the crowded eighth floor was completely ablaze.

For those who reached the windows, there seemed to be a chance for safety. The *New York World* describes people balancing on window sills, nine stories up, with flames scorching them from behind, until firemen arrived: "The nets were spread below with all promptness. Citizens were commandeered into service, as the firemen necessarily gave their attention to the one engine and hose of the force that first arrived. The catapult force that the bodies gathered in the long plunges made the nets utterly without avail. Screaming girls and men, as they fell, tore the nets from the grasp of the holders, and the bodies struck the sidewalks and lay just as they fell. Some of the bodies ripped big holes through the life nets."

One reporter who witnessed the fire remembered how:

A young man helped a girl to the window sill on the ninth floor. Then he held her out deliberately, away from the building, and let her drop. He held out a second girl the same way and let her drop. He held out a third girl who did not resist. They were all as unresisting as if he were helping them into a street car instead of into eternity. He saw that a terrible death awaited them in the flames and his was only a terrible chivalry. He brought around another girl to the window. I saw her put her arms around him and kiss him. Then he held her into space—and dropped her. Quick as a flash, he was on the window sill himself. His coat fluttered

upwards—the air filled his trouser legs as he came down. I could see he wore tan shoes.

Those who had rushed to the fire escape found the window openings rusted shut. Several precious minutes were lost in releasing them. The fire escape itself ended at the second floor, in an airshaft between the Asch Building and the building next door. But too frantic to notice where it ended, workers climbed on to the fire escape one after another until, in one terrifying moment, it collapsed from the weight, pitching the workers to their death.

Those who had made their way to the elevators found crowds pushing to get into the cars. When it became obvious that the elevators could no longer run, workers jumped down the elevator shafts, landing on the tops of the cars, or grabbing for cables to ease their descent. Several died, but incredibly, some did manage to save themselves this way. One man was found, hours after the fire, beneath an elevator car in the basement of the building, nearly drowned by the rapidly rising water from the firemen's hoses.

Several people, among them Triangle's two owners, raced to the roof, and from there were led to safety. Others never had that chance. "When Fire Chief Croker could make his way into the [top] three floors," states one account of the fire, "he found sights that utterly staggered . . . he saw as the smoke drifted away bodies burned to the bare bones. There were skeletons bending over sewing machines."

The day after the fire, the *New York Times* announced that "the building was fireproof. It shows hardly any signs of the disaster that overtook it. The walls are as good as ever, as are the floors: nothing is worse for the fire except that furniture and 14 [sic] of the 600 men and girls that were employed in its upper three stories."

The building *was* fireproof. But there had never been a fire drill in the factory, even though the management had been warned about the possible hazard of fire on the top three floors. Owners Max Blanck and Isaac Harris had chosen to ignore these warnings in spite of the fact that many

An unsafe work environment at the Triangle Waist Company caused the deaths of 146 workers when a fire broke out in the building in 1911. The tragedy brought labor issues to national attention.

of their employees were immigrants who could barely speak English, which would surely mean panic in the event of a crisis.

The *New York Times* also noted that Leonora O'Reilly of the League had reported Max Blanck's visit to the WTUL during the shirtwaist strike, and his plea that the girls return to work. He claimed a business reputation to maintain and told the Union leaders he would make the necessary improvements right away. Because he was the largest manufacturer in the business, the League reported, they trusted him and let the girls return.

But the improvements were never made. And there was nothing that anybody could or would do about it. Factory doors continued to open in instead of out, in violation of fire regulations. The doors remained bolted during working hours, apparently to prevent workers from getting past the inspectors with stolen merchandise. Triangle had

only two staircases where there should have been three, and those two were very narrow. Despite the fact that the building was deemed fireproof, it had wooden window frames, floors, and trim. There was no sprinkler system. It was not legally required.

These were the same kinds of conditions which existed in factories throughout the garment industry; they had been cited repeatedly in the complaints filed with the WTUL. They were not unusual nor restricted to Triangle; in fact, Triangle was not as bad as many other factories.

But it was at Triangle that the fire took place.

The *Jewish Daily Forward* mourned the dead with sorrowful stories, and its headlines talked of "funerals instead of weddings" for the dead young girls. The entire Jewish immigrant community was affected, for it seemed there was scarcely a person who was not in some way touched by the fire. Nearly everyone had either been employed at Triangle themselves, or had a friend or relative who had worked there at some time or another. Most worked in factories with similar conditions, and so everyone identified with the victims and their families.

Many of the dead, burned beyond recognition remained unidentified for days, as searching family members returned again and again to wait in long lines to look for their loved ones. Many survivors were unable to identify their mothers, sisters, or wives; the confusion of handling so many victims and so many survivors who did not understand what was happening to them and to their dead led to even more anguish for the community. Some of the victims were identified by the names on the pay envelopes handed to them at quitting time and stuffed deeply into pockets or stockings just before the fire. But many bodies remained unclaimed for days, with bewildered and bereaved survivors wandering among them, trying to find some identifying mark.

Charges of first- and second-degree manslaughter were brought against the two men who owned Triangle, and Leon Stein's book artfully depicts the subtle psychological and sociological implications of the powerful against the oppressed, and of the Westernized, German-Jewish immigrants against those still living their old-world, Eastern European heritage. Ultimately, Triangle owners Blanck and Harris were acquitted of the charges against them, and in due time they collected their rather sizable insurance.

The shirtwaist, popularized by Gibson girls, had come to represent the new-found freedom of females in America. After the fire, it symbolized death. The reaction of the grief-stricken Lower East Side was articulated by socialist lawyer Morris Hillquit:

The girls who went on strike last year were trying to readjust the conditions under which they were obliged to work. I wonder if there is not some connection between the fire and that strike. I wonder if the magistrates who sent to jail the girls who did picket duty in front of the Triangle shop realized last Sunday that some responsibility may be theirs. Had the strike been successful, these girls might have been alive today and the citizenry of New York would have less of a burden upon its conscience.

For the first time in the history of New York's garment industry there were indications that the public was beginning to accept responsibility for the exploitation of the immigrants. For the first time, the establishment seemed to understand that these were human beings asking for their rights, not merely trouble-making anarchists.

The day after the Triangle fire a protest meeting was held at the Women's Trade Union League, with representatives from twenty leading labor and civic organizations. They formed "a relief committee to cooperate with the Red Cross in its work among the families of the victims, and another committee . . . to broaden the investigation and research on fire hazards in New York factories which was already being carried on by the League."

The minutes of the League recount the deep indignation that members felt at the indifference of a public which had ignored their pleas for safety after the Newark fire. In an attempt to translate their anger into constructive action, the League drew up a list of forceful resolutions that included a plan to gather delegates from all of the city's unions to make a concerted effort to force safety changes in factories. In addition, the League called upon all workers to inspect factories and then report any violations to the proper city authorities and to the WTUL. They called upon the city to immediately appoint organized workers as unofficial inspectors. They resolved to submit the following fire regulations suggestions: compulsory fire drills, fireproof exits, unlocked doors, fire alarms, automatic sprinklers, and regular inspections. The League called upon the legislature to create the Bureau of Fire Protection and finally, the League underscored the absolute need for all workers to organize themselves at once into trade unions so that they would never again be powerless.

The League also voted to participate in the funeral procession for the unidentified dead of the Triangle fire.

The city held a funeral for the dead who were unclaimed. "More than 120,000 of us were in the funeral procession that miserable rainy April day," remembered Rose Schneiderman. "From ten in the morning until four in the afternoon we of the Women's Trade Union League marched in the procession with other trade-union men and women, all of us filled with anguish and regret that we had never been able to organize the Triangle workers."

Schneiderman, along with many others, was absolutely determined that this kind of tragedy would never happen again. With single-minded dedication, they devoted themselves to unionizing the workers. The searing example of the Triangle fire provided them with the impetus they needed to gain public support for their efforts.

They dramatized and emphasized and capitalized on the scandalous working conditions of the immigrants. From all segments of the community came cries for labor reform. Stephen S. Wise, the prestigious reform rabbi, called for the formation of a citizens' committee. Jacob H. Schiff, Bishop David H. Greer, Governor John A. Dix, Anne Morgan (of *the* Morgans) and other leading civic and religious leaders collaborated in a mass meeting at the Metropolitan Opera House on May 2 to protest factory conditions and to show support for the workers.

Several people spoke at the meeting on May 2, and many in the audience began to grow restless and antagonistic. Finally, 29-year-old Rose Schneiderman stepped up to the podium.

In a whisper barely audible, she began to address the crowd.

I would be a traitor to these poor burned bodies, if I came here to talk good fellowship. We have tried you good people of the public and we have found you wanting. The old Inquisition had its rack and its thumbscrews and its instruments of torture with iron teeth. We know what these things are today: the iron teeth are our necessities, the thumbscrews the

high-powered and swift machinery close to which we must work, and the rack is here in the fireproof structures that will destroy us the minute they catch on fire.

This is not the first time girls have burned alive in the city. Every week I must learn of the untimely death of one of my sister workers. Every year thousands of us are maimed. The life of men and women is so cheap and property is so sacred. There are so many of us for one job it matters little if 140-odd are burned to death.

We have tried you, citizens, we are trying you now, and you have a couple of dollars for the sorrowing mothers and daughters and sisters by way of a charity gift. But every time the workers come out in the only way they know to protest against conditions which are unbearable, the strong hand of the law is allowed to press down heavily upon us.

Public officials have only words of warning to us—warning that we must be intensely orderly and must be intensely peaceable, and they have the workhouse just back of all their warnings. The strong hand of the law beats us back when we rise into the conditions that make life bearable.

I can't talk fellowship to you who are gathered here. Too much blood had been spilled. I know from my experience it is up to the working people to save themselves. The only way they can save themselves is by a strong working-class movement.

Her speech has become a classic. It is more than just an emotional picture of persecution; it reflects the persuasive sadness and profound understanding that comes from knowing, finally, the cruel realities of life, the perspective of history, and the nature of human beings.

The devastation of that fire and the futility of the seemingly successful strike that had preceded it seemed to impart an undeniable truth to Rose Schneiderman: they could not fail again. The events of 1911 seemed to have made her, and many others, more keenly aware than they had ever been that the workers' fight for reform was absolutely essential. If they did not do it, it would not be done.

In a sense, the fire touched off in Schneiderman an awareness of her own responsibility in the battle for industrial reform. This fiery socialist worker had been transformed into a highly effective labor leader.

The influential speech she gave did help swing public opinion to the side of the trade unions, and the fire itself had made the workers more aware of the crucial need to unionize. Widespread support for labor reform and unionization emerged. Pressure from individuals, such as Rose Schneiderman, as well as from groups like the Women's Trade Union League and the International Ladies' Garment Workers' Union, helped form the New

York State Factory Investigating Commission, the New York Citizens' Committee on Safety, and other regulatory and investigatory bodies. The League and Local 25 (the Shirtwaist Makers' Union of the ILGWU) were especially instrumental in attaining a new Industrial Code for New York State, which became "the most outstanding instrument for safeguarding the lives, health, and welfare of the millions of wage earners in New York State and . . . in the nation at large."

It took years for these changes to occur, and labor reform did not rise majestically, Phoenix-like, from the ashes of the Triangle fire. But that fire, and Rose Schneiderman's whispered plea for a strong working-class movement, had indeed become the loud, clear call for action.

Study Questions

1. How successful had workers at the Triangle Waist Company been in gaining better working conditions before the fire? What had been their major successes and failures?

2. What were the major labor concerns of the female immigrant workers?

3. Why did the fire lead to so many deaths? How did the design of the building contribute to the tragedy?

4. What was the Jewish community's reaction to the fire? How did the funeral help unify reform-minded people in New York City?

5. What role did Rose Schneiderman play in the aftermath of the tragedy? How did the fire influence the American labor movement?

Bibliography

As Mitelman indicates, the best treatment of the tragedy is Leon Stein, *The Triangle Fire* (1962). For a recent interpretation of the events, see David Von Drehle, *Triangle: The Fire That Changed America* (2003). Leslie Woodcock Tentler, *Wage-Earning Women: Industrial Work and Family Life in the United States, 1900–1930* (1979), treats the difficulties faced by working women. Useful treatments of the same theme are Susan Estabrook Kennedy, *If All We Did Was to Weep at Home: A History of White Working Class Women in America* (1979), and Barbara Mayer Wertheimer, *We Were There: The Story of Working Women in America* (1977). Meredith Tax, *The Rising of the Women: Feminist Solidarity and Class Conflict, 1880–1917* (1982) examines the successes and failures of middle-class and working-women to unite female laborers. Two excellent introductions to general issues that concerned workers are Herbert Gutman, *Work, Culture and Society in Industrializing America* (1977), and David Montgomery, *Workers' Control in America: Studies in the History of Work, Technology, and Labor Struggles* (1979). Moses Rischin, *The Promised City: New York's Jews, 1870-1940* (1970); Arthur S. Goren, *New York Jews and the Quest for Community: The Kehillah Experiment, 1908-1922* (1970); and Irving Howe, *World of our Fathers: The Journey of the Eastern European Jews to America and the Life They Found and Made* (1976), treat the Jewish experience in America.

READING 10

★ ★ ★

Jack Johnson Wins the Heavyweight Championship

Randy Roberts

For the most part, the Progressive movement was a for-whites-only affair. During the first twenty years of the twentieth century, Asian and black Americans faced open and violent discrimination. On the West Coast, Japanese and Chinese immigrants confronted a humiliating series of discriminatory laws, while in the South and even North blacks were equally hard-pressed. Neither presidents Theodore Roosevelt nor Woodrow Wilson made any attempt to alter the social structure of the Jim Crow South, where the lives of the blacks were unequal to the lives of the whites. Although blacks retained some political and civil rights in the North, they still suffered from social and economic discrimination.

Some blacks responded to the injustice. Booker T. Washington was willing to forego social and political equality for economic opportunities. W. E. B. Du Bois demanded more; he worked for full equality. Other blacks lodged less articulate protests through their actions. They refused to live within the narrow borders proscribed for them by white society. Often these blacks were labeled "bad niggers." White authorities hated and punished them, but in black communities they were regarded as heroes and legends. The most famous of these real-life renegades was Jack Johnson, the first black heavyweight champion. He defeated white boxers, married white women, enraged white authorities, and lived by his own laws. In the following selection, historian Randy Roberts uses Johnson's fight with Tommy Burns as an opportunity to examine the racial attitudes of the early twentieth century.

Afterwards concerned whites said it should never have taken place. John L. Sullivan, who by 1908 had quit drinking and become a moral crusader, said, "Shame on the money-mad Champion! Shame on the man who upsets good American precedents because there are Dollars, Dollars, Dollars in it." A dejected sports columnist wrote, "Never before in the history of the prize ring has such a crisis arisen as that which faces the followers of the game tonight." The sadness these men felt could only be expressed in superlatives—greatest tragedy, deepest gloom, saddest day, darkest night. The race war had been fought. Armageddon was over. The Caucasian race had lost. Twenty years after the event, and after a few more such Armageddons, Alva Johnston tried to explain the mood of the day: "The morale of the Caucasian race had been at a low ebb long before the great blow fell in 1908. The Kaiser had been growing hysterical over the Yellow Peril. Africa was still celebrating the victory of Emperor Menelik of Abyssinia over the Italians. Dixie was still in ferment because Booker T. Washington . . . had had a meal at the White House. Then . . . Jack Johnson won the World Heavyweight Championship from Tommy Burns. The Nordics had not been so scared since the days of Tamerlane."

Black ghetto dwellers and sharecroppers rejoiced. In cities from New York to Omaha, blacks smiled with delight. "Today is the zenith of Negro sports," observed a *Colored American Magazine* editor. Other black publications felt such qualifications were too conservative. The *Richmond Planet* reported that "no event in forty years has given more genuine satisfaction to the colored people of this country than has the signal victory of Jack Johnson." Joy and pride spilled over into arrogance, or so some whites believed. The cotton-buying firm of Logan and Bryan predicted that Johnson's victory would en-

courage other blacks to enter boxing, thereby creating a shortage of field labor. Independent of Logan and Bryan's report, the black writer Jim Nasium counseled black youths to consider seriously a boxing career—where else could they face whites on an equal footing? In that last week of 1908 social change seemed close at hand. The implication of most reports was that Jack Johnson had started a revolution.

How had it all come about? When Burns arrived in Perth in August 1908, the world did not seem in any immediate danger. He was treated like a conquering hero. From Perth to Sydney he was cheered and fêted. Mayors and members of Parliament courted Burns as if he were visiting royalty. When the train made its normal 6 A.M. stop at Abury, men stood shivering in the cold to greet Burns. And at Sydney, at a more civilized hour, more than 8,000 people cheered the champion. Speeches were made and applause modestly received. An Australian politician, Colonel Ryrie, extolled the virtues of boxing, telling the gathering that the sport produced sturdy young men needed for battle, "not those milksops who cry out against it."

At these August occasions Burns was frequently asked about Johnson. Would he fight the black champion? If so, where? When? Burns patiently answered the questions like a saint repeating a litany. He would fight Johnson when the right purse was offered. The place was not important. In fact, Australia was as good as—if not better than—any other place. As Burns told a Melbourne reporter: "There are a lot of newspaper stories that I don't want to fight Johnson. I do want to fight him, but I want to give the white boys a chance first." And since the early English settlers had exterminated the Tasmanians, there were a lot of white boys in Australia.

Listening to Burns was an ambitious promoter. Hugh D. "Huge Deal" McIntosh was an American success story with an Australian setting. As a boy he worked in the Broken Hill mines and as a rural laborer, but early in life he realized that a man could make more money using his brain than his back. His fortune was made as a pie salesman in

Reprinted with the permission of The Free Press, a division of Simon & Schuster from *Papa Jack: Jack Johnson and the Era of White Hopes* by Randy Roberts. Copyright © 1983 by The Free Press.

Australian parks and sporting events, but his career included tours as a racing cyclist, a boxer, a waiter, a newspaper publisher, a member of parliament, a theatrical impresario, and other assorted jobs. All these stints equipped him with enough gab and gall to become a first-rate boxing promoter. It was McIntosh who had invited Burns to Australia to defend his title against Aussie boxers. A student of maps and calendars, he knew that when Teddy Roosevelt's Great White Fleet, then cruising about the Pacific, dropped anchor in Australia a heavyweight championship fight would prove a good draw. With this in mind, he rented a market garden at Rushcutter's Bay, on the outskirts of Sydney, and built an open-air stadium on it. By mid-summer he was ready for Burns.

In June he matched Burns against Bill Squires, whom the champion had already knocked out twice, once in the United States and once in France. In defense of Squires, however, it was noted by the press that in his second fight with Burns he had lasted eight rounds, seven longer than the first fight. On his home continent Squires did even better. He was not knocked out until the thirteenth round. Though the fight was not particularly good, the overflowing stadium pleased McIntosh mightily. More than 40,000 people showed up for the fight, including American sailors from the Great White Fleet, but only 15,000 could be seated in the stadium. The 25,000 others milled about outside, listening to the noise made by lucky spectators watching the fight.

Less than two weeks later Burns again defended his title, this time against Bill Lang in Melbourne before 19,000 spectators. Like the stadium at Rushcutter's Bay, South Melbourne Stadium had been hurriedly constructed on McIntosh's orders—it was built in twelve days—and the result had been worth the effort. In the two fights Burns made more than $20,000 and McIntosh grossed about $100,000, half of which was clear profit. In addition, both fights had been filmed, and revenue from this pioneering effort was much greater than anticipated. Burns, McIntosh, and the Australian boxing public were all exceedingly pleased.

In late October Johnson arrived, and the pulse of Australia picked up a beat. The fight had already been arranged. McIntosh guaranteed Burns $30,000. Before such a sum the color line faded. Therefore, when Johnson landed at Perth he was in an accommodating mood. "How does Burns want it? Does he want it fast and willing? I'm his man in that case. Does he want it flat footed? Goodness, if he does, why I'm his man again. Anything to suit; but fast or slow, I'm going to win." After eight years of trying Johnson was about to get his chance to fight for the heavyweight title.

Short of money, Johnson and Fitzpatrick set up their training quarters in the inexpensive Sir Joseph Banks Hotel in Botany, far less plush than the Hydro Majestic Hotel at Medlow Bath, where Burns trained. Yet Johnson, like Burns, trained in earnest. Johnson looked relaxed—he joked, smiled, made speeches, and played the double bass—but the men and women who watched him train failed to notice that he was also working very hard. Each morning he ran; each afternoon he exercised and sparred with Bill Lang, who imitated Burns's style. Johnson knew that Burns—short, inclined toward fatness, addicted to cigars and strong drink—was nonetheless a very good boxer. In Bohum Lynch's opinion, Burns was a "decidedly good boxer" who, though unorthodox, had a loose and easy style. And in the weeks before the fight Johnson showed by his training that he did not take Burns lightly.

Nor did he disregard the power of Australian racism. He feared that in the emotionally charged atmosphere of an interracial championship fight he might not be given an even break. His concern was not unfounded. An editorial in Sydney's *Illustrated Sporting and Dramatic News* correctly indicated the racial temper of Australian boxing fans: "Citizens who have never prayed before are supplicating Providence to give the white man a strong right arm with which to belt the coon into oblivion." But of more concern to Johnson than white men's prayers were his suspicions of McIntosh as promoter and self-named referee. Several times the two quarreled in public, and they nearly came to blows when Johnson greeted the promoter with "How do, Mr. McIntosh? How do you drag yourself away from Tahmy?" McIntosh, a big, burly, muscular man, thereafter began carrying a lead pipe wrapped in sheet music. As he told his friend Norman Lindsay, it was in case "that black bastard" ever "tries any funny business."

As the bout drew closer, the racial overtones destroyed the holiday atmosphere. It seemed as if all Australia were edgy. In the name of civilization, Protestant reformers spoke words that fell on deaf ears. The fight, said the Sydney Anglican Synod, with "its inherent brutality and dangerous nature" would surely "corrupt the moral tone of the community." But the community was worried less about being corrupted than about the implication of a Johnson victory. Lindsay, whom McIntosh hired to draw posters to advertise the fight, visually portrayed the great fear. Across Sydney could be seen his poster showing a towering black and a much smaller white. As Richard Broome has suggested, "Thus must have evoked the deepest feelings Australians held about the symbols of blackness and whiteness and evoked the emotiveness of a big man versus a small man and the populous coloured races versus the numerically smaller white race." Clearly, the *Australian Star* editors had this in mind when they printed a cartoon showing the fight being watched by representatives of the white and black races. Underneath was a letter that predicted that "this battle may in the future be looked back upon as the first great battle of an inevitable race war. . . . There is more in this fight to be considered than the mere title of pugilistic champion of the world."

Racial tension was nothing new to Australia. Race had mattered since the colony's founding. Partly it was an English heritage, passed down from the conquerors of Ireland, Scotland, and Wales—and absolute belief in the inferiority of everything and everyone non-English. In Australia, however, it had developed its own unique characteristics. There common English prejudices had been carried to extremes, and when confronted with dark-skinned natives, the Australians did not shrink from the notion of geno-

cide. The most shocking example of racial relations was the case of the small island of Tasmania off the southeast coast of Australia. When the English first settled the island there were perhaps a few thousand Tasmanians. Short but long-legged, these red-brown people were described as uncommonly friendly natives. But the friendliness soon died, as British colonists hunted, raped, enslaved, abducted, or killed the Tasmanians. Slowly the race died off, until in 1876 Truganini, the very last survivor, died. Her passing struck many Australians as sad—but inevitable. As a correspondent for the *Hobart Mercury* wrote, "I regret the death of the last of the Tasmanian aborigines, but I know that it is the result of the *fiat* that the black shall everywhere give place to the white."

For Australia the problem was that other darker races had not given way fast enough in the generation after the death of Truganini. Though Social Darwinists preached the virtues of the light-skinned, by 1909 Australians felt threatened by the "lower" races. Increasingly after 1900 Australians demonstrated anxiety over their Oriental neighbors. Immigration restrictions aimed at keeping the country white were proposed and adopted. So bitter had the struggle become that in 1908, the year of the Johnson-Burns fight, the *Australia Bulletin* changed its banner from "Australia for Australians" to "Australia for the white men."

Johnson and Burns became both an example of and a contribution to the fears of white Australians. Small, white Burns became the symbol of small, white Australia, nobly battling against the odds. Burn's defense was his brain and pluck, his desire to stave off defeat through intelligence and force of will. Johnson became the large, vulgar, corrupt, and sensual enemy. Reports said that he ignored training and instead wenched and drank. He had strength and size but lacked heart—in fact, he *should* win but probably would not. This last report gave rise to the rumor that the fight was fixed. Even the *New York Times* endorsed this view, as did the betting line that made Burns a 7 to 4 favorite.

Cool rains washed Sydney on Christmas night, the eve of the fight. To allow filming, the fight was not scheduled to begin until 11 A.M., but by 6 A.M. an orderly crowd of more than 5,000 was waiting at the gate. The stadium would be filled to capacity; yet interest was much more widespread. Throughout Australia men milled around newspaper offices hoping to hear a word about the progress of the fight. Inside the stadium at Rushcutter's Bay all Christmas cheer had vanished. The mood and tone of the day, from the gray, overcast sky to the uneasy quiet of the spectators, was eulogistic.

Johnson entered the ring first. Despite his dull gray robe his mood was almost carefree. There were a few cheers—though not many—as he slipped under the upper strand of the ropes, but calls of "coon" and "nigger" were more common. He smiled, bowed grandly, and threw kisses in every direction. He liked to strut the stage, and the vicious insults did not outwardly affect him. If anything, his smile became broader as he was more abused. In a country exhilarated by the discovery of gold, Johnson's gold-toothed smile ironically attracted only hate. Satisfied that he was not the crowd's favorite, he retired to his corner, where Sam Fitzpatrick massaged his shoulders and whispered words of assurance into an unlistening ear.

By contrast, when Burns climbed into the ring, the stadium was filled with sound. Burns did not seem to notice. For a time it looked as if he had come into the ring expecting something other than a fight. He was dressed in a worn blue suit, more appropriate for a shoe salesman than the heavyweight champion. Methodically he removed the suit, folded it neatly, and put it in a battered wicker suitcase. Yet even in his short, tight boxing trunks he looked out of place. Jack London, covering the fight for the *New York Herald,* wrote that Burns looked "pale and sallow, as if he had not slept all night, or as if he had just pulled through a bout with fever." Pacing nervously in his corner, he avoided looking across the ring at Johnson.

Burns examined the bandages on Johnson's hands. He did this carefully, looking for hard tape or other unnatural objects. Satisfied, he returned to his corner. Johnson, however, was upset by the tape on Burns's elbows. He asked Burns to re-

move it. Burns refused. Johnson—suddenly serious—said he would not fight until the tape was removed. Still Burns refused. McIntosh tried to calm the two fighters. He was unsuccessful. The crowd, sensing an unexpected confrontation but not aware of the finer details, sided with Burns and used the moment as a pretext to shout more insults at Johnson, who smiled as if complimented on a new necktie but still refused to alter his protest. Finally, Burns removed the tape. Johnson nodded, satisfied.

McIntosh called the fighters to the center of the ring. He went over the do's and don'ts and the business of what punches would or would not be allowed. Then he announced that in the event that the police stopped the fight, he would render a decision based on who was winning at the time. The unpopular "no decision" verdict would not be given. Both Johnson and Burns had earlier agreed to this procedure. The fighters returned to their corners. A few moments later the bell rang. The color line in championship fights was erased.

Watching films of Johnson boxing is like listening to a 1900 recording of Enrico Caruso played on a 1910 gramophone. When Johnson fought Burns, film was still in its early days, not yet capable of capturing the subtleties of movement. Nuance is lost in the furious and stilted actions of the figures, which move about the screen in a Chaplinesque manner, as if some drunken cutter had arbitrarily removed three of every four frames. When we watch fighters of Johnson's day on film, we wonder how they could have been considered even good. That some of them were champions strains credulity. They look like large children, wrestling and cuffing each other, but not actually fighting like real boxers, not at all like Ali captured in zoom-lensed, slow-motion, technological grace. But the film misleads.

It was no Charlie Chaplin that shuffled out of his corner in round one to meet Tommy Burns. It was a great boxer who at age thirty was in his physical prime. No longer thin, Johnson was well-muscled, with a broad chest and thick arms and legs. His head was shaved in the style of the eighteenth-century bare-knuckle fighters, and his high cheekbones gave his face a rounded appearance. Although he had fought often, his superb defensive skills had kept his face largely unmarked. Like his mother he had a broad, flat nose and full lips, but his eyes were small and oddly Oriental when he smiled. He was famous for his clowning, but this stereotype of a black man obscured the more serious reality. He was often somber, and even when he smiled and acted like a black-faced minstrel, he could be serious. What he thought, he believed, was his own affair. His feelings could not be easily read on his face.

Both boxers began cautiously. Johnson flicked out a few probing jabs, designed more to test distance than to do any physical damage. Although Burns was much smaller than Johnson, he was considered a strong man with a powerful punch. Johnson clinched, tested Burns's strength, then shifted to long-range sparring. He allowed Burns to force the action, content to parry punches openhanded. Burns tried to hit Johnson with long left hooks, which fell short. Johnson feinted a long left of his own, but in the same motion he lowered his right shoulder, pivoted from the waist, stepped forward with his right foot, and delivered a perfect right uppercut. It was Johnson's finest weapon, and some ring authorities claim there never has been a fighter who could throw the punch as well as Johnson. Burns was caught flatfooted, leaning into the punch. His momentum was stopped and he fell backward. His head hit heavily on the floor. He lay still. The referee started to count.

"The fight," Jack London wrote only hours after it ended, "there was no fight. No Armenian massacre could compare with the hopeless slaughter that took place in the Sydney stadium today." From the opening seconds of the first round it was clear who would win. At least it was clear to London. It was a fight between a "colossus and a toy automation," between a "playful Ethiopian and a small and futile white man," between a "grown man and a naughty child." And through it all, London and the 20,000 white supporters of Burns watched in horror as their worst fears materialized.

"Hit the coon in his stomach." Burns needed no reminder. After surviving the first-round knockdown, he shifted to a different strategy, one he had thought about before. In the days before the fight, when reporters asked about his battle plan, he had smiled knowingly at his white chroniclers and said he would move in close and hit the black fighter where all black fighters were weak—in the stomach. This theory was hardly novel; it had long been considered axiomatic that black boxers had weak stomachs and hard heads. So thoroughly was the view accepted that black boxers took it for granted that white fighters would attack the body. Peter Jackson once told Fred Dartnell, "They are all after my body. Hit a nigger in the stomach and you'll settle him, they say, but it never seems to occur to them that a white man might just as quickly be beaten by a wallop in the same region." Sam Langford agreed: blacks hated to be hit by a hard punch to the stomach, but so too did whites.

Boxing was not immune to the scientific explanations of the day. Polygenists believed—and Darwinists did not deny—that the black race was an "incipient species." Therefore, whites maintained, physically blacks and whites were very different. Burns, for example, assumed that Johnson not only had a weak stomach but lacked physical endurance. So he believed that the longer the fight lasted the better were his chances. Behind these stereotypes rested the science of the day. Writing only a year before in the *North American Review,* Charles F. Woodruff claimed that athletes raised in Southern climates lacked endurance: "The excessive light prods the nervous system to do more than it should, and in time such constant stimulation is followed by irritability and finally by exhaustion." Only athletes from the colder Northern latitudes had enough stamina to remain strong during the course of a long boxing match. Therefore, Burns, a Canadian, had reason to remain hopeful. By contrast, Johnson, raised about as far south as one could travel in the United States and only a generation or two removed from Africa, had to win quickly or not at all. At least, this was what Burns and his white supporters hoped.

Burns's strategy was thus founded on the racist belief that scientists, armed with physiological and climatological evidence, had proved that blacks were either inferior to whites, or—as in the case of harder heads—superior because of some greater physiological inferiority; that is to say, blacks had thicker skulls because they had smaller brains. Burns never questioned that his abdominal strength and his endurance were superior to Johnson's. Nor did he doubt that his white skin meant that his desire to win and willingness to accept pain were greater than Johnson's. But above all, he was convinced that as a white he could outthink Johnson, that he could solve the problems of defense and offense more quickly than his black opponent. Burns's faith, in short, rested ultimately on the color of his skin.

Burns forgot, however, that he was facing a boxer liberated from the myths of his day. Johnson's stomach was not weak, and, more important, he knew it was not. As the fight progressed, he exposed the fallacy of Burns's theory. He started to taunt Burns. "Go on, Tommy, hit me here," Johnson said pointing to his stomach. When Burns responded with a blow to Johnson's midsection, Jack laughed and said to try again. "Is that all the better you can do, Tommy?" Another punch. "Come on, Tommy, you can hit harder than that, can't you?" And so it continued; Johnson physically and verbally was destroying the white man's myths.

Burns fought gamely, but without success. Johnson did not try for a knockout; he was content to allow the fight to last until the later rounds. Partly his decision was based on economics. The bout was being filmed, and few boxing fans in America would pay to watch pictures of pressmen, seconds, and other boxers for five minutes as a build-up for a fight that lasted only half a minute. But more important was Johnson's desire for revenge. He hated Burns and wanted to punish him. And he did. By the second round Burns's right eye was discolored and his mouth was bloody. By the middle rounds Burns was bleeding from a dozen minor facial cuts. Blood ran over his shoulders and stained the canvas ring. Before the

The first African American man to gain the heavyweight boxing championship of the world was Jack Johnson, who held the title from 1908 to 1915.

white audience, Johnson badly punished Burns. And he enjoyed every second of it.

But punishment was not enough. Johnson wanted also to humiliate Burns. He did this verbally. From the very first round Johnson insulted Burns, speaking with an affected English accent, so that "Tommy" became "Tahmy." Mostly what Johnson said was banal: "Poor little Tahmy, who told you you were a fighter?" Or, "Say little Tahmy, you're not fighting. Can't you? I'll have to show you how." Occasionally, when Burns landed a punch, Johnson complimented him: "Good boy, Tommy; good boy, Tommy." In almost every taunt Johnson referred to Burns in the diminutive. It was always "Tommy Boy"; or "little Tommy." And always a derisive smile accompanied the words.

Sometimes Johnson sought to emasculate Burns verbally. Referring to Burns's wife, Johnson said, "Poor little boy, Jewel won't know you when she gets you back from this fight." Once when Burns landed what looked to be an effective punch, Johnson laughed: "Poor, poor Tommy. Who taught you to hit? Your mother? You a woman?" Crude, often vulgar and mean, Johnson's verbal warfare was nevertheless effective.

Burns responded in kind. Bohum Lynch, who was a great fan of Burns, admitted that his champion's ring histrionics included baleful glaring, foot stomping, and mouth fighting. He often called Johnson a "cur" or a "big dog." At other times, when he was hurt or frustrated, he said, "Come on and fight, nigger. Fight like a white man." Burns's comments, however, were self-defeating. When Johnson insulted Burns, the champion lost control and fought recklessly. But Burns's taunts pleased Johnson, who responded by fighting in an even more controlled way than before. Johnson gained particular strength from Burns's racist statements. It was like playing the Dozens, where accepting abuse with an even smile and concealing one's true emotions were the sign of a sure winner.

When Johnson was not insulting Burns, he was talking to ringsiders. Usually he just joked about how easy the fight was and what he would do with the money he won from betting on the bout. That the ringsiders hated Johnson and screamed racial insults did not seem to bother him. Only rarely did Johnson show his disgust with the white audience. Once as he moved from his corner at the start of a round he spat a mouthful of water toward the press row, but such actions were unusual. More common was the smile—wide, detached, inscrutable. In describing the grin, Jack London came closest to the truth: it was "the fight epitomized." It was the smile of a man who has mastered the rules to a slightly absurd game.

After a few rounds the only question that remained unanswered was not who would win but how much punishment Burns could take. By the middle rounds that too was evident—he could survive great amounts of punishment. His eyes were bruised and discolored, his mouth hung open, his jaw was swollen and looked broken, and his body was splotched with his own blood. In the corner between rounds his seconds sponged his face with champagne, which was popularly believed to help revive hurt fighters. It did not help Burns. Yet at the bell he always arose to face more punishment and insults. For the white spectators, Burns's fortitude was itself inspiring. As Bohum Lynch wrote, "To take a beating any time, even from your best friend, is hard work. But to take a beating from a man you abhor, belonging to a race you despise, to know that he is hurting you and humiliating you with the closest attention to detail, and the coldest deliberation . . . this requires pluck."

By the thirteenth round everyone but Burns and Johnson was surfeited with the carnage. Spectators, left with nothing and nobody to cheer, now yelled for the fight to be stopped. After the thirteenth round police entered the ring. They talked with McIntosh, then with Burns. The white champion refused to concede. He insisted that he could win. But in the fourteenth Burns was again severely punished. A hard right cross knocked him to the canvas. He arose at the count of eight but was wobbly. Again policemen climbed into the ring, only this time there was no talking. The fight was stopped, although Burns—dazed, covered with blood, but still game—screamed at the police to give him another chance.

Everywhere was a stunned silence as the spectators accepted that the inevitable was now the actual. It had happened. A black man now wore the crown that had once belonged to Sullivan, Corbett, and Jeffries. As far as Australia was concerned, an "archetypal darkness" had replaced sweetness and light; the barbarian had defeated the civilized man. As the *Daily Telegraph* observed in doggerel:

And yet for all we know and feel,
For Christ and Shakespeare,
  knowledge, love,

We watch a white man bleeding reel,
We cheer a black with bloodied glove.

The imagery in which the fight was reported clearly reflects the white Australian attitude toward Johnson. He was portrayed as a destructive beast. *Fairplay,* the liquor trades weekly, called Johnson "a huge primordial ape," and the *Bulletin's* cartoons likened him to a shaven-headed reptile. He was the discontented black and yellow masses that haunted the Australian mind. Journalist Randolph Bedford, perhaps the most unabashedly racist reporter at the fight, depicted it in ominous terms: "Yet the white beauty faced the black unloveliness, forcing the fight, bearing the punishment as if it were none . . . weight and reach were ebbing against intrepidity, intelligence and lightness. . . . His courage still shone in his eyes; his face was disfigured and swollen and bloodied. He was still beauty by contrast—beautiful but to be beaten; clean sunlight fighting darkness and losing."

In America the fight was not viewed in quite so maudlin a manner. Certainly the white American press was not pleased by the result, but it generally tried to dismiss it in a light-hearted mood. Perhaps, reporters reasoned, all was not lost. "Br'er Johnson is an American anyway," commented a reporter for the *Omaha Sunday Bee.* Then, too, boxing had declined so much in recent years that some experts wondered if the fight meant anything at all. Though John L. Sullivan criticized Burns for fighting Johnson, he added that "present day bouts cannot truly be styled prize fights, but only boxing matches." A fine distinction, but Sullivan believed it was enough to invalidate Johnson's claim as heavyweight champion. And certainly even if Johnson were the champion, reporters all agreed that he was far below the likes of Sullivan, Corbett, or Jeffries.

Though the mood had not yet reached a crisis stage, the fight's portent was still most unsettling to American whites. This was especially true about the manner in which blacks celebrated Johnson's victory. It was reported that the Manassas Club, a Chicago organization of wealthy blacks who had white wives, hired white waiters to serve the food at their banquet. And one of their members said that "Johnson's victory demonstrates the physical superiority of the black over the Caucasian. The basis of mental superiority in most men is physical superiority. If the negro can raise his mental standard to his physical eminence, some day he will be a leader among men." In other parts of the country blacks were reported as acting rude to whites and being swelled by false pride.

Johnson's actions in Australia did little to calm Caucasian fears. Turning against the sportsmanlike tradition of praising one's opponent, Johnson openly said that Burns was a worthless boxer: "He is the easiest man I ever met. I could have put him away quicker, but I wanted to punish him. I had my revenge." Nor was Johnson discreet about the company with whom he was seen in public. Hattie McClay, his companion who had remained in the background during the weeks before the fight, was now prominently on display. Dressed in silk and furs, she seemed as prized a possession of Johnson's as his gold-capped teeth.

Johnson now seemed more apt to emphasize racial issues that irritated whites. Interviewed during the days after the fight, he told reporters that he had the greatest admiration for the aboriginal Australians. Commenting on their weapons, he said, "Your central Australian natives must have been men of genius to have turned out such artistic and ideal weapons." Nor, he hinted, was he any less a genius. He understood human nature: because he defeated Burns he could expect to be hated by all whites. But, he added, he could find solace in his favorite books—*Paradise Lost, Pilgrim's Progress* and *Titus Andronicus.* His comments achieved their purpose; everywhere white Australians snorted in disgust. But his choice of books certainly did not reflect his own attitude. Unlike Milton's Adam, Johnson did not practice the standard Christian virtues.

Burns left Australia soon after the fight. A richer man by some $30,000, he nevertheless was bitter and filled with hatred. Johnson, however, decided to stay for a while in Australia. His side of the purse, a mere $5,000, was hardly enough to make the venture profitable. He hoped instead to capitalize on his fame by touring Australia as a vaudeville performer. It was common for any famous boxer to make such tours. In 1908 he had toured in America and Canada with the Reilly and Woods Big Show and had enjoyed the experience. He loved the limelight and, unlike other boxers, put on a good show. He demonstrated a few boxing moves, sang several songs, danced, and played the bass fiddle. During his Australian tour he actually made more money than he had in his fight with Burns. Not until mid-February was he ready to go home.

He had changed. The Johnson who left Australia in February was not the same man who had arrived in October. Inwardly, perhaps, he was much the same. But outwardly he was different. He was more open about his beliefs and his pleasures, less likely to follow the advice of white promoters and managers. Undoubtedly he believed the title of world champion set him apart from others of his race. And in this he was right. He would never be viewed as just another black boxer. But he was wrong in his assumption that the crown carried with it some sort of immunity against the dictates of whites and traditions of white society. Now more than ever Johnson was expected to conform. And now more than ever Johnson felt he did not have to. The collision course was set.

Study Questions

1. How did the promoters of the Johnson-Burns fight use racism to build up the gate? How did the racial attitudes of white Australians compare with those of white Americans?

2. How did Burns demonstrate racial stereotypes by the manner in which he fought Johnson?

3. What was the reaction of white Australians and Americans to Jack Johnson's victory?

4. What was Johnson's attitude toward white society?

5. How else might one use sports or popular culture to demonstrate racial attitudes?

Bibliography

The section is taken from Randy Roberts, *Papa Jack: Jack Johnson and the Era of White Hopes* (1983). Finis Farr, *Black Champion: The Life and Times of Jack Johnson* (1965), provides a readable popular history of the boxer, and Al-Tony Gilmore, *Bad Nigger! The National Impact of Jack Johnson* (1975), traces the newspaper reaction to Johnson. Johnson's image in black folklore is treated by William Wiggins, "Jack Johnson as Bad Nigger: The Folklore of His Life," *Black Scholar* (1969), and Lawrence W. Levine, *Black Culture and Black Consciousness: Afro-American Folk Thought from Slavery to Freedom* (1977). A number of books trace the evolution of white attitudes toward blacks. Among the best are George M. Fredrickson, *The Black Image in the White Mind: The Debate on Afro-American Character and Destiny, 1817-1914* (1971); Thomas F. Gossett, *Race: The History of an Idea in America* (1965); and John S. Haller, Jr., *Outcasts from Evolution: Scientific Attitudes of Racial Inferiority, 1859-1900* (1971).

READING 11

★ ★ ★

The Trench Scene

Paul Fussell

For the generation that fought it, World War I was the Great War. It came after almost one hundred years of general European peace, and it shattered not only nations and people but also a system of thought, a world view. Before the Great War, intellectuals talked seriously and earnestly about human progress and the perfectability of societies and individuals. Men and women, they agreed, were reasonable creatures, fully capable of ordering their lives and environment. The terrible slaughter of Verdun and the Somme, the mud and lice and rats of the trenches, the horrors of poison gases and bullet-torn bodies draped over barbed-wire barriers—these unspeakable barbarities silenced talk of progress. Ernest Hemingway spoke for his generation when he wrote about the impact of the Great War: "I was always embarrassed by the words *sacred, glorious,* and *sacrifice* and the expression *in vain* . . . I had seen nothing sacred, and the things that were glorious had no glory and the sacrifices were like the stockyards at Chicago if nothing was done with the meat except to bury it. There were many words that you could not stand to hear and finally only the names of places had dignity. . . . Abstract words such as *glory, honor, courage,* or *hallow* were obscene beside the concrete names of villages, the number of roads, the names of rivers, the numbers of regiments and the dates."

   In the following essay, literary historian Paul Fussell discusses the Great War as experienced by millions of soldiers who served time in the trenches of the Western Front. In these ditches some 7,000 British soldiers were killed or wounded daily between 1914 and 1918. Though not in such horrendous numbers, Americans too died in the trenches of France, and the experience of mass death transformed American society. The United States went into the war to "make the world safe for democracy" but emerged from the war pessimistic, cynical, and discouraged. As Fussell observes, "To be in the trenches was to experience an unreal, unforgettable enclosure and constraint, as well as a sense of being unoriented and lost." This was the aspect of the Great War that changed the temper of Western culture.

The idea of "the trenches" has been assimilated so successfully by metaphor and myth ("Georgian complacency died in the trenches") that it is not easy now to recover a feeling for the actualities. *Entrenched,* in an expression like *entrenched power,* has been a dead metaphor so long that we must bestir ourselves to recover its literal sense. It is time to take a tour.

From the winter of 1914 until the spring of 1918 the trench system was fixed, moving here and there a few hundred yards, moving on great occasions as much as a few miles. London stationers purveying maps felt secure in stocking "sheets of 'The Western Front' with a thick wavy black line drawn from North to South alongside which was printed 'British Line.'" If one could have gotten high enough to look down at the whole line at once, one would have seen a series of multiple parallel excavations running for 400 miles down through Belgium and France, roughly in the shape of an *S* flattened at the sides and tipped to the left. From the North Sea coast of Belgium the line wandered southward, bulging out to contain Ypres, then dropping down to protect Béthune, Arras, and Albert. It continued south in front of Montidier, Compiégne, Soissons, Reims, Verdun, St. Mihiel, and Nancy, and finally attached its southernmost end to the Swiss border at Beurnevisin, in Alsace. The top forty miles—the part north of Ypres—was held by the Belgians; the next ninety miles, down to the river Ancre, were British; the French held the rest, to the south.

Henri Barbusse estimates that the French front alone contained about 6,250 miles of trenches. Since the French occupied a little more than half the line, the total length of the numerous trenches occupied by the British must come to about 6,000 miles. We thus find over 12,000 miles of trenches on the Allied side alone. When we add the trenches of the Central Powers, we arrive at a figure of about 25,000 miles, equal to a trench sufficient to circle the earth. Theoretically it would have been possible to walk from Belgium to Switzerland entirely below ground, but although the lines were "continuous," they were not entirely seamless: occasionally mere shell holes or fortified strongpoints would serve as a connecting link. Not a few survivors have performed the heady imaginative exercise of envisioning the whole line at once. Stanley Casson is one who, imagining the whole line from his position on the ground, implicitly submits the whole preposterous conception to the criterion of the "normally" rational and intelligible. As he remembers, looking back from 1935:

Our trenches stood on a faint slope, just overlooking German ground, with a vista of vague plainland below. Away to right and left stretched the great lines of defense as far as eye and imagination could stretch them. I used to wonder how long it would take for me to walk from the beaches of the North Sea to that curious end of all fighting against the Swiss boundary; to try to guess what each end looked like; to imagine what would happen if I passed a verbal message, in the manner of the parlor game, along to the next man on my right to be delivered to the end man of all up against the Alps. Would anything intelligible at all emerge?

Another imagination has contemplated a similar absurd transmission of sound all the way from north to south. Alexander Aitken remembers the Germans opposite him celebrating some happy public event in early June, 1916, presumably either the (ambiguous) German success at the naval battle of Jutland (May 31–June 1) or the drowning of Lord Kitchener, lost on June 5 when the cruiser *Hampshire* struck a mine and sank off the Orkney Islands. Aitken writes, "There had been a morning in early June when a tremendous tin-canning and beating of shell-gongs had begun in the north and run south down their lines to end, without doubt, at Belfort and Mulhausen on the Swiss frontier." Impossible to believe, really, but in this mad setting, somehow plausible.

The British part of the line was normally populated by about 800 battalions of 1,000 men each. They were concentrated in the two main sectors of the British effort: the Ypres Salient in Flanders and the Somme area in Picardy. Memory has given these two sectors the appearance of two distinguishable worlds. The Salient, at its largest point about nine miles wide and projecting some four miles into the German line, was notable for its terrors of concentrated, accurate artillery fire. Every part of it could be covered from three sides, and at night one saw oneself almost surrounded by the circle of white and colored lights set up by the Germans to illuminate the ground in front of their trenches or to signal to the artillery behind them. The "rear area" at Ypres was the battered city itself, where the troops harbored in cellars or in the old fortifications built by Vauban in the seventeenth century. It was eminently available to the German guns, and by the end of the war Ypres was flattened to the ground, its name a byword for a city totally destroyed. Another war later, in 1940, Colin Perry—who was not born until four years after the Great War—could look at the ruins of London and speak of "the Ypres effect of Holborn." If the character of the Ypres sector was concentration and enclosure, inducing claustrophobia even above ground, the Somme was known—at least until July 1, 1916—for its greater amplitude and security. German fire came generally from only one direction; and troops at rest could move further back. But then there was the Somme mud; although the argument about whether the mud wasn't really worse at Ypres was never settled.

Each of these two sectors had its symbolic piece of ruined public architecture. At Ypres it was the famous Cloth Hall, once a masterpiece of medieval Flemish civic building. Its gradual destruction by artillery and its pathetic final dissolution were witnessed by hundreds of thousands, who never forgot this eloquent emblem of what happens when war collides with art. In the Somme the memorable ruined work of architecture, connoting this time the collision of the war with religion and the old pieties, was the bat-

tered Basilica in the town of Albert, or "Bert," as the troops called it. The grand if rather vulgar red and white brick edifice had been built a few years before the war, the result of a local ecclesiastic's enthusiasm. Together with his townsmen he hoped that Albert might become another Lourdes. Before the war 80,000 used to come on pilgrimages to Albert every year. The object of veneration inside the church was a statue of the Virgin, said to have been found in the Middle Ages by a local shepherd. But the statue of the Virgin never forgotten by the hordes of soldiers who passed through Albert was the colossal gilded one on top of the battered tall tower of the Basilica. This figure, called Notre Dame des Brebiéres, originally held the infant Christ in outstretched arms above her; but now the whole statue was bent down below the horizontal, giving the effect of a mother about to throw her child—in disgust? in sacrifice?—into the debris-littered street below. To Colonel Sir Maurice Hankey, Secretary of the War Committee, it was "a most pathetic sight." Some said that the statue had been bent down by French engineers to prevent the Germans from using it to aim at. But most—John Masefield among them—preferred to think it a victim of German artillery. Its obvious symbolic potential (which I will deal with later) impressed itself even on men who found they could refer to it only facetiously, as "The Lady of the Limp."

The two main British sectors duplicated each other also in their almost symbolic road systems. Each had a staging town behind: for Ypres it was Poperinghe (to the men, "Pop"); for the Somme, Amiens. From these towns troops proceeded with augmenting but usually well-concealed terror up a sinister road to the town of operations, either Ypres itself or Albert. And running into the enemy lines out of Ypres and Albert were the most sinister roads of all, one leading to Menin, the other to Bapaume, both in enemy territory. These roads defined the direction of ultimate attack and the hoped-for breakout. They were the goals of the bizarre inverse quest on which the soldiers were ironically embarked.

But most of the time they were not questing. They were sitting or lying or squatting in places below the level of the ground. "When all is said and done," Sassoon notes, "the war was mainly a matter of holes and ditches." And in these holes and ditches extending for ninety miles, continually, even in the quietest times, some 7,000 British men and officers were killed and wounded daily, just as a matter of course. "Wastage," the Staff called it.

There were normally three lines of trenches. The front-line trench was anywhere from fifty yards or so to a mile from its enemy counterpart. Several hundred yards behind it was the support trench line. And several hundred yards behind that was the reserve line. There were three kinds of trenches: firing trenches, like these; communication trenches, running roughly perpendicular to the line and connecting the three lines; and "saps," shallower ditches thrust out into No Man's Land, providing access to forward observation posts, listening posts, grenade-throwing posts, and machine gun positions. The end of a sap was usually not manned all the time: night was the favorite time for going out. Coming up from the rear, one reached the trenches by following a communication trench sometimes a mile or more long. It often began in a town and gradually deepened. By the time pedestrians reached the reserve line, they were well below ground level.

A firing trench was supposed to be six to eight feet deep and four or five feet wide. On the enemy side a parapet of earth or sandbags rose about two or three feet above the ground. A corresponding "parados" a foot or so high was often found on top of the friendly side. Into the sides of trenches were dug one- or two-man holes ("funk-holes"), and there were deeper dugouts, reached by dirt stairs, for use as command posts and officers' quarters. On the enemy side of a trench was a fire-step two feet high on which the defenders were supposed to stand, firing and throwing grenades, when repelling attack. A well-built trench did not run straight for any distance: that would have been to invite enfilade fire. Every few yards a good trench zigzagged. It had frequent

traverses designed to contain damage within a limited space. Moving along a trench thus involved a great deal of weaving and turning. The floor of a proper trench was covered with wooden duckboards, beneath which were sumps a few feet deep designed to collect water. The walls, perpetually crumbling, were supported by sandbags, corrugated iron, or bundles of sticks or rushes. Except at night and in half-light, there was of course no looking over the top except through periscopes, which could be purchased in the "Trench Requisites" section of the main London department stores. The few snipers on duty during the day observed No Man's Land through loopholes cut in sheets of armor plate.

The entanglements of barbed wire had to be positioned far enough out in front of the trench to keep the enemy from sneaking up to grenade-throwing distance. Interestingly, the two novelties that contributed most to the personal menace of the war could be said to be American inventions. Barbed wire had first appeared on the American frontier in the late nineteenth century for use in restraining animals. And the machine gun was the brainchild of Hiram Stevens Maxim (1840–1916), an American who, disillusioned with native patent law, established his Maxim Gun Company in England and began manufacturing his guns in 1889. He was finally knighted for his efforts. At first the British regard for barbed wire was on a par with Sir Douglas Haig's understanding of the machine gun. In the autumn of 1914, the first wire Private Frank Richards saw emplaced before the British positions was a single strand of agricultural wire found in the vicinity. Only later did the manufactured article begin to arrive from England in sufficient quantity to create the thickets of mock-organic rusty brown that helped give a look of eternal autumn to the front.

The whole British line was numbered by sections, neatly, from right to left. A section, normally occupied by a company, was roughly 300 yards wide. One might be occupying front-line trench section 51; or support trench S 51, behind it; or reserve trench SS 51, behind both. But a less formal way of identifying sections of trench was

Trench warfare was a common practice during World War II. Here, U.S. troops set up trench artillery in France.

by place or street names with a distinctly London flavor. *Piccadilly* was a favorite; popular also were *Regent Street* and *Strand;* junctions were *Hyde Park Corner* and *Marble Arch*. Greater wit—and deeper homesickness—sometimes surfaced in the naming of the German trenches opposite. Sassoon remembers "Durley's" account of the attack at Delville Wood in September, 1916: "Our objective was Pint Trench, taking Bitter and Beer and clearing Ale and Vat, and also Pilsen Lane." Directional and traffic control signs were everywhere in the trenches, giving the whole system the air of a parody modern city, although one literally "underground".

The trenches I have described are more or less ideal, although not so ideal as the famous exhibition trenches dug in Kensington Gardens for the edification of the home front. These were clean, dry, and well furnished, with straight sides and sandbags neatly aligned. R. E. Vernède writes his wife from the real trenches that a friend of his has just returned from viewing the set of ideal ones. He "found he had never seen anything at all like it before." And Wilfred Owen calls the Kensington Gardens trenches "the laughing stock of the army." Explaining military routines to civilian readers, Ian Hay labors to give the impression that the

real trenches are identical to the exhibition ones and that they are properly described in the language of normal domesticity a bit archly deployed:

The firing-trench is our place of business—our office in the city, so to speak. The supporting trench is our suburban residence, whither the weary toiler may betake himself periodically (or, more correctly, in relays) for purposes of refreshment and repose.

The reality was different. The British trenches were wet, cold, smelly, and thoroughly squalid. Compared with the precise and thorough German works, they were decidedly amateur, reflecting a complacency about the British genius for improvisation. Since defense offered little opportunity for the display of pluck or swank, it was by implication derogated in the officers' *Field Service Pocket Book*. One reason the British trench system was so haphazard and ramshackle was that it had originally taken form in accord with the official injunction: "The choice of a [defensive] position and its preparation must be made with a view to economizing the power expended on defense in order that the power of offense may be increased." And it was considered really useless to build solid fortifications anyway: "An occasional shell may strike and penetrate the parapet, but in the case of shrapnel the damage to the parapet will be trifling, while in the case of a shell filled with high explosive, the effect will be no worse on a thin parapet than on a thick one. It is, therefore, useless to spend time and labor on making a thick parapet simply to keep out shells." The repeatedly revived hopes for a general breakout and pursuit were another reason why the British trenches were so shabby. A typical soldier's view is George Coppard's:

The whole conduct of our trench warfare seemed to be based on the concept that we, the British, were not stopping in the trenches for long, but were tarrying awhile on the way to Berlin and that very soon we would be chasing Jerry across country. The result, in the long term, meant that we lived a mean and impoverished sort of existence in lousy scratch holes.

In contrast, the German trenches, as the British discovered during the attack on the Somme, were deep, clean, elaborate, and sometimes even comfortable. As Coppard found on the Somme, "Some of the [German] dugouts were thirty feet deep, with as many as sixteen bunk-beds, as well as door bells, water tanks with taps, and cupboards and mirrors." They also had boarded walls, floors, and ceilings; finished wooden staircases; electric light; real kitchens; and wallpaper and overstuffed furniture, the whole protected by steel outer doors. Foreign to the British style was a German dugout of the sort recalled by Ernst Jünger:

At Monchy . . . I was master of an underground dwelling approached by forty steps hewn in the solid chalk, so that even the heaviest shells at this depth made no more than a pleasant rumble when we sat there over an interminable game of cards. In one wall I had a bed hewn out. . . . At its head hung an electric light so that I could read in comfort till I was sleepy. . . . The whole was shut off from the

outer world by a dark-red curtain with rod and rings. . . .

As these examples suggest, there were "national styles" in trenches as in other things. The French trenches were nasty, cynical, efficient, and temporary. Kipling remembered the smell of delicious cooking emanating from some in Alsace. The English were amateur, vague, *ad hoc,* and temporary. The German were efficient, clean, pedantic, and permanent. Their occupants proposed to stay where they were.

Normally the British troops rotated trench duty. After a week of "rest" behind the lines, a unit would move up—at night—to relieve a unit in the front-line trench. After three days to a week or more in that position, the unit would move back for a similar length of time to the support trench, and finally back to the reserve. Then it was time for a week of rest again. In the three lines of trenches the main business of the soldier was to exercise self-control while being shelled. As the poet Louis Simpson has accurately remembered:

*Being shelled is the main work of an infantry soldier, which no one talks about. Everyone has his own way of going about it. In general, it means lying face down and contracting your body into as small a space as possible. In novels [*The Naked and the Dead *is an example] you read about soldiers, at such moments, fouling themselves. The opposite is true. As all your parts are contracting, you are more likely to be constipated.*

Simpson is recalling the Second War, but he might be recalling the First. While being shelled, the soldier either harbored in a dugout and hoped for something other than a direct hit or made himself as small as possible in a funk-hole. An unlucky sentry or two was supposed to be out in the open trench in all but the worst bombardments, watching through a periscope or loophole for signs of an attack. When only light shelling was in progress, people moved about the trenches freely, and we can get an idea of what life there was like if we posit a typical twenty-four hours in a front-line trench.

The day began about an hour before first light, which often meant at about 4:30. This was the moment for the invariable ritual of morning stand-to (short for the archaic formal command for repelling attack, "Stand to Arms"). Since dawn was the favorite time for launching attacks, at the order to stand-to everyone, officers, men, forward artillery observers, visitors, mounted the fire-step, weapon ready, and peered toward the German line. When it was almost full light and clear that the Germans were not going to attack that morning, everyone "stood down" and began preparing breakfast in small groups. The rations of tea, bread, and bacon, brought up in sandbags during the night, were broken out. The bacon was fried in mess-tin lids over small, and if possible smokeless, fires. If the men were lucky enough to be in a division whose commanding general permitted the issue of the dark and strong government rum, it was doled out from a jar with the traditional iron spoon, each man receiving about two tablespoonsful. Some put it into their tea, but most swallowed it straight. It was a precious thing, and serving it out was almost like a religious ceremonial, as David Jones recalls in *In Parenthesis,* where a corporal is performing the rite:

> *O have a care—don't spill the precious*
> *O don't jog his hand—ministering; do*
>   *take care.*
> *O please—give the poor bugger elbow*
>   *room.*

Larger quantities might be issued to stimulate troops for an assault, and one soldier remembers what the air smelled like during a British attack: "Pervading the air was the smell of rum and blood." In 1922 one medical officer deposed before a parliamentary committee investigating the phenomenon of "shell shock": "Had it not been for the rum ration I do not think we should have won the war."

During the day the men cleaned weapons and repaired those parts of the trench damaged during the night. Or they wrote letters, deloused themselves, or slept. The officers inspected, encouraged, and strolled about looking nonchalant to inspirit the men. They censored the men's letters and dealt with the quantities of official inquiries brought them daily by runner. How many pipe-fitters had they in their company? Reply immediately. How many hairdressers, chiropodists, bicycle repairmen? Daily "returns" of the amount of ammunition and the quantity of trench stores had to be made. Reports of the nightly casualties had to be sent back. And letters of condolence, which as the war went on became form letters of condolence, had to be written to the relatives of the killed and wounded. Men went to and fro on sentry duty or working parties, but no one showed himself above the trench. After evening stand-to, the real work began.

Most of it was above ground. Wiring parties repaired the wire in front of the position. Digging parties extended saps toward the enemy. Carrying parties brought up not just rations and mail but the heavy engineering materials needed for the constant repair and improvement of the trenches: timbers, A-frames, duckboards, stakes and wire, corrugated iron, sandbags, tarpaulins, pumping equipment. Bombs and ammunition and flares were carried forward. All this ant-work was illuminated brightly from time to time by German flares and interrupted very frequently by machine gun or artillery fire. Meanwhile night patrols and raiding parties were busy in No Man's Land. As morning approached, there was a nervous bustle to get the jobs done in time, to finish fitting the timers, filling the sandbags, pounding in the stakes, and then returning mauls and picks and shovels to the Quartermaster Sergeant. By the time of stand-to, nothing human was visible above ground anywhere, but every day each side scrutinized the look of the other's line for significant changes wrought by night.

Flanders and Picardy have always been notorious for dampness. It is not the least of the ironies of the war for the British that their trenches should have been dug where the water-table was the highest and the annual rainfall the most copious. Their trenches were always wet and often flooded several feet deep. Thigh-boots or waders were issued as standard articles of uniform. Wilfred Owen writes his mother from the Somme at the beginning of 1917: "The waders are of course indispensable. In 2 1/2 miles of trench which I waded yesterday there was not one inch of dry ground. There is a mean depth of two feet of water." Pumps worked day and night but to little effect. Rumor held that the Germans not only could make it rain when they wanted it to—that is, all the time—but had contrived some shrewd technical method for conducting the water in their lines into the British positions—perhaps piping it underground. Ultimately there was no defense against the water but humor. "Water knee deep and up to the waist in places," one soldier notes in his diary. "Rumors of being relieved by the Grand Fleet." One doesn't want to dwell excessively on such discomforts, but here it will do no harm to try to imagine what, in these conditions, going to the latrine was like.

The men were not the only live things in the line. They were accompanied everywhere by their lice, which the professional delousers in rest positions behind the lines, with their steam vats for clothes and hot baths for troops, could do little to eliminate. The entry *lousy* in Eric Partridge's *Dictionary of Slang and Unconventional English* speaks volumes: "Contemptible; mean; filthy. . . . Standard English till 20th C, when, especially after the Great War, colloquial and used as a mere pejorative." *Lousy with,* meaning *full of,* was "originally military" and entered the colloquial word-hoard around 1915: "That ridge is lousy with Fritz."

The famous rats also gave constant trouble. They were big and black, with wet, muddy hair. They fed largely on the flesh of cadavers and on dead horses. One shot them with revolvers or coshed them to death with pick handles. Their hunger, vigor, intelligence, and courage are recalled in numerous anecdotes. One officer notes from the Ypres Salient: "We are fairly plagued with rats. They have eaten nearly everything in the mess, including the tablecloth and the operations orders! We borrowed a large cat and shut it up at night to exterminate them, and found the place empty next morning. The rats must have eaten it up, bones, fur, and all, and dragged it to their holes."

One can understand rats eating heartily there. It is harder to understand men doing so. The stench of rotten flesh was over everything, hardly repressed by the chloride of lime sprinkled on particularly offensive sites. Dead horses and dead men—and parts of both—were sometimes not buried for months and often simply became an element of parapets and trench walls. You could smell the front line miles before you could see it. Lingering pockets of gas added to the unappetizing atmosphere. Yet men ate three times a day, although what they ate reflected the usual gulf between the ideal and the actual. The propagandist George Adam announced with satisfaction that "the food of the army is based upon the conclusions of a committee, upon which sat several eminent scientists." The result, he asserted, is that the troops are "better fed than they are at home." Officially, each man got daily: 1 1/4 pounds fresh meat (or 1 pound preserved meat), 1 1/4 pounds bread, 4 ounces bacon, 3 ounces cheese, 1/2 pound fresh vegetables (or 2 ounces dried), together with small amounts of tea, sugar, and jam. But in the trenches there was very seldom fresh meat, not for eating, anyway; instead there was "Bully" (tinned corned-beef) or "Maconochie" (ma-cón-o-chie), a tinned meat-and-vegetable stew named after its manufacturer. If they did tend to grow tedious in the long run, both products were surprisingly good. The troops seemed to like the Maconochie best, but the Germans favored the British corned beef, seldom returning from a raid on the British lines without taking back as much as they could carry. On trench duty the British had as little fresh bread as fresh meat. "Pearl Biscuits" were the substitute. They reminded the men of dog biscuits, although, together with the Bully beef, they were popular with the French and Belgian urchins, who ran (or more often strolled) alongside the railway trains bringing troops up to the front, soliciting gifts by shouting, "Tommee! Bull-ee! Bee-skee!" When a company was out of the line, it fed better. It was then serviced by its company cookers—stoves on wheels—and often got something approaching the official ration, as it might also in a particularly somnolent part of the line, when hot food might come up at night in the large covered containers known as Dixies.

Clothing and equipment improved as the war went on, although at the outset there was a terrible dearth and improvisation. During the retreat from Mons, as Frank Richards testifies, "A lot of us had no caps: I was wearing a handkerchief knotted at the four corners—the only headgear I was to wear for some time." Crucial supplies had been omitted: "We had plenty of small-arm ammunition but no rifle-oil or rifle-rag to clean our rifles with. We used to cut pieces off our shirts . . . and some of us who had bought small tins of vaseline . . . for use on sore heels or chafed legs, used to grease our rifles with that." At the beginning line officers dressed very differently from the men. They wore riding-boots or leather puttees; melodramatically cut riding breeches; and flare-skirted tunics with Sam Browne belts. Discovering that this costume made them special targets in attacks (German gunners were instructed to fire first at the people with the thin knees), by the end they were dressing like the troops, wearing wrap puttees; straight trousers bloused below the knee; Other Ranks' tunics with inconspicuous insignia, no longer on the cuffs but on the shoulders; and Other Ranks' web belts and haversacks. In 1914 both officers and men wore peaked caps, and it was rakish for officers to remove the grommet for a "Gorblimey" effect. Steel helmets were introduced at the end of 1915, giving the troops, as Sassoon observed, "a Chinese look." Herbert Read found the helmets "the only poetic thing in the British Army, for they are primeval in design and effect, like iron mushrooms." A perceptive observer could date corpses and skeletons lying on disused battlefields by their evolving dress. A month before the end of the war, Major P. H. Pilditch recalls, he

spent some time in the old No Man's Land of four years' duration. . . . It was a morbid but intensely interesting occupation tracing the various battles amongst the hundreds of skulls, bones and remains scattered thickly about. The progress of our successive attacks could be clearly seen from the types of equipment on the skeletons, soft cloth caps denoting the 1914 and early 1915 fighting, then respirators, then steel helmets marking attack in 1916. Also Australian slouch hats, used in the costly and abortive attack in 1916.

To be in the trenches was to experience an unreal, unforgettable enclosure and constraint, as well as a sense of being unoriented and lost. One saw two things only: the walls of an unlocalized, undifferentiated earth and the sky above. Fourteen years after the war J. R. Ackerley was wandering through an unfrequented part of a town in India. "The streets became narrower and narrower as I turned and turned," he writes, "until I felt I was back in the trenches, the houses upon either side being so much of the same color and substance as the rough ground between." That lost feeling is what struck Major Frank Isherwood, who writes his wife in December, 1914. "The trenches are a labyrinth, I have already lost myself repeatedly. . . . You can't get out of them and walk about the country or see anything at all but two muddy walls on each side of you." What a survivor of the Salient remembers fifty years later are the walls of dirt and the ceiling of sky, and his eloquent optative cry rises as if he were still imprisoned there: "To be out of this present, everpresent, eternally present misery, this stinking world of sticky, trickling earth ceilinged by a strip of threatening sky." As the only visible theater of variety, the sky becomes all-important. It was the sight of the sky, almost alone, that had the power to persuade a man that he was not already lost in a common grave.

Study Questions

1. What was the effect of World War I on the landscape of Europe?

2. In theory, how were the trenches supposed to be constructed? What was life supposed to be like in the ideal trench? How did reality differ from theory?

3. What national differences were there in the construction and maintenance of trenches? What do the differences tell us about the different national characters and war aims?

4. Describe the sights, sounds, and smell of life in the trenches. How did trench life affect the soldiers?

5. What does Fussell mean when he describes the experience as "unreal"? How did trench life breed "a sense of being unoriented and lost"?

Bibliography

The above selection is taken from Fussell's award-winning *The Great War and Modern Memory* (1975), the best discussion of the impact of the war on modern culture. Robert Wohl, *The Generation of 1914* (1979), recreates the experiences of the men who fought and wrote about the war. Three good military overviews of the war are James L. Stokesbury, *A Short History of World War I* (1981); B. H. Liddell Hart, *The Real War, 1914-1918* (1930); and Cyril Falls, *The Great War* (1959). S. B. Fay, *The Origins of World War* (2 vols., 1928-1930); L. Albertini, *The Origins of the War of 1914* (3 vols., 1952-1957); and Fritz Fischer, *Germany's Aims in the First World War* (1967), discuss the complex origins of the war. The best studies of America's entry into the war are E. R. May, *The First World War and American Isolation* (1957); P. Devlin, *Too Proud to Fight: Woodrow Wilson's Neutrality* (1975); and Barbara Tuchman, *The Zimmerman Telegram* (1958). Tuchman's *Guns of August* (1994) chronicles the first thirty days of the war. Military studies that give the reader a sense of the problems faced by the typical soldier include Martin Middlebrooks, *The First Day on the Somme* (1971); Alister Horne, *The Price of Glory: Verdun, 1916* (1962); Leon Wolff, *In Flanders Field* (1958); Barrie Pitt, *The Last Act* (1962); and John Keegan, *The Face of Battle: A Study of Agincourt, Waterloo, and the Somme* (1976). Two recent books are especially good: John Keegan, *The First World War* (2000) and Gary Mead, *The Doughboys: America and the First World War* (2000).

Heroes and Society
in the 1920s

The year 1920 ushered in a decade that historians steadfastly refuse to discuss in anything less than superlative terms. The decade brings to mind Charles Dickens's description of the revolutionary years of the eighteenth century in his novel *A Tale of Two Cities:* "It was the best of times, it was the worst of times . . . it was the season of Light, it was the season of Darkness, it was the spring of hope, it was the winter of despair, we had everything before us, we had nothing before us." If a decade may be said to have a personality, then the 1920s had the personality of a child; sometimes laughing and playful, at other times brooding, brutal, and ugly.

The first and perhaps most widely read book about the decade was Frederick Lewis Allen's *Only Yesterday: An Informal History of the 1920s.* Published in 1931 during the midst of the Great Depression, *Only Yesterday* describes a carefree decade that began with the end of the Great War and ended with the stock market crash. Allen paints a decade that roars with excitement, a decade brimming with bathtub gin, bootleg liquor, and bubbling champagne. Gangsters, movie sex goddesses, athletic heroes, and fabulous moneymakers seem to come alive on the pages of *Only Yesterday.* In sweeping terms Allen examines the "revolution in manners and morals," the "aching disillusionment" of intellectuals, and the crass materialism of millions of Americans.

Allen was not necessarily wrong. The sexual mores of the youth were changing, and there was evidence of intellectual disillusionment and crass materialism. The problem with the book is that its sweeping generalizations are simply too sweeping. In addition, too much of the activity of the decade is left out. The economic plight of rural Americans, the rise of the Ku Klux Klan, urban-rural tensions, racial injustice, nativism, and religious revivalism are just a few of the subjects that Allen does not treat. As a result, *Only Yesterday* is a flawed and unbalanced classic.

THE AMERICAN
FLAPPER · 1927

In recent years historians have explored the areas where Allen did not venture. And they have presented a different view of the 1920s, viewing the decade as a period of transition where older rural and newer urban attitudes uneasily coexisted. Although the country was becoming increasingly urban and bureaucratic, many Americans clung tightly to the more traditional values of their parents and grandparents. In an effort to preserve these values, they supported a variety of movements such as the Society for the Preservation of New England Antiquities, the Ku Klux Klan, and the National Origins Act of 1924.

If rural America resisted change, most of urban America accepted it. Spectators filled movie theaters and athletic stadiums to watch others perform, and entertainment became a product that was packaged and marketed by business executives. Millions of Americans worshipped at the altar of business efficiency and organization. Even crime became more organized and efficient. By 1929 the debate between rural and urban America was decided. The future belonged to the cities.

READING 12

★ ★ ★

The Mood of the People

Roderick Nash

No decade in American history has been more studded with heroes and idols than the 1920s. Such athletic heroes as Babe Ruth, Jack Dempsey, Red Grange, Bill Tilden, and Bobby Jones are still household names. In Hollywood, they were rivaled by stars such as Rudolph Valentino, Mary Pickford, Douglas Fairbanks, Clara Bow, and Charlie Chaplin. Heroes even came from the worlds of business, finance, and government. Herbert Hoover and Edward Bok demonstrated the appeal of self-made millionaires. The greatest hero, however, was Charles Lindbergh, who captured the public's imagination in 1927 by making the first solo flight across the Atlantic.

Nor has there been a decade that has been more acclaimed for its literary output. Novelists F. Scott Fitzgerald and Ernest Hemingway and poets e. e. cummings, T. S. Eliot, and Edna St. Vincent Millay are among the most talented America ever produced. More people, however, read the stories of such popular novelists as Gene Stratton-Porter, Harold Bell Wright, Zane Grey, and Edgar Rice Burroughs.

In the following essay, historian Roderick Nash probes the meaning behind the heroes people chose and the novels they read. Heroes, Nash claims, reflect the "mood of the people"; they mirror the aspirations, longings, and fears of millions of unheralded Americans. Similarly, popular novelists' success depends on their ability to interpret and tap the mood of the nation. That mood, Nash feels, was not bold and carefree, as Frederick Lewis Allen believed, but rather timid and nervous. Americans chose heroes and read novels that glorified their rural past and eased their minds concerning their urban future.

Heroes abounded in the American 1920s. Their names, especially in sports, have been ticked off so frequently they have become clichés. Less often have commentators paused to probe for explanations. Why were the twenties ripe for heroism? And why did the heroics follow a predictable pattern? Such questions lead to an understanding of the mood of the people, because heroism concerns the public as well as the individual. It depends on achievement but even more on recognition. In the final analysis the hopes and fears of everyday Americans create national heroes.

The nervousness of the post-World War I generation provided fertile soil for the growth of a particular kind of heroism. Many Americans felt uneasy as they experienced the transforming effects of population growth, urbanization, and economic change. On the one hand, these developments were welcome as steps in the direction of progress. Yet they also raised vague fears about the passing of frontier conditions, the loss of national vigor, and the eclipse of the individual in a mass society. Frederick Jackson Turner and Theodore Roosevelt, among others, had pointed to the liabilities of the transformation at the turn of the century. World War I underscored the misgivings and doubts. By the 1920s the sense of change had penetrated to the roots of popular thought. Scarcely an American was unaware that the frontier had vanished and that pioneering, in the traditional sense, was a thing of the past. Physical changes in the nation were undeniable. They occurred faster, however, than intellectual adjustment. Although Americans, in general, lived in a densely populated, urban industrial civilization, a large part of their values remained rooted in the frontier, farm, and village. Exposure of this discrepancy only served to increase the tightness with which insecure people clung to the old certainties. Old-style pioneering was impossible, but Americans proved ingenious in finding equivalents. The upshot in the twenties was the cult of the hero—the man who provided living testimony of the power of courage, strength, and honor and of the efficacy of the self-reliant, rugged individual who seemed on the verge of becoming as irrelevant as the covered wagon.

Sports and the star athlete were the immediate beneficiaries of this frame of mind. The American sports fan regarded the playing field as a surrogate frontier; the athletic hero was the twentieth-century equivalent of the pathfinder or pioneer. In athletic competition, as on the frontier, people believed, men confronted tangible obstacles and overcame them with talent and determination. The action in each case was clean and direct; the goals, whether clearing forests or clearing the bases, were easily perceived and immensely satisfying. Victory was the result of superior ability. The sports arena, like the frontier, was pregnant with opportunity for the individual. The start was equal and the best man won. Merit was rewarded. True or not, such a credo was almost instinctive with Americans. They packed the stadiums of the 1920s in a salute to time-honored virtues. With so much else about America changing rapidly, it was comforting to find in sports a ritualistic celebration of the major components of the national faith.

Writing in the *North American Review* for October 1929, A. A. Brill, a leading American psychologist of the Freudian school, took a closer look at the meaning of athletics. Why, he wondered, do men play and why do they select the particular kinds of play they do? Brill was also interested in the reasons spectators came to games. His main point was that sports were not idle diversions but intensely serious endeavors rooted in the values and traditions of a civilization. "The ancestry of sport," Brill declared, "is written very plainly in the fact that the first games among all nations were simple imitations of the typical acts of warriors and huntsmen." The primary motivation of play, according to Brill, was the "mastery impulse"—and inherent aggressiveness in man stemming from the Darwinian struggle for existence. Modern man had largely transcended direct physical struggle, but the need for it persisted in the human psyche. Sports were contrived as substitutes for actual fighting, mock struggles that satisfied the urge to conquer. Brill did not suggest a relationship between American sports and the American frontier, but his argument suggested one. So did the fact that the rise of mass spectator sports and the decline of the frontier were simultaneous in the United States.

By the 1920s the nation went sports crazy. It seemed to many that a golden age of sport had arrived in America. Football received a large portion of the limelight. As they had in the declining days of Rome, fans thronged the stadiums to witness contact, violence, bloodshed, man pitted against man, strength against strength. The vicarious element was invariably present. For a brief, glorious moment the nobody in the bleachers *was* the halfback crashing into the end zone with the winning touchdown. For a moment he shared the thrill of individual success and fought off the specter of being swallowed up in mass society.

Big-time professional football began on September 17, 1920, when the American Football Association was organized with the great Indian athlete Jim Thorpe as its first president. When the Green Bay Packers joined the Association in 1921, the saga of pro football was solidly launched. Attendance rose dramatically. On November 21, 1925, the presence on the playing field of the fabled Harold "Red" Grange helped draw 36,000 spectators to a game. A week later 68,000 jammed the Polo Grounds in New York to watch Grange in action. The names of the pro teams were suggestive. As on the frontier of old, it was cowboys versus Indians, or giants versus bears—with the names of cities prefixed.

The twenties was also the time of the emergence of college football on an unprecedented scale. Heroes appeared in good supply: Red Grange at Illinois, Knute Rockne's "Four Horsemen" at Notre Dame in 1924, Harold "Brick" Muller who began a dynasty at California that extended through fifty consecutive victories in the

seasons 1919 through 1925. Hundreds of thousands attended the Saturday games, an estimated twenty million during the season. Millions more followed the action over their radios and made a Sunday morning ritual of devouring the newspaper accounts of the games of the previous day. To accommodate the crowds colleges and universities built huge new stadiums. Yale's and California's seated eighty thousand; Illinois, Ohio State, and Michigan were not far behind. The number of Americans who attended games doubled between 1921 and 1930. A *Harper's* writer caught the spirit of college football in 1928: "It is at present a religion, sometimes it seems to be almost our national religion." So, once, had been westward expansion.

Despite its popularity, football tended to obscure the heroic individual. It was, after all, a team sport. Even Red Grange received an occasional block on his long runs. But in sports pitting man against man or against the clock, the heroism latent in competition achieved its purest expression. Americans in the 1920s had a glittering array of well-publicized individuals from which to choose their idol. In golf Robert T. "Bobby" Jones, Walter Hagen, and Gene Sarazen were the dominant figures. Tennis had "Big" Bill Tilden and "Little" Bill Johnson whose epic duels on the center court at Forest Hills filled the stands. The competition was even more direct in boxing with its "knockout," the symbol of complete conquest. During the twenties promoters like Tex Rickard built boxing into a big business. Jack Dempsey and Gene Tunney proved so attractive to the sporting public that a ticket sale of a million dollars for a single fight became a reality. By the end of the decade the figure was two million. Fifty bouts in the twenties had gates of more than $100,000. More than 100,000 fans came to Soldiers' Field in Chicago on September 22, 1927, to see the second Dempsey-Tunney fight with its controversial "long count" that helped Tunney retain the championship and earn $990,000 for thirty minutes of work. In a nation not oblivious to the approach of middle age, it was comforting to count the heavyweight champion of the world among the citizenry. Here was evidence, many reasoned, that the nation remained strong, young, and fit to survive in a Darwinian universe. Record-breaking served the same purpose, and in Johnny Weismuller, premier swimmer, and Paavo Nurmi, Finnish-born track star, the United States had athletes who set world marks almost every time they competed. Gertrude Ederle chose a longer course when she swam the English Channel in 1926, but she too set a record and was treated to one of New York's legendary ticker-tape parades.

And there was the Babe. No sports hero of the twenties and few of any decade had the reputation of George Herman Ruth. Baseball was generally acknowledged to be the national game, and Ruth played with a superb supporting cast of New York Yankees, but when he faced a pitcher Babe Ruth stood as an individual. His home runs (particularly the 59 in 1921 and the 60 in 1927) gave him a heroic stature comparable to that of legendary demigods like Odysseus, Beowulf, or Daniel Boone. Ruth's unsavory background and boorish personal habits were nicely overlooked by talented sportswriters anxious to give the twenties the kind of hero it craved. The payoff was public adulation of the Babe and of baseball.

The twenties also saw the public exposure of corruption in baseball and confronted Americans with the necessity of reviewing their entire hero complex. On September 28, 1920, three members of the Chicago White Sox appeared before a grand jury to confess that they and five other players had agreed to throw the 1919 World Series to Cincinnati for a financial consideration. Gradually the unhappy story of the "Black Sox" unfolded. Big-time gamblers had persuaded selected players to make sure that a bet on the underdog Cincinnati team would pay off. Some of the greatest names in the game were involved, preeminently that of "Shoeless" Joe Jackson. An illiterate farm boy from South Carolina, Jackson's natural batting eye helped him compile a .356 average in ten seasons as a major leaguer. In the process he became one of the most idolized players in baseball. It was Jackson's exit from the grand jury chamber on September 28 that allegedly precipitated the agonized plea from

a group of boys: "Say it ain't so, Joe!" According to the newspapers, Jackson, shuffling, head down, replied, "Yes, boys, I'm afraid it is."

Reaction to the Black Sox testified to the importance baseball had for many Americans. One school of thought condemned the "fix" in the strongest terms and agitated for the restoration of integrity to the game. It was a serious matter. The Philadelphia *Bulletin* compared the eight players with "the soldier or sailor who would sell out his country and its flag in time of war." Suggesting the link between sports and the national character, the *New York Times* declared that bribing a ballplayer was an offense "which strikes at the very heart of this nation." If baseball fell from grace, what could be honest in America? The question haunted journalists and cartoonists. *Outlook* for October 13, 1920, carried a drawing of a crumpled statue of a ballplayer whose torn side revealed a stuffing of dollar bills. The statue bore the inscription "The National Game." A small boy wept in the foreground; the caption to the cartoon read "His Idol."

Baseball officials and club owners were similarly dismayed at the revelation of corruption and determined to clean up the game. Charles A. Comiskey, owner of the Chicago White Sox, led the way with a public statement that no man involved in the fix would ever wear the uniform of his club again. Other owners followed suit until all organized baseball, even the minor leagues, was closed to the Black Sox. On November 12, 1920, Kenesaw Mountain Landis, a former federal judge, was appointed commissioner of baseball with full control over the game and a charge to safeguard its integrity.

The everyday fans' response to the fix differed sharply from that of the sportswriters and owners. Many Americans seemed determined to deny the entire affair; more precisely, they didn't *want* to believe anything could be wrong with something as close to the national ideal as baseball. Like the boys of the "say it ain't so" episode, they begged for evidence that the old standards and values still applied. Especially in 1920 in the United States sports heroes were needed as evidence of the virtues of competition, fair play, and the self-reliant individual. Consequently, when confronted with the scandal, the average American simply closed his eyes and pretended nothing was wrong. The heroes remained heroes. When the Black Sox formed an exhibition team, it received enthusiastic support. Petitions were circulated in the major league cities to reinstate the players in organized baseball. But the most remarkable demonstration of the public's feeling came at the conclusion of the Black Sox trial on August 2, 1921. After deliberating two hours and forty-seven minutes, the jury returned a verdict of *not guilty*. According to the *New York Times* reporter at the scene, the packed courtroom rose as one man at the good news, cheering wildly. Hats sailed and papers were thrown about in the delirium. Men shouted "hooray for the clean sox." The bailiffs pounded for order until, as the *Times* reported, they "finally noticed Judge Friend's smiles, and then joined in the whistling and cheering." Finally the jury picked up the acquitted ballplayers and carried them out of the courtroom on their shoulders!

Baseball officials and journalists regarded the acquittal of the Black Sox as a technical verdict secured by the lenient interpretation of the Illinois statute involved. The fans in the courtroom, however, and, presumably, many elsewhere were on the side of the players regardless, and viewed the verdict as a vindication. They were not prepared to believe that baseball or its heroes could become tarnished. The game was too important to the national ego. Following baseball gave Americans an opportunity to pay tribute to what many believed was the best part of their heritage. The game was a sacred rite undertaken not merely to determine the winner of league championships but to celebrate the values of a civilization. As one newspaper account of the scandal put it, to learn that "Shoeless" Joe Jackson had sold out the world series was like discovering that "Daniel Boone had been bought by the Indians to lose his fights in Kentucky."

In the gallery of popular heroes in the United States the only rival of the frontiersman and his

athletic surrogate was the self-made man. In the 1920s the archetype was Herbert Hoover, a hero-President hewn out of the traditional rags-to-riches mold. Left an orphan in 1884 at the age of ten, Hoover launched an international career in mining that made him rich. During World War I he became famous, heading the American Relief Commission abroad and the Food Administration at home. A genius in matters of large-scale efficiency, Hoover neatly executed apparent miracles. After the decline of Woodrow Wilson in the wake of the Versailles Treaty, Hoover was easily the foremost American beneficiary of war-caused popularity. In 1922, while Secretary of Commerce under Warren G. Harding, he set forth his creed in a slender book entitled *American Individualism.* Apparently oblivious of the doubts that beset intellectuals at the time, Hoover professed his "abiding faith in the intelligence, the initiative, the character, the courage, and the divine touch in the individual." But he also believed that individuals differed greatly in energy, ability, and ambition. Some men inevitably rose to the top of the heap, and for Hoover this was entirely right and proper. It was necessary, moreover, if society were to progress. Hoover's philosophy was the old American one of rugged individualism and free enterprise that the Social Darwinists had decorated with scientific tinsel after the Civil War. Intellectually, Hoover was a bedfellow with Benjamin Franklin and William Graham Sumner.

Hoover's social, political, and economic ideas followed from these assumptions. He staunchly defended the unregulated profit system. Society and government owed the people only three things: "liberty, justice, and equality of opportunity." Competition took care of the rest, carrying the deserving to their just rewards and the failures to deserved defeat. Any interference, such as philanthropy to the poor or favoritism to the rich, only dulled *"the emery wheel of competition."* To be sure, Hoover paid lip service to restricting the strong in the interest of the society, but the main thrust of his thought awarded the victors their spoils. Critics were disarmed with three words—"equality of opportunity." The state should interfere to preserve it; otherwise, hands off! An exponent of the gospel of efficiency in economic affairs, Hoover believed that the road to the good life lay in the direction of more and better production. His mind equated material success with progress.

In the concluding chapter of *American Individualism,* Hoover drew the connection between his philosophy and the frontier. "The American pioneer," he declared, "is the epic expression of . . . individualism and the pioneer spirit is the response to the challenge of opportunity, to the challenge of nature, to the challenge of life, to the call of the frontier." Undismayed by the ending of the geographical frontier in the United States, Hoover declared that "there will always be a frontier to conquer or to hold to as long as men think, plan, and dare. . . . The days of the pioneer are not over."

When Hoover was elected President in 1928, these ideals were accorded the nation's highest accolade. They dominated popular thought as they had for three centuries of American history. In fact, all the men who occupied the Presidency from 1917 to 1930 were distinctly old-fashioned in their beliefs and in their public image. The traits are so familiar as to require listing only: Wilson the moralist and idealist; Harding the exemplar of small-town, "just folks" normalcy; Coolidge the frugal, farm-oriented Puritan; and Hoover the self-made man. If there was any correlation between a people's taste and its Presidents, then the record of this period underscored nostalgia.

Rivalling Hoover in the public mind of the early 1920s as an exponent of self-help and individualism was Edward Bok, the Dutch boy who made good and wrote about it in *The Americanization of Edward Bok* (1920). The book described Bok's immigration from Holland in 1870 at the age of six and his rise from a fifty-cents-a-week window cleaner to editor of the magazine with the largest circulation in the nation, the *Ladies Home Journal.* Bok's autobiography reads as a paean to the American ideal of success. Through luck, pluck, and clean living, he became a confidant and friend of Presidents. Thrift and determination made him rich. Bok played the rags to riches theme to the hilt. "Here was a little Dutch boy," he wrote in his preface, "unceremoniously set down in America . . . yet, it must be confessed, he achieved." His book, Bok promised, would describe "how such a boy, with every disadvantage to overcome, was able . . . to 'make good.'"

In the final chapters of his autobiography, Bok stepped back to comment on the liabilities and advantages of America. He did not slight the former, yet in "What I Owe to America" Bok brushed all debits aside in order to celebrate America's gift of "limitless opportunity: here a man can go as far as his abilities will carry him." For anyone "endowed with honest endeavor, ceaseless industry, and the ability to carry through, . . . the way is wide open to the will to succeed."

The public reception of *The Americanization of Edward Bok* suggests how much Americans in the 1920s wanted to confirm old beliefs. Bok was a hero in the Benjamin Franklin-Horatio Alger mold. His success story demonstrated that passing time and changing conditions had not altered hallowed ideals. His pages suggested no troubling doubts, and, after receiving the Pulitzer Prize for biography in 1921, Bok's book became a bestseller. An inexpensive eighth edition issued in July 1921 enabled it to attain third place on the 1922 lists. But the primary reason for Bok's popularity as hero-author was his ability to tell a nervous generation what it wanted to hear.

It has long puzzled students of the Great Crash of 1929 why even the most informed observers in education and government as well as business did not recognize and heed the prior economic danger signals that in retrospect seem so apparent. Part of the explanation possibly lies in the depth of the general commitment to the ideals of rugged individualism and free enterprise that Hoover and Bok articulated and symbolized. This commitment, in turn, lay in the nervousness of the American people. So much about the twenties was new and disturbing that Americans tended to cling tightly to familiar economic forms. They just could not bear to admit that the old business premises based on individualism and free enterprise might be fraught with peril. With Herbert

Hoover leading the way, they chose to go down with the economic ship rather than question and alter its suicidal course.

Respect for the old-time hero was evident in other aspects of postwar thought. The vogue of the Boy Scouts is an example. Although the movement began in 1910, the twenties was the time of its flowering. There were 245,000 Scouts at the beginning of 1917, 942,500 at the end of 1929. In addition, 275,000 adults volunteered their services as leaders. No youth club and few adult organizations matched this record. The Boy Scout Handbook, a manual of ideals and instruction, sold millions of copies. Scouting, apparently, tapped fertile soil in its embodiment of the old-time idea of good citizenship and expertise in the outdoors. The Scout, standing straight in his shorts or knickers and doing the daily good deed that his oath required, was the epitome of the traditional American model of heroic young manhood.

In the late 1920s the Boy Scout Handbook featured an unusual drawing. In the foreground was a clean-cut Scout, eyes fixed on adventure. Behind him, signifying the heritage from which he sprang, were the figures of Daniel Boone, Abraham Lincoln, and Theodore Roosevelt, men who were staples in the annals of American heroism. But there was also a new face, that of Charles A. Lindbergh of Minnesota. At the age of just twenty-five Lindbergh rose to the status of an American demigod by virtue of a single feat. On May 20, 1927, he took off in a tiny single-engine airplane from New York City and thirty-three hours later landed in Paris. The nonstop, solo run across the Atlantic catapulted the average American into a paroxysm of pride and joy. Overnight Lindbergh became the greatest hero of the decade. There was but little exaggeration in the contention of one journalist that Lindbergh received "the greatest ovation in history." Certainly his return from Paris to the United States generated a reception extraordinary even for an age that specialized in ballyhoo. The *New York Times* devoted more space to Lindbergh's return than it had to the Armistice ending World War I. A virtual national religion took shape around Lindbergh's person. A 1928 poll of schoolboys in a typical American town on the question of whom they most wanted to be like produced the following results: Gene Tunney, 13 votes; John Pershing, 14; Alfred E. Smith, 16; Thomas A. Edison, 27; Henry Ford, 66; Calvin Coolidge, 110; Charles A. Lindbergh, 363. If the amount of national adulation is meaningful, adults everywhere would likely have responded in similar proportions.

The explanation of Lindbergh's popularity lies less in his feat (pilots had flown across the Atlantic before) and more in the mood of the people at the time it occurred. The typical American in 1927 was nervous. The values by which he ordered his life seemed in jeopardy of being swept away by the force of growth and change and complexity. Lindbergh came as a restorative tonic. He reasserted the image of the confident, quietly courageous, and self-reliant individual. He proved to a generation anxious for proof that Americans were still capable of pioneering. Even in an age of machines the frontier was not dead— a new one had been found in the air.

The reaction to Lindbergh's flight in the national press stressed these ideas. "Lindbergh served as a metaphor," wrote one commentator in *Century*. "We felt that in him we, too, had conquered something and regained lost ground." A writer in *Outlook* made the point more explicitly: "Charles Lindbergh is the heir of all that we like to think is best in America. He is the stuff out of which have been made the pioneers that opened up the wilderness first on the Atlantic coast, and then in our great West." A newspaper cartoon showed a covered wagon leaving for California in 1849 and next to it Lindbergh's plane taking off for Paris in 1927. Colonel Theodore Roosevelt, the son of the President, remarked that Lindbergh "personifies the daring of youth. Daniel Boone, David Crockett, and men of that type played a lone hand and made America. Lindbergh is their lineal descendant." Calvin Coolidge, who personally welcomed Lindbergh home, simply said that he was "a boy representing the best traditions of this country."

In an age of mechanization, Charles Lindbergh represented a comforting continuation of the pioneering spirit and of self-reliance. His flight was well publicized, and Lindbergh returned to a wildly enthusiastic America as a popular hero.

For one journalist the most significant part of the Lindbergh phenomenon was not the flight but the character of the man: "his courage, his modesty, his self-control, his sanity, his thoughtfulness of others, his fine sense of proportion, his loyalty, his unswerving adherence to the course that seemed right." His unassuming manner fit the traditional hero's mold. Many observers of the postflight celebration noted how the hero refused to capitalize financially on his popularity. It was telling evidence as an essayist put it, that the American people "are *not* rotten at the core, but morally sound and sweet and good!" The generalization from the individual to society was easily acceptable because Americans in 1927 desperately wanted to keep the old creed alive. Lindbergh's flight was popularly interpreted as a

flight of faith—in the American experience and in the American people.

Looking back over the 1920s F. Scott Fitzgerald remembered in 1931 that "in the spring of 1927, something bright and alien flashed across the sky. A young Minnesotan who seemed to have nothing to do with his generation did a heroic thing, and for a moment people set down their glasses in country clubs and speakeasies and thought of their old best dreams." Also in 1931 Frederick Lewis Allen recalled that Lindbergh had been "a modern Galahad for a generation which had foresworn Galahads." Both Fitzgerald and Allen were right in their assessment of the public reaction to Lindbergh's flight, but wrong about the dreams he engendered being foreign to the 1920s. Fitzgerald notwithstanding, Lindbergh had a great deal to do with his generation. Allen to the contrary, the Lindbergh craze was not a case of Americans returning to ideals they had forsaken; they had never left them.

Popular books as well as heroes revealed the American mind in the 1920s, and the great majority of the best-sellers of the decade were decidedly old-fashioned. Frontier and rural patterns of thought and action dominated the popular novels. Their plots and protagonists operated according to time-honored standards of competition, loyalty, and rugged individualism. Complications were few and usually resolved, in the final pages, with an application of traditional morality. The total effect was a comforting reaffirmation of the old American faith. Such novels, to be sure, made slight contribution to serious American literature. But they were read—by millions! And they both influenced and reflected the mood of Americans who had never even heard of Fitzgerald and Hemingway. Indeed in comparison to best-selling authors, the Fitzgeralds and Hemingways were highly esoteric.

Exact figures are elusive, but it would be difficult to dispute Gene (Geneva) Stratton-Porter's claim to preeminence among popular novelists in the first three decades of the twentieth century. Her vogue began with *Freckles* in 1904 and continued right through the war, into the twenties, and beyond. In 1932 a *Publisher's Weekly* survey of the best-selling novels of the century revealed Porter in the top four positions with *Freckles, The Girl of the Limberlost* (1909), *The Harvester* (1911), and *Laddie* (1913). Each had sold well over a million copies. With other titles Porter made the "top ten" list in 1918, 1919, 1921, and 1925. Most of her sales were in fifty-cent reprint editions, suggesting that her public consisted of relatively unsophisticated readers.

Gene Stratton-Porter found a publishing bonanza by articulating the values to which a large part of the American reading public subscribed. Chief among them was a belief in the virtue of close association with nature. As a girl Porter ran in the swamps, woods, and fields around Wabash, Indiana, and the characters in her novels do like-

wise. The experience was represented as inspirational in the highest sense. Nature was not only a source of beauty and contentment but a repository of moral and religious truth. The outdoors provided a constant backdrop in Porter's stories. Indeed the margins of her books were sometimes adorned with pen and ink drawings of birds, animals, and flowers. *The Harvesters* was dedicated to Henry David Thoreau.

Second only to nature in Porter's scale of values was cheerfulness. Her stories expound the benefits of optimism, confidence, courage, and keeping a stiff upper lip. Typically the plots involve the protagonist, frequently a child, in a series of adversities. But looking for the silver lining and heeding the teachings of nature eventually resolve all problems. *Freckles,* for instance, describes a boy who believes himself an orphan, wanders in the Limberlost swamp, and is ultimately found and claimed by his wealthy father. Eleanora of *A Girl of the Limberlost* defies poverty by selling the moths she collected in the swamp. In *Michael O'Halloran* Porter copied the Horatio Alger formula, taking a little newsboy up the success ladder on the wings of determination and pluck.

Porter's novels appealed to the kind of American whose eyes glazed and even dampened when they thought of the good old days when life was simple and generally lived in close proximity to nature. In Porter one basked momentarily in an uncomplicated world where virtue triumphed and right prevailed. Much of Porter's public seemed to consist of people displaced or crushed by modern American civilization. Letters of appreciation poured in to her from sanitariums, rest homes, reform schools, and jails. But in a larger sense the uncertainties and nervousness of the age in general provided a milieu in which her kind of writing could flourish.

William Lyon Phelps once wrote of Gene Stratton-Porter, "She is a public institution, like Yellowstone Park, and I should not think she would care any more than a mountain for adverse criticism." In fact, Porter did care. She habitually replied to her unfavorable reviewers in lengthy letters. In one she responded to a critic who had labeled her writing "molasses fiction." This was really a compliment, rejoined Porter: "Molasses is more necessary to the happiness of human and beast than vinegar. . . . I am a molasses person myself. . . . So I shall keep straight on writing of the love and joy of life . . . and when I have used the last drop of my molasses, I shall stop writing." She closed the letter with a hint of conceit: "God gave me a taste for sweets and the sales of the books I write prove that a few other people are similar to me in this."

Harold Bell Wright rivaled Gene Stratton-Porter as a dispenser of wholesomeness, optimism, and the arcadian myth. His *The Winning of Barbara Worth* (1911) had a half million copies in print within a month of its initial publication and maintained sufficient popularity to rank fifth, behind Porter's four books, in the 1932 best-selling novels of the century poll. After *Barbara Worth* Wright produced a novel every other year for two decades, Americans seemed as eager to buy and read his books after the war as before. His first twelve books enjoyed an average sale of nearly 750,000 each.

A sometime minister, Wright sermonized constantly in his novels. Until the final typing no character in any had a name except that of his main trait—Hypocrisy, Greed, Ambition, and so on. Wright's message was the familiar one: clean living, hard work, and contact with God's great open spaces could save a man from the physical and moral deterioration city life engendered. *When a Man's a Man* of 1916, for example, features a millionaire who goes west to escape the effete, artificial, decadent East. Its setting on an Arizona cattle ranch reflected Wright's own enthusiasm for the Southwest that led him to make his home there. Wright also loved Missouri's Ozark Mountains, and the region figured in a number of his stories. *The Re-Creation of Brian Kent*, third on the best-seller list for 1920, employs an Ozark setting to tell the story of a human wreck who is redeemed by the beauty of nature, the challenge of work, and a woman's love. An elderly schoolmarm, identified only as Auntie Sue, supervises the transformation and extracts the moral.

The stereotyped plots and characters, the wooden dialogue, and the commonplace preach-ing in Wright's books elicited a barrage of unfavorable criticism. According to one reviewer in 1924, Wright was guilty of perpetuating "the shibboleths and superstitions of our fathers, making old creeds and antique fables sacred in the eyes of all." And so he did. Yet his stories sold millions of copies. A large number of American readers found his message comfortable and meaningful. "Harold," one critic punned, "is always Wright." But for the popular mind of the teens and twenties ethical certainty was highly valued, and traditional mores seemed the most certain. The intellectuals might scoff, but Wright, like Porter, found the goldmine of popular favor.

The western novel, which Owen Wister introduced into American writing in 1902 with *The Virginian,* increased in popularity as the nation moved increasingly further from frontier conditions. The foremost practitioner of the art in the decade after World War I was a one-time dentist from Zanesville, Ohio, named Zane Grey. Blending minor literary talent with a keen sense of the public taste, Grey produced over fifty westerns and provided the basis for dozens of motion pictures, many of which were produced in the early 1920s before the advent of sound tracks. The total sale of all his writings approaches twenty million. From 1917 to 1924 Grey was never *off* the national list of the top ten best-sellers. Twice, 1918 and 1920, he ranked first. He may well have been the most widely read author in the American twenties.

The Zane Grey magic was a blend of violence, heroism, and the frontier. His stories lacked sophistication, but they juxtaposed good and evil in unmistakable terms. Titanic struggles might be waged, but the issues were always clearly defined and the outcome, as Grey fans came to learn, never really in doubt. A simple code of conduct suffused Grey's books. It emphasized courage, self-reliance, fair play, and persistence—the traditional frontier virtues. Those who violated the code always paid the price.

As a mythmaker for the multitudes in the 1920s, Zane Grey became as legendary as his protagonists. Many people believed he spoke for the best parts of the national heritage. John Wanamaker, the department store mogul, addressed him directly: "Never lay down your pen, Zane Grey. . . . You are distinctively and genuinely American. You have borrowed none of the decadence of foreign writers. . . . The good you are doing is incalculable." Even the critics treated Grey more tolerantly than they did Porter and Wright. "We turn to him," one commentator wrote, "not for insight into human nature and human problems nor for refinements of art, but simply for crude epic stories, as we might to an old Norse skald, maker of the sagas of the folk."

The concept of escape from the present, so important in the appeal of many of the best-selling popular novels in the twenties, reached a climax in the writing of Edgar Rice Burroughs. A failure for years in business and pulp magazine writing, Burroughs turned to a new theme in 1914 and struck pure gold. *Tarzan of the Apes* has probably sold more copies to date (over five million) than any other American book. Over thirty other stories of the English orphan reared in the African jungle by apes followed. As early as 1920 the Tarzan cult was nationwide. Burroughs was syndicated in newspapers; his motion pictures reached millions of people. With his superhuman prowess and his mate, Jane, Tarzan entered public thought and speech to an astonishing degree. For people vaguely repressed by civilization, Tarzan was a potent symbol of freedom, power, and individuality. A new wild man on a new frontier, Tarzan helped sustain traditional American values.

American readers seemed to have an insatiable appetite for nature novels for the first three decades of the twentieth century. In addition to Porter, Wright, Grey, and Burroughs, a host of others rode the theme to publishing successes that were minor only in comparison. The names of Rex Beach, Peter B. Kyne, Emerson Hough, and James Oliver Curwood were quite familiar to readers and moviegoers of the postwar decade even if they are not to most literary historians. Curwood, for instance, published between 1908 and 1926 twenty-six novels that dramatized the theme of courage in the wilderness. The motion pictures made from his books, such as *Back to God's Country* (1919), were intended, so an advertisement ran, for those who "love God's great out-of-doors, the land of frozen forests and everlasting snows where the gaunt wolf stalks its prey, where men loom large and life is big." In 1923 Hough's *The Covered Wagon* became the basis for the most famous western movie of the decade. Stewart Edward White rivaled both Curwood and Hough with books such as *The Blazed Trail, The Silent Places,* and *The Rules of the Game.* And that was it precisely—the game had rules that were at once easily perceived and rooted in the national character. If changing conditions were eroding the old certainties, that was only more reason to grasp them more tightly.

In popular fiction Americans of the 1920s were still inhabitants of the nineteenth century. The sexy novels of flaming youth and the risqué movies satisfied only part of the taste of the twenties. The other, and larger, part thrilled to old-time heroics such as those provided by the man Douglas Durkin sketched in *The Lobstick Trail* of 1922: "His blood was clean, his body knit of fibre woven in God's out-of-doors, his mind fashioned under a clear sky in a land of wide horizons."

Study Questions

1. What caused the nervousness that many American experienced in the 1920s?

2. What values were characteristic of America's pioneering past? How did the heroes of the 1920s demonstrate these values?

3. Why were sports so popular during the decade? How did athletic heroes help ease Americans' minds about the national character?

4. How were the popular images of Herbert Hoover and Charles Lindbergh similar? Why were both men considered heroes during the 1920s?

5. What were the characteristics of many popular novels during the 1920s? What types of stories did people enjoy reading?

6. How were the novels of Gene Stratton-Porter, Harold Bell Wright, Zane Grey, and Edgar Rice Burroughs similar or different?

Bibliography

The selection comes from Roderick Nash, *The Nervous Generation: American Thought, 1917–1930* (1970), which presents a view of the 1920s vastly different from Frederick Lewis Allen's. A good overview of the role of the hero in American culture is Leo Lowenthal, *Literature, Popular Culture and Society* (1961). The most important athletic heroes of the decade are discussed in Randy Roberts, *Jack Dempsey: The Manassa Mauler* (1979); Robert Creamer, *Babe: The Legend Comes to Life* (1992); Robert Creamer, *Babe* (1974); Marshall Smelser, *The Life that Ruth Built* (1975); Paul Gallico, *The Goddess People* (1965); and Frank Deford, *Big Bill Tilden: The Triumphs and the Tragedy* (1975). John W. Ward, "The Meaning of Lindbergh's Flight," *American Quarterly,* 10 (1958), is a classic study of the importance of heroism in the 1920s. On Lindbergh also see Walter S. Ross, *The Last Hero Charles Lindbergh* (1976) and Randy Roberts and David Welky eds., *Charles A. Lindbergh: The Power and Peril of Celebrity, 1927–1941.*

READING 13

★ ★ ★

The Black Sox Scandal

Dean Smith

Every few years or so, fat-bellied, middle-aged journalists start complaining that base-ball "isn't what it used to be," that the American pastime is "in trouble," that the game is "in a crisis from which it may never recover." And yet, in spite of their nostalgic re-flections about "the good old days," baseball is alive and well. Men's and women's softball leagues fill city recreation parks every night of the week, and Little Leaguers are playing more baseball than ever before. Fantasy baseball groups have sprouted in small towns and large cities all over the country, and junior high school boys have turned baseball cards into big business. America still loves baseball.

But there was a time when baseball was in real trouble. In 1921, headlines in news-papers across the country let Americans know that eight members of the Chicago White Sox were accused of conspiring to lose the 1919 World Series. The ensuing in-vestigation and trial became symbolic of American life in the post-World War I years, when doubts about the country's future seemed endemic. It became known as the Black Sox Scandal, and in the following article Dean Smith describes the controversy and its significance in the 1920s.

When Jim Crusinberry, the *Chicago Tribune's* ace baseball writer, entered the lobby of the Sinton Hotel in Cincinnati that evening of September 30, 1919, he stumbled onto one of the most remarkable scenes of his career.

Perched atop a chair in the lobby was a wildly gesturing man whom he immediately recognized as Abe Attell, former world featherweight boxing champion and consort of New York gamblers. Attell had $1,000 bills in both hands and he was screaming his head off to anyone who would listen, offering to bet on the Cincinnati Reds to beat the Chicago White Sox—any amount, and at even money—in the World Series which was to open the following day at Redland Park.

Crusinberry's nose for news twitched like a bloodhound's. Even in those free-wheeling days of American sport, gamblers usually exercised more discretion than Attell was displaying. And why was he betting against the White Sox? The awesome Sox, one of the finest teams ever assembled up to that time, were top-heavy favorites to crush the so-so Reds in the Series. In most quarters, one had to offer at least 4-to-1 odds to bet on Chicago. Yet here was Attell betting big on Cincinnati, and at even money!

For most of the next two years, Crusinberry pursued his big story. Although thwarted repeatedly by baseball officialdom, underworld silence, and his cautious sports editor, he put the pieces together at last. With other tenacious reporters, he forced a Chicago grand jury to investigate the case that exploded over the sporting world as the Black Sox Scandal.

For nearly six decades American sports buffs have been discussing and analyzing the Black Sox legend, and still the complete story may never be told. What has been established is that eight members of the 1919 White Sox team conspired with two combinations of gamblers to throw the World

---

"The Black Sox Scandal" by Dean Smith. This article is reprinted from the January 1977 issue of *American History Illustrated* 11, pp. 16–25, with the permission of Cowles History Group, Inc. Copyright *American History Illustrated* magazine.

Series to the Reds, and that the White Sox did indeed lose, five games to three. None of the sinning players, forever tarred in history as the Black Sox, ever received all the money promised for the fix, and several may have gotten no money at all.

What they did get was lifetime exile from organized baseball—an edict decreed and enforced by Commissioner Kenesaw Mountain Landis—despite the fact that the jury in a Cook County trial found them all innocent.

The Black Sox Scandal had an immense impact on a nation struggling to resume "normalcy" in the wake of World War I. To many Americans in that era of innocence, baseball was an almost religious rite, and the World Series was its most holy sacrament. The heroes of the Great American Game were assumed to be as pure as saints—despite considerable evidence to the contrary—and the heresy of desecrating the game for gambler's gold was unthinkable. When the stink of the Black Sox sellout fouled the air, an entire nation was sickened.

This early 20th-century scandal did incalculable damage to America's self-image as a moral nation, disillusioned millions of youthful fans, and helped set the tone for the licentious decade of the 1920's. Teapot Dome, the Prohibition era, corruption in high places, and the public acceptance of "everybody's doing it" raised questions about the value of personal integrity that remain to the present.

To reconstruct the story of the Black Sox tragedy, return to the Sinton Hotel and September 30, 1919. Jim Crusinberry was only one of many who had heard the rumor of an impending White Sox sellout. Hugh Fullerton, syndicated columnist of the Chicago Herald and Examiner, wired this cryptic warning to his newspaper clients: "Don't bet on Series. Ugly rumors afloat."

Jack Doyle, whose New York billiard academy was one of the nation's biggest gambling centers, estimated that $2,000,000 was wagered in his establishment the night before the Series opener. "You couldn't miss it . . . the thing had an odor," he said later. "I saw smart guys take even money on the Sox who should have been asking for 5-to-1 odds."

The Series fix was one of the worst-kept secrets in the history of infamy. As the betting odds shifted dramatically, Cincinnati was buzzing with rumors. Chick Gandil, the Chicago first baseman and admitted ringleader of the sellout, recalled in a *Sports Illustrated* confession nearly four decades later that even a clerk in a downtown stationary store whispered to him on the eve of the opener, "I have it firsthand that the Series is in the bag."

Everybody knew, and yet nobody knew for sure. Who was bribing whom—and to do what? To complicate the situation, a story popped up that some Chicago gamblers were out to insure a White Sox victory by getting ace Cincinnati pitcher Dutch Ruether drunk the night before the opener.

The White Sox should have needed no help at all. Owner Charles Comiskey, revered as "The Old Roman," had built a magnificent ball club in Chicago. There was Eddie Collins, probably the best second baseman in baseball, and Buck Weaver, without a peer at third base. "Shoeless Joe" Jackson was a virtual illiterate, but there was no better hitter and left fielder in the game. Happy Felsch in center and Shano Collins in right rounded out a great Chicago outfield. Chick Gandil at first base was so tough he could play his position without a glove. And Swede Risberg was one of the great shortstops of the era. Behind the plate was the superb Ray Schalk.

The pitching staff was a little thin, especially with Red Faber on the injured list, but Eddie Cicotte, Claude Williams, and Dickie Kerr were a match for anything Cincinnati could throw against them. As for manager Kid Gleason, he was a canny veteran who knew the game inside out and did a passable job of welding his moody and contentious athletes into a team that had dominated the American League.

The first post-World War Series had been lengthened to best five games of nine to insure a bigger box office take (it was returned to best four-of-seven shortly thereafter), and a nation weary of war and sacrifice was eager for the spectacle to begin.

The tragic prelude to the opener at Cincinnati on October 1, 1919, is still difficult to piece together. Conflicting grand jury and court testimony, countless published revelations and "authentic" analyses—but a paucity of reliable source material—combine to create a knotty problem for the historian. Eliot Asinof's *Eight Men Out,* generally regarded as the most comprehensive book on the subject, says the Black Sox plot had its beginning when Gandil contacted Boston gambler Joseph (Sport) Sullivan some three weeks before the 1919 Series and offered to "put the Series in the bag" for $80,000. Gandil, in his 1956 revelation, declared it was Sullivan who first suggested to him that the Series might be fixed.

At any rate, Gandil first enlisted pitcher Eddie Cicotte in the plot and then shortstop Swede Risberg and pitcher Claude Williams. The team's top three hitters—Buck Weaver, Joe Jackson, and Happy Felsch—were reluctant enlistees. Gandil felt sure that those seven could guarantee a White Sox defeat. They could ground out in crucial spots, feed a fat pitch to a slugger with men on base, barely miss a fly ball—all without detection. The seven were soon joined by an eighth conspirator through sheer accident. Utility infielder Fred McMullin, a man hardly in a position to affect the Series outcome, was lying behind a locker one afternoon and overheard Gandil discussing the plan with Risberg. McMullin demanded a part of the action, and he was included to buy his silence.

Consorting with gamblers was not a new occupation for Gandil, who for years had sold information on starting pitchers and other useful baseball tips to the betting fraternity. "We all mixed with gamblers," Gandil explained later, "and most of them were honest." Such shady associations were a fact of baseball life in 1919, and nobody seemed to care very much.

The eight Chicago players assembled in Gandil's room at the Ansonia Hotel in New York City on the evening of September 21st to discuss strategy. The eight were not particularly good friends and were united on only one subject: their common hatred for Comiskey, whom they regarded as a tight-fisted tyrant who paid his players less than did any other owner in major league baseball.

"Shoeless" Joe Jackson and seven other players on the Chicago White Sox were charged with accepting money to throw the 1919 World Series.

Gandil and Felsch, for example, were earning only a little more than $4,000 a year; Cicotte's 1919 salary was about $5,000 (and he a 29-game winner with an earned run average of 1.82!); and the great Jackson, batting .375 for the season, earned only $6,000—compared with the $10,000 Cincinnati paid its leading hitter, Ed Roush.

The eight agreed to deal with the gamblers, although Weaver is said to have suggested that they take the fix money and win the Series, anyhow. The evidence is conclusive that the superlative third baseman never threw a game or received a dime from the gamblers. He spent the rest of his life protesting his innocence and trying to restore his good name.

Even before arrangements could be made with Sullivan, word of the fix attempt leaked out. Cicotte was approached by gambler William T. (Sleepy Bill) Burns, a former pitcher who had made money in Texas oil, to let him bid on the action. Soon two gambling combinations—unknown to each other—were negotiating with the Chicago eight.

It was common knowledge in the far-flung American gambling community that only one man, Arnold Rothstein of New York City, could put up enough money to engineer a project as grandiose as the fixing of a World Series. Burns hurriedly consulted with a small-time gambler named Billy Maharg in Philadelphia, and together they rushed to Rothstein with the proposition.

Rothstein would not see them personally, but told his ambitious lieutenant, Abe Attell, to check it out. Attell was entranced with the sheer audacity of the idea, so Rothstein agreed to discuss the matter with Burns. But the gambling king, known far and wide as "The Big Bankroll," turned Burns down flat and advised him to forget this wild scheme.

Attell could not put the lucrative idea out of his mind, however, and he decided to step into the big time on his own. He called Burns and told him a lie that could have bought Abe a concrete casket: Rothstein had changed his mind, said Attell, and would put up $100,000 if Burns could get the eight White Sox to go along. It was sheer bluff on

Attell's part. Certainly he could not lay his hands on the money the players were demanding, but he put up a confident front and prayed he could get the cash somewhere.

Meanwhile, Sullivan was busy, too. He also sought out Rothstein and somehow made a better impression on the shrewd New Yorker than had Burns. Rothstein assigned an aide named Nat Evans to work out the details of the Series fix with Sullivan and the players.

So Gandil and his co-conspirators began their comic opera dealings with two sets of gamblers, holding clandestine meetings in hotel rooms and hoping the rival fixers would never meet. The players demanded cash in advance, but the gamblers were untrusting souls who refused payment except after each game Chicago lost. Only Cicotte held out for his money beforehand, so Sullivan gave Gandil $10,000 to clinch the deal. The money mysteriously appeared under Cicotte's pillow at the Sinton Hotel the night before the Series opener.

According to the Black Sox legend, Rothstein demanded that Cicotte "give a sign" that the fix was on by hitting the first Cincinnati batter with a pitch. Whether or not Cicotte agreed, we will never know for sure, but for whatever reason— the heat of the 90-degree afternoon, the screaming throng of 30,500 in Redland Park, nerves made jumpy by his Judas role, or a shouted threat from the stands that "there's a guy looking for you with a rifle"—Cicotte's second pitch to Cincinnati leadoff hitter Maurice Rath strayed inside and hit him in the small of the back.

It was not Cicotte's day. He was driven from the mound in the fourth inning as the Reds waltzed to a 9–1 victory. Even the Cincinnati pitcher, Dutch Ruether, connected for two triples to the humiliation of the proud Sox. The next day Claude Williams, a left-hander famous for his control, was shockingly wild and the Reds won again, 4–2.

Meanwhile, rumors of the fix had reached manager Gleason and owner Comiskey. Late at night after the first game, according to one version of the story, Comiskey woke John Heydler, president of the National League and a member of baseball's National Commission, and poured out his fears that the White Sox had sold out to the gamblers. Heydler then woke Ban Johnson, president of the American League and a bitter enemy of Comiskey's, and relayed the Chicago owner's apprehensions.

"That's the yelp of a beaten cur!" sneered Johnson, who terminated the conversation abruptly and went back to bed.

The gamblers were equally indisposed to conversation. Sullivan disappeared after the first game. Attell was in town, but he was very vague about specifics of the payoff to Gandil. "The money is all out on bets," he told the ringleader. "You'll have to give me another day."

According to Asinof's version, Attell did come up with $10,000 after the second game, the money going to Gandil. Gandil later denied receiving any of the money for himself, but he did manage somehow to buy a big new car immediately after the Series.

Chicago had lost the first two games and, aside from Gandil and Cicotte, none of the White Sox conspirators had received so much as a "thank you" from either gambling combination. Understandably, they were now ready to forget the entire arrangement and play to win. With rookie Dickie Kerr pitching a three-hit shutout before 29,126 rabid fans at Chicago's Comiskey Park, the White Sox cruised to a 3–0 triumph. Gandil himself drove in two of the Chicago runs.

Unfortunately for Attell, Burns, and their colleagues, the news of the White Sox rebirth of spirit had not reached them. As they ruefully reported later, they lost all their previous winnings betting on the Reds in the third game and had no further participation in the Series machinations. But Sullivan was still very much in the game. Fearful that the White Sox players had revolted, he came up with $20,000, part of the bankroll reportedly supplied by Rothstein.

Now it was time for the fourth game and Cicotte's chance to redeem himself. The spitball ace pitched a strong five-hitter, but his mates were powerless at the plate and Cincinnati walked away with a 2–0 win. Williams gave up only four hits in the fifth game, but again the White Sox bats were silent and the Reds had their fourth victory, 5–0.

At this point Sullivan made the last of the gamblers' payments, this one purportedly $15,000.

Only one game away from losing the Series, the White Sox miraculously returned to their regular season form in the sixth game. Kerr won it, 5–4, with Gandil's hit providing the winning margin in the 10th inning. Cicotte was brilliant in the seventh game, winning 4–1, and suddenly the White Sox looked like winners again.

The gamblers were more than a little nervous, even with the paid-off Williams slated to pitch the eighth game in Chicago. To be sure of his position, Sullivan (according to Williams' wife) employed a professional persuader to remind Williams of the unpleasant consequences in store for him and his family if he should win.

A well-known gambler telephoned reporter Fullerton before the game and told him to "watch out for the biggest first inning you ever saw." It arrived on schedule, with Williams surrendering four runs in the first frame. The fired-up Reds raced off to a 10–1 lead before Chicago scored four in the eighth to close the final Cincinnati victory margin to 10–5.

The lowly Reds had pulled off the baseball upset of the decade. But had they really outplayed the White Sox, or had the eight Chicago conspirators handed the Series to them in return for tainted money?

The debate continues to this day.

One of the leading advocates of the "no fix" theory, Victor Luhrs, in his book *The Great Baseball Mystery,* declares the indications are overwhelming that Cincinnati would have won the Series anyhow. In his summary Luhrs admits that Williams' poor pitching cost the White Sox the second and eighth games and that he quite probably was an intentional loser. Gandil and Risberg, he says, did not give their best efforts and McMullin (who appeared only twice as a pinch hitter) did not play enough to permit a judgment. But he stoutly defends Jackson, Weaver, Felsch, and Cicotte, crediting all four with playing their best.

Dr. Harold Seymour, in his book *Baseball— The Golden Age,* concluded that the box scores

do not indicate that the Series was thrown. "In fact," says he, "the Black Sox on the whole actually made a better showing in the games than the Clean Sox (the other Chicago players)."

Joe Jackson, for example, led both teams at the plate with a .375 average, and Weaver ended with a .324 batting effort. Gandil's timely hitting won two games, and both Weaver and Jackson played errorless ball. Clean Eddie Collins, on the other hand, made two errors and batted an anemic .224; the other unblemished Chicago regulars did little better.

The rumors of a fix continued for many months, despite the best efforts of investigative reporters to dig out the truth. Comiskey offered a $20,000 reward (soon reduced to $10,000) for information on any skullduggery. But he ignored tips supplied by at least one gambler and never answered a letter from the remorseful Jackson, written by his wife, offering to tell what he knew. Apparently baseball officialdom had decided to sweep the dirt under the rug and hope it would be forgotten.

But the Chicago *Tribune's* Jim Crusinberry would not forget.

Crusinberry devoted every spare moment to tracking down leads, and at last—on a rainy New York afternoon in July 1920—the first crack in the wall of silence appeared. The telephone rang in the hotel room when Crusinberry was relaxing with columnist Ring Lardner. It was Kid Gleason, and he spoke in an excited whisper.

"I'm at Dinty Moore's," he told Crusinberry, "and Abe Attell is at the bar, drinking and starting to talk. Come on over and get close enough to listen." Within minutes, Crusinberry and Lardner were eavesdropping on a fascinating conversation.

"So it was Arnold Rothstein who put up the dough for the fix," they heard Gleason say. "That was it, Kid," answered Attell. "You know, Kid, I hated to do that to you, but I thought I was going to make a lot of money and I needed it, and then the big guy doublecrossed me, and I never got but a small part of what he promised."

Attell rambled on for half an hour, naming the participants. At last Crusinberry had the information for his block-busting story. But his sports editor, wary of a libel suit, refused to print it. Frustrated and angry, Crusinberry decided to take matters into his own hands. He wrote an open letter to the *Tribune,* demanding a grand jury investigation of the Series fix, and persuaded Chicago businessman Fred M. Loomis to sign it. The strategy worked. The Cook County grand jury agreed to the probe, and on September 21, 1920 subpoenas were sent to baseball owners, managers, players, writers, and gamblers.

Six days later the first sensational revelation hit the newspapers. Enterprising Jimmy Isaminger, a writer for the Philadelphia *North American,* tracked down gambler Billy Maharg—a cohort of Burns and Attell—and got him to talk. Maharg knew only part of the story, of course, but his statement exploded like a bombshell. He implicated Cicotte as the chief fixer, said Attell had betrayed Burns and himself, and declared that the first, second, and eighth Series games had been thrown by the Chicago eight—who immediately became known as the Black Sox.

The ink was still damp on the Isaminger story when Gleason sought out the tormented Cicotte and persuaded him to confess. Weeping through much of his sensational testimony before the grand jury the following day, Cicotte admitted receiving $10,000, confessed that he had served up pitches that anyone could hit, and said he did it for his wife and children.

Jackson next took the stand, nervously admitting that he got $5,000 of the $20,000 promised him. As he was leaving the courthouse following his testimony, the most poignant incident of the whole sordid scandal took place. Several ragged youngsters crowded around him and one asked pleadingly, "Say it ain't so, Joe!"

All America fervently joined in that plea.

Historians may note with some amusement that the original Associated Press quote of the remark was a more grammatical "It isn't true, is it, Joe?" But several other reporters who were there quoted it in the street jargon in which it was probably uttered.

Williams testified next, admitting that he got $5,000 for his part in the fix. Then came Felsch, who also confessed $5,000, but insisted that he had done nothing to throw any of the games.

Although the White Sox were battling for the American League pennant in the final week of the season, Comiskey immediately suspended all seven active players. (Gandil had "retired" from baseball before the start of the 1920 season.) With the Chicago team decimated, Cleveland breezed to the league championship.

The grand jury indicted all eight Chicago players, along with gamblers Attell, Burns, Hal Chase, and "Rachael Brown," the name used by Rothstein aide Nat Evans. Rothstein himself escaped indictment. The New York gambling king made an appearance before the grand jury, storming in outraged innocence, and somehow convinced everyone that he had not participated in any way.

When the Black Sox trial finally began, on June 27, 1921, the prosecution made an electrifying announcement: All the players' signed confessions had mysteriously disappeared from the files! American League President Ban Johnson accused Rothstein of paying $10,000 to arrange the theft, upon which Rothstein threatened him with a $250,000 slander suit. He never carried out the threat.

Free of the damning confessions, the players all denied their earlier testimony and pleaded innocent. None testified during the trial.

All through a blazing hot July the sensational trial dragged on in the sweltering Chicago courtroom. The defense was conducted by several of the most expensive lawyers of the day (who paid them was never proved), and the crowded courtroom was noisily in support of the players. Burns turned state's evidence, and the other gamblers all avoided prosecution through legal maneuvers.

The outcome teetered in the balance as the mountain of testimony piled up. Then, on August 2, both legal teams rested their cases and Judge Hugo Friend made his charge to the jury:

The State must prove that it was the intent of the ballplayers and gamblers charged with conspiracy through the throwing of the World Series to defraud the public and others, and not merely to throw ball games.

The tricky bit of semantics was all the jury needed. The judge said taking bribes was not enough—throwing ball games was not enough. To be legally guilty, the players must have intended to defraud the public. How could anybody prove that?

In just two hours, forty-seven minutes the jury brought in "not guilty" verdicts on all concerned. The hushed courtroom erupted in wild cheering and, incredibly, members of the jury hoisted several of the Black Sox to their shoulders and paraded them triumphantly around the courtroom. Flushed with victory, Gandil spotted Ban Johnson, rushed to his side, and declared: "Goodbye, good luck, and to hell with you!"

The Black Sox celebrated their triumph at an Italian restaurant after the verdict was read—the same restaurant, incidentally, where the jurors dined and congratulated themselves—and toasted the immediate resumption of their baseball careers. But they did not reckon with the stern morality of white-haired Judge Kenesaw Mountain Landis, who had been installed as Commissioner of Baseball following the grim days of the grand jury investigation. Landis had said upon taking office that the Black Sox would never play again, but that was before the trial. Surely, the players reasoned, the judge would not dare to overrule a court of law.

But he did just that. Landis's statement after the trial was a verdict of doom:

Regardless of the verdict of juries, no player that throws a ball game . . . [or] sits in a conference with a bunch of crooked players and gamblers where the ways and means of throwing games are planned and discussed, and does not promptly tell his club about it, will ever play professional baseball.

He added one more shocker: In addition to the eight Black Sox, he slapped a lifetime ban on Joe Gedeon of the St. Louis Browns, who had told the grand jury he made money betting on Cincinnati at the suggestion of Swede Risberg.

The players screamed, hired lawyers, and got petitions signed—but all to no avail. None of them ever played in organized baseball again. Landis was as unbending as iron, and many years later he went so far as to deny Jackson's petition to manage the Greenville, South Carolina, club in the low-low minors.

Part of the Black Sox legend is that Landis's stiff punishments saved baseball in its darkest hour. A glance at the soaring major league gate receipts in 1920 and 1921, however, seems to show that the sporting public would have supported the game whether or not the Black Sox had been punished. But the old judge's decision undoubtedly discouraged future cozy dealings between players and gamblers. Baseball never has suffered another scandal.

So the chastened Black Sox were cast out to make a living the best way they could. Weaver ran a Chicago drug store. Cicotte farmed near Detroit and then worked at an automobile plant. Williams ran a Chicago poolroom for a time and then started a nursery business in California. Felsch opened a tavern in Milwaukee. Risberg worked on a Minnesota dairy farm before opening a tavern in northern California. Gandil became a plumber in California. McMullin took one job and then another. Jackson operated a restaurant, and later a liquor store, in South Carolina.

All eight are now dead.

Though most of them protested varying degrees of innocence throughout their lives, Gandil declared in his 1956 confession, "To this day, I feel that we got what we had coming."

Baseball survived and thrived, but it was never again the gloriously pure American rite it once had been. Too many little boys—of all ages—had suffered sobering disillusionment.

Perhaps Nelson Algren, who had idolized Swede Risberg, said it best many years later in his superb short story "The Silver-Colored Yesterday":

I traded off my Risberg bat . . . and I flipped the program from that hot and magic Sunday when Cicotte was shutting out everybody forever, and a triumphant right-hander's wind had blown all the score cards across home plate, into the Troy Street gutter. I guess that was one way of learning what Hustletown, sooner or later, teaches all its sandlot sprouts. "Everybody's out for The Buck. Even big leaguers."
Even Swede Risberg.

Study Questions

1. Why did the little boy's comment "Say it ain't so, Joe" come to symbolize the public's reaction to the entire scandal?

2. What actually happened? Did the players really throw the World Series?

3. Who were the major characters in the scandal?

4. What decision did Judge Landis reach? Do you agree with the decision?

5. How would you compare the punishment given to the players in 1921 with contemporary professional athletes who gamble or find themselves with drug problems?

Bibliography

In recent years the history of sport in the United States has enjoyed increasing scholarly respectability. For a general survey, see Benjamin Rader, *American Sports: From the Age of Folk Games to the Age of Spectators* (1983). Stephen Reiss, *Touching Base: Professional Baseball and American Culture in the Progressive Era* (1980) is an especially useful examination of baseball in early twentieth-century America. Also see David Q. Voigt, *American Baseball, Vol. 1: From Gentlemen's Sport to the Commissioner System* (1966). On the scandal itself, see Eliot Asinof, *Eight Men Out: The Black Sox and the 1919 World Series* (1963). For a discussion of the mood of the 1920s in the United States, see Roderick Nash, *The Nervous Generation: American Thought, 1917–1930* (1970). Organized crime in the 1920s has also generated a scholarly literature. Herbert Asbury, *Sucker's Progress: An Informal History of Gambling in America* (1938) is a good, if dated, survey. Also see Jenna Joselit, *Our Gang: Jewish Crime and Politics in One American Community* (1983) and Humbert S. Nelli, *The Business of Crime: Italians and Syndicate Crime in the United States* (1981). For a discussion of the Black Sox Scandal, see Robert C. Cottrell, *Blackball, the Black Sox, and the Babe: Baseball's Crucial 1920 Season* (2001); and Daniel A. Nathan, *Saying It's So: A Cultural History of the Black Sox Scandal* (2003).

Organized Crime in Urban Society: Chicago in the Twentieth Century

Mark Haller

In 1919 Congress adopted the Eighteenth Amendment, which prohibited "the manufacture, sale, or transportation of intoxicating liquors." Prohibition, however, did not stop Americans from manufacturing, selling, or transporting alcohol; it simply made the actions illegal. During the 1920s and early 1930s, criminals rather than businessmen supplied the public's thirst, and often the distinction between the two occupations grew fuzzy. As "Scarface" Al Capone once noted, "I make my money by supplying a public demand. If I break the law, my customers, who number hundreds of the best people in Chicago, are as guilty as I am. . . . Everybody calls me a racketeer. I call myself a businessman. When I sell liquor it's bootlegging. When my patrons serve it on a silver tray on Lake Shore Drive, it's hospitality."

For many Americans, Capone's point was well taken. As a result, criminals achieved a certain social respect and were able to spread their influence into legitimate business. A 1926 congressional investigation demonstrated that organized crime had made significant inroads into the worlds of labor unions, industry, and city governments. By 1933 when Congress repealed the Eighteenth Amendment, organized crime had become a permanent part of the American scene.

In the following essay, historian Mark H. Haller examines the role of crime in ethnic communities and urban society. Like sports and entertainment, crime served as an avenue out of the ethnic ghettoes and played an important role in the complex urban environment.

Many journalists have written exciting accounts of organized crime in American cities and a handful of scholars have contributed analytical and perceptive studies. Yet neither the excitement in the journalistic accounts nor the analysis in the scholarly studies fully captures the complex and intriguing role of organized criminal activities in American cities during the first third of the twentieth century. The paper that follows, although focusing on Chicago, advances hypotheses that are probably true for other cities as well. The paper examines three major, yet interrelated, aspects of the role of organized crime in the city: first, the social worlds within which the criminals operated and the importance of those worlds in providing social mobility from immigrant ghettos; second, the diverse patterns by which different ethnic groups became involved in organized criminal activities and were influenced by those activities; and third, the broad and pervasive economic impact of organized crime in urban neighborhoods, and the resulting influence that organized crime did exert.

Crime and Mobility

During the period of heavy immigrant movement into the cities of the Northeast and Midwest, organized crime provided paths of upward mobility for many young men raised in ethnic slums. The gambling kings, vice lords, bootleggers and racketeers often began their careers in the ghetto neighborhoods; and frequently these neighborhoods continued to be the centers for their entrepreneurial activities. A careful study of the leaders of organized crime in Chicago in the late 1920s found that 31 percent were of Italian background, 29 percent of Irish background, 20 percent Jewish, and 12 percent black; none were native white of native white parents. A recognition

"Organized Crime in Urban Society: Chicago in the Twentieth Century" by Mark Haller, from *Journal of Social History 5* (Winter, 1971-1972). pp. 210-234. Copyright © 1971 by The Regents of the University of California. Reprinted by permission.

of the ethnic roots of organized crime, however, is only a starting point for understanding its place in American cities.

At a risk of oversimplification, it can be said that for young persons in the ethnic ghettos three paths lay open to them. The vast majority became, to use the Chicago argot, "poor working stiffs." They toiled in the factories, filled menial service and clerical jobs, or opened mom-and-pop stores. Their mobility to better jobs and to homeownership was, at best, incremental. A second, considerably smaller group followed respectable paths to relative success. Some of this group went to college and entered the professions; others rose to management positions in the business or governmental hierarchies of the city.

There existed, however, a third group of interrelated occupations which, although not generally regarded as respectable, were open to uneducated and ambitious ethnic youths. Organized crime was one such occupational world, but there were others.

One was urban machine politics. Many scholars have, of course, recognized the function of politics in providing mobility for some members of ethnic groups. In urban politics, a person's ethnic background was often an advantage rather than a liability. Neighborhood roots could be the basis for a career that might lead from poverty to great local power, considerable wealth, or both.

A second area consisted of those businesses that prospered through political friendships and contacts. Obviously, construction companies that built the city streets and buildings relied upon government contracts. But so also did banks in which government funds were deposited, insurance companies that insured government facilities, as well as garbage contractors, fraction companies and utilities that sought city franchises. Because political contacts were important, local ethnic politicians and their friends were often the major backers of such enterprises.

A third avenue of success was through leadership in the city's labor unions. The Irish in Chicago dominated the building trade unions and most of the other craft unions during the first

25 years of this century. But persons of other ethnic origins could also rise to leadership positions, especially in those unions in which their own ethnic group predominated.

Another path of mobility was sports. Boxing, a peculiarly urban sport, rooted in the neighborhood gymnasiums, was the most obvious example of a sport in which Irish champions were succeeded by Jewish, Polish and black champions. Many a fighter, even if he did not reach national prominence, could achieve considerable local fame within his neighborhood or ethnic group. He might then translate this local fame into success by becoming a fight manager, saloon keeper, politician or racketeer.

A fifth area often dominated by immigrants was the entertainment and night life of the city. In Chicago, immigrants—primarily Irish and Germans—ran the city's saloons by the turn of the century. During the 1920s, Greek businessmen operated most of the taxi-dance halls. Restaurants, cabarets and other night spots were similarly operated by persons from various ethnic groups. Night life also provided careers for entertainers, including B-girls, singers, comedians, vaudeville and jazz bands. Jewish comedians of the 1930s and black comedians of our own day are only examples of a larger phenomenon in which entertainment could lead to local and even national recognition.

The organized underworld of the city, then, was not the only area of urban life that provided opportunities for ambitious young men from the ghettos. Rather, it was one of several such areas. Part of the pervasive impact of organized crime resulted from the fact that the various paths were interrelated, binding together the worlds of crime, politics, labor leadership, politically related businessmen, sports figures and the night life of the city. What was the nature of the interrelationships?

To begin with, organized crime often exerted important influences upon the other social worlds. For aspiring politicians, especially during the early years after an ethnic group's arrival in a city, organized crime was often the most important source of money and manpower. (By the turn of the century, an operator of a single policy wheel in Chicago could contribute not only thousands of dollars but also more than a hundred numbers writers to work the neighborhoods on election day.) On occasion, too, criminals supplied strongarm men to act as poll watchers, they organized repeat voters, and they provided other illegal but necessary campaign services. Like others engaged in ethnic politics, members of the organized underworld often acted from motives of friendship and common ethnic loyalties. But because of the very nature of their activities, criminal entrepreneurs required and therefore sought political protection. It would be difficult to exaggerate the importance of organized crime in the management of politics in many of the wards of the city.

Furthermore, it should not be thought that the politics of large cities like Chicago was peculiarly influenced by organized crime. In a large and heterogeneous city, there were always wards within which the underworld exercised little influence and which could therefore elect politicians who would work for honest government and law enforcement. But in the ethnic and blue-collar industrial cities west or southwest of Chicago, the influence of organized crime sometimes operated without serious opposition. In Cicero, west of Chicago along major commuting lines, gambling ran wide open before the 1920s; and after 1923 Capone's bootlegging organization safely had its headquarters there. In other towns, like Stickney and Burnham, prostitution and other forms of entertainment often operated with greater openness than in Chicago. This symbiotic relationship, in which surrounding blue-collar communities provided protected vice and entertainment for the larger city, was not limited to Chicago. Covington, Kentucky, had a similar relationship to Cincinnati, while East St. Louis serviced St. Louis.

The organized underworld was also deeply involved in other areas of immigrant mobility. Organized criminals worked closely with racketeering labor leaders and thus became involved in shakedowns, strike settlements and decisions concerning union leadership. They were participants in the night life, owned many of the night spots in the entertainment districts, and hired and promoted many of the entertainers. (The comedian Joe E. Lewis started his career in Chicago's South Side vice district as an associate and employee of the underworld; his case was not atypical.) Members of the underworld were also sports fans and gamblers and therefore became managers of prize fighters, patrons at the race tracks and loyal fans at ball games. An observer who knew many of Chicago's pimps in the 1920s reported:

The pimp is first, last and always a fight fan. He would be disgraced if he didn't go to every fight in town. . . .
  They hang around gymnasiums and talk fight. Many of them are baseball fans, and they usually get up just about in time to go to the game. They know all the players and their information about the game is colossal. Football is a little too highbrow for them, and they would be disgraced if they played tennis, but of late the high grade pimps have taken to golf, and some of them belong to swell golf clubs.

However, criminals were not merely sports fans; some ran gambling syndicates and had professional interests in encouraging sports or predicting the outcome of sports events. Horse racing was a sport conducted primarily for the betting involved. By the turn of the century, leading gamblers and bookmakers invested in and controlled most of the race tracks near Chicago and in the rest of the nation. A number of successful gamblers had stables of horses and thus mixed business with pleasure while becoming leading figures in horse race circles. At a less important level, Capone's organization in the late 1920s owned highly profitable dog tracks in Chicago's suburbs.

The fact that the world of crime exerted powerful influences upon urban politics, business, labor unions, sports and entertainment does not adequately describe the interrelations of these worlds. For many ambitious men, the worlds were tied together because in their own lifetimes

they moved easily from one area to another or else held positions in two or more simultaneously. In some ways, for instance, organized crime and entertainment were barely distinguishable worlds. Those areas of the city set aside for prostitution and gambling were the major entertainment districts of the city. Many cabarets and other night spots provided gambling in backrooms or in rooms on upper floors. Many were places where prostitutes solicited customers or where customers could find information concerning local houses of prostitution. During the 1920s, places of entertainment often served liquor and thus were retail outlets for bootleggers. In the world of entertainment, the distinction between legitimate and illegitimate was often blurred beyond recognition.

Take, as another example, the career of William Skidmore. At age fourteen, Billie sold racing programs at a race track near Chicago. By the time he was twenty-one, in the 1890s, he owned a saloon and cigar store, and soon had joined with others to operate the major policy wheels in Chicago and the leading handbook syndicate on the West Side. With his growing wealth and influence, he had by 1903 also become ward committeeman in the thirteenth ward and was soon a leading political broker in the city. In 1912 he was Sergeant-at-Arms for the Democratic National Convention and, afterwards, aided Josephus Daniels in running the Democratic National Committee. Despite his success as gambler and politician, his saloon, until well into the 1920s, was a hangout for pickpockets and con men; and "Skid" provided bail and political protection for his criminal friends. In the twenties Skidmore branched into the junk business and made a fortune selling junk obtained through contracts with the county government. Not until the early 1940s did he finally go to prison, the victim of a federal charge of income tax evasion. In his life, it would be impossible to unravel the diverse careers to determine whether he was saloon keeper, gambler, politician or businessman.

The various social worlds were united not simply by the influence of organized crime and by interlocking careers; the worlds also shared a common social life. At local saloons, those of merely local importance met and drank together. At other restaurants or bars, figures of wider importance had meeting places. Until his death in 1920, Big Jim Colossimo's restaurant in the South Side vice district brought together the successful from many worlds; the saloon of Michael (Hinky Dink) Kenna, first ward Alderman, provided a meeting place in the central business district. Political banquets, too, provided opportunities for criminals, police, sports figures and others to gather in honor of a common political friend. Weddings and funerals were occasions when friends met to mark the important passages through life. At the funeral of Colossimo—politician, vice lord and restauranteur—his pallbearers included a gambler, two keepers of vice resorts, and a bailbondsman. Honorary pallbearers were five judges (including the chief judge of the criminal courts), two congressmen, nine resort keepers or gamblers, several aldermen and three singers from the Chicago Opera. (His good friend, Enrico Caruso, was unable to be present.) Such ceremonial events symbolized the overlapping of the many worlds of which a man like Colossimo was a part.

Thus far we have stressed the social structure that linked the criminal to the wider parts of the city within which he operated. That social world was held together by a system of values and beliefs widely shared by those who participated in crime, politics, sports and the night life of the city. Of central importance was the cynical—but not necessarily unrealistic—view that society operated through a process of deals, friendships and mutual favors. Hence the man to be admired was the smart operator and dealer who handled himself well in such a world. Because there was seen to be little difference between a legal and an illegal business, there was a generally tolerant attitude that no one should interfere with the other guy's racket so long as it did not interfere with one's own. This general outlook was, of course, widely shared, in whole or in part, by other groups within American society so that there was no clear boundary be-

tween the social world of the smart operators and the wider society.

In a social system held together by friendships and favors, the attitude toward law and legal institutions was complex. A basic attitude was a belief that criminal justice institutions were just another racket—a not unrealistic assessment considering the degree to which police, courts and prosecutor were in fact used by political factions and favored criminal groups. A second basic attitude was a belief that, if anyone cooperated with the law against someone with whom he was associated or to whom he owed favors, he was a stoolpigeon whose behavior was beneath contempt. This does not mean that criminal justice institutions were not used by members of organized crime. On a day-to-day basis, members of the underworld were tied to police, prosecutors and politicians through payments and mutual favors. Criminal groups often used the police and courts to harass rival gangs or to prevent the development of competition. But conflicts between rival groups were also resolved by threats or violence. Rival gambling syndicates bombed each others' places of business, rival union leaders engaged in bombing and slugging, and rival bootlegging gangs after 1923 turned to assassinations that left hundreds dead in the streets of Chicago. The world of the rackets was a tough one in which a man was expected to take his knocks and stand up for himself. Friendship and loyalty were valued; but so also were toughness and ingenuity.

Gangsters, politicians, sports figures and entertainers prided themselves for being smart guys who recognized how the world operated. They felt disdain mixed with pity for the "poor working stiffs" who, ignorant of how the smart guys operated, toiled away at their menial jobs. But if they disdained the life of the working stiffs, they also disdained the pretensions of those "respectable" groups who looked askance at the world within which they operated. Skeptical that anyone acted in accordance with abstract beliefs or universalistic principles, the operators believed that respectable persons were hypocrites. For instance,

Ben Shahn's "Prohibition Alley" portrays whiskey barrels, delivered by ship, being stacked under a portrait of Chicago gangster Al Capone, a victim of gang warfare at lower left, and patrons outside a speakeasy at lower right.

when Frank J. Loesch, the distinguished and elderly lawyer who headed the Chicago Crime Commission, attacked three criminal court judges for alleged political favoritism, one politician declared to his friends:

Why pick on these three judges when every judge in the criminal court is doing the very same thing, and always have. Who is Frank Loesch that he should holler? He has done the same thing in his day. . . . He has asked for plenty of favors and has always gotten them. Now that he is getting older and is all set and doesn't have to ask any more favors, he is out to holler about every one else. . . . There are a lot of these reformers who are regular racketeers, but it won't last a few years and it will die out.

In short, the world view of the operators allowed them to see their world as being little different from the world of the respectable persons who looked down upon them. The whole world was a racket.

Ethnic Specialization

Some have suggested that each ethnic group, in its turn, took to crime as part of the early adjustment to urban life. While there is some truth to such a generalization, the generalization obscures more than it illuminates the ethnic experiences and structure of crime. In important respects, each ethnic group was characterized by different patterns of adjustment; and the patterns of involvement in organized crime often reflected the particular broader patterns of each ethnic group. Some ethnic groups—Germans and Scandinavians, for instance—appear not to have made significant contributions to the development of organized crime. Among the ethnic groups that did contribute, there was specialization within crime that reflected broader aspects of ethnic life.

In Chicago by the turn of the century, for example, the Irish predominated in two areas of organized crime. One area was labor racketeering, which derived from the importance of the Irish as leaders of organized labor in general.

The second area of Irish predominance was the operation of major gambling syndicates. Irish importance in gambling was related to a more general career pattern. The first step was often ownership of a saloon, from which the owner might move into both politics and gambling. Many Irish saloon keepers ran handbooks or encouraged other forms of gambling in rooms located behind or over the saloon. Those Irishmen who used their saloon as a basis for electoral politics continued the gambling activities in their saloons and had ties to larger gambling syndicates. Other saloon keepers, while sometimes taking important but backstage political positions such as ward committeeman, developed the gambling syndicates. Handbooks required up-to-the-minute information from race tracks across the country. By establishing poolrooms from which information was distributed to individual handbooks, a single individual could control and share in the profits of dozens or even hundreds of handbooks.

The Irish also predominated in other areas of gambling. At the turn of the century they were the major group in the syndicates that operated the policy games, each with hundreds of policy writers scattered in the slum neighborhoods to collect the nickels and dimes of the poor who dreamed of a lucky hit. They also outfitted many of the gambling houses in the Loop which offered roulette, faro, poker, blackjack, craps and other games of chance. Furthermore, many top police officers were Irish and rose through the ranks by attaching themselves to the various political factions of the city. Hence a complex system of Irish

politicians, gamblers and police shared in the profits of gambling, protected gambling interests and built careers in the police department or city politics. Historians have long recognized the importance of the Irish in urban politics. In Chicago, at any rate, politics was only part of a larger Irish politics-gambling complex.

The Irish politics-gambling complex remained intact until about World War I. By the 1920s, however, the developing black ghetto allowed black politicians and policy operators to build independent gambling and political organizations linked to the Republicans in the 1920s and the Democratic city machine in the 1930s. By the 1920s, in addition, Jewish gamblers became increasingly important, both in the control of gambling in Jewish neighborhoods and in operations elsewhere. Finally, by the mid-1920s, Italian bootleggers under Capone took over gambling in suburban Cicero and invested in Chicago gambling operations. Gambling had become a complex mixture of Irish, Negro, Jewish and Italian entrepreneurship.

Although the Irish by the twentieth century played little direct role in managing prostitution, Italians by World War I had moved into important positions in the vice districts, especially in the notorious Levee district on the South Side. (Political protection, of course, often had to be arranged through Irish political leaders.) Just as the Irish blocked Italians in politics, so also they blocked Italians in gambling, which was both more respectable and more profitable than prostitution. Hence the importance of prohibition in the 1920s lay not in initiating organized crime (gambling continued both before and after prohibition to be the major enterprise of organized crime); rather, prohibition provided Italians with an opportunity to break into a major field of organized crime that was not already monopolized by the Irish.

This generalization, to some extent, oversimplifies what was in fact a complex process. At first, prohibition opened up business opportunities for large numbers of individuals and groups, and the situation was chaotic. By 1924, however, shifting coalitions had emerged. Some bootlegging gangs were Irish, including one set of O'Donnell brothers on the far West Side and another set on the South Side. Southwest of the stockyards, there was an important organization, both Polish and Irish, coordinated by "Pollack" Joe Saltis. And on the Near North Side a major group—founded by burglars and hold-up men—was led by Irishmen . . . and Jews. . . . There were, finally, the various Italian gangs, including the Gennas, the Aiellos, and, of course, the Capone organization.

The major Italian bootlegging gang, that associated with the name of Al Capone, built upon roots already established in the South Side vice district. There John Torrio managed houses of prostitution for Big Jim Colossimo. With Colossimo's assassination in 1920, Torrio and his assistant, Capone, moved rapidly to establish a bootlegging syndicate in the Loop and in the suburbs south and west of the city. Many of their associates were persons whom they had known during humbler days in the South Side vice district and who now rose to wealth with them. Nor was their organization entirely Italian. Very early, they worked closely with Irishmen like Frankie Lake and Terry Druggan in the brewing of beer, while Jake Guzik, a Jew and former South Side pimp, became the chief business manager for the syndicate. In the bloody bootlegging wars of the 1920s, the members of the Capone organization gradually emerged as the most effective organizers and most deadly fighters. The success of the organization brought wealth and power to many ambitious Italians and provided them with the means in the late 1920s and early 1930s to move into gambling, racketeering and entertainment, as well as into a broad range of legitimate enterprises. Bootlegging allowed Italians, through entrepreneurial skills and by assassination of rivals, to gain a central position in the organized underworld of the city.

Although Jewish immigrants in such cities as Cleveland and Philadelphia were major figures in bootlegging and thus showed patterns similar to Italians in Chicago, Jews in Chicago were somewhat peripheral figures. By World War I, Chicago Jews, like Italians, made important inroads into vice, especially in vice districts on the West Side. In the 1920s, with the dispersal of prostitution, several Jewish vice syndicates operated on the South and West Sides. Jews were also rapidly invading the world of gambling. Although Jews took part in vice, gambling and bootlegging, they made a special contribution to the organized underworld by providing professional or expert services. Even before World War I, Jews were becoming a majority of the bailbondsmen in the city. By the 1920s, if not before, Jews constituted over half the fences who disposed of stolen goods. (This was, of course, closely related to Jewish predominance as junk dealers and their importance in retail selling.) Jews were also heavily overrepresented among defense attorneys in the criminal courts. It is unnecessary to emphasize that the entrepreneurial and professional services of Jews reflected broader patterns of adaptation to American urban life.

Even within relatively minor underworld positions, specialization by ethnicity was important. A study of three hundred Chicago pimps in the early 1920s, for instance, found that 109 (more than one-third) were black, 60 were Italian, 47 Jewish and 26 Greek. The large proportion of blacks suggests that the high prestige of the pimp among some elements of the lower-class black community is not a recent development but has a relatively long tradition in the urban slum. There has, in fact, long been a close relationship of vice activities and Negro life in the cities. In all probability, the vice districts constituted the most integrated aspect of Chicago society. Black pimps and madams occasionally had white girls working for them, just as white pimps and madams sometimes had black girls working for them. In addition, blacks held many of the jobs in the vice districts, ranging from maids to entertainers. The location of major areas of vice and entertainment around the periphery and along the main business streets of the South Side black neighborhood gave such activities a pervasive influence within the neighborhood.

Black achievements in ragtime and jazz had their roots, at least in part, in the vice and entertainment districts of the cities. Much of the early history of jazz lies among the talented musicians—black and white—who performed in the famous resorts in the Storyville district of New Orleans in the 1890s and early 1900s. With the dissolution of Storyville as a segregated vice district, many talented black musicians carried their styles to Chicago's South Side, to Harlem, and to the cabarets and dance halls of other major cities. In the 1920s, with black performers like King Oliver and Louis Armstrong and white performers like Bix Beiderbecke, Chicago was an important environment for development of jazz styles. Just as Harlem became a center for entertainment and jazz for New Yorkers during prohibition, so the black and tan cabarets and speakeasies of Chicago's South Side became a place where blacks and whites drank, danced and listened to jazz music—to the shock of many respectable citizens. Thus, in ways that were both destructive and productive, the black experience in the city was linked to the opportunities that lay in the vice resorts, cabarets and dance halls of the teeming slums. In the operation of entertainment facilities and policy rackets, black entrepreneurs found their major outlet and black politicians found their chief support.

Until there has been more study of comparative ethnic patterns, only tentative hypotheses are possible to explain why various ethnic groups followed differing patterns. Because many persons involved in organized crime initiated their careers with customers from their own neighborhood or ethnic group, the degree to which a particular ethnic group sought a particular illegal service would influence opportunities for criminal activities. If members of an ethnic group did not gamble, for instance, then ambitious members of that ethnic group could not build gambling syndicates based upon local roots. The general attitude toward law and law enforcement, too, would affect

opportunities for careers in illegal ventures. Those groups that became most heavily involved in organized crime migrated from regions in which they had developed deep suspicions of government authority—whether the Irish fleeing British rule in Ireland, Jews escaping from Eastern Europe, Italians migrating from southern Italy or Sicily, or blacks leaving the American South. Within a community suspicious of courts and government officials, a person in trouble with the law could retain roots and even respect in the community. Within a community more oriented toward upholding legal authority, on the other hand, those engaged in illegal activities risked ostracism and loss of community roots.

In other ways, too, ethnic life styles evolved differently. Among both Germans and Irish, for instance, friendly drinking was part of the pattern of relaxation. Although the Irish and Germans by 1900 were the major managers of Chicago's saloons, the meaning of the saloon was quite different for the two groups. German saloons and beer gardens were sometimes for family entertainment and generally excluded gambling or prostitution; Irish saloons, part of an exclusively male social life, often featured prostitution or gambling and fit more easily into the world of entertainment associated with organized crime. Finally, it appears that south Italians had the highest homicide rate in Europe. There was, in all probability, a relationship between the cultural factors that sanctioned violence and private revenge in Europe and the factors that sanctioned the violence with which Italian bootleggers worked their way into a central position in Chicago's organized crime.

There were, at any rate, many ways that the immigrant background and the urban environment interacted to influence the ethnic experience with organized crime. For some ethnic groups, involvement in organized crime was not an important part of the adjustment to American urban life. For other groups, involvement in the organized underworld both reflected and influenced their relatively unique patterns of acculturation.

Economic Impact

The economic role of organized crime was an additional factor underlying the impact of organized crime upon ethnic communities and urban society. Organized crime was important because of the relatively great wealth of the most successful criminals, because of the large numbers of persons directly employed by organized crime, and because of the still larger numbers who supplemented their income through various part-time activities. And all of this does not count the multitude of customers who bought the goods and services offered by the bootleggers, gambling operators and vice lords of the city.

During the first thirty or forty years after an immigrant group's arrival, successful leaders in organized crime might constitute a disproportionate percentage of the most wealthy members of the community. In the 1930s at least one-half of the blacks in Chicago worth more than $100,000 were policy kings; Italian bootleggers in the 1920s may have represented an even larger proportion of the very wealthy among immigrants from southern Italy. The wealth of the successful criminals was accompanied by extensive political and other contacts that gave them considerable leverage both within and outside the ethnic community. They had financial resources to engage in extensive charitable activities, and often did so lavishly. Projects for improvement of ethnic communities often needed their support and contacts in order to succeed. Criminals often invested in or managed legitimate business enterprises in their communities. Hence, despite ambiguous or even antagonistic relations that they had with "respectable" members of their ethnic communities, successful leaders in organized crime were men who had to be reckoned with in the ethnic community and who often represented the community to the outside world.

In organized crime, as in other economic activities, the very successful were but a minority. To understand the economic impact of crime, it is necessary to study the many persons at the middle and lower levels of organization. In cities like Chicago the number of persons directly employed in the activities of organized crime was considerable. A modest estimate of the number of full-time prostitutes in Chicago about 1910 would be 15,000—not counting madams, pimps, procurers and others in managerial positions. Or take the policy racket. In the early 1930s an average policy wheel in the black ghetto employed 300 writers; some employed as many as 600; and there were perhaps 6,000 policy writers in the ghetto. The policy wheels, in this period of heavy unemployment, may have been the major single source of employment in the black ghetto, a source of employment that did not need to lay off workers or reduce wages merely because the rest of the economy faced a major depression. Finally, during the 1920s, bootlegging in its various aspects was a major economic activity employing thousands in manufacture, transportation and retailing activities.

Yet persons directly employed constituted only a small proportion of those whose income derived from organized crime. Many persons supplemented their income through occasional or part-time services. While some prostitutes walked the streets to advertise their wares, others relied upon intermediaries who would direct customers in return for a finder's fee. During certain periods, payments to taxi drivers were sufficiently lucrative so that some taxi drivers would pick up only those passengers seeking a house of prostitution. Bellboys, especially in the second-class hotels, found the function of negotiating between guests and prostitutes a profitable part of their service. (Many of the worst hotels, of course, functioned partly or wholly as places of assignation.) Bartenders, newsboys and waiters were among the many helpful persons who provided information concerning places and prices.

Various phases of bootlegging during the 1920s were even more important as income supplements. In the production end, many slum families prepared wine or became "alky cookers" for the bootlegging gangs—so much so that after the mid-1920s, explosions of stills and the resulting fires were a major hazard in Chicago's slum neighborhoods. As one observer reported:

During prohibition times many respectable Sicilian men were employed as "alky cookers" for the Capones, the Aiellos or for personal use. Many of these people sold wine during prohibition and their children delivered it on foot or by streetcar without the least fear that they might be arrested. . . .

During the years of 1927 to 1930 more wine was made than during any other years and even the "poorest people" were able to make ten or fifteen barrels each year—others making sixty, seventy, or more barrels.

Other persons, including policemen, moonlighted as truck drivers who delivered booze to the many retail outlets of the city. Finally, numerous persons supplemented their income by retailing booze, including bellboys, janitors in apartment buildings and shoe shine boys.

The many persons who mediated between the underworld and the law were another group that supplemented its income through underworld contacts. Large numbers of policemen, as well as bailiffs, judges and political fixers, received bribes or political contributions in return for illegal cooperation with the underworld. Defense attorneys, tax accountants and bailbondsmen, in return for salaries or fees, provided expert services that were generally legal.

For many of the small businessmen of the city, retailing the goods or services of the underworld could supplement business income significantly. Saloons, as already mentioned, often provided gambling and prostitution as an additional service to customers. Large numbers of small businesses were outlets for handbooks, policy, baseball pools, slot machines and other forms of gambling. A substantial proportion of the cigar stores, for example, were primarily fronts for gambling; barber shops, pool halls, newsstands, and small hotels frequently sold policy or would take bets on the horses. Drug stores often served as outlets for cocaine and, during the 1920s, sometimes sold liquor.

The organized underworld also influenced business activity through racketeering. A substantial minority of the city's labor unions were racketeer-controlled; those that were not often used the assistance of racketeer unions or of strongarm gangs during strikes. The leaders of organized crime, as a result, exercised control or influence in the world of organized labor. Not so well known was the extensive racketeering that characterized small business organizations. The small businesses of the city were generally marginal and intensely competitive. To avoid cutthroat competition, businessmen often formed associations to make and enforce regulations illegally limiting competition. The Master Barbers Association, for example, set minimum prices, forbad a shop to be open after 7:30 P.M., and ruled that no shop could be established within two blocks of another shop. Many other types of small businesses formed similar associations: dairies, auto parts dealers, garage owners, candy jobbers, butcher stores, fish wholesalers and retailers, cleaners and dyers, and junk dealers. Many of the associations were controlled, or even organized, by racketeers who levied dues upon association members and controlled the treasuries; they then used a system of fines and violence to insure that all businessmen in the trade joined the association and abided by the regulations. In return for control of the association's treasury, in short, racketeers performed illegal services for the association and thereby regulated much of the small business activity of the city.

Discussion of the economic influence of organized crime would be incomplete without mentioning the largest group that was tied economically to the underworld, namely, the many customers for the illegal goods and services. Like other retailers in the city, some leaders of organized crime located their outlets near the center of the city or along major transportation lines and serviced customers from the entire region; others were essentially neighborhood businessmen with a local clientele. In either case, those providing illegal goods and services usually attempted to cultivate customer loyalty so that the same customers would return on an ongoing basis and advertise among their friends. Organized crime existed because of wide customer demand, and a large proportion of the adult population of the city was linked to organized crime on a regular basis for purchase of goods and services.

Heroism and Ambiguity

Because of the diverse ways that successful criminal entrepreneurs influenced the city and ethnic communities, many of them became heroes—especially within their own communities. There were a variety of reasons for the admiration that they received. Their numerous philanthropies, both large and small, won them reputations as regular guys who would help a person in need. Moreover, they were often seen as persons who fought for their ethnic communities. They aided politicians from their communities to win elections in the rough and often violent politics of the slums and thereby advanced their ethnic group toward political recognition. Sometimes they were seen as fighters for labor unions and thus as friends of labor. And, on occasion, they fought directly for their ethnic group. There was, for instance, the case of the three Miller brothers from Chicago's West Side Jewish ghetto. In typical ghetto pattern, one became a boxer, one a gangster and one a policeman. The boxer and gangster were heroes among Jews on the West Side, where for many years Jewish peddlers and junk dealers had been subjected to racial slurs and violent attacks by young hoodlums from other ethnic groups. "What I have done from the time I was a boy," Davy Miller told a reporter,

was to fight for my people here in the Ghetto against Irish, Poles or any other nationality. It was sidewalk fighting at first. I could lick any five boys or men in a sidewalk free-for-all.

When the Miller brothers and their gang protected the Jews of the West Side, the attacks against them abated.

Particularly for youngsters growing up in the ghettos, the gangsters were often heroes whose exploits were admired and copied. Davy Miller modestly recognized this when he said:

Maybe I am a hero to the young folks among my people, but it's not because I'm a gangster. It's because I've always been ready to help all or any of them in a pinch.

An Italian student at the University of Chicago in the early 1930s remembered his earlier life in the Italian ghetto:

For 26 years I lived in West Side "Little Italy," the community that has produced more underworld limelights than any other area in Chicago. . . .
    I remember these men in large cars, with boys and girls of the neighborhood standing on the running board. I saw them come into the neighborhood in splendor as heroes. Many times they showered handfuls of silver to youngsters who waited to get a glance at them—the new heroes—because they had just made headlines in the newspapers. Since then I have seen many of my playmates shoot their way to the top of gangdom and seen others taken for a ride.

Nevertheless, despite the importance of gangsters and the world within which they moved, their relations to ethnic groups and the city were always ambiguous. Because many of their activities were illegal, they often faced the threat of arrest and, contrary to common belief, frequently found themselves behind bars. Furthermore, for those members of the ethnic community who pursued respectable paths to success, gangsters gave the ethnic group a bad name and remained a continuing source of embarrassment. St. Clair Drake and Horace R. Cayton, in their book on the Chicago black ghetto, describe the highly ambiguous and often antagonistic relations of the respectable black middle class and the policy kings.

In his book on Italians in Chicago, Humbert S. Nelli explains that in the 1920s the Italian language press refused to print the name of Al Capone and covered the St. Valentine's Day massacre without suggesting its connection with bootlegging wars.

The respectable middle classes, however, were not the only ones unhappy about the activities or notoriety of gangsters. Organized crime sometimes contributed to the violence and fear of violence that pervaded many of the ghetto neighborhoods. Often local residents feared to turn to the police and lived with a stoical acceptance that gangs of toughs controlled elections, extorted money from local businesses and generally lived outside the reach of the law. Some immigrant parents, too, resented the numerous saloons, the open prostitution and the many gambling dens— all of which created a morally dangerous environment in which to raise children. Especially immigrant women, who watched their husbands squander the meager family income on liquor or gambling, resented the activities of organized crime. Within a number of neighborhoods, local churches and local leaders undertook sporadic campaigns for better law enforcement.

Organized crime, then, was an important part of the complex social structure of ethnic communities and urban society in the early twentieth century. For certain ethnic groups, organized crime both influenced and reflected the special patterns by which the groups adjusted to life in urban America. Through organized crime, many members of those ethnic groups could achieve mobility out of the ethnic ghettos and into the social world of crime, politics, ethnic business, sports, and entertainment. Those who were successful in organized crime possessed the wealth and contacts to exercise broad influence within the ethnic communities and the city. The economic activities of the underworld provided jobs or supplemental income for tens of thousands. Despite the importance of organized crime, however, individual gangsters often found success to be ambiguous. They were not always able to achieve secure positions or to translate their positions into respectability.

Study Questions

1. What were the primary occupational paths out of the ghetto for uneducated but ambitious ethnic youths? How were the paths interrelated?

2. How did organized crime exert influence upon other social worlds? What in particular was the relationship between organized crime and urban politics?

3. What social values did criminals share with the leaders in politics, sports, labor unions, entertainment, and business? What was the attitude of the men in these professions toward law and legal institutions?

4. What does Haller mean by "ethnic specialization" in crime? What factors account for the criminal specialization of the different ethnic groups?

5. What was the economic impact of organized crime on the ethnic and urban environment?

6. Why did a number of criminals become ethnic heroes? What role did the "criminal heroes" play in their ethnic neighborhoods?

Bibliography

Because of the secretive nature of organized crime, it has proven an elusive subject for scholars. Nevertheless historians and sociologists have produced several valuable studies. Andrew Sinclair, *Prohibition: The Era of Excess* (1962), examines the impact of the Eighteenth Amendment on the rise of organized crime. Works by Humbert S. Nelli, *The Italians in Chicago, 1880-1930: A Study in Ethnic Mobility* (1970) and *The Business of Crime* (1976), deal admirably with the subject of ethnic crime. John A. Gardiner, *The Politics of Corruption: Organized Crime in the American City* (1970), is also valuable. William F. Whyte, *Street Corner Society: The Social Structure of an Italian Slum* (1955), is a classic sociological study of an ethnic urban environment. Finally, Daniel Bell, *The End of Ideology* (1961), considers crime as a means of social and economic mobility. Thomas Reppetto, *American Mafia: A History of Its Rise to Power* (2004), seeks to dispel common myths of mafia action and connect organize crime to political power struggles.

Depression and War

Despite all the talk about prosperity and progress in the 1920s, there were disturbing signs that the economy was not as healthy as people assumed. Throughout the decade, agricultural prices steadily declined as production rose, in what many called a "poverty of abundance." In face of high protective tariffs, foreign trade gradually declined, and the production of durable, domestic goods peaked in 1927. When the bubble burst with the crash of the stock market in October 1929, most Americans were shocked. The shock soon turned to despair as banks failed in record numbers, small businesses closed their doors, and unemployment reached unheard-of levels. How could it have been? For three centuries the world viewed America as the land of opportunity. Suddenly, people were losing their jobs, homes, and life savings. The American dream had become a nightmare.

Bewildered with their plight, most Americans were desperate for answers. Socialists and Communists blamed capitalism, arguing that, just as Karl Marx had predicted, the system was collapsing under the weight of its own corruption and exploitation. The technocrats claimed that industrialization had run its course and that a new social order, based on science and technology, would soon emerge out of the rubble of the Depression. Businessmen blamed politicians for the trouble. Farmers saw bogeymen in bankers and commodities speculators. Some Americans even blamed Jews for the collapse. Abandoning laissez-faire economics, Hoover modestly tried to reorganize the federal government to fight the Depression, but his efforts failed. In the next presidential election, Americans put Franklin D. Roosevelt into the White House.

Roosevelt was an unlikely hero for an impoverished nation. Born to old wealth and raised in splendor, he had little understanding of economics and no empathy for poverty. But he did have keen political instincts and few philosophical inhibitions. In a whirlwind of activity, the New Deal greatly increased relief spending, attacked specific problems in the money markets, and tried, usually in a haphazard way, to stimulate an industrial recovery. Although it took World War II to finally lift the country out of the Depression, Franklin D. Roosevelt nevertheless became one of the most beloved presidents in American history, popular enough to win reelection in 1936,

1940, and 1944. People remembered him for the spark in his eye, his smiling face and cocked head, and his uncompromising exuberance. To men working on government projects, it was Roosevelt who took them away from the soup lines. To farm wives living in poverty, it was Roosevelt who brought the electric transmission lines, the subsidy check, and the refinanced mortgage. To mass production workers, it was Roosevelt who sanctioned their labor unions and brought minimum wages. And to old people, it was Roosevelt who provided for their futures with Social Security.

But just as Roosevelt was easing fears about the economic future, political developments in Europe were bringing new tensions to a weary nation. Adolf Hitler's designs on Austria, Czechoslovakia, and Poland in 1938 and 1939 convinced many that another war was imminent and that the problems of the Depression, as bad as they were, would only be child's play compared to a new global conflagration. Hitler's conquest of France and the Low Countries in 1940, the assault on Great Britain, and the invasion of the Soviet Union in 1941 only confirmed those fears. For a brief time, the United States was caught between its historic need for isolation and its responsibilities as a global leader. On December 7, 1941, Japan resolved America's uncertain position.

READING 15

★ ★ ★

The Sad Irons

Robert A. Caro

For millions of older Americans, the Great Depression remains a vivid memory, a haunting reminder of the time when the promise of prosperity failed. For their descendants, the Great Depression is a chapter or two in a textbook, marked by pictures of gaunt faces and skinny Texas panhandle farmers leaning into the fierce winds of the Dust Bowl. Most descriptions of the Great Depression and New Deal revolve around images of what was lost and what was regained, of how the nation underwent the glittering but superficial prosperity of the 1920s, the poverty of the 1930s, and the boom years of World War II, and how public policymakers struggled to gain control of vast economic forces.

But there is another side of the New Deal. While economic recovery was the primary objective of the Roosevelt administration, the New Deal also introduced some sections of the country to modern technology. In the nineteenth century, the Industrial Revolution began its transformation of American life, bringing people together in large cities, organizing life into bureaucracies and interest groups, and relieving drudgery through technology. By the 1920s, the nation had become intoxicated with the marvels of the light bulb, the internal combustion engine, and the electric motor, all of which revolutionized the way people lived. But millions of people were still unable to take advantage of the new gadgets. Instead, they lived as their ancestors had, tied to the soil in backbreaking, relentless labor. In "The Sad Irons" Robert Caro describes the Hill Country of Central Texas before the Rural Electrification Administration brought farm families into the modern age. The extension of electric transmission lines into the remote corners of the Hill Country transformed their lives, and for the next fifty years they remembered the New Deal as their savior.

Obtaining the financing and the authorization for the four dams being built along the Lower Colorado had been difficult. Now Lyndon Johnson undertook a task more difficult still. By ensuring completion of the dams, he had ensured the creation of electric power, which would be generated by the fall of water through dam penstocks. Now he was going to try to get the power to the people. He was going to try to bring electricity to the Hill Country.

Electricity had, of course, been an integral part of life in urban and much of small-town America for a generation and more, lighting its streets, powering the machinery of its factories, running its streetcars and trolleys, its elevated trains and subways, moving elevators and escalators in its stores, and cooling the stores with electric fans. Devices such as electric irons and toasters (which were in widespread use by 1900), refrigerators (which were widely sold beginning in 1912), and vacuum cleaners, dishwashers, hot plates, waffle irons, electric stoves and automatic washing machines for clothes had freed women from much of the drudgery of housework. In the evenings, thanks to electricity, there were the movies, and by 1922, forests of radio antennae had sprouted on tenement roofs. By 1937, when Lyndon Johnson went to Congress, electricity was so integral a part of life that it was hard to remember what life had been like without it.

It was not a part of life in the Hill Country. In Lyndon Johnson's congressional district, the sole source of power had been Texas Power & Light, a subsidiary of the New York-based utility holding giant, Electric Bond & Share. TP&L had, in 1927, agreed to "electrify" a handful of Hill Country towns (Johnson City was one), but not with power from its central generating station at Marble Falls; according to TP&L, which put the cost of building electric lines at $3,000 per mile, the limited use such small communities would make of electric power would never justify the investment

required to build lines across the wide spaces of the Edwards Plateau. The TP&L "power plant" in each of these towns was, therefore, no more than a single thirty-horsepower diesel engine; it generated only enough voltage for ten-watt bulbs, which were constantly dimming and flickering—and which could not be used at all if an electric appliance (even an electric iron) was also in use. Since the "power plant" operated only between "dark to midnight," a refrigerator was useless. To most of the residents in these towns, such problems were academic: so high were TP&L's rates that few families hooked up to its lines. And in any case, the diesel engine was constantly breaking down under the strain placed on it. On the rare occasions on which a movie was shown, there was as much suspense in the audience over whether the electricity would hold out to the end of the film as there was in the film itself. Recalls Lucille O'Donnell of Burnet: "I'd be watching *The Perils of Pauline* and I'd just be about to see whether or not the train was going to run over her and the lights would go out." And the residents of these towns were the only inhabitants of the Hill Country with any electricity at all. TP&L refused even to consider building lines to the area's tens of thousands of individual farms and ranches.

As a result, although the electric milking machine had been invented almost two decades before, the Hill Country farmer had to milk his cows by hand—arising at three-thirty or four o'clock in the morning to do so, because milking was a time-consuming chore (more than two hours for twenty cows) and it had to be finished by daylight: every hour of daylight was needed for work in the fields. Milking was done by the dim light of kerosene lanterns; although Sears, Roebuck was boasting in 1937 that a new, deluxe kerosene lamp provided as much illumination as a forty-watt electric bulb, the lamps in use in the Hill Country furnished—at most—twenty-five watts of light. Or it was done in the dark. And there was a constant danger of fire with kerosene lamps, and even a spark could burn down a hay-filled barn, and destroy a farmer's last chance of holding on to his place, so many farmers were afraid to use a lantern in the barn. "Winter mornings," recalls one, "it would be so dark . . . you'd think you were in a box with the lid shut." Because without electricity there could be no refrigerator, the milk was kept on ice. The ice was expensive and farmers had to lug it from town at enormous cost in time. Though they kept it underground—covered with sawdust—it still, as farmer Chester Franklin of Wimberley puts it, "melted away so quick." And often even the ice didn't help. Farmers would have to take the milk out of their pit and place it by the roadside to be picked up by the trucks from Austin dairies, but often—on those unpaved Hill Country roads on which flat tires were a constant occurrence—the trucks would be late, and the milk would sit outside in the Hill Country heat. Even if it was not actually spoiled, the dairy would refuse to accept it if its temperature was above fifty degrees Fahrenheit—and when the truck driver pulled his thermometer out of the milk, a farmer, seeing the red line above fifty, would know that his hours of work in the barn in the dark had been for nothing.

Because there was no electricity, moreover, a Hill Country farmer could not use an electric pump. He was forced not only to milk but to water his cows by hand, a chore that, in dry weather, meant hauling up endless buckets from a deep well. Because he could not use an electric auger, he had to feed his livestock by hand, pitchforking heavy loads of hay up into the loft of his barn and then stomping on it to soften it enough so the cows could eat it. He had to prepare the feed by hand: because he could not use an electric grinder, he would get the corn kernels for his mules and horses by sticking ears of corn—hundreds of ears of corn—one by one into a corn sheller and cranking it for hours. Because he could not use electric motors, he had to unload cotton seed by hand, and then shovel it into the barn by hand; to saw wood by hand, by swinging an axe or riding one end of a ripsaw. Because there was never enough daylight for all the jobs that had to be done, the farmer usually finished after sunset, ending the day as he had begun it, stumbling around the barn milking the cows in the dark, as farmers had done centuries before.

But the hardness of the farmer's life paled beside the hardness of his wife's.

Without electricity, even boiling water was work.

Anything which required the use of water was work. Windmills (which could, acting like a pump, bring water out of a well into a storage tank) were very rare in the Hill Country; their cost—almost $400 in 1937—was out of the reach of most families in that cash-poor region, and the few that had been built proved of little use in a region where winds were always uncertain and, during a drought, non-existent, for days, or weeks, on end. And without electricity to work a pump, there was only one way to obtain water: by hand.

The source of water could be either a stream or a well. If the source was a stream, water had to be carried from it to the house, and since, in a country subject to constant flooding, houses were built well away from the streams, it had to be carried a long way. If the source was a well, it had to be lifted to the surface—a bucket at a time. It had to be lifted quite a long way: while the average depth of a well was about fifty feet in the valleys of the Hill Country, in the hills it was a hundred feet or more.

And so much water was needed! A federal study of nearly half a million farm families even then being conducted would show that, on the average, a person living on a farm used 40 gallons of water every day. Since the average farm family was five persons, the family used 200 gallons, or four-fifths of a ton, of water each day—73,000 gallons, or almost 300 tons, in a year. The study showed that, on the average, the well was located 253 feet from the house—and that to pump by hand and carry to the house 73,000 gallons of water a year would require someone to put in during that year 63 eight-hour days, and walk 1,750 miles.

A farmer would do as much of this pumping and hauling as possible himself, and try to have his sons do as much of the rest as possible (it was Lyndon Johnson's adamant refusal to help his mother with the pumping and hauling that touched off the most bitter of the flareups with his father during his youth). As soon as a Hill

Members of the Peterson family in Travis County, Texas. These farm women of the Hill Country had to haul wood and water for washing and cooking day in and day out until the end of the 1930s.

Country youth got big enough to carry the water buckets (which held about four gallons, or thirty-two pounds, of water apiece), he was assigned the job of filling his mother's wash pots before he left for school or the field. Curtis Cox still recalls today that from the age of nine or ten, he would, every morning throughout the rest of his boyhood, make about seven trips between his house and the well, which were about 300 feet apart, on each of these trips carrying two large buckets, or more than sixty pounds, of water. "I felt tired," he says. "It was a lot of water." But the water the children carried would be used up long before noon, and the children would be away—at school or in the fields—and most of the hauling of water was, therefore, done by women. "I would," recalls Curtis' mother, Mary Cox, "have to get it, too—more than once a day, more than twice; oh, I don't know how many times. I needed water to wash my floors, water to wash my clothes, water to

cook. . . . It was hard work. I was always packing [carrying] water." Carrying it—after she had wrestled off the heavy wooden lid which kept the rats and squirrels out of the well; after she had cranked the bucket up to the surface (and cranking—lifting thirty pounds fifty feet or more—was very hard for most women even with a pulley; most would pull the rope hand over hand, as if they were climbing it, to get their body weight into the effort; they couldn't do it with their arms alone). Some Hill Country women make wry jokes about getting water. Says Mrs. Brian Smith of Blanco: "Yes, we had running water. I always said we had running water because I grabbed those two buckets up and ran the two hundred yards to the house with them." But the joking fades away as the memories sharpen. An interviewer from the city is struck by the fact that Hill Country women of the older generation are noticeably stooped, much more so than city women of the same age. Without his asking for an explanation, it is given to him. More than once, and more than twice, a stooped and bent Hill Country farm wife says, "You see how round-shouldered I am? Well, that's from hauling the water." And, she will often add, "I was round-shouldered like this well before my time, when I was still a young woman. My back got bent from hauling the water, and it got bent when I was still young."

The Hill Country farm wife had to haul water, and she had to haul wood.

Because there was no electricity, Hill Country stoves were wood stoves. The spread of the cedar brakes had given the area a plentiful supply of wood, but cedar seared bone-dry by the Hill Country sun burned so fast that the stoves seemed to devour it. A farmer would try to keep a supply of wood in the house, or, if he had sons old enough, would assign the task to them. (Lyndon Johnson's refusal to chop wood for his mother was another source of the tension between him and Sam.) They would cut down the trees, and chop them into four-foot lengths that could be stacked in cords. When wood was needed in the house, they would cut it into shorter lengths and split the pieces so they could fit into the stoves. But as with the water, these chores often fell to the women.

The necessity of hauling the wood was not, however, the principal reason so many farm wives hated their wood stoves. In part, they hated these stoves because they were so hard to "start up." The damper that opened into the firebox created only a small draft even on a breezy day, and on a windless day, there was no draft—because there was no electricity, of course, there was no fan to move the air in the kitchen—and a fire would flicker out time after time. "With an electric stove, you just turn on a switch and you have heat," says Lucille O'Donnell, but with a wood stove, a woman might have to stuff kindling and wood into the firebox over and over again. And even after the fire was lit, the stove "didn't heat up in a minute, you know," Lucille O'Donnell says—it might in fact take an hour. In part, farm wives hated wood stoves because they were

so dirty, because the smoke from the wood blackened walls and ceilings, and ashes were always escaping through the grating, and the ash box had to be emptied twice a day—a dirty job and dirtier if, while the ashes were being carried outside, a gust of wind scattered them around inside the house. They hated the stoves because they could not be left unattended. Without devices to regulate the heat and keep the temperature steady, when the stove was being used for baking or some other cooking in which an even temperature was important, a woman would have to keep a constant watch on the fire, thrusting logs—or corncobs, which ignited quickly—into the firebox every time the heat slackened.

Most of all, they hated them because they were so hot.

When the big iron stove was lit, logs blazing in its firebox, flames licking at the gratings that held the pots, the whole huge mass of metal so hot that it was almost glowing, the air in the kitchen shimmered with the heat pouring out of it. In the Winter the heat was welcome, and in Spring and Fall it was bearable, but in the Hill Country, Summer would often last five months. Some time in June the temperature might climb to near ninety degrees, and would stay there, day after day, week after week, through the end of September. Day after day, week after week, the sky would be mostly empty, without a cloud as a shield from the blazing sun that beat down on the Hill Country, and on the sheet-iron or corrugated tin roofs of the box-like kitchens in the little dog-run homes that dotted its hills and valleys. No matter how hot the day, the stove had to be lit much of the time, because it had to be lit not only for meals but for baking; Hill Country wives, unable to afford store-bought bread, baked their own, an all-day task. (As Mrs. O'Donnell points out, "We didn't have refrigerators, you know, and without refrigerators, you just about have to start every meal from scratch.") In the Hill Country, moreover, Summer was harvest time, when a farm wife would have to cook not just for her family but for a harvesting crew—twenty or thirty men, who, working from sun to sun, expected three meals a day.

Harvest time, and canning time.

In the Hill Country, canning was required for a family's very survival. Too poor to buy food, most Hill Country families lived through the Winter largely on the vegetables and fruit picked in the Summer and preserved in jars.

Since—because there was no electricity—there were no refrigerators in the Hill Country, vegetables or fruit had to be canned the very day they came ripe. And, from June through September, something was coming ripe almost every day, it seemed; on a single peach tree, the fruit on different branches would come ripe on different days. In a single orchard, the peaches might be reaching ripeness over a span as long as two weeks; "You'd be in the kitchen with the peaches for two weeks," Hill Country wives recall. And after the peaches, the strawberries would begin coming ripe, and then the gooseberries, and then the blueberries. The tomatoes would become ripe before the okra, the okra before the zucchini, the zucchini before the corn. So the canning would go on with only brief intervals—all Summer.

Canning required constant attendance on the stove. Since boiling water was essential, the fire in the stove had to be kept roaring hot, so logs had to be continually put into the firebox. At least twice during a day's canning, moreover—probably three or four times—a woman would have to empty the ash container, which meant wrestling the heavy, unwieldy device out from under the firebox. And when the housewife wasn't bending down to the flames, she was standing over them. In canning fruit, for example, first sugar was dropped into the huge iron canning pot, and watched carefully and stirred constantly, so that it would not become lumpy, until it was completely dissolved. Then the fruit—perhaps peaches, which would have been peeled earlier—was put in the pot, and boiled until it turned into a soft and mushy jam that would be packed into jars (which would have been boiling—to sterilize them—in another pot) and sealed with wax. Boiling the peaches would take more than an hour, and during that time they had to be stirred constantly so that they would not stick to the pot.

And when one load of peaches was finished, another load would be put in, and another. Canning was an all-day job. So when a woman was canning, she would have to spend all day in a little room with a tin or sheet-iron roof on which a blazing sun was beating down without mercy, standing in front of the iron stove and the wood fire within it. And every time the heat in that stove died down even a bit, she would have to make it hotter again.

"You'd have to can in the Summer when it was hot," says Kitty Clyde Ross Leonard, who had been Johnson's first girlfriend. "You'd have to cook for hours. Oh, that was a terrible thing. You wore as little as you could. I wore loose clothing so that it wouldn't stick to me. But the perspiration would just pour down my face. I remember the perspiration pouring down my mother's face, and when I grew up and had my own family, it poured down mine. That stove was so hot. But you had to stir, especially when you were making jelly. So you had to stand over that stove." Says Bernice Snodgrass of Wimberley: "You got so hot that you couldn't stay in the house. You ran out and sat under the trees. I couldn't stand it to stay in the house. Terrible. Really terrible. But you couldn't stay out of the house long. You had to stir. You had to watch the fire. So you had to go back into the house."

And there was no respite. If a bunch of peaches came ripe a certain day, that was the day they had to be canned—no matter how the housewife might feel that day. Because in the fierce Hill Country heat, fruit and vegetables spoiled very quickly. And once the canning process was begun, it could not stop. "If you peeled six dozen peaches, and then, later that day, you felt sick, you couldn't stop," says Gay Harris. "Because you can't can something if it's rotten. The job has to be done the same day, no matter what." Sick or not, in the Hill Country, when it was time to can, a woman canned, standing hour after hour, trapped between a blazing sun and a blazing wood fire. "We had no choice, you see," Mrs. Harris says.

Every week, every week all year long—every week without fail—there was washday.

The wash was done outside. A huge vat of boiling water would be suspended over a larger, roaring fire and near it three large "Number Three" zinc washtubs and a dishpan would be placed on a bench.

The clothes would be scrubbed in the first of the zinc tubs, scrubbed on a washboard by a woman bending over the tub. The soap, since she couldn't afford store-bought soap, was soap she made from lye, soap that was not very effective, and the water was hard. Getting farm dirt out of clothes required hard scrubbing.

Then the farm wife would wring out each piece of clothing to remove from it as much as possible of the dirty water, and put it in the big vat of boiling water. Since the scrubbing would not have removed all of the dirt, she would try to get the rest out by "punching" the clothes in the vat—standing over the boiling water and using a wooden paddle or, more often, a broomstick, to stir the clothes and swish them through the water and press them against the bottom or sides, moving the broom handle up and down and around as hard as she could for ten or fifteen minutes in a human imitation of the agitator of an automatic—electric—washing machine.

The next step was to transfer the clothes from the boiling water to the second of the three zinc washtubs: the "rinse tub." The clothes were lifted out of the big vat on the end of the broomstick, and held up on the end of the stick for a few minutes while the dirty water dripped out.

When the clothes were in the rinse tub, the woman bent over the tub and rinsed them, by swishing each individual item through the water. Then she wrung out the clothes, to get as much of the dirty water out as possible, and placed the clothes in the third tub, which contained bluing, and swished them around in *it*—this time to get the bluing all through the garment and make it white—and then repeated the same movements in the dishpan which was filled with starch.

At this point, one load of wash would be done. A week's wash took at least four loads: one of sheets, one of shirts and other white clothing, one of colored clothes and one of dish towels. But for the typical, large, Hill Country farm family, two loads of each of these categories would be required, so the procedure would have to be repeated eight times.

For each load, moreover, the water in each of the three washtubs would have to be changed. A washtub held about eight gallons. Since the water had to be warm, the woman would fill each tub half with boiling water from the big pot and half with cold water. She did the filling with a bucket which held three or four gallons—twenty-five or thirty pounds. For the first load or two of wash, the water would have been provided by her husband or her sons. But after this water had been used up, part of washday was walking—over and over—that long walk to the spring or well, hauling up the water, hand over laborious hand, and carrying those heavy buckets back. Another part of washday was also a physical effort: the "punching" of the clothes in the big vat. "You had to do it as hard as you could—swish those clothes around and around and around. They never seemed to get clean. And those clothes were heavy in the water, and it was hot outside, and you'd be standing over that boiling water and that big fire—you felt like you were being roasted alive." Lifting the clothes out of the vat was an effort, too. A dripping mass of soggy clothes was heavy, and it felt heavier when it had to be lifted out of that vat and held up for minutes at a time so that the dirty water could drip out, and then swung over to the rinsing tub. Soon, if her children weren't around to hear her, a woman would be grunting with the effort. Even the wringing was, after a few hours, an effort. "I mean, wringing clothes might not seem hard," Mrs. Harris says. "But you have to wring every piece so many times—you wring it after you take it out of the scrub tub, and you wring it after you take it out of the rinse tub, and after you take it out of the bluing. Your arms got tired." And her hands—from scrubbing with lye soap and wringing—were raw and swollen. Of course, there was also the bending—hours of bending—over the rub boards. "By the time you got done washing, your back was broke," Ava Cox says. "I'll tell you—of the things of my life that I will never forget, I will never forget how much my back hurt on washdays." Hauling the water, scrubbing, punching, rinsing: a Hill Country farm wife did this for hours on end—while a city wife did it by pressing the button on her electric washing machine.

Says Mary Cox, in words echoed by all elderly Hill Country farm wives: "Washing was hard work, but ironing was the worst. Nothing could be as hard as ironing."

The Department of Agriculture finds that "Young women today are not aware of the origin of the word 'iron,' as they press clothes with lightweight appliances of aluminum or hollow stainless steel." In the Hill Country, in the 1930s an iron was *iron*—a six- or seven-pound wedge of iron. The irons used in the Hill Country had to be heated on the wood stove, and they would retain their heat for only a few minutes—a man's shirt generally required two irons; a farm wife would own three or four of them, so that several could be heating while one was working. An iron with a wooden handle cost two dollars more than one without the handle, so Hill Country wives did their weekly loads of ironing—huge loads because, as Mary Cox puts it, "in those days you were expected to starch and iron almost everything"—with irons without handles. They would either transfer a separate wooden handle from one iron to another, or they would protect their hands with a thick pot holder.

Since burning wood generates soot, the irons became dirty as they sat heating on the stove. Or, if any moisture was left on an iron from the sprinkled clothes on which it had just been used, even the thinnest smoke from the stove created a muddy film on the bottom. The irons had to be cleaned frequently, therefore, by scrubbing them with a rag that had been dipped in salt, and if the soot was too thick, they had to be sanded and scraped. And no matter how carefully you checked the bottom of the irons, and sanded and scraped them, there would often remain some little spot of soot—as you would discover when you rubbed it over a clean white shirt or dress. Then you had to wash that item of clothing over again.

Nevertheless, the irons would burn a woman's hand. The wooden handle or the searing metal against her flesh; by noon, she might have blister atop blister—on hands that had to handle the rag that had been dipped in salt. Ironing always took a full day—often it went on into Tuesday evening—and a full day of lifting and carrying six- or seven-pound loads was hard on even these hardy Hill Country women. "It would hurt so bad between the shoulders," Elsie Beck remembers. But again the worst aspect of ironing was the heat. On ironing day, a fire would have to be blazing in the wood stove all day, filling the kitchen, hour after hour, with heat and smoke. Ironing had to be done not only in the Winter but in the Summer—when the temperature outside the kitchen might be ninety or ninety-five or one hundred, and inside the kitchen would be considerably higher, and because there was no electricity, there was no fan to so much as stir the air. In a speech in Congress some years later, Representative John E. Rankin described the "drudgery" a typical farm wife endured, "burning up in a hot kitchen and bowing down over the washtub or boiling the clothes over a flaming fire in the summer heat." He himself remembered, he said, "seeing his mother lean over that hot iron hour after hour until it seemed she was tired enough to drop." Rankin was from Mississippi, but his description would have been familiar to the mothers of the Edwards Plateau. The women of the Hill Country never called the instruments they used every Tuesday "irons," they called them "sad irons."

Washing, ironing—those were chores that were performed every week. Then, of course, there were special occasions—harvest time and threshing time, when a woman had to cook not just for her family but for a crew of twenty or thirty men; the shearing, when, because there was no electricity and her husband had to work the shears, she had to crank the shearing machine, pedaling as if she were pumping a bicycle up a steep hill, pedaling, with only brief pauses, hour after hour; "He was always yelling 'Faster, faster,' Mrs. Walter Yett of Blanco recalls. "I could hardly get up the next morning, I was so tired after that." Washing, ironing, cooking, canning, shearing, helping with the plowing and the picking and the picking and the sowing, and, every day, carrying the water and the wood, and because there was no electricity, having to do everything by hand by the same methods that had been employed by her mother and grandmother and great-great-great-grandmother before her—"They wear these farm women out pretty fast," wrote one observer. In the Hill Country, as many outside observers noted, the one almost universal characteristic of the women was that they were worn out before their time, that they were old beyond their years, old at forty, old at thirty-five, bent and stooped and tired.

A Hill Country farm wife had to do her chores even if she was ill—no matter how ill. Because Hill Country women were too poor to afford proper medical care, they often suffered perineal tears in childbirth. During the 1930s, the federal government sent physicians to examine a sampling of Hill Country women. The doctors found that, out of 275 women, 158 had perineal tears. Many of them, the team of gynecologists reported, were third-degree tears, "tears so bad that it is difficult to see how they stand on their feet." But they *were* standing on their feet, and doing all the chores that Hill Country wives had always done—hauling the water, hauling the wood, canning, washing, ironing, helping with the shearing, the plowing and the picking.

Because there was no electricity.

The lack of electricity meant that the days of the people of the Hill Country were filled with drudgery; at night they were denied the entertainment—movies, radio—that would have made the drudgery more bearable. The radio could, moreover, have ended the area's isolation. The feeling of the Hill Country youngsters of the 1920s—Lyndon Johnson's generation—that "we were completely cut off out here," that "we were back in the woods, compared to the rest of the world," that "everything had already happened before we found out about it," was the feeling of the 1930s generation as well. Because there was no electricity, the only radios in the Hill Country

were the occasional crystal sets with earphones and poor reception. Amos 'n' Andy, Lum 'n' Abner, Ma Perkins—theirs were voices familiar to most of America; it was a rare inhabitant of the Edwards Plateau who had not heard them even once. "What we missed most was the fireside chats," says Mary Cox. "I mean, we loved Franklin D. Roosevelt in this country, and we kept reading about these wonderful fireside chats. But we never got to hear them."

Even reading was hard.

Evening was often the only time in which Hill country farm couples could read ("There was no other time," says Lucille O'Donnell. "There was never a minute to read during the day, it seemed"), but the only light for reading came from kerosene lamps. In movies about the Old West, these lamps appear so homey that it is difficult for a city dweller to appreciate how much—and why—some farm dwellers disliked them so passionately.

Lighting the kerosene lamp was a frustrating job. "You had to adjust the wick just right," says Curtis Cox of Bryan. "If you turned it too high, it would flame up and start to smoke. The chimney—that's the glass part—would get all black, and your eyes would start to smart." Keeping it lit was even more frustrating. It burned straight across for only a moment, and then would either flare up or die down to an inadequate level. Even when the wick was trimmed just right, a kerosene lamp provided only limited illumination. The approximately twenty-five watts of light provided by most such lamps was adequate for children doing their homework—although surveys would later find that the educational level of rural children improved markedly immediately upon the introduction of electricity—but their parents, whose eyes were not so strong, had more difficulty. Mary Cox says that she couldn't read with their lamp for more than a short period: "I always loved to read," she recalls. "But I couldn't enjoy it on the farm. It was hard on the eyes, a strain on the eyes. I had to force myself to read at night." Lucille O'Donnell came to Burnet from Virginia, where she had liked to read in bed; she couldn't do that on her farm, she says, because she couldn't afford the kerosene. When she did read at night, she couldn't read in bed. Her husband, Tom, "would be asleep," she recalls, "and I would put the lamp beside him on the bed, and sit on that little stool and read in the most awkward position." Pointing to deep vertical lines between her eyebrows, more than one Hill Country farm wife says: "So many of us have these lines from squinting to read."

The circle of light cast by a kerosene lamp was small, and there were seldom enough lamps in the home of an impoverished farm family. If a family had so many children that they completely surrounded the one good lamp while studying, their mother could not do her sewing until they were finished. And outside the small circles of light, the rooms of a farmhouse were dark. "The house looked scary," says Mary Cox. "If I was alone at night, it was awfully lonely." And, of course, there were no lamps in the outhouse. Many a Hill country farm wife echoes the words of Betty MacDonald: "I had a horrible choice of either sitting in the dark and not knowing what was crawling on me or bringing a lantern and attracting moths, mosquitoes, nighthawks and bats."

No radio; no movies; limited reading—little diversion between the hard day just past and the hard day just ahead. "Living was just drudgery then," says Carroll Smith of Blanco. "Living—just *living*—was a problem. No lights. No plumbing. Nothing. Just living on the edge of starvation. That was farm life for us. God, city people think there was something fine about it. If they only knew . . ."

So many conveniences taken for granted in American cities were unknown on the Edwards Plateau: not just vacuum cleaners and washing machines but, for example, bathrooms, since, as a practical matter, indoor plumbing is unfeasible without running water, which requires an electric pump. In the Summer, bathing could be done in the creek (when the creek wasn't dry); in the Winter, it entailed lugging in water and heating it on the stove (which entailed lugging in wood) before pouring it into a Number Three washtub. Because bathing was so hard, "you bathed about once a week," Bernice Snodgrass says. Children

went barefoot, so "we'd make them wash their feet [at the pump outside] you know. We [adults] would wash our face and hands and ears in washpans but we didn't take a bath but once a week." There were few toilets, and most Hill Country outhouses were the most primitive sort. Many had no pit dug under them. "It would just drop on the ground," Guthrie Taylor recalls. "No, it wouldn't be cleared away"; every so often the flimsy little shelter would just be moved to another spot. Since toilet paper was too expensive, pages from a Sears, Roebuck catalogue, or corncobs, were used. And some families did not have outhouses. When the Snodgrasses moved to Mount Gaynor from Austin, Bernice Snodgrass says, "We were the only people in the neighborhood that had one. You know what everybody else did? They went out behind the barn, or behind a tree, or something." Frederick Law Olmsted had found the same situation—houses at which there was "no other water-closet than the back of a bush or the broad prairies"—on his journey through the Hill Country in 1857. He had been shocked then, because the America he knew had advanced beyond such primitive conditions. Now it was 1937; four more generations had been living in the Hill Country—with no significant advance in the conditions of their life. Many of the people of Lyndon Johnson's congressional district were still living in the same type of dwelling in which the area's people had been living in 1857: in rude "dog-run" shelters one board thick, through which the wind howled in the winter. They were still squatting behind a bush to defecate. Because of their poverty, they were still utterly bereft not only of tractors and feed grinders, but of modern medical assistance—and were farming by methods centuries out of date.

Although they understood that, as Louise Casparis says, "we were behind the rest of the world," natives of the Hill Country did not realize how *far* behind the rest of the world.

How could they be expected to realize? Without many books to read—or, in general, newspapers, either, except for those pathetic four-page local weeklies; without radio to listen to, with only an occasional movie to watch—how was news of advances in the rest of the world to reach them? Since many of them never saw that world for themselves—an astonishing high proportion of Hill Country residents would never visit even Austin or San Antonio—the Hill Country's awareness of the outside world was dim. The life of Hill Country natives was, moreover, the same life that their mothers and fathers—and grandmothers and grandfathers—had lived; how were they to know, except in general, vague terms, that there was another kind of life? When they heard about the wonders of electricity, they thought electricity was the electricity they saw in Johnson City, the dim, flickering lights hardly better than lamplight; the wonders they imagined were the electric iron and the radio, little more; "I remember when someone started telling me about these washing machines," recalls Ava Cox. "A machine that *washed*? I couldn't picture that *at all*!" Even the concept of the toilet was difficult for them to accept completely; when Errol Snodgrass, newly arrived in Mount Gaynor, began not only to build an outhouse but to dig a pit underneath it, a neighbor asked him: "What do you want that pit for?" And when he explained, Bernice Snodgrass recalls, the reaction of the neighborhood was, "They're so highfalutin that they have to have a toilet. They thought an outhouse with a pit under it—they thought that that was what people meant when they spoke about a toilet!" Natives of the Hill Country couldn't understand why families that had moved away from the Hill Country never returned. It is not, therefore, by lifelong residents of the Hill Country that the contrast between life there and in the outside world is most clearly enunciated, but by newcomers: from families which, due to economic necessity, moved to the Hill Country in the 1930s.

The Depression had cost Brian and Mary Sue Smith their home and their once-profitable automobile-repair shop in Portland, Texas, a town near Corpus Christi. In 1937, they moved with their three children to the Hill Country—to a fifty-three-acre farm near Blanco—because "that was

the only place where land was cheap enough so we could buy a farm."

Portland had electricity—had had it for years. "You never even thought about electricity," Mrs. Smith says. "I just accepted it. I mean, if I thought about it, I suppose I would have thought, 'Doesn't *everyone* have electricity?' "

Now she found out that not everyone did.

The Smiths had brought their radio, a big black Atwater Kent with an amplifying horn on top, to their new home, but it could not be played. "You know, it was very lonely on that farm," Mrs. Smith says. "The quiet was nice sometimes. But sometimes it was so quiet it hurt you." They had brought their washing machine, but that could not work, either. Mrs. Smith loved to read, but "The light was hard on your eyes. My eyes just weren't good enough to read at night." In Portland, she had crocheted at night, but she found the light was too dim for her to do that at night. And, of course, there was no time to do it during the day; what time wasn't consumed by her household chores was taken up husking, shelling and grinding corn by hand for feed for the 150 hens whose eggs she was selling; by cranking the sheep-shearing machine. Soon after she arrived on the farm, her husband became very ill, and for more than a year she had to care for the livestock too, and to plow behind a pair of mules—although she had never plowed before. "Up before daylight. Build the fire in the wood range. Put on the biscuits. Go out and milk the cows. Breakfast. Work was all there was. It was a bare existence."

Getting the water, from a well some 200 yards from the house, was the chore that bothered her most. "The children had had running water in Portland, of course, and they acted like they still had it," she says. When she started meeting other Hill Country women, she noticed that many of them were round-shouldered, and they told her it was from carrying heavy buckets of water. She didn't want to be round-shouldered. But there seemed no solution. "Carry and carry. Back and forth. Sometimes I would get awfully discouraged. When I first moved there [to the Hill Country], I felt like a pioneer lady, like one of the women who had come here in covered wagons. I said, if they could do it, I could, too. But it was very hard. After you spent all morning lugging those big buckets back and forth, you felt more like an ox or a mule than a human being. Portland was just a little town. It was no great metropolis. But moving from Portland into the Hill Country was like moving from the twentieth century back into the Middle Ages."

Study Questions

1. Why had electric transmission lines never been built in large areas of the Hill Country?

2. Why was the lot of these women so difficult before the arrival of electricity?

3. Why was water such a critical item to Hill Country women? Describe the efforts required to get water into the typical home in this area.

4. Why did Hill Country women hate their stoves?

5. How did these women iron clothes? Why did they hate the chore of ironing?

6. When electricity arrived at a Hill Country farm, what changes did it bring in the way people lived?

Bibliography

For the best description of the Hill Country, see Robert A. Caro, *The Years of Lyndon Johnson, The Path to Power* (1982). Also see John Graves, *Hard Scrabble* (1974) and *Texas Heartland: A Hill Country Year* (1975). The best descriptions of southern agriculture during the New Deal years are Richard S. Kirdendall, *Social Scientists and Farm Politics in the Age of Roosevelt* (1966) and David Conrad, *The Forgotten Farmers* (1965). The latter deals with those who did not benefit from the Agricultural Adjustment Administration. On the problem of poverty in the South, see Paul Mertz, *The New Deal and Southern Rural Poverty* (1978). The best discussion of the Rural Electrification Administration is D. Clayton Brown, *Electricity for Rural America: The Fight for REA* (1980).

READING 16

★ ★ ★

The Black Blizzards Roll In

Donald Worster

Early in 1935, clouds black as night began to rumble across the southern plains. These waves of dirt rose from the ground, sometimes to a height of 7,000 or 8,000 feet, and they obscured the sun. They filled streets and houses with dirt, sand-blasted paint from automobiles, covered the exposed faces of men and women with a layer of grime. All the while they kept moving, some making their way to the Atlantic seaboard and the ocean beyond. The year before they had dumped millions of pounds of dirt on Boston, New York, Washington, and Atlanta; ship captains 300 miles out in the Atlantic reported decks coated with dust. They were part of the worst ecological disaster in the 1930s—the "dirty thirties"—part of what came to be known simply as the Dust Bowl.

Nature helped form the Dust Bowl, but humans made it. The ecology of the high plains had always been fragile, but farmers had moved into the area and exploited the land, transforming millions of acres of grasslands into wheat fields. They overplanted, used the wrong sort of plows, and prayed for plenty of rain. But in an area known more for drought than rain, they badly miscalculated. Soon strong winds lifted the dry top soil and sent it east, leaving dust pneumonia, ruined crops, and shattered lives in its wake.

While Franklin D. Roosevelt's New Deal confronted the economic and physical costs of the Dust Bowl, artists focused on the human suffering. Pare Lorentz's documentary *The Plow That Broke the Plains,* Woody Guthrie's song "The Great Dust Bowl," Alexandre Hogue's painting "Drouth Survivors," and John Steinbeck's novel *The Grapes of Wrath* were all inspired by the Dust Bowl. In the following essay, historian Donald Worster eloquently describes what the dust storms looked, tasted, smelled, and felt like. People who lived through such a storm, where as one writer observed, "Lady Godiva could ride thru the streets without even the horse seeing her," did not soon forget the experience.

The thirties began in economic depression and in drought. The first of those disasters usually gets all the attention, although for the many Americans living on farms drought was the more serious problem. In the spring of 1930 over 3 million men and women were out of work. They had lost their jobs or had been laid off without pay in the aftermath of the stock market crash of the preceding fall. Another 12 million would suffer the same fate in the following two years. Many of the unemployed had no place to live, nor even the means to buy food. They slept in public toilets, under bridges, in shantytowns along the railroad tracks, or on doorsteps, and in the most wretched cases they scavenged from garbage cans—a Calcutta existence in the richest nation ever. The farmer, in contrast, was slower to feel the impact of the crash. He usually had his own independent food supply and stood a bit aloof from the ups and downs of the urban-industrial system. In the twenties that aloofness had meant that most farm families had not fully shared in the giddy burst of affluence—in new washing machines, silk stockings, and shiny roadsters. They had, in fact, spent much of the decade in economic doldrums. Now, as banks began to fail and soup lines formed, rural Americans went on as before, glad to be spared the latest reversal and just a little pleased to see their proud city cousins humbled. Then the droughts began, and they brought the farmers to their knees, too.

During the spring and summer of 1930, little rain fell over a large part of the eastern United States. A horizontal band on the map, from Maryland and Virginia to Missouri and Arkansas, marked the hardest hit area of wilting crops, shrinking groundwater supplies, and uncertain income. Over the summer months in this drought band the rainfall shortage was 60,000 tons for each 100-acre farm, or 700 tons a day. Seventeen million people were affected. In twelve states the drought set record lows in precipitation, and

among all the Eastern states only Florida was above normal. Three years earlier the Mississippi River had overflowed its banks and levees in one of the most destructive floods in American history. Now captains there wondered how long their barges would remain afloat as the river shrank to a fraction of its average height.

During the thirties serious drought threatened a great part of the nation. The persistent center, however, shifted from the East to the Great Plains, beginning in 1931, when much of Montana and the Dakotas became almost as arid as the Sonoran Desert. Farmers there and almost everywhere else watched the scorched earth crack open, heard the gray grass crunch underfoot, and worried about how long they would be able to pay their bills. Around their dried-up ponds the willows and wild cherries were nearly leafless, and even the poison ivy dropped. Drought, of course, is a relative term: it depends upon one's concept of "normal." But following the lead of the climatologists of the time, we can use a precipitation deficiency of at least 15 percent of the historical mean to qualify as drought. By that standard, of all the American states only Maine and Vermont escaped a drought year from 1930 to 1936. Twenty states set or equaled record lows for their entire span of official weather data. Over the nation as a whole, the 1930s drought was, in the words of a Weather Bureau scientist, "the worst in the climatological history of the country."

Intense heat accompanied the drought, along with economic losses the nation could ill afford. In the summer of 1934, Nebraska reached 118 degrees, Iowa, 115. In Illinois thermometers stuck at over 100 degrees for so long that 370 people died—and one man, who had been living in a refrigerator to keep cool, was treated for frostbite. Two years later, when the country was described by *Newsweek* as "a vast simmering caldron," more than 4,500 died from excessive heat, water was shipped into the West by diverted tank-cars and oil pipelines, and clouds of grasshoppers ate what little remained of many farmers' wheat and corn—along with their fence posts and the washing on their clotheslines. The financial cost of the

From *The Dust Bowl: Southern Plains 1930's* by Daniel Worster, © 1979 Oxford University Press, Inc. Used by permission of the publisher.

1934 drought alone amounted to one-half the money the United States had put into World War I. By 1936, farm losses had reached $25 million a day, and more than 2 million farmers were drawing relief checks. Rexford Tugwell, head of the Resettlement Administration, who toured the burning plains that year, saw "a picture of complete destruction"—"one of the most serious peacetime problems in the nation's history."

As the decade reached its midpoint, it was the southern plains that experienced the most severe conditions. During some growing seasons there was no soil moisture down to three feet over large parts of the region. By 1939, near Hays, Kansas, the accumulated rainfall deficiency was more than 34 inches—almost a two-year supply in arrears. Continued long enough in such a marginal, semiarid land, a drought of that magnitude would produce a desert. Weathermen pointed out that there had been worse single years, as in 1910 and 1917, or back in the 1890s, and they repeatedly assured the people of the region that their records did not show any modern drought lasting more than five years, nor did they suggest any long-range adverse climatic shift. But farmers and ranchers did not find much comfort in statistical charts; their cattle were bawling for feed, and their bank credit was drying up along with the soil. Not until after 1941 did the rains return in abundance and the burden of anxiety lift.

Droughts are an inevitable fact of life on the plains, an extreme one occurring roughly every twenty years, and milder ones every three or four. They have always brought with them blowing dust where the ground was bare of crops or native grass. Dust was so familiar an event that no one was surprised to see it appear when the dry weather began in 1931. But no one was prepared for what came later: dust storms of such violence that they made the drought only a secondary problem—storms of such destructive force that they left the region reeling in confusion and fear.

"Earth" is the word we use when it is there in place, growing the food we eat, giving us a place to stand and build on. "Dust" is what we say when it is loose and blowing on the wind. Nature en-

compasses both—the good and the bad from our perspective, and from that of all living things. We need the earth to stay alive, but dust is a nuisance, or, worse, a killer. On a planet such as ours, where there is much wind, where there are frequent dry spells, and where we encounter vast expanses of bare soil, dust is a constant presence. It rises from the hooves of animals, from a wagon's wheels, from a dry riverbed, from the deserts. If all the continents were an English greensward, there would be no dust. But nature has not made things so. Nor has man, in many times and places.

Dust in the air is one phenomenon. However, dust storms are quite another. The story of the southern plains in the 1930s is essentially about dust storms, when the earth ran amok. And not once or twice, but over and over for the better part of a decade: day after day, year after year, of sand rattling against the window, of fine powder caking one's lips, of springtime turned to despair, of poverty eating into self-confidence.

Explaining why those storms occurred requires an excursion into the history of the plains and an understanding of the agriculture that evolved there. For the "dirty thirties," as they were called, were primarily the work of man, not nature. Admittedly, nature had something to do with this disaster too. Without winds the soil would have stayed put, no matter how bare it was. Without drought, farmers would have had strong, healthy crops capable of checking the wind. But natural factors did not make the storms—they merely made them possible. The storms were mainly the result of stripping the landscape of its natural vegetation to such an extent that there was no defense against the dry winds, no sod to hold the sandy or powdery dirt. The sod had been destroyed to make farms to grow wheat to get cash. But more of that later on. It is the storms themselves we must first comprehend: their magnitude, their effect, even their taste and smell. What was it like to be caught in one of them? How much did the people suffer, and how did they cope?

Weather bureau stations on the plains reported a few small dust storms throughout 1932, as many as 179 in April 1933, and in November of that year a large one that carried all the way to Georgia and New York. But it was the May 1934 blow that swept in a new dark age. On 9 May, brown earth from Montana and Wyoming swirled up from the ground, was captured by extremely high-level winds, and was blown eastward toward the Dakotas. More dirt was sucked into the airstream, until 350 million tons were riding toward urban America. By late afternoon the storm had reached Dubuque and Madison, and by evening 12 million tons of dust were falling like snow over Chicago—4 pounds for each person in the city. Midday at Buffalo on 10 May was darkened by dust, and the advancing gloom stretched south from there over several states, moving as fast as 100 miles an hour. The dawn of 11 May found the dust settling over Boston, New York, Washington, and Atlanta, and then the storm moved out to sea. Savannah's skies were hazy all day 12 May; it was the last city to report dust conditions. But there were still ships in the Atlantic, some of them 300 miles off the coast, that found dust on their decks during the next day or two.

"Kansas dirt," the New York press called it, though it actually came from farther north. More would come that year and after, and some of it was indeed from Kansas—or Nebraska or New Mexico. In a later spring, New Hampshire farmers, out to tap their maples, discovered a fresh brown snow on the ground, discoloration from transported Western soil. Along the Gulf Coast, at Houston and Corpus Christi, dirt from the Llano Estacado collected now and then on windowsills and sidewalks. But after May 1934 most of the worst dust storms were confined to the southern plains region; less frequently were they carried by those high-altitude currents moving east or southeast. Two types of dusters became common then: the dramatic "black blizzards" and the more frequent "sand blows." The first came with a rolling turbulence, rising like a long wall of muddy water as high as 7,000 or 8,000 feet. Like the winter blizzards to which they were compared, these dusters were caused by the arrival of a polar continental air mass, and the atmospheric

electricity it generated helped lift the dirt higher and higher in a cold boil, sometimes accompanied by thunder and lightning, other times by an eerie silence. Such storms were not only terrifying to observers, but immensely destructive to the region's fine, dark soils, rich in nutrients. The second kind of duster was a more constant event, created by the low sirocco-like winds that blew out of the southwest and left the sandier soils drifted into dunes along fence rows and ditches. Long after New York and Philadelphia had forgotten their taste of the plains, the people out there ate their own dirt again and again.

In the 1930s the Soil Conservation Service compiled a frequency chart of all dust storms of regional extent, when visibility was cut to less than a mile. In 1932 there were 14; in 1933, 38; 1934, 22; 1935, 40; 1936, 68; 1937, 72; 1938, 61—dropping as the drought relented a bit— 1939, 30; 1940, 17; 1941, 17. Another measure of severity was made by calculating the total number of hours the dust storms lasted during a year. By that criterion 1937 was again the worst: at Guymon, in the panhandle of Oklahoma, the total number of hours that year climbed to 550, mostly concentrated in the first six months of the year. In Amarillo the worst year was 1935, with a total of 908 hours. Seven times, from January to March, the visibility there reached zero—all complete blackouts, one of them lasting eleven hours. A single storm might rage for one hour or three and a half days. Most of the winds came from the southwest, but they also came from the west, north, and northeast, and they could slam against windows and walls with 60 miles-per-hour force. The dirt left behind on the front lawn might be brown, black, yellow, ashy gray, or, more rarely, red, depending upon its source. And each color had its own peculiar aroma, from a sharp peppery smell that burned the nostrils to a heavy greasiness that nauseated.

In the memory of older plains residents, the blackest year was 1935, particularly the early spring weeks from 1 March to mid-April, when the Dust Bowl made its full-blown debut. Springtime in western Kansas can be a Willa Cather world of meadowlarks on the wing, clean white curtains dancing in the breeze, anemones and wild verbena in bloom, lilacs by the porch, a windmill spinning briskly, and cold fresh water in the bucket—but not in 1935. After a February heat wave (it reached 75 degrees in Topeka that month), the dust began moving across Kansas, Oklahoma, and Texas, and for the next six weeks it was unusual to see a clear sky from dawn until sundown. On 15 March, Denver reported that a serious dust storm was speeding eastward. Kansans ignored the radio warnings, went about their business as usual, and later wondered what had hit them. Small-town printer Nate White was at the picture show when the dust reached Smith Center: as he walked out the exit, it was as if someone had put a blindfold over his eyes; he bumped into telephone poles, skinned his shins on boxes and cans in an alleyway, fell to his hands and knees, and crawled along the curbing to a dim houselight. A seven-year-old boy wandered away and was lost in the gloom; the search party found him later, suffocated in a drift. A more fortunate child was found alive, tangled in a barbed wire fence. Near Colby, a train was derailed by dirt on the tracks, and the passengers spent twelve dreary hours in the coaches. The Lora-Locke Hotel in Dodge City overflowed with more than two hundred stranded travelers; many of them bedded down on cots in the lobby and ballroom. In the following days, as the dust kept falling, electric lights burned continuously, cars left tracks in the dirt-covered streets, and schools and offices stayed closed. A reporter at Great Bend remarked on the bizarre scene: "Uncorked jug placed on sidewalk two hours, found to be half filled with dust. Picture wires giving way due to excessive weight of dust on frames. Irreparable loss in portraits anticipated. Lady Godiva could ride thru streets without even the horse seeing her."

The novelty of this duster, so like a coffee-colored winter snow, made it hard for most people to take it seriously. But William Allen White, the Emporia editor, called it "the greatest show" since Pompeii was buried in ashes. And a Garden City woman described her experience for the *Kansas City Times:*

All we could do about it was just sit in our dusty chairs, gaze at each other through the fog that filled the room and watch that fog settle slowly and silently, covering everything— including ourselves—in a thick, brownish gray blanket. When we opened the door swirling whirlwinds of soil beat against us unmercifully. . . . The door and windows were all shut tightly, yet those tiny particles seemed to seep through the very walls. It got into cupboards and clothes closets; our faces were as dirty as if we had rolled in the dirt; our hair was gray and stiff and we ground dirt between our teeth.

By the end of the month conditions had become so unrelenting that many Kansans had begun to chew their nails. "Watch for the Second Coming of Christ," warned one of Topeka's unhinged, "God is wrathful." Street-corner sects in Hill City and other towns warned pedestrians to heed the signs of the times. A slightly less frenetic Concordian jotted in her log: "This is ultimate darkness. So must come the end of the world." The mood of the people had begun to change, if not to apocalyptic dread in every case, at least to a fear that this was a nightmare that might never end.

By 24 March southeastern Colorado and western Kansas had seen twelve consecutive days of dust storms, but there was worse to come. Near the end of March a new duster swept across the southern plains, destroying one-half the wheat crop in Kansas, one-quarter of it in Oklahoma, and all of it in Nebraska—5 million acres blown out. The storm carried away from the plains twice as much earth as men and machines had scooped out to make the Panama Canal, depositing it once again over the East Coast states and the Atlantic Ocean. Then the wind slackened off a bit, gathering strength, as it were, for the spectacular finale of that unusual spring season— Black Sunday, 14 April.

Dawn came clear and rosy all across the plains that day. By noon the skies were so fresh and blue that people could not remain indoors; they remembered how many jobs they had been postponing, and with a revived spirit they rushed outside to get them done. They went on picnics, planted gardens, repaired henhouses, attended funerals, drove to the neighbors for a visit. In midafternoon the summery air rapidly turned colder, falling as many as 50 degrees in a few hours, and the people noticed then that the yards were full of birds nervously fluttering and chattering—and more were arriving every moment, as though fleeing from some unseen enemy. Suddenly there appeared on the northern horizon a black blizzard, moving toward them; there was no sound, no wind, nothing but an immense "boogery" cloud. The storm struck Dodge City at 2:40 P.M. Not far from there John Garretson, a farmer in Haskell County, Kansas, who was on the road with his wife, Louise, saw it coming, but he was sure that he could beat it home. They had almost made it when they were engulfed; abandoning the car, they groped for the fencewire and, hand over hand, followed it to their door. Down in the panhandle Ed and Ada Phillips of Boise City, with their six-year-old daughter, were on their way home too, after an outing to Texline in their Model A Ford. It was about five o'clock when the black wall appeared, and they still had fifteen miles to go. Seeing an old adobe house ahead, Ed realized that they had to take shelter, and quickly. By the time they were out of the car the dust was upon them, making it so dark that they nearly missed the door. Inside they found ten other people, stranded, like themselves, in a two-room hut, all fearing that they might be smothered, all unable to see their companions' faces. For four hours they sat there, until the storm let up enough for them to follow the roadside ditch back to town. By then the ugly pall was moving south across the high plains of Texas and New Mexico.

Older residents still remember Black Sunday in all its details—where they were when the storm hit, what they did then. Helen Wells was the wife of the Reverend Rolley Wells, the Methodist minister in Guymon. Early that morning she had helped clean the accumulated dust from the church pews, working until she was choking and exhausted. Back in the parsonage she switched on the radio for some inspiring music, and what she heard was the hymn "We'll Work Till Jesus Comes." "I just had to sit down and laugh," she recalls; she had worn out her sweeper but still had a broom if that was needed. Later that day her husband, partly to please two visiting *Saturday Evening Post* reporters, held a special "rain service," which concluded in time for the congregation to get home before the dust arrived.

A Kansas cattle dealer, Raymond Ellsaesser, almost lost his wife that day. She had gone into Sublette with her young daughter for a Rebekah lodge meeting. On the way home she stopped along the highway, unable to see even the winged hood ornament on her car. The static electricity in the storm then shorted out her ignition, and, foolishly, she determined to walk the three-quarters of a mile home. Her daughter plunged ahead to get Raymond's help, and he quickly piled into a truck and drove back down the road, hallooing out the window. Back and forth he passed, but his wife had disappeared into the fog-like dust, wandering straight away from the car into the field, where she stumbled about with absolutely no sense of direction. Each time she saw the truck's headlights she moved that way, not realizing her husband was in motion too. It was only by sheer luck that she found herself at last standing in the truck's beams, gasping for air and near collapse.

The last of the major dust storms that year was on 14 April, and it was months before the damages could be fully calculated. Those who had been caught outside in one of the spring dusters were, understandably, most worried about their lungs. An epidemic of respiratory infections and something called "dust pneumonia" broke out across the plains. The four small hospitals in Meade County, Kansas, found that 52 percent of their April admissions were acute respiratory cases—thirty-three patients died. Many dust victims would arrive at a hospital almost dead, after driving long distances in a storm. They spat up clods of dirt, washed the mud out of their mouths, swabbed their nostrils with Vaseline, and rinsed their bloodshot eyes with boric acid water. Old people and babies were the most vulnerable to the dusters, as were those who had chronic asthma, bronchitis, or tuberculosis, some of whom had moved to the plains so they might breathe the high, dry air.

Doctors could not agree on whether the dust caused a new kind of pneumonia, and some even denied that there were any unusual health problems in their communities. But the Red Cross thought the situation was so serious that it set up six emergency hospitals in Kansas, Colorado, and Texas, and it staffed them with its own nurses. In Topeka and Wichita volunteers worked in high school sewing rooms to make dust masks of cheesecloth; over 17,000 of those masks were sent to the plains, especially to towns where goggles had been sold out. Chewing tobacco was a better remedy, snorted some farmers, who thought it was too much of a bother to wear such gadgets when driving their tractors. But enough wore the Red Cross masks or some other protection to make the plains look like a World War I battlefield, with dust instead of mustard gas coming out of the trenches.

On 29 April the Red Cross sponsored a conference of health officers from several states. Afterward the representatives of the Kansas Board of Health went to work on the medical problem in more detail, and eventually they produced a definitive study on the physiological impact of the dust storms. From 21 February to 30 April they counted 28 days of "dense" dust at Dodge City and only 13 days that were "dust free." Dirt deposited in bakepans during the five biggest storms gave an estimated 4.7 tons of total fallout per acre. Agar plate cultures showed "no pathogenic organisms" in the accumulation, only harmless soil bacteria, plant hair, and microfungus spores. But the inorganic content of the dust was mainly fine silicon particles, along with bits of feldspar, volcanic ash, and calcite; and "silica," they warned, "is as much a body poison as is lead"—"probably the most widespread and insidious of all hazards in the environment of mankind," producing, after sufficient contact, silicosis of the lungs. These scientists also found that a measles outbreak had come with the black blizzards, though why that happened was not clear; in only five months there were twice as many cases as in any previous twelve-month period. The death rate from acute respiratory infections in the 45 western counties

of Kansas, where the dust was most intense, was 99 per 100,000, compared with the statewide average of 70; and the infant mortality was 80.5, compared with the state's 62.3.

The medical remedies for the dust were at best primitive and makeshift. In addition to wearing light gauze masks, health officials recommended attaching translucent glasscloth to the inside frames of windows, although people also used cardboard, canvas, or blankets. Hospitals covered some of their patients with wet sheets, and housewives flapped the air with wet dish towels to collect dust. One of the most common tactics was to stick masking tape, felt strips, or paraffin-soaked rags around the windows and door cracks. The typical plains house was loosely constructed and without insulation, but sometimes those methods proved so effective that there was not enough air circulation inside to replenish the oxygen supply. Warren Moore of southwestern Kansas remembers watching, during a storm, the gas flame on the range steadily turn orange and the coal-oil lamp dim until the people simply had to open the window, dust or no dust. But most often there was no way to seal out the fine, blowing dirt: it blackened the pillow around one's head, the dinner plates on the table, the bread dough on the back of the stove. It became a steady part of one's diet and breathing. "We thrived on it," claim some residents today; it was their "vitamin K." But all the same they prayed that they would not ingest so much it would maim them for life, or finish them off, as it had a neighbor or two.

Livestock and wildlife did not have even those crude defenses. "In a rising sand storm," wrote Margaret Bourke-White, "cattle quickly become blinded. They run around in circles until they fall and breathe so much dust that they die. Autopsies show their lungs caked with dust and mud." Newborn calves could suffocate in a matter of hours, and the older cattle ground their teeth down to the gums trying to eat the dirt-covered grass. As the dust buried the fences, horses and cattle climbed over and wandered away. Where there was still water in rivers, the dust coated the surface and the fish died too. The carcasses of jackrabbits, small birds, and field mice lay along roadsides by the hundreds after a severe duster; and those that survived were in such shock that they could be picked up and their nostrils and eyes wiped clean. In a lighter vein, it was said that prairie dogs were now able to tunnel upward several feet from the ground.

Cleaning up houses, farm lots, and city stores after the 1935 blow season was an expensive matter. People literally shoveled the dirt from their front yards and swept up bushel-basketfuls inside. One man's ceiling collapsed from the silt that had collected in the attic. Carpets, draperies, and tapestries were so dust-laden that their patterns were indiscernible. Painted surfaces had been sandblasted bare. Automobile and tractor engines operated in dust storms without oil-bath air cleaners were ruined by grit, and the repair shops had plenty of business. During March alone, Tucumcari, New Mexico, reported over $288,000 in property damage, although most towns' estimates were more conservative than that: Liberal, Kansas, $150,000; Randall County, Texas, $10,000; Lamar, Colorado, $3,800. The merchants of Amarillo calculated from 3 to 15 percent damage to their merchandise, not to mention the loss of shoppers during the storms. In Dodge City a men's clothing store advertised a "dust sale," knocking shirts down to 75 cents. But the heaviest burdens lay on city work crews, who had to sweep dirt from the gutters and municipal swimming pools, and on housewives, who struggled after each blow to get their houses clean.

The emotional expense was the hardest to accept, however. All day you could sit with your hands folded on the oilcloth-covered table, the wind moaning around the eaves, the fine, soft, talc sifting in the keyholes, the sky a coppery gloom; and when you went to bed the acrid dust crept into your dreams. Avis Carlson told what it was like at night:

A trip for water to rinse the grit from our lips. And then back to bed with washcloths over our noses. We try to lie still, because every turn stirs the dust on the blankets. After a while, if we are good sleepers, we forget.

After 1935 the storms lost much of their drama; for most people they were simply a burden to be endured, and sometimes that burden was too heavy. Druggists sold their supplies of sedatives quickly. An Oklahoman took down his shotgun, ready to kill his entire family and himself—"we're all better off dead," he despaired. That, to be sure, was an extreme instance, but there were indeed men and women who turned distraught, wept, and then, listless, gave up caring.

The plains people, however, then as now, were a tough-minded, leather-skinned folk, not easily discouraged. Even in 1935 they managed to laugh a bit at their misfortunes. They told about the farmer who fainted when a drop of water struck him in the face and had to be revived by having three buckets of sand thrown over him. They also passed around the one about the motorist who came upon a ten-gallon hat resting on a dust drift. Under it he found a head looking at him. "Can I help you some way?" the motorist asked, "Give you a ride into town maybe?" "Thanks, but I'll make it on my own," was the reply, "I'm on a horse." They laughed with Will Rogers when he pointed out that only highly advanced civilizations— like ancient Mesopotamia—were ever covered over by dirt, and that California would never qualify. Newspaper editors could still find something to joke about, too: "When better dust storms are made," the *Dodge City Globe* boasted, "the Southwest will make them." Children were especially hard to keep down; for them the storms always meant adventure, happy chaos, a breakdown of their teachers' authority, and perhaps a holiday. When darkness descends, as it did that April, humor, bravado, or a childlike irresponsibility may have as much value as a storm cellar.

Whether they brought laughter or tears, the dust storms that swept across the southern plains in the 1930s created the most severe environmental catastrophe in the entire history of the white man on this continent. In no other instance was there greater or more sustained damage to the American land, and there have been few times when so much tragedy was visited on its inhabitants. Not even the Depression was more devastating, economically. And in ecological terms we have nothing in the nation's past, nothing even in the polluted present, that compares. Suffice it to conclude here that in the decade of the 1930s the dust storms of the plains were an unqualified disaster.

At such dark times the mettle of a people is thoroughly and severely tested, revealing whether they have the will to go on. By this test the men and women of the plains were impressive, enduring, as most of them did, discouragements the like of which more recent generations have never had to face. But equally important, disasters of this kind challenge a society's capacity to think—require it to analyze and explain and learn from misfortune. Societies that fail this test are sitting ducks for more of the same. Those that pass, on the other hand, have attained through suffering and hardship a more mature, self-appraising character, so that they are more aware than before of their vulnerabilities and weaknesses. They are stronger because they have been made sensitive to their deficiencies. Whether the dust storms had this enlarging, critical effect on the minds of southern plainsmen remains to be seen.

Study Questions

1. When did the dust storms begin and when did they end? What areas of the country did they affect the most?

2. Describe the size, color, and smell of the dust storms. How long did they last? Were they uniform?

3. Describe the impact that the dust storms had on humans and animals. How did people cope with them?

4. What kinds of destruction did the dust storms cause?

Bibliography

The above selection is from Donald Worster, *Dust Bowl: The Southern Plains In the 1930s* (1979), an award-winning study that combines passion and outrage with scholarly distance and fine writing. Also valuable are Paul Bonnifield, *The Dust Bowl: Men, Dirt, and Depression* (1979); R. Douglas Hurt, *The Dust Bowl: An Agricultural and Social History* (1981); and James N. Gregory, *American Exodus: The Dust Bowl Migration and Oke Culture in California* (1991). An outstanding overview of the Great Depression is Robert S. McElvaine, *The Great Depression* (1984). For a new perspective on the Depression, see Gene Smiley, *Rethinking the Great Depression* (2003). In their own ways, the works of John Steinbeck, Pare Lorentz, Woody Guthrie, and Alexandre Hogue also document the era of the Dust Bowl and the Depression.

READING 17

★ ★ ★

Night of the Martians

Edward Oxford

It's a truism today that the mass media influences the lives of Americans. Society is constantly barraged with questions and criticism about such issues as the quality of children's television programming, the political bias of newscasters, the ethics of television advertising, the domination of political campaigns by the media, and the decline of literacy and the written word. More than any other technological innovation, the development first of radio and then of television has transformed American life, changing the way people live and relate to one another. The first radio station in the United States began broadcasting out of Pittsburgh in 1920. Three years later there were more than 500 stations doing the same thing, and by 1929 more than 12 million families listened to the radio at home every night. The communications revolution that radio stimulated contributed to the creation of a mass, national culture.

The influence of the radio, however, did not immediately dawn on people. In 1927 the National Broadcasting Company became the first national network, and by 1933 President Franklin D. Roosevelt was effectively using the radio for his famous "fireside chats." But it was not until 1938, when Orson Welles broadcast his famous "War of the Worlds" program, that Americans realized the potential of radio to shape public attitudes. With Adolf Hitler making his designs on Czechoslovakia well known, Americans were worried that another global conflict was in the making. Battered by the frustration of the Great Depression and nervous about the safety of the world, millions of people panicked when Orson Welles described over national radio an invasion of the East Coast by Martians. In the following essay, historian Edward Oxford describes the broadcast and the controversy it inspired.

A little after eight P.M. on Halloween eve 1938, thirteen-year-old Dick Stives, his sister, and two brothers huddled around their family's radio. They were in the dining room of their grandfather's farmhouse near the hamlet of Grovers Mill, four miles east of Princeton, New Jersey. Their mother and father had dropped them off there and gone to the movies.

Dick worked the radio dial, hunting for the station that carried the *Chase and Sanborn Hour,* his—and the nation's—favorite Sunday evening program. As he scanned the airwaves, Dick tuned in the local affiliate of the Columbia Broadcasting System (CBS). A commanding voice—that of Orson Welles—riveted his attention.

". . . across an immense ethereal gulf, minds that are to our minds as ours are to the beasts of the jungle, intellects vast, cool, and unsympathetic, regarded this earth with envious eyes and slowly and surely drew their plans against us. . . . "

Dick Stives turned the dial no further. Instead, during the next hour he and millions of other listeners sat glued by their radios, convinced by an alarming series of "news bulletins" that monster aliens from Mars were invading America. Dick's village of Grovers Mill—the supposed landing site for these invaders—became the focal point of a panic wave that rapidly swept across the nation.

The program—the *Mercury Theatre on the Air* adaptation of H. G. Welles's *The War of the Worlds*—would later be remembered as the most extraordinary radio show ever broadcast. And Orson Welles, its brilliant young producer, director, and star, would be catapulted to nationwide fame overnight.

As the wonder boy of the performing arts, Orson Welles had by age twenty-three already appeared on the cover of *Time* magazine; built a considerable reputation as a radio actor; set the stage world on its ear with a *Julius Caesar* set in Fascist Italy, an all-black *Macbeth,* and a production of Marc Blitzstein's opera *The Cradle Will Rock;* and founded—with his partner-in-drama John Houseman—the revolutionary and often controversial Mercury Theatre.[1]

In midsummer 1938, the Columbia Broadcasting System, impressed by Welles's meteoric success, offered him and his repertory company a grand stage, radio—"the Broadway of the entire United States"—on which to deliver a sixty-minute dramatization each week.

Broadcast from the twenty-second floor of the CBS building in midtown Manhattan, the *Mercury Theatre on the Air* had no commercial sponsor. The show was subsidized by the CBS network, and its bare-bones budget provided no money for expensive, original plays. "We offered the audience classic works from the public domain— *Julius Caesar, Oliver Twist, The Heart of Darkness, Jane Eyre,* and such," recalls John Houseman. "Orson and I would select the book. Sometimes it was my task to fashion the original into a workable radio script."

For the last program of October, the seventeenth in their series, Welles and Houseman wanted to "throw in something of a scientific nature." They settled on an adaptation of *The War of the Worlds,* a science-fiction novel written in 1898 by British author H. G. Wells. Houseman assigned the script to a recent addition to the company, writer Howard Koch.

For the fall season CBS had moved the *Mercury Theatre on the Air* from Monday evening to the Sunday night eight-to-nine-o'clock slot, an "unsold" time period. During this hour much of America tuned in to the competing NBC Red network for the *Chase and Sanborn Hour,* which featured ventriloquist Edgar Bergen and his wooden-headed "dummy" Charlie McCarthy. The

---

"Night of the Martians" by Edward Oxford. This article is reprinted from the October 1988 issue of *American History Illustrated* 23, pp. 14–23, 47–48 with the permission of Cowles History Group, Inc. Copyright *American History Illustrated* magazine.

[1]Up to this time Welles was probably best known to radio audiences as "Lamont Cranston," alias "The Shadow," on the popular Sunday afternoon mystery program of the same name. But he also appeared frequently on many other shows including "The March of Time," and was said to be earning $1,000 a week from his radio commitments alone.

Crossley ratings of listenership gave Charlie Mc-Carthy a "thirty-five" (roughly 35 percent of radio listeners at that hour tuned in), while the *Mercury* usually scored about "three."

During the week before the October 30 broadcast, Welles nonchalantly put in his own typically frantic week while Houseman, Koch, and the cast struggled to ready the show. Welles spent much of his time not in the CBS studios at 485 Madison Avenue, but on the stage of the Mercury Theatre on West 41st Street, rehearsing his repertory company for the opening of a new play. He hurried back to CBS at odd hours to try out some of his lines, listen to run-throughs by the radio show's cast, and render his inimitable revisions.

Welles and his company spent much of Sunday amid a litter of sandwiches and coffee cups in Studio One, adding final touches to their version of *The War of the Worlds* and conducting a dress rehearsal with full music and sound effects.

Just before eight P.M., Eastern Standard Time, Welles, conductor-like, stood poised on his platform in the middle of the studio. He had at his command not only his loyal band of actors, but also a small symphony orchestra. Wearing a headset, the multifaceted genius was prepared to read his own lines, cue the other actors, signal for sound effects, summon the orchestra, and also keep in touch with the control room.

At the stroke of eight o'clock, he gave the cue for the start of the *Mercury* theme—the Tchaikovsky Piano Concerto No. 1 in B-Flat Minor.

For the next unforgettable hour, Dick Stives at Grovers Mill, along with several million other Americans, sat transfixed as the airwaves brought word of weird and almost incomprehensible events that seemed to unfold with terrifying reality even as they listened.

It was not as though listeners hadn't been warned. Most simply didn't pay close attention to the program's opening signature (or tuned in a few seconds late and missed it altogether): "The Columbia Broadcasting System and its affiliated stations present Orson Welles and the Mercury Theatre on the Air in *The War of the Worlds* by H. G. Wells. . . ."

Many in the radio audience failed to associate what they heard with prior newspaper listings of the drama. And, by the time a single station break came late in the hour with reminders that listeners were hearing a fictional story, many others were too agitated to comprehend that they had been deceived.

Skillfully choreographed by Welles and Houseman, the program—a play simulating a montage of real-life dance band "remotes" and news bulletins—began with deliberate calm. Millions of listeners, conditioned by recent news reports of worldwide political turmoil—and by their inherent trust in the medium of radio—believed what they heard.

Just two minutes into the show, audience perception between fantasy and reality began to blur when, following Welles's dramatic opening monologue, the microphone shifted to a "network announcer" reading an apparently routine report from the "Government Weather Bureau."

Programming then shifted to "Ramon Raquello and his orchestra" in the "Meridian Room" at the "Hotel Park Plaza" in downtown New York City.

During rehearsals for the show, Welles had insisted—over the objections of his associates—on increasing the broadcast time devoted to the fictional orchestra's soothing renditions of "La Cumparsita" and "the ever-popular 'Stardust.'" As he had anticipated, the resulting "band remote" had a disarming air of reality—and provided emotional contrast to the intensity of later news bulletins.[2]

Just when Welles had calculated that listeners might start tuning out the music in search of something more lively, an announcer broke in with a bulletin from the "Intercontinental Radio News": "Professor Farrell of the Mount Jennings Observatory" near Chicago had reported observing "several explosions of incandescent gas occurring at regular intervals on the planet Mars. . . .

---

[2]The format was a familiar one to radio listeners. "Big band remotes"—network broadcasts featuring America's best-known dance bands as they played at one-night stands in ballrooms from coast to coast—were a staple of broadcasting during the 1930s.

The spectroscope indicates the gas to be hydrogen and moving towards the earth with tremendous velocity."

The dance music resumed, only to be interrupted repeatedly during the next several minutes by other bulletins. The tempo of events—and listeners' interest—began to intensify.

From a "remote pickup" at the "Princeton Observatory," reporter "Carl Phillips" interviewed famous astronomer "Richard Pierson" (played by Welles). As the clockwork of mechanism of his telescope ticked in the background, Professor Pierson described Mars as a red disk swimming in a blue sea. He said he could not explain the gas eruptions on that planet. But skeptical of anything that could not be explained by logic, the astronomer counted the chances against living intelligence on Mars as being "a thousand to one."

Then Phillips read a wire that had just been handed to Pierson: a seismograph at the "Natural History Museum" in New York had registered a "shock of almost earthquake intensity occurring within a radius of twenty miles of Princeton." Pierson played down any possible connection with the disturbances on Mars: "This is probably a meteorite of unusual size and its arrival at this particular time is merely a coincidence."

Again the program returned to music, followed by yet another bulletin: an astronomer in Canada had observed three explosions on Mars, confirming "earlier reports from American observatories."

"Now, nearer home," continued the announcer, "comes a special announcement from Trenton, New Jersey. It is reported that at 8:50 P.M. a huge, flaming object, believed to be a meteorite, fell on a farm in the neighborhood of Grovers Mill, New Jersey, twenty-two miles from Trenton. The flash in the sky was visible within a radius of several hundred miles and the noise of impact was heard as far north as Elizabeth."

Listeners leaned closer to their sets. In Grovers Mill, Dick Stives stared at the radio and gulped.

Again the broadcast returned to dance music—this time to "Bobby Millette and his orchestra" at the "Hotel Martinet" in Brooklyn. And again the music was interrupted by a news flash. Having just arrived at the scene of "impact" on the "Wilmuth farm" near Grovers Mill, reporter Carl Phillips, accompanied by Professor Pierson, beheld police, state troopers, and onlookers crowding around what appeared to be a huge metallic cylinder, partially buried in the earth.

About this time, some twelve minutes into the broadcast, many listeners to the *Chase and Sanborn Hour,* momentarily bored by a guest musical spot, turned their dials. A lot of them stopped in sudden shock as they came upon the CBS wavelength. The events being described seemed real to listeners—quite as real to them as reports, not many months before, that Adolf Hitler's troops had marched into Austria.

"I wish I could convey the atmosphere . . . the background of this . . . fantastic scene," reported Phillips. "Hundreds of cars are parked in a field back of us. . . . Their headlights throw an enormous spot on the pit where the object is half-buried. Some of the more daring souls are venturing near the edge. Their silhouettes stand out against the metal sheen. . . . "

Professor Pierson described the object as "definitely extraterrestrial . . . not found on this earth. . . . This thing is smooth and, as you can see, of cylindrical shape." Then Phillips suddenly interrupted him:

"Just a minute! Something's happening! Ladies and gentlemen, this is terrific! The end of the thing is beginning to flake off! The top is beginning to rotate like a screw! The thing must be hollow! [shouts of alarm] Ladies and gentlemen, this is the most terrifying thing I have ever witnessed. . . . Wait a minute! Someone's crawling out of the hollow top. Someone or . . . something. I can see peering out of that black hole two luminous disks—are they eyes? Good heavens, something's wriggling out of the shadow like a gray snake. . . . I can see the thing's body. It's large as a bear and it glistens like wet leather. But that face. It . . . it's indescribable. I can hardly force myself to keep looking at it. The eyes are black and gleam like a serpent. The mouth is V-shaped with saliva dripping from its rimless lips that seem to quiver and pulsate. . . . "

Thirty state troopers, according to the reporter, now formed a cordon around the pit where the object rested. Three policemen carrying a white handkerchief of truce walked toward the cylinder. Phillips continued:

"Wait a minute . . . something's happening. [high-pitched, intermittent whine of machinery] A humped shape is rising out of the pit. I can make out a small beam of light against a mirror. . . . What's that? There's a jet of flame springing from the mirror, and it leaps right at the advancing men! It strikes them head on! Good Lord, they're turning into flame! [screams and shrieks] Now the whole field by the woods has caught fire! [sound effects intensify] The gas tanks, tanks of automobiles . . . it's spreading everywhere! It's coming this way now! About twenty yards to my right [abrupt silence]."[3]

Now terror was afoot. A series of voices—fictional "announcers," "militia commanders," "network vice presidents," and "radio operators"—took up the narrative. At least forty people, according to the radio bulletins, lay dead at Grovers Mill, "their bodies burned and distorted beyond all possible recognition." And in a Trenton hospital, "the charred body of Carl Phillips" had been identified.

A current of fear flowed outward across the nation. Real-life police switchboards, first in New Jersey, then, steadily, throughout the whole Northeast, began to light up: "What's happening?" "Who's attacking America?" "When will they be here?" "What can we do?" "Who are they—these Martians?"

By now, according to the broadcast, "eight battalions of infantry" had surrounded the cylinder, determined to destroy it. A "Captain Lansing" of the "Signal Corps"—calm and confident at first, but with obviously increasing alarm—described what happened next:

---

[3]Phillip's narrative bore a perhaps-not-coincidental resemblance to a famous eyewitness report by Chicago radio newsman Herb Morrison, who on May 6, 1937, had described the explosion and destruction of the German dirigible Hindenburg as it was about to moor at Lakehurst, New Jersey.

"Well, we ought to see some action soon. One of the companies is deploying on the left flank. A quick thrust and it'll all be over. Wait a minute, I see something on top of the cylinder. No, it's nothing but a shadow. . . . Seven thousand armed men closing in on an old metal tube. Tub, rather. Wait, that wasn't a shadow. It's something moving . . . solid metal. Kind of a shield-like affair rising up out of the cylinder! It's going higher and higher! Why, it's . . . standing on legs! Actually rearing up on a sort of metal framework! Now it's reaching above the trees and searchlights are on it! Hold on [abrupt silence]."

In a matter of moments, a studio "announcer" gave America the incredible news:

". . . Those strange beings who landed in the Jersey farmlands tonight are the vanguard of an invading army from the planet Mars. The battle which took place tonight at Grovers Mill has ended in one of the most startling defeats ever suffered by an army in modern times; seven thousand men armed with rifles and machine guns pitted against a single fighting machine of the invaders from Mars. One hundred and twenty known survivors. The rest strewn over the battle areas from Grovers Mill to Plainsboro crushed and trampled to death under the metal feet of the monster, or burned to cinders by its heat ray. . . . "

Grovers Mill's couple of hundred real-life residents hardly knew what to make of it all. Young Dick Stives was stunned. He and his sister and brothers pulled down the shades in the farmhouse. Their grandfather shoved chairs against the doors.

Teen-aged Lolly Dey, who heard about the "invasion" while attending a church meeting, consoled herself by saying: "I am in the Lord's House." Another resident, seeing what he thought to be a Martian war machine among the trees (actually a water tower on a neighbor's property), peppered it with shotgun blasts. One man packed his family into the car, bound for parts unknown. He backed right through his garage door. "We're never gonna be needing that again anyway," he muttered to his wife.

"The monster is now in control of the middle section of New Jersey," proclaimed the voice on the radio. "Communication lines are down from Pennsylvania to the Atlantic Ocean. Railroad tracks are torn and service from New York to Philadelphia discontinued. . . . Highways to the north, south, and west are clogged with frantic human traffic. Police and army reserves are unable to control the mad flight. . . ."

Life was soon to imitate art. A wave of terror, unprecedented in its scope and rapidity, swept across New Jersey. A New Brunswick man, bound for open country, had driven ten miles when he remembered that his dog was tied up in the backyard of his home. Daring the Martians, he drove back to retrieve the dog.

A West Orange bar owner pushed customers out into the street, locked his tavern door, and rushed home to rescue his wife and children.

Twenty families began to move their belongings out of a Newark apartment house, their faces covered by wet towels to repel Martian rays. Doctors and nurses volunteered to come to hospitals to help handle the "war casualties."

At Princeton University, the chairman of the geology department packed his field equipment and headed into the night to look for whatever it was that was out there. The governor of Pennsylvania offered to send troops to help New Jersey. A Jersey City man called a bus dispatcher to warn him of the fast-spreading "disaster." He cut their conversation short with: "The world is coming to an end and I have a lot to do!"

Meanwhile, on the radio, the "Secretary of the Interior," speaking in a voice much like that of President Franklin D. Roosevelt, announced that he had faith in the ability of the American military to vanquish the Martians.[4] He solemnly intoned:

". . . placing our trust in God we must continue the performance of our duties each and

every one of us, so that we may confront this destructive adversary with a nation united, courageous, and consecrated to the preservation of human supremacy on this earth."

A Trenton store owner ran out screaming, "The world is ending! The world is ending!" Another man dashed into a motion-picture theater in Orange, crying out that "the state is being invaded! This place is going to be blown up!" The audience hurriedly ran out to the street.

A woman in a Newark tenement just sat and cried. "I thought it was all up with us," she said. A man driving westward called out to a patrolman: "All creation's busted loose! I'm getting out!"

More grim reports issued from the radio. Scouting planes, according to the broadcast, had sighted three Martian machines marching through New Jersey. They were uprooting power lines, bridges, and railroad tracks, with the apparent objectives of crushing resistance and paralyzing communications. In swamps twenty miles south of Morristown, coon hunters had stumbled upon a second Martian cylinder.

In the Watchung mountains, the "22nd Field Artillery" set down a barrage against six tripod monsters—to no avail. The machines soon let loose a heavy black poisonous gas, annihilating the artillerymen. Then eight army bombers from "Langham Field, Virginia," attacked the tripod machines, only to be downed by heat rays.

Thousands of telephone calls cascaded into radio stations, newspaper offices, power companies, fire houses, and military posts throughout the country. People wanted to know what to do . . . where to go . . . whether they were safer in the cellar or the attic.

Word spread in Atlanta that a "planet" had struck New Jersey. In Philadelphia, all the guests in one hotel checked out. Students at a college in North Carolina lined up at telephones to call their parents for the last time. When a caller reached the CBS switchboard, the puzzled operator, asked about the end of the world, said: "I'm sorry, we don't have that information."

Radio listeners soon heard an "announcer," said to be atop the "Broadcasting Building" in Manhattan, describe a doomed New York City:

---

[4]Network censors, concerned that the drama might sound too factual, had earlier requested more than thirty changes in the script. Thus, although he still sounded like Franklin Roosevelt, the "President" became the "Secretary of the Interior." The "U.S. Weather Bureau" was changed to the "Government Weather Bureau," the "National Guard" became the "State Militia," etc.

"The bells you hear are ringing to warn the people to evacuate the city as the Martians approach. Estimated in last two hours three million people have moved out along the roads to the north. . . . No more defenses. Our army wiped out . . . artillery, air force, everything wiped out. . . . We'll stay here to the end."

Something like madness took hold among radio listeners in New York City. People stood on Manhattan street corners hoping for a glimpse of the "battle." Thirty men and women showed up at a Harlem police station wanting to be evacuated. A woman had her husband paged at a Broadway theater and told him of the Martian landings; word spread quickly and a throng of playgoers rushed for the exits.

The radio voice continued: "Enemy now in sight above the Palisades! Five great machines. First one is crossing the river . . . wading the Hudson like a man wading through a brook. . . . Martian cylinders are falling all over the country. One outside Buffalo, one in Chicago, St. Louis. . . . Now the first machine reaches the shore! He stands watching, looking over the city. His steel, cowlish head is even with the skyscrapers. He waits for the others. They rise like a line of new towers on the city's west side. . . . "

A Bronx man dashed into the street and saw people running in all directions. One New Yorker claimed he heard the "swish" of Martian flying vehicles. Another told of machine-gun fire. Atop a midtown Manhattan building, a man with binoculars "saw" the firing of weapons. In Brooklyn, a man called the police station: "We can hear the firing all the way here, and I want a gas mask. I'm a taxpayer."

An NBC executive was upset because *his* network wasn't carrying the ultimate news event. One man sped at eighty miles an hour to reach a priest before the "death rays" overtook him; his car flipped over twice, but he lived.

The program played out the drama of doom right to its end.

From atop his fictional building, the "broadcaster" continued his "eyewitness" report: "Now they're lifting their metal hands. This is the end now. Smoke comes out. . . . People in the streets see it now. They're running towards the East River . . . thousands of them, dropping in like rats. . . . It's reached Times Square. . . . People trying to run away from it, but it's no use. They . . . they're falling like flies. . . . "

Meanwhile, in real life, Boston families gathered on rooftops and thought they could see a glow in the sky as New York burned. A horrified Pittsburgh husband found his wife with a bottle of poison, screaming: "I'd rather die this way than that!"

People called the electric company in Providence, Rhode Island, to turn off all the city lights to make it a less visible target. A motorist rode through the streets of Baltimore, Paul Revere-fashion, blowing his horn and warning of the Martian invasion.

The staff of a Memphis newspaper readied an extra edition on rumored landings in Chicago and St. Louis. In Minneapolis, a woman ran into a church yelling: "This is the end of the world! I heard it on the radio!"

Back on the broadcast, the forlorn announcer carried on: "Now the smoke's crossing Sixth Avenue . . . Fifth Avenue . . . [coughing] a hundred yards away . . . it's fifty feet . . . [thud of falling body, then only sound of ships' whistles]."

In Salt Lake City, people started to pack before heading into the Rocky Mountains. One man, in Reno for a divorce, started to drive east, hoping to aid his estranged wife. A man and woman who'd run out of gas in northern California just sat and held hands, expecting any minute to see the Martian war machines appear over the tops of trees. Electric power failed in a village in Washington; families started to flee.

In Hollywood, John Barrymore downed a drink, went to his kennels and released his Great Danes. "Fend for yourselves!" he cried.

Then, from the radio, came the mournful call of a "radio operator": "2X2L calling CQ . . . New York. Isn't there anyone on the air? Isn't there anyone?"

Forty minutes into the broadcast, Welles gave his distraught audience a breather—a pause for station and program identification.

In the control room, CBS staffer Richard Goggin was startled as telephones there began to ring.

That would only happen in an emergency. "Tension was becoming enormous in Studio One," he later recalled. "They had a tiger by the tail and couldn't let go."

For those brave enough to stay tuned, Welles was able to match the program's stunning first portion with an equally remarkable concluding sequence. In what amounted to a twenty-minute soliloquy, he, in the role of Professor Pierson, chronicled the events that followed the Martians' destruction of New York City. Welles's spellbinding voice—magnetic, doom-filled, stirring—held listeners mesmerized.[5]

In the script, a stoic Pierson, still alive in the rubble, made his solitary way toward the ruins of New York, hiding from the invaders as he went.

Along the way he met a "stranger," a former artilleryman. This survivor feared that the Martians would cage and enslave any humans still alive. The stranger was determined to outwit and outlast the Martians and, in time, to turn the heat-rays back on the invaders and even—if need be—upon other humans. And so, one day, new leaders would rule a new world.

Pierson, unwilling to join the stranger's cause, continued his lonely journey. Entering Manhattan through the now-empty Holland Tunnel, he found a lifeless city:

"I wandered up through the Thirties and Forties . . . stood alone on Times Square. I caught sight of a lean dog running down Seventh Avenue with a piece of dark brown meat in his jaws, and a pack of starving mongrels at his heels. . . . I walked up Broadway . . . past silent shop windows, displaying their mute wares to empty sidewalks. . . ."

There seemed to be little hope left for the human race. Then Pierson "caught sight of the hood of a Martian machine, standing somewhere in Central Park, gleaming in the late afternoon sun":

"I rushed recklessly across Columbus Circle and into the park. I climbed a small hill above the pond at Sixtieth Street, and from there I could see standing in a silent row along the mall, nineteen of those great metal Titans, their cowls empty, their steel arms hanging listlessly by their sides. I looked in vain for the monsters that inhabit those machines. Suddenly my eyes were attracted to the immense flock of black birds that hovered directly below me . . . and there before my eyes, stark and silent, lay the Martians, with the hungry birds pecking and tearing brown shreds of flesh from their dead bodies."

The mighty Martians had fallen: ". . . it was found that they were killed by the putrefactive and disease bacteria against which their systems were unprepared . . . slain, after all man's defenses had failed, by the humblest thing that God in His wisdom put upon this earth."

In a sprightly epilogue, Welles then explained away the whole unsettling broadcast as the Mercury Theatre's "way of 'dressing up in a sheet and saying Boo!' . . . We annihilated the world before your very ears, and utterly destroyed the CBS. You will be relieved, I hope, to learn that we didn't mean it, and that both institutions are still open for business."

He tried cheerily to dispel the darkness: "So goodbye everybody, and remember . . . the terrible lesson you learned tonight. . . . And if your doorbell rings and nobody's there, that was no Martian . . . it's Hallowe'en."

The joke was on the listeners. More than one hundred and fifty stations affiliated with CBS had carried the broadcast. About twelve million people had heard the program. Newspapers estimated that at least a million listeners, perhaps many more, had thought the invasion real.

Back in Grovers Mill, disenchantment began to take hold. Twenty-year-old Sam Goldman and three pals had been playing cards when they heard that the Martians were on the move down by the mill. They had thrown down their cards and jumped into a car, ready to face the invaders. "We got there and looked around," Sam said, "and nothing was going on."

---

[5]Welles's closing narrative, fictionally dramatic in style and compressing months of events into twenty minutes, contrasted sharply with the realism of the first portion of the program. Nevertheless, many listeners apparently remained convinced that Martians had landed.

A squad of New Jersey state troopers equipped with riot guns had deployed near the crossroads. They found little more than the dilapidated old mill itself.

Nearby, in their grandfather's farmhouse, Dick Stives, his sister, and brothers talked excitedly about the "men from Mars." Then their mother and father came home from the movies and told the children about the "make believe" on radio that everyone was talking about. Dick, more confused than ever, went upstairs to go to sleep, still half-sure that what he heard was "really real."

For the players who had inadvertently just made radio history, the next hours turned into a nightmare. As soon as Welles left the twenty-second-floor studio, he was called to a telephone. He picked it up, to hear the irate mayor of Flint, Michigan, roar that his city was in chaos because of the program and that he, the mayor, would soon be on his way to New York to punch one Orson Welles in the nose.

"By nine o'clock several high-ranking CBS executives had arrived or were in full flight toward 485 Madison. We were in trouble," recalled Larry Harding, a CBS production supervisor for the *Mercury Theatre* show.

Policemen hurried into the CBS building. Welles, Houseman, and the cast were held under informal house arrest. Staffers hastily stashed scripts, memoranda, and the sixteen-inch acetate disks upon which the show had been recorded.

Welles was taken to a room on the seventeenth floor, where reporters battered him with questions about whether he knew of the deaths and suicides his broadcast had caused (none have ever been documented), whether he knew ahead of time how devastating an effect his show would have (he said he didn't), and whether he had planned it all as a publicity stunt (he said he hadn't).

Finally, at about one o'clock Monday morning, Welles and the cast were "released," free to go out into the streets of New York where not a Martian was stirring. Welles walked a half-dozen blocks to the Mercury Theatre, where, even at that hour, members of the stage company were still rehearsing their new play.

Welles went up on stage, where news photographers were lurking. They caught him with his eyes raised, his arms outstretched. The next day his photograph appeared in newspapers throughout the country, over a caption that blurted: "I Didn't Know What I Was Doing!", or words to that effect.

The next morning headlines in major city newspapers reported the hoax: "Radio Listeners in Panic, Taking War Drama as Fact" (*New York Times*); "U.S. Terrorized by Radio's 'Men From Mars' " (*San Francisco Chronicle*); "Radio Drama Causes Panic" (*Philadelphia Inquirer*); "Listeners Weep and Pray, Prepare for End of World" (*New Orleans Times-Picayune*).

Many of the listeners who had been deluded laughed good-naturedly at one another—and at themselves. Some professed not to have been taken in by what one woman called "that Buck Rogers stuff." But others turned their wrath on Welles, on the network, and on the medium that had turned their Sunday evening into a time of unsolicited terror.

CBS apologized to the public, but also pointed out that during the program no fewer than four announcements had been made stating that it was a dramatic presentation, not a news broadcast.

A subdued Welles, believing his career was ruined, dutifully followed suit. "I don't think we will try anything like this again," he stated.

For two or three days, the press would not let Welles, nor radio, off the front page. Media rivalry played its part; newspaper publishers seemed anxious to portray radio—and Welles—as villains. The clipping bureau that served CBS delivered condemnatory editorials by the pound.

While newsmen "tsk-tsked," government officials fumed. Senator Clyde Herring of Iowa, reflecting the anger of many citizens, stated his support for legislation to curb such "Halloween bogymen." The Federal Communications Commission (FCC), flooded with complaint letters,

Orson Welles, besieged by reporters after the 1938 brodcast of War of the Worlds.
*Welles expressed amazement and regret that his dramatization had created panic
among millions of radio listeners.*

tried to find a philosophical stance somewhere
between imposing severe censorship and permit-
ting unbridled expression.

Novelist H. G. Wells cabled his disregards from
London. Although he had given CBS permission
to air his novel, he complained that "it was not explained to me that this dramatization would be
made with a liberty that amounts to a complete
reworking of *The War of the Worlds.*"

But some columnists and editorialists began to
perceive significant merit in the program. Essayist
Heywood Broun interpreted the broadcast as a
cautionary tale: "Jitters have come home to roost.
The peace of Munich hangs heavy over our heads
like a thundercloud." *Variety,* under a headline
stating "Radio Does U.S. A Favor," described the
program as a warning to Americans of the danger
of unpreparedness.

In a column that turned the tide of public
opinion in favor of Welles and company,
Dorothy Thompson called the broadcast "the

news story of the century—an event which made
greater contribution to an understanding of Hit-
lerism, Mussolinism, Stalinism, anti-Semitism,
and all the other terrorism of our time than all
the words about them that have been written by
reasonable men."

Welles, to his relief, soon learned that he would
not be consigned to durance vile. "Bill Paley, the
head of CBS, brought Orson and me up on the carpet and gave us a reprimand," Houseman later recalled. "But there was ambivalence to it. The
working stiffs thought we were heroes. The executives thought of us as some sort of anarchists. But
reason—and revenues—prevailed. A few days
after the broadcast, when it was announced that
Campbell's Soup had become a sponsor, the boys
at the top began to think of us as heroes, or at least
as employable persons, as well."

Some critics continued to decry the credulity
of the American people. They spoke of the compelling power of the human voice emanating

from the upper air. Radio, ominously, seemed able to reduce an entire country to the size of one room; it exerted unexpected power over susceptible millions.

For a book-length study titled *The Invasion from Mars,* Princeton University psychology professor Hadley Cantril interviewed scores of persons who had listened to the program. Speaking with them shortly after "that night," he received responses ranging from insecure to phobic to fatalistic.

"The coming of the Martians did not present a situation where the individual could preserve one value if he sacrifices another," Professor Cantril concluded from his research. "In this situation the individual stood to lose all his values at once. Nothing could be done to save any of them. Panic was inevitable."

Did Welles intend the panic? Had he hoped, by means of his magnificent dramatic powers, to gain all those headlines?

Houseman dismisses such conjecture as "rubbish." He declares: "Orson and I had no clear presense of the mood of the audience. *The War of the Worlds* wasn't selected as a parable of invasion and war in the 1930s, but just as an interesting story unto itself. Only after the fact did we perceive how ready and resonant the world was for the tale. Our intent was theatre, not terror."

Welles and his players could not know that they had portrayed the shape of things to come. The program was, in a way, quite prophetic. Barely two weeks later, German foreign minister Joachim von Ribbentrop chillingly commented: "I would not be surprised if in the United States eyewitness reports are under consideration in which the 'Giants from Mars' marched up in brown shirts waving swastika flags."

Sooner than the peoples of the world could guess, a true nightmare—that of World War II—would be upon them.

Welles, of course, went on to memorable successes in motion pictures and theater. And his *War of the Worlds* broadcast became the most famous radio program of all time.

These days, the crossroads village of Grovers Mill is much the way it was that spectral night half a century ago. There are, however, signs of strangers nearby—new homes sprouting up among what had been potato fields. And futuristic shapes—sleek, glass-walled, high-technology industrial buildings—stand amid the trees.

But the old mill itself is still at the intersection of Millstone and Cranbury roads—a dot east of Princeton on the highway map. The weatherworn wooden structure, with a few of its millstones scattered about, stands lonely vigil.

Here fate tossed its random lightning-bolt. Here the "Martians" made their landing on what is now a municipal park. Nearby, ducks glide on a big, placid pond.

The former Wilson farm (the script spoke of the "Wilmuth" farm, but sightseers made do with the Wilson place) has long since been cut up into smaller properties. Here Martian-hunters once tramped across the cornfields looking for traces of the invaders.

Wayfarers from all parts of the world still occasionally wander the roads and fields of Grovers Mill. They know they will see no Martians, find no burn marks on the earth left by war machines from outer space, nor come upon charred ruins wrought by the aliens' devastation. Still, drawn by curiosity, they come and look and wonder.

Not all Grovers Mill residents find such doings fascinating. The proprietor of a nearby gas station, for example, remembers the night of the "invasion", but didn't think much of it then and thinks as little of it now. "It doesn't make sense," he says with disdain. "Never has. Never will."

But for Dick Stives, now sixty-three, the "panic broadcast" till holds disquieting memories. Not long ago he walked around the "Martian landing ground."

"When I was a kid," he recalled, "I would crawl down near the wheel of the old mill, just by the pond there, and shuck my clothes and go in swimming. It was just a pond on a farm. But now, looking at it, I have to wonder why people still come so far to find a place where something that was supposed to happen didn't happen."

"I still remember," he said, "how I felt that night, up there in the bedroom in my granddad's place, in the dark, trying to sleep, thinking about what we had heard on the radio. The nighttime would make me think about how almost anything, just about anytime, could happen anywhere—even in Grovers Mill. Things in the shadows. Things I didn't understand."

Study Questions

1. Describe the early career of Orson Welles. Did he realize that his "War of the Worlds" broadcast would create such a controversy?

2. Describe how the show was structured to create tension and heighten suspense.

3. How did Americans react to the broadcast? What do their reactions suggest about the power of radio?

4. In your opinion, was the broadcast unethical or dangerous?

5. How did the struggles going on in Europe affect how Americans received the broadcast?

Bibliography

For discussions of the role of advertising in the 1920s, see Stuart Ewen, *Captains of Consciousness* (1976) and Roland Marchand, *Advertising the American Dream: Making Way for Modernity, 1920-1940* (1986). The influence of films on American culture is ably portrayed in Robert Sklar, *Movie-Made America: A Cultural History of American Movies* (1975) and Larry May, *Screening Out the Past* (1980). Paul Carter's *Another Part of the Twenties* (1977) is an excellent description of popular social attitudes during the infancy of the radio industry. Although there is not much literature on the history of radio, see Erik Barnouw, *A Tower of Babel: A History of Broadcasting in the United States* (1966), Francis Chase, *Sound and Fury: An Informal History of Broadcasting* (1942); Michele Hilmes and Jason Loviglio eds., *Radio Reader: Essays in the Cultural History of Radio* (2001). The broadcast itself is discussed in Howard Koch, *The Panic Broadcast* (1970) and Barbara Leaming, *Orson Welles* (1985).

READING 18

★ ★ ★

Superman in Depression and War

David Welky

In the comic book, Superman may have been born on the doomed planet of Krypton, but in reality, he was a product of the Great Depression. He was the creation of Jerry Siegel and Joe Shuster, two sons of Jewish immigrants. In the midst of the Depression Siegel and Shuster maintained their faith in the American Dream, and Superman expressed that faith. The most appealing quality of Superman is that he was both average and extraordinary. As Clark Kent, the mild-mannered reporter, he was the American common man, a person who blended anonymously into a crowd. As Superman, however, he was endowed with the power to avenge wrongs, eradicate evils, and triumph over inequities. Superman debuted in DC's *Action Comics* in June 1938. He was the "champion of the oppressed," an action hero for a country that desperately needed action, and as a commercial venture a super success. As historian David Welky shows, however, Superman also expressed the anxieties and fears, as well as the hopes and dreams, of Americans during the crisis years of the Depression and World War II. At a time when Adolf Hitler spoke of a Nazi superman, America's Superman became a democratic hero.

Yes, Superman, strange visitor from another planet, a handsome man in red boots and cape with one lock of dark hair curling across his forehead and a bold "S" emblazoned upon his chest. Even the most cultured and all but the most ignorant Americans know who is faster than a speeding bullet and more powerful than a locomotive, and few can honestly say that they have never tied a towel around their neck, thrust out their arms, and run around a room in an approximation of flight. From his obscure origins on the doomed planet Krypton, Kal-El, or Superman, has achieved a level of popularity here on Earth greater than any other figure in mass culture save perhaps Mickey Mouse. He has fought for truth, justice, and the American way in films, cartoons, comic strips, a Broadway musical, television shows, novels, and a radio program, and his image has been emblazoned on products ranging from T-shirts to moccasins to peanut butter. He has even had his own exhibit at the Smithsonian Institute.

Superman emerged during the depths of the Great Depression of the 1930s. The decade's economic dislocation was not only unprecedented, it also occurred against a backdrop of wrenching social and political transformations. Many worried that Franklin Roosevelt's ambitious New Deal marked the first step toward an American dictatorship. The rise of Hitler and Mussolini, the specter of Joseph Stalin, and the growth of militarism in Japan seemed to confirm that totalitarianism was on the march and democracy was on the run. This climate of fear, uncertainty, and suffering raised loud calls for sweeping changes in American life. Proletarian authors like James T. Ferrell, Michael Gold, and John Dos Passos produced novels that vividly portrayed the psychological, economic, and social damage done by the Depression. Much more common and much more popular, however, was literature that upheld long-standing American values and insisted that there was no need for dramatic reforms. Middle-class magazines, newspapers, and books demon-

strated the continuing relevance of the rags-to-riches ethos of hard work, upheld traditional gender roles, and expressed suspicion of foreigners and outsiders. They also envisioned a homogenous society without class divisions and assured Americans that their country was still uniquely blessed and had a distinct Way of Life. This middlebrow ideology had deep roots in the past and offered comforting and familiar landmarks to a nation reeling from domestic and overseas disasters.

Although Superman did not appear until 1938, his instant popularity and strong identification with many common Depression-era themes make him a valuable figure to study. He is also noteworthy because, perhaps more than any other figure in popular culture, he transmitted many of the themes of middlebrow ideology to the next generation of Americans. And yet he ignited a firestorm of controversy when he first appeared. Although his early adventures were far from radical, they often challenged the status quo and called for social revision. His rebellious side attracted the notice of parental and educational groups, who launched a very public campaign to quiet him and the new medium he represented, the comic book, which violated accepted ideals of childrearing and awakened fears for the future of democracy in an age of dictatorship. Superman rapidly evolved in response to these attacks, shifting from a culturally marginal figure known only to children to a mainstream character and a lucrative cash cow for his corporate handlers. He dropped his dangerous elements and completely embraced the safety of tradition. Just as Clark Kent transformed himself into the Man of Steel, Superman shed his reformer role to become a booster of middle-class Americanism, providing a notable example of how cultural products alter their messages when they move from the periphery to the center of the popular consciousness. The adventures of Superman are also instructive for those who argue for the primacy of radicalism in 1930s-era culture. The forces of respectability and the lure of profits made it impossible for culture to be both popular and subversive. The pressures to conform were too powerful even for Superman to resist. They were the kryptonite that weakened his original message and rendered him socially harmless.

Superman arrived at a time when his young readers desperately needed someone to admire. The comic magazine's primary audience, boys aged eight to twelve, had never known good times. Their lives had been marked by want and militarism, and disorder seemed the normal state of affairs. Economic dislocation exacted a psychological toll on many children. They often lost respect for fathers who were unemployed or had trouble providing for the family. The accompanying damage to family status made many more self-conscious and often led to withdrawal, under-achievement, and feelings of shame. The belief that their parents had failed led many children and young adults to look beyond them for positive examples. Younger children typically use older peers and siblings as role models, but comic-book readers often had little reason to admire big brother, for teenagers keenly felt their own economic shortcomings. Even well-educated teenagers struggled to find work and felt that they were a drag on their families. Many unsuccessful jobseekers left home for the life of a transient or grew apathetic toward their own lives and events in the outside world. With their parents and older siblings proving inadequate role models and with only hardship looming in

the future, it is no wonder that children wanted a hero who spoke directly to them and offered hope for a better tomorrow.

That hero came not from Washington, D.C. and not even from the United States, but rather from the faraway planet of Krypton. Superman was the brainchild of Jerry Siegel and Joe Shuster, two youths who were as obscure and hopeless as millions of others in their generation. Had their formative years not been so bleak, it is unlikely that the Man of Steel would have arrived on Earth, for Superman was not just the creation of two inventive minds. He was the product of and the answer to the problems of a troubled generation, a hero sent from above who helped to alleviate the anxieties spawned by a world in turmoil.

Jerry Siegel was an awkward introvert who spent much of his life in a world of his own imagination. Born into a lower-middle-class family in Cleveland in 1914, the "slightly built, slope-shouldered" boy seemed bound for nowhere. He was a poor student who usually showed up late for school, often still wearing his pajamas beneath his clothes, and made few close friends. But the mediocre student had what comic book historian Dennis Dooley called "the soul of a D'Artagnon imprisoned in the body of an undernourished delivery boy." Siegel secretly loved dime detective novels and adventure stories and devoured Edgar Rice Burroughs, Jules Verne, and H. G. Wells novels. He also adored action films and fantasy comic strips like *Tarzan, Buck Rogers,* and *Flash Gordon.* Philip Wylie's 1930 novel, *Gladiator,* featuring a hero who could leap forty feet, lift cars, and deflect bullets with his body, heavily influenced the young man. He considered becoming a writer or a newspaper reporter, but his future was still very much in question when he met Joe Shuster in 1930.

Also born in 1914, Shuster was as unremarkable as his future collaborator. He moved with his family from Toronto to Cleveland when he was ten, settling in a run-down area just twelve blocks from Siegel's modest home. He was as awkward as Siegel and resembled an "undernourished, bewildered schoolboy of sixteen" despite his earnest efforts to bulk up. Burdened with the additional handicap of thick-lensed glasses, he was painfully shy around girls. Schuster shared Siegel's interest in science fiction, but he was more attracted to pictures than words. He drew comic strips for his school newspaper, including one prophetically titled *Jerry the Journalist.* The strip's author introduced Shuster to his cousin, Jerry Siegel, when he learned of their common love.

Siegel and Schuster were on the fringe of American life. They were poor, socially inept, and far from the culture centers of New York and Hollywood. They both sensed that they were misfits and outsiders, and the two hit it off instantly. Their relationship was, Siegel later remarked, "like the right chemicals coming together." Thrilled to have found kindred spirits, they dreamed of launching a comic strip and submitted innumerable proposals with no success. They started a fantasy pulp of sorts in 1933, a mimeographed publication entitled *Science Fiction.* One of their best stories, "The Reign of the Superman," in which a bald, villainous megalomaniac gains super powers and threatens to conquer the earth, appeared in the third issue. But their work accomplished little, and *Science Fiction* died after five issues. They graduated from high school with no career prospects and worked odd jobs to pay for postage for comic-strip submissions. Shuster was so poverty-stricken that he had to draw their proposals on brown wrapping paper or on the back of wallpaper.

Their lives could have gone the way of a proletarian novel. They could have grown disaffected and radical. They could have ended up drunk and penniless in a dank urban pool hall like James Farrell's antihero Studs Lonigan. But as Jerry Siegel lay in bed one summer night in 1933, he was struck by a simple yet profound epiphany. "I conceive[d]," he later wrote, of "a character like Samson, Hercules, and all the strong men I ever heard of rolled into one. *Only more so.*" He got Shuster to give his inspiration a visual form the next morning. Schuster drew a powerful man, clad in a T-shirt and jeans, holding a thug over his head as another futilely fired a machine gun at him. A one-word logo arched across the top of the page, each

letter getting smaller as it gently descended to the right: "SUPERMAN." Unlike the "Superman" from their *Science Fiction* story, he was a hero, not a villain (an "infinitely more commercial" proposition, remarked Siegel). The two fleshed out their creation in the Shusters' unheated apartment through 1933 and 1934. Superman shed his civilian garb in favor of a garish, skintight outfit, complete with a flowing cape and the trademark "S" on his chest. After properly outfitting him, Siegel and Shuster developed Superman's mild-mannered alter ego, named for two of their favorite actors, Clark Gable and Kent Taylor, and loosely modeled in looks and personality on the film comedian Harold Lloyd. They also gave Superman a home, named in honor of Fritz Lang's 1926 science-fiction film *Metropolis.*

Siegel and Shuster had not designed a character for the middle-class America of the *Saturday Evening Post* and the *Ladies' Home Journal.* They consciously created a character who spoke to the disaffected and the disenfranchised and bore direct relevance to the current economic crisis. "Both of us were children of the Depression," Siegel once remarked, "so we knew how the people felt who were having a rough time of it." Siegel deeply sympathized with those in need and felt a powerful sense of "compassion . . . for the downtrodden." Seeing nothing but dislocation at home and growing discord abroad, he pondered how he could make the world a better place for them. "What would I do," he asked, "if I weren't so meek and mild, and if I were stronger than anyone else on Earth?" Superman was Siegel and Shuster's gift to America, a fictional figure who did more to restore hope than his creators ever could on their own. They wanted him to be the protector of the little man, the defender of common folk struggling in a world gone mad. He also marked the ultimate expression of "wish fulfillment." As Clark Kent, he was no more remarkable than his creators—shy, bespectacled, and awkward around women. But suddenly and without warning, this mild-mannered reporter became the most powerful being on Earth, saving lives and catching crooks while maintaining a nonchalant air towards the women who worshiped him—most notably, the ever-adoring Lois Lane. Superman addressed the inadequacies of a hopeless generation by instilling a belief that ordinary people could be special, that they could succeed in an unforgiving world that offered little hope for the future. In a way it was a very traditional message that incorporated the dreams of hundreds of years of Americans, the dream of finding a special gift that will make you an extraordinary person. By pitching his appeal to the underclass, however, Superman would end up making many conservative thinkers very uncomfortable.

The budding cartoonists labored for five years to get Superman into the public eye. They sent samples to numerous comic-strip syndicates to no avail. Superman seemed too marginal and immature for these engines of middlebrow culture. Finally accepting that *Superman* would not appear in newspapers any time soon, Siegel and Shuster pursued employment in a new and little-known medium—the comic magazine.

The comic-book industry was not much of an industry. Comic books had existed since the turn of the century, but publications like *Yellow Kid Magazine* (1897), *Comic Monthly* (1922), and *Famous Funnies* (1934) contained reprints of newspaper comics rather than original material. Some appeared on newsstands and others served as giveaway premiums—purchasers of Phillips' Dental Magnesia, for example, received a free copy of *Skippy Comics*. *New Comics* broke new ground in 1935 by including original material. That same year, *New Fun Comics* (later renamed *More Fun Comics*) followed its lead and became the first regularly issued comic to feature all-new work.

The shift from reprints to first-run comics created a pressing need for artists and storywriters. Drawing from a large pool of unemployed, often-inexperienced, and sometimes-incompetent artists and writers, companies established assembly lines that focused on quantity rather than quality of output. Artist Will Eisner recalled that employees "worked buttock-to-buttock and communicated like cell-block inmates" as they performed their assigned tasks—inking, lettering, drawing backgrounds or main characters—for about one dollar per page. It was not always pleasant work, but it was work. When asked why he worked in such conditions, Eisner responded: "malnutrition."

The two youngsters from Cleveland traveled to New York in 1935 to get a toehold in this still-primitive business. *Superman* came with them, but no publisher wanted to use such an absurd feature in their book. Siegel and Shuster convinced National Allied Publishing (later DC Comics) head Major Malcolm Wheeler-Nicholson to run their "Henri Duval," the story of a swashbuckling adventurer (submitted on brown wrapping paper), in *New Fun Comics*. The pair later contributed "Federal Men," which followed the lives of G-Men, and "Dr. Occult the Ghost Detective" to Wheeler-Nicholson's comics. Dr. Occult's superhuman powers, long cape, and triangular chest insignia indicate that Superman had not left their minds. The duo's wisecracking vigilante sleuth, "Slam Bradley," became a fan favorite in National's new *Detective Comics* and gave them enough clout to get the Man of Steel in print. In 1938, National featured Superman in the first issue of *Action Comics*. Conceived during the first days of the New Deal, Superman was finally born at the bottom of the Roosevelt Recession. He appeared at exactly the time when Americans began a quest to discover strength in the ordinary citizen. Like Steinbeck's Tom Joad and Capra's Jefferson Smith, he was an average-looking man who could do great things for the country, a vivid expression of the capabilities of the everyday American riled in support of a just cause.

Action Comics had an instant impact upon the business. Kids snatched up the first edition of 200,000 and dealers begged for more. The fourth installment of *Action Comics* sold almost 500,000 issues, far more than any other comic on the market. Surveys revealed that kids bought the magazine mostly because of the Man of Steel. It was not *Action Comics* they wanted, it was *Superman Comics*. National gave the buyers what they wanted; the first issue of *Superman*, featuring four stories about the man from Krypton, hit newsstands in early 1939, making him the first comic character to have his own magazine. The quarterly *Superman* moved about 1.25 million copies per issue by the next year, while sales of the monthly *Action Comics* skyrocketed to about 900,000 copies per issue, far outreaching their closest competitors. Both magazines reached far larger audiences than sales indicate. Far from being a private commodity, kids treated comic books as "a sort of currency," exchanging them with peers for ones that they had not yet read. Statisticians estimated that about three children read each comic book.

Superman and the other "costumed characters" who soon cropped up around him—Batman, Captain America, Green Arrow, Hawkman, Wonder Woman—put the business upon solid financial footing. But Superman was clearly the star of the medium. Superman deserves most of the credit for this. Comic-book insider Carmine Infantino argued that he "literally *created* this industry. . . . He's the key, the granddaddy of them all."

Comic books are built on fantasy, and there were of course differences between the comic world and the real world. Obviously, there were no caped superheroes patrolling the skies over Depression-era America, and much of the technology in Superman comics went far beyond contemporary capabilities. But more interesting are the ways that they twisted the reality of American demographics to better conform to conservative traditions. Although it was more willing to show the lower class than many other publications, the comic offered a world populated almost entirely by WASPy whites, who accounted for the bulk of comic book sales. Not one African American appeared in the pre-war issues of *Superman* and *Action Comics*. Although a few stories included native peoples, they rarely had personalities and acted primarily as colorful backdrops for Superman's exploits. Siegel and Shuster appealed to their largely male, youthful audience by including very few women in their stories, most notably Lois Lane. Lois was a career woman—a rarity in 1930s literature—but her job serves mostly as a gateway to trouble. Her journalistic efforts generally get her kidnapped or into some other scrape

that Superman has to extract her from. One wonders if she would have been better off at home, and her constant fawning over the Man of Steel makes one wonder if she would have chosen a man over a career.

Superman upheld other conservative priorities. Though he is a unique figure, he embodies many of the attributes Americans traditionally ascribed to themselves. Superman continued a tradition of superheroes that stretched back to the ancient Babylonians, whose Gilgamesh epic told the story of a half-human, half-god creature, but the cowboy, who embodied independence and rugged individualism as he created order out of lawlessness in the Old West, was a much more important influence for Superman's creators. Pulp characters like Doc Savage propelled the ideals of the cowboy into a modern, urban environment, and Superman carried them into the realm of science fiction. Like all white Americans, he was an immigrant, and he quickly shed any vestige of his alien nature to blend seamlessly into the mainstream. He applied his talents to lift himself from an obscure Midwestern town to become nationally renowned, and he works to preserve the social order, preventing chaos and disaster from wracking the lives of the innocent.

Even though the comic was in many ways aligned with the conservative tradition, its social rebelliousness placed it beyond respectability. Unlike most middlebrow sources, it realistically depicted the country's economic woes and pinned blame for them squarely upon the business class, which was in turn tied to notorious criminals and devious foreigners—even America's most famous immigrant shared the nation's traditional suspicion of outsiders. Restoring tranquility meant shattering the capitalist class' stronghold on power. In one story, Superman investigates the murder of Paul Dorgan, a prominent sociologist who believed that "sinister persons or forces" wanted to "stave off the return of national prosperity." Superman learns that Dorgan's killers work for J. F. Curtis, a powerful industrialist whose henchmen are hard at work sabotaging factories and sowing labor discord.

Superman digs further and discovers that a "foreign nation" has promised to give Curtis "important concessions if he'll wreck America's economic structure" by crashing the stock market. Superman visits the capitalist, who inhospitably tries to electrocute him. But the current has no effect on the Man of Tomorrow. He grabs Curtis as it surges through him, "instantly electrocuting" him and allowing the United States to resume its "march toward prosperity."

Another story posits an even more sinister plot to devastate America. With the country in the midst of "the worst depression" in history, the *Daily Planet* dispatches Clark Kent to interview some leading financiers. Not unlike Herbert Hoover, they all assure Clark that the downturn is just "a temporary panic." Clark overhears one of them laughing with his cronies about the profits he is making "while the rest of the country goes bankrupt." Changing into Superman, he follows the "ruthless financial giant" to a strange meeting headed by his mortal enemy, Lex Luthor, who uses a "narcotic incense" to control the capitalists' minds and pocketbooks. They have been manipulating the stock market while under his influence, creating huge profits for Luthor and driving the rest of the country to ruin. Superman breaks up Luthor's ring and knocks his airplane from the sky when he flees, presumably ending his career in crime. With Luthor gone, Clark assures his publisher that "the menace is removed" and "the nation" will soon return "to its former prosperity."

Metropolis's moguls engaged in an array of dubious ventures that were not directly tied to the Depression but nevertheless wreaked havoc on ordinary people. Businessmen masterminded numerous stock swindles and had a nasty habit of using low-grade materials in construction projects. Thornton Blakely was the most repulsive of the lot. Workers at the Blakely Coal Mine had long complained about unsafe conditions. The boss, however, paid little heed to their concerns and the miners had to either stay on or starve. Their fears are confirmed when a shaft collapses and traps a miner. Superman saves his life, but the accident leaves the miner crippled. Blakely

blames the accident on the worker's "own carelessness" in an interview with Clark Kent and offers a mere fifty dollars in severance pay. Angrily denying charges that he is running an unsafe business, he retorts that even if there are "safety hazards" in the mine, they are not his problem. "I'm a business man, not a humanitarian," he remarks. That night, Clark disguises himself as a miner and crashes a party at the boss's mansion. Watchmen capture him and bring him before Blakely. Inspired by this unexpected arrival, the host decides to move the gathering into the mine. After the assembly dutifully troops beneath the earth to continue the fete, their new miner friend interrupts their revelry by yanking down the supports holding up their shaft and imprisoning them. Blakely remains calm until he discovers that the alarms that signal the world above have broken due to years of neglect. His party assails the "blasted skin-flint" for his greed. "If you'd have had the mine equipped with proper safety-precautions," screams one tuxedo-clad prisoner, "we might have gotten out alive!" They futilely claw at the rubble, exhausting themselves without making any progress. Superman finally frees the panicked group, and when Clark visits Blakely for a follow-up interview, he discovers a changed man. "Henceforth," he insists, "my mine will be the safest in the country, and my workers the best treated."

The various crimes of corrupt businessmen were one part of a bleak picture painted by the first Superman comics. Siegel and Shuster placed their hero in a gritty urban landscape full of vice, crime, and official ineptitude, a blasted-out mockery of America's City on a Hill. It was an image that stretched all the way back to Thomas Jefferson, but anti-city rhetoric found many expressions in Depression-era mass culture. Hollywood issued a spate of films portraying the city as a seedbed of corruption and moral decay, populated by devious slicksters, shyster lawyers, and politicians on the take. Urbanites like radio's Amos and Andy lived in a world full of tricksters and con-artists. Countless B-Westerns identified the city with greedy businessmen and bankers eager to cheat common folk out of their money. Even though middle-class sources generally avoided this world, the marginalized comic-book industry identified much more with John Wayne than the *Saturday Evening Post.* Batman and other comic-book heroes existed in climates similar to Superman's, but none were as good at uncovering and crushing wickedness as the Man of Steel.

Malicious capitalists were not the only threat to social tranquility in this malevolent environment. Murders and kidnappings occur with frightening regularity. Racketeers impose protection schemes on innocent storekeepers and cab drivers. Many of the institutions designed to expose and halt crime are ineffective or, even worse, assist the bad guys. Although Clark Kent's *Daily Planet* remains squeaky-clean, the tabloid *Morning Herald* cooperates with crooks to get lurid scoops, and its equally yellow competitor, the *Morning Pictorial,* uses its influence to denounce critics of its politician-owner, Alex Evell (who could very easily be viewed as a caricature of William Randolph Hearst), who plans to dominate the city for his own benefit. The police are always at least one step behind the Man of Tomorrow and repeatedly prove incapable of solving a crime without his help. Further, even with all the confessions he extracts and all of the felons he deposits at Police Headquarters, the cops still consider him an enemy. Figuring that anyone who is around so many crimes must be involved somehow, they spend more time trying to capture Superman than tracking down criminals.

In Superman's world, inept police officers were indicative of larger failings. He resolved to do something about the problems in local government in late 1940. An opening caption shrieks the setup:

Crooked politics sabotages the very foundations of democratic government! When **SUPERMAN** *finds the city of Metropolis infested by evil, conniving public officeholders, he begins a clean-up campaign which for sheer thoroughness and unorthodox procedure has never before been witnessed in the annals of representative government!*

Clark and Lois suspect that city prosecutor Ralph Dale is "working hand-in-hand with the underworld" and convince the *Daily Planet* to endorse opposition candidate Bert Runyan in the upcoming election. The evildoings of Nat Burly, a "corrupt political boss" whose shady regime depends upon Dale's lax prosecution of criminals, hampers Runyan's campaign. Superman thwarts Burly's efforts to bump him off and to use corrupt police officers to frame and discredit him. Runyan keeps up his attacks on Burly, who retaliates by using "strongarm men" to bust up his rallies. Prosecutor Dale wins the election with the help of some vigorous ballot-box stuffing, but Superman, infuriated by this perversion of democracy, forces a pivotal pro-Burly ward leader to confess his chicanery on the radio, thereby nullifying the fraudulent results and returning "good government" to Metropolis. Good government was apparently tough to preserve. Superman was again battling "crooked politicians" with links to organized crime by mid 1941.

The little guy needed help in this brutal world, so Superman dedicated much of his energy to assisting ordinary citizens who were down on their luck. Just because the Man of Steel was superpowerful did not mean that he always concentrated on super-important issues; no problem is too small for the man in the sky. In one early story, he helps a washed-up boxer regain his form and win the title. In another, he takes the place of a bench-warming college football player, partly to bring down a crooked coach and partly to help the second-stringer keep his girlfriend from running off with another athlete. In a third tale, he poses as a strongman to drum up business for the struggling Jordan Circus. Mr. Jordan is a kindly old man who maintains "an optimistic front" despite facing "bitter disappointment and certain defeat." "A guy like that," Superman concludes, "deserves a break." And what a break. Superman's remarkable feats of strength pack the big top and save Mr. Jordan from bankruptcy.

His desire to help those in need and his drive for social reform reach an interesting peak in *Action Comics* #8, cover-dated January 1939 but written on the heels of the Roosevelt Recession. The story, which shows the influence of social-problem films like *Dead End* (1937) and *Angels With Dirty Faces* (1938), again revolves around children. Always on the lookout for a story, Clark watches as Frankie Marello, a hardened street urchin of perhaps twelve, is found guilty of assault and battery. He listens intently as Frankie's mother begs the court for leniency. "He's my only son," she tells the judge. "He might have been a good boy, except for his environment." The reporter agrees with Frankie's distraught mother but notes that "if I know the court of law . . . her plea hasn't a chance!" Sure enough, the judge sentences Frankie to two years in the reformatory. Clark discovers that Frankie was part of a child-crime syndicate straight from the pages of *Oliver Twist,* with "Gimpy," a "loathsome corrupter of youth," standing in for Dickens's Fagin. Appalled by the scheme, Superman roughs up Gimpy and exiles him from Metropolis, then scares the slum kids straight. He is satisfied that they will live "clean an' honest" lives yet hopes to do more. "It's not entirely your fault that you're delinquent," he explains, "these slums—your poor living conditions" are the real culprit. He sends the children through the slums to tell residents to gather their possessions and leave the area, then rips down dilapidated buildings and single-handedly clears the slum while ignoring the gunfire of troops brought in to stop him. After the dust settles, emergency crews replace the tenements with decent apartments, allowing the children to live in "splendid housing conditions" and putting a major dent in juvenile crime.

As this story implies, Superman did not merely fight crime. He instead took a proactive approach by reforming the environment and misguided morals that led to felonious behavior. Nor was he reluctant to use force to get what he wanted. The May 1939 edition of *Action Comics* presented the most violent and dictatorial vision of Superman during the pre-war era. Clark Kent arrives at a crash scene to find that a negligent driver has killed a friend of his. The ineffective mayor refuses to improve the city's traffic situation, so he takes the matter into his own hands. Bursting through the door of a radio station, the Man of Tomorrow snatches the microphone from a startled announcer and proclaims that "the auto-accident death rate of this community . . . should shame us all! It's constantly rising and due entirely to reckless driving and inefficiency! . . . From this moment on, I declare war on reckless drivers—Henceforth, homicidal drivers answer to *ME!*" He "systematically" destroys every vehicle in the city's impound lot as he chuckles about his "private little war." Next, he accuses the owner of the Bates Motor Company, whose cars are involved in more accidents than any other make, of using inferior parts to save money at the cost of human lives, then dismantles the entire factory without a thought for the jobs to be lost. Finally, he catches the mayor himself driving recklessly. Hurling himself into the car, Superman grabs the wheel and mashes the accelerator. The mayor panics as the car lurches forward. "Do you want to kill us?" he screams. "Why not?" Superman replies. "You didn't worry much about killing the others! . . . By not seeing to it that the speed laws were strictly enforced." He yanks the mayor out of the vehicle a split second before it collides with a boulder and drags him to the morgue to show him the bodies of recent auto-accident victims. Shaken by Superman's actions, the mayor agrees to "rigidly" enforce the traffic laws. Clark finds a parking ticket on his car soon after, proving the effectiveness of his tactics and demonstrating that sometimes people need a strongman, not a bureaucracy, to set them right.

Superman's social ethos set him apart from other comic-book heroes. He outmuscled all of his comic competitors, but this was merely a matter of shading. Batman, Captain Marvel, Wonder Woman, and the other superheroes could approach Superman physically. None, however, were nearly as committed to helping the unfortunate as the self-proclaimed "champion of the weak and helpless," and none were so concerned with improving morals and standards of conduct. Cosmo, the Phantom of Disguise, mostly helped rich people and never explained why he was so eager to help. Batman, Superman's closest rival in sales, was less interested in the welfare of others than in satisfying his own dark and mysterious urges. He wanted vengeance, not a better world.

As the leading voice in a marginal industry, Superman challenged authority, demonized the rich, exposed class differences, demanded social reform, and worked on behalf of common people. But by making the comic book a phenomenon among American youth, he also brought it to the attention of adult critics who viewed it as a threat to children and even to the nation.

Parents, educators, and librarians agreed that "virtually no child escape[d] the influence of the comics," and set about to combat the menace. *Chicago Daily News* literary editor Sterling North contributed one of the most vociferous attacks against the genre with a 1940 editorial entitled "A National Disgrace," in which he denounced the comic book as "a poisonous mushroom growth" growing upon the American social body. These "sex-horror serials" pushed "mayhem, murder, torture and abduction" into impressionable minds, making children more likely to live reckless lives. They imbalanced "young nervous systems" by portraying an unnaturally tinted landscape and crudely drawn characters that ruined "the child's natural sense of color." Comics also prevented children from discovering the "better" class of literature that all educated people should be acquainted with. Ultimate blame for the comic menace lay not with kids, but rather with adults and, by implication, society:

The shame lies largely with the parents who don't know and don't care what their children are reading. It lies with unimaginative teachers who force stupid, dull twaddle down eager young throats, and, of course, it lies with the completely immoral publishers of the 'comics'— guilty of a cultural slaughter of the innocents.

Over forty newspapers and magazines reprinted North's jeremiad. Preachers read it from pulpits, teachers posted it on schoolhouse walls, and concerned adults nationwide wrote in its support.

Most who commented on comic books seconded North's argument. Literary critic Lovell Thompson found the comics to be brutal, sadistic, and fantastic, and wondered how kids would ever "learn concentration on such a reading diet." The *Wilson Library Bulletin* declared that any child "conditioned by the jerky, jiggling, inflamed world of the comics is a damaged child." Writing in the *Horn Book,* Louise Bechtel urged parents to blunt the comics' appeal by reading their children more mind-expanding books and taking a more active interest in their schooling. Parents should feel "ashamed that in an America which above all cares for education, such a phenomenon as Superman should be so successful." Perhaps the most trenchant analysis came from James Frank Vlamos, one of the few commentators who actually studied his subject before assaulting it. Writing in the *American Mercury* in 1941, he expressed his concerns in terms that reflected a profound concern for the traditional social and political fabric of America and an awareness of how events in Europe could unravel that fabric. "You can't go through an issue of a 'comic' magazine," he declared,

without realizing that the lawful processes of police and courts have disappeared and that only the heroism of superheroes keep us from being annihilated by divers[e] disasters and crimes. The 'hero' has no hesitancy, in these tracts for the kiddies, in subjecting the 'villain' to third-degree tortures and mental terror. . . . His methods may be those of a bully, but his alleged motives make him a hero. He is a law unto himself, this super-hero. . . . 'Politician' in these child stories means 'crook' and 'policeman' means 'idiot.' Expressions like 'racketeering union' and 'war-mongering industrialist' and 'Fifth Columnist' are used indiscriminately. If any hope for normal democratic society exists at all, it is in the goodness and might of some superman."

Vlamos worried that figures such as Superman subverted respect for traditional institutions of authority without offering any appropriately American substitute. Superheroes, who settled problems without strictly adhering to the law, seemed anti-democratic at a time when democracy desperately needed defending.

The anxieties raised by comic books reflected broader social attitudes toward the youth and youth leisure. Critics who connected comic books to totalitarianism tapped into widespread worries for the future of America's youth. Herbert Hoover feared that continued deprivation would cause the youth to lose faith in democracy and Americanism. Roosevelt shared Hoover's concern and established several agencies designed to neutralize impoverished young people's rebelliousness. The National Youth Administration (NYA) and the Civilian Conservation Corps (CCC) furnished jobs and job training for adolescents and young adults, provided an introduction to middle-class values of thrift and hard work, and acted as a primer course on Americanism. These programs, explained NYA executive Charles Taussig, existed to teach the young to adopt a "democratic approach" to the world.

But government programs did not alleviate Americans' fears of and for their children. The spread of fascism only enhanced adults' suspicions that dictators would seduce their children. Thatcher Winslow noted the prominent role that young people played in elevating Hitler and Mussolini to power and concluded that there was "no reason to suppose" that American youth would prove "any more immune to the appeal of the dictator than the youth of other countries." George Lawton, a psychologist writing for *Scholastic Magazine,* proposed a similar argument. Because of the difficulty in finding jobs, adolescents could not become independent adults and instead remained in a sort of perpetual childhood. Their frustration made them more susceptible to the false charms of demagogues who promised them the chance to "play an active part in our economic and social system," even if that meant the "sacrifice of democracy." In this climate of fear, Superman appeared as an enabling figure, a benevolent *Übermensch* who could facilitate a generational switch in allegiance from democracy to dictatorship.

Comic books also offended current attitudes toward recreation. Many in the 1930s echoed a sentiment that first gained strength in the Progressive-era Playground Movement by arguing that play should be organized and meaningful, not unstructured and anarchistic. The federal government contributed to this effort by spending hundreds of millions of dollars constructing playgrounds, swimming pools, and athletic fields where play could take place under adult direction. Supervised contests in which nobody kept score or declared a winner offered excellent opportunities to instill "socially desirable conduct" in children by teaching them teamwork and cooperation. Proper recreation developed social skills, physical prowess, and creativity, and produced "useful citizens" by teaching kids "justice and fair play." Games that relied on teamwork and cooperation trained children to serve as the next generation of leaders. Children who did not spend their free time properly would likely suffer from a stunted mind and body and never reach "the full stature of manhood." No wonder the perceived rise of more passive and solitary forms of recreation dismayed experts. Instead of absorbing valuable social lessons, kids sat alone and listened to the radio, watched movies, and read comic books—one survey revealed that nine- to fourteen-year-olds spent three-quarters of their leisure time reading comic books—that did not teach kids how to get along in society or assist in acquiring the skills necessary to ensure the smooth development of an American community. Many feared that the next generation would be "soft" and socially inept, resulting in a nation of weak individuals who had no sense of togetherness or ability to lead.

Superman and the fledgling comic-book industry were therefore open to assault on several fronts, and a business just able to stand on its own had no stomach for a vigorous counterattack that would at best leave it marginalized and unstable and at worst demonized and bankrupt. Sales of *Superman* and *Action Comics* were bringing in big money, and DC was finding ways to milk their hero for even more. It could use Superman's endorsement to sell other comics in its line or new toys like the "Krypto Ray Gun." As the medium's standard bearer, Superman had to harmonize his focus with middle-class morality to deflect criticisms that could cut into sales and sink the trade. In response to these pressures, DC Comics hired an advisory board of child psychiatrists, social workers, and educators, and watered down the content of comic books. "With millions of parents ready to ban Superman from the house should his high moral sense falter," noted the *Saturday Evening Post,* "the company takes its civic responsibilities seriously." DC also changed the personnel behind Superman. The strain of churning out artwork day after day overwhelmed Joe Shuster, who was so near-sighted that he almost had to press his face onto the paper to see the pages on his desk. His staff did most of the drawing by mid-1940. Once free to develop plots from his office in Cleveland, Jerry Siegel found himself attending more policy meetings in New York and facing tougher editing of story proposals. The B-movie-style class conflict was no longer acceptable. No more destruction of private property, unless absolutely necessary. No more deaths, unless absolutely necessary. No more evil capitalists, unless absolutely necessary. After the start of 1941, it was rarely necessary. A new Superman emerged, one palatable to a middle-class audience. He abandoned his concerns for social reform and the common man and became a super-patriot, proudly selling Americanism for ten cents a shot. It was now the Man of Steel's job to bring young people into tune with the trend of middle-class culture as it prepared to face the global challenge to the American Way of Life.

This shift began almost as soon as Superman landed in children's hands. He started to embrace his role as the bringer of traditional values when DC Comics formed the Supermen of America Club in 1939. The Club allowed the Man of Steel to directly share his views with readers while making his handlers a few extra dollars. For a dime, enrollees received a certificate of membership, a Supermen of America pin, and a decoder ring. DC also set aside a special "Supermen of America" page in *Action Comics* and *Superman*

in which the Man of Steel personally addressed his fans. Anyone could read the page, but only members, about 250,000 of them by 1941, had the decoder rings necessary to read the encrypted message included in each edition. He created an air of intimacy with readers by signing his note, "Sincerely, Clark Kent"—although everyone knew that it was Superman speaking. "I regard each and every one of you as a real part of my family," he told them. He sometimes used this page to promote a new contest or giveaway ("I will soon announce a gigantic contest for Superman club members only," read one secret directive), but typically used it to imbue readers with the values that he considered important. In 1940, Superman cautioned kids to "remember to play fair and live honestly," a theme he returned to many times in his notes. He often built his messages around the three central principles of the club—strength, courage, and justice—arguing that one needed equal shares of each to be a true Superman. He also offered kids advice on physical conditioning—critical, since "mental health" was "inextricably linked with physical health." Perhaps, with good diet, moderate exercise, lots of sleep, and clean living, they too could be Supermen.

The new Superman stopped talking about the economy and social change and focused more and more of his attention on the looming threat to democracy and Americanism. To do this, he had to renounce some of his earlier views. The first two Superman adventures, which appeared about the time that Germany annexed Austria, contain an unmistakably anti-war message. Clark is sent to cover a war in the tiny South American country of San Monte but, for reasons left unclear, instead hastens to Washington, D. C., where he finds the powerful Senator Barrows cohorting with Alex Greer, "the slickest lobbyist in Washington." His suspicions aroused, the "champion of the oppressed" overhears the Senator agreeing to Greer's plan to embroil the United States in a war and net themselves a tidy profit. The enraged Superman kidnaps the lobbyist and demands to know who is behind the plot. The terrified Greer confesses that he is the pawn of "munitions magnate" Emil

Norvell. The Man of Steel releases Greer and hunts down Norvell, then drags the arms dealer to San Monte and forces him to enlist in the army. Norvell cowers as bombs explode around him. His nerves in tatters, he begs Superman to let him go home. "Let me return to the U.S.," he pleads, "I've grown to hate war. . . . From now on, the most dangerous thing I'll manufacture will be a firecracker!" Superman next kidnaps the leaders of the rival armies and demands that they settle their differences with a one-on-one fistfight ("Or I'll clean up on both of you myself!"). But the two generals quickly discover that they have no real differences and no good reason for fighting. Sensing their bewilderment, he explains that it is "obvious you've been fighting only to promote the sale of munitions!" They agree to end the war, bringing peace to the beleaguered nation and ending the rule of the arms dealers.

Superman's anti-war philosophy supported the findings of the 1934 Nye Committee investigation of the causes of World War I, but middle-class culture had evolved since then, and the new Man of Steel followed the flow. As Roosevelt guided the United States closer to intervention, Superman paralleled other middle-class reading by loudly voicing the merits of Americanism. Once a critic of the status quo, he reinvented himself as "patriot number one." He used his "Supermen of America" column to inspire readers to become true believers in America's cause. More and more, his messages focused on patriots like Washington and Lincoln and on the greatness of democracy, "the best and truest form of government." He informed kids of the wonders of a free society and contrasted it with life in fascist nations. With freedom, however, comes obligations. The Man of Steel reminded readers to do their part to make their families and communities stronger, for "in these crucial days each of us, young or old, has responsibilities to be shouldered." He warned them not to take their own loyalty for granted, but rather work to keep "the fierce fires of love of country and liberty alive" within them by upholding democratic principles and living up to the ideals

of the Supermen of America Club: strength, courage, and justice. Taking loyalty and duty to country lightly, he cautioned, would bring dire consequences upon America—in Superman's mind, France fell because its citizens had taken democracy "so much for granted that they allowed the forces of fascism within France herself to betray their nation." Small wonder then, that his Secret Message for August 1941 read: "True Americanism becomes more important to us all every day."

Making it clear that "sinister forces" wanted to "impede America's effort to arm itself," he spent much of 1941 battling saboteurs, fifth columnists, and other "secret foes of our nation." Nothing was safe from terrorists, who targeted factories, individuals, and even the *Daily Planet*. Superman prevented these strikes from succeeding, but they were frightening nonetheless. What was most unsettling is that anyone, no matter their public reputation, could be a spy—prominent patriots and "ultra-respectable" citizens headed many of the espionage rings that Superman busted up. The "traitorous activities of fifth columnists," however, were usually directed by highly-visible members of the anti-war movement, who were in turn guided by fascists. In early 1941, Superman attended a meeting of the "Volunteers for Peace," an anti-war group led by Stuart Pemberton. He looks on in disgust as the crowd, in a scene reminiscent of Hitler's rallies, "goes berserk in fanatical applause" when Pemberton urges the crowd to oppose rearmament. Superman later spies on a meeting of the group's leaders and is horrified to learn that they are in league with "Nation X," which is plotting an immediate strike against the United States. The Volunteers plan to "prepare the way by sabotaging important strategic centers." Superman foils Nation X's attempts to destroy a train, poison the water supply, and bomb Metropolis, then goes after the traitorous Pemberton, who has taken over a radio station and proclaimed that "democracy's death is at hand!" Unwilling to submit to a foreign dictatorship, the Man of Steel captures the rogue and puts both his organization and Nation X's invasion out of commission.

Superman's writers made Germany their primary enemy. Spies resembled northern Europeans, and insignia on enemy weaponry often imitated the markings on Nazi arms. A story from *Superman* #10 (May/June, 1941) cleared up any lingering doubts as to who was America's most dangerous foe. The *Daily Planet* sends Clark and Lois to cover a sports festival pitting American athletes against a team from Dukalia, a country whose relations with the United States have been strained in recent years. The tall and blond Dukalian athletes epitomize the Aryan ideal. The crowd notes the symbol they wear on their chests (which resembles a cross with an extra set of arms) and their extended right-arm salute as they enter the stadium. Convinced that these sportsmen actually represent "an organization fomenting unamerican activities," Clark listens as Karl Wolff, the Dukalian Consul, regales the crowd with a speech taken straight from *Mein Kampf.* "Present here," he intones, "is the flower of Dukalian youth! You have seen them perform physical feats which no other human beings can. Proof, I tell you, that we Dukalians are superior to any other race or nation! Proof that we are entitled to be the masters of America!" Sensing "a menace to American democracy," Clark changes into Superman and leaps onto the field to find out "just how superior you **really** are!" Superman proves that Americans are not so inferior after all, hurling the Dukalian shotput champion farther than his record throw, lifting the pole-vault champion over his record height, dragging the sprint champion on a two-second hundred-yard dash, and carrying the hurdler champion over the whole course with one great leap. Finally, with total disregard for the niceties of diplomacy, he seizes Wolff and deposits him on top of a flagpole. But the Man of Steel is not finished. After some top-notch spy work, he foils a Dukalian plot to use their newest weapon, an invisible submarine that is also capable of flight, to blow up the Panama Canal.

Superman's subversive spirit was gone, not to return until the more permissive 1960s. He had always illustrated some elements of the conservative American tradition, but social, political, and economic pressures forced him to jettison any controversial or divisive story lines. Gone were the socially incendiary plots of his first few years, replaced by patriotic stories that never opposed the status quo. He exchanged his class-based social vision for one that stressed the unified agenda of all Americans, neatly folding himself into the middle-class tradition of imagining a classless and essentially homogenous society. He also accepted the mainstream's insistence that America was a special and unique nation with a divinely granted mission to spread its ideals around the globe. Superman faced a career crisis in the early 1940s. He could preserve his original principles and remain condemned to the fringes of American culture, or abandon his convictions and join the cultural center by becoming middle class. His continuing presence provides ample evidence of his ultimate decision and demonstrates the coercive power of the middlebrow tradition in American life.

Study Questions

1. What social and economic conditions best describe America when the Superman character was introduced to the American public?

2. What does the age of Superman's creators and audience reveal about the impact of the Great Depression on young America?

3. What attributes of American society did Superman embody?

4. What ailments of American society did Superman strive to correct?

5. The author tells us that Superman changed over the years. Why did he change and what do these changes reflect about American politics, economy, and society from the Great Depression through World War II?

Bibliography

The scholarship on the role of comic books in American society has proliferated over the past few decades. Bradford W. Wright, *Comic Book Nation: The Transformation of Youth Culture in America* (2001) impressively outlines the connections between the genre and one element of American society. For general histories of the comic book in American society, see Joseph Witek, *Comic Book as History* (1989) and Michael Benton, *The Comic Book in America* (1989). Historians are also beginning to examine the role of children in American society. For a good recent overview of the changing place of children in the twentieth century, see Judith Sealander, *The Failed Century of the Child: Governing America's Young in the Twentieth Century* (2003). See also Eric Rauchway, *The Refuge of Affections: Family and American Reform Politics, 1900–1920* (2001).

READING 19

★ ★ ★

Okinawa: Of Mud and Maggots

E. B. Sledge

Okinawa was one of the final steps on the route to Japan. Lying about 330 miles southwest of Japan, the long, narrow island was perfectly situated for what the United States Pacific forces needed: an air and supply base to launch an invasion of the Japanese home islands. It had airfields, harbors, and Japanese defenders determined to give their lives, if necessary, to keep Americans from capturing the island. The Japanese were not the only obstacles for Americans. Like so many other Pacific islands where Americans and Japanese soldiers fought, Okinawa was a hothouse of spiders, mosquitoes, black flies, leeches, lizards, centipedes, crabs, and other small, biting, sucking, and stinging pests. It was a terrain overgrown with ferns, vines, and mushrooming growth, drenched by rain and all but empty of comfort. Battle on such islands was simply terrible, a hellish place of nightmares.

American forces stormed the beaches of Okinawa on Easter Sunday, April 1, 1945. At first the Marine and Army troops encountered limited opposition, but when they reached the defensive Shuri line on the southern end of the island, they faced the full force of the Japanese resistance. The Japanese were dug in, surrounded by valleys and gorges that they used to their advantage. American soldiers literally fought for every yard of territory. Before the battle ended in an American victory, 107,000 Japanese and 15,500 Americans were dead. Those numbers do not even approximate the reality of Okinawa. E. B. Sledge fought there and recounts what the battle was like for the soldiers of the war.

The boundary between the III Amphibious Corps (Marines) and the XXIV Corps (Army) ran through the middle of the main Japanese defensive position on the heights of Shuri. As the Marines moved southward, the 1st Marine Division remained on the left in the III Amphibious Corps' zone of action with the 6th Marine Division on the right. Within the 1st Marine Division's zone of action, the 7th Marines occupied the left flank and the 5th Marines the right. The 1st Marines was in reserve.

Beyond Awacha-Dakeshi, the Marines next faced Wana Ridge. On the other side of Wana Ridge lay Wana Draw, through which meandered the Asato Gawa. Forming the southern high ground above Wana Draw was yet another ridge, this one extending eastward from the city of Naha and rising to the Shuri Heights. This second ridge formed a part of the main Japanese defensive positions, the Shuri Line.

Wana Draw aimed like an arrow from the northwest directly into the heart of the Japanese defenses at Shuri. Within this natural avenue of approach, the Japanese took advantage of every difficult feature of terrain; it couldn't have provided a better opportunity for their defense if they had designed it. The longest and bloodiest ordeal of the battle for Okinawa now faced the men of the 1st Marine Division.

For the attack against Wana on 15 May 1945, the 5th Marines sent 2/5 forward with 3/5 in close support. The 1st Battalion came behind in reserve.

Before 2/5's attack began, we moved into a position behind that battalion. We watched tanks firing 75s and M7s firing 105s thoroughly shell the draw. The tanks received such heavy Japanese fire in return that the riflemen of 2/5 assigned to attack with the tanks had to seek any protection they could in ditches and holes while they covered the tanks from a distance; no man on his feet could have survived the hail of shells the enemy fired at the tanks. And the tanks couldn't move safely beyond the cover the riflemen provided be-

cause of Japanese suicide tank-destroyer teams. Finally, we saw the tanks pull back after suffering some hits. Our artillery and naval gunfire threw a terrific barrage at the Japanese positions around the draw. Shortly after that the tanks withdrew. Then an air strike was made against the draw. The bombardment of the draw seemed very heavy to us, but it wasn't anything compared to what was to become necessary before the draw was taken.

We moved from one position to another behind 2/5 until I was so confused I had no idea where we were. Late in the afternoon, we halted temporarily along a muddy trail running along the treeless slope of a muddy ridge. Marines of 2/5 moved past us going the other direction. Japanese shells whistled across the ridge and burst to the rear. Our artillery roared and swished overhead, the explosions booming and thundering out in the draw across the ridge.

Nearby our regimental Protestant chaplain had set up a little altar made out of a box from which he was administering Holy Communion to a small group of dirty Marines. I glanced at the face of a Marine opposite me as the file halted. He was filthy like all of us, but even through a thickly mudcaked dark beard I could see he had fine features. His eyes were bloodshot and weary. He slowly lowered his light machine gun from his shoulder, set the handle on his toe to keep it off the mud, and steadied the barrel with his hand. He watched the chaplain with an expression of skepticism that seemed to ask, "What's the use of all that? Is it gonna keep them guys from gettin' hit?" That face was so weary but so expressive that I knew he, like all of us, couldn't help but have doubts about his God in the presence of constant shock and suffering. Why did it go on and on? The machine gunner's buddy held the gun's tripod on his shoulder, glanced briefly at the muddy little communion service, and then stared blankly off toward a clump of pines to our rear—as though he hoped to see home back there somewhere.

"Move out," came along their file.

The machine gunner hoisted the heavy weapon onto his shoulder as they went slipping and sliding around a bend in the trail into the gathering dusk.

E. B. Sledge, *With the Old Breed: At Peleliu and Okinawa* (New York: Oxford University Press, 1990).

We were told to spread out, take cover, and await further orders. Some of us found holes. Others scooped out what they could. Soon several Japanese shells exploded not far from me. I heard a shout for a corpsman and then, "Hey, you guys, Doc Caswell got hit!"

I forgot about the shells and felt sick. I ran in the direction of the shout to look for Kent Caswell, praying with every step that he wasn't hurt badly. Several other Marines were already with Doc, and a fellow corpsman was bandaging his neck. Doc Caswell lay back in the foxhole and looked up at me as I bent over him and asked him how he was doing (no doubt a stupid question, but my throat was constricted with grief). He opened his lips to speak, and blood trickled out from between them. I was heartbroken, because I didn't see how he could possibly survive. I feared that vital blood vessels in his neck had been severed by the shell fragments.

"Don't talk Doc, they'll get you outa here, and you'll be OK," I managed to stammer.

"OK you guys, let's get him outa here," the corpsman said as he finished his aid.

As I said so long to Doc and got up to leave, I noticed a cloverleaf of 60mm mortar shells lying on the side of the foxhole. A shell fragment had sliced a gash through the thick black metal endplate. I shuddered as I wondered whether it had passed first through Doc's neck.[1]

Our massive artillery, mortar, naval gunfire, and aerial bombardment continued against Wana Draw on our front and Wana Ridge on our left. The Japanese continued to shell everything and everybody in the area, meeting each tank-infantry attack with a storm of fire. A total of thirty tanks, including four flamethrowers, blasted and burned Wana Draw. Our artillery, heavy mortars, ships' guns, and planes then plastered the enemy positions all over again until the noise and shock made me wonder what it was like to be in a quiet place. We had been under and around plenty of "heavy stuff" at Peleliu, but not on nearly so massive a scale or for such unending periods of time as at Wana. The thunderous American barrages went on and on for hours and then days. In return, the Japanese threw plenty of shells our way. I had a continuous headache I'll never forget. Those thunderous, prolonged barrages imposed on me a sense of stupefaction and dullness far beyond anything I ever had experienced before.

It didn't seem possible for any human being to be under such thunderous chaos for days and nights on end and be unaffected by it—even when most of it was our own supporting weapons, and we were in a good foxhole. How did the Japanese stand up under it? They simply remained deep in their caves until it stopped and then swarmed up to repulse each attack, just as they had done at Peleliu. So our heavy guns and air strikes had to knock down, cave in, or otherwise destroy the enemy's well-constructed defensive positions.

At some time during the fight for Wana Draw, we crossed what I supposed was the draw itself, somewhere near its mouth. To get to that point, we fought for days. I had lost count of how many. Marines of 2/5 had just gone across under fire, while we waited in an open field to move across. We eased up to the edge of the draw to cross in dispersed order. An NCO ordered three men and me to cross at a particular point and to stay close behind the 2/5 troops directly across the draw from us. The other side looked mighty far away. Japanese machine guns were firing down the draw from our left, and our artillery was swishing overhead.

"Haul ass, and don't stop for anything til you get across," said our NCO. (We could see other Marines of our battalion starting across on our right.) He told me to leave my mortar ammo bag and that someone else would bring it. I had the Thompson (submachine gun) slung over my shoulder.

We left the field and slid down a ten-foot embankment to the sloping floor of the draw. My feet hit the deck running. The man ahead of me was a Company K veteran whom I knew well, but the other two were replacements. One I knew by name, but the other not at all. I ran as fast as I

---

[1]Some time later we learned that Doc had survived the trip to the aid station with the stretcher team and that he would live. He returned to his native Texas where he remains one of my most faithful friends from our days in K/3/5.

A U.S. Marine of the 1st Division takes aim and fires with his machine gun at a Japanese sniper as his comrade ducks for cover, during the division's advance to take Wana Ridge near the town of Shuri, on Okinawa, in 1945. (AP Photo)

could, and was glad I was carrying only my Tommy, pistol, and combat pack.

The valley sloped downward toward a little stream and then upward to the ridge beyond. The Japanese machine guns rattled away. Bullets zipped and snapped around my head, the tracers like long white streaks. I looked neither right nor left, but with my heart in my throat raced out, splashed across the little stream, and dashed up the slope to the shelter of a spur of ridge projecting out into the draw to our left. We must have run about three hundred yards or more to get across.

Once behind the spur I was out of the line of machine-gun fire, so I slowed to a trot. The veteran ahead of me and a little to my right slowed

up, too. We glanced back to see where the two new men were. Neither one of them had made more than a few strides out into the draw from the other side. One was sprawled in a heap, obviously killed instantly. The other was wounded and crawling back. Some Marines ran out, crouching low, to drag him to safety.

"Jesus, that was close, Sledgehammer," said the man with me.

"Yeah," I gasped. That was all I could say.

We went up the slope and contacted a couple of riflemen from 2/5.

"We got a kid right over there just got hit. Can you guys get him out?" one of them said. "There's some corpsmen set up in a ravine along the ridge there." He pointed out the location of the casualty and then the dressing station.

We hailed two Company K men coming along the ridge, and they said they would help. One ran back along the ridge to get a stretcher. We other three moved up the ridge and into some brush where we found the wounded Marine. He lay on his back still clutching his rifle. As we came up he said, "Boy, am I glad to see you guys."

"You hit bad?" I asked as I knelt beside him.

"Look out you guys! Nips right over there in the bushes."

I unslung my Tommy and, watching where he indicated the Japanese were, I talked to him. My two buddies knelt beside us with their weapons ready, watching for enemy soldiers through the brush while we waited for the stretcher.

"Where you hit?" I asked the wounded Marine.

"Right here," he said, pointing to the lower right portion of his abdomen.

He was talkative and seemed in no pain—obviously still shocked and dazed from his wound. I knew he would hurt badly soon, because he was hit in a painful area. I saw a smear of blood around a tear in his dungaree trousers, so I unhooked his cartridge belt and then his belt and his trousers to see how serious the wound was. It wasn't the round, neat hole of a bullet, but the gash characteristic of a shell fragment. About two inches long, it oozed a small amount of blood.

"What hit you?" I asked.

"Our company sixty mortars," answered the wounded Marine.

I felt a sharp twinge of conscience and thought some 60mm mortarman in the poor guy's own company fouled up and dropped some short rounds.

Almost as though he had read my thoughts, he continued, "It was my own damn fault I got hit, though. We were ordered to halt back there a way and wait while the mortars shelled this area. But I saw a damn Nip and figured if I got a little closer I could get a clear shot at the sonofabitch. When I got here the mortars came in, and I got hit. Guess I'm lucky it wasn't worse. I guess the Nip slipped away."

"You better take it easy now," I said as the stretcher came up.

We got the young Marine on the stretcher, put his rifle and helmet alongside him, and moved back down the ridge a little way to a corpsman. Several corpsmen were at work in a deep ravine cut into the ridge by erosion. It had sheer walls and a level floor and was perfectly protected. About a dozen wounded, stretcher cases, and walking wounded were there already.

As we set our casualty onto the floor of the ravine, he said, "Thanks a lot you guys; good luck." We wished him luck and a quick trip to the States.

Before we left, I paused and watched the corpsmen a moment. It was admirable how efficiently they handled the wounded, with more coming in continuously as stretcher teams left for evacuation centers with those already given field first-aid.

We split up, moved apart a little, and sought shelter along the slope to await orders. I found a commodius two-man standing foxhole commanding a perfect wide view of the draw for a long distance right and left. It obviously had been used as a defensive position against any movement in the draw and probably had sheltered a couple of Japanese riflemen or perhaps a light machine gunner. The hole was well dug in dry clay soil; the ridge sloped up steeply behind it. But the hole and its surroundings were devoid of any enemy equipment or trash of any kind. There wasn't so much as an empty cartridge case or ammo carton to be seen. But there were enemy tracks in the soft soil thrown out of the hole, tracks of tabi sneakers and hobnail-sole field shoes.

The Japanese had become so security conscious they not only removed their dead when possible but sometimes even picked up their expended "brass" just as we did on a rifle range. Sometimes all we found were blood-stains on the ground where one had been killed or wounded. They removed everything they could when possible to conceal their casualties. But when they removed even empty cartridge cases, and we found only tracks, we got an eerie feeling—as though we were fighting a phantom enemy.

During their battle on the Motobu Peninsula in April, Marines of the 6th Division had seen evidence of increased security consciousness on the part of the Japanese. But we had seen nothing like it on Peleliu, and Guadalcanal veterans had told me nearly every Japanese they "field stripped" had a diary on him. The same was said about Gloucester.

After sitting out another thunderous barrage of friendly artillery fire, the three of us shouldered our weapons and moved along the ridge to rejoin Company K. Once together, our company formed into extended file and headed westward toward the regimental right flank. (I lost track of the date, as we moved about for several days.) The shell-blasted terrain was treeless and increasingly low and flat. We dug in, were shelled off and on, and were thoroughly bewildered as to where we were, other than we were said to be still somewhere in Wana Draw. Shuri loomed to our left front.

About that time Burgin was wounded. He was hit in the back of the neck by a shell fragment. Fortunately, he wasn't killed. Burgin was a Texan and as fine a sergeant as I ever saw. He was a Gloucester veteran whose luck had run out. We would miss him from the mortar section, and were delighted when he returned later after eighteen days of convalescence.

The weather turned cloudy on 21 May, and the rains began. By midnight the drizzle became a deluge. It was the beginning of a ten-day period of torrential rains. The weather was chilly and mud, mud, mud was everywhere. We slipped and slid along the trails with every step we took.

While the 1st Marine Division was fighting the costly, heartbreaking battle against the Wana positions, the 6th Marine Division (on the right and slightly forward) had been fighting a terrible battle for Sugar Loaf Hill. Sugar Loaf and the surrounding pieces of prominent terrain— the Horse Shoe and Half Moon—were located on the main ridge running from Naha to Shuri. Like Wana, they were key Japanese defensive positions in the complex that guarded the Shuri Heights.

During the morning of 23 May, the boundary between the 1st Marine Division and the 6th Marine Division shifted to the right (west) so the latter could rearrange its lines. The 3d Battalion, 5th Marines went into line on the right to take over the extended front.

I remember the move vividly, because we entered the worst area I ever saw on a battlefield. And we stayed there more than a week. I shudder at the memory of it.

We shouldered our weapons and gear and the column telescoped its way circuitously through muddy draws, slipping and sliding along the slopes of barren hills to avoid observation and consequent shelling by the enemy. It rained off and on. The mud got worse the farther we went. As we approached our destination, the Japanese dead, scattered about in most areas since 1 May, became more numerous.

When we had dug in near enemy dead and conditions permitted, we always shoveled soil over them in a vain effort to cut down the stench and to control the swarming flies. But the desperate fighting for ten days against and around Sugar Loaf Hill and the continued, prolonged Japanese artillery and mortar fire had made it impossible for the Marine units there to bury the enemy dead.

We soon saw that it also had been impossible to remove many Marine dead. They lay where they had fallen—an uncommon sight even to the veterans in our ranks. It was a strong Marine tradition to move our dead, sometimes even at considerable risk, to an area where they could be covered with a poncho and later collected by the graves registration people. But efforts to remove many Marines killed in the area we entered had been in vain, even after Sugar Loaf Hill had been captured following days of terrible fighting.

The rains had begun 21 May, almost as soon as Sugar Loaf Hill had been secured by men of the 6th Marine Division. Because of the deep mud, the able-bodied could scarcely rescue and evacuate their wounded and bring up vital ammo and rations. Regrettably, the dead had to wait. It couldn't have been otherwise.

We slogged along through a muddy draw around the base of a knoll. On our left we saw six Marine corpses. They were lying face down against a gentle muddy slope where they apparently had hugged the deck to escape Japanese shells. They were "bunched up"—in a row, side by side, scarcely a foot apart. They were so close together that they probably had all been killed by the same shell. Their browning faces lay against the mud in an even row. One could imagine the words of fear or reassurance that had been passed among them as they lay under the terror of the shelling. Each clutched a rusting rifle, and every sign indicated that those tragic figures were new replacements, fresh to the shock of combat.

The first man's left hand was extended forward, palm down. His fingers clutched the mud in a death grip. A beautiful, shiny gold watch was held in place around the decaying wrist by an elaborate gold metal stretch band. (Most of the men I knew—and myself—wore plain, simple luminous-dial, waterproof, shockproof wristwatches with a plain green cloth wristband.) How strange, I thought, for a Marine to wear a flashy, conspicuous watch while on the front lines, stranger still that some Japanese hadn't slipped out during a dark night and taken it.

As we filed past the dead Marines, each of my buddies turned his head and gazed at the horrible spectacle with an expression that revealed how much the scene inwardly sickened us all.

I had heard and read that combat troops in many wars became hardened and insensitive to the sight of their own dead. I didn't find that to be the case at all with my comrades. The sight of dead Japanese didn't bother us in the least, but the sight of Marine dead brought forth regret, never indifference.

Half Moon Hill

While the artillery swished and whined overhead in both directions, we moved to our new positions in the westernmost extension of Wana Draw. By twos and threes, the Company K men forming the front line eased onto a barren,

muddy, shell-torn ridge named Half Moon Hill and into the foxholes of the company we were relieving. Our mortar section went into place behind a low rise of ground below the ridge and about a hundred yards back of the front lines. The terrain between us and Half Moon was nearly flat. The little elevation behind which we emplaced our guns was so low that when we stood up beside the gun pit, we could see clearly up to the company's forward lines on the ridge.

Readily visible beyond that, to the left front, were the still higher, smoke-shrouded Shuri Heights, the heart of the Japanese defensive system. That ominous and formidable terrain feature was constantly under bombardment of varying intensity from our artillery, heavy mortars, and gunfire support ships. No matter, though. It didn't seem to deter the enemy observers from directing their artillery and heavy mortars in shelling our whole area frequently, every day and every night.

We faced south on Half Moon. A narrow-gauge railroad track lay a short distance to our right and ran south through a flat area between Half Moon and a ridge to our right known as the Horse Shoe. Beyond that it swung westward toward Naha. An officer told us that the ridge to our right (west) and slightly to our rear across the railroad was Sugar Loaf Hill.

Company K was on the right flank of 3/5 and moved up onto the western part of the base of Half Moon. The Japanese still occupied caves in both of the southward-pointing tips of the crescent. The right-flank foxhole of our company was dug on the crest at the western edge of the end of the base of Half Moon. Below it to the right the ridge dropped away to low flat ground.

Our company CP was situated in the sunken railroad bed to the right of our mortar section's position. A nice tarpaulin was stretched over the CP from one side of the railroad embankment to the other. This kept the post snug and dry while torrents of chilly rain kept shivering riflemen, machine gunners, and mortarmen soaked, cold, and miserable day and night in open foxholes. The rain greeted us as we moved into our assigned area.

The almost continuous downpour that started on 21 May turned Wana Draw into a sea of mud and water that resembled a lake. Tanks bogged down and even amtracs could not negotiate the morass. Living conditions on the front lines were pitiful. Supply and evacuation problems were severe. Food, water, and ammunition were scarce. Foxholes had to be bailed out constantly. The men's clothing, shoes, feet, and bodies remained constantly wet. Sleep was nearly impossible. The mental and physical strain took a mounting toll on the Marines.

Making an almost impossible situation worse were the deteriorating bodies of Marines and Japanese that lay just outside the foxholes where they had fallen during the five days of ferocious fighting that preceded Company K's arrival on Half Moon. Each day's fighting saw the number of corpses increase. Flies multiplied, and amoebic dysentery broke out. The men of Company K, together with the rest of the 1st Marine Division, would live and fight in that hell for ten days.

We dispersed our guns and dug gun pits as best we could in the mud. Snafu and I took compass readings and set aiming stakes based on the readings from our observer. As soon as we fired a couple of rounds of HE to register in my gun, it was obvious we had a bad problem with the base plate of our mortar being driven farther into the soft soil with the recoil of each shell. We reasoned the rain would soon stop, however, or if it didn't, a couple of pieces of ammo box under the base plate would hold it firm. What a mistake!

After digging in the gun, registering in on the aiming stakes, and preparing ammo for future use, I had my first opportunity to look around our position. It was the most ghastly corner of hell I had ever witnessed. As far as I could see, an area that previously had been a low grassy valley with a picturesque stream meandering through it was a muddy, repulsive, open sore on the land. The place was choked with the putrefaction of death, decay, and destruction. In a shallow defilade to our right, between my gun pit and the railroad, lay about twenty dead Marines, each on a stretcher and covered to his ankles with a poncho—a commonplace, albeit tragic, scene to every veteran. Those bodies had been placed there to await transport to the rear for burial. At least those dead were covered from the torrents of rain that had made them miserable in life and from the swarms of flies that sought to hasten their decay. But as I looked about, I saw that other Marine dead couldn't be tended properly. The whole area was pocked with shell craters and churned up by explosions. Every crater was half full of water, and many of them held a Marine corpse. The bodies lay pathetically just as they had been killed, half submerged in muck and water, rusting weapons still in hand. Swarms of big flies hovered about them.

"Why ain't them poor guys been covered with ponchos?" mumbled my foxhole buddy as he glanced grimly about with a distraught expression on his grizzled face. His answer came the moment he spoke. Japanese 75mm shells came whining and whistling into the area. We cowered in our hole as they crashed and thundered around us. The enemy gunners on the commanding Shuri Heights were registering their artillery and mortars on our positions. We realized quickly that anytime any of us moved out of our holes, the shelling began immediately. We had a terrible time getting our wounded evacuated through the shell fire and mud without the casualty- and stretcher-bearers getting hit. Thus it was perfectly clear why the Marine dead were left where they had fallen.

Everywhere lay Japanese corpses killed in the heavy fighting. Infantry equipment of every type, U.S. and Japanese, was scattered about. Helmets, rifles, BARs, packs, cartridge belts, canteens, shoes, ammo boxes, shell cases, machine-gun ammo belts, all were strewn around us up to and all over Half Moon.

The mud was knee deep in some places, probably deeper in others if one dared venture there. For several feet around every corpse, maggots crawled about in the muck and then were washed away by the runoff of the rain. There wasn't a tree or bush left. All was open country.

Shells had torn up the turf so completely that ground cover was nonexistent. The rain poured down on us as evening approached. The scene was nothing but mud; shell fire; flooded craters with their silent, pathetic, rotting occupants; knocked-out tanks and amtracs; and discarded equipment—utter desolation.

The stench of death was overpowering. The only way I could bear the monstrous horror of it all was to look upward away from the earthly reality surrounding us, watch the leaden gray clouds go skudding over, and repeat over and over to myself that the situation was unreal—just a nightmare—that I would soon awake and find myself somewhere else. But the everpresent smell of death saturated my nostrils. It was there with every breath I took.

I existed from moment to moment, sometimes thinking death would have been preferable. We were in the depths of the abyss, the ultimate horror of war. During the fighting around the Umurbrogol Pocket on Peleliu, I had been depressed by the wastage of human lives. But in the mud and driving rain before Shuri, we were surrounded by maggots and decay. Men struggled and fought and bled in an environment so degrading I believed we had been flung into hell's own cesspool.

Not long after 3/5 took over Half Moon, several of us were on a work party, struggling through knee-deep mud to bring ammo from the rear up to the mortar positions. We passed near the company CP in the railroad bed.

"Hey, you guys, looka there; Stumpy's in bad shape!" said a Marine in an excited low voice. We all stopped and looked toward the CP. There was our CO, Stumpy Stanley, just outside the edge of the tarpaulin, trying to stand by himself. But he had to be supported by a man on each side. He looked haggard and weary and was shaking violently with malarial chills. He could barely hold up his head. The men supporting him seemed to be arguing with him. He was objecting as best he could. But it was a feeble effort, because he was so sick.

"Po' Stumpy got that goddamn bug so bad he can't hardly stand up. But looka there; he's all man, by God. He don't wanna be 'vacuated,'" said Snafu gravely.

"He's a damn good Joe," someone else said.

We thought highly of Stumpy and respected him greatly. He was a good skipper, and we had confidence in him. But malaria made him too ill to stay on his feet. The chilly rain, the emotional stress, and the physical exertion and strain of those days were enough to make a well man collapse. Obviously those who had malarial infections couldn't possibly keep going. So, for the second time in May, we lost our commanding officer. Stumpy was the last of our Peleliu officers, and his evacuation ended an era for me. He was the last tie to Capt. Andy Haldane. For me, Company K was never the same after that day.

As we feared, Shadow became the CO. It's best that I don't record what we said about that.

At daybreak the morning after we took over the line on Half Moon, George Sarrett and I went up onto the ridge to our observation post. Half Moon was shaped like a crescent, with the arms pointing southward. Our battalion line stretched along the crest of the ridge as it formed the base of the crescent. The arms extended outward beyond our front lines, and Japanese occupied caves in the reverse slopes of those arms, particularly the one on the left (east). They made our line a hot spot.

To our front, the ridge sloped down sharply from the crest then more gently all the way to a big road embankment approximately three hundred yards out and running parallel to our lines. A large culvert opened toward us through the embankment. The area to our front was well drained and as bare as the back of one's hand. It wasn't heavily cratered. Two shallow ditches about fifty yards apart ran across the area between the southern tips of the Half Moon. These ditches were closer to the road embankment than to our lines. The sloping area leading to the culvert resembled an amphitheater bordered by the base of the crescent (where we were) to the north, the arms of the crescent extending southward, and the high road embankment running east and west at the southern end. Our visibility within the amphitheater was perfect (except for the reverse slopes of the arms of the crescent).

Marines of 2/4 had warned us as they departed that the Japanese came out of the caves in the reverse slopes of the crescent's arms at night and generally raised hell. To combat that, our ships kept star shells aloft, and our 60mm mortars kept flares burning in the wet sky above the ridge all night every night we were there.

As the dawn light grew brighter, we could see the lay of the land through the drizzle and thin fog. So we registered the mortar section's three guns with an aiming stake on one of each of three important terrain features. We had one gun register in on the reverse slope of the left-hand extension of the Half Moon. A second mortar we registered on the reverse slope of the road embankment. We registered the third gun to cover the area around the mouth of the culvert.

No sooner had we registered the guns than we got a reaction. Big 90mm Japanese mortar shells began crashing along the crest of the ridge. They came so thick and so fast we knew an entire enemy mortar section was firing on us, not an isolated gun. They were zeroed in on the ridge and traversed along the crest from my left to the far right end of the company's line. It was an awful pounding. Each big shell fluttered and swished down and went off with a flash and an ear-splitting crash. Shrapnel growled through the air, and several men were wounded badly. Each shell threw stinking mud around when it exploded. The wounded were moved down behind the ridge with great difficulty because of the slippery, muddy slopes. A corpsman gave them aid, and they were carried to the rear—shocked, torn, and bleeding.

An uneasy quiet then settled along the line. Suddenly, someone yelled, "There goes one." A single Japanese soldier dashed out of the blackness of the culvert. He carried his bayoneted rifle and wore a full pack. He ran into the open, turned, and headed for shelter behind the tip of the southern end of the crescent arm on our left front. It looked as though he had about a thirty-yard dash to make. Several of our riflemen and BARmen opened up, and the soldier was bowled over by their bullets before he reached the shelter of the ridge. Our men cheered and yelled when he went down.

As the day wore on, more Japanese ran out of the culvert in ones and twos and dashed for the shelter of the same ridge extension. It was obvious they wanted to concentrate on the reverse slope there from where they could launch counterattacks, raids, and infiltration attempts on our front line. Obviously, it was to our best interest to stop them as quickly as possible. Any enemy soldier who made it in behind that slope might become one's unwelcome foxhole companion some night.

When the Japanese ran out of the culvert, our men fired on them and nearly always knocked them down. The riflemen, BARmen, and machine gunners looked on it as fine target practice, because we received no return small-arms fire, and the Japanese mortars were quiet.

I kept busy with the field glasses, observing, adjusting range, and calling fire orders onto the slope and the road embankment. I had the Tommy with me, but it wasn't as steady and accurate at the two- to three-hundred-yard range as an M1 Garand rifle. We had an M1 and an ammo belt in our OP, though, and I wanted to throw down that phone and the field glasses and grab up that M1 every time an enemy popped into view. As long as our mortar section was firing a mission, I had no choice but to continue observing.

The Japanese kept up their efforts to move behind the slope. Some made it, because our men missed them. Our 60mm mortar shells crashed away steadily on the target areas. We could see Japanese emerge from the culvert and be killed by our shells.

The longer this action continued without our receiving any return fire, the more relaxed my buddies became. The situation began to take on certain aspects of a rifle range, or more likely, an old-fashioned turkey shoot. My buddies started making bets about who had hit which Japanese. Lively arguments developed, but with rifles, BARs and several machine guns firing simultaneously, no one could tell for sure who hit which enemy soldier.

The men yelled and joked more and more in one of their few releases from weeks of tension under the pounding of heavy weapons. So they began to get careless and to miss some of the

Japanese scurrying for the slope. Shadow saw this. He ran up and down our firing line cursing and yelling at everybody. Then the men settled down and took more careful aim. Finally the enemy stopped coming, and I received orders to call "cease firing" to our mortars. We sat and waited.

During the lull, I moved over into the machine-gun emplacement next to our mortar OP to visit with the gunner. It contained a Browning .30 caliber water-cooled heavy machine gun manned by a gunner who had joined Company K as a replacement after Peleliu. On Pavuvu, he and I had become good friends. We called him "Kathy" after a chorus girl he knew in California. He was married and very much in love with his wife, so he bore a heavy burden of guilt because he had had an affair with Kathy on his way overseas and couldn't get her out of his mind.

As we sat alone in the machine-gun pit, he asked me whether I wanted to see a picture of Kathy. I said yes. He carefully and secretively picked up his rain-soaked combat pack and took out a waterproof plastic map holder. Folding back the canvas cover, he said, "Here she is."

My eyes nearly popped out of my head. The eight- by ten-inch photo was a full-length portrait of one of the most beautiful girls I ever saw. She was dressed, or undressed, in a scanty costume which exposed a good portion of her impressive physical endowments.

I gasped audibly, and "Kathy" said, "Isn't she a beauty?"

"She really is!" I told him, and added, "You've got a problem on your hands with a girl like that chorus girl and a wife you love." I kidded him about the possible danger of getting the letters to his wife and his girl crossed up and in the wrong envelopes. He just laughed and shook his head as he looked at the photo of the beautiful girl.

The scene was so unreal I could barely believe it: two tired, frightened young men sitting in a hole beside a machine gun in the rain on a ridge, surrounded with mud—nothing but stinking mud, with so much decaying human flesh buried or half buried in it that there were big patches of wriggling fat maggots marking the spots where Japan-ese corpses lay—looking at the picture of a beautiful seminude girl. She was a pearl in a mudhole.

Viewing that picture made me realize with a shock that I had gradually come to doubt that there really was a place in the world where there were no explosions and people weren't bleeding, suffering, dying, or rotting in the mud. I felt a sense of desperation that my mind was being affected by what we were experiencing. Men cracked up frequently in such places as that. I had seen it many times by then. In World War I they had called it shell shock or, more technically, *neuresthenia.* In World War II the term used was combat fatigue.

Strange that such a picture provoked such thoughts, but I vividly recall grimly making a pledge to myself. The Japanese might kill or wound me, but they wouldn't make me crack up. A peaceful civilian back home who sat around worrying about losing his mind probably didn't have much to occupy him, but in our situation there was plenty of reason for the strongest-willed individuals to crack up.

My secret resolve helped me through the long days and nights we remained in the worst of the abyss. But there were times at night during that period when I felt I was slipping. More than once my imagination ran wild during the brief periods of darkness when the flares and star shells burned out.

"There comes another one," somebody yelled. "Kathy" quickly stowed his picture in his pack, spun around, gripped the machine-gun handle in his left hand, poised his trigger finger, and grabbed the aiming knob with his right hand. His assistant gunner appeared from out of nowhere and jumped to his post to feed the ammo belt into the gun. I started back to the OP hole but saw that George had phone in hand, and the mortars were still "secured." So I grabbed up an M1 rifle "Kathy" had in the machine-gun emplacement.

I saw enemy soldiers rushing out of the culvert. Our line started firing as I counted the tenth Japanese to emerge. Those incredibly brave soldiers formed a skirmish line abreast, with a few yards between each other, and started trotting silently toward us across open ground about three hundred yards away. Their effort was admirable but so hopeless. They had no supporting fire of any kind to pin us down or even to make us cautious. They looked as though they were on maneuvers. They had no chance of getting close to us.

I stood up beside the machine gun, took aim, and started squeezing off shots. The Japanese held their rifles at port arms and didn't even fire at us. Everybody along our line was yelling and firing. The enemy soldiers wore full battle gear with packs, which meant they had rations and extra ammo, so this might be the beginning of a counterattack of some size.

Within seconds, eight of the ten enemy soldiers pitched forward, spun around, or slumped to the deck, dead where they fell. The remaining two must have realized the futility of it all, because they turned around and started back toward the culvert. Most of us slackened our fire and just watched. Several men kept firing at the two retreating enemy soldiers but missed, and it looked as though they might get away. Finally one Japanese fell forward near one of the shallow ditches. The surviving soldier kept going.

Just as "Kathy" got his machine-gun sights zeroed in on him, the order "cease firing" came along the line. But the machine gun was making so much noise we didn't hear the order. "Kathy" had his ammo belts loaded so that about every fifth cartridge was a tracer. He squeezed off a long burst of about eight shots. The bullets struck the fleeing Japanese soldier in the middle of his pack and tore into him between his shoulders.

I was standing directly behind "Kathy," looking along his machine-gun barrel. The tracers must have struck the man's vertebrae or other bones and been deflected, because I clearly saw one tracer flash up into the air out of the soldier's right shoulder and another tracer come out of the top of his left shoulder. The Japanese dropped his rifle as the slugs knocked him face down into the mud. He didn't move.

"I got him; I got the bastard." Kathy yelled, jumping around slapping me on the back, and

shaking hands with his assistant gunner. He had reason to be proud. He had made a good shot.

The enemy soldier who fell near the ditch began crawling and flopped into it. Some of the men started firing at him again. The bullets kicked up mud all around the soldier as he slithered desperately along in the shallow ditch which didn't quite hide him. Machine-gun tracers ricocheted off the ground like vicious red arrows as the Japanese struggled along the shallow ditch.

Then, on one of the rare occasions I ever saw compassion expressed for the Japanese by a Marine who had to fight them, one of our men yelled, "Knock it off, you guys. The poor bastard's already hit and ain't got a snowball's chance in hell."

Someone else yelled angrily, "You stupid jerk; he's a goddamn Nip ain't he? You gone Asiatic or something?"

The firing continued, and bullets hit the mark. The wounded Japanese subsided into the muddy little ditch. He and his comrades had done their best. "They died gloriously on the field of honor for the emperor," is what their families would be told. In reality, their lives were wasted on a muddy, stinking slope for no good reason.

Our men were in high spirits over the affair, especially after being pounded for so long. But Shadow was yelling, "Cease firing, you dumb bastards." He came slipping and sliding along the line, cursing and stopping at intervals to pour out storms of invective on some smiling, muddy Marine. He carried his helmet in his left hand and periodically took off his cap and flung it down into the mud until it was caked. Each man looked glum and sat or stood motionless until Shadow had finished insulting him and moved on.

As Shadow passed the machine-gun pit, he stopped and screamed at "Kathy," who was still jumping around in jubilation over his kill. "Knock it off, you goddamn fool!" Then he glared at me and said, "You're supposed to be observing for the mortars; put that goddamn rifle down, you bastard."

I wasn't impetuous, but, had I thought I could get away with it, I would certainly have clubbed him over the head with that M1 rifle.

I didn't, but Shadow's asinine conduct and comment did make me rash enough to say, "The guns are secured, sir. We were all sent out here to kill Nips, weren't we? So what difference does it make what weapon we use when we get the chance?"

His menacing expression turned into surprise and then doubt. With a quizzical look on his face, he cocked his head to one side as he pondered my remark, while I stood silently with the realization that I should have kept my mouth shut. The fine sergeant accompanying Shadow half glared and half smiled at me. Suddenly, without another glance, Shadow strode off along the ridge crest, cursing and yelling at the Marines in each foxhole as he passed them. I resolved to keep my mouth shut in the future.

As daylight waned, I looked out to our front through the drizzling rain falling through the still, foul air. A wisp of smoke rose straight up from the pack of the Japanese soldier "Kathy" had shot. The tracers had set something on fire. The thin finger of smoke rose high and then spread out abruptly to form a disc that appeared to rest on the column. So delicate and unreal, the smoke stood in the stagnant, fetid air like a marker over the corpse. Everything out there was motionless, only death and desolation among the enemy bodies.

George and I got orders to return to our mortar gun pits. Someone else would man the OP for the night. Getting back to the mortar emplacements from the company's front line was a major effort and an extremely dangerous one. From the moment we stepped to the rear of the crest of the ridge to descend the muddy slope, it was like trying to walk down a greased slide.

A large and unknown number of Japanese all over the ridge had been killed during the early counterattacks. They had been covered with soil as soon as possible. And Japanese were still being killed out front. Infiltrators also were being killed all along the ridge at night. Our men could only spade mud over them.

The situation was bad enough, but when enemy artillery shells exploded in the area, the eruptions of soil and mud uncovered previously buried Japanese dead and scattered chunks of corpses. Like the area around our gun pits, the ridge was a stinking compost pile.

If a Marine slipped and slid down the back slope of the muddy ridge, he was apt to reach the bottom vomiting. I saw more than one man lose his footing and slip and slide all the way to the bottom only to stand up horror-stricken as he watched in disbelief while fat maggots tumbled out of his muddy dungaree pockets, cartridge belt, legging lacings, and the like. Then he and a buddy would shake or scrape them away with a piece of ammo box or a knife blade.

We didn't talk about such things. They were too horrible and obscene even for hardened veterans. The conditions taxed the toughest I knew almost to the point of screaming. Nor do authors normally write about such vileness; unless they have seen it with their own eyes, it is too preposterous to think that men could actually live and fight for days and nights on end under such terrible conditions and not be driven insane. But I saw much of it there on Okinawa and to me the war was insanity.

Study Questions

1. What tactics did the Japanese use to hide casualties, and what was its psychological impact on U.S. soldiers?

2. How did the author and other American soldiers cope with the dead and wounded—both Japanese and American?

3. What impact did the island's geography and weather conditions have on the mentality of soldiers?

4. How had the fighting near Sugar Loaf Hill and Half Moon Hill changed the landscape?

5. How do you explain the difference in soldier attitudes between times of combat and periods of lull in battle?

6. What different ways did soldiers resolve to remember life back home in the states?

7. What attitudes did soldiers hold toward the enemy?

Bibliography

This piece first appeared in E. B. Sledge, *With the Old Breed: At Peleliu and Okinawa* (1981). John W. Dower, *War Without Mercy: Race and Power in the Pacific War* (1986), details the feelings of soldiers who fought in the Pacific. Hiromichi Yahara, *The Battle for Okinawa* (1997), is the personal account from a Japanese soldier and provides an interesting counterpoint to Sledge. John Frayn Turner, ed., *Fight for the Sea: Naval Adventures from World War II* (2001), is a collection of American reminiscences of the war in the Pacific. Other good personal narratives and firsthand accounts of World War II are Studs Terkel, ed., *The Good War: An Oral History of World War Two* (1984); and Jack Stenbuck, ed., *Typewriter Battalion: Dramatic Front-Line Dispatches from World War II* (1995). For a general overview of the battles for Iwo Jima and Okinawa, see Roy Appleman, *Okinawa: The Last Battle* (1948); and Robert Leckie, *Okinawa: The Last Battle of World War II* (1995). John Keegan, *The Second World War* (1989), is an excellent place to begin study of World War II.

★ ★ ★

America in the Age of
Anxiety: 1945-1960

The fallout of Hiroshima lasted many years. The most immediate result of the atomic bombs that America dropped on Japan on August 6 and August 9, 1945, was the end of World War II. V-J Day was celebrated with an emotional outpouring of relief. Most Americans believed that the United States had saved the world from the totalitarian threat of the Axis Powers. They also assumed that America would now return to its traditional foreign policy posture of isolationism. Such was not the case. World War II had made the United States the most powerful country in the world. Retreat into isolationism was impossible. During the next few years, America accepted the responsibilities that went with being a world power and replaced Great Britain as the globe's police force.

Almost as soon as the war was over, the Soviet Union emerged as America's leading rival. Joseph Stalin, Russia's leader, was by nature suspicious, and the complexities and uncertainties of Soviet politics made him even more so. He resented America and Great Britain for delaying the second front against Germany during World War II. He was also upset that the United States refused to share its nuclear secrets with the Soviet Union. Fears, anxieties, and ambitions degenerated into a new type of power conflict. Called the Cold War, the object was to control, either through economic or military means, as much of the world as possible.

America originated the policy of containment as a strategy for the Cold War. The policy was essentially defensive in nature, and it forced America to react to Soviet movements. Although the policy scored several notable successes—particularly in Turkey, Greece, and Western Europe—it had a number of real weaknesses. Most important, it committed American troops to prevent the expansion of Communism. In Korea and later in Vietnam, Americans came to understand the limitations and constraints of the containment doctrine.

The Cold War and the fear of a nuclear confrontation shaped domestic politics as well as foreign affairs. If Americans distrusted Stalin's motives, they also questioned the actions of their own leaders. They asked pointed and complex questions, yet sought simple answers. Why had Stalin gained so much territory at Yalta? How was Russia able to develop its own atomic weapons so rapidly? Who lost China? Politicians such as Senator Joseph McCarthy of Wisconsin and Congressman Richard Nixon of California provided easy answers. They said that Communist sympathizers in the American government had worked to ensure the success of the Soviet Union. The publicity lavished on the trials of Alger Hiss and Julius and Ethel Rosenberg and the activities of McCarthy and the House Un-American Activities Committee increased the public's distrust of its own officials.

In the following section, the essays deal with the fallout of Hiroshima and the Cold War. Although they examine very different subjects—race questions, sexual anxieties, cigarette smoking, and television scandals—they contain a unifying theme. They all discuss Americans' attitudes toward themselves. The underlying assumption was that something deep and troubling was happening, that the American character had changed for the worse. The search for exactly what was wrong took many different turns and helped illuminate the psychological, cultural, and social landscape of the 1950s.

READING 20

★ ★ ★

The Man Who Changed His Skin

Ernest Sharpe, Jr.

For millions of African Americans the early 1960s were years of pain mixed with glimpses of promise. Compared to white Americans, they faced a grim set of statistics. The 1960 census reported that African Americans died seven years younger than did white Americans, had half the chance of completing high school, one-third the chance of finishing college, and one-third the chance of entering a profession. On the average, African Americans earned half as much as whites and were twice as likely to be unemployed. Yet events like the *Brown v. The Board of Education* decision, the Montgomery bus boycott, and the various Freedom Rides, "sit-ins," "wade-ins," "pray-ins," and "apply-ins" sent the message that the time to change was at hand. For demanding no more than what was guaranteed them by the Constitution of the United States and a general sense of decency, African Americans were hosed, set on by dogs, arrested, beaten, and even murdered, yet they continued their march toward justice.

How ironic then, with so many examples of injustice and inhumanity toward African Americans, that many white Americans had to be told by another white American what it was like to be black. In 1959 John Howard Griffin chemically darkened his skin, shaved his head, and traveled through the heart of Dixie as a black man. He experienced humiliations large and small, occasionally feared for his life, and came to know racism on very personal terms. After a few months he returned to his white world and wrote a book about his experiences. Published in 1961, *Black Like Me* became a national sensation, selling over five million copies, angering millions of white Americans and opening the eyes of millions more. On television shows and radio programs, Griffin heard variations of the same line by whites: "I never knew what it was like to be black."

Probably Griffin never did either. In "The Man Who Changed His Skin," Ernest Sharpe, Jr. explores the life of the unusual man who passed for a brief time as black.

On a sunny November day in 1959, a tall, brown-haired Texan entered the home of a New Orleans friend. Five days later an unemployed, bald black man walked out. The name of both was John Howard Griffin, and the journey he began that Louisiana evening was to take him to a country farther than any he had ever been in, one bordered only by the shade of its citizens' skin.

For four weeks Griffin, his skin chemically darkened, posed as an itinerant black. He wandered the South, hitchhiking, seeking work, and talking and listening to people black and white. His journal of those weeks became a series of magazine articles and then a book, *Black Like Me.* In passionate first-person prose it brought home to millions of American whites the misery and injustice daily endured by American blacks. It opened eyes and seized hearts and changed minds.

It also changed lives, including Griffin's own. Abandoning a promising literary career, he devoted the next eight years to the civil rights movement. He saw authorship of a single book eclipse all his other achievements. He became for the rest of his life the man who had turned himself black. But *Black Like Me* was only the most prominent event in a life filled with drama and transformation. By the time of his death, in 1980, Griffin had left behind the sloughed skins of a dozen careers and identifies. Born to a middle-class Dallas family, he was schooled in France, where he joined in the soirées of European aesthetes and aristocrats. He served in the French Resistance and soldiered in the South Pacific, where he lived for a year as an aborigine islander. He converted to Catholicism, and he thirsted for a life of prayer and chastity even while he wrote a novel banned in Detroit for its sexual explicitness. He lost his sight, lived for ten years as a blind man, and then miraculously recovered his vision. He was a musical scholar, a religious intellectual, a working journalist, a live-

stock breeder, a professional photographer, a social activist, and a controversial novelist.

And, of course, for a few weeks in 1959 he was a black man.

Griffin was a product of two disparate cultures, Texan and French, and was never totally at home in either. He was born on June 16, 1920, the second of four children. His father was a religious, hardworking wholesale-grocery salesman utterly devoted to his refined, delicate wife. Years later Griffin recalled waking each morning to the sound of his mother practicing the piano sonatas of Mozart and Schubert and Bach preludes and fugues.

When Griffin was fifteen, he came upon a magazine ad for the Lycée Descartes, a boarding school in France, and wrote to the headmaster begging for admission. He had no money, he confessed, but he would do anything to pay his way, even scrub floors. Several weeks later a reply came back: If the young man wanted to learn so badly, he was by all means welcome. Griffin presented the letter to his flabbergasted parents; they responded predictably, but he was already a person of considerable will, and he was soon aboard an ocean liner.

Griffin was a gifted student. He graduated from the lycée, then stayed in France to study medicine and the humanities. He spent his seventeenth summer at the country home of a wealthy French family. Evenings he played Ravel, Debussy, and Schubert on the phonograph or lay in bed reading Balzac, Gide, and Rabelais.

By the spring of 1939 his future seemed bright. Having decided on a career in psychiatry, he began work after his first year of medical school as an "extern" at the Tours insane asylum. A student of religious music, he conducted experiments using Gregorian chants as therapy for patients considered beyond cure. Then, in September, Germany invaded Poland. France declared war, and virtually all the medical staff at the asylum was immediately conscripted. Griffin was placed in charge of the hospital's female wing, responsible, along with eight nuns, for 120 patients. He was nineteen years old.

It was a harrowing time. He was often dragged from his bed to treat wounded soldiers trucked

"The Man Who Changed His Skin" by Ernest Sharpe, Jr. in *American Heritage,* Vol. 40/No. 1, February 1989, pp. 44–55. Reprinted by permission of *American Heritage* Magazine, a division of Forbes, Inc. © Forbes, Inc., 1989.

from the front. German and Austrian Jews began trickling into the city; officially enemy aliens, many did not speak French and most lacked safe-conduct papers. As the French fell back, the young American volunteered to help the refugees. He strapped them into strait-jackets and smuggled them in an asylum ambulance to the port of St.-Nazaire for passage to England. Their faces haunted him: he never forgot the encounter with racism.

After the French surrender in 1940, Griffin himself fled. He returned to the United States and joined the Army Air Corps. Leaving for what would become a three-year stint in the Pacific, he stuffed his duffel bag full of books by Molière and Racine and scores by Mozart and Beethoven. His initial assignments were light. For a while he served as a disc jockey, broadcasting classical concerts to front-line troops. Bored, he volunteered for a post on a remote island, to set up liaison in the event of an American occupation.

He lived on Nuni, as the natives called it, for a year. His charge was not only to learn the local tongue but to gain the islanders' trust. To do so, he became one of them: fishing with the men, chewing betel nut, observing tribal customs and ceremonies, and even taking a wife. "They were one of the few truly primitive tribes left in the world," he later wrote, "in a land where there was no sense of time or goal." But life there was far from innocent. Behind the apparent languor Griffin discovered a harsh existence where children sometimes perished in brutal rites of initiation. When his year was up, he was ready to leave.

He was reassigned to Morotai, a tiny spot of land in the Moluccas close to several islands held by the Japanese. Manning the radar tent there alone one night, he was caught in an air raid and artillery barrage. He described the scene in his unpublished autobiography: "A shell shrieked downward and I threw myself to the ground. . . . The shell exploded nearby and shrapnel whizzed unseen around me. Relief and exhaustion overwhelmed my senses. . . . I wanted to lie still and rest, to ignore some gigantic urgency in the atmosphere. A new wave

of mortars, ackack explosions and shell screeches swept toward me. I hurried to my feet to run ahead of it." He didn't make it; knocked unconscious, he was at first taken for dead by medics and later rescued by an alert burial crew.

Griffin regained consciousness, apparently suffering from nothing worse than a concussion, and except for sensitivity to light and difficulty reading his mail, he quickly recovered. Sick of the service and fearful of a prolonged hospital stay, he kept his vision problems to himself. Back in the United States he was given a last physical, including a cursory eye exam. Unable to make out the results on his discharge papers, he asked another soldier to read them to him. He was staggered to learn that his vision was 20/200. He was legally blind.

He soon realized that his blindness would be more than legal. He was losing his sight completely. Specialists were unable to help; he had apparently suffered some kind of brain damage. They outfitted him with thick, dark spectacles, but they weren't strong enough. Wanting to hide his affliction, he took to reading with the help of a small, easily hidden magnifying glass.

Medicine was obviously no longer a viable profession, so in 1946 Griffin returned to France to pursue a career as a musicologist. He spent the summer at the conservatory at Fontainebleau. Each day his eyes were a little worse, but still he told no one: "I felt that losing my sight was a thing I had to do alone."

In the fall he left for Paris to visit an old school friend who had become a monk in a Dominican convent. At first he found the monastery dismal, reeking of "the odors of cabbages and onions and mop water," but distaste gradually turned to respect, and respect to reverence. "The poverty of my unlighted cell warmed with delight," he wrote. "I had imagined that men seeking union with God more or less languished in a state of mystical trauma, soaring above the baser aspects of their own daily living. But here men lived in intimacy with the things of the earth—cold, fasting, labor. . . . I saw they were men like me. I lived with them, saw them bleary-eyed at dawn, smelled them sweating after labors, and yet sanctity lay there within them."

It was to be five years before Griffin left the Episcopal Church for the Catholic, but by the time he departed the Couvent St. Jacques he was already very much converted. Moreover, he had discovered a part of himself that yearned for the devotional solitude of a monastic life. In the years to come he would often retreat to the sanctuary of monastery walls.

From Paris Griffin went to the Abbey of Solesmes, to research medieval church music. When he returned to the United States in the spring of 1947, he was twenty-six and totally blind. He was also engaged. During his year in France he had fallen in love with a woman several years his senior named Françoise Longuet.

The two faced obvious obstacles; the first was Griffin's physical helplessness. Françoise decided to remain in France for the time being. Back in Texas Griffin and his parents escaped the city's noise and hazardous traffic by moving to a farm outside Mansfield, a small town near Fort Worth. To earn an income, Griffin turned from musicology to animal husbandry. After some tutoring by teachers at Texas A&M, he purchased four Ohio Improved Chester sows and began breeding them. He also began tutoring local children in advanced piano. One of his first students was the thirteen-year-old daughter of a local insurance agent, Clyde Holland. Elizabeth Holland—"Piedy" to friends and family—was already a talented pianist. She proved an apt pupil and was soon a regular visitor to the Griffin farm.

By 1949 Griffin was earning a respectable income as a breeder of prize livestock, but his yeoman days were already numbered. That spring he met the New York drama critic John Mason Brown, who was in Texas on a lecture tour. Brown suggested that Griffin try his hand at writing; he certainly talked like a writer. Griffin, intrigued, asked how he should start. You get some paper and write, Brown curtly replied. Griffin did just that, converting a room in the barn behind his parents' house into an office. It was a cramped space, "about three long steps each way," but it

suited Griffin's anchoritic temperament. It also suited his subject, a novel about a young American man studying Gregorian chant in a French monastery. Neglecting his hogs, Griffin sometimes worked all night, dictating in French on a wire recorder and later transcribing his dictation in English on his mother's ancient Underwood. In seven weeks he had completed a first draft and launched a new career for himself.

He had also precipitated a series of events that eventually changed the law of the land. He called the book *The Devil Rides Outside,* borrowing from a French proverb: "The devil rides outside the monastery walls." The six-hundred-page novel is a study of the struggle between faith and temptation, a raw, sprawling work that seems to have sprouted like a mushroom in the garden of Texas letters. In 1981 the novelist Larry McMurtry wrote of it as "a strange, strong book whose verbal energy . . . still seems remarkable after almost 30 years. In the mostly all-too-healthy and sunlit world of Texas fiction, the book remains an anomaly, dark, feverish, introverted, claustrophobic, tortured."

Issued by a fledgling Fort Worth publisher, *The Devil Rides Outside* received surprising attention for a first novel by an unknown. Reviews were mixed. "Most of the novel's sound and fury is bound up with the medieval notion that sex is the domain of Satan," complained the *Atlantic Monthly,* but the noted literary critic Maxwell Geismar was impressed. He called the book one of the best novels of the decade and dubbed its author "a Texas Balzac."

The Legion for Decent Literature, a Catholic organization, succeeded in getting *The Devil Rides Outside* banned in Detroit on the grounds that it was unfit for children and adolescents. While little in the book would shock a contemporary reader, the novel was daring for the fifties. It contains a pair of passages that describe in exactly the same language sexual climax and spiritual rapture.

Postwar censorship laws were a welter of local and state statutes, many of which, despite the historic 1934 circuit court ruling on *Ulysses,* still banned whole works based on isolated passages.

In the spring of 1954 the book's paperback publisher, Pocket Books, arranged to challenge the Detroit ban. A bookstore manager was arrested for selling a copy to a police inspector; the court convicted, the bookseller appealed, and *Butler v. Michigan* began a two-and-a-half-year march to the Supreme Court.

Despite the praise and attention, the fall of 1952 found the thirty-two-year-old Griffin utterly miserable. After six years of delay Françoise had bitterly broken their engagement. In his grief he received solace from an unexpected source, Piedy Holland, now a seventeen-year-old high school senior. Despite Griffin's disability and the gap in their ages, the two found themselves increasingly drawn to each other. After a genteel courtship of several months, he proposed to Piedy at midnight mass on Christmas Eve. She happily accepted, and the two were married the following June after Griffin received dispensation from the Vatican for his Pacific marriage. They moved into a cottage behind the Hollands' house, and Griffin went to work on a second novel.

That fall Griffin noticed a growing numbness in his fingers. The doctor diagnosed malaria, a souvenir of his days in the tropics. The numbness progressed until by December he was not only blind but confined to a wheelchair, effectively paralyzed except in his left arm. He began taking minute doses of strychnine as a stimulant, but the prognosis was uncertain. To compound his troubles, he had been diagnosed as diabetic.

Despite these afflictions, he continued to labor on *Nuni,* a Robinson Crusoe tale of a middle-aged English professor struggling for survival on an island of savages. In his journal he wrote: "I am aware perhaps that I am putting the problems of my life into the lap of Professor Harper and I am desperate for him to solve them. I am stripping him of everything that men generally consider necessary to a man's ability to function at the human level."

Professor Harper overcame his predicament, and so, after a long ordeal, did Griffin. By May 1956, when *Nuni* was published, he was not only fully recovered from the malaria but perhaps

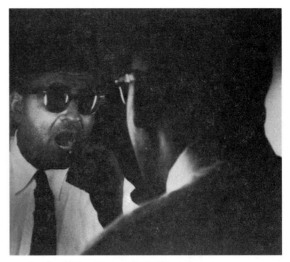

Portrait of John Howard Griffin

more content than he had ever been. *Nuni* was receiving favorable reviews, translations of his first novel were selling well in Europe, and he was close to finishing a third. He was the happy husband of a loving wife and the doting father of two small children. He seemed finally to have achieved a measure of peace.

All that changed one morning the following January. As with everything in his life, he described it in his daily journal:

"Wednesday, four days ago, I was walking to the house for lunch. Redness swirled in front of my eyes. Then I thought I saw the back door, cut in portions, dancing at crazy angles. I stood dumbfounded. Angles continued to dance and there was pain in the eyes and head.

"I stumbled inside, found the telephone. Some how I got the number dialed. I heard my wife's voice.

"'I think . . .' I began, and then collapsed into weeping.

"'What is it? What's happening?' she asked.

"'I think I can see.'" He could. By the time Piedy and the family physician reached the farmhouse, he was able to make out forms and colors. He was euphoric. The sight of his two-year-old daughter was "like looking at the sun—blinding me to everything else."

The strychnine, he was told, had apparently unstopped blocked blood vessels. The flow of blood in turn had unknotted twisted vessels. A month later he wrote to a friend: "We have, on this near-lethal dosage . . . brought my vision to a plu-perfect 20/15 in each eye. I am overwhelmed by details seen with the utmost clarity—every glass flaw, every pebble."

The singularity of his recovery brought Griffin national attention and some local gibes. Many in Mansfield had never taken to Griffin's cosmopolitan background and cultured air, and some suggested that maybe he had never been blind at all. *Time,* echoing the skeptics, reported in its medicine section that Griffin's recovery was unprecedented, but his blindness might have been "mainly, if not entirely, hysterical."

On February 25, 1957, a little more than a month after he regained his sight, the sun broke on Griffin again. The Supreme Court of the United States unanimously struck down the Michigan law banning *The Devil Rides Outside.* Speaking for the Court, Justice Felix Frankfurter wrote, "The state insists that, by thus quarantining the general reading public against books not too rugged for grown men and women in order to shield juvenile innocence it is exercising its power to promote the general welfare. Surely this is to burn the house to roast the pig." The decision effectively reversed an 1868 British ruling that for almost a century had remained the principal guide to Anglo-American jurisprudence on censorship and obscenity.

Moral triumphs do not pay bills, however, and the income from his novels was not enough to support Griffin and his growing family. Several months before his sight returned, he had found employment in Fort Worth as a staff writer at *Sepia,* a black monthly modeled loosely after *Life.* Griffin fit in easily at the magazine, whose publisher, George Levitan, practiced a policy of equal opportunity long before it became a national slogan.

In the fall of 1959 he began research on a piece about the high suicide rate among Southern blacks. He sent out questionnaires to black professionals, but the few who responded simply returned them blank. The article stalled. He vented his frustration on Adelle Martin, the magazine's editorial director. Why wouldn't Negroes trust him? He was on their side. Mrs. Martin, black herself, responded bluntly: Negroes knew that no matter how he tried, he would never understand. The only way he could know what it was like to be a Negro was by being one.

The remark triggered the return of an old, odd thought: If a white man became a Negro in the Deep South, what adjustments would he have to make? A few days later he proposed a series of articles to Levitan. He would dye his skin and travel the South. He wouldn't change his name or hide his background or education. He would still be John Howard Griffin—author, teacher, musicologist—but with one difference: he would be black.

The publisher warned Griffin of the dangers involved, but he couldn't hide his enthusiasm. Go ahead, he told Griffin; *Sepia* would foot the bill. Piedy was less enthusiastic. It sounded dangerous, but if he felt he had to do it, then he should. He would be gone for a month.

Two days later Griffin flew to New Orleans. He arranged to stay at the house of a friend, and the next morning he explained his project to a sympathetic dermatologist. The physician prescribed Oxsoralen, a drug usually used to treat vitiligo, a condition that causes milky patches on the skin. The process would take a couple of months. Griffin explained there wasn't time, so the physician suggested a higher dosage coupled with exposure to a sunlamp; the drug worked through reaction to ultraviolet light. There was some chance of liver damage, but as long as Griffin was monitored through frequent blood tests, he was probably safe.

For four days Griffin lay in his room under a sunlamp, his eyes protected by cotton pads. The Oxsoralen produced lassitude and nausea and didn't entirely work; by the evening of the fourth day his skin was dark but mottled. Determined to see the project through, he touched up the light patches with vegetable dye and then shaved his head. The whole process took hours. Finally he was done.

"Turning off all the lights, I went into the bathroom and closed the door. I stood in the darkness before the mirror, my hand on the light switch. I forced myself to flick it on.

"In the flood of light against white tile, the face and shoulders of a stranger—a fierce, bald, very dark Negro—glared at me from the glass. He in no way resembled me.

"The transformation was total and shocking. I had expected to see myself disguised, but this was something else. I was imprisoned in the flesh of an utter stranger, an unsympathetic one with whom I felt no kinship. All traces of the John Griffin I had been were wiped from existence."

Toting a pair of duffel bags, Griffin stepped out of the house and walked to the corner to catch a streetcar to downtown New Orleans. Trembling, he bought a ticket and moved down the aisle to take a seat in the back. No one gave him a glance. After a few moments he sighed with relief; he had passed the first test of his new identity.

He stayed the night in a shabby hotel, and the next morning he made a confidant of a street-corner shoe shine boy. The "boy," a gray-haired World War I veteran named Sterling Williams, cackled with delight at Griffin's charade. He agreed to let the writer work at his stand for a few days. Then he pointed at the giveaway brown hair on Griffin's hands. Griffin grabbed a razor from his duffel and scurried for the nearest lavatory. In his haste he almost entered a whites' washroom, forgetting he was black even as he rushed to eliminate the last sign of his whiteness.

Griffin worked as a shoe-shine boy for several days, learning when to smile, when to laugh, when to shrug, and when to be silent. One of his earliest lessons was that the friendliest customers were those looking for black women. "When they want to sin, they're very democratic," his mentor observed. After gaining some confidence, Griffin began searching for a regular job, applying for clerical work at local businesses. The responses were polite but consistent. After three days he had failed to obtain even an interview. At the end of each day he plodded back to the shine stand, and as Williams dolloped out a supper of raccoon stew, Griffin told the old man what he already knew: nobody would hire a black man for anything but manual labor.

After a week in New Orleans, Griffin decided to travel to Mississippi, where, despite massive evidence collected by the FBI, a grand jury had recently refused to return indictments in a race lynching. New Orleans had proved outwardly affable, but as he bought a ticket at the Greyhound station, Griffin had his first encounter with the "hate stare," a cold, irrational gaze long familiar to blacks that struck Griffin like a blow in the face. It was on the bus ride that he first experienced the petty tyranny regularly visited on Southern blacks. Pulling into a small town for a rest stop, the driver let out the white passengers but ordered the blacks to stay in their seats. They grumbled and objected but complied. Griffin saw that one of the unexpected requirements of blackness was an impressive ability to hold one's urine.

He stayed in Mississippi only a few days. Overwhelmed by the oppressive poverty and climate of violence, he returned to New Orleans and then took a bus along the Gulf to Biloxi. From Biloxi he hitchhiked to Mobile, traveling beside miles of white, sandy beaches forbidden to blacks. In Mobile he again sought work and also spent much of his time seeking out the things he had once taken for granted: "a place to eat, or somewhere to find a drink of water, a rest room, somewhere to wash my hands." He had no better luck with jobs there than in New Orleans. "No use trying down here," one plant foreman told him. "We're gradually getting you people weeded out. . . . We're going to do our damndest to drive every one of you out of the state."

Unable to find a room one evening, Griffin accepted the offer of an elderly black preacher to share a thin mattress in his small, bare room. Night had come to be a time of comfort for Griffin. The strain of the day was over, and he could, like blacks throughout the South, relax in darkness's enveloping anonymity. The two men lay under quilts, gazing at the ceiling and chatting about Bible miracles. The old man was especially fond of the raising of Lazarus. When it came to prospects for Southern blacks, however, his faith was less secure. He had two sons who had gone north. He hoped they would never return.

From Mobile Griffin hitchhiked to Montgomery. The white men who gave him lifts were friendly, but invariably they turned the conversation to the same topic: "All but two picked me up the way they would pick up a pornographic photograph or book. . . . Some were shamelessly open, some shamelessly subtle. All showed morbid curiosity about the sexual life of a Negro, and all had, at base, the same stereotyped image of the Negro as an inexhaustible sex machine with oversized genitals and a vast store of experiences, immensely varied."

The situation might almost have been comic had not Griffin, despite the earthiness of his writing, possessed an almost nineteenth-century sense of modesty. He found the conversations increasingly loathsome and grew increasingly curt, a dangerous tone for a black in rural Alabama. One farmer asked Griffin if he was one of those out-of-state "troublemakers." Griffin replied that he was just passing through. The farmer patted the shotgun by his knee and gestured at the swampy forest on either side of the road. "You can kill a nigger and toss him into that swamp and no one will ever know what happened to him." Griffin nodded, "Yes, sir."

Arriving in Montgomery, Griffin found the atmosphere electric with racial tension. Blacks there seemed less passive and deferential than in other towns. The difference, he decided, was due to the influence of the city's prominent black minister, Martin Luther King, Jr. But if Montgomery's blacks seemed less defeated, its whites seemed more actively hostile. Griffin saw the hate stare everywhere. Looking into a washroom mirror, he discovered a change in his own gaze: "My face had lost animation. In repose, it had taken on the strained, disconsolate expression that is written on the countenance of so many Southern Negroes. My mind had become the same way, dozing empty for long periods."

The strain of Griffin's appropriated identity was taking its toll. He began having nightmares. Then he stopped taking the Oxsoralen pills, and his skin began daily turning lighter. His hair grew to a heavy fuzz. He decided to see if he could

cross the border back into whiteness. He scrubbed off the vegetable dye, donned a dark shirt to stand off against his lightening skin, and headed for the city's white section. He strolled into a segregated restaurant and ordered a meal. "I ate the white meal, drank the white water, received the white smiles and wondered how it all could be. What sense could a man make of it?"

He returned to the black section and discovered that blacks had a subtle but definite hate stare of their own. He reapplied the dye and found himself once again accepted by one race, spurned by the other. He began zigzagging back and forth across Montgomery, shifting skins like a chameleon, deliberately testing the limits of his disguise. It was, he sadly concluded, impenetrable. He gave up and boarded the bus for Atlanta, the last station in his tracing of the black cross.

Atlanta was a surprise for Griffin. Leaving Montgomery, he had given up hope for the lot of Southern blacks, but Georgia's capital changed his mind. The city, he found, had made "great strides." He professed to see hope for the South in Atlanta, but his optimism sounds forced. Despite thoughtful interviews with black and white civic leaders and a tour of black colleges, Griffin's picture of Atlanta is overwhelmed by the shadows of New Orleans, Mississippi, and Alabama.

Nearly three decades have gone by since Griffin made his journey through the South, but *Black Like Me*'s power to move and outrage remains undiminished. Still in print, it has sold more than twelve million copies and been translated into fourteen languages. Most recently it was published in South Africa. Part of its enduring appeal comes from what seems the very transparency of the author's imposture.

It is hard to imagine a person worse suited than Griffin to pass for black. A cultural epicure who had spent his adolescence in France and lived a blind, sheltered existence for the previous decade, Griffin had remarkably little in common with most Southern whites, let alone with blacks. In the book his relations with blacks are cordial but never intimate. He practically shudders every time his ears are assaulted by jazz or the blues. Griffin was able to change his color, but not his heritage.

Which makes it all the harder to see how he pulled it off. Naturally he fooled whites; whites didn't look at blacks. But how did he dupe blacks? Surely somebody should have seen through such a thin disguise. No one did. His transformation was skin-deep, but neither whites nor blacks ever looked deeper. As readers we are in on the secret. Griffin's voice—courtly, refined, educated—is so evident throughout the book that we are amazed at the blindness of bus drivers and shopkeepers and all the others. We hear him secretly wail, "I'm just like you," at each new indignity or abuse, and we cannot believe that no one else hears him.

It is on this level of moral protest that *Black Like Me* is best known and most celebrated, as a work of civil rights advocacy and a tract on man's inhumanity to man. But also it was one of the first works of a new kind of journalism—what was called in the sixties the New Journalism—with its personal, participatory, novelistic approach. In fact, the book is arguably the genre's first masterpiece, even though Griffin was really less a journalist than a personal essayist. Judged as reporting, *Black Like Me* is an imperfect work. There is too much of the author, too little of others; too much earnest discussion of issues and too little personal observation and encounter. Assuming they had Griffin's bull-headed courage, one can imagine other writers—Norman Mailer, Tom Wolfe—rendering the experience with more nuanced insight and elegance of style.

What one cannot imagine is these masters of irony abandoning their strategic distance for the raw, racked emotion that powers Griffin's prose. *Black Like Me* is not simply a record of oppression and injustice; it is an account of painful personal discovery. Griffin began his experiment as an adventure. He assumed he would find racism, but he did not expect to find it everywhere, least of all in himself. By the end of his four weeks, he ached with hurt and humiliation. The adventure had turned into an ordeal. In discovering the brutal reality of

racism, however, he also discovered compassion for the fierce stranger he had first seen three weeks before, the one with whom he had felt no kinship.

"I switched on the light and looked into a cracked piece of mirror bradded with bent nails to the wall. The bald Negro stared back at me from its mottled sheen. I knew I was in hell. Hell could be no more lonely or helpless. . . .

"I heard my voice, as though it belonged to someone else, hollow in the empty room, detached, say: 'Nigger, what you standing up there crying for?'

"I saw tears slick on his cheeks in the yellow light."

The initial installment of Griffin's series appeared in *Sepia* in April 1960, two months after the first lunch-counter sit-in and seven months before Kennedy's election. It was an instant sensation. Griffin went to New York for television interviews with Dave Garroway, Mike Wallace, and other hosts. Letters poured in—six thousand of them, mostly from Southern states, and only nine hostile.

Closer to home, friends and a few townspeople were warmly congratulatory, but most of Mansfield was silent. One night in April an effigy of Griffin— half black, half white, a yellow stripe down its back—was hung next to the downtown traffic light. A few days later a cross was burned in front of the town's predominantly black elementary school. Anonymous phone calls warned Griffin that "they" were coming to castrate him. Griffin's father came to the house to keep watch with a shotgun.

For a month the Griffins hid out in the homes of friends; in August he decided to move to Mexico. There he worked on a book version of the *Sepia* articles. Published in 1961, *Black Like Me* became an immediate best seller and was soon sold to Hollywood. (The film, a mediocre melodrama starring James Whitmore, was released in 1964.)

Griffin stayed in Mexico for nine peaceful months and began a scholarly history of the Tarascan Indians. Then, in the spring of 1961, anti-American riots erupted near his home in Morelia, and the Griffins were forced to take refuge in a Benedictine monastery. They returned north to Fort Worth.

Soon Griffin was swallowed up in the civil rights movement. He had an authority among whites and a credibility among blacks that made him a persuasive and much sought-after speaker. He lectured, marched, investigated, worked as a mediator, argued against violence, and grieved with the families of those claimed by violence. To the dismay of his literary friends, he shelved his autobiography and two nearly finished novels. What time he had for writing he devoted to essays and articles on racism, culminating with his book *The Church and the Black Man,* an outspoken criticism of the failure of the Christian churches to act on their creeds.

During this time Griffin met Thomas Merton, the Trappist monk and author of the best-selling *The Seven Storey Mountain.* The two had much in common. Both were French-educated and Catholic converts: Merton a contemplative with a lively interest in the world outside, Griffin an activist with a yearning for the cloister. Not surprisingly, a close friendship blossomed.

After Merton's death, in 1968, the Merton Legacy Trust asked Griffin to write the monk's official biography. He accepted the task gladly. Recurrent foot tumors and bone deterioration from diabetes kept him largely confined to a wheelchair, and he welcomed a return to purely literary labor. He spent the next nine years working on the book. As he had done before, he sought to understand his subject by slipping inside his skin. For nearly three years he spent two weeks out of every month at Merton's Kentucky hermitage, faithfully observing the monastic routine, a Spartan schedule of prayer and work beginning each morning at three. He discovered a tranquillity there that made these among the happiest days of his life.

By 1973 Griffin was too ravaged by diabetes to work away from home. As his health declined, the work proceeded more and more slowly. He missed his first deadline and then a second. Finally, in 1978, despite Griffin's pleadings, the Merton Legacy Trust named Michael Mott as Merton's official biographer. To compound Griffin's woes, his publisher demanded the return of its substantial advance. The settlement left him virtually bankrupt.

For the last two years of his life, Griffin was tortured by pain and despair. Emotionally he never recovered from the loss of what he thought would be his masterpiece, his contribution to the world's spiritual literature. Physically he suffered from kidney trouble, lung congestion, impaired circulation, and regular heart attacks, sometimes several a week. A bearish man, he dwindled to a hundred and fifty pounds. In 1979 his left leg was amputated and he was confined to bed.

He, Piedy, and their youngest daughter were forced to live on overextended credit cards and Piedy's secretarial job. When he could, Griffin worked on his thirty years of daily journals, with an eye toward eventual publication. Sometimes he rallied to give interviews or entertain friends or even cook a meal. But more often he had neither the wind nor the fire to do more than rest and reflect.

He died on September 9, 1980. When a friend asked the cause, Piedy said simply, "Everything." In the years since his death, a myth has spread that Griffin died from cancer cause by the Oxsoralen he had taken years before. He did not, and the suggestion of martyrdom would have offended him. He was in pain, though, in his last days, and perhaps he often thought of a favorite poem by Langston Hughes. He had used it for his most famous title:

Rest at pale evening . . .
A tall slim tree . . .
Night coming tenderly
Black like me.

Study Questions

1. What experiences and adventures contributed to the development of John Howard Griffin's racial attitudes? What obstacles in life did he personally face?

2. What does the novel *The Devil Rides Outside* tell us about Griffin's inner world and American society in the early 1950s?

3. Why did Griffin decide to temporarily change his skin color to better understand discrimination? Why did some people consider his experiment dangerous?

4. What conclusions did Griffin reach? What privations, small and large, did he experience? How did skin color alter the way he was received and treated by both races?

5. What impact did *Black Like Me* have on American society and American journalism?

Bibliography

The best place to start a search for John Howard Griffin is in his book *Black Like Me* (1961). A good starting point for literature on the general struggles and everyday life of African Americans during the late 1950s and early 1960s is Taylor Branch, *Parting the Waters: America in the King Years* (1988). Also insightful are John Dittmer, *Local People: The Struggle for Civil Rights in Mississippi* (1994); Eric R. Burner, *And Gently He Shall Lead Them: Robert Parris Moses and Civil Rights in Mississippi* (1994); William H. Chafe, *Civilities and Civil Rights* (1980); David Garrow, *Bearing the Cross: Martin Luther King, Jr. and the Southern Christian Leadership Conference* (1986); Doug McAdam, *Freedom Summer* (1988); and Stephen Oates, *Let the Trumpet Sound: The Life of Martin Luther King, Jr.* (1982). Anne Moody, *Coming of Age in Mississippi* (1968), is also a deeply moving document of the period.

READING 21

★ ★ ★

The Scientist as Sex Crusader: Alfred C. Kinsey and American Culture

Regina Markell Morantz

During the late 1940s and early 1950s, a series of unsettling events shocked Americans and disturbed their sense of postwar complacency and optimism. Communism—its spread and increased dangerousness—inspired much of the fear. In late 1949, the Nationalist leader Chiang Kai-shek and his followers fled mainland China for sanctuary on Formosa. In Chiang's place came Communist Mao Tse-tung. Although Mao's victory was predictable and the result of internal Chinese forces, Americans tended to view the fall of China as a victory for Soviet foreign policy. Other shocks came rapidly. In September 1949, President Truman announced that the Russians had detonated a nuclear device, thus ending the American monopoly of the bomb. And throughout the period, the trials of Alger Hiss raised questions about the loyalty of American government officials.

No less sensational and disturbing was the publication of Alfred Kinsey's *Sexual Behavior in the Human Male* (1948), which quickly sold over 275,000 copies. For many Americans, Kinsey's message was as insidious as those of Marx and Lenin. He told Americans about themselves, about their sexual practices, fears, and desires. And what Kinsey said was not what most Americans wanted to believe. In the following essay, historian Regina Markell Morantz discusses the reception, influence, and implications of Kinsey's scientific pioneering work. She demonstrates the limits of Kinsey's scientific objectivity and the nature of his liberalism. More importantly, however, Morantz uses the findings of Kinsey and more recent sex researchers to explore the changing character and behavior of millions of Americans. As she suggests, sex has become less a liberating, revolutionary force than simply another aspect of America's consumer economy.

In January 1948, Robert Latou Dickinson, noted gynecologist and sex researcher, dashed off a note to his friend and colleague Alfred Charles Kinsey. Dickinson's copy of the newly published *Sexual Behavior in the Human Male,* which he had awaited "with one of the keenest anticipations of a lifetime," had arrived. "I have my copy at last of SBHM!" he informed Kinsey. "Glory to God!" In a lively correspondence throughout the 1940s the two men shared enthusiasm for Kinsey's studies in human sexuality, their mutual respect enhanced by appreciation of the social significance of this work. Given the chance to see Kinsey's labors in print, Dickinson's excitement grew: "Dear ACE:" he wrote Kinsey in February, "In sex education, and marriage counsel [*sic*] and v.d. and prostitution attacks . . . we would, in America, hereafter, speak of the Pre-Kinsey and Post-Kinsey eras."

The press, the public, and expert opinion subsequently confirmed Dickinson's assessment. Writers dubbed *Sexual Behavior in the Human Male* "the most talked about book of the twentieth century." Others ranked it with *Das Kapital, The Origin of Species, and Wealth of Nations.* Indeed, the reception accorded Kinsey's work was unprecedented. Although Kinsey's publishers authorized an inadequate first printing of 5,000 copies, less than two months after publication *Sexual Behavior in the Human Male* had sold 200,000 copies and stood in second place on the non-fiction best-seller list. George Gallup reported that one out of every five Americans had either read or heard about the book, while five out of six of those interviewed judged its publication "a good thing." Multiple reviews appeared in literary periodicals. Medical and lay organizations held symposia to assess its impact. Overnight "Kinsey" became a household word, his name forever embedded in popular culture.

Response to the Kinsey report testified more than anything else to the revolution in sexual

"The Scientist as Sex Crusader: Alfred C. Kinsey and American Culture" by Regina Markell Morantz, from *American Quarterly XXIX* (Winter, 1977). Published by permission of *American Quarterly* and the author.

mores that its text, charts, and statistical tables so laboriously documented. No one would now dispute that a generation of Americans who had come of age in the first decades of the twentieth century had begun to lift the mantle of fear and shame from their sexual activities. Since 1913 American newspapers had been hailing what one headline writer called "sex o'clock in America." Even the scientific study of sex had gotten underway years before Kinsey: The Male Report cites 19 prior investigations of human sexuality. But journalists who wrote about America's sex obsession before World War I rarely elaborated on what factors underlay the new freedom in manners, while post-war professionals who had begun to analyze its components increasingly avoided sharing their findings with a popular audience. What made Kinsey different—indeed, what made him unique—was his confidence that Americans were ready for a confrontation with their own sexuality. In dispassionate prose he laid bare the facts.

Most of his contemporaries understood Kinsey's research to be a monumental achievement of twentieth-century science. He managed where others had failed to discuss sexual matters before a public still ignorant and uncomfortable with the subject. His own liberalism was grounded in the conviction that nothing human should be alien to the realm of science.

Of course Kinsey's detractors were vindictive. Some disputed his findings, questioning his evidence and doubting his methods; others condemned him for publicizing his facts. But though Kinsey may have underestimated the reaction of those ill-equipped to handle his candor, his faith in the American people was not misplaced. Accepting the legitimacy of his research with respect they afforded all science, they rapidly made his work part of the conventional wisdom. After summarizing the origins of sex research in America, this essay will attempt to analyze this process of acceptance. It will focus on Kinsey the man, the content of his reports and the critical response they evoked, and the larger cultural meaning of Kinsey's work.

Victorian aversion to the investigation of sexual matters relegated sex to the backroom almost

Dr. Alfred C. Kinsey, shown here with his family, pioneered sex research in two studies (1948 and 1953) that brought sex out of the bedroom and into America's parlor.

as effectively in 1900 as in the previous century. Scientists and physicians either shared their society's view of what was proper, or else kept quiet about it. Research into the socially taboo took courage; chastisement was often swift and forceful. When the distinguished Chicago physician, Denslow Lewis, proposed in 1899 to speak to the American Medical Association on the "Gynecological Consideration of the Sexual Act," he was denounced by Howard A. Kelly of Johns Hopkins. "The discussion of the subject," Kelly asserted, "is attended with filth and we besmirch ourselves by discussing it in public." Characteristically, the Association refused to publish Lewis' paper.

Nineteenth-century moralism gradually succumbed in the first decades of the twentieth century to the combined attack of purity advocates (including feminists, clergymen, and social re-

formers), idealistic physicians inspired by bacteriological discoveries facilitating the control of venereal disease, and the diverse but insistent proponents of the Freudian revolution. Social and economic factors also underlay the emergence of new sexual attitudes. As early as 1907 Simon Patten predicted the gradual economic shift away from austerity and production to a concern with consumption. An interest in leisure and luxury fostered pleasure and personal fulfillment as positive goods, and undermined Victorian prescriptions of thrift, self-denial, and personal control. Urbanization eroded community and religious controls on behavior. In addition, the increasingly visible women joining the labor force were freed from some of the constraints of home and family.

Though sex was discussed in the Progressive era, sex research remained controversial. Not until 1921 did scientists and social reformers organize a two-day conference under the auspices of the National Research Council to examine the status of American sex research. Acknowledging the importance of such investigation, conference members decried the "enshrouding of sex relations in a fog of mystery, reticence and shame." Sensing the national faith in science, participants argued that scientists were best qualified to study sex because "their standing in the community would prevent fears that their findings would be put to propaganda purposes." The meetings resulted in the formation of a Committee for Research on Problems in Sex chaired by Yale psychologist Robert Yerkes and connected with the National Research Council. Funded largely by the Rockefeller Foundation, and working closely with the Bureau of Social Hygiene, another Foundation project, the Committee directed most sex studies in the next two decades. Alfred Kinsey turned to this committee for financial support in 1939. Aid for this project opened the door to a new and controversial era in sex research.

While the Committee for the Study of Problems in Sex quietly encouraged research on sexuality in the 1920s and 1930s, Kinsey built his career as a leading expert on the gall wasp. Twenty-six years old in 1920, Kinsey came to Indiana University as an assistant professor of zoology. For the next two decades he taught courses in entymology, general biology, and insect taxonomy, and by the mid-thirties he had published two specialized books, numerous articles, and an innovative high school biology text.

Few facts are available to explain Kinsey's subsequent interest in sex. His own sexual history, like those of the people he interviewed, will presumably remain locked forever in the confidential files at the Institute for Sex Research. Though he spoke little of his past, it is clear that his parents were strict and puritanical. The product of a deeply religious home, Kinsey suffered as a youngster because of his proficiency in the natural sciences and his fascination with Darwinian evolution. When Kinsey rebelled, science offered him a set of values which emotionally rivaled his

juvenile commitment to religion. His sympathetic attitude toward the sexual dilemmas of the young may have grown out of the memories of his own pain, frustration, and ignorance; science granted him the tools to make his sympathy more objective. But cloaked in the unbiased empiricism of the dispassionate scientist lay the emotional preferences of a moral crusader.

Kinsey's involvement with sex research began quietly in 1938 when he was chosen as the faculty coordinator of a newly established marriage course. The course consisted of interdisciplinary guest lecturers, with Kinsey lecturing on biology. His class notes reveal sophistication with published works on sex. Indeed, in a letter to Robert Latou Dickinson written in 1941, he admitted: "It was your own work which turned my attention to the purposes of research in this field some ten or twelve years ago although circumstances were not propitious for starting the work until three years ago." In a talk he delivered in 1935 to a faculty discussion club he had proved himself familiar with previous sex studies by G. V. Hamilton and Katherine B. Davis. The lectures displayed his concern with both the influence of social institutions on sexual behavior and the "sexual conflicts of youth." Significantly, he reflected that such conflicts arose because of the "long frustration of the normal sexual activities."

Kinsey emphasized the central importance of sexual adjustment to stable unions. "I know of no evidence," he stated flatly, "that this biological basis can be completely sidestepped and still lead to a successful home." He accused modern education "through its system of mores, laws, and ethics," of conditioning attitudes toward sex which were "wrong in the sense that they interfere with the successful consummation of the marriage . . . [and] develop the sexual maladjustments that appear most often after marriage. Our ignorance of copulatory techniques," he continued, "which is the direct outcome of the impressions that are imprinted on the young, our ignorance of satisfactory contraceptive devices above all, produce attitudes which make our concepts of sex wrong." By delaying sexual activity until marriage, he argued, young people only made the achievement of successful marriage more problematic. Responses repressed for ten or twelve years after an individual is first capable of sexual activity could hardly be changed by a marriage ceremony. Distorted attitudes formed in adolescence required years of adjustment after marriage. "Why offer a marriage course?" Kinsey asked his listeners. "Society," he answered, "has been responsible for interfering with what would have been normal biological development. . . . It behooves us to make amends to society by taking you as you approach the time of marriage and giving you the results of scholarly thinking on these several problems." Repeatedly, Kinsey the scientist would side with biology when it conflicted with accepted social mores.

In the summer of 1938 Kinsey began taking the sex histories of his students and within a year had scheduled interviews outside the university to vary his sampling. Aware of their potential significance, he termed these histories "a scientific goldmine" and wondered to a colleague if they would not account "for the largest volume of research I will yet publish." Under mounting pressure from conservative elements of the community, Kinsey terminated his connection with the marriage course in 1940. Soon afterward he received his first grant from the Committee for Research in Problems of Sex. Abandoning his interest in the gall wasp, he prepared to devote himself solely to the study of human sexual behavior.

The current permissiveness surrounding sex research should not obscure the fact that thirty years ago Kinsey's findings disturbed, shocked, and threatened not just ordinary men and women but professionals as well. A good deal of the hostile criticism directed at Kinsey's work had little to do with its scientific value. Princeton University president Harold Dodds likened the Male volume to "the work of small boys writing dirty words on fences." The Chicago *Tribune* termed Kinsey a "menace to society." The Reverend Henry Van Dusen, president of Union Theological Seminary and a member of the Rockefeller Foundation, called for a "spontaneous ethical re-

vulsion from the premises of the study," and chided the Foundation for its sponsorship. Kinsey's work, he lamented, revealed "a prevailing degradation of American morality approximating the worst decadence of the Roman era." Harvard sociologist Carle C. Zimmerman labeled the Male volume an "attack on the Western family," and accused Kinsey of irresponsibility in making it public. Millicent McIntosh, indomitable president of Barnard College and mother of five, worried in 1954 that Kinsey's books had already contributed "to the difficulties encountered by young people in establishing a good relationship between the sexes."

Hysteria reached Congress when New York Representative Louis B. Heller called upon the Postmaster General to bar the Female Report from the mails until it could be investigated, charging Kinsey with "hurling the insult of the century against our mothers, wives, daughters and sisters." Soon rumors spread that the Special House Committee founded during the McCarthy era to inquire into the use of funds by tax-exempt foundations would ask Kinsey to testify regarding financial aid from the Rockefeller Foundation. Others accused Kinsey of aiding communism. Shortly thereafter the Rockefeller Foundation informed Kinsey that his grant would not be renewed.

Much of the criticism of Kinsey's work, however, was not hysterical. Most commentators admired his research and welcomed its publication. Yet serious critics also offered objections. The debate centered on two issues: the possibility of conducting a scientific investigation that was value-free (and whether Kinsey had done so); and the extent to which a behavioristic approach could solve fundamental questions of human existence.

Kinsey never admitted publicly that scientists based their investigations on cultural assumptions. He remained deaf to the charge that his work reflected his own biases. Yet his objectivity was itself polemical: his research subverted the status quo specifically because it examined individual deviance dispassionately. Many critics were repelled by the idea of studying sexual nonconformity objectively. By definition norms are not always rational. Kinsey's non-judgmental approach aligned him with the twentieth-century rebels against Victorian repression. Though many critics shared the Progressive faith that the truth would make men free, they resisted applying this conviction to sex research. In this instance the truth was dangerous and might help destroy the American value system. Reinhold Niebuhr passionately argued this point of view when he declared that Kinsey's assumptions represented "a therapy which implies a disease in our culture as grievous or more grievous than the sickness it pretends to cure."

Soon after the publication of the Male volume, Lionel Trilling wrote of Kinsey and his coauthors that "nothing comes more easily to their pens than the criticism of the subjectivity of earlier writers on sex, yet their own subjectivity is sometimes extreme." A retrospective reading of both volumes reveals why Kinsey was an easy mark for Trilling's pen. In neither book did he disguise either his admiration for the sexually active or his suspicion of the sexually repressed. His statistical interpretations fell invariably on the side of sexual liberalism. In a chapter on the onset of male puberty, for example, he recorded his approval of men who began their sexual activities early. On scant evidence he asserted that early-adolescent males were often "the more alert, energetic, vivacious, spontaneous, physically active, socially extrovert, and/or aggressive individuals in the population," while late-maturing males tended to be "slow, quiet, mild in manner, without force, reserved, timid, taciturn, introvert, and/or socially inept." He revealed his own biases most clearly when he linked the aggressive, success-oriented personality type—and American paragon—to vigorous sexuality.

Equally controversial were Kinsey's interpretations of the data concerning the relationship between premarital intercourse and marital adjustment. Although he admitted that premarital petting contributed "definitely to the effectiveness of the sexual relations after marriage," he nevertheless remained contemptuous of the hypocrisy involved in adolescent petting behavior. "It is amazing," he wrote,

to observe the mixtures of scientifically supported logic, and utter illogic, which shapes the petting behavior of most of these youths. That some of them are in some psychic conflict over their activities is evidenced by the curious rationalizations which they use to satisfy their consciences. They are particularly concerned with the avoidance of genital union. The fact that petting involves erotic contacts which are as effective as genital union, and that it may even involve contacts which have been more taboo than genital union, including some that have been considered perversions, does not disturb the youth so much as actual intercourse would. By petting, they preserve their virginities, even though they may achieve orgasm by doing so.

Coupled with his disdain for this hypocrisy was his finding of a "marked, positive correlation between experience in orgasm obtained from premarital coitus [for women], and the capacity to reach orgasm after marriage." Over half the female sample who had experienced premarital coital orgasm had reached sexual climax in nearly all of their coitus during the first year of marriage. Only 29 percent of women without such premarital experience were able to achieve regular orgasm during the first year.

Kinsey dismissed selective factors as accounting for the correlation, and emphasized that almost half of those women sampled who had premarital intercourse had it exclusively with their fiancés. This figure led some critics to question whether such behavior could properly be termed "premarital coitus" at all. Kinsey found that the overall number of women achieving orgasm *at least occasionally* within the first year of marriage was as high as 75 percent. Indeed, the percentage rose steadily according to the number of years married. What Kinsey's statistics seemed to indicate was that reaching orgasm for women was a *learned* skill that took time to develop. Kinsey's data, critics argued, could or could not be interpreted to justify premarital intercourse.

Kinsey nevertheless used his findings to suggest that traditional mores regarding premarital intercourse were outmoded. In an impassioned paragraph, he made his sympathies clear. His carefully selected phrases, typical of numerous passages in the books, bristled with an aggressive undertone barely couched in the language of scientific neutrality: "The attempt," he wrote

to ignore and suppress the physiologic needs of the sexually most capable of the population, has led to more complications than most persons are willing to recognize. This is why so many of our American youth, both females and males, depend upon masturbation instead of coitus as a premarital outlet. Restraints on premarital heterosexual contacts appear to be primary factors in the development of homosexual activities among both females and males. . . .

The considerable development of petting, which many foreigners consider one of the unique aspects of the sexual pattern in this country, is similarly an outgrowth of this restraint on premarital coitus.

The law specifies the right of the married adult to have regular intercourse, but it makes no provision whatsoever for the approximately 40 per cent of the population which is sexually mature but unmarried. Many youths and older unmarried females and males are seriously disturbed because the only sources of sexual outlet are either legally or socially disapproved.

Such statements challenged the 1950s social and sexual standards. Most marriage manuals still preached the virtues of premarital chastity, while only a few professionals had given serious thought to the problems of sexual adjustment for the unmarried.

Kinsey's detractors feared that his premises implied an animalistic philosophy of sex devoid of emotional and social content. They accused him of a crude behaviorism that failed to place sexual activity within the larger context of human values. Thoughtful reviewers, many of them psychiatrists and psychologists, chided him for his recurrent

neglect of the psycho-dynamics of sex. Denying that as a biologist Kinsey was equipped to examine complex psycho-social questions, analysts decried his measure of sex activity in terms of outlet and orgasm. By reducing sex to the mechanistic Kinsey ignored motivation. Should orgasm in and of itself, they asked, be the goal of human sexual behavior? Where was the place of love in Kinsey's universe? Speaking of sex solely in terms of outlet negated its relationship to the creative, integrative, and inspirational aspects of human life. Sexuality, though important, remained only one dimension of the human personality. "It was Freud's idea," wrote Karl Menninger, "that sexuality in the broad sense, the life instinct, was represented not nearly so much by orgasm as by human love, and that the goal of all sexual behavior was better integration, better inter-human concern, and thereby less mutual destructiveness."

The psychoanalytic case against Kinsey extended beyond his failure to consider the emotional content of the sex act. Kinsey avoided placing sexuality within a developmental framework. Except for confirming infantile sexuality, he refused to see any substantiation for other central tenets of psychoanalytic theory. His animus toward psychoanalysts remained clear. He denied that "normal" psycho-sexual development preceded from narcissism through homosexual to heterosexual activities. In a final affront to Freudian theory, he questioned the significance to women of such concepts as penis envy, castration fear, defense against incestuous wishes, and fixation at the clitoral stage. "The psycho-sexual pattern in the human animal," he wrote, "originates in indiscriminate sexual responses which as a product of conditioning and social pressures, become increasingly restricted in the directions of traditional interpretations of what is normal or abnormal in sexual behavior. . . . It is simply a picture of physiologic response and psychologic conditioning in terms that are known to the biologist and psychologist." Psychoanalysts found this approach simplistic. "Frigidity," argued Marie Robinson, "is in the vast majority of cases, essentially a psychological problem. No amount of mechanical manipulation can make a difference. Anybody who tells you differently," she cautioned her patients, "is . . . wrong." "Kinsey's credo," wrote Edmund Bergler and William S. Kroger, "amounts to naiveté of the first order. . . . It overlooks the complex mechanisms of inner-unconscious-conscious. . . . Sex, though biologically present in every human being, goes through complicated (not simple) transformations before maturity is reached."

While psychoanalysts worried over Kinsey's behaviorism, theologians accused him of materialism. Kinsey's animal analogy represented a conscious tool in his revolt against Victorian sexual attitudes which for a century had exalted ecstasy of the spirit and devalued the pleasures of the flesh. In contrast, Kinsey embraced man's mammalian heritage. Admiring Freud for reasserting the primacy of physical drives, Kinsey believed that man's pretensions to uniqueness had accounted for untold sexual unhappiness. As a biologist he took for granted that, in the long run, physiological factors were more effective than man-made regulations in determining patterns of human behavior. Reinhold Niebuhr read him correctly when he charged Kinsey with referring consistently to analogies between man and the sex practices of infrahuman species "without once calling attention to uniquely human characteristics of man's sexual life."

This alleged materialism led Kinsey to the controversial assumption that the prevalence of certain types of behavior indicated both their mammalian origins and their biological normality. The frequency of types of behavior socially labelled "deviant" testified to the persistence of biologic over cultural determinants. Such a view demanded a reevaluation of homosexuality. Regarding the "normality" of such behavior Kinsey wrote:

In view of the data which we now have on the incidence and frequency of the homosexual, in particular on its coexistence with the heterosexual in the lives of a considerable portion of the male population, it is difficult to maintain the view that psycho-sexual reactions between *individuals of the same sex are rare and therefore abnormal or unnatural, or that they constitute within themselves evidence of neuroses or even psychoses.*

Theologians and other humanists united in their revulsion against this view of sex. Man, they reminded their readers, was not just a little above the apes, but a little below the angels. The difference between human beings and animals lay in the capacity of men to control their instincts, to use language, and to develop creativity, imagination, and culture. In the end, critics maintained, sex was a social activity, culturally and psychologically influenced.

Many of Kinsey's difficulties with the humanists may have arisen from his narrow philosophy of science. He often argued that as a scientist he reserved the right to limit his investigation in any way he saw fit. Though he never denied the significance of the social and psychologic components of human behavior, he insisted that science was "by its method limited to the consideration of material phenomena. The accumulation of scientific data depends upon the reduction of such material to quantifiable units which can be measured." He implied that any other order of facts or values than his could be explored only by non-scientific or ultra-scientific means. He accused psychiatrists studying Freudian stages in psycho-sexual development of investigating "mystic impulses." Theologians, and those "concerned with the moral values of sexual behavior" he considered to be antagonistic to science altogether.

Kinsey's refusal to answer the criticism of the humanists also revealed his shortcomings as a sexual theorist. Kinsey's work is peculiarly joyless. "If someone," wrote Karl Stern in *Commonweal*, "attempted to set the stage for a dehumanized, depersonalized society, for the great beehive—he would start out with things like the Kinsey Report." Ironically, the Victorians themselves had been accused of joy-lessness, though for different reasons. Kinsey, it seemed to some, represented a new kind of puritan. "There is in all this," Stern remarked with considerable irony, "a subtle, hidden despising of nature."

In the present period of sexual permissiveness, the arguments of the humanists loom more salient than they did thirty years ago. A general theory of sexuality cannot remain grounded in only one academic discipline, but must seek to integrate the methods and findings of many. Undoubtedly Kinsey would have renounced the role of sexual theorist. He died too soon for us to speculate on whether subsequent research would have led him beyond a crude empiricism. Yet in stubbornly labelling even thoughtful critics as Victorian moralists in disguise, perhaps Kinsey had a point. His findings may not have helped to cure the sexually neurotic, but, given the prevailing atmosphere surrounding the public discussion of sex, his behavioristic approach may have liberated sexually active men and women still haunted with Victorian prudery. *Look* magazine recognized this therapeutic effect: "What they [the authors] have learned and will learn may have a tremendous effect on the future social history of mankind. For they are presenting facts. They are revealing not what *should be,* but what is. For the first time data on human sex behavior is entirely separated from questions of philosophy, moral values, and social customs."

The fact that Kinsey himself had been raised under the canons of sexual puritanism probably made him sensitive to the problems of ordinary men and women. Certainly his democratic tendencies convinced him that for most people questions concerning the ultimate significance of sexuality were not only unimportant, they were irrelevant. The first task was to unshackle a generation from its repressive past. Relieving guilt and reassuring readers that everyone had similar sexual impulses, Kinsey's books contributed to a changing sexual climate in which ordinary people lived and worked. They probably had the same emancipating effect on the unpsychoanalyzed masses that Freud's work achieved for generations of intellectuals.

Not long after the publication of the Female volume, Kinsey's health began to deteriorate. For over a decade he had maintained a schedule which left him little free time. The emotional criticism that accompanied the release of his second book hurt him deeply. Cessation of foundation backing left the future of his research in the balance; for three years he struggled to reestablish the Institute for Sex Research on a solid financial footing. In 1956, at the age of 64, he died of a heart attack.

In the years between the publication of the Male Report and his premature death, Kinsey grew petrified of yellow journalism and the danger of misinterpretation. The importance of his scientific approach in achieving acceptance for his work cannot be overstressed. Indeed, his insistence on the legitimacy of his research and his scientific credentials eventually made him a heroic figure, even in the eyes of his enemies. Nowhere was this fact more poignantly demonstrated than in the following obituary published in the *Catholic Record,* one of his most severe critics:

The death of Dr. Kinsey, famous Indiana University zoologist, and compiler of the controversial studies on human sex life, removes a truly dedicated scholar from the Bloomington campus. Few could disagree more strongly than we with Dr. Kinsey's views or deplore more deeply the evil influence such views could have on individuals and society. Yet one cannot deny that Dr. Kinsey's unremitting efforts, his patient, endless search, his disregard for criticism and ridicule, and his disinterest in financial gain should merit him high marks as a devoted scholar. While we have hurled our share of brick-bats at some of Dr. Kinsey's ideas when he was living, and still hold these ideas to be poisonously wrong, we must admit that we would welcome on our side many more scholars with something of Kinsey's devotion to knowledge and learning.

Kinsey hoped that his work would be widely publicized and that its effect would be educational, not trivializing. Contemporary observers credited him with achieving his goal. Donald B. Hileman's study of magazine coverage of the Female volume in 1953 found that Kinsey had already forced a reorientation of attitudes toward sexual matters among journalists. *Time* magazine agreed. Kinsey's biggest impact, they argued, was "conversational." Despite the increase in talk about sex after World War I, printed and public discussion remained taboo. "No single event," they concluded, "did more for open discussion of sex than the Kinsey Report, which got such matters as homosexuality, masturbation, coitus and orgasm into most papers and family magazines."

Though some critics feared that the reports would have an immediate adverse effect on public behavior, there is little evidence that such fears were justified. On the other hand, studies undertaken soon after publication suggested that Kinsey's work did liberalize attitudes, especially among the young. His findings publicized not only the sexual diversity but also the gap between ideals and reality in America. Such information about the prevalence of certain "questionable" practices tended to alter attitudes in the direction of tolerance. In this sense Kinsey's books probably were a catalyst. With consummate skill he dispelled ignorance about changes in sexual mores which had already taken place, *sub rosa,* since World War I. In presenting Americans with a *fait accompli,* his work demanded more realistic, more human sex mores. He forced a public debate over the meaning of sex in modern life as no other author had except Freud.

Marriage counselors and sex therapists hailed the report's role in alleviating guilt and promoting understanding between the sexes. For over a generation liberal therapists had struggled with their own ignorance and the greater ignorance of their patients. Lack of sexual harmony was deemed the most frequent cause of family disruptions. Dr. Lena Levine, director of the Margaret Sanger Research Bureau, recalled the early period of marriage counseling "with no nostalgia whatever."

We had no authorities to turn to, no reference books to give the women. We listened to the same story over and over again, and we counseled patients as best we could on technique. The worst job was to get the message across to the husbands, who were usually at fault,

chiefly because they hadn't the slightest idea how a woman was put together and what she needed in the way of stimulation.

Kinsey paved the way for modern approaches to sex therapy. Masters and Johnson built on the groundwork laid by their more controversial predecessor.

Ironically, Kinsey's friends as well as his enemies responded only to the obvious Kinsey: the broad-minded, democratic rebel, the sexual libertarian. While he was surely all of these things, there was another side to this complex and subtle man, more easily understood only in historical retrospect. In many ways Kinsey remained bound to his Victorian past. Despite his studied neutrality concerning the various forms of sexual outlet, his acceptance of homosexuality, and his tolerance of extramarital sexuality, Kinsey was not a social revolutionary. His revolt against his society's outmoded sexual mores did not lead him to question other aspects of the value structure. Like most of his contemporaries, he had an attachment to happy, stable marriages, and he expected his research to ease the majority of Americans into a permanent monogamy so satisfying that social stability would be guaranteed. His data suggesting that sexual liberation had not destroyed cherished social institutions should have reassured his detractors, had they been composed enough to pay careful attention. It was no accident that Kinsey admired other personality traits of sexually precocious youths—their aggressive energy, their drive and spontaneity. Here he is most candid and also most reactionary: sexual abandon is coupled with the time-honored assumptions of enterprising capitalistic society.

Kinsey's faith in this social order is evident in his lecture notes for the 1938 marriage course, and in his special relationship with the American Association of Marriage Counselors. For many years an associate member, Kinsey was made an affiliate in 1952. Many critics erroneously interpret the failure to treat reproductive issues in the two reports as evidence of Kinsey's lack of interest. Yet approximately ten percent of Kinsey's standard interview was devoted to this subject and his silence on these matters reflects anything but indifference. He withheld his statistics on pregnancy, contraception, and abortion because the AAMC had convinced him to devote an entire book to these questions. Thus Masters and Johnson have only followed in the direction that Kinsey led. Like him they emerge as resolute foes of guilt and shame; like him they do not champion the cause of premarital chastity. But their ideal sexual order, like Kinsey's, leads to a retreat into privatism. They link greater sexual permissiveness with happier marriages, and they conceive of sexual life in terms of "enduring, heterosexual relationships of substantial affection."

Thus the cultural and intellectual revolution that Kinsey touched off was archetypically American: its purpose was to keep basic institutions the same, especially at a time when, in the aftermath of world war, they might have been fundamentally altered.

In the thirty years since Kinsey published his volumes, his data have become a rich potential source for measuring social change. Unfortunately, historians have yet to mine his findings with any persistence. Used primarily to verify the "sexual revolution" in the first decades of this century, Kinsey's work has been virtually ignored by students interested in broader social and cultural issues. Few commentators, for example, have explored the implications of Kinsey's discovery that men from different classes exhibit divergent sexual behaviors. The report maintained that lower- and working-class males had a decidedly higher incidence of premarital intercourse than college-educated men, tended to frown on extended foreplay in intercourse as "unnatural," were less likely to make love in the nude, masturbated less frequently, and viewed sex more as an uncontrollable impulse, less as a question of right and wrong. Middle-class and college-educated youths were moralistic; they tended to be virgins at marriage, although they petted and masturbated more often. The upwardly or downwardly mobile male, moreover, tended to form such attitudinal and behavioral patterns *long before he moved into his destined class.*

Kinsey's findings raise questions about the relationship of sex behavior, character structure, social mobility, and class, some of which might be read back into the past. Indeed, his data suggest a connection between twentieth-century middle-class behavior patterns and the emergence of the "modern" temperament, a primary attribute of which seems to be, at least for the nineteenth century, the ability to defer present gratification for future rewards. Historians of the nineteenth century have been struggling to link Victorian sexual repression to the emergence of a personality type comfortable with industrial capitalism. Thrift in semen, they argue, mirrored the injunction to be frugal materially. The ability to control passion and the denigration of personal pleasure as a goal created men and women who fit the demands of the take-off period of industrialization, when production, economy, and austerity took precedence over consumption. Marx eloquently characterized this stage in capitalistic growth:

Political economy, the science of wealth, is therefore, at the same time, the science of renunciation, of privation and of saving. . . . The science of a marvelous industry is at the same time the science of asceticism. . . . The less you eat, drink, buy books, go to the theater or to balls, or to the public house, and the less you think, love, theorize, sing, paint, fence, etc. the more you will be able to save. . . .

Historians have based their theories about nineteenth-century sexuality on evidence drawn from the prescriptive literature—advice books, political and social writings, medical treatises. Surely Kinsey's statistics give us some hard evidence that the repressive Victorian sexual theory was somehow linked to the behavior patterns of an upwardly mobile middle class.

Yet when we examine Kinsey's data more closely we must qualify Marx's contention that deferred gratification was always a prerequisite for capitalistic growth. By the 1920s, at least, it seems clear that middle-class youths were no longer deferring *gratification*; they were merely delaying *copulation.* The upwardly mobile petted and masturbated frequently despite guilt. Kinsey's figures for *total* sexual outlet (achieving orgasm by any means) showed only minor class differences. Presumably, the mature industrial economy no longer requires the full repression of sexual desires, it merely demands that those desires be gratified in particular ways. Thus, middle-class youths, in order to contribute to the system, deferred not necessarily sexual pleasure, but intercourse, marriage, children, and family obligations. Lower-class men, on the other hand, postponed neither early copulation, nor marriage, nor large families, all of which probably helped to insure their docility, if not contentedness, in the factory.

Recent sex surveys report that the behavioral gap between men of different classes has substantially narrowed since Kinsey. Probably because of the widespread dissemination of effective contraceptive devices, premarital intercourse has increased among college-educated males, while sex behavior among the lower classes has differentiated to include nudity, extended foreplay, and increasing oral-genital contacts. Indeed, it appears that in an economy characterized by abundance and oriented toward the production of luxury items and consumer goods, sexual pleasure has become a means of recreation for all classes. Character structure and child rearing practices have shifted accordingly, away from an emphasis on autonomous self-control and toward the rational acceptance of pleasure, personal fulfillment, and happiness. Education, mass media, and the increase in leisure time among all social strata have tended to homogenize popular culture and narrow behavioral differences between social groups.

These developments suggest that we have entered a third phase of capitalistic growth. As yet we have proved incapable of dealing with problems of overproduction. The goal of the system remains consumption, and sexual liberation is encouraged primarily through advertising, as a means of orienting people toward new *things,* new ideas, new forms of luxury and pleasure. The encouragement of hedonism in all spheres seems essential for the affluent society. Thus sexual freedom has not been tied to social revolution. Championing privatism and the concern with individual adjustment, the new permissiveness has focused on self-fulfillment, not social change. Social historians interested in generational shifts in personality structure would do well to explore the implications of these changes in sexual behavior.

Kinsey's findings also indicate that knowledge of female sexuality has gradually become more sophisticated. If a sexual revolution has occurred, its base has been changes in female attitudes and behavior. While male trends shifted only minimally between generational cohorts in Kinsey's sample, women moved steadily toward the male standard. The evidence of the Female Report that women born after 1900 were more likely to reach orgasm in marriage, and that educated middle-class women achieved greater sexual satisfaction than their lower-class sisters deserves special attention. It would seem that sexual liberation, fostered by greater educational opportunities, presupposes and encourages the development of individuality and autonomy among women.

On the other hand, students of lower-class sexual patterns have found that among the less educated "both husbands and wives feel that sexual gratification for the wife is much less important than for the husband." Lower-class lovemaking tends to be less "technically versatile," lacking in the extended foreplay intended to facilitate the wife's satisfaction. Lower-class women, perhaps as a consequence, view sex primarily as a duty. Yet although they enjoy sex less they rarely refuse intercourse. Sociologist Lee Rainwater links these sexual patterns to a patriarchal family structure, a radical separation between male and female spheres, and a lack of meaningful communication between sexual partners, all characteristic of lower-class groups. Recent work on nineteenth-century sex roles has pictured a similar family structure exhibiting the same well-defined differentiation between male and female culture. One is tempted to use Kinsey's statistics to posit the prevalence among the middle class in the last century of contemporary lower-class patterns of lovemaking, oriented toward male satisfaction. For an age which barely accepted the legitimacy of female pleasure and still linked intercourse with reproduction, such a thesis appears plausible and is borne out by Kinsey's data revealing a gradual increase in female orgasm in the twentieth century.

The evolution of consciousness over the last century has altered expectations concerning what is sexually natural and possible. Human needs diversify with changing social and cultural conditions, and things become desirable merely because they are suddenly possible. Kinsey's data offer us an insight into this transformation in the meaning of marriage and sexual relations. His findings suggest that this century has witnessed a merging of spiritual love and passion in a novel way. His evidence indicates that middle-class lovemaking techniques are a recent dimension of the popular imagination. The emergence of almost universal petting in the 1920s and 1930s represents a new psycho-sexual intimacy. The increasing sexual responsiveness of middle-class women may be a function of this.

It has become fashionable to mourn the passing of the old sexual order in which the omnipresence of guilt, anxiety, and dread over the violation of taboos guaranteed at least that life would be interesting. "If . . . nothing is grave," a recent commentator has written, satire cannot bite and tragedy gives way to the social illness of maladjustment. For many, human life under such conditions would lose its music." Such an attitude offers further proof of the distance we have travelled from the sexual culture of Kinsey's generation. Privy to the tragic ways in which people's sexual lives were blighted by society, Kinsey welcomed a new order while he helped bring it about. We are the richer for Kinsey's conviction that human beings should get more joy out of all sexual activity.

Yet Kinsey was no revolutionary. Though he wished that the world would be a better place because of his books, his vision required no fundamental social or economic changes. He understood neither the revolutionary nor the disintegrative potentialities inherent in sexual liberation. In the end, Kinsey's hedonism has become a conservative force, and he himself the unwitting agent of an increasingly callous and wasteful society.

Study Questions

1. What factors explain the remarkable popular success of *Sexual Behavior in the Human Male*?

2. What characterized the study of sexual behavior before Kinsey? How did Kinsey's study change people's beliefs and attitudes?

3. What does Regina Morantz mean when she describes Kinsey as "the scientist as sex crusader?" Did the passionate or dispassionate side of Kinsey's personality influence his life?

4. How did the American people react to the publication of *Sexual Behavior in the Human Male*? What were the major issues raised by the debate over Kinsey's book?

5. How were Kinsey's research and results culturally biased? How was his sexual liberalism demonstrated in his work? How did he challenge the 1950s social and sexual standards? What place did love play in Kinsey's study of sexual relations?

6. How did Kinsey's work set the stage for dehumanized, depersonalized society? What long-range effects did Kinsey's writing have on society? Was Kinsey a social revolutionary? Why or why not?

7. What links are there between sexual activity and economic and class behavior?

Bibliography

The fullest biography of Kinsey is James H. Jones, *Alfred Kinsey: A Public/Private Life* (1997). Jonathon Gatharne-Hordy, *Sex the Measure of All Things: A Life of Alfred C. Kinsey* (2000) also explores Kinsey's life. Two pieces that consider Kinsey's work, its effects, and its context are David Halberstam, "Discovering Sex," *American Heritage* 44 (1993): 39–58 and David Allyn, "Private Acts/Public Policy: Alfred Kinsey, The American Law Institute and the Privatization of American Sexual Morality," *Journal of American Studies* 30 (1996): 405–428. For general sexual history, see John D'Emilio and Estelle Freedman, *Intimate Matters* (1997), Martha Hodes, ed., *Sex, Love and Race* (1999).

READING 22

★ ★ ★

Intellect on Television: The Quiz Show Scandals of the 1950s

Richard S. Tedlow

In 1854, Henry David Thoreau wrote, "We are in great haste to construct a magnetic telegraph from Maine to Texas; but Maine and Texas, it may be, have nothing important to communicate." More than one hundred years later, Thoreau's observation, greatly expanded, is still valid. Possessing the technological means of communication is no guarantee of meaningful communication. Nowhere is this situation more evident than in the commercial television industry. In the following essay, Richard S. Tedlow examines the problems inherent in commercial broadcasting, especially as they relate to the television quiz scandals of the late 1950s. The picture he presents is not a flattering one; the object of commercial television is quite simply to sell products, not to educate or uplift its audience. The result is an industry dominated by monetary values and generally oblivious to all ethical or moral consideration. In the specific case of quiz shows, television has produced an additional side effect: it has cheapened the meaning of education and intelligence. As Tedlow cogently observed, "If any crime had been committed in the quiz show episode, it was surely the broad conspiracy to portray as genuine intellectual activity the spouting of trivia." In today's America where books of lists and trivia make the best-sellers list, Tedlow's discussion of the quiz shows has a haunting familiarity.

On the seventh of June, 1955, *The $64,000 Question* made its debut on the CBS television network. No programming idea could have been more thoroughly foreshadowed by previous shows. Since the mid-1930s radio had been exploiting the American passion for facts with contests and games. For years, small amounts of cash or manufacturer-donated merchandise had been given away through various formats. What was new about *Question* was the size of the purse. The giveaway had taken a "quantum jump"; losers received a Cadillac as a consolation prize.

Question's format was simple. The producers selected a contestant who chose a subject about which he or she answered increasingly difficult questions which were assigned monetary values ranging from $64 to $64,000. The contestants could quit without attempting the succeeding plateau, but if he chose to continue and missed, he forfeited his winnings and was left with only his Cadillac.

By a few deft touches, the producers heightened the aura of authenticity and tension. The questions used were deposited in a vault of the Manufacturers Trust Company and brought to the studio by a bank officer flanked by two armed guards. As the stakes increased, the contestant entered a glass-enclosed "isolation booth" on stage to the accompaniment of "ominous music which hinted at imminent disaster" in order to prevent coaching from the audience. Since the contestant returned week after week rather than answering all the questions on one broadcast, the audience was given time to contemplate whether he would keep his winnings or go on to the next plateau and also a chance to worry about how difficult the next question might be.

The program became an immediate hit. In September, an estimated 55 million people, over twice as many as had seen the Checkers speech, viewing 84.8 percent of the television sets in operation at

Richard S. Tedlow, "Intellect on Television: The Quiz Show Scandals of the 1950s" in *American Quarterly,* Vol. 27/No. 4 (Fall, 1979). © The Johns Hopkins University Press. Reprinted by permission.

the time, saw Richard S. McCutchen, a 28-year-old Marine captain whose category was gourmet foods, become the first grand prize winner.

Most early contestants were seemingly average folks who harbored a hidden expertise in a subject far removed from their workaday lives. Thus McCutchen was asked about *haute cuisine* rather than amphibious assault. This separation was no accident. Its purpose was not only to increase the novelty of the show by providing something odd to the point of being freakish but also to integrate the viewer more intimately into the video melodrama. Everyone who had ever accumulated a store of disconnected, useless information could fantasize about transforming it into a pot of gold.

In a few months, *Question* had created a large new "consumption community," Daniel Boorstin's label for the nonideological, democratic, vague, and rapidly shifting groupings which have characterized twentieth-century American society. Suddenly, a third of the country had a common bond about which total strangers could converse. Paradoxically, in order to belong to this community, the individual had to isolate himself physically from others. Families stayed at home to watch the show, rather than celebrating it in the company of a large crowd. Movie theaters reported a precipitous decline in business, and stores and streets were empty when it came on the air.

Everyone whose life was touched by the show seemed to prosper. In addition to their prize money, some contestants received alluring offers to do public relations work for large companies or to star in movies. *Question's* creator, an independent program packager named Louis Cowan, became president of CBS-TV, an indication of how pleased the network executives were to present so successful a show. Even the banker who brought the sealed questions from the vault found himself promoted to a vice presidency. But the greatest beneficiary was the sponsor.

In March of 1955, the show was purchased by Revlon, which soon began reaping the rewards of well-constructed advertising on a popular television program. Several products quintupled their sales, and advertising for one had to be discontinued because it sold out nationally. George F. Abrams, the company's vice president in charge of advertising, gloated that *Question* " . . . is doing a most fantastic sales job. It certainly is the most amazing sales success in the history of the cosmetics industry. There isn't a single Revlon item that hasn't benefitted. . . ." Net sales for 1955 increased 54 percent over the previous year, and in 1956 they soared another 66 percent. When Revlon shares were first offered on the New York Stock Exchange at the end of 1955, the issue's success was "so great it was almost embarrassing."

Question's greatest liability was its own success; it spawned imitators around the world. In the United States, a spate of programs featuring endless variations of gift-giving for answering questions further retarded "TV's already enfeebled yearning to leaven commercialism with culture." Most of these have mercifully been consigned to oblivion, but one rivaled *The $64,000 Question* in the impact it made upon the nation.

The *21* program was developed by another firm of independent program packagers, Barry and Enright, Inc. The format was different, especially in having two contestants compete against each other and no limit on their winnings, but the basic idea was the same. Questions were given point values, and the points were worth money. Once again, the "wiles of a riverboat gambler" were combined with the memory of sundry bits of information which was passed off as intellectual acumen, with the result a spectacularly profitable property.

Barry and Enright leased the show to Pharmaceuticals, Inc., now known as the J. B. Williams Company, and it first appeared on NBC on October 12, 1956. Pharmaceuticals, whose most well-known product was Geritol, soon had good reason to be pleased with its quiz show. *21* did not attain quite the ratings of *Question,* but it competed successfully against *I Love Lucy,* one of the most popular programs in television history, and attracted much notice. Although its advertising director was reluctant to give complete credit to the program for the increased sales of Geritol, it

could hardly have hurt. Sales in 1957 bettered the previous year's mark by one-third.

Unlike *Question, 21* did not shun the highly educated, and one of its contestants became a symbol to the nation of the profitability of intellectual achievement. Charles Van Doren provided evidence that an intellectual could be handsome, that he could get rich, and that he could be a superstar. Like a football player, the intellectual athlete could win fame and wealth. Van Doren's family could lay genuine claim to membership in an American aristocracy of letters. Descended from seventeenth-century Dutch immigrants, Van Doren's uncle Carl was a literary critic whose 1939 biography of Benjamin Franklin won a Pulitzer Prize. His father Mark won the Prize for poetry the following year, and he was equally famous for his accomplishments in the classroom as a professor of English at Columbia. The wives of the Van Doren brothers were also literary, rounding out a remarkably cultivated quartet. Van Doren's family divided its time between a country estate in Connecticut and a Greenwich Village townhouse where guests over the years included Sinclair Lewis, Mortimer Adler, Joseph Wood Krutch, and Morris Ernst. The family was the symbol of intellectual vitality.

Van Doren established himself on the program by defeating the swarthy, seemingly impoverished previous champion Herbert Stempel on December 5, 1956, after having played three tie matches with Stempel on November 28. It was smooth sailing for the weeks that followed.

On the TV screen [Eric Goldman has written] he appeared lanky, pleasant, smooth in dress and manner but never slick, confident but with an engaging way of understating himself. The long, hard questions would come at him and his eyes would roll up, squeeze shut, his forehead furrow and perspire, his teeth gnaw at his lower lip. Breathing heavily, he seemed to coax information out of some corner of his mind by talking to himself in a kind of stream-of-consciousness. Like a good American, he fought hard, taking advantage of every rule. . . . Like a good American, he won without crowing. And, like a good American, he kept on winning, drowning corporation lawyers or ex-college presidents with equal ease on questions ranging from naming the four islands of the Balearic Islands to explaining the process of photosynthesis to naming the three baseball players who each amassed more than 3,500 hits. Charles Van Doren was "the new All-American boy," the magazines declared, and to millions he was that indeed. . . .

Van Doren's victories on the quiz show brought him greater rewards than had accrued to any of his predecessors. He received thousands of letters from parents and teachers around the world, thanking him for popularizing the life of the mind. Little services such as dry cleaning, which he had had to pay for when supporting himself on his $4,400 yearly salary as an English instructor at Columbia, were now donated *gratis* by star-struck shopkeepers. Several colleges expressed an interest in hiring him away from Columbia, and he found himself referred to in print as "Doctor" despite not yet having earned his Ph.D. And then, of course, there was the money. Van Doren won $129,000 during his 14 weeks on *21.* Soon after he left, he was awarded a $50,000 contract to appear on the *Today* show, where for five minutes each morning he would speak of science, literature, history. "I think I may be the only person," he once remarked, "who ever read seventeenth-century poetry on a network television program—a far cry from the usual diet of mayhem, murder, and rape."

Rumors of improper practices surfaced soon after the quiz shows made their debut. By the end of 1956, articles were appearing in the trade and general circulation press discussing the "controls" exercised by the producers to keep popular contestants alive and eliminate the unpopular. "Are the quiz shows rigged?" asked *Time* magazine in the spring of 1957, a year in which the networks were investing a small fortune in them. The answer: producers could not "afford to risk collusion with contestants," and yet, because of

pretesting, they were able to ask questions which they knew the contestants would or would not know. They could thus manipulate the outcome "far more effectively than most viewers suspect." The report noted, however, that Van Doren "feels certain that no questions were being formfitted to his phenomenal mind."

A number of contestants had been disappointed at their treatment on the shows. The most important of these, and the John Dean of this piece, was the man Van Doren first defeated, Herbert Stempel.

Stempel's motives were very mixed. One was money. He had quickly squandered his winnings and had failed in an attempt to blackmail more out of producer Dan Enright. A more important reason was his bruised ego. Stempel had been forced to portray himself as a poor boy from Brooklyn, when in fact he had married into a well-to-do family and was from Queens. Enright insisted that he wear ratty suits and a cheap wristwatch to project this image and that he address the emcee, Jack Barry, deferentially as Mr. Barry while other contestants called him Jack. He had an I.Q. of 170 and was infuriated by having to "miss" answers he knew "damn well." And he was beside himself at the unearned praise accorded to Van Doren. Here was " . . . a guy that had a fancy name, Ivy League education, parents all his life, and I had the opposite. . . ." He would hear passing strangers remark that he was the man who had lost to this child of light, and he could not stand it. But it was more than greed or envy that prompted Stempel to turn state's evidence. Even before he was ordered to "take a dive" and before he had ever heard of Charles Van Doren, he was telling friends that the show was fixed. Stempel knew all the real answers about the quiz shows, and he was bursting to show the nation how smart he was.

In 1957, Stempel tried to interest two New York newspapers in the truth, but both papers refused to print what would have been one of the biggest scoops of the decade because they feared libel action. It is a commentary on the state of investigative journalism at the time that not until August, 1958, after the discovery that a giveaway show called *Dotto* was fixed, was Stempel able to make his charges in public. At this time also, New York Country District Attorney Frank Hogan began an investigation, and the inexorable process of revelation had been set in motion. For almost a year, the grand jury interviewed about 150 witnesses. The producers tried to arrange a cover-up by persuading the show's alumni to perjure themselves. Many of the most well known did just that. It was one thing to fix a quiz show, however, and quite another to fix a grand jury probe. Realizing that the day of reckoning was at last approaching, the producers hurried back to change their testimony. This they did without informing the contestants, leaving them, to put it mildly, out on a limb.

For reasons which remain unclear, the judge sealed the grand jury's presentment, but the Subcommittee on Legislative Oversight (over the FCC) of the House Interstate and Foreign Commerce Committee determined to get to the bottom of the matter. Its public hearings, held in Washington in October and November of 1959, attracted worldwide attention.

On October 6, a bitter Herbert Stempel exposed the whole sordid story of *21*. He had originally applied to take part in what he thought was an honest game but was approached by Enright who talked him into becoming an actor rather than a riverboat gambler. Every detail of his performances was prearranged: his wardrobe, his diffidence, his hesitations, and his answers. He was instructed on the proper way to mop his brow for maximum effect, and he was guaranteed to sweat because the air conditioning in the isolation booth was purposely kept off. From his testimony, it became clear that Van Doren was implicated as well. On the following two days, other contestants, producer Enright, and his assistant Albert Freedman testified to the fix. No one contradicted Stempel.

In the months preceding the hearings Van Doren had consistently and ever more vehemently proclaimed that no matter what others had done, his appearances on *21* had been strictly legitimate. When Stempel's charges were first published in the papers, Van Doren was " . . . horror struck. . . . I couldn't understand why Stempel should want to proclaim his own involvement." A representative of D. A. Hogan interviewed him toward the end of the year, and he denied everything. He retained a lawyer, to whom he lied about his involvement, and then proceeded to perjure himself before the New York County Grand Jury in January, 1959. He was assured by Enright and Freedman that they too would cover up.

Van Doren's day of reckoning came on November 2, 1959, before the subcommittee. Herb Stempel hurried down from New York City to get a seat from which he could clearly see his former adversary. Pale and jittery, Van Doren walked into the crowded hearing room and delivered himself of one of the most pathetic confessions in the history of American public speech.

He wished that he could erase the past three years but realizing the past may be immutable resolved to learn from it. When he had first contacted Barry and Enright, he had assumed that their programs were honest. Before his appearance on *21,* Albert Freedman summoned him to his apartment and, talking him into the bedroom, explained that Stempel had to be defeated in order to make the show more popular. Van Doren asked to go on the air honestly, but Freedman said he had no chance to defeat the brilliant Stempel. "He also told me that the show was merely entertainment and that giving help to quiz contestants was a common practice and merely a part of show business." Besides, said Freedman, Van Doren had an opportunity to help increase respect for intellectual life and education. "I will not," said Van Doren, "bore this committee by describing the intense moral struggle that went on inside me." The result of that struggle was history. Freedman coached him on how to answer questions to increase suspense and several times gave him a script to memorize. When Van Doren missed the questions which were slated for the evening, Freedman " . . . would allow me to look them up myself. A foolish sort of pride made me want to look up the answers when I could, and to learn as much about the subject as possible."

As time went on the show ballooned beyond my wildest expectations. . . . [F]rom an unknown college instructor I became a celebrity. I received thousands of letters and dozens of requests to make speeches, appear in movies, and so forth—in short, all the trappings of modern publicity. To a certain extent this went to my head.

He realized, however, that he was misrepresenting education and was becoming more nervous about the show. He urged the producers to let him quit, but it was only after they could arrange a sufficiently dramatic situation that he was defeated.

Van Doren's brief testimony was the climax of the subcommittee's investigation as it was of this scandal as a whole. Nevertheless, the hearings continued, including an investigation of *The $64,000 Question. Question* was also fixed, and although the details differed from the *21* case, the deception was no less pervasive.

It is no exaggeration to say that the American public was transfixed by the revelation of quiz show fraud. A Gallup poll found the highest level of public awareness of the event in the history of such surveys. Questioned about the shows at successive news conferences, President Eisenhower said he shared "the American general reaction of almost bewilderment" and compared the manipulations to the Black Sox scandal of 1919. The quiz show episode affords an opportunity to discuss feelings toward Van Doren, the hero unmasked, and also the general arguments which swirled around television at decade's turn.

For Van Doren, humiliation came in the wake of confession. Just as institutions had been happy to associate themselves with quiz show geniuses, they hurried to dissociate themselves when the geniuses turned out to be hustlers. NBC fired Van Doren, while Columbia "accepted his resignation." The actions of these two institutions were scrutinized along with those of Van Doren in the period following his confession.

From the first, both NBC and CBS had maintained the highly implausible stand that they were fooled about the shows along with the public. They unquestionably could have uncovered the rigging had they really wanted to, and in the end they were left holding the bag. They had lost millions of dollars and, what was worse, had suffered what at the time loomed as a potentially mortal blow to a very pleasant way of making a lot of money. The popular uproar threatened to force government to restrict the broadcasting prerogatives of management. In this state of affairs, Van Doren had to go. CBS took the next step, eliminating quiz shows altogether, from which NBC refrained.

Few were surprised by NBC's stand. The network was, after all, a business, and Van Doren had become a liability. Columbia's treatment of him aroused different issues. Some students had no patience with him, but hundreds rallied to his defense with petitions and demonstrations. They pointed out that his teaching was excellent and that having made public relations capital out of his victories, Columbia would be craven to desert him now. The Columbia College dean, however, maintained, "The issue is the moral one of the honesty and integrity of teaching." The dean found Van Doren's deceptions contrary to the principles a teacher should have and should try to instill in his students.

The academic community holds in especial contempt, as *Love Story* author Erich Segal was to discover, those "willing to play the fool" for limitless publicity. In defense of Columbia's action, political scientist Hans J. Morgenthau published two essays purporting to show that Van Doren had actually violated "the moral law" as handed down from Moses, Plato, Buddha, and other worthies. Apparently no such law would have been violated had Van Doren's participation in what thinking people very well knew was a cheap stunt been unrigged. If any crime had been committed in the quiz show episode, it was surely the broad conspiracy to portray as genuine intellectual activity the spouting of trivia. But while the shows were on and winning high ratings, there was neither from Morgenthau nor Columbia a peep of protest.

The most devastating but also perhaps the fairest indictment of Van Doren's role was penned by a Columbia colleague, Lawrence S. Hall, who demonstrated that Van Doren's confession had been as thoroughly fraudulent as his conduct on *21*. He had not confessed because of a letter from a fan of his on the *Today* show as he had claimed but only because of a congressional subpoena. "To the very end he never did perform the ethical free act of making up his mind. . . . Van Doren did not *decide* to tell the truth; what he did was adapt himself to the finally inescapable necessity of telling it." Worst of all, asserted Hall, was his "concealing under [the] piously reflexive formulas" of his silken prose "the most maudlin and promiscuous ethical whoredom the soap opera public has yet witnessed."

Unlike Hall the average American seemed rather sympathetic. A Sindlinger poll asked respondents to rate those most blameworthy for the fixes. Asked to assess the responsibility of network, sponsor, producer, and Van Doren, only 18.6 percent blamed Van Doren the most while 38.9 percent blamed him the least. A substantial number even favored a continuation of the shows, rigged or not. Many man-in-the-street interviewees said they would have done no differently, and most newspaper editorials treated him extraordinarily gently.

Investigators discovered not a single contestant on *21,* and only one on *The $64,000 Question,* who refused to accept money once they learned the shows were fixed. Most were quite "blithe" about it. Pollsters at the end of the 1950s were finding the belief widespread that the individual did not feel it was his place to condemn. Moral relativism, it seemed, rather than adherence to Professor Morgenthau's moral absolutism, was the rule. So many people lived polite lies that though it may have been titillating to discover them, they were hardly worth preaching about.

Other factors, in addition to this general willingness to partake in a fraud such as the quiz shows, help explain why the outrage was muted and transient. First, as Boorstin has pointed out, television unites many people in a community, but their union is tenuous and easily forgotten. Secondly, although many were taken in by the seeming reality of the shows, they had believed and been disabused so many times in the past that the shock soon wore off. For underneath the belief in the shows there probably lingered skepti-

cism. Robert Merton observed in 1946 that cynicism about public statements from any source, political or commercial, was pervasive. Television was a new medium which some may have thought was simply too big to play by the rules of the old-time newspaper patent medicine advertiser. The quiz shows taught them that it was not, and some critics asserted that it was the naked selfishness of commercial radio and television, more than the machinations of particular producers or contestants, that was truly to blame. The quiz shows excited to a new pitch of intensity long-running arguments about commercial broadcasting and the public interest.

The growth of commercial broadcasting cannot be explored here at length, but suffice it to say that it was opposed every step of the way by intellectuals, educators, and journalists who deplored what they saw as the perversion of a medium of great potential for the sake of the desire of private business to push products. As early as the 1920s, when radio was first coming into its own, articulate voices spoke up against its use for advertising. Bruce Bliven thought such "outrageous rubbish" should be banned from the air, and at least one congressman considered introducing legislation to that end. Herbert Hoover, whose Commerce Department supervised the granting of broadcast licenses, felt that radio would die if it allowed itself to be "drowned in advertising chatter," but he favored self-regulation rather than government action. The Radio Act of 1927 demanded that licensees operated their stations not solely for profit but with due regard for the "public interest, convenience, and necessity."

As charted by broadcasting's foremost historian, Erik Barnouw, the ascendancy of commercial programming was established in a fit of absence of mind. "If such a system [as exists today] had been outlined in 1927 or 1934, when our basic broadcasting laws were written," he concluded, "it certainly would have been rejected." Critics believed that the quiz shows and the radio "payola" scandals that followed proved that broadcasting was too important to be left in the hands of those whose primary, if not sole, motive was to turn a profit for the stockholders.

Television executives insisted that the scandals were the exception in a generally well run industry, but critics thought they were the tip of the iceberg. In themselves, the scandals were relatively unimportant, held the *New Republic.* "A real investigation would center on the simple question: why is television so bad, so monstrous?" It was the thirst for profit which forced the industry to a state of thralldom to the ratings. It was profit which mandated such dreadful children's programming. Advertising agencies and their clients, with profit always uppermost in mind, forced absurd restrictions on what could be broadcast. When commentators complained about the astounding amount of violence on the tube, defenders warned of the danger of censorship. Critics replied that the most stultifying censorship was already being exercised in behalf of the manufacturers of the pointless nostrums of an overindulgent society. In its quest for ratings, television seemed consistently to avoid satisfying the intelligent minority.

The industry had now been caught red-handed, Walter Lippmann wrote, in " . . . an enormous conspiracy to deceive the public in order to sell profitable advertising to the sponsors." The situation which had made this shameful occurrence possible could not be allowed to survive intact. Television had "to live up to a higher, but less profitable, standard." What America needed was prime time TV produced "not because it yields private profits but because it moves toward truth and excellence." What was needed, said Lippmann, was public service television.

Industry spokesmen had traditionally defended themselves as true democrats. The president of CBS, Frank Stanton, soon after *The $64,000 Question* was first aired, declared, "A program in which a large part of the audience is interested is by that very fact . . . in the public interest." By such a standard, the quiz shows can be seen not as "cynical malpractices . . . in one corner of television," as Robert Sarnoff tried to represent them, but rather as the perfect expression of the industry.

Sarnoff recognized the charges being hurled at TV in 1959 and 1960 as the "long-familiar [ones] of mediocrity, imbalance, violence, and overcommercialism." These charges had been unjustified

in the past and were unjustified in 1960, but because " . . . those who press them are now armed with the cudgels represented by the quiz-show deceptions" they could not be sloughed off. Sarnoff's response was to promise careful scrutiny of such programs in the future and vigorous self-regulation. As a special bonus to the viewing public in a gesture to wipe the slate clean, he offered to donate time for a series of debates between the major Presidential candidates of 1960, which eventually resulted in the televised confrontations between Kennedy and Nixon.

Sarnoff's offer was enthusiastically welcomed by such politicians as Stewart Udall, who had been working for a suspension of equal time regulations in order to permit broadcast debates between Democratic and Republican Presidential nominees in the upcoming election. Paradoxically, the four "Great Debates" which ensued showed unmistakably the influence of the supposedly discredited quiz programs. The similarity in formats was obvious. As in *21,* two adversaries faced each other and tried to give point-scoring answers to questions fired at them under the glare of klieg lights. The debates bore as little relationship to the real work of the presidency as the quiz shows did to intellectuality. Boorstin has remarked on how successful they were " . . . in reducing great national issues to trivial dimensions. With appropriate vulgarity, they might have been called the $400,000 Question (Prize: a $100,000-a-year job for four years)." No President would act on any question put to him by the reporters without sustained and sober consultation with trusted advisors. But the American people, conditioned by five years of isolation booth virtuosity, expected the "right" answer to be delivered pithily and with little hesitation. They did not want to be told that some questions did not have simple answers—or any answers at all.

The technological advances which led to radio and television grew out of the tinkerings of amateur experimenters. These two new forms of mass communication, with unprecedented drama and immediacy, developed independently of the desire to say anything. In 1854, Henry David Thoreau wrote, "We are in great haste to con-

Charles Van Doren, winner of $129,000 in a rigged TV quiz show, pleaded guilty to perjury in his testimony to the New York County Grand Jury and received a suspended sentence in 1962.

struct a magnetic telegraph from Maine to Texas; but Maine and Texas, it may be, have nothing important to communicate." This observation has been yet more relevant during the last half century. Except for the military, which was always seeking more direct means for locating ships at sea and soldiers on the battlefield, no one knew what to broadcast and telecast. The federal government, dominated by the ideology of free enterprise, declined to fill this void. To be sure, regulations did prohibit certain messages over the air, but there has never been a national statement on the positive purposes of the new media which the industry was obliged to take seriously.

Businessmen soon discovered that broadcasting was a powerful instrument for increasing sales. Those advertisers who had financed the print media, including manufacturers of patent medicines, cosmetics, and cigarettes, quickly adopted the same role with radio and television. Left to their own devices, they sought programs which would constitute a congenial frame for their selling message. They soon hit upon the idea, among others, of parlor games, of which the quiz shows were direct descendants.

Such programs had been popular since the thirties, but in the 1950s, clever producers learned how to make them even more so. They combined large sums of money with the American fondness for facts, dressed up as intellectuality, and the result was *The $64,000 Question* and *21*. When these programs were exposed as frauds, a jaded public, inured to mendacity, was quick to forgive.

Critics have often complained, as they did with vigor after the scandals, that television—"a medium of such great potential"—was being so ill-used. But no one seems to have a clear vision of what that potential is. The lack of direction which characterized the early years of American broadcasting has never been overcome. Commentators such as Lippmann have won their public broadcasting system, but commercial television has not upgraded its fare in order to compete. If anything, public TV may act as a lightning rod deflecting complaints about the commercial industry by providing an outlet for those demanding alternative viewing.

For its part, the industry has usually ignored what enlightened guidance has been available in favor of traditional forms of entertainment guaranteed not to distract the viewer from the advertisements. Thus, recently, quiz and game shows have made a comeback. There has even been talk of resurrecting *The $64,000 Question,* despite the risk of reviving along with it memories of past chicanery. Such programming represents a distressing devotion to Philistinism and a failure of imagination, the solution for which is not in sight.

Study Questions

1. What is implied by the concept of a "consumption community"? How is this sort of a community different from any other community?

2. Compare how Charles Van Doren and Herbert Stempel were presented on the television quiz show *21.* Why was Stempel told to appear poor and deferential on the show? Is there a political statement in the images of both men?

3. How did most Americans respond to the disclosure that *21* and other quiz shows were rigged?

4. What does Tedlow mean by the concept of "moral relativism"? Is morality ever absolute?

5. What issues are involved in the debate between advocates of commercial broadcasting and proponents of public service broadcasting?

6. How were the Nixon-Kennedy television debates in 1960 similar to or different from the format of the television quiz show *21?* What does this say about the importance of television in a political campaign?

Bibliography

The television industry has received far less historical attention than the film industry. This is perplexing, considering that television "touches" more people—American as well as non-American—than the movies. The fact that some movie directors have consciously cultivated reputations as "artists" undoubtedly has something to do with academic interest in their product that is not apparent with television. There are, however, several very good books on television. Among the best are Erik Barnauw, *The Golden Web* (1968) and *The Image Empire: A History of Broadcasting in the United States* (1970); Raymond Williams, *Television: Technology and Cultural Form* (1975); and Robert Sklare, *Prime-Time America: Life on and Behind the Television Screen* (1980). Also of interest are two books by Daniel Boorstin, *The Americans: The Democratic Experience* (1974) and *The Image: A Guide to Pseudo-Events in America* (1961). The Van Doren case is dealt with in Kent Anderson, *Television Fraud* (1978), and Eric Goldman, *The Crucial Decade and After: America, 1945–1960* (1960). Douglas Miller and Marian Novak discuss social and cultural developments in the 1950s in *The Fifties: The Way We Really Were* (1977) as does Karal Ann Marling *As Seen on TV: The Visual Culture of Everyday Life in the 1950s* (1996).

READING 23

★ ★ ★

Smoking and Cancer

James T. Patterson

For Americans who watched television in the 1960s or leafed through magazines for much of the rest of the decade, the image of a nameless man is etched in their minds. A rugged outdoorsmen, handsome and strong, framed against the equally rugged, equally strong, equally handsome American West, the land of snow-capped mountains and parched cattle country and pure virility. The man is often astride a horse, reins in his hands, a cowboy hat covering his eyes, a cigarette between his lips. The Marlboro Man, riding through the fantasies of American men and women, riding across a purely mythic American landscape toward a universal nightmare. In the early 1950s, Marlboro was a brand of cigarettes produced by Philip Morris and targeted for women. It came in a white soft pack, had a red "beauty tip" filter to camouflage lipstick, and sold under the slogan, "Mild as May." In the mid-1950s, advertiser Leo Burnett took over the Marlboro account and targeted a new audience. He dumped the white soft pack for a red hard pack, got rid of the "beauty tip" and "Mild as May" slogan, and tapped into Western iconography for the Marlboro Man. Pure West, pure American. Burnette's campaign became the most financially successful in advertising history.

By the time of Burnett's campaign, most Americans, of course, had at least a vague sense that cigarettes were related to cancer. But the tobacco industry was grimly determined to blur the growing medical evidence of the harmful effects of cigarette smoking and to tie their product to American fantasies of sex and virility. As much as any two industries, tobacco and advertising went hand and glove, each helping the other to mature and profit. In the following essay, historian James T. Patterson looks at the unglamorous side of cigarette smoking, tracing the growth of medical evidence against the habit.

No pleasure can exceed the smoking of the weed," proclaimed an advertisement from the nineteenth century. Millions of Americans agreed—among them Mark Twain, who said, "It's easy to stop smoking. I know because I've done it thousands of times." A hundred years later, Americans are bombarded with reasons for giving up the pleasure of "the smoking of the weed":

Country-western songwriter and entertainer Sollie "Tex" Williams, a heavy smoker best known for his tune, "Smoke, Smoke, Smoke That Cigarette," died after a year-long battle with cancer, his daughter said . . . her father, who was diagnosed a year ago as having cancer, smoked two packs of cigarettes a day, dropping to about a pack a day before he died. "He tried to quit, but he couldn't," she said.

Smoking causes lung cancer, heart disease, emphysema and may complicate pregnancy.

Quitting smoking now greatly reduces serious risks to your health.

Smoking by pregnant women may result in fetal injury, premature birth and low birth weight.

Cigarette smoke contains carbon monoxide.

Cigarette smoking is clearly identified as the chief, single, avoidable cause of death in our society and the most important public health issue of our time.

Cigarette consumption per person over age eighteen rose from 151 per year in 1910 to 1,485 in 1930 to a high if 4,286 in 1963; since then it has decreased, mainly after 1975, to 3,378 in 1985. Between 1935 and 1980 more than one million Americans died of lung cancer caused by smoking. Lung cancer, one medical historian commented, is "the most remarkable epidemic of the twentieth century." Government officials say that cigarette-induced ailments cost $65 billion a year by the mid-1980s, more than $22 billion for medical expenses and the rest attributed to losses of

wages, productivity, and taxes. Lung cancer deaths—at least 80 percent caused by smoking—were estimated to total 126,000 in 1985, as opposed to but 2,300 in 1930 and 7,100 in 1940. These 126,000 deaths were 23 percent of cancer mortality in the United States. (Mortality from cancers of the rectum and colon, estimated at 60,000 in 1985, ranked second.) An additional 22,000 Americans died in 1985 from tobacco-induced cancers elsewhere in the body, 20,000 from pulmonary disease, and 225,000 from tobacco-related cardiovascular ailments. The grand total of nearly 400,000 represented more than 1,000 premature deaths linked to smoking a day. As one cancer researcher has commented, "it is almost as if Western societies had set out to conduct a vast and fairly well controlled experiment in carcinogenesis bringing about several million deaths and using their own people as experimental animals."

Without the increase in lung cancer, epidemiologists pointed out, age-adjusted mortality rates from malignant tumors would have declined slightly since the 1930s. But lung cancers caused aggregate age-adjusted rates in the United States to climb slowly. The villain, almost all experts agreed, was tobacco—described by John Cairns as a "fifth column in our midst." Surgeon General C. Everett Koop said in 1986 that people who smoked two packs a day had a rate of lung cancer that was as much as twenty-five times greater than the rate for nonsmokers.

If there were any promising statistics to be found in these numbers, they had to do with the tobacco habits of men. For years men had been the main consumers of cigarettes: from the mid-1920s through the early 1960s more than 50 percent of adult American males smoked. In 1985, 87,000 of the estimated 126,000 lung cancer deaths afflicted men. After the mid-1960s the percentage of adult males who smoked declined considerably—to around 33 percent in 1985—and mortality from lung cancer among white males began in 1984 to decrease for the very first time. But women, who had entered the tobacco culture later, were smoking more by this time. In the mid-1930s fewer than 20 percent of adult fe-

James T. Patterson, *The Dread Disease: Cancer and Modern American Culture* (1987), pp. 201–222.

males smoked in the United States, but during and after World War Two they, too, took up the habit in large numbers. The percentage of adult women who smoked peaked at approximately 33 percent between 1955 and 1975 and declined only to around 28 percent by 1985. By then lung cancer (at more than 38,000) for the first time seemed about to replace breast tumors as the leading source of cancer mortality among women. The American Cancer Society, drawing on evidence that had accumulated since the 1950s, reported that women who smoked while pregnant were more likely to have miscarriages, stillbirths, and premature deliveries, and to give birth to infants with serious mental and physical ailments.

These dramatic developments in smoking, and the consequent rise in mortality from lung cancer, can be traced to profound social, economic, and cultural forces in twentieth-century American life: the rise of large tobacco corporations, the flowering of mass cigarette advertising, the anxieties of world wars, the quest for masculinity, the pressure of peers, the addictive power of nicotine, the spread of female employment, the gospel of women's liberation, sheer pleasure. These and other forces helped to explain why nearly one-third of adult Americans, more than 50 million people, in the mid-1980s persisted in maintaining a habit that substantially increased their risk of premature death.

The persistence of the smoking habit is remarkable. It flourished, after all, during the very years that most Americans expressed great concern for good health, fear of death, and dread of cancer. The tobacco habit, a known risk, clashed sharply with these values. But the contradiction is not altogether surprising. Some who continued to smoke had no choice—they were addicted. Many others simultaneously celebrated competing values, such as the pursuit of personal pleasure and the quest for good health. Quitting, an investment in future gains, was a renunciation of immediate gratification. To some the sacrifice was not worth it.

The clash of values over smoking also revealed—as reactions to diseases often had—significant differences in the attitudes of America's social classes toward health, illness, and the medical profession. Since the 1950s the clash has featured on one level a noisy battle between two well-organized interest groups—tobacco companies and health professionals. But on another level it has been a struggle between a mainly middle-class and professional alliance against smoking and a rearguard action especially strong among blue-collar and lower-class people, many of whom continue to have scant access to or faith in scientific medicine. With characteristically American independence of mind, millions of people have felt they ought to be allowed to do as they pleased, even if experts said otherwise.

In the 1920s and early 1930s, the wilderness years of cancer control, various researchers cited tobacco as a carcinogen. Their reports reinforced a popular opinion, widespread since before [President] Grant's time, that smoking was unhealthy. Grant's death, indeed, was often used (by Frederick Hoffman, among others) as proof enough of the argument. But the main concern was cancer of the mouth or throat; lung cancer was very rare.

Only in the early 1930s did many doctors begin to encounter the ailment. And only then did surgeons and pathologists start to make the connection between smoking and lung cancer. One of the first was Dr. William McNally of Rush Medical College, who stated in 1932 that "cigarette smoking is an important factor in the increase of cancer of the lungs." In 1938 Dr. Raymond Pearl, a distinguished professor of biometry, claimed in *Science* that smoking was "statistically associated with an impairment of life duration." In the same year the *Science News Letter* carried an article by Drs. Alton Ochsner and Michael DeBakey of New Orleans that asserted, "more persons are dying of cancer of the lung than ever before, probably because more persons are smoking and inhaling tobacco smoke than ever before."

Not everyone, however, agreed. James Tobey, in his popular, sensible book on cancer in 1932, spoke for many who distrusted the "rabid antitobacco literature" and the "fanatical reform bodies" who lobbied against smoking just as they had done—with such controversial results—against drinking. "An example of the banal attacks on tobacco," he said, "is the frequent assertion that President Grant suffered from cancer of the throat merely because he smoked to excess." "There is no scientific evidence," he concluded, "to show that My Lady Nicotine has any deleterious effect."

Many doctors in the 1930s agreed with Tobey. Some asserted that the incidence of lung cancer only seemed to be increasing—the result of better diagnoses from X-rays and bronchoscopies. Others thought the increases real, but blamed them on atmospheric pollution or from delayed reactions to the great flu epidemic of 1918-19. Still others believed that lung cancer, which seemed mainly to afflict men, could not be caused by cigarettes, because women also smoked. And many, articulating the contemporary emphasis on "irritation," maintained that tobacco could provoke cancer only among those who overindulged and who were genetically predisposed. If there was a common denominator to these varied views, it was that cigarettes did not do too much harm if smoked in moderation. Clarence Little, summing up the evidence in 1939, concluded on behalf of the cancer society that "the more common use of tobacco is blamed by some for the frequency of lung cancer . . . It is impossible to say how accurate these opinions are."

While the experts debated, the way remained open for proponents of tobacco to push their products. In 1933 Congress approved legislation guaranteeing price supports—and long-range economic security—for tobacco farmers. This step advanced a powerful network of tobacco interests that joined the producers and marketers with governments—federal, state, and local—which derived substantial income from taxes on tobacco products.

Paramount among the tobacco lobby were the cigarette manufacturers, who spent ever increasing amounts on advertising—an estimated $50 million by 1940—to sell their wares. The new mass-circulation magazines such as *Time* and *Newsweek* became heavily dependent on cigarette advertising for revenue. The *Journal of the*

Reprinted with permission from Katz and Harrison, Attorneys at Law, 1986.

American Medical Association carried cigarette ads as late as the 1950s. The battle over smoking in modern America involved considerably more than skirmishes over scientific findings; important economic interests were also at stake.

Beginning in the late 1920s, many ads broke with the past by appealing directly to women. Cigarettes, the ads said in raising the banner of female emancipation, were "torches of freedom." Albert Lasker's "Reach for a Lucky instead of a Sweet," aimed at women's weight-consciousness. Many ads dwelt on romance and sex: "Blow Some My Way," a woman purred as she looked longingly at her man puff on a cigarette. As early as 1934 Eleanor Roosevelt showed her independence by smoking publicly. In the late 1930s women's handbags and compacts were routinely designed to hold cigarette packs. By then prominent women gladly posed for full-page color cigarette ads in the magazines. Alice Roosevelt Longworth, Theodore's daughter, praised the virtues of Luckies. "They're a light smoke," kind to the throat, she said. The syndicated columnist Dorothy Kilgallen promoted Camels. The actress Carole Lombard favored Luckies—"they're easier on the throat."

The ads, moreover, tried to make smoking look attractive: cigarettes made women sexually alluring, young men tough and masculine. The American Tobacco Company pushed a brand named "Stud," and John Wayne (who later died of lung cancer) promoted Camels. A cigarette dangled from the lips of Humphrey Bogart playing Sam Spade in "The Maltese Falcon" (1941). A sultry Lauren Bacall made her entrance in "To Have or Have Not" (1944) with the line, "Anybody got a match?" Betty Grable, the ultimate pin-up girl of the forties, posed alluringly for tobacco ads. "With the boys," she said, "it's Chesterfields." Promotions for Luckies used the acronym "LSMFT" to make the sexual connection more explicit. Lucky Strike, the ads said, "Means Fine Tobacco—so round, so firm, so fully packed."

Cigarette consumption jumped enormously during World War Two and in the late 1940s— from 1,976 to 3,552 annually per adult American during the decade. Though some of this increase reflected the growing consumption by women, many of whom broke with traditional roles to enter the labor market, much of it was accounted for by men in the armed services. Young, far from home, often afraid, soldiers turned to cigarettes—which came with C rations— for solace amidst the pressures of war and military discipline.

So taken for granted were cigarettes to American culture in these years that the rapidly rising incidence of lung cancer, which caused 15 percent of cancer deaths by 1950, received relatively little public attention. Neither did the warnings by Ochsner and others. Many doctors, on the contrary, continued to smoke and to dismiss such warnings. As late as 1948 the *Journal of the American Medical Association* stated that "more can be said in behalf of smoking as a form of escape from tension than against it . . . there does not seem to be any preponderance of evidence that would indicate the abolition of the use of tobacco as a substance contrary to the public health."

While the AMA remained reluctant to confront the tobacco lobby for many years thereafter, others jumped in during the 1950s to forge an increasingly aggressive alliance against tobacco. Leaders in this struggle were physicians and epidemiologists who began to publish statistics connecting cigarette smoking and cancer.

One of the earliest to show concern over lung cancer was Dr. Evarts Graham, a surgeon and professor at Washington University in St. Louis. Observing great increases in lung cancers in the mid-1930s, he and his students—including Ochsner—feared a virtual epidemic of carcinoma of the lung. But Graham, a smoker himself, was slow to blame tobacco. "Yes," he told Ochsner, "there is a parallel between the sale of cigarettes and the incidence of cancer of the lung, but there is also a parallel between the sale of nylon stockings and cancer of the lung." Graham's skepticism mirrored contemporary bewilderment about the causes of lung cancer.

But Ernst Wynder, another of Graham's students, was not to be put off. He strongly suspected that tobacco was the villain, and in the

1940s he and Graham launched an epidemiological study of the subject. At the same time a group of British doctors and statisticians embarked on similar research. Both studies were "retrospective," selecting cancer patients (and others without cancer) and then asking both groups about their habits. When these studies were published in 1950, they documented significant statistical correlations between cigarette smoking and lung cancer. "Extensive and prolonged use of tobacco, especially cigarettes," Wynder and Graham concluded, "seems to be an important factor in the inducement of bronchiogenic carcinoma." The British researchers added that "smoking is a factor and an important factor, in the production of carcinoma of the lung."

Because these were careful studies, each involving hundreds of cases of lung cancer, they attracted a fair amount of attention in medical circles. But the researchers tended to stop short of asserting a causal connection between smoking and lung cancer. Other factors, they noted, might also cause the disease. Moreover, Graham and others admitted that they did not know what was carcinogenic about tobacco. Some people wondered if the carcinogenic effect came from insecticides, not from the tobacco itself. The researchers also faced criticism of their methods, for retrospective studies depend heavily on the recollections of patients. For all these reasons the early studies fell short of persuading the doubters.

But the studies were too alarming to be ignored, and over the next few years laboratory researchers showed that tars from tobacco were carcinogenic in animals. Epidemiologists, meanwhile, began conducting "prospective" studies, one of which was funded by the American Cancer Society starting in 1951. These studies used volunteers to locate hundreds of thousands of smokers and nonsmokers and to track their health over time. As early as 1952 the researchers were shocked by the incidence of lung cancer among the smokers, and in 1954 they published the first of many reports. They found that age-adjusted death rates from lung cancer were at least three times higher among male smokers than among nonsmokers, and at least five times higher among heavy smokers.

These researchers, too, conceded that other carcinogens, such as soot or automobile fumes, might also be causing lung cancer. But they were convinced by the study that cigarettes were the major cause of the disease. E. Cuyler Hammond and Daniel Horn, the ACS researchers, had both been cigarette smokers, but they quickly dropped the habit, taking up pipes, when the statistics started coming in. "We believe," they said in 1954, "the associations found between regular cigarette smoking and diseases of the coronary arteries, and between smoking and cancer, reflect cause-and-effect relationships." The ACS joined in by urging smokers to cut consumption. By 1957 Hammond was still more certain. He asserted that people who persisted in smoking two packs a day or more died seven years earlier on the average than nonsmokers and that cigarette smoking increased the chance of fatal coronary attack by 50 percent. In that same year Evarts Graham—though he cut back in 1953 to a pack a day—died from lung cancer.

By this time a few federal officials began to join the slowly developing alliance against smoking. Among these were members of the House Committee on Governmental Operations, which conducted an investigation in 1957 of tobacco advertising, especially ads proclaiming the supposed benefits of newly marketed filter cigarettes. Led by Congressman John Blatnik of Minnesota (who was a smoker), the committee reported in 1958 that "cigarette manufacturers have deceived the American public through their advertising of cigarettes." This kind of pressure encouraged the Federal Trade Commission (which in 1955 had taken steps against ads that implied medical endorsement of smoking) to negotiate a voluntary agreement with the tobacco companies in 1960. The FTC attempted to put an end to exaggerated claims for filter cigarettes.

Perhaps more important to the antitobacco alliance was the gradual participation of the Public Health Service. Under the cautious stewardship of Surgeon General Leroy Burney, the PHS in 1956 established a scientific study group involving the NCI, the National Heart Institute, the ACS, and the American Heart Association. In 1957 the group announced that "there is an increasing and consistent body of evidence that excessive cigarette smoking is one of the causative factors in lung cancer." Venturing further in 1959, Burney singled out cigarettes as the major cause of lung cancer. The cooperation of the PHS—and under it of the NCI—with the ACS suggested that the long-standing professional alliance against cancer was gradually lining up against cigarettes.

To some extent popular magazines lined up, too. As early as 1952 *Reader's Digest,* which refused to carry tobacco ads, ran a scare story entitled "Cancer by the Carton." When laboratory scientists demonstrated the carcinogenic nature of tobacco tars in 1953, *Time* stated that they had proved "beyond any doubt" that smoking caused cancer. A month later *Life* carried a story headed SMOKE GETS IN THE NEWS. It cautioned that the findings of Graham and Wynder, whose research on cigarette tars involved animals, should not induce people to "promptly quit smoking, for this might create nervous ailments." But the article also made it clear that tar from tobacco had caused cancer in mice. It added that statistics on tobacco consumption correlated with significant increases in lung cancer among human beings. Other magazines—*Nation, New Republic, U.S. News and World Report*—also refused to take cigarette advertisements. *Time, Life,* and *Newsweek,* while profiting from big ads, reported the damaging findings of the epidemiologists and the warnings of government officials.

Through these various outlets the alliance succeeded in conveying their arguments to the public. Opinion polls as early as 1954 revealed that 90 percent of respondents had read news stories linking smoking and cancer. Polls also showed ever increasing pluralities of people agreeing that "cigarette smoking is one of the causes of lung cancer." As early as 1954 a lung cancer patient sued the tobacco companies, and the store where he bought his cigarettes, claiming that they had advertised death-dealing products.

Though he lost the case, his effort received a fair amount of publicity. Suits like this one signified the rise of hostility already being directed at tobacco companies.

Perhaps the most striking insight into popular attitudes came from opinion polls taken after publication of Hammond's findings in 1957. Of those polled 77 percent claimed to have heard about them. Half of these respondents said that smoking caused cancer, a quarter that it did not, and the rest that they did not know. At that time, 42 percent of the adult population (52 percent of men, 34 percent of women) were smokers. Even this group (by a margin of 38 percent to 36 percent, with 26 percent undecided) thought smoking caused cancer.

These polls made two important things unmistakably clear: first, that smokers were more likely than nonsmokers to reject the warnings about cancer; second, that substantial majorities of the population as a whole recognized that cigarettes were unhealthy. Those who smoked, then and later, did not always know the full extent of the dangers of tobacco. Smokers who were not addicted, however, were making a conscious choice to ignore the expert advice of the alliance against cancer. Their behavior says much about conflicting values in American society.

The opponents of the antismoking campaign included first of all some determined and well-financed economic interests. In 1954, following the damaging publicity surrounding the prospective studies (which temporarily depressed cigarette sales), the tobacco companies banded together to establish the Tobacco Industry Research Committee (later renamed the Council for Tobacco Research—U.S.A.). Founders of the committee recognized that they had to fight expertise with expertise, and they contacted Clarence Little, who had been running the Jackson Laboratory in Maine since leaving the ACS. Little agreed to serve (for an annual salary of $20,000) as scientific director.

Why Little joined the committee was never entirely clear—probably it was because his scientific training in genetics led him to associate cancer with genetic predisposition. Whatever the reasons, Little, who stayed at this post until his re-tirement in 1971, tried to give the committee sci-entific respectability. He received very consider-able resources. Under his direction the tobacco lobby spent an estimated $7 million on research between 1954 and 1964. Most of this work, whose findings had little to do with the effect of cigarettes on health, evoked contempt from inde-pendent scientists.

In 1958 the cigarette lobby also formed the To-bacco Institute, Inc., headed by George Allen, for-mer director of the United States Information Agency. Relying on the skill of Hill and Knowlton, a leading public-relations firm, the institute issued a steady stream of releases refuting claims that smoking caused cancer. "We are not on a crusade either for or against tobacco," it announced. "If we have a crusade, it is a crusade for research." Allen elevated tobacco to the status of national symbol. "Through the years," he said,

tobacco is poetry and plays, novels, and essays. Tobacco is painting and sculpture for great artists. Tobacco has been comfort for the com-bat soldier, from Valley Forge to Korea. Tobacco is the ambassador of good will around the world. Tobacco is millions of men and women on the farms, in the factories, in stores and of-fices. Tobacco is a moment of relaxation from today's stress . . . For Franklin Roosevelt, it was a cigarette in a jaunty holder, for Churchill a long cigar, for Einstein, a heavy curved pipe.

Meanwhile, the tobacco companies stepped up their advertising campaigns, the costs of which rose to an estimated $148 million in 1959 (and to $314 million by 1970). Huge as these ex-penditures were, they were worth it to an indus-try whose sales were $7 billion in 1960. By then much of the advertising extolled the virtues of fil-ter cigarettes, which the tobacco companies began emphasizing in the 1950s. The tobacco companies sponsored many of the most expen-sive prime-time TV shows of the 1950s and 1960s—"Arthur Godfrey and His Friends," "The Chesterfield Supper Club," "Stop the Music," and

"Your Lucky Strike Theatre." "It was just like wiring the slot machine to keep paying out a per-petual jackpot," one happy advertiser exulted. "My boy, it was like *printing money.*"

Allen, an experienced Washington insider, de-veloped an effective political coalition to counter the enemies of smoking. This coalition included many advertising executives, magazine and news-paper publishers, and the National Association of Broadcasters, who depended heavily on cigarette ads and whose good will was valued by politicians. Some advertisers were on the board of the ACS and resisted the efforts of Hammond and others to involve the society in the crusade against smoking.

Many doctors, too, abetted the tobacco coali-tion. Some were heavy smokers who could not bring themselves to believe the epidemiological evidence. Others attributed the rise in lung can-cer to better diagnosis. Although the AMA journal opened its pages to Hammond and other re-searchers, top officials of the association refused to accept the causal relationship between smok-ing and lung cancer or heart disease. Critics charged that the association's refusal arose from its consuming fear of national health insurance: if the AMA had opposed the tobacco interests, it would have antagonized well-placed congress-men who were needed in the fight against "so-cialized medicine."

The "Smoke Ring," as enemies of the coalition called it, was especially strong in Congress. Its core consisted of politicians from the tobacco-producing and -manufacturing states. Their allies on the Hill included most southerners, who joined the coalition to demonstrate their regional solidarity; Republicans, who had long worked harmoniously with southern Democrats; and con-servatives, who were fearful on principle of gov-ernmental regulation. Against this formidable combination, the alliance against smoking made little political headway in the 1950s.

Furthermore, some respected researchers con-tinued to doubt the conclusions of the epidemio-logical studies. Wilhelm Hueper, who still headed the environmental cancer section of the NCI, con-sidered smoking an "unhealthy habit" but concentrated his efforts on the chemical and automobile companies. He thought the air pollution caused by these companies and their products was correlated with the rise in lung cancer. Many laboratory scientists, like Harold Stewart, chief pathologist of the NCI, refused to accept the epidemiological data until it was thoroughly confirmed by experimental research. They accepted the fact that tars from cigarettes, when rubbed into the skin of animals, were carcinogenic. But they insisted that no experiments had yet connected cigarette smoke (as opposed to tars) to cancer in animals, let alone in human beings. Doubts within the NCI itself led Surgeon General Burney and John Heller, director of the institute, to move cautiously until the late 1950s.

Another prominent cancer expert who moved cautiously was Charles Cameron, medical and scientific director of the ACS. Though he accepted the epidemiological data, he resisted the argument that cigarette smoking by itself caused cancer. Like many others at the time, he was troubled by the fact that the vast majority of smokers did not seem to develop the disease—and that a few who did not smoke also were afflicted by it. He wondered if the root cause of lung cancer lay in some predisposing factor, such as genetic makeup. Perhaps the same predisposition led many people to the habit of smoking and—independently—to a susceptibility to cancer.

The defenders of tobacco seized quickly on these and other doubts about the epidemiological case. Again and again they emphasized several points: that only a small minority of smokers ever developed lung cancer (experts later estimated that consistent smokers had between a one in four and a one in ten chance of developing it); that tobacco-induced tumors in animals differed from lung cancer in human beings; that the evidence (such as it was) connecting smoking and lung cancer rested mainly on statistical associations, not on laboratory science; and that the increased incidence of lung cancer stemmed from the aging of the population, not from tobacco. Epidemiological studies pointing a finger at cigarettes, they insisted, were flawed, in part because

their findings did not fully consider the health histories or places of residence of their subjects. Little explained in 1954, "I do not feel that a definite cause-and-effect relationship between smoking and human lung cancer has been established on a basis that meets the requirements of definiteness, extent, and specificity of data, which the seriousness and implications of the problem deserve."

While Little ordinarily assumed the high road of scientific proof, he was prepared to join Allen and others in appealing to popular feelings. The scare over cigarettes, they said, was but one of many—over packaged foods, pollution, even Coca-Cola—aroused by meddlesome reformers who had nothing better to do with their time and who resorted, Little charged, to "expensive and pressure propaganda" and "personal misrepresentations and attacks." Cigarettes, tobacco spokesmen added, calmed the nerves. If people were prevented from smoking, they would fall victim to tics, or even beat their wives. Why pick on cigarettes? they asked—after all, many things kill people!

The spokesmen for tobacco devoted special emphasis to the importance of preserving personal freedom. Smokers, they pointed out, were well aware of the "propaganda" against tobacco, yet they continued to enjoy the habit. That was not because smokers were ignorant of warnings; the polls clearly showed otherwise. Nor was it because cigarettes were addictive—this was an argument that tobacco spokesmen dismissed out of hand. Rather, it was because cigarettes gave people pleasure. Millions of Americans concurred. They stressed that they loved the taste, that cigarettes set off their meals, that smoking helped them relax. Their passion for the habit sometimes recognized no bounds. One smoker exclaimed, "they can outlaw cigarettes, label 'em poison, raise the tax, jail everyone that smokes and hang everyone that raises tobacco; but people are gonna smoke."

Indeed, the tobacco lobby implied, smokers knew better than the arrogant, patronizing "experts" who were trying to run people's lives. This was a nicely calculated, populist appeal to the enduring skepticism of many Americans about professional claims for expertise. The defenders of tobacco, like many others who had resisted the medical alliance against cancer in the past, portrayed themselves as embattled Americans resisting dictation from above. The "experts," the tobacco forces said, were obstructing the right of people to do as they pleased.

As arguments like these show, the controversy over smoking involved more than a strictly medical debate over theories and therapies, more than a struggle between well-organized interest groups. It was in a way a debate over culturally ingrained life styles and cherished values. Just as the battle against cancer in America had long been characterized by social and ideological conflict, so too were the postwar arguments over smoking and health.

The debate intensified greatly following publication in January 1964 of *Smoking and Health: Report of the Advisory Committee to the Surgeon General of the Public Health Service.* This landmark document, ordinarily known as the surgeon general's report on smoking, placed the federal government unambiguously in the camp of the alliance against smoking and prompted increasingly vocal counterattacks by the tobacco coalition in the next two decades.

Luther Terry, the surgeon general in 1964, was hardly a crusader. Until 1962 he had shown little desire to combat the tobacco interests. But he faced increasing pressure for action from a number of organizations, including the ACS, the American Heart Association, the National Tuberculosis Association, and the American Public Health Association. In response he agreed to set up an advisory committee on smoking and health. In doing so Terry acted with political sagacity. To ensure that the committee would have broad support he gave the Tobacco Institute the chance to veto prospective appointees. The ten experts finally named to the committee were chosen from a list of some 150 nominees sent in by health organizations, government agencies, and tobacco interests. None of the ten had taken a public stand on the issue. Three smoked cigarettes, two others smoked pipes and cigars.

The committee, aided by hundreds of consultants, worked diligently and secretly for a year and

a half. When it was ready to issue its findings, Terry staged a televised press conference behind closed doors in the State Department auditorium. The thoroughness that went into preparation of the report, together with the theatrics surrounding its publication, assured that the document would attract wide attention in the media.

The committee members were acutely aware of the need to speak with scientific precision and carefully noted the problems involved in talking about a "cause" or "major cause" of fatal diseases. Ailments such as cancer or heart disease, they acknowledged, exhibit the "multiple etiology of biological processes." But this was practically the only sop thrown to the tobacco interests, whose contentions the committee forcefully struck down. Cigarette smoking, the report said, "contributed substantially to mortality from certain specific diseases and to the overall death rate." Cigarette smoking was "causally related to lung cancer in men; the magnitude of the effect of cigarettes far outweighs all other factors. The data for women, though less extensive, point in the same direction." The committee concluded that cigarettes were a "health hazard of sufficient import in the United States to warrant appropriate remedial action."

The committee's conclusions inevitably received wide coverage in the press. *Newsweek,* speaking for most of the magazines and newspapers, called the report "monumental." Alarmed consumers cut back sharply (though temporarily) on cigarette consumption. Other organizations, moreover, demanded governmental action against tobacco. The World Health Organization called for "restriction of advertisements for cigarettes" and "regulations to curb smoking in all places of public entertainment." The ACS, able at last to pinpoint a specific cause of a major cancer, said that "the reduction of cigarette smoking offers greater possibilities than any other available medical or public health measure for the prevention of cancer, of serious illness, of physical disability, of suffering and of premature death in this country—an astounding statement, but true."

The Federal Trade Commission, which had cooperated with the surgeon general's office in preparing the report, showed special zeal for regulating tobacco. Within a week of the report's appearance the FTC requested public hearings on a proposed trade regulation requiring warnings on cigarette ads and packages. It proposed two possible wordings. One read, "CAUTION—CIGARETTE SMOKING IS A HEALTH HAZARD: The Surgeon General's Advisory Committee on Smoking and Health has found that 'cigarette smoking contributes substantially to mortality from certain diseases and to the overall death rate.'" The other said, "caution: Cigarette smoking is dangerous to health. It may cause death from cancer and other diseases." The FTC recommended a ban on "words, pictures, symbols, devices or demonstrations, or any combination thereof that would lead the public to believe that cigarette smoking promotes good health or physical well-being."

In pressing its case the FTC had the support of many in the anticancer alliance, but some influential groups either fought the FTC or stood by on the sidelines. The Agriculture Department not only refused to oppose supports for tobacco farmers but also asserted that it would need much more evidence about the role of tobacco smoke before it would think about recommending health warnings on cigarette packages. The Advertising Federation of America and the American Newspaper Publishers Association joined the cigarette companies in opposing the proposed regulations. The AMA, which accepted a $10 million research grant from the Tobacco Institute to study the health effects of cigarettes, declined to endorse either the report or the FTC's ambitious plans for regulating advertising.

The Tobacco Institute protected its flanks in other ways, too. It hired the prestigious Washington law firm of Arnold, Porter, and Fortas to defend its interests and named as its chief strategist Earle Clements, a former senator from Kentucky. Clements had been campaign coordinator for Lyndon Johnson's presidential bid in 1960. His daughter was press secretary to the first lady. As a former solon Clements had floor privileges in the Senate. He was shrewd, conciliatory, and very influential on the Hill.

Clements played for time. Matters of such import, he explained, ought to be decided by popular representatives in Congress, not by faceless bureaucrats in the FTC. Meanwhile, the Tobacco Institute announced, the cigarette companies would undertake to police themselves. Henceforth cigarette ads would not be aimed at people under twenty-one years of age or placed in college or school media. The companies' new advertising code emphasized that commercials would not "represent that cigarette smoking is essential to social prominence, distinction, success, or sexual attraction."

Accepting such assurances, Congress contented itself with passage of the Federal Cigarette Labelling and Advertising Act of 1965. This legislation authorized federal spending on a National Clearinghouse on Smoking and Health, which later proved helpful to foes of cigarettes. The law also required cigarette manufacturers to place a health warning on packages. But it was a watered-down warning: "Caution: Cigarette Smoking May Be Hazardous to Your Health." As critics pointed out, it had little if any impact on per capita cigarette sales, which were higher in 1965–66 than they had been in 1964. If anything, the warnings on packages might protect cigarette manufacturers against law suits by cancer victims and their families. (As of early 1987 the companies had won all these suits.)

Advocates of regulation especially deplored Congress's response to the contentious issue of cigarette advertising. The act not only failed to police such advertising; it also forbade governmental agencies to require any health warnings in cigarette ads for the next four years, during which time—it was hoped—the advertising code of the companies would have stilled the controversy. To the foes of tobacco, who thoroughly distrusted the companies, this was a bitter pill. The journalist Elizabeth Drew expressed this bitterness in an article entitled "The Quiet Victory of the Cigarette Lobby—How It Found Its Best Filter Yet—Congress." She called the legislation an "unabashed act to protect private industry from government regulation."

To no one's surprise the tobacco companies' advertising code had little impact on the nature of cigarette commercials. The enemies of smoking thereby intensified their efforts after 1965. A young New York lawyer, John Banzhaf 3d, was instrumental in getting the Federal Communications Commission to apply the so-called Fairness Doctrine to cigarette commercials. Though many opponents of smoking showed little enthusiasm for this effort—even the ACS, which relied on broadcasters for free air time, was cool to his plans—Banzhaf and the antismoking lobby persevered. After extended legal maneuvering, the FCC agreed in 1967 to act. Henceforth, the commission ruled, radio and television stations would have to run one anticigarette message for every three aired by the tobacco companies.

At first Banzhaf and his newly formed lobby, Action on Smoking and Health (ASH), found that broadcasters simply evaded the rule. The FCC, with only a small staff, could not begin to monitor the stations. ASH therefore concentrated on monitoring one station, WNBC-TV of New York, whose messages ran closer to ten to one on behalf of cigarettes; the antismoking spots mainly appeared between 2 and 6:30 A.M. When ASH shared its findings with the FCC in 1968, the agency stepped up its pressure. Forewarned, WNBC and other stations made a better effort, especially after courts affirmed the Fairness Doctrine in late 1968.

For the next two years the FCC ruling greatly heartened the foes of tobacco. The ACS and other health organizations created anticigarette messages, which were broadcast in what was estimated to be more than $40 million in free air time. The ads were meant to be hard-hitting. One ran a caption, "This is life," next to a group of people having fun. Then someone lit up a cigarette. The fun ended abruptly, and a new caption read, "This cuts it short." Another depicted a tough Marlboro man coughing uncontrollably as he stood at the bar of a saloon. A clean-cut, nonsmoking cowboy then pushed him aside. The word cancer appeared on the screen, accompanied by the voice-over, "Cigarettes—they're killers."

Perhaps the most moving of these messages came from the actor William Talman, the gravel-voiced district attorney on the Perry Mason television show. In a prerecorded message Talman introduced his family to television viewers, revealed that he had lung cancer, and warned people not to smoke. "If you haven't smoked," he said, "don't start. If you do smoke, quit! Don't be a loser." By the time the message appeared on the air, Talman had died, one of many prominent Americans—Nat King Cole, Edward R. Murrow, and Walt Disney were three others—to succumb to lung cancer between 1964 and 1970.

To the tobacco lobby these antismoking spots were extraordinarily threatening. For the first time in modern history the annual per-capita cigarette consumption of American adults moved downward for an extended period of time—from 4,197 in 1966 to 3,969 in 1970. The foes of tobacco then set out to toughen the 1965 law by changing the message on cigarette packs from "Caution: Cigarette Smoking May Be Hazardous to Your Health" to "Warning: The Surgeon General Has Determined That Cigarette Smoking Is Dangerous to Your Health and May Cause Cancer and Other Diseases."

The foes of smoking also took steps to include in new legislation a ban on radio and television cigarette advertising. As in 1965, however, they underestimated the Tobacco Institute. Deeply worried by the anticigarette messages on radio and television, the tobacco forces resolved to compromise. It was better, they thought, to surrender their radio and television commercials than to allow continued airing of the opposing point of view. They recognized that such a ban would not affect their appeals on billboards or in the print media, which happily anticipated much increased advertising revenue. Though the broadcasters fought the proposed ban, their allies deserted them, and the ban passed the Congress in 1970. It went into effect on January 2, 1971, a date established so as to permit cigarette advertising—for the last time—during broadcasts of the football games on New Year's Day.

The legislation also required the companies to relabel their packages. The new message was slightly more explicit than the caution which had been required since 1965, but less alarming than the one desired by the antitobacco forces. It read: "Warning: The Surgeon General Has Determined That Cigarette Smoking Is Dangerous to Your Health." The companies had managed to prevent mention in the warning of the dread word "cancer"—or of any other smoking-related diseases.

This hotly contested legislation, the Public Health Cigarette Smoking Act of 1970, clearly indicated the political and economic power of the tobacco lobby. The cigarette companies were now free from worry about antismoking messages on radio and television. Relieved, they increased their advertising on billboards and in magazines and newspapers. *Life's* first three issues in 1971 carried 22 pages of cigarette advertising, all in color. The companies also employed slightly more sophisticated and subtle appeals, such as promoting Virginia Slims tennis tournaments. Perhaps because of these changes, cigarette consumption moved upward again after the decline in the Fairness Doctrine years. Between 1971 and 1976 annual consumption averaged nearly 4,100 per adult, compared to the low of 3,969 in 1970. Total sales increased from 534 billion cigarettes in 1970 to 610 million in 1976.

Study Questions

1. What influences brought about the emergence, decline, and reemergence of cigarette smoking in America?

2. How have individual rights and community responsibility shaped the debate on smoking and health?

3. The author argues that tobacco use persists despite common knowledge about the dangers of smoking. What allows this?

4. Is there an "American" way to smoke?

Bibliography

For opposing views on tobacco and public opinion, see Jacob Slocum, *For Your Own Good: The Anti-Smoking Crusade and the Tyranny of Public Health* (1998) and Philip J. Hilts, *Smokescreen: The Truth Behind the Tobacco Industry Cover-up* (1996). General works on tobacco include Jordan Goodman, *Tobacco in History: The Cultures of Dependence* (1994); Victor G. Kiernan, *Tobacco: A History* (1991); Richard Kluger, *Ashes to Ashes: America's Hundred-Year Cigarette War, the Public Health, and the Unabashed Triumph of Philip Morris* (1997); and Iain Gately, *Tobacco: A Cultural History of How an Exotic Plant Seduced Civilization* (2001). Stephen Lock, L.A. Reynolds, and E.M. Tansey present a global collection of essays on smoking in *Ashes to Ashes: The History of Smoking and Health* (1998).

★ ★ ★

Coming Apart:
1960-2000

The era began innocently enough. In an extremely close election, John F. Kennedy defeated Richard M. Nixon for the presidency and quickly became one of the most admired men in the country. Blessed with brains, charisma, money, and a lovely young family, Kennedy epitomized America, particularly the rise and triumph of the immigrant. In public rhetoric, he cultivated a tough idealism, one that offered a courageous challenge to the Russians and hope for democracy and prosperity in the rest of the world. When Kennedy assumed the presidency in 1961, Americans believed their moral hegemony would last forever. They believed that their values deserved to govern the world by virtue of their success—an equality of opportunity and a standard of living unparalleled in human history. In closing his inaugural address, Kennedy even invoked the divine by claiming that "God's work must truly be our own."

What few people realized was that Kennedy was sitting on a powder keg, both at home and abroad. His liberal idealism, so self-righteous and yet so naive, barely survived his own life. From the mid-1960s through the mid-1970s, the country passed through a period of intense turmoil and doubt. Smug convictions about the virtues of equality and opportunity in the United States succumbed to the shrill criticisms of racial, ethnic, and gender groups. Beliefs in the virtues, safeguards, and stability of the American government were shattered by the lies exposed in the controversies over Watergate and the Pentagon Papers. By the late 1960s and early 1970s, the explosion in oil prices, the appearance of stagflation, and the worries about the future of the environment all undermined the prevailing confidence about the American economy. Finally, the moral complacency so endemic to Kennedy liberalism died in the jungles of Southeast Asia. Like few other events in American history, the Vietnam War tore the country apart. At home, America was characterized by bitterness, demonstrations, and widespread disaffection from the country's leaders. A counter culture of young people scornful of conventional values appeared, and the symbols of their rebellion were drugs and rock and roll. As far as world opinion was concerned, the country seemed to be a superpower out of control, employing the latest military technology in a futile effort to impose democracy on a nation barely out of the stone age.

Between 1964 and 1977, four American presidents struggled with these overwhelming problems. Lyndon Johnson's Great Society was eventually destroyed by what he called "that bitch of a war." Richard Nixon left the White House in disgrace after the Watergate tapes proved his complicity in perjury and obstructing justice. Gerald Ford failed in his WIN campaign—whip inflation now—and then watched helplessly as the last Americans, fleeing the invading North Vietnamese troops, took off in helicopters from the roof of the United States embassy in Saigon. Jimmy Carter left the White House in 1977 after trying unsuccessfully to get Americans to accept the idea of austerity, shortages, and reduced expectations. The hostage crisis in Iran seemed the final symbol of American impotency. Not until the late 1980s, with Vietnam receding into history, oil prices dropping, inflation subsiding, and Ronald Reagan in the White House, did the United States recapture its legendary optimism about the future.

READING 24

★ ★ ★

Why the Shirelles Mattered

Susan J. Douglas

Rock and roll in the 1950s and 1960s was charged with testosterone. Sung by Elvis Presley, Chuck Berry, Jerry Lee Lewis, and the Beatles, it emphasized rebellion and sexuality. Rockers dressed in leather, rejected bourgeois culture, and viewed monogamy as a capital crime. Women, though occasionally idealized, were generally treated as objects designed for the satisfaction of males. Consider a few of Presley's Gold records—"I Want You, I Need You, I Love You," "Don't Be Cruel," "Love Me Tender," "Any Way You Want Me," "Treat Me Nice," "It's Now or Never," "Surrender," "Are You Lonesome Tonight." The titles suggest sex but not marriage, satisfaction but not commitment. They act as windows to a world of male fantasies—selfish, aching, insistent.

In the 1960s, Top 40 radio stations also gave females' fantasies air time. Such groups as the Bobbettes, the Chantels, the Crystals, the Marvelettes, the Chiffons, the Shangri-Las, the Supremes, the Ronettes, and the Shirelles—collectively know as "girl groups"—recorded songs that spoke to the dreams and fears of teenage girls. In such songs as "Will You Love Me Tomorrow?" "He's So Fine," "Sweet Talkin' Guy," "I Will Follow Him," "I Wanna Be Bobby's Girl," and "Wishin' and Hopin'," female singers address female audiences, asking questions about sex, independence, and longings. In the following selection from her book *Where the Girls Are: Growing Up Female with the Mass Media,* Susan J. Douglas presents an insightful reading of the girl groups, suggesting that they were a bridge toward an important liberation movement.

OK—here's a test. Get a bunch of women in their thirties and forties and put them in a room with a stereo. Turn up the volume to the "incurs temporary deafness" level and play "Will You Love Me Tomorrow" and see how many know the words—all the words—by heart. If the answer is 100 percent, these are bona fide American baby boomers. Any less, and the group has been infiltrated by impostors, pod people, Venusians. But even more interesting is the fact that non–baby boomers, women both older and younger than my generation, adore this music too, and cling to the lyrics like a life raft.

Why is it that, over thirty years after this song was number one in the country, it still evokes in us such passion, such longing, such euphoria, and such an irresistible desire to sing very loudly off key and not care who hears us? And it's not just this song, it's girl group music in general, from "He's So Fine" to "Nowhere to Run" to "Sweet Talkin' Guy." Today, the "oldies" station is one of the most successful FM formats going, in no small part because when these songs come on the radio, baby boomers get that faraway, knowing, contented look on their faces that prompts them to scream along with the lyrics while running red lights on the way home from work. None of this is silly—there's a good reason why, even on our deathbeds, we'll still know the words to "Leader of the Pack."

First of all, girl group music was really about us—girls. When rock 'n' roll swiveled onto the national scene in the mid-1950s and united a generation in opposition to their parents, it was music performed by rebellious and sexually provocative young men. Elvis Presley was, of course, rock 'n' roll's most famous and insistently masculine star—in 1956, five of the nine top singles of the year were by Elvis. At the same time,

Susan J. Douglas, *Where the Girls Are: Growing Up Female With the Mass Media* (NY: Random House, 1994) .

there would be weeks, even months, when no woman or female group had a hit among the top fifteen records. When women in the fifties did have hits, they were about the moon, weddings, some harmless dreamboat, like Annette's "Tall Paul," or maybe about kissing. But they were never, ever about doing the wild thing.

Then, in December 1960, the Shirelles hit number one with "Will You Love Me Tomorrow"; it was the first time a girl group, and one composed of four black teenagers, had cracked the number one slot. And these girls were not singing about doggies in windows or old Cape Cod. No, the subject matter here was a little different. They were singing about whether or not to go all the way and wondering whether the boyfriend, so seemingly full of heartfelt, earnest love in the night, would prove to be an opportunistic, manipulative, lying cad after he got his way, or whether he would, indeed, still be filled with love in the morning. Should the girl believe everything she'd heard about going all the way and boys losing respect for girls who did? Or should she believe the boy in her arms who was hugging and kissing her (and doing who knows what else) and generally making her feel real good?

Even though this song was about sex, it didn't rely on the musical instrument so frequently used to connote sex in male rockers' songs, the saxophone. Saxes were banished, as were electric guitars; instead, an entire string section of an orchestra provided the counterpoint to Shirley Owens's haunting, earthy, and provocative lead vocals. The producer, Luther Dixon, who had previously worked with Perry Como and Pat Boone, even overlaid the drumbeats with violins, so it sounded as if the strings gave the song its insistent, pulsing rhythm. While Owens's alto voice vibrated with teen girl angst and desire, grounding the song in fleshly reality, violin arpeggios fluttered through like birds, and it was on their wings that our erotic desires took flight and gained a more acceptable spiritual dimension. It was this brilliant juxtaposition of the sentimentality of the violins and the sensuality of the voice that made the song so perfect, because it was simultaneously lush and spare,

In the 1960s, the Shirelles used the cross-over look and lyrics that spoke to young female listeners to climb the pop charts.

conformist and daring, euphemistic yet dead-on honest. The tens of millions of girls singing along could be starry-eyed and innocent, but they could also be sophisticated and knowing. They could be safe and sing about love, or dangerous and sing about sex. "Will You Love Me Tomorrow" was about a traditional female topic, love, but it was also about female longing and desire, including sexual desire. And, most important, it was about having a choice. For these girls, the decision to have sex was now a choice, and *this* was new. This was, in fact, revolutionary. Girl group music

gave expression to our struggles with the possibilities and dangers of the Sexual Revolution.

What were you to do if you were a teenage girl in the early and mid-1960s, your hormones catapulting you between desire and paranoia, elation and despair, horniness and terror? You didn't know which instincts to act on and which ones to suppress. You also weren't sure whom to listen to since, by the age of fourteen, you'd decided that neither your mother nor your father knew anything except how to say no and perhaps the lyrics to a few Andy Williams songs. For answers—real answers—many of us turned to the record players, radios, and jukeboxes of America. And what we heard were the voices of teenage girls singing about—and dignifying—our most basic concern: how to act around boys when so much seemed up for grabs. What were you to do to survive all those raging hormones? Why, dance, of course.

There's been a lot of talk, academic analysis, and the like about how Elvis Presley and rock 'n' roll made rebelliousness acceptable for boys. But what about the girls? Did girl group music help *us* become rebels? Before you say "no way" and cite "I Will Follow Him," "Chapel of Love," and "I Wanna Be Bobby's Girl" to substantiate your point, hear me out. Girl group music has been denied its rightful place in history by a host of male music critics who've either ignored it or trashed it. Typical is this pronouncement, by one of the contributors to *The Rolling Stone History of Rock & Roll:* "The female group of the early 1960s served to drive the concept of art completely away from rock 'n' roll. . . . I feel this genre represents the low point in the history of rock 'n' roll." Nothing could be more wrong-headed, or more ignorant of the role this music played in girls' lives. It would be ideal if this section of the book were accompanied by a customized CD replaying all these fabulous songs for you. Since that's not possible, I do urge you to listen to this music again, and to hear all the warring impulses, desires, and voices it contained.

By the late 1950s, Tin Pan Alley realized that Perry Como, Doris Day, and Mantovani and his orchestra weren't cutting it with the fastest-growing market segment in America, teenagers. Even Pat Boone was hopelessly square, having foisted on us the insufferable "April Love" and his goody-two-shoes advice book to teens, *'Twixt Twelve and Twenty,* which said kissing "for fun" was dangerous. Music publishers and producers grasped two key trends: rock 'n' roll was here to stay, and there was this flourishing market out there, not just boys, but girls, millions of them, ready and eager to buy. And they were not buying the Lennon Sisters or Patti Page. At the same time, the proliferation of transistor radios meant that

this music could be taken and heard almost everywhere, becoming the background music for our desires, hopes, and fears, the background music to our individual and collective autobiographies.

Teenage songwriters like Carole King and Ellie Greenwich got jobs in the Brill Building in New York, the center of pop music production in America, and in the aftermath of the Shirelles hit, all kinds of girl groups and girl singers appeared, from the pouf-skirted Angels ("My Boyfriend's Back") to the cute and innocent Dixie Cups to the eat-my-dirt, in-your-face, badass Shangri-Las. There was an explosion in what has come to be called "girl talk" music, the lyrics and beat of which still occupy an inordinately large portion of the right—or is it the left?—side of my brain.

The most important thing about this music, the reason it spoke to us so powerfully, was that it gave voice to all the warring selves inside us struggling, blindly and with a crushing sense of insecurity, to forge something resembling a coherent identity. Even though the girl groups were produced and managed by men, it was in their music that the contradictory messages about female sexuality and rebelliousness were most poignantly and authentically expressed. In the early 1960s, pop music became the one area of popular culture in which adolescent female voices could be clearly heard. They sang about the pull between the need to conform and the often overwhelming desire to rebel, about the tension between restraint and freedom, and about the rewards—and costs—of prevailing gender roles. They sang, in other words, about getting mixed messages and about being ambivalent in the face of the upheaval in sex roles. That loss of self, the fusing of yourself with another, larger-than-life persona that girls felt as they sang along was at least as powerful as what they felt in a darkened movie theater. And singing along with one another, we shared common emotions and physical reactions to the music.

This music was, simultaneously, deeply personal and highly public, fusing our neurotic, quivering inner selves with the neurotic, quivering inner selves of others in an effort to find strength and confidence in numbers. We listened to this music in the darkness of our bedrooms, driving around in our parents' cars, on the beach, making out with some boy, and we danced to it—usually with other girls—in the soda shops, basements, and gymnasiums of America. This music burrowed into the everyday psychodramas of our adolescence, forever intertwined with our most private, exhilarating, and embarrassing memories. This music exerted such a powerful influence on us, one that we may barely have recognized, because of this process of identification. By superimposing our own dramas, from our own lives, onto each song, each of us could assume an active role in shaping the song's meaning. Songs that were hits around the country had very particular associations and meanings for each listener, and although they were mass-produced they were individually interpreted. The songs were ours—but they were also everyone else's. We were all alone, but we weren't really alone at all. In this music, we found solidarity as girls.

Some girl group songs, like "I Will Follow Him," allowed us to assume the familiar persona *Cinderella* had trained us for, the selfless masochist whose identity came only from being some appendage to a man. As we sang along with Dionne Warwick's "Walk On By," we were indeed abject martyrs to love, luxuriating in our own self-pity. But other songs addressed our more feisty and impatient side, the side unwilling to sit around and wait for the boy to make the first move. In "tell him" songs like "Easier Said Than Done," "Wishin' and Hopin'," and, of course, "Tell Him," girls were advised to abandon the time-wasting and possibly boy-losing stance of passively waiting for *him* to make the first move. We were warned that passivity might cost us our man, and we were urged to act immediately and unequivocally, before some more daring girl got there first. Girls were urged to take up a previously male prerogative—to be active agents of their own love lives and to go out and court the boy. Regardless of how girls actually behaved—and I know from personal experience that what was derisively called "boy chasing" was on the rise—now there were lyrics in girls' heads that said, "Don't be passive, it will cost you."

Was being cautious too safe? Was being daring too risky? Girl group music acknowledged—even celebrated—our confusion and ambivalence. Some of us wanted to be good girls, and some of us wanted to be bad. But most of us wanted to get away with being both, and girl group music let us try on and act out a host of identities, from traditional, obedient girlfriend to brassy, independent rebel, and lots in between. We could even do this in the same song, for often the lead singer represented one point of view and the backup singers another, so the very wars raging in our own heads about how to behave, what pose to strike, were enacted in one two-minute hit single.

Few songs capture this more perfectly than one of the true girl group greats, "Sweet Talkin' Guy" by the Chiffons. Here we have a tune about a deceitful and heartless charmer who acts like he loves you one day and moves on to another girl the next. Nonetheless, since he's "sweeter than sugar" (ooh-ooh) with "kisses like wine (oh he's so fine)," this heel is irresistible. The lead singer warns other girls to stay away from such a boy, since he'll only break their hearts, but she also confesses he is "my kinda guy." The female chorus backs her up, acknowledging that it is indeed understandable to be swept up by such a cad.

On the face of it, we have lyrics about the unrequited love of a young woman with, no doubt, a few masochistic tendencies. But the song achieves much more. With the layering of voices over and against one another, some of them alto and some of them soprano, we have a war between resisting such boys and succumbing to them. The music, with its driving beat and a tambourine serving as metronome, is dance music. At the end of the song the layered vocal harmonies run ecstatically up the octaves, like girls running jubilantly across a field, ending with a euphoric chord that suggests, simultaneously, that young female love will win in the end and that it will transcend male brutishness. Singing along to a song like this, girls could change voice, becoming singing ventriloquists for different stances toward the same boy, the same situation. As altos, sopranos, or both, back and forth, we could love and denounce such boys, we could warn against our own victimization, yet fall prey to its sick comforts. We could feel how desire—irresistible, irrational, timeless—was shaping our destinies. The euphoric musical arrangement made us feel even more strongly that the power to love and to dream would enable us somehow to burst through the traps of history. In "Sweet Talkin' Guy," being divided against yourself is normal, natural, true: the song celebrates the fact not just that girls *do* have conflicting subjective stances but that, to get by, they *must*. Yes, we can't help loving them, even when they're bastards, but we have to be able to name how they hurt us, and we must share those warnings with other girls. And if we're dancing while we do it, moving our bodies autonomously, or in unison with others girls, well, maybe we'll escape after all.

Girl group songs were, by turns, boastful, rebellious, and self-abnegating, and through them girls could assume different personas, some of them strong and empowering and others masochistic and defeating. As girls listened to their radios and record players, they could be martyrs to love ("Please Mr. Postman"), sexual aggressors ("Beechwood 4-5789"), fearsome Amazons protecting their men ("Don't Mess with Bill" and "Don't Say Nothin' Bad About My Baby"), devoted, selfless girlfriends ("My Guy," "I Will Follow Him"), taunting, competitive brats ("Judy's Turn to Cry," "My Boyfriend's Back"), sexual sophisticates ("It's in His Kiss"), and, occasionally, prefeminists ("Don't Make Me Over" and "You Don't Own Me"). The Shirelles themselves, in hit after hit, assumed different stances, from the faithful romantic ("Soldier Boy," "Dedicated to the One I Love") to knowing adviser ("Mama Said," "Foolish Little Girl") to sexual slave ("Baby, It's You"). The songs were about escaping from yet acquiescing to the demands of a male-dominated society, in which men called the shots but girls could still try to give them a run for their money. Girls in these songs enjoyed being looked at with desire, but they also enjoyed looking with desire themselves. The singers were totally confident; they were abjectly insecure. Some songs

said do and others said don't. Sometimes the voice was of an assertive, no-nonsense girl out to get the guy or showing off her boyfriend to her friends. At other times, the voice was that of the passive object, yearning patiently to be discovered and loved. Often the girl tried to get into the boy's head and imagined the boy regarding her as the object of his desire. Our pathetic struggles and anxieties about popularity were glamorized and dignified in these songs.

In girl group music, girls talked to each other confidentially, primarily about boys and sex. The songs took our angst-filled conversations, put them to music, and gave them a good beat. Some songs, like "He's So Fine" (doo lang, doo lang, doo lang), picked out a cute boy from the crowd and plotted how he would be hooked. In this song the choice was clearly hers, not his. Songs also recreated images of a clot of girls standing around in their mohair sweaters assessing the male talent and, well, looking over boys the way boys had always looked over girls. Other songs, like "Playboy" or "Too Many Fish in the Sea," warned girls about two-timing Romeo types who didn't deserve the time of day, and the sassy, defiant singers advised girls to tell boys who didn't treat them right to take a hike. Opening with a direct address to their sisters—"Look here, girls, take this advice"—the Marvelettes passed on what sounded like age-old female wisdom: "My mother once told me something/And every word is true/Don't waste your time on a fella/Who doesn't love you." Urging the listener to "stand tall," the lead singer asserted, "I don't want nobody that don't want me/Ain't gonna love nobody that don't love me."

The absolute necessity of female collusion in the face of thoughtless or mystifying behavior by boys bound these songs together, and bound the listeners to the singers in a knowing sorority. They knew things about boys and love that they shared with each other, and this shared knowledge—smarter, more deeply intuitive, more worldly wise than any male locker room talk—provided a powerful bonding between girls, a kind of bonding boys didn't have. And while boys were often identified as the love object, they were also identified as the enemy. So while some of the identities we assumed as we sang along were those of the traditional, passive, obedient, lovesick girl, each of us could also be a sassy, assertive, defiant girl who intended to have more control over her life—or at least her love life. In numerous advice songs, from "Mama Said" to "You Can't Hurry Love," the message that girls knew a thing or two, and that they would share that knowledge with one another to beat the odds in a man's world, circulated confidently.

Other songs fantasized about beating a different set of odds—the seeming inevitability, for white, middle-class girls, of being married off to some boring, respectable guy with no sense of danger or adventure, someone like David Nelson or one of Fred MacMurray's three sons. Here we come to the rebel category—"Leader of the Pack," "Uptown," "He's a Rebel," "Give Him a Great Big Kiss," and "He's Sure the Boy I Love." Academic zeros, on unemployment, clad in leather jackets, sporting dirty fingernails, and blasting around on motorcycles, the boy heroes in these songs were every suburban parent's nightmare, the boys they loved to hate. By allying herself romantically and morally with the rebel hero, the girl singer and listener proclaimed her independence from society's predictable expectations about her inevitable domestication. There is a role reversal here, too—the girls are gathered in a group, sharing information about their boyfriends, virtually eyeing them up and down, while the rebel heroes simply remain the passive objects of their gaze and their talk. And the girls who sang these songs, like the Shangri-Las, dressed the part of the defiant bad girl who stuck her tongue out at parental and middle-class authority. The Ronettes, whose beehives scraped the ceiling and whose eyeliner was thicker than King Tut's, wore spiked heels and skintight dresses with slits up the side as they begged some boy to "Be My Baby." They combined fashion rebellion with in-your-face sexual insurrection.

In "Will You Love Me Tomorrow," Shirley Owens asked herself, Should she or shouldn't she? Of course, the question quickly became Should I or shouldn't I? The answer wasn't clear, and we heard plenty of songs in which girls found themselves smack in the grip of sexual desire. Sexuality emerged as an eternal ache, a kind of irresistible, unquenchable tension. But in the early 1960s, sex and sexual desire were still scary for many girls. The way many of these songs were produced—orchestrated with violins instead of with electric guitars or saxophones—muted the sexual explicitness and made it more romantic, more spiritual, more safe. "And Then He Kissed Me" alluded to some kind of new kiss tried on the singer by her boyfriend, one she really liked and wanted to have a lot more of. In "Heat Wave," Martha Reeves sang at the top of her lungs about being swept up in a sexual fever that just wouldn't break, and the whispering, bedroom-voiced lead in "I'm Ready" confessed that she didn't really know quite what she was supposed to do but that she was sure ready to learn—right now. Claudine Clark desperately begged her mother to let her go off to the source of the "Party Lights," where one helluva party was happening, and she sounded like someone who had been in Alcatraz for twenty years and would simply explode if she didn't get out.

The contradictions of being a teenage girl in the early and mid-1960s also percolated from the conflict between the lyrics of the song and the beat of the music. Girl group music had emerged at the same time as all these new dance crazes that redefined how boys and girls did—or, more accurately, did not—dance with each other. Chubby Checker's 1960 hit "The Twist" revolutionized teenage dancing, because it meant that boys and girls didn't have to hold hands anymore, boys didn't have to lead and girls didn't have to follow, so girls had a lot more autonomy and control as they danced. Plus, dancing was one of the things girls usually did much better than boys. As the twist gave way to the locomotion, the Bristol stomp, the mashed potatoes, the pony, the monkey, the slop, the jerk, and the frug, the dances urged us to loosen up our chests and our butts, and learn how to shimmy, grind, and thrust. This was something my friends and I did with gleeful abandon.

Many of us felt most free and exhilarated while we were dancing, so bouncing around to a song like "Chains" or "Nowhere to Run" put us smack-dab between feelings of liberation and enslavement, between a faith in free will and a surrender to destiny. Both songs describe prisoners of love, and if you simply saw the lyrics without hearing the music, you'd think they were a psychotherapist's notes from a session with a deeply paranoid young woman trapped in a sadomasochistic relationship. Yet with "Chains," sung by the Cookies, girls were primed for dancing from the very beginning by the hand clapping, snare drums, and saxophones, so that the music worked in stark contrast to the lyrics, which claimed that the girl couldn't break free from her chains of love. Then, in a break from the chorus, the lead singer acknowledged, "I wanna tell you pretty baby/Your lips look sweet/I'd like to kiss them/But I can't break away from all of these chains." At least two personas emerge here, coexisting in the same teenager. One is the girl who loves the bittersweet condition of being hopelessly consumed by love. The other is the girl who, despite her chains, has a roving and appreciative eye for other boys. The conflict between the sense of entrapment in the lyrics and the utter liberation of the beat is inescapable. The tension is too delicious for words.

It was the same for one of the greatest songs ever recorded, "Nowhere to Run." The opening layers of drums, horns, and tambourines propelled us out onto the dance floor—I mean, you couldn't not dance to this song. While we were gyrating and bouncing around to a single about a no-good boy who promised nothing but heartache yet had us in his sadistic grip, we were as happy as we could be. The best part was the double entendre lyrics in the middle, which we belted out with almost primal intensity. "How can I fight a love that shouldn't be?/When it's so deep—so deep—it's deep inside of me/My love reaches so high I can't get over it/So wide, I can't get around it, no." In the face of our entrapment, Martha Reeves made us sweat, and celebrated the capacity of girls to love like women. She also articulated a sophisticated knowingness about how

sexual desire overtakes common sense every time, even in girls. In a very different kind of song, the effervescent "I Can't Stay Mad at You," Skeeter Davis told her boyfriend that he could treat her like dirt, make her cry, virtually grind her heart under the heel of his boot, and she'd still love him anyway, and all this between a string of foot-tapping, butt-bouncing shoobie doobie do bops. So even in songs seemingly about female victimization and helplessness, the beat and euphoria of the music put the lie to the lyrics by getting the girl out on the dance floor, moving on her own, doing what she liked, displaying herself sexually, and generally getting ready for bigger and better things. Dancing to this music together created a powerful sense of unity, of commonality of spirit, since we were all feeling, with our minds and our bodies, the same enhanced emotions at the same moment.

While a few girl groups and individual singers were white—the Angels, the Shangri-Las, Dusty Springfield—most successful girl groups were black. Unlike the voices of Patti Page or Doris Day, which seemed as innocent of sexual or emotional angst as a Chatty Cathy doll, the vibrating voices of black teenagers, often trained in the gospel traditions of their churches, suggested a perfect fusion of naivete and knowingness. And with the rise of the civil rights movement, which by 1962 and 1963 dominated the national news, black voices conveyed both a moral authority and a spirited hope for the future. These were the voices of exclusion, of hope for something better, of longing. They were not, like Annette or the Lennon Sisters, the voices of sexual repression, of social complacency, or of homogenized commercialism.

From the Jazz Age to rap music, African American culture has always kicked white culture upside the head for being so pathologically repressed; one consequence, for black women, is that too often they have been stereotyped as more sexually active and responsive than their white-bread sisters. Because of these stereotypes, it was easier, more acceptable, to the music industry and no doubt to white culture at large that black girls, instead of white ones, be the first teens to give voice to girls' changing attitudes toward sex. But since the sexuality of black people has always been deeply threatening to white folks, black characters in popular culture also have been desexualized, the earth-mother mammy being a classic example. The black teens in girl groups, then, while they sounded orgiastic at times, had to look feminine, innocent, and as white as possible. Berry Gordy, the head of Motown, knew this instinctively, and made his girl groups take charm school lessons and learn how to get into and out of cars, carry their handbags, and match their shoes to their dresses. They were trapped, and in the glare of the spotlight, no less, between the old and new definitions of femininity. But under their crinolined skirts and satin cocktail dresses, they were also smuggling into middle-class America a taste of sexual liberation. So white girls like me owe a cultural debt to these black girls for straddling these contradictions, and for helping create a teen girl culture that said, "Let loose, break free, don't take no shit."

The Shirelles paved the way for the decade's most successful girl group, the Supremes, who had sixteen records in the national top ten between 1964 and 1969. But of utmost importance was the role Diana Ross played in making African American beauty enviable to white girls. As slim as a rail with those cavernous armpits, gorgeous smile, and enormous, perfectly made-up eyes, Diana Ross is the first black woman I remember desperately wanting to look like, even if some of her gowns were a bit too Vegas. I couldn't identify with her completely, not because she was black, but because when I was fourteen, she seemed so glamorous and sophisticated. Ross has taken a lot of heat in recent years as the selfish bitch who wanted all the fame and glory for herself, so it's easy to forget her importance as a cultural icon in the 1960s. But the Supremes—who seemed to be both girls and women, sexy yet respectable, and a blend of black and white culture—made it perfectly normal for white girls to idolize and want to emulate their black sisters.

Another striking trend that grew out of the girl group revolution was the proliferation of the male falsetto. From Maurice Williams in "Stay" to

Lou Christie in "Two Faces Have I" to Roy Orbison in "Crying" and Randy and the Rainbows in "Denise" (ooo-be-ooo), and most notably with The Four Seasons and The Beach Boys, boys sang in high-pitched soprano ranges more suited for female than for male sing-along. What this meant was that girls belting out lyrics in the kitchen, in the car, or while watching *American Bandstand* had the opportunity to assume *male* roles, male subjective stances as they sang, even though they were singing in a female register.

This was nothing less than musical cross-dressing. While the male falsettos sang of their earnest love for their girls, about how those girls got them through the trials and tribulations of parental disputes, loneliness, drag-car racing ("Don't Worry Baby"), or being from the wrong side of the tracks, girls could fantasize about boys being humanized, made more nurturing, compassionate, and sensitive through their relationships with girls. This is an enduring fantasy, and one responsible for the staggeringly high sales of romance novels in America. It was a narcissistic fantasy that the girl was at the center of someone's universe, that she did make a difference in that universe, and that that difference was positive. This practice of assuming male voices later enabled girls to slip in and out of male points of view, sometimes giving girls a temporary taste of power. Several years later, in a song much maligned by feminists, "Under My Thumb," girls could and did sing not as the one under the thumb but as the one holding the thumb down.

While girl group music celebrated love, marriage, female masochism, and passivity, it also urged girls to make the first move, to rebel against their parents and middle-class conventions, and to dump boys who didn't treat them right. Most of all, girl group music—precisely because these were groups, not just individual singers—insisted that it was critically important for girls to band together, talking about men, singing about men, trying to figure them out.

What we have here is a pop culture harbinger in which girl groups, however innocent and commercial, anticipate women's groups, and girl talk anticipates a future kind of women's talk. The consciousness-raising groups of the late sixties and early seventies came naturally to many young women because we'd had a lot of practice. We'd been talking about boys, about loving them and hating them, about how good they often made us feel and how bad they often treated us, for ten years. The Shirelles mattered because they captured so well our confusion in the face of changing sexual mores. And as the confusion of real life intersected with the contradictions in popular culture, girls were prepared to start wondering, sooner or later, why sexual freedoms didn't lead to other freedoms as well.

Girl group music gave us an unprecedented opportunity to try on different, often conflicting, personas. For it wasn't just that we could be, as we sang along first with the Dixie Cups and then the Shangri-Las, traditional passive girls one minute and more active, rebellious, even somewhat prefeminist girls the next. Contradiction was embedded in almost all the stances a girl tried on, and some version, no matter how thwarted, of prefeminism, constituted many of them. We couldn't sustain this tension forever, especially when one voice said, "Hey, hon, you're equal" and the other voice said, "Oh no, you're not."

The Shirelles and the other girl groups mattered because they helped cultivate inside us a desire to rebel. The main purpose of pop music is to make us feel a kind of euphoria that convinces us that we can transcend the shackles of conventional life and rise above the hordes of others who do get trapped. It is the euphoria of commercialism, designed to get us to buy. But this music did more than that; it generated another kind of euphoria as well. For when tens of millions of young girls started feeling, at the same time, that they, as a generation, would not be trapped, there was planted the tiniest seed of a social movement.

Few symbols more dramatically capture the way young women in the early 1960s were pinioned between entrapment and freedom than one of the most bizarre icons of the period, the go-go girl dancing in a cage. While African American performers like the Dixie Cups or Mary Wells sang on *Shindig* or *Hullabaloo,* white girls in white go-go boots pranced and shimmied in their cages in the background. Autonomous yet objectified, free to dance by herself on her own terms yet highly choreographed in her little prison, seemingly indifferent to others yet trapped in a voyeuristic gaze, the go-go girl seems, in retrospect, one of the sicker, yet more apt, metaphors for the teen female condition during this era. It's not surprising that when four irreverent, androgynous, and irresistible young men came over from England and incited a collective jailbreak, millions of these teens took them up on it. For we had begun to see some new kinds of girls in the mass media—some perky, some bohemian, some androgynous—who convinced us that a little anarchy was exactly what we, and American gender roles, needed.

Study Questions

1. What were Americans' popular views on sexuality in the late 1950s and early 1960s?

2. How did the lyrics and beat of music in the early and mid-1960s reflect contradictions of being a teenage girl?

3. Why did African American females become the popular choice for the voice and look of the new sexualized music?

4. What was it about girl groups, like the Shirelles or Supremes, that attracted young white female audiences?

5. How did girl groups of the 1960s pave the way for other music in that decade?

Bibliography

This piece came from Susan J. Douglas, *Where the Girls Are: Growing Up Female with the Mass Media* (1994). For more on the Shirelles and other girl groups of this period, see Charolette Greig, *Will You Still Love Me Tomorrow* (1989). Susan McClary, *Feminine Endings: Music, Gender, and Sexuality* (1991), provides an impressive examination of the interconnections between female artists and sexuality in this period. Nelson George, *Where Did Love Go?: The Rise and Fall of the Motown Sound* (1985) and Suzanne Smith, *Dancing in the Street: Motown and the Cultural Politics of Detroit* (1999), present wonderful studies on the conditions of African American artists in the 1950s and 1960s. Several excellent general overviews of the history of rock and roll have been published in recent years, including Paul Friedlander, *Rock and Roll: A Social History* (1996) and David P. Szatmary, *Rockin' in History: A Social History of Rock and Roll* (2000). For a general overview of the 1960s, see Alexander Broom, ed., *"Takin's It to the Streets": A Sixties Reader* (2004).

READING 25

★ ★ ★

Oliver Stone and Vietnam

Randy Roberts and David Welky

In today's video culture, how do we learn history? From the Alamo to the *Titanic,* from Gettysburg to the Watergate break-in, most Americans have learned the essentials of important historical events on television or at the movies. Such documentary film makers as Ken Burns and such television outlets as the History Channel have provided a classroom where millions of Americans have learned about their history. For much of his film making career, Oliver Stone has labored to explain the Vietnam War to a movie-going public. In such films as *Platoon* (1986), *Born on the Forth of July* (1989), *JFK* (1991), *Heaven and Earth* (1993), and *Nixon* (1995), he has addressed the American culture and politics that lead to the war, the nature of the conflict, and the human price of the engagement. A Vietnam veteran, Stone spent decades trying to come to terms with and to understand the war. In the process, he became the most famous public historian of the war. The following essay examines what Stone's films have taught viewers about the conflict.

To me the '60s were very hard—my parents got divorced, I went to Vietnam.

If it's a movie worth making, you should make it. If you can convey that passion, it should all be open. Anything is permitted.

Vietnam is not over, although some people say it is. Vietnam is a state of mind that continues all over the world—as long as m[a]n in his quest for power interferes in the affairs of other men.

Part of me is scared, and wants to say, let's pull back, let's make a film that is understandable to everyone, that's sweeter, that the whole country can believe in, like Forrest Gump.

—*Oliver Stone*

I n September 1967, Oliver Stone departed the United States on a transport bound for Vietnam. Behind him he left his life—an unhappy childhood; frustrating, lonely years at Hill School and Yale; a long, rejected novel manuscript. He might have been Ernest Hemingway heading for Italy, or Joseph Conrad bound for the sea. Perhaps his mind was already tracking film images, imagining what might have been and what would be. Perhaps Vietnam was more of an escape than a mission. Whatever the case, the country would soon take hold of him, and it would occupy his thoughts and his creativity for much of the next thirty years. Few artists would delve so completely into the nature, texture, and causes of the Vietnam War. Fewer still would produce such a dazzling body of work. And at the heart of it all would be biography—Stone's and America's.

For Oliver Stone, exploring Vietnam would become a sacred mission. As a young man, he served two tours in the country—one as a civilian, the other as a soldier. These experiences changed him and set his artistic agenda. For the next twenty-five years he would return repeatedly to

Vietnam for inspiration. The conflict became his touchstone; it provided him with both an avenue for personal exploration and a tool for understanding larger historical questions. In a series of brilliant films about America and Vietnam, Stone moved from autobiographical observations about the nature of war, to a sociological analysis of the American culture that led to the war, to historical investigation of the political causes and course of the war. In the process, Stone became the most influential historian of America's role in Vietnam. But to understand Stone's position, one has to come to terms with Stone himself.

Considering his career as a writer and director of powerful films that deal with war, it is perhaps not surprising that, had it not been for World War II, Oliver Stone's parents would never have met. Louis Stone, Oliver's father, was a Wall Street stockbroker and the scion of a wealthy family. He met Jacqueline Goddet, a poor nineteen-year-old beauty, shortly after V-E Day, while he was serving as a financial officer for General Eisenhower in Paris. After some initial hesitation, Jacqueline wed Louis in November 1945. By the time the couple returned to New York City, Jacqueline was preg-

Randy Roberts and David Welky, "A Sacred Mission: Oliver Stone and Vietnam" in Robert Trent Toplin, ed., *Oliver Stone's USA: Film History, and Controversy* (Lawrence: University Press of Kansas, 2003).

nant with what would be their only child. William Oliver Stone was born on September 15, 1946.

The future critic of the establishment grew up within its comfortable embrace. Despite being prone to making poor financial decisions, his father generally proved to be a good provider, enabling Oliver to lead, by his own admission, "a sheltered existence." Oliver lived in a large townhouse complete with a nanny and a butler, dressed stylishly, studied piano, and listened to classical music and Broadway show tunes. After finishing eighth grade at Manhattan's Trinity School, his parents shipped him to the exclusive Hill School, an all-boys academy in Pottstown, Pennsylvania. Oliver knew that Hill was the first step that would probably lead to Yale and Wall Street, the path his father had taken.

Oliver's childhood was pampered, but hardly happy. Both his parents were distant. His mother seemed more interested in New York's party scene than in him, and his father was a "dark and pessimistic" man who had a hard time expressing his emotions. Oliver's closest family may have been his grandparents in France. As a youth, he spent his summers in Europe, raptly listening to his grandfather tell stories about the Great War and happily playing army with his cousins on the battlefields where millions of men had lost their lives. He passed summer days writing plays, many about war, that willing locals performed.

But the carefree summers ended, and he faced the unappealing prospect of returning to the States and school. Although he was intellectually curious and fascinated with American and European history, he was uncomfortable at Hill. A self-proclaimed "outsider," he made few friends, chafed under the strict discipline of the boarding school, and resented its efforts to impose a rigid "orthodoxy" upon him. Like many adolescents, Oliver was extremely "self-conscious," living in constant fear of being ridiculed by fellow students. Burdened with feelings of isolation, he pursued his interest in writing, primarily as a means of "retreat[ing] from reality."

His family life got even lonelier. In 1962, when he was fifteen, the headmaster of Hill called him to his office to inform him that his parents were separating. The news shocked him; he had failed or refused to see any signs of discord in his parents' relationship. In fact, the split surprised few others. Louis had had a string of affairs, and Jacqueline, fully aware of her husband's philandering, coped by partying, popping uppers, and, finally, taking lovers of her own. By the early 1960s, the Stones' marriage existed solely on paper. Now, when Oliver most needed attention, his parents reinforced his sense of isolation by refusing to visit him. Oliver wanted to take a leave from school, but his father would not hear of it, claiming that he was too busy at work to attend to anyone else. Jacqueline was even more remote— she left for Europe, expressing no interest in seeing her son. Oliver received another shock when he learned that Jacqueline's free-spending habits had driven the family into debt. Louis moved, with Oliver's possessions, from their spacious town house to a cramped hotel room. Oliver was devastated. His parents' actions taught him that "adults were dangerous" and "not to be trusted."

Abandoned by his parents, he accepted the grind at Hill. Unsure of his future, he struggled through his last tedious years of high school. World events seemed remote. Certainly, he did not see his destiny in the assassination of President Kennedy. Raised a staunch Republican by his conservative father (Oliver voted for Barry Goldwater in 1964), he has only vague memories of being "on a lunch break or something" when he heard of the president's death. Although he was never a "Kennedy lover when he was alive," Stone was shocked by the crime, but no more than others. He was not burdened with concerns for America's future, only "stunned" that "a young, handsome president could be killed like that." He fully accepted the Warren Commission's finding that Kennedy had been killed by Lee Harvey Oswald alone.

Personal concerns were more pressing. In accordance with his father's wishes, in 1964 he enrolled at Yale. He quickly realized that college would be more of "the same crap" that Hill had been. Even more than before, he desperately searched for meaning in his life, longing to break out of the constricting East Coast conservative mold that his father had crammed him into. Books provided a means of escape. He devoured Joseph Conrad's writings and was especially drawn to *Lord Jim,* with Conrad's dark view of human nature and his lush depictions of the exotic Orient. The idea of living in a primitive land, unsullied by civilization, consumed him, and he began inquiring about possibilities for overseas employment. After several rejections, he was finally accepted by the Free Pacific Institute in Taiwan, a church-based organization that operated a number of schools. The Institute offered him a position as an English teacher at a school in Cholon, the Chinese suburb of Saigon. In 1965, he dropped out of Yale and headed for Vietnam.

Saigon, with its gambling, drugs, and prostitution, was no Yale. It "was like Dodge City." Hookers stalked busy street corners, drunks spilled out from numerous bars, and guns and violence were common. The hot sun and the nearby ocean lent a sense of romance to the chaotic scene. Stone felt alive. After the suffocating depths of Hill School and Yale, Saigon was like coming up for air. He plunged into his new job, working hard and living a spartan life, but loving it all.

But an immediate, itchy restlessness persisted. Travel had gotten into his blood, and he wanted to see more of the world. He quit his teaching position after two semesters and joined the merchant marine, where he passed his days cleaning toilets and engine rooms. After a long voyage from Vietnam to Oregon, the nineteen-year-old Stone drifted south to Mexico to write a novel. The manuscript, which he called "A Child's Night Dream," grew into a 1,400-page stream-of-consciousness look at the psyche of a bright, troubled youth. The largely autobiographical story followed the protagonist through his experiences in Asia and the merchant marine. Stone worked furiously through much of 1966 at what he thought was a literary masterpiece, eventually feeling confident enough to return to New York City and the harsh judgment of his father, who desperately wanted his son to return to Yale and a buttoned-down life. Stone finally gave in and reenrolled, but unenthusiastically. "Night Dream" continued to occupy his thoughts and his energy. He worked on his novel at a punishing pace, skipping classes and writing about ten hours every day. Not surprisingly, his return to Yale was brief and inglorious. He was expelled but, undaunted, returned to New York to finish his book. The incredible effort he poured into the novel only made it more painful when publishers panned the manuscript. Frustrated, he threw hundreds of pages into the East River and decided to take a drastic step. He would visit Vietnam again, this time as a soldier.

Because he was a well-educated white male, the army offered Stone a position at Officer Candidate School. He refused and requested infantry duty. His decision to go to war appears rash but actually stemmed from a number of factors. To be sure, he had been hurt by the series of personal and literary rejections. But he was equally upset by the grand literary pretensions he had harbored. In a sense, his decision to enlist was an act of atonement for his perceived character flaws; he yearned to "obliterate" the ego he had created and, after a long bout with individualism, become an "anonymous" grunt. Though he often considered suicide, he could not bring himself to "pull the trigger." Instead, he resolved to let someone else pull it for him on a battlefield.

But perhaps more than anything else, Stone went to Vietnam simply because he believed in the war. Like many other Americans who grew up during the 1950s, he had learned to "fear Russians and hate Communism." He fully believed that communism needed to be stopped in order to preserve American democracy, and he felt it was his duty to fight. His father had served during World War II, his grandfather during World War I. Now it was his turn to serve his country and, by doing so, to announce that he was "a man." Imbued with both pathos and patriotism, Private Bill Stone (he opted to enlist using his first name, fearing that "Oliver" was too effeminate) left for Vietnam on September 14, 1967, and was assigned to the second platoon of Bravo Company, Third Battalion, 25th Infantry, stationed near the Cambodian border.

Naive optimism and idealism soon crumbled under the weight of reality. Vietnam was not the same place it had been in 1965. By 1967, many Vietnamese had gone from loving to loathing the occupying Americans. Corruption ran rampant as noncombatants lived high, far behind the lines, and unscrupulous sergeants stole supplies to sell on the black market. Stone quickly discovered that Vietnam was not a people's conflict but a politicians' war fought by the poorest Vietnamese and Americans. Just as disconcerting for him were the unexpected attitudes of his new comrades in arms, who made it clear to him that he was as "expendable" as a piece of "raw meat." Very quickly he realized that enlisting had been "a terrible mistake" and that he was "in deep." One of his only pleasures was writing long, introspective letters to his grandmother, Adele Goddet, in France.

Stone was given little time to adjust to his new surroundings. After only a week, he found himself on point in a night ambush. He struggled through nearly a week of field duty without confronting the enemy. His greatest adversaries were the incessant swarms of mosquitoes that kept him awake at night, the spiders that crawled in his shirt, and the fifty pounds of equipment on his back that nearly overwhelmed him as he humped through the jungle. One night he fell asleep during his watch, waking to discover that the Vietcong (VC) were practically on top of the platoon. "Scared shitless" and numbed with fear, he forgot his training and silently stared. A comrade opened fire on the oncoming troops, jolting Stone out of his stupor. He pulled the trigger, but had forgotten to take the safety off his M-16. Eventually, he regained his bearings and the platoon beat back the VC approach, but not before at least one American was severely wounded. Stone received a flesh wound in the neck during the melee and was briefly out of action.

His first taste of battle improved his combat sense. It also, despite his mistake during the ambush, put him more at ease with the other members of the platoon. He could not, however, com-

pletely fit in. The differences in background between him and the other grunts were obvious. He enjoyed classical music and serious literature, while they favored Hank Williams and Motown, hard liquor and serious drugs. One of Stone's comrades later recalled that he was "a quiet person who kept to himself." At first, he did not drink, spending his leisure hours writing stories of his experiences. Slowly, however, the war changed him. As his tour dragged on, he felt himself becoming disconnected from his civilized roots and becoming a "jungle animal," operating less on reason than "instinct." Increasingly, he sided with the progressive element of the platoon, who preferred Motown and drugs to the country music and alcohol that fueled the platoon's other faction. Stone's association with this group, composed mostly of lower-class blacks and whites from small towns, expanded his horizons and exposed him to the social injustice and prejudice of American life.

Then came 1968. There was nothing happy about Stone's new year. On January 1, he and 700 other U.S. soldiers were attacked by some 2,000 VC troops at Firebase Burt. The enemy lobbed mortars into the American entrenchment before beginning a ground assault at one in the morning. The American perimeter collapsed, and Stone's platoon was thrown into the counterattack. The VC inched forward, taking bunker after bunker, and the battle quickly devolved into brutal hand-to-hand combat. But the fighting came to an abrupt close when American planes dropped bombs directly on the American position, killing friend and foe without discrimination. The incident embittered Stone. As he watched bulldozers push lifeless Vietnamese bodies into a mass grave, he wondered if the American force had been no more than bait, a dab of honey designed to lure the antlike VC army into the open.

But Stone had little time to ponder. Just two weeks later, Bravo Company was hit again, this time while on patrol a few miles from Firebase Burt. Bravo's third platoon stumbled into a VC bunker complex and got pinned down. The first platoon faced a similar predicament. It was up to

Stone and the second platoon to extricate the men from the morass. But Stone's jungle instincts let him down; he got caught in a trip-wire explosion and received shrapnel in his leg and his rear. Medics shot him full of morphine, packed him on a stretcher, and loaded him on a helicopter. Bravo Company took about thirty casualties without inflicting any. Stone's rehabilitation kept him off the field during the Tet Offensive, which further devastated Bravo. By the time he returned to duty, he barely recognized anyone in his largely reconstructed platoon.

After another brief stint on combat duty, he was transferred to a military police auxiliary battalion in Saigon, where he guarded barracks and trolled for miscreants. The new duty bored Stone, and he numbed the tedium with drugs. The jungle beckoned. He wanted to get back into the heat of battle and got his wish after brawling with a rear-duty sergeant. In order to avoid having his tour extended as punishment, Stone opted in April 1968 to volunteer for the First Cavalry Division's reconnaissance and minesweeping detail.

The transfer proved portentous for his later career. While in the First Cavalry, Stone met a large black man from a small town in Tennessee who would later become the basis for "King" in *Platoon.* He also met a half-Spanish, half-Apache sergeant named Juan Angel Elias, who fascinated him. Elias, recalls Stone, "was like a rock star in the body of a soldier." Rather than terrify, the compassionate Elias inspired his men. He was a heavy drug user who was loathed by the lifers and juicers. Stone stayed close to Elias, learning how to rely on his senses, not his intellect, during combat. For the first time, Stone believed that it was possible to be both a good soldier and a good person.

By now, Stone had become a veteran, a fact he demonstrated in August 1968 when the platoon got pinned down by a North Vietnamese Army (NVA) soldier with a machine gun in a foxhole. With his fellow soldiers trapped under a hail of bullets, Stone lost contact with reality and functioned on pure instinct. With reckless abandon, he charged the bunker and, while on the run, lobbed a grenade directly into the hole, thus buying time for the platoon to be rescued. He is still at a loss to explain what happened to him. "Something went crazy in my head," he explains. "I flipped out." He received the Bronze Star for his heroism/confusion.

As the war dragged on, Stone sensed a loss of basic humanity. Yet another transfer brought him under the influence of Platoon Sergeant Barnes. Barnes had become something of an army legend. He had been wounded six or seven times, and one shot over the eye had left a large, sickle-shaped scar down the left side of his face. A passionate soldier, he volunteered to return to combat after every wound. In contrast to Elias, Barnes was "a very frightening man" with a "cold stare" that grunts felt "all the way down to [their] balls." Stone and the other awestruck soldiers were terrified yet intrigued by the grizzled warrior. From Barnes, Stone learned how to suppress his emotions, kill, and become a disciplined, mechanized soldier. Death came to concern him no more than life, and his sense of right and wrong eroded. He burned villages on "a steady basis." He watched uncaringly as frustrated U.S. troops sprayed mosquito repellent on their feet to make them sore so they could avoid marching and as they committed random acts of violence against Vietnamese civilians. He coolly stood by as one soldier, who would become "Bunny" in *Platoon,* bashed an old woman's head in with his rifle butt. In one village, Stone lost control and began shooting at an old man's feet because "he wouldn't stop smiling" at him. He could not, however, bring himself to kill the old man. Finally, he was shaken out of his complacency when he witnessed two U.S. soldiers raping a young village girl. He broke up the incident and decided that it was time to reassert his humanity. Looking at the world around him, he noticed the natural beauty of Vietnam. He purchased a 35mm Pentax and took the first of hundreds of snapshots of the country. For the first time, he thought of the war in visual terms.

Stone received his discharge orders in late November 1968. In fifteen months, he had earned a Bronze Star and a Purple Heart with an Oak Leaf Cluster for his multiple wounds. Yet even now there was sadness. Just before he was shipped home, he learned that Sergeant Elias had been killed, possibly by an errant American grenade. Stone was eager to leave the heat, insects, fatigue, jungle rot, and frustration behind, but he was still uncertain about his future. He thought that the war was "rotten and corrupt" and lacked "moral purpose" and integrity, but he did not feel that he could challenge the system. Burned out and drugged up, the twenty-two-year-old private returned to the United States with no immediate plans.

He was not prepared to return to New York—his father's New York, a city of commerce, commitment, and respectability. So, without even letting his parents know that he had come back from the war, he fled to Mexico. He found the experience unsatisfying and headed north after only a few days. But his homecoming would not be a happy one. American authorities busted Stone at the border for carrying two ounces of Vietnamese marijuana and threw him into a federal jail in San Diego. He faced the unpleasant prospect of five to twenty years behind bars. It was two weeks before prison officials allowed him to call his dad, but once Louis put up $2,500 for his son's defense, the public attorney suddenly took an interest in Stone's case, and he was soon released. The experience convinced him that nobody in America cared about Vietnam veterans and served to further radicalize him. Having seen injustice abroad, conditions in the prison alerted him to injustice at home. The jail was as horrible as those in Saigon. Inmates were stuffed "in every fucking nook and cranny," and 5,000 prisoners, mostly young blacks and Hispanics, had to sleep on the floor.

Life outside of prison was not much better. Stone returned to New York and life with his father. Louis, however, complained about Oliver's drug use and ghetto speech. Further, Oliver felt estranged from his old acquaintances. His friends had avoided the war, and most of his Vietnam buddies went back to the small, southern towns they came from. Americans' lack of interest in the war, their "mass indifference," stung him. Nobody wanted to hear his stories of Vietnam's hor-

rors; they were much more interested in "the business of making money." Even the antiwar movement troubled and disgusted him. He felt that it was not really serious about becoming "militarized and politicized" in order to force a peace and served only as a means for pampered college students to blow off steam.

Deciding that he would never be at peace with himself until he had written about Vietnam, Stone began writing a screenplay called *Break,* a story that moved on a symbolic level but contained characters that would later become Rhah, King, Bunny, Lehner, Barnes, and Elias in *Platoon.* After working slavishly on the script, he sent it to Jim Morrison of the Doors, whom he envisioned as the star. Though he never heard back from the singer, the experience convinced him that he could be a filmmaker. He was accepted at New York University's film school and studied under Martin Scorsese, who believed that, despite his penchant for cinematic excess, Stone showed potential as a filmmaker. He was particularly impressed with his student's first film, *Last Year in Vietnam,* a touching appraisal of the trials and tribulations of a Vietnam vet coming home. But Stone did not blend well with the other students. He was older than most and a loner by nature, leading many to believe that he was arrogant. Similarly, he found himself unable to participate in NYU's political scene. While other students marched, Stone advocated "a fucking revolution." He wanted to push beyond "bullshit meetings and conferences" and called for an armed march on Washington.

Stone's marriage in 1971 to Najwa Sarkis, a Lebanese woman who worked for the Moroccan Mission to the United Nations, seemed to calm him a bit. She made enough to support them both and encouraged him to work on writing screenplays. He completed his degree in September 1971 and began to bounce from job to job. While he wrote screenplays, he earned money as a Xerox boy for a copy pool, a messenger, and a cabdriver. By mid-1976, he had written eleven scripts and even directed one, *Seizure,* on a shoestring budget in Canada but failed to attract much critical or popular attention. It seemed he was going nowhere at a frantic pace. His marriage fell apart, he quit one job after another, and success continued to elude him. As America celebrated its bicentennial, Oliver Stone was a marginally employed twenty-five-year-old living in a cheap apartment in New York City.

Had Stone been a movie character, he would have been *Taxi Driver's* Travis Bickle. He had lost all faith in the government, largely due to the trauma of Watergate. Oddly, he admired Nixon, whose toughness, conservatism, and emotionlessness reminded him of his father, but the scandal destroyed any respect he may have had for the president. Watergate also convinced him that the government was "a lie" and "hammered home the point" that it had "lied to us about Ho Chi Minh and it lied to us about the Vietnam War." His depression was magnified when his grandmother died in 1976. Instead of adding to his rootlessness, however, her death inspired Stone to rededicate himself to making something of his life. Armed with this newfound conviction, he turned once again to Vietnam—the real Vietnam this time, not a symbolic one. In a few weeks of furious typing he produced the screenplay for *Platoon*.

Stone started shopping *Platoon* around Hollywood and attracted the attention of Stan Kamen of the William Morris Agency. Encouraged, he moved to Los Angeles, but no studio expressed interest in the film. The writing, however, was powerful enough that Columbia Pictures hired him to write a treatment of Billy Hayes's autobiography, *Midnight Express*. His screenplay won an Academy Award for best adapted screenplay of 1978 and brought more opportunities his way, including an offer from producer Marty Bergman (*Serpico, Dog Day Afternoon*) to write a screenplay for Ron Kovic's book, *Born on the Fourth of July*. Al Pacino was set to star, and William Friedkin was to direct. The releases of *The Deer Hunter* and *Coming Home*, however, threatened to overload the market for Vietnam films, and *Born*'s funding fell through three days before shooting was to begin.

But work was now easier to find. Stone wrote and directed *The Hand* (1981), a low-budget thriller starring Michael Caine, and produced an early version of the script for *Conan the Barbarian* (1982). In Hollywood, he was earning a reputation for writing violent, right-wing screenplays, a charge that gained strength from his scripts for *Scarface* (1983), *Year of the Dragon* (1985), and *8 Million Ways to Die* (1986). He resented the stereotype and found inspiration in Warren Beatty's *Reds,* a film that proved to him that a Hollywood movie could be both big-budget and leftist. Then, in 1984, Dino DeLaurentis agreed to finance *Platoon*. Once again, however, funding fell through at the last moment. It was not until after the surprise success of *Salvador* (1986), which did well on video despite being underpromoted, that he received solid backing for *Platoon,* and then only by Hemdale, a British-based operation.

Part of Stone's problem with getting the funding for *Platoon* had to do with Hollywood's suspicion that Vietnam War films were both too controversial and too economically risky. This notion began to take form while Stone himself was still serving in Vietnam. In 1967, John Wayne filmed *The Green Berets* at Fort Benning, Georgia. Released in 1968 after the Tet Offensive, the hawkish, pro-American film provoked a violent left-wing critical response. "Unspeakable . . . stupid, . . . rotten, . . . false, . . . vile and insane," commented Renata Adler in the *New York Times*. "Immoral . . . racist," agreed Michael Korda in *Glamour*. "Childishly sleazy," added Frank Mararella in *Cinema Magazine*. Although the film found its audience and made money, Hollywood producers who did not have Wayne's clout with moviegoers decided that the war was simply too hot.

For the next decade, filmmakers treated the war as little more than a reference or a source of inspiration. The WAR—that bloody, passionate creature sitting in America's living room— was not mentioned. Then came the first tentative steps. In 1978, *Coming Home* and *The Deer Hunter* explored the mentality of soldiers returning from the war, with mixed critical and financial results. The same year, *Go Tell the Spartans,* a fine film, was all but ignored. In 1979, Francis Ford Coppola released *Apoca-*

lypse Now, a film buried beneath so much myth and symbol that critics read it as both hawkish and dovish. Its profound ambivalence—or perhaps its psychological complexity—may have penetrated to the heart of war's darkness, but it failed to say much about the everyday nature of combat.

During the Reagan era, Hollywood retrieved, dusted off, and modestly updated stock war-film materials. Once again, combat became a heroic enterprise, corrupted only by politicians. The *Rambo* films and the *Missing in Action* series captured the big bucks. Americans wanted to watch winners, not agonize over what happened or why it happened. They desired action, not introspection; results, not meaning. They wanted heroes for their next wars, not victims of lost crusades.

But Oliver Stone had his own agenda, which smacked against the political currents of Hollywood and Washington. Much of *Platoon* is an echo, not only to the themes of *Apocalypse Now* but also to the antiwar literature of World War I. Sergeant Barnes, the scarred figure from both Stone's own tour in Vietnam and *Platoon,* recalls Hemingway's injured hero Jake Barnes in *The Sun Also Rises.* And the use of Charlie Sheen as not only the protagonist but also the narrative guide serves the same purpose as Martin Sheen did in *Apocalypse Now.* The twin references announced that *Platoon* would explore both coming of age and the futility of modern war.

The strength of *Platoon* emerged from Stone's passion for and his palpable understanding of the subject. Like Hemingway, war was the defining experience in his life. He enlisted, he fought, he killed, he was injured; he believed, he questioned, he lost faith. He suffered the full range of emotions, entertained the gamut of thoughts. And when he turned to the subject, it was not like Francis Ford Coppola, Sylvester Stallone, or Chuck Norris, filmmakers and actors who embraced the war as a commercial vehicle rather than a biographical necessity. Stone, unlike others who depicted Vietnam on-screen, viewed the war as the central event not only in his life but also in the "soul" of America "and the world."

From the beginning of the *Platoon* project, he insisted on absolute realism. Anything less than fidelity would have betrayed his memory and experiences—although the U.S. Department of Defense refused to cooperate on the film because it believed that it was a "totally unrealistic" depiction of the war. Stone maintained that the film was not about larger issues; it was about "boys in the field." To ensure that his actors were as knowledgeable and competent as the real men of Bravo Company, he imposed a rigorous, two-week-long boot camp in the Philippine jungles under the dictatorial supervision of Captain Dale Dye, a twenty-year marine and a Vietnam veteran. Captain Dye subjected the cast to long marches with sixty-pound packs, cold army rations, and uncomfortable nights in foxholes, punctuated by sudden bursts of explosions to guarantee that no one would sleep. By the time filming began, the actors had the "tired, don't-give-a-damn attitude" that Stone had hoped to achieve. In a short time, Stone and Dye had made soldiers out of actors.

To maintain faith with his past, Stone set *Platoon* in a real time and a real place—his time, his place. The film details the activities of 25th Bravo Company, operating near the Cambodian border, in 1967. The film's central character, Chris Taylor (Charlie Sheen), views the war from a perspective similar to Stone's. Like Stone, Taylor is a white, upper-middle-class kid who went to Vietnam to escape from the boredom and rigors of civilized life. His experiences in Vietnam mirror Stone's—one reason why the film is so realistic and personal.

The film's initial impression of Vietnam focuses on the landscape, perhaps the overriding presence in the film. It is, in the fullest sense, a world without vision, a land of eight-foot elephant grass, overgrown virginal forests, and lush jungles. It is a landscape that one needs a machete to hack through. Much of the tension of the film originates in its confining setting; danger always seems to threaten from behind the next tree.

Daily discomforts add to the tension. Stone's Vietnam is a place where a grunt cannot relax. Mosquitoes swarm, ants bite, and leeches cling.

Insects maintain a perpetual hum in the background, constantly reminding the viewer and the soldier of their presence. The product of a wealthy family, Chris finds it difficult to adjust to Vietnam's fatal environment; he staggers under the weight of his pack, gags at the sight of a dead body, and attracts the ants and leeches like a magnet. Making matters worse, night seems to conspire with the harsh environment to deny rest to the weary Americans. Bombs explode, flares light up the sky, ambushers lurk everywhere. "You never really sleep," observes Chris in a voice-over, as his year-long tour of Vietnam assumes the dimensions of an 8,760-hour day.

The language in *Platoon* is similarly authentic. Fresh soldiers are "cherries" and "newbies"; Vietnam is "the Nam," and America is "the world"; pot smokers are "heads" that meet in the "underworld." The film is also littered with obscenities, as Stone refused to pull any verbal punches. The music the soldiers listen to and the words they use reflect Stone's own experiences. The use of Motown hits like "Tracks of My Tears" alongside country classics like "Okie from Muskogee" adds to the realistic aura and helps to divide the platoon into two hostile camps—the "heads" and the "juicers"—just as it was in Stone's platoon. They are his people, "guys nobody really cares about" from small towns and villages, "the bottom of the barrel," the undereducated and the uneducated.

It is in the realistic portrayal of the platoon itself that the film departs most radically from the traditional war genre. The classic World War II film upholds the ideal of the melting pot: out of many, one. Multiethnic, multireligious, and multiregional, the platoon is a smorgasbord of Italians, Poles, and Irish; Protestants, Jews, and Catholics; Brooklyn sharpies, southern Rebs, and midwestern rubes. Yet they all pull together toward a common goal. No such comfortable—and comforting—arrangement is present in *Platoon*. Stone observed a clear "moral division" in his platoon when he served in Vietnam, and Bravo's cinematic counterpart is faithful to Stone's memory. On a symbolic level, the film centers on the two sergeants, Elias and Barnes. For Barnes, all civilians are potential Vietcong and are liable to ruthless treatment. Elias, however, takes a more compassionate "hearts and minds" approach to the war. He wants to save Vietnam; Barnes merely wants to destroy the country.

But the platoon is split over more than war aims. Unlike traditional war films, Stone shows how race divided soldiers in Vietnam. In the base camp, African Americans are usually by themselves, shunted off to one side. Black soldiers are aware that they are being treated unfairly. One complains that they have to take extra turns on ambush patrol because of racial "politics," and another objects to "always being fucked by the rich." They are not, however, passive victims. Junior, a black grunt, for example, is not afraid to order Chris around. "Hey, white boy!" he shouts, before encouraging him to dig a foxhole with a little more enthusiasm. The only place blacks and whites can comfortably coexist is in the underworld, where, supervised by Sergeant Elias, they dance together in a drug-induced haze to the sounds of Smokey Robinson. In 1967, a year that saw vicious race riots in Detroit and other cities and heard former Student Nonviolent Coordinating Committee chairman Stokely Carmichael call for a black revolution, race was as much of an issue in Vietnam as it was in America. Stone, unlike other filmmakers, brought this reality to the screen. By doing so, he added a deeper, more nuanced understanding of America.

Despite their divisions, soldiers have to pull together when they are in combat. It is in these sequences that Stone achieves the greatest sense of realism in the film. Stone's war is the grunt's war, a war without maps, red and blue arrows, or a grand design. Men fight because they are attacked, not for any lofty goal or territorial objective, and battles often end as inconclusively as they begin. In such contests, "winning" loses any elevated meaning; soldiers fight to survive. Period.

The mise-en-scène of the battle sequences underscores Stone's idea of combat. His camera work captures Karl von Clausewitz's notion of the "fog of war." The camera becomes Chris's eyes—jerking back and forth, seeing nothing distinctly, and blindly reacting to threats both perceived and real. Violence erupts suddenly and brutally, often without warning or meaning. Death and injury are neither noble nor ignoble, they just are. The best answer to the suffering and violence is given early in the film by Barnes. In true Hemingway fashion, he clamps his hand over a screaming, dying man and demands that he "take the pain."

Premiering in New York and Los Angeles in December 1986, *Platoon* created an international sensation and propelled Stone into the forefront of American directors. *Time* proclaimed that Stone's effort portrayed "Viet Nam as It Really Was," and the *New York Times*'s Vincent Canby called the film "a succession of found moments"—that is, it had rediscovered the lost reality of the war. More importantly for Hollywood and Oliver Stone, *Platoon* was a massive commercial success as well. Made for a paltry $6.5 million, the film grossed $136 million in U.S. box office receipts. Video sales pushed the total gross to a staggering $250 million. For now, Stone believed that he had exorcised the demons of Vietnam, and he looked forward to new projects. Having suddenly become a famous director, he planned to move to a lighter subject for his next film. In 1987, he remarked that he "would love to do a comedy."

Had Oliver Stone been Francis Ford Coppola or even Sylvester Stallone, perhaps he could have jumped genres and made a quick transition to another project. But the whole point of *Platoon* was that it was not just a film project; it was Stone—his biography, his vision, his nightmare. He could no more set Vietnam aside than Hemingway could forget his war or Ahab abandon his whale. *Platoon* had not ended his dialogue with America about the war; it had only started it.

After *Platoon,* Stone made two movies, *Wall Street* and *Talk Radio,* before returning to Vietnam with a version of Ron Kovic's autobiography, *Born on the Fourth of July.* He had been interested in the project since 1980, but there was no money in Hollywood for a film about a paraplegic Vietnam veteran who discovers that all his country's cherished ideals are false and that the war in Vietnam was a sham. In a Hollywood marked by escape and fantasy, and a Washington following in lockstep, Kovic and Stone were as warmly embraced as repo men. They were pounding on the door, trying to get inside to claim their America, but nobody was at home. The financial success of *Platoon,* however, gave Stone the sledge he needed to break down the door.

Born on the Fourth of July centers on America's fatal flaw, the culture that conditions and indoctrinates young men to go to war. It is a brutal culture, life-hating, joy-denying, pleasure-destroying. In the film, Stone labors to subvert that culture, and by casting Tom Cruise in the lead, he moved far in that direction. By the mid-1980s, Cruise had become America's smile, the charming good-bad boy of *Top Gun* and *Risky Business.* Stone took Cruise's chiseled good looks and spit-shined image and caked them with mud. "Tom had the classical facial structure of an athlete," noted Stone. "He's the kid off a Wheaties box. I wanted to yank the kid off that box and mess with his image—take him to the dark side."

Seldom in the American cinema has the dark side initially seemed so benign. The opening sequences of the film are infused with a soft, golden light, and falling autumn leaves create a snow-globe effect. Everything about Kovic's Massapequa has a Norman Rockwell familiarity—small town and safe streets, boys playing war in the woods and men mouthing platitudes about the need to serve, rippling flags and firecrackers on the Fourth of July, baseball games and Yankee caps, wrestling matches and first loves. Kovic is his mother's "little Yankee Doodle Boy," born on the Fourth of July and raised with loving care. Yet something is out of whack in his comfortable, middle-class America. A parading World War II veteran flinches at the sound of an exploding firecracker, a coach's quest for victory borders on obsession, a mother's religious faith merges into zealotry. Kovic is taught not only to be upright, courteous, reverent, and clean but also that winning is everything, God hates quitters, communists are banging on our doors, and Uncle Sam needs you. As America's perfect son, he moves naturally from the Boy Scouts to the marines.

For Kovic and Stone, the culture of winning, violence, and unquestioning loyalty was America's dark side. It was a culture that despised softness and sensitivity and created a god out of John Wayne—in the book, Kovic writes that he resented having to give his "dead dick for John Wayne." These forces—family, community, school—imbued Kovic and Stone with a cold war mentality and the idea that manliness could be found only on a battlefield. The power of the culture makes Kovic's disillusionment all the more wrenching. After being wounded and returning home, he blames his country for making him go to Vietnam. "They told us to go," he cries, implicating the faceless establishment for perpetrating an immoral war.

Kovic's story also shows how easily this dark side can be foisted onto the next generation. As he rides through a crowd during a Fourth of July parade, his eyes come to rest on a boy who looks much as he once did. The child's Yankees cap and his toy gun suggest that little has changed since his own youth. By exposing America's dark side, Stone pushes his analysis of Vietnam beyond that presented in *Platoon.* Unlike *Platoon,* which made no effort to explain the larger issues behind the war, *Born on the Fourth of July* suggests that Vietnam, and war in general, are a product of America's own moral deficiencies, a theme that he would further explore in later films.

Kovic's and Stone's disillusionment is fueled by outrage, because they believed that they had been duped by their country's martial culture. The film implies that only the true believers, boys like Kovic born on the Fourth of July, evinced a willingness to fight and die for their country. Most of Kovic's high school classmates cannot understand why he wants to enlist; they do not feel particularly threatened by communists, and they are not moved by any overwhelming impulse to be "part of history." They seek only normal lives and a chance to prosper financially. When Kovic returns from Vietnam in a wheelchair, his friends have moved on with their lives. They are husbands, fathers, budding entrepreneurs, as distant as people can be from what he experienced on the other side of the world. Perhaps even more than his injuries, his friends' apathy gnaws at him. While he is consumed with the war, they could not care less. A hospital orderly tells him, "You can take your Vietnam and shove it up your ass." "They don't give a shit about the war," his friend Stevie adds. Even his mother switches the television station to *Laugh In* when a story about a Vietnam War protest comes on the news.

Stone shared Kovic's attitude toward America and his desire to shake his sleeping countrymen. The messages of *Born on the Fourth of July* are don't forget and get involved. America fought and lost the wrong war in the wrong place at the wrong time. It was a needless, senseless war, the product of a military culture and blind ideological faith. And unless Americans begin to question that culture and that faith, it will happen again. On this point, Stone and Kovic are products of the late 1960s and early 1970s political radicalization. Conservatives argue that protest movements had no effect. Stone disagreed. "That's why making *Born* was a particular thrill, 'cause it was flying in the face of that shit," he said. "People were outraged, I'd get letters saying . . . there was no protest, no hatred, why are you bringing up all this divisiveness? But I remember the late '60s as a very rough time. . . . A lot of people can't face their past, you know."

Stone felt so strongly about the message of the film that he allowed it to interrupt the narrative flow. Most of the film deals with Kovic's coming to terms with the forces that shaped him, a struggle that is largely internal and intellectual. The film ends, however, with sketchy scenes of Kovic's political activism, and the manipulation of historical footage to put Cruise/Kovic at the 1972 Republican Convention contrasts sharply with the camera work of the rest of the film. But the transition from internal search to external activism—personal to political—is the message of *Born on the Fourth of July.*

Stone's concern for America's involvement in the war runs even deeper, however. It was not enough for the director just to show the impact of the war on an individual—on Ron Kovic, Chris

Taylor, or Oliver Stone. It was not enough just to be the cinematic Hemingway of the Vietnam War. Stone wanted to be the war's historian as well. As a historian of the war, Stone moves on two levels: personal and political. *Platoon* and *Born on the Fourth of July* are primarily personal statements, though the political lurks beneath the surface. Both films were huge critical and commercial successes (*Born on the Fourth of July* was nominated for eight Academy Awards and won four, including an Oscar for Stone for best director).

Heaven and Earth (1994) is also largely a personal film of self-discovery, although it too has a historical and political message. The war, Stone says, was not only, or even mostly, about the United States. The overwhelming majority of people who were killed in the war were Vietnamese, and most of them were civilians. It was their land that was destroyed, their economy that was shattered, and their culture that was threatened with ruin. Stone commented that he made the film for two reasons—first, to explore the themes of Buddhist spirituality, reverence for ancestors, and respect for the land, and second,

to respond to, in part, the blind militarism and mindless revisionism of the Vietnam War as typified by a certain odious brand of thinking that has snaked its way into our culture over the past decade or so, in which the conflict is refought in comic-book style by American superheroes, with a brand new ending . . . we win! Within the moronic context of these ideas, hundreds of nameless, faceless, Vietnamese are blithely and casually shot, stabbed, and blown to smithereens, utterly without the benefit of human consideration. Entire villages are triumphantly laid to waste, with not one microsecond of thought or care given to those inside the little bamboo hamlets being napalmed. Who were they?

In his attempt to give "the reverse angle" of the war, Stone succeeds. He depicts Phang Thy Le Ly Hayslip's world in loving detail, from the agricultural cycle to the serene beauty of the land to the peaceful stability of village and religious life. Seldom has a commercial filmmaker devoted so much attention to the undramatic nature of a third-world culture. When Stone finally turns his attention to Americans, he portrays them as rich, barbaric invaders. They intrude into the Vietnamese civil war, overlay it with an alien ideological meaning, then take it over, destroying or corrupting everything they touch. They disrupt nature by destroying entire villages, defoliating forests, and severing the rice cycle. American forces turn Le Ly's "most beautiful village on earth" into a scene from Dante's *Inferno*. Culturally, American capitalism corrupts the country, sending villagers to cities and bases where they become pimps, prostitutes, and black marketeers. Drawing not only on Le Ly's memoirs but also on his own experiences as an MP, Stone is at his best when showing American GIs at their worst.

Stone even contends that Americans are at their worst when they are trying to be at their best. In one scene, South Vietnamese soldiers—American allies—use honey donated by the United States and angry ants to torture Le Ly. On a metaphoric level, Stone uses Steve Jones (Tommy Lee Jones) as the representative American. A twisted, misguided killer, Steve attempts to atone for his own sins by showering Le Ly with gifts and by taking her out of her natural environment and dropping her in the United States. But just as the relationship between the United States and the Republic of South Vietnam rotted, so the unnatural union of Steve and Le Ly turns exploitive and violent. Steve's suicide reinforces Stone's view of the results of the American mission in Vietnam.

Heaven and Earth differed from *Platoon* and *Born on the Fourth of July* in its public reception. Expensive to make, it failed miserably at the box office. Production costs exceeded the combined costs of *Platoon* and *Born on the Fourth of July,* but *Heaven and Earth* grossed only $6 million in the United States. Although it was critically applauded—one reviewer called it "Stone's ultimate war film"—it failed to reach the audience the director intended it for. It had a message for all Rambo-cheering, Reagan-voting Americans, but few people paid it even passing attention.

After the success of *Born on the Fourth of July* and before the debacle of *Heaven and Earth,* Stone moved on to new topics. Instead of fulfilling his dream of making a comedy, he decided to catalogue the life of his musical hero, Jim Morrison. But even before *The Doors* was completed, he had laid the foundations for a bold return to the Vietnam genre. By the late 1970s, he had decided that the assassination of John F. Kennedy had drastically altered the course of the war and America's future, but it was not until 1988, when book publisher Ellen Ray gave him a copy of Jim Garrison's *On the Trail of the Assassins* in an elevator in Havana, that he became convinced that Lee Harvey Oswald had not acted alone. Stone devoured Garrison's work, buying the rights to the book with his own money. He then immersed himself in the "serious research" required of any historian. He read every book on JFK and the assassination that he could lay his hands on and, along with screenwriter Zachary Sklar and coproducer A. Kitman Ho, conducted over 200 interviews with conspiracy theorists and other people with knowledge of the case.

Stone's conception of the film soon outgrew the mere circumstances of the assassination. "The central historical question" that courses through the movie centers on neither Jim Garrison nor the identity of the president's killers. Instead, Stone used the murder as a means of exploring the event that was central to both his and, he believed, his nation's life—Vietnam. In this way, he was building on issues he had explored in his previous films. *Platoon* was an autobiographical study that showed how the everyday horrors of the war affected a young man. *Born on the Fourth of July* carried the war home by examining how indifference, misunderstanding, and the perverted nature of American life affected Ron Kovic's life. But now, Stone cast an even wider net. *JFK* is a biography of America since World War II, with Vietnam serving as the defining event for the period.

Stone begins *JFK* by rehabilitating the slain president's image. A narrator informs the viewer that Kennedy represented "change and upheaval" in American government. We see Kennedy as he wanted to be seen, making conciliatory speeches toward the Soviets and frolicking with his family. Most importantly, we learn that Kennedy, through no fault of his own, found himself "embroiled" in a war in Southeast Asia. After the assassination, a stricken black maid, perhaps the mother of a grunt, sobs as she tells a reporter what "a fine man" Kennedy was. Meanwhile, Guy Banister (Ed Asner) cheers the killing, ripping Kennedy for letting the "niggers vote." Those who supported and those who objected to Kennedy are neatly delineated. Stone seems intent on transforming Kennedy into the stained-glass hero that the Vietnam War never had.

Vietnam barely ripples the surface of the first half of the film. As New Orleans district attorney Jim Garrison (Kevin Costner) initially becomes obsessed with the assassination, there is little indication that the war plays a pivotal role in anything. Instead, the war appears, as it did in the mid-1960s, as background noise—always present, but rarely commented on. A brief clip shows Lyndon Johnson declaring his intent to vigorously prosecute the war. Another quick mention informs us that Johnson is asking for more money and more men to fight the war.

As Garrison unearths more information, however, Vietnam becomes increasingly central to the story. The pivotal scene comes when Garrison travels to Washington, D.C., to meet "Mr. X" (Donald Sutherland). Mr. X gives him the broader perspective that the DA could never have unearthed on his own. Mr. X cannot tell Garrison who killed Kennedy, although he suggests that top government officials were involved—when he refers to "the perpetrators" and calls the killing a "coup d' état," Stone flashes images of LBJ. He can, however, give Garrison information on the more important issue—*why* "they" killed Kennedy. Kennedy had irritated powerful militarists with his refusal to invade Cuba and his decision to eliminate the CIA's power to conduct covert activities during peacetime. The central issue, however, was Vietnam. Kennedy wanted to pull out of Vietnam by 1965, a decision clearly unacceptable to the military and the big arms dealers, who stood to make a killing if the killing continued. Somehow, these forces colluded, perhaps in combination with others, to remove the offending executive and replace him with the more hawkish Johnson, who was "personally committed" to Vietnam. Once Kennedy was out of the way, the war could start "for real." Kennedy's murder and the continuation of the war marked the final triumph of the military-industrial complex, a powerful junta that could run roughshod over any elected official. The personalized war Stone presented in *Platoon* had thus grown into a critical event that marked a decisive shift in the power structure of the United States.

JFK was a mortar lobbed at the establishment, and it set off a firestorm of controversy. Many critics ignored Stone's central thesis, seizing instead on the idea that he had proposed a "grand conspiracy" involving the CIA, FBI, elements of the military, anti-Castro Cubans, New Orleans homosexuals, the Dallas police department, and God only knows who else. Others blasted Stone for lionizing Garrison, who had, in real life, used some questionable methods (including truth serum and questioning hypnotized subjects) to gather his evidence, and for presenting speculation and composite figures as factual. Indeed, *JFK* attains the highest level of realism in any of Stone's films. As in *Platoon,* the camera acts as an eye, as fallible as any human's. The camera jerks as we see something out of the corner of our eye. Did we really see what we thought was there? Stone never provides an answer. Further, Stone has mastered the technique (first seen in the 1972 Republican Convention scene in *Born on the Fourth of July*) of combining documentary and new footage into a seamless unity. His realistic approach went too far for many of his detractors, one of whom referred to *JFK* as "the cinematic equivalent of rape."

Stone responded to the furor surrounding his film. He was willing to give way on most issues. He freely admitted that *JFK* was intended as "entertainment" and that he had taken "dramatic license" with the facts. *JFK* was not supposed to tell the truth about the assassination; Stone simply wanted to present a "paradigm of possibilities" that would point out the shortcomings of the Warren Commission's report. He noted where he had fictionalized or created composite characters and agreed that he had made his Garrison "better" than the real person. He was even willing to negotiate his portrayal of Kennedy. Stone was aware of Kennedy's faults—the pattern of "sex" and "drug use" that marked his life, his "stealing the election in '60," and his penchant for saying "one thing to the public" and doing "another thing behind their backs." In his defense, Stone correctly maintained that three hours was insufficient time to fully develop Kennedy's character and that, in any case, there was "a larger issue at stake."

On the "larger issue," however, Stone would not budge. He continued to insist that, had Kennedy lived, he would have ended the Vietnam War. Stone firmly believed that Kennedy had been reevaluating Vietnam and the cold war throughout 1963. Citing national security memoranda and statements made by Robert McNamara, Kennedy's secretary of defense, Stone claimed that Kennedy was only waiting to be reelected before withdrawing from Southeast Asia. Instead, he was murdered, thus putting "an abrupt end to a period of innocence and great idealism."

Though passionately and eloquently argued, Stone's position, however ardently held, does not stand up to scrutiny. There was, in fact, little to suggest that Kennedy wanted to end either Vietnam or the cold war, unless it was on America's terms. The conciliatory speeches that Stone quotes were anomalous. Even the speech he was to give in Dallas on November 22, 1963, took a hard-line stance on communism. McNamara may have believed that Kennedy would have pulled out of Vietnam (even though he wrote to Kennedy in October 1963 that the "security of South Vietnam" was "vital to United States security"), but Kennedy advisers McGeorge Bundy and Robert Kennedy did not. Only three weeks before he was killed, Kennedy approved the overthrow of South Vietnam's president, Ngo Dinh Diem, on the grounds that a new government was needed to save South Vietnam from communism. Kennedy's National Security Memorandum (NSAM) 263, which Stone cites, did call for the withdrawal of 1,000 U.S. troops, but this was merely giving notice to Diem that the United States was not pleased with his corrupt regime. At no point did Kennedy plan to abandon Vietnam. Lyndon Johnson's NSAM 273, which Stone claimed was a radical departure from Kennedy's position, was nothing of the sort. In fact, the document appears in *The Pentagon Papers* as an "Order by Johnson Reaffirming Kennedy's Policy on Vietnam" and stated that the United States' "objectives" remained identical to those stated by Kennedy.

If Stone has been flexible on other issues, why does he remain so steadfast in his assertion that Kennedy would have ended the Vietnam War? To do otherwise would be to undermine all that he has done in the last twenty years. In his films, he has constructed an explanation for an unexplainable war, reducing a complex swirl of ideology and global politics to a simple cause-and-effect relationship. Further, his theory supports his contention that the war had "no moral purpose." In *JFK,* Vietnam resulted from the cowardly murder by a group of vicious, power-hungry warmongers of a benevolent "king" who was trying to bring peace to the world. A more despicable beginning could hardly be imagined, tainting the war with evil before it even began in earnest. Finally, placing Kennedy's death within the context of Vietnam gives Stone and other veterans a hero in a war without acknowledged heroes. Kennedy represents the only hope that America could escape from the clutches of "the Beast" that has held the reins of power since 1963. If Kennedy did not offer hope in the 1960s, what chance is there that any future leader would be inclined to give power back to the people?

In showing how a corrupted American society created Vietnam, Stone returned to the theme of *Born on the Fourth of July.* In earlier films, he showed how a culture of violence, manifested in both public and private institutions, caused one young man to go to war. *JFK* maintains the same image of America but makes a quantum leap in in-

terpretation. Instead of exploring the effects of this culture on one person, he demonstrates how one manifestation of violence affected the course of the entire nation. Whereas Chris Taylor and Ron Kovic may have been naive individuals with no direct relation to viewers, the events in *JFK,* with Vietnam as its centerpiece, implicate all Americans who remain complacent and refuse to challenge the system.

Having, for the first time, explored the origins of the Vietnam War and situated it within a particular view of how American history operates, Stone was prepared to show how the war ended. Although it is impossible to say what he will do in the future, it may be that *Nixon* will mark Stone's final cinematic statement on the war. Although *Nixon* lacks some of the stridency of his earlier films, it reinforces the themes posited by Stone's other Vietnam War films. Instead of merely discussing the end of the war, he continues his bold explorations of the conflict's impact on both American and global history.

Even while he was president, Richard Nixon had intrigued Stone. Stone saw his father in the blunt and withdrawn executive, and the shame of Watergate helped turn Stone into a critic of America. Nixon, along with Kennedy, "shaped the era in which [he] grew up," and Stone eagerly plunged into the task of bringing the story of "the dominant figure in the latter part of this century" to the screen. Again, as with *JFK,* he engaged in the basic research required of any historian. He read "everything there was" on the ex-president and spoke with many of the people who would be portrayed on-screen. Stone also listened to some of Nixon's presidential tapes that had not yet been released to the public. Still smarting from critics' accusations that he had created characters and evidence for *JFK,* Stone released an advance copy of the script for *Nixon,* complete with hundreds of footnotes listing books, interviews, tapes, and oral histories.

At over three hours, *Nixon* is a lengthy yet compelling portrait of a complex politician. Stone's Nixon (Anthony Hopkins) is a master of detail, yet prone to confusion; a caring yet cold person; a man with a bold vision of the future who is haunted by the past. Nixon's greatest demon is the memory of JFK. Nixon resents Kennedy as only a hardscrabble, self-made man can resent a person who has been handed everything. At the same time, he maintains that he and the man from Massachusetts were like "brothers." Not content to merely expose this contradiction, Stone digs deep to explore the roots of Nixon's guilt, suggesting that he was indirectly responsible for Kennedy's death. Nixon, he says, was in charge of a program called "Track Two," a covert program to assassinate Fidel Castro, and may also have been involved in the Bay of Pigs in some way. By participating in this effort, Nixon unwittingly helped create the culture of violence that, as detailed in *JFK*, led to Kennedy's death and, as seen in *Born on the Fourth of July*, inspired Ron Kovic and others to go to war.

Although there is no evidence that Nixon knew of the plot to kill Kennedy, Stone shows him near the scene of the crime and explicitly links Kennedy's death to the Vietnam War. In the film, we see Nixon in Dallas in November 1963, meeting with a group of far-right businessmen headed by Jack Jones (Larry Hagman). As Nixon uncomfortably banters with high-class prostitutes, Jones and others urge Nixon to run for president in 1964. The wealthy businessmen are displeased with how Kennedy is handling Vietnam and promise Nixon "a shit-pot" of money and a victory in the South in exchange for a more militant foreign policy. Nixon demurs, claiming that Kennedy is unbeatable. But what if, one of the extremists asks, Kennedy does not run in 1964? Nixon is unnerved by the implications of this statement and beats a hasty retreat. Although he was clearly not responsible for Kennedy's death, Nixon's association with the forces that killed the president haunted him. Stone beautifully captures this mood by drenching the White House in a stormy, almost gothic atmosphere. In a very real sense, *Nixon* assumed the quality of a horror film.

Besides deepening his explanation of the causes of the war, Stone continues to expand his vision of how the war affected the world. *JFK* treats Vietnam as an event of national importance. *Nixon,* however, goes beyond this, and shows how the war played a critical role in the development of the global cold war. At times, Nixon seems to prosecute the war solely to salve his own bruised masculinity; he refuses to be pushed around by a smaller country. But, for the first time, we also see how Vietnam was but one aspect of a larger scene; Nixon refuses to back down in the face of a communist alliance. When he is in control of events, Nixon realizes that he has to continue to vigorously prosecute the war in order to gain concessions from the Soviets and the Chinese. He is successful in this endeavor. Stone shows Nixon's success in his meetings with Mao Zedong and Leonid Brezhnev. But, he argues, simply demonstrating Vietnam's importance in international politics does not make it a worthwhile war. Instead, Vietnam is reduced to a mere pawn in a global game. In January 1968, Private Stone's platoon acted as human bait to draw out a larger Vietnamese force. Other Vietnam veterans served the same purpose, only their job was to lure the world's major communist countries into negotiations with the United States. In Stone's view, the war was a chess game with one king and many pawns.

Finally, the Vietnam War comes to a close. It does not, however, reach either a glorious end or a satisfying resolution. After learning that the North Vietnamese are prepared to sign a treaty, an exhilarated Nixon calls a press conference to announce the conclusion of a successful war. He believes that he has finally negotiated a "peace with honor" and is prepared to join the country in celebration. But the press conference quickly turns hostile. One reporter challenges the president, claiming that the last several years of the war accomplished nothing, that the terms Nixon got were little different from those offered in 1968. As the president stammers, reporters bombard him with questions. Much to his surprise, they are less interested in the end of the war than in the breaking Watergate scandal. Vietnam has become a footnote in the history of the cold war. For Nixon and America, the war did not end so much as just fade away. There were no parades, no celebrations, and, for Stone and others, no closure. This stands as the final insult for a generation of soldiers and forced at least one to begin writing about his experiences. The lack of closure in 1973 led Stone to follow a twenty-year-long path to find redemption. In ending the war on-screen, Stone has taken us to the beginning of his own life as a filmmaker.

In a 1991 *Rolling Stone* interview, journalist David Breskin asked Oliver Stone if he felt like a great artist. "I never doubted it, from day one," Stone replied. "When I was eighteen, I just felt like I had a call. . . . And living up to that call has been the hardest part." From the first, Vietnam was an integral part of that calling. As a nineteen-year-old, he began a long, sprawling manuscript entitled "A Child's Night Dream." As a twenty-three-year-old film student at NYU, his first picture was entitled *Last Year in Vietnam.* At the age of forty, his first great commercial success as a director was *Platoon.* The circle closed eleven years later when *A Child's Night Dream,* heavily edited and slimmed down, was published by St. Martin's Press. The link between the nineteen-year-old would-be Hemingway and the fifty-one-year-old established artist was a passion for America's involvement in Vietnam—why we went, how we fought, what were the results and the implications.

In the process of becoming an artist, Stone also became the most successful and controversial historian of the war. For him, the past had an irresistible pattern, one woven with lost opportunities, conspiracies, fallen heroes, personal biographies, and impersonal forces. "I'm looking for a very difficult pattern in our history," he said. "What I see in 1963, with Kennedy's murder at high noon in Dallas, to 1974, with Nixon's removal, is a pattern." It is a pattern of promise and betrayal, vision and death, from John and Robert Kennedy to Martin Luther King, Jr., and Richard Nixon. "These four men came from different political perspectives, but they were pushing the envelope, trying to lead America to new levels. We posit that, in some way, they pissed off what we

call 'the Beast,' the Beast being a force (or forces) greater than the presidency."

Stone's burden is to be history's witness. For him, the past is a very real, painful, and unresolved phenomenon. Like William Faulkner, he believes that "the past is never dead." In fact, "it's not even past." But Stone's view of history contains inherent problems. It indicts an entire culture but suggests that members of that culture can make a lasting difference. For example, in *Born on the Fourth of July,* Stone contends that a martial culture packed Ron Kovic off to Vietnam, but in *JFK* he argues that Kennedy would have ended the war and that his promise died with him. But on a higher level, Stone realizes that the duty of the historian is to keep the past alive. It is the tension between his desire to teach and entertain and his desire to be taken seriously as an arbiter of the past that makes Stone such a controversial figure. Always reluctant to accept the work of popular historians (which Stone certainly is), academics have resisted embracing his vision of the past. And yet, his Vietnam films seem to have touched a nerve in the American public. To his credit, as his fame has grown, he has consistently adopted more sophisticated methods of exploring the past. Beginning in 1986 with an insulated, autobiographical view of history, Stone has expanded his analysis to incorporate the broader themes and movements that lay behind his own experience in Vietnam. In doing this, he uses the methods of a professional historian, going so far as to issue footnotes to accompany his work. Still, Stone remains true to his vision above all else; the details must be subservient to the big picture, the facts must support the conclusion. As Stone wrote, "Elie Wiesel reminds us that survivors are all charged with a sacred mission: to serve as witnesses and teachers of what they suffered, thereby preventing such catastrophes from occurring again." It is this goal, this quest for relevance, that drives Oliver Stone's pursuit of the past, separates his work from that of academic historians, and forces Americans to decide which is more important: a truthful rendition of the facts, or facts rendered in such a way as to illustrate the truth.

Study Questions

1. Oliver Stone grew up in a conservative home and seldom challenged the status quo as a youth. What events in his early life altered his views of American society? Specifically, how did his experience in Vietnam influence these changes?

2. What did Stone do when he returned from Vietnam, and what events in America provoked him to become more radical in his political beliefs?

3. How would you best describe the character of Vietnam War films at the time when Stone fought to gain funding for *Platoon* in the 1970s and 1980s?

4. What made Stone's film different from previous Vietnam War movies?

5. How does Oliver Stone's interpretation of Kennedy's political philosophy in the movie *JFK* connect to Stone's personal feelings about the United State's involvement in Vietnam?

Bibliography

This essay is taken from Robert Brent Toplin, ed., *Oliver Stone's USA: Film, History, and Controversy* (2000). James Riordan, *Stone: The Controversies, Excesses, and Exploits of a Radical Filmmaker* (1994) provides bibliographic information on Oliver Stone. For information on Vietnam War veterans and their positions on the war after returning home, see Murray Polner, *No Victory Parades: The Return of the Vietnam Veteran* (1971); David Cortright, *Soldiers in Revolt: The American Military Today* (1975); and Richard Moser, *The New Winter Soldiers: GI and Veteran Dissent during the Vietnam War* (1996). There is a wealth of information on the impact of the Vietnam War on film and television. See Albert Auster and Leonard Quart, *How the War Was Remembered: Hollywood and Vietnam* (1984); Peter T. Rollins, "The Vietnam War: Perceptions Through Literature, Film, and Television," *American Quarterly* 36 (Fall 1984), 419–432. For a good overview of the Vietnam War, see Gary Hess, *Vietnam and the United States* (1990).

READING 26

★ ★ ★

Ms. America: Jane Fonda

Peter Braunstein

Jane Fonda was the daughter of a major Hollywood star and the sister of a minor one. As a child John Wayne bounced her on his knee, Jimmy Stewart was a household fixture, and she was familiar with many of the leading actors and actresses of the day. It was natural that after a stint at Vassar, a brief career in modeling, and an education at the Actors' Studio, she too became an actress, making her debut in 1960 in an innocent piece of fluff entitled *Tall Story*. She played the cheerleader girlfriend of her college's basketball star, and she demonstrated a wonderful screen presence. During the next forty years, she played a series of roles. She was a sex goddess in *Barbarella* (1968), a fragile, destructive call girl in *Klute* (1971), a disillusioned Vietnam veteran's wife in *Coming Home* (1978), and an alcoholic in *The Morning After* (1986). Off the screen, she has also played a series of very public roles, from the political activist wife of radical Tom Hayden to video workout guru to the oddly "traditional" wife of conservative media mogul Ted Turner. Historian Peter Braunstein asks the right question about Jane Fonda: "Who *is* she?" In fact, in her ability to continually reinvent herself, she is a classic example of modern culture.

On the cusp of turning 60 in 1997, Jane Fonda decided to compile a video of highlights in her notably eventful life to present to guests at her forthcoming birthday party. In search of a guiding concept, she turned to her daughter Vanessa and asked for her input. She wasn't prepared, however, for her daughter's reply. "She said to me, 'Why don't you just get a chameleon and let it crawl across the screen?'," Fonda recounts. "Ouch. And so I thought to myself, Is that true. Am I simply a chameleon that changes color according to the times and the men in my life?" Of course, compared with some of the things Jane Fonda has been called, cultural chameleon is positively mild—even flattering. After all, most celebrities enjoy a relatively brief vogue before disappearing from the cultural landscape. By contrast, Jane Fonda's unusual staying power as an active public figure stems from her uncanny ability to adopt the foliage of successive eras of American culture. She was libertine in the mid-sixties, radical by decade's end, progressive in the seventies, entrepreneurial in the eighties, and corporate *grande dame* in the nineties.

It is in fact possible to trace the vicissitudes of American history over the past four decades simply by watching Fonda's public persona multiply and subdivide like so many stock splits. Her nineties incarnation as "Mrs. Ted Turner" might seem an apotheosis, but it was just another identity pit stop for a public figure who is part Zeitgeist receptacle, part historical timeline, and part cultural encyclopedia.

Fonda's tendency to intersect with the larger forces of history may be hereditary. The ancestors of her actor father Henry Fonda were among the first Dutch settlers of what is now upstate New York, where the town of Fonda still stands today. The family of Frances Fonda, Jane's mother, claimed direct descent from Edward Seymour, Duke of Somerset, whose sister, Lady Jane Seymour, was the third of King Henry VIII's unfortunate wives. So infatuated was Frances with her

regal ancestry that when the Fondas' baby girl was born, in December 1937, Frances christened her Jane Seymour Fonda. It wasn't long before the tomboyish girl rejected her "Lady Jane" epithet because, as she recalls, "It made me feel different."

When Henry Fonda announced in late 1949 that he was leaving his wife for a much younger woman, Frances had a nervous breakdown and was institutionalized in a sanitarium, where she committed suicide. Because Jane was 12 at the time, and her brother, Peter, 10, Henry thought it best to tell them that their mother had died of a heart attack. Jane learned the truth a year later, when a classmate leafing through a movie magazine stumbled on the real story. "I was very powerful for the first 10 years of my life," she recalls today. "I was feisty, I was brave, I had ambition. Then, at the beginning of puberty, it disappeared, and you could have put what was left of me in a thimble."

While Peter learned to act out his childhood trauma, Jane followed her father's lead and dissembled. During her adolescence, she nursed tightly packed emotions that might be let out at a moment's notice—a psychological foundation fit for the soon-to-be actress. She entered Vassar College in the fall of 1955 and quickly earned a reputation as what one observer called a "sophisticated delinquent." Her college antics, such as sneaking off to spend time with boys at Yale, seem mild enough today, but that hasn't kept a rumor from circulating among subsequent generations of Vassar students. It holds that Fonda was once barred from the daily afternoon tea service at Rose Hall because she wasn't wearing the requisite white gloves and pearls, so she promptly left the scene and returned wearing gloves, pearls—and nothing else. "Totally untrue," Fonda insists. Still, it wouldn't be the last time that Fonda's subsequent notoriety would be retroactively projected onto the rest of her life.

Fonda's ongoing habitation of the American moment began in 1958. Having dropped out of college after her second year, she toyed with the idea of becoming an actress and soon found a teacher in Lee Strasberg, the famous dean of the

Peter Braunstein "Ms. America," *American Heritage* (July/August 2001).

Actors Studio. Strasberg's "Method" acting regime was at the zenith of its cultural visibility, having influenced such film stars as Montgomery Clift, Paul Newman, and Anne Bancroft. Aspiring actors clamored for entry into the Studio, which accepted only five new members a year for every thousand applicants. Many settled for Strasberg's more accessible private classes, which were seen as a way to get one's foot in the Studio door. Fonda met Strasberg while he was working with Marilyn Monroe, his favorite protégé, on *Some Like It Hot.* After a short interview, she was accepted into the Strasberg fold. "The only reason I took her," Strasberg said, "was her eyes. There was such panic in her eyes."

Strasberg's approach to acting has often been criticized for producing a generation of mumbling, self-enclosed islands of subjectivity, Marlon Brando being a chief example. Yet despite its excesses, Strasberg's philosophy centered on the belief that actors shouldn't play a role so much as inhabit it. As he put it in a 1956 *New York Times Magazine* article, "I stress the difference between the actor who thinks acting is an imitation of life and the actor who feels acting is living. Unless the actor onstage really comes alive, really lives a character, he gives a superficial interpretation." The Method emphasized the importance of empathy, not imitation: One student who was to play a prostitute in a movie was told to go out and sleep with sailors. It was very possibly under Strasberg's tutelage—part dramatic training and part group psychoanalysis—that Fonda mastered the two elements that would make her such an effective harbinger and exemplar of her times: empathy and exhibitionism. The technique that allowed her intuitively to appropriate someone else's subjectivity for the purposes of a screen role would later enable her to conform to, and inhabit, the changing configurations of American culture—to "become" the culture, as it were.

From the high-minded rigor of the Actors Studio, Fonda descended in 1960 into a morass of shallow, forgettable roles, playing a cheerleader in her debut, *Tall Story,* and a "bad girl" in *Walk on the Wild Side.* Fearful of becoming just another Hollywood studio player, she made a bold career move in 1963: She accepted the director René Clément's offer to star in a French film, *Joy House,* opposite Alain Delon. Although eager to work with Clément, Fonda worried about the repercussions of a cinematic identity crafted abroad. "Nobody's ever heard of an American actress making a name for herself by taking off to Europe," her future husband Roger Vadim recalled her saying at the time. But as it turned out, she had unwittingly located the pulse of 1960s cinema.

Fonda chose Paris, which at the time was the capital of New Wave filmmaking, the home of the avant-garde directors Jean-Luc Godard and François Truffaut. "Hollywood had already embarked on a desperate effort to become Europeanized," notes her biographer Thomas Kiernan. "In their attempt to recover their audiences, American films rapidly became infiltrated by the mannerisms of the French style."

One of the masters of the "French style" was the director Roger Vadim, who had launched the career of his wife Brigitte Bardot in the 1956 film *And God Created Woman.* Vadim's entire cultural mission seemed to center on provoking audiences with movies about sexual frankness. He had mastered the art of embedding risqué adult content in scenarios drawn from classic French novels, thereby coating it with a varnish of respectability. As a result, his movies gained distribution in France and the United States under the guise of "art films." Interwoven with his film work was Vadim's reputation as the self-described "pope of hedonism," a reputation reinforced by his fathering children with two of France's most famous female stars, Bardot and Catherine Deneuve. Vadim mused on his ability to attract high-profile women in his notorious autobiography *Bardot Deneuve Fonda:* "For some, the secret was my performance in bed; for others, I was only a vehicle for success; and for still others, I was a Svengali capable of bewitching innocent young girls and molding them as I wished." Repulsed by and then attracted to Vadim for precisely these reasons, Jane Fonda married him in 1965—which also meant starring in his films and serving as iconographic ammunition in Vadim's ongoing crusade against bourgeois sexual morality. "I needed someone to teach me how to be a woman," Fonda remarks today with a laugh, "and I was stupid enough—no, I take that back—superficial enough to think that Vadim would do it. And he taught me a lot, but it's a certain version of womanhood."

It was during the Vadim years that Fonda became, in both France and America, a kind of shorthand signifier for hedonism, decadence, and public nudity. Although she bore no resemblance to Brigitte Bardot either physically or stylistically, the French press quickly dubbed Fonda "la BB americaine" and, fond of animal metaphors, described her as "a young wild thing, galloping too fast" and "the black panther I used to watch in the zoo."

The films she made in France, while successfully endowing her with sought-after European cachet, also tended to reinforce her association with free-loving nudism. American critics like Judith Crist ignored the plot of Vadim's 1966 film *The Game Is Over* and dwelled instead on the near-nudity, dubbing Fonda a "Miss Screen Nude of '67." (Fonda later remarked that, in the United States, "if you do a Dostoyevsky film and take your bra off, you're a sex symbol.") The American distributors of another Vadim/Fonda movie, *Circle of Love,* placed an eight-story-high billboard of a nude Fonda atop a Broadway theater, an image not even drawn from the film itself. "What shocked me personally was that the poster was extremely ugly," remarked the relentlessly casual Vadim.

Another example of the almost subliminal association made between Jane Fonda and the new morality was *Newsweek*'s decision to feature a barebacked photo of the actress for a cover story titled "The Permissive Society," evoking her as the child of Eros even though the article barely mentioned her. Questioned by the press about whether she had exhibitionist tendencies, Fonda spontaneously realized that she had been Method living—applying Method acting to the entirety of her life. "I do in life exactly what I do when I act," she admitted, "talking like the character, and so on—as an experi-

ment." The fact that the American public and media conflated her with her vixenish film roles, that she tended to "become" her onscreen self in real life, and that her films reflected the sexual libertinism of the sixties, produced a unique synergy in which Jane Fonda the actress, the person, and the cultural phenomenon all melded into one entity. This fusion of self, image, and culture took hold at the very moment *Barbarella* was released, in 1968.

Barbarella, the kitschy sci-fi hit about a sexually uninhibited space woman, emblazoned her sex-symbol image forever after in the public mind. While *Barbarella* wasn't a "movement movie" like *Bonnie and Clyde,* its free-love ethic implicated it in the cultural revolt sweeping the United States in the form of the hippie counterculture. Looking back on his *Barbarella*-era theories of sexual revolution from the vantage point of the 1980s, Vadim recalled the "aura of intoxication" of the late sixties, where "ancestral rules were on shaky ground," and concluded, "Jane and I were guinea pigs of an unstable era, and we did not know it." As it turned out, it was this very instability that would separate Fonda from Vadim and launch her into the most controversial phase of her life/career.

She had spent several years justifying American foreign policy to Vadim and his French friends, all of whom relentlessly criticized America's intervention in Vietnam. Indeed, she had once been bestowed the title of "Miss Army Recruiting of 1962," whereupon she gave an animated acceptance speech on America's need for a strong military. "I was very defensive," she recalls. "My father had fought in World War II, and I really believed that if our flag was flying somewhere, what we were doing in the name of the flag must be noble." But gradually she came to oppose the Vietnam war. In 1968, pregnant with her first child, Vanessa, during the near-collapse of the de Gaulle government in France, she underwent an epiphany: "In the streets there was revolution, and then there was my own revolution—which childbirth is. I was seeing people in the United States putting their lives on the line to try to end the war, and I realized I wanted to be there." Taking her newborn child with her, she abruptly terminated the French phase of her life, returning to a Hollywood brimming with radical activism.

Nineteen sixty-nine was the year of the radical celebrity in Hollywood. Fonda's brother, Peter, starred in *Easy Rider,* the youth-culture hit that expressed hippie fears of a silent-but-deadly majority, while actors like Marlon Brando and Paul Newman lent support to groups ranging from the Black Panthers to antiwar activists and Native Americans. Fonda landed on U.S. soil and dove headfirst into radical politics, holding press conferences for Huey Newton, visiting Native Americans who had seized Alcatraz, and devoting particular attention to the G.I. Coffeehouse movement, which was attempting to instill antiwar sentiment in U.S. soldiers. This abrupt shift in personas was replicated onscreen. At her most campy and frivolous in *Barbarella,* her next part was that of misanthropic, suicidal Gloria in *They Shoot Horses, Don't They,* perhaps the most brutally realistic role of her film career. In a prescient commentary, the film critic Pauline Kael wrote, "Jane Fonda stands a good chance of personifying American tensions and dominating our movies in the seventies as Bette Davis did in the thirties." Nominated Best Actress for her harrowing performance, Fonda flashed a Black Panther fist-salute as she strode into the Oscars.

Despite her attempts to distance herself from the frivolity of the Vadim years, the public perceived her newfound radicalism through the prism of her immediately preceding incarnation. "Jane Fonda represented unrestrained sexuality to American audiences," observed the historian David Farber, author of *The Age of Great Dreams: America in the 1960s,* "and now supporters of the war found that sexuality turned against them." Tom Hayden, the antiwar activist whom Fonda married in 1973, theorized that her sex-kitten image, combined with her radical antiwar activism, had left her open to charges of "sleeping with the enemy"—both literally and metaphorically: "All these people expected her to be a certain kind of person who occupied, probably, a large part of their fantasies, and when your fantasy life is threatened, and Barbarella becomes revolutionary, it's very upsetting."

Apart from her being perceived as a Barbarella-gone-bad, much anti-Fonda animus stemmed from the fact that her immersion in radical politics transcended and defied the public roles traditionally assigned to celebrities, film stars, pin-up girls, daughters of famous people, and women in general. Of course, for Fonda herself, this broadening of her public persona was quite intentional— "being a movie star," she was fond of saying at the time, "is not a purpose"—but others believed she had ventured into forbidden territory. Henry Fonda took to referring to her as "my alleged daughter," while Vadim made it clear that she had violated his version of womanhood: "I prefer to be married to a soft and vulnerable woman rather than to an American Joan of Arc." A sardonic 1971 *Life* magazine profile depicted her as a bubble-headed dilettante whose superficial espousal of left-wing politics was everything one would expect from a sex kitten–turned–radical. The misogynist article, entitled "Nag, Nag, Nag! Jane Fonda has become a nonstop activist," ended with the derisory summation, "If Jane Fonda only had a sense of humor, a sense of history and a power base, she could cause a real commotion."

As it turned out, Fonda caused quite a commotion during her infamous visit to Hanoi in the summer of 1972. The trip, conceived as a mission to uncover whether the Nixon administration was in fact bombing the dikes of North Vietnam, ended up as the crucible of her public life. Subjected to routine bombing by American planes, and awed by the determination of the North Vietnamese people, she went completely Method; she "became" North Vietnam. All the earmarks of her actress training came into play: a radical immersion in the subject experience resulting in profound empathy, followed by an exhibitionist portrayal of this newly adopted perspective. But this time, Jane completely forgot about the audience. In one fateful moment, she was photographed laughing with her North Vietnamese hosts while seated on an antiaircraft gun. On the index of self-inflicted

Ironically, in Barbarella *Jame Fonda struck blows for both the sexual revolution and the feminist movement.*

character assassination by photograph, the Hanoi image ranked somewhere between the *Life* magazine cover photo of Oswald holding the rifle and the 1988 footage of a helmeted Dukakis inside the Army tank. "The worst thing I ever did in my life" is how Fonda assesses that moment today. "It's the most stupid, naive thing I could have done. I was so swept up in what was happening that I didn't even think that there were photographers there and how it could be interpreted. I will go to my grave regretting that—not going to North Vietnam," she qualifies, "but that photograph."

She returned to an enraged nation. Several states immediately began introducing legislation that would have made "Hanoi Jane" *persona non grata* within their borders. The conservative Manchester (N.H.) *Union-Leader* urged that she be tried for treason and, if found guilty, shot. Some congressmen took this proposal to heart and at-

tempted to prosecute her for treason, sponsoring a House bill—unofficially called the Fonda Amendment to the 1950 Internal Security Act—that would have made it a felony for any citizen to visit a country at war with the United States. Such initiatives foundered on the question of whether the United States was constitutionally at war with Vietnam; nonetheless, Fonda's Hanoi trip transformed her from a wayward celebrity to a permanently controversial national figure.

Whereas the explicit phase of Jane Fonda's activism can be regarded as the death rattle of sixties-era New Left radicalism, her political career during the liberal sunset of the Carter years testified to a burgeoning political maturity. By the mid-1970s, a more pragmatic, less impulsive Fonda now characterized herself as a "progressive Democrat"; this repositioning was consistent with the new ambitions of former sixties radicals who now sought a place in the "system," be it electoral or corporate. Her husband Tom Hayden even bought a suit and ran (unsuccessfully) for the Senate in 1976 with the slogan "The radicalism of the 1960s is becoming the common sense of the 1970s." To fund the political arm of the Fonda-Hayden alliance, called the Campaign for Economic Democracy (CED), Fonda launched her own film production company, IPC (for Indochina Peace Campaign).

"If you want to send a message," the film mogul Samuel Goldywn once said about political movies, "use Western Union." Fonda's cinematic successes of the late seventies proved, quite to the contrary, that message films could ride high at the box office. The key was subtlety and audience appeal. "You can't propagandize," she insisted, cognizant of her mistakes earlier in the decade. "It has to be a good, well-told story. If you don't have that, people won't go." Having learned the hard way that audiences took her onscreen persona as her real one, she mastered the art of casting herself against type, playing apolitical characters onscreen and thereby confounding her reputation as a left-wing rabble-rouser. Her film roles belied her public image, enabling her to finesse her political agenda for easy, almost subliminal consumption by a mass audience. In IPC's first feature film,

Coming Home (1978), she played the politically neutral wife of a career Army officer who falls in love with a handicapped veteran who comes to oppose the war. The film's implicit message—that an antiwar conscience actually translates into a superior masculinity—was conveyed through the two men, not through Fonda, but her performance earned her a second Oscar for Best Actress.

This calibration of her political and cinematic identities netted her critical acclaim and box-office success even while rehabilitating her public image. At the same time, her political concerns had a knack for shadowing, and at times even anticipating, the cultural and political permutations of the late seventies. In 1979 she coproduced *The China Syndrome,* cannily playing a politically apathetic, career-minded TV reporter who accidentally witnesses a meltdown while visiting a nuclear power plant. No sooner had the film opened than a real-life nuclear accident occurred in Pennsylvania, producing a bizarre convergence in which audiences went to see *The China Syndrome* in order to understand Three Mile Island. Fonda's antinuke message was so effective that the "father of the H-bomb," Edward Teller, actually blamed her for the heart attack he suffered at the time. The 1980 hit *Nine to Five* took on the issues of sexual harassment and women's workplace grievances through the easily palatable formula of slapstick comedy, and Fonda cast the film's players with the strategic care of a presidential candidate choosing a running mate. Knowing that "there are still a lot of people out there who would like to see me dead," especially in more conservative regions of the country, she picked Dolly Parton because "Dolly gets us the South."

By 1980, the year her political nemesis Ronald Reagan was elected President, Jane Fonda had staged a remarkable comeback: a Gallup poll ranked her among the world's 10 most admired women. But despite the success of her films, she foresaw the diminished earning potential she could expect as an actress in her mid-forties and worried about securing new funding sources for the CED. As it turned out, the answer to her financial concerns would launch her next, and

most lucrative, cultural incarnation. "This was at the height of Lyndon Larouche, and I discovered that he funded his organization through a computer business," Fonda recalls. "So I said to Tom, 'Let's borrow a page from the right wing and figure out a business that we can start.' Now, I'm about as far from a businesswoman as anybody could possibly be. But one day it just hit me: There's one thing I understand, and that's exercise. I know what works, and I know what it can do for a woman. Why don't I turn it into a business?" Drawing from an exercise routine she had developed over the past twenty years that built on her early ballet training, she launched the "Workout," an interdisciplinary regimen that incorporated calisthenics, dance, and aerobics.

Once again, Jane Fonda had tapped the spirit of the age. She opened her first Workout center in Beverly Hills, in 1979, and the concept took off. Workout centers spread to other cities, and *Jane Fonda's Workout Book* sold nearly two million copies in its first year. Not only did her newest endeavor mesh with, as well as fortify, the fitness craze of the 1980s, it also helped jump-start the infant home-video industry. When the entrepreneur Stuart Karl persuaded her to release a video version of the Workout, her videocassettes quickly became bestsellers. By 1982 her fitness empire had taken in an astonishing $20 million. Like a vertically integrated corporation, the diversification of her professional identities now had a mutually reinforcing, synergistic effect. Showing off her fit, middle-aged body onscreen promoted her Workout routine; the Workout and film roles subsidized Hayden's successful campaign for California State Assembly in 1982. At the same time, Jane Fonda the "political actress" now mutated into an emblem of the fitness-crazed, body-conscious, "say no to drugs" eighties.

It might seem paradoxical that she found her greatest mainstream appeal during the Reagan era, but Jane Fonda's Workout rhetoric also proclaimed a return to a strenuous life and a code of self-discipline that aptly, if perversely, meshed with the President's neoconservative philosophy. Indeed, Fonda once defended her Workout regimen—deemed too rigorous by some critics—by articulating a "zero tolerance" approach to fitness wimpiness worthy of a White House press conference: "I shed no tears for the Beverly Hills matron who cries and drinks and takes drugs. You have the ability to get off your butt and find out what life is about. If you don't, that's your problem, not someone else's."

Part Murphy Brown, part Teddy Roosevelt, the eighties Fonda was a solid role model for entrepreneurial feminists and career moms. But the nineties Fonda was perplexing. Fresh on the heels of her breakup with Hayden after 16 years of marriage, she met the media baron Ted Turner and married him in 1991. Despite their disparate cultural orbits, Fonda and Turner shared a high-profile public presence and similar family tragedies; Turner's father, like Fonda's mother, had taken his own life, when Ted was 24. Fonda chose this turning point to retire gracefully from cinema, her financial independence having spared her from the lesser roles normally allotted to older actresses. She still devoted her time to an array of causes, particularly the Georgia Campaign for Adolescent Pregnancy Prevention. The nineties Fonda also embraced Christianity, after a lifetime of agnosticism. Yet even these ostensibly conservative turns were enacted with characteristic Fonda bravura. In true Civil Rights–era fashion, she frequently attends a black Baptist church. Her inner permutations, though less publicly visible than before, also contributed to the recent disintegration of her marriage. She attributes the rupture with Turner to a continuing pursuit of personal growth and self-definition. "You can lose a marriage when you find your voice," Fonda says, "if you didn't have a voice when you got into the marriage."

Any summation of Jane Fonda's life must begin with the question: Who *is* she? Indeed, in the kaleidoscope of identities that constitute her past, many observers and detractors still attempt to reduce her to one of her many incarnations. Hanoi Jane, for some, is the quintessential Fonda, while others attempt to explain her life through her successive marriages. But she eludes all such interpretations. Vadim titled his autobiography *Bardot Deneuve Fonda,* thereby boiling his life down to the women in it; a Fonda autobiography called *Vadim Hayden Turner* would surely sell, but it wouldn't explain the complexity of her public image. If one factor does stand out, it is that Fonda had her formative training as a Method actress and approached her subsequent personae—from libertine to disciplinarian—like sought-after roles that accorded her a vivid and all-encompassing, if temporary, identity. Yet this only brings us back to her daughter's chameleon remark, and begs the question: Was Fonda's life merely a series of performances, each played with Oscar-worthy conviction?

She herself has trouble answering such questions. "It's like my whole life has been a quest for growing up," she muses. "I had no mother, my father was remote, I had to invent myself, and I used men to do it." What is unique, however, is that Fonda also used the shifting configurations of our culture to assemble her identities. One consequence of this symbiosis with great national currents is that Fonda the historical figure now affords us a guided tour of nearly 40 years of American history. This unique historical utility, in turn, points to what is perhaps the greatest meaning of her life.

During the making of *Klute,* in 1970, Fonda's antiwar militancy placed her at odds with much of the film's crew, and one day she arrived to find the set decorated with American flags. Still, by the end of the shoot she had won over the crew because, as the director, Alan Pakula, put it, "above all else, she is quintessentially an American." When one adds up all of her incarnations—sixties sex kitten, seventies feminist, eighties fitness drill sergeant, nineties church lady—and factors in her ability to thrive in conservative and radical times alike, what emerges is a highly visible existence that has managed to encompass the country's moral, cultural, and political contradictions without being overwhelmed by them. Whether evinced in her moralistic politics, her entrepreneurial zeal, her thirst for novelty, or her capacity for self-reinvention, the larger message of Jane Fonda's life may just be: Jane Fonda is America.

Study Questions

1. How did Jane Fonda's youth influence her adulthood?

2. How did Americans react to Fonda's early film career in Paris?

3. What was America like in 1968 when Fonda returned to the United States? What were other actors, in the States, doing?

4. How did Fonda's career in the 1970s reflect her real life? How had she changed since the 1960s?

5. How did Jane Fonda's rise as a workout icon reflect national attitudes in the 1980s and the growth of neoconservatism?

6. Why has the author argued that Jane Fonda reflects American life throughout the past four decades?

Bibliography

This piece came from *American Heritage* (July/August, 2001). Much has been written on the Fonda family and their role in Hollywood. For an overview of the Fonda family's legacy, see Jack Stewart, *The Fabulous Fondas: Henry, Jane, and Peter* (1976); and Peter Collier, *The Fondas: A Hollywood Dynasty* (1991). For Fonda's journey to Vietnam, see Henry Mark Holzer and Erica Holzer, *"Aid and Comfort": Jane Fonda in North Vietnam* (2002) and Russell Sorto, *Jane Fonda: Political Activism* (1991). For a general biography of Jane Fonda, see Bill Davidson, *Jane Fonda: An Intimate Biography* (1990). For a good overview of the sixties, see Alexander Broom, ed., *"Takin' It to the Streets": A Sixties Reader* (2004); for the seventies, Brice Schulman, *The Seventies: The Great Shift in American Culture, Society, and Politics* (2001); and the eighties, Gilbert Sewall, ed., *The Eighties: A Reader* (1997).

READING 27

★ ★ ★

Liberalism Overthrown

Matthew Dallek

In 1964 Barry Goldwater, a Republican senator from Arizona, ran for the presidency on a platform that seemed singularly out of step with the times. At a moment in American history when liberalism was nearing its high point, when more government was seen as the answer to the country's many problems, Goldwater called for a drastic reduction in the size and scope of the federal government. The government in Washington, he suggested, had already become too big, too fat, and too complacent, and he meant to change all of that. "I have little interest in streamlining government or making it more efficient, for I mean to reduce its size," he wrote. "I do not undertake to promote welfare, for I propose to extend freedom. My aim is not to pass laws, but to repeal them."

His Democratic opponent Lyndon Johnson scoffed at Goldwater's proposals. He promised a Great Society, with Washington playing the role of Big Daddy. "I just want to tell you this—we're in favor of a whole lot of things and we're against mighty few," Johnson said in speech after speech. He favored federal dollars for Medicare, Medicade, regional redevelopment, urban renewal, and education. Responding to his measured tones—and perhaps frightened by Goldwater's seeming stridency—Americans voted in large numbers for Johnson. As Johnson carried over 60 percent of the popular vote, journalists wrote obituaries for Goldwater's conservative movement. A *Time* magazine writer prophesied, "The conservative cause whose championship Goldwater assumed suffered a crippling setback. . . . The humiliation of their defeat was so complete that they will not have another shot at party domination for some time to come."

But the movement was not dead. As Matthew Dallek shows in "Liberalism Overthrown," the election of 1964 just showed the conservative movement how to win. In 1966 a new candidate—polished smooth by years in Hollywood and a sharp staff of advisors—assumed the lead of the movement. In that year in California conservatism and liberalism battled once again for domination.

The rain had been pelting for hours when the mourners gathered in St. Cecilia's Roman Catholic Church, in the Sunset district, but now the skies cleared as four National Guard helicopters clattered overhead in a "missing man" formation as scores of dignitaries—governors and representatives, senators and aides from Sacramento and Washington, Los Angeles and New York—stared gravely at the casket, draped in the red and white state flag. It was February 17, 1996, and Edmund G. ("Pat") Brown, the liberal former governor of California, was being buried in San Francisco.

The mourners were burying more than a man; they were burying a political era. The decades-long liberal consensus that had begun with the New Deal had faded years before. But Brown's passing offered friends and foes alike a chance to reflect upon that time.

As word of his death spread, the telephone at the Brown family home rang with calls from around the nation. Kathleen Kelly, one of Pat Brown's ten grandchildren, walked outside the modest three-bedroom house in Benedict Canyon to address the reporters gathered in front. "My grandfather, I think, represented to so many people a compassion and a justice that we are just not seeing in this political era," Kelly said. A political commentator named Sherry Bebitch Jeffe had been in New Hampshire covering the Republican presidential primary when she heard of Pat Brown's death. "This place today," she said, "is one million light-years away from where California politics and government were back then. Here I am following a group of men, including the incumbent, who are competing against everything that Pat Brown stood for . . . active government, government that could make civic life better for everyone. That is all under deconstruction right now, on all sides of the political spectrum."

Why did liberalism fail? For the past thirty years that question has dominated many discus-

sions of American politics, and the search for answers has become something of a national obsession. Conservative politicians, such as Newt Gingrich, tend to blame student radicals and pushy minorities for wanting too much too fast. Liberals generally either fault a white racist backlash or, when the issue is raised, act as if they were discussing sexual matters with their teenagers: They prefer to avoid the subject (remember Michael Dukakis in 1988?).

Scholars and journalists have also offered numerous explanations, and their studies of the civil rights movement, the Great Society, the New Left, and Vietnam have done much to answer the question, but most have missed a central reason: the rise as early as the 1960s of a well-organized, popular conservative movement bent on winning political power.

The best studies of the 1960s—Allen Matusow's *The Unraveling of America,* John Morton Blum's *Years of Discord,* and William Chafe's *The Unfinished Journey*—pay little or no attention to the rise of the right, one of the most important developments of the decade. Instead, these books divide the politics of those years into neat categories, describing, in order, the triumph of New Deal and Great Society liberalism, left-wing challenges to liberalism, and the disintegration of the liberal coalition. If they mention conservatism at all, it is usually only after 1968, and the one serious study that deals with both liberals and conservatives—Thomas Byrne Edsall's *Chain Reaction*—minimizes the role conservatives played in their own victories and argues that racial backlash was the main key to the rise of the right.

Previous interpretations of liberalism's collapse are not wrong, but they are incomplete: None of them capture the complexity of the political transformations that took place in the 1960s. The decline of liberalism and the rise of the right were not, as many have suggested, two separate developments. Rather, they were inextricably intertwined, and to understand the sudden, dramatic shift, we need to examine how liberal failures and conservative successes worked hand in hand to reverse a long-standing political balance of power.

"Liberalism Overthrown" by Matthew Dallek in *American Heritage,* Vol. 47/No. 6, October 1996, pp. 39-60. Reprinted by permission of *American Heritage* Magazine, a division of Forbes, Inc. © Forbes, Inc., 1996.

We also need to look back past the convulsions of the last thirty years and revisit a time that was so different—politically, ideologically, socially—from our own that it seems, as Pat's son, Jerry, put it, "like a different country." The time was 1966; the place, California. That year Pat Brown was being challenged by a bumptious political upstart from Southern California, Ronald Reagan.

Brown should have won. He should have won because he was a popular two-term incumbent, the economy was booming, migrants were thronging the West, hailing his state as the promised land, and he had accomplished more than any of his predecessors. In previous races he had defeated two of the Republican party's political titans, the Senate minority whip William Knowland and former Vice President Richard Nixon. That last victory had earned him the nickname "the Giant Killer."

And Ronald Reagan, his likely opponent in the 1966 general election, was no Richard Nixon. A fervent right-winger, a mediocre actor, and, most encouraging, a political novice, Reagan seemed easy prey for the Giant Killer. Surely, the governor thought, his constituents would never put someone with such scant experience and such shallow, extreme views in charge of the most populous state in the nation, would never reject a liberal, progressive philosophy for an antiquated conservatism more appropriate to the nineteenth century. The forces of history seemed once again to be on his side.

Pat Brown was a Catholic, a Californian, and a career politician. Above all, he was a liberal. But he hadn't always been one. Born in San Francisco in 1905, a year before the great earthquake razed the city, Edmund G. Brown early developed an interest in politics. In the seventh grade he delivered a "give me liberty or give me death" speech on behalf of World War I Liberty bonds so rousing that classmates started calling him Pat, short for Patrick Henry. The name stuck.

In 1928 Brown ran for the state assembly as a Calvin Coolidge Republican. Soundly defeated, he returned to his fledgling law practice in San Francisco. A few years later, as the Great Depression settled on the nation, he began to question the wisdom of his laissez-faire philosophy. His high school chum Matthew Tobriner (a future state supreme court justice) told Brown to wake up; F.D.R.'s victory was no ordinary political event but the beginning of a new political era. Tobriner gave Brown copies of *The New Republic* and quoted the columnist Walter Lippmann on the need for economic reform. In 1934, with farm prices at record lows and twenty million Americans out of work, Pat Brown became a Roosevelt New Dealer.

The switch was not unusual. Like many young men of his generation, Brown had come to believe that the ideas of Coolidge, Harding, and Hoover held little hope for the unemployed millions. Those ideas, Brown said years later, represented "an appeal for human selfishness. . . . I never regretted the change, not for a minute."

He had little reason to. As a moderate Democrat he built a political résumé second to none: In 1943 he was elected San Francisco district attorney, seven years later he became the state attorney general and earned a reputation as a tough law-and-order man, and in 1958 he became governor of California—just the second Democrat to hold that post in the twentieth century.

Although his predecessors were virtually all Republicans, they were also, like him, liberals. Hiram Johnson, the progressive governor who dominated California politics from 1911 to 1917, was one of the great crusaders of the era; he rid the state of the corrupting influence of the Southern Pacific Railroad and won passage of such landmark-political reforms as the referendum, recall, and initiative. During his tenure brothels were banned, racetrack gambling outlawed, workmen's compensation laws enacted, and eight-hour days adopted. Earl Warren shared Johnson's vision. Governor from 1943 to 1954—the longest tenure in state history—Warren built highways, housing, schools, prisons, mental health facilities, and parks, and in so doing met the needs of the three million new residents who moved to California during his incumbency.

But in California no one more incarnated the forces of liberalism than Pat Brown. He helped build the largest and most prestigious state university system in the country as well as the California water system, which each day brought two billion gallons of the precious liquid from the rainy north to the arid south. He won passage of fair housing legislation, established a Fair Employment Practices Commission, reformed state labor laws, increased unemployment insurance, and expanded welfare benefits. He believed in the ability of government to improve the human condition—a central tenet of postwar liberalism—and he brought the state into unprecedented areas of California society.

"Think big," Pat exhorted fellow Californians in his 1962 race against Richard Nixon. In the boom years of post-World War II America, many politicians thought big. But in vision and public works, none thought bigger than Pat Brown.

In early 1966 Brown felt so good about his chances against Ronald Reagan that he did what many politicians in his position would have done: He played dirty to help Reagan get the Republican nomination. George Christopher, the moderate Republican former mayor of San Francisco, who was challenging Reagan in the primary, had been convicted in 1940 of violating milk-pricing laws. It was a minor transgression and had done little damage to Christopher's political career. Until 1966. The Brown campaign got wind of the scandal, and in the two months before the June primary Brown's people spoon-fed the story to reporters. In early May the governor's team hit pay dirt when the syndicated columnist Drew Person wrote two ferocious articles about the milk control law violation. "Pearson's putrid piece . . . ," one prominent Christopher supporter said, "can be laid right at the door step of Pat Brown's political outhouse. Brown, of course, wants to . . . destroy George Christopher, and thus have Ronald Reagan nominated." Don Bradley, one of Brown's top campaign aides, responded: "Mr. Christopher is a cry baby. . . . George Christopher's arrest record . . . [is a matter] of public record which Mr. Christopher has yet to explain adequately. Mr. Christopher has been ducking the truth for years." It was a blow

from which Christopher's candidacy never recovered.

It was also a classic miscalculation. In the 1950s and 1960s liberal politicians and journalists dismissed conservatives as "kooks" and "crackpots" with no hope of winning political power. "Republicans," a typical article read in 1966, "try to make the voters afraid of the world." Right-wingers, another explained, like to "complain about the twentieth century." Pat Brown could not have agreed more. In 1964, during the fight over Proposition 14, a move to repeal the Brown-endorsed Rumford Fair Housing Act, the governor described his conservative opponents as fascists: "There have been echoes in this state of another hate binge which began more than thirty years ago in a Munich beer hall. These echoes come from a minority of the angry, the frustrated, the fearful. They do not represent California or its people. But what they do represent—the spasm reaction of hatred—does exist not only in California but elsewhere in our nation and in our world."

When Brown heard Reagan might oppose him, he was at once incredulous and delighted: "Ronald Reagan for Governor of California?" Brown wrote in 1970. "We thought the notion was absurd and rubbed our hands in gleeful anticipation of beating this politically inexperienced, right-wing extremist and aging actor in 1966." In January 1965 one of Brown's secretaries sent Jack Burby, his press secretary, an article predicting that Reagan would run for governor. "Bring him on," Burby scribbled in the margin.

But before Brown could do battle with Reagan, he had to contend with Sam Yorty, the maverick mayor of Los Angeles, who was running against Brown in the Democratic primary. Yorty was the George Wallace of California politics, an acid-tongued conservative Democrat, who had become known for his scalding attacks on liberal elites. In early 1966 Yorty concentrated his fire on Pat Brown: The governor coddled left-wing radicals, did nothing to halt the proliferation of drugs, stood by while Communist agitators fomented riots on campus, and had lost touch with the common man.

Worst of all, Brown had failed to crack down on black rioters in Watts. Imposing law and order,

Yorty thundered, was the only way to quash the violence in South Central L.A. Yorty's police chief backed him all the way. "We are interested," Chief William Parker declared, "in maintaining order." When Watts erupted, Parker explained the disorder this way: "One person throws a rock and then, like monkeys in a zoo, others started throwing rocks." Yorty returned the favor to the chief posthumously when at Parker's funeral in 1966 he crooned, "God may not be dead, but his finest representative on earth has just passed away."

Berkeley was also a favorite subject of the mayor. During the campaign a reporter asked Yorty what he thought of a report on the situation there recently issued by a state senate committee. He hadn't had a chance to analyze it, Yorty responded; then, said the San Francisco *Chronicle,* he "launched into a lengthy dissertation on 'filth' on the campus."

There are times in American history when events are so unsettling, so disruptive to the normal patterns of social interaction, that they shake the political foundation to its core. In 1919 race riots, widespread labor unrest, the battle over women's suffrage, and the rejection of Wilson's cherished Versailles Treaty helped end two decades of progressive reform and usher in the new era of retrenchment that Warren G. Harding called a "return to normalcy." Normalcy ended in 1932, when Franklin D. Roosevelt, with no firm ideas about how to govern, began to forge a new political coalition that brought workers, blacks, and Southern whites together in the belief that government had the capacity to improve their lives. And in 1966 the third great political upheaval of this century began.

In California the new era might be said to have begun on October 1, 1964, when police at the University of California, Berkeley, arrested Jack Weinberg, a former student, for setting up a civil rights table on campus. The police were about to drive Weinberg off to jail when several hundred students surrounded their car. The standoff lasted for thirty-two hours, and it not only launched the Free Speech Movement but also marked the beginning of almost a decade of student protest. Ten

months later, on a scorching summer day, the black ghetto of Watts some three hundred miles south of Berkeley exploded in violence. When the riots finally subsided, the statistics told the story: thirty-four dead, one thousand injured, four thousand arrested, two hundred million dollars in property damage, and sixteen thousand law enforcement officials deployed.

Watts and Berkeley were the two most visible issues in California in the mid-sixties, but there were plenty of others to reinforce the sense that disorder and immorality were taking over. In 1965, just one year after Californians had voted overwhelmingly to repeal Pat Brown's Fair Housing Act, the state supreme court declared the repeal measure unconstitutional and reinstated the antidiscrimination law. At Berkeley protests against the Vietnam War popped up, and a short-lived Filthy Speech Movement, in which students took turns shouting "F—!" over loudspeakers in Sproul Plaza, raised the specter of "educational anarchy." Residents read stories about LSD, saw photos of unkempt hippies parading the streets of San Francisco, and were told that their state had the good fortune to be producing 60 percent of the nation's "booming smut trade." One conservative activist vividly summed up many Californians' feelings about the last: "This crud falls into the hands of teenagers and younger persons . . . and the worst stuff comes in books like 'Seed of the Beast,' which describes sexual intercourse between animals and humans, and 'Queer Daddy,' which contains vivid descriptions of almost every other kind of perversion. . . . The message . . . is that if you haven't practiced homosexuality, you just haven't lived."

The polls showed that nine out of ten Californians disapproved of antiwar demonstrations; they identified "crime, drugs, juvenile delinquency" as the most pressing issue confronting their state; "racial problems" came in second; "student discipline at the University of California," sixth.

Berkeley was a particular sore point. Tuition was free there, and the university was widely seen as the crown jewel in the state's educational system. So when *The Saturday Evening Post*— that citadel of middle-class values—reported that "on the sunny, seemingly serene Berkeley campus, rebellion is fashionable and it is widely believed that half the student body has experimented with marijuana," tax-payers were upset. Berkeley Citizens United, a local conservative group, issued a mock U.C. curriculum in which the entering class could look forward to taking "Riot 101, Russian Language 101, and Dirty Books 101," while sophomores were required to devote two minutes per week to "Personal Hygiene" and eleven hours to "Draft Dodging, Troop Train Delaying, and Composition (4-Letter Words)." Those fortunate enough to make it to their junior years could take "Police Car Sit-In 331, Car Burning Lab, and Public Speaking Lab (Yelling and Shouting)."

At other times—say, in the 1950s—Sam Yorty might have come across as a mere hooligan, flinging wild political charges that bore little relation to the larger scene. But in the mid-1960s his attacks on the liberal establishment rang true for increasing number of Californians.

In the early weeks of the primary Brown simply ignored Yorty. Then, when the mayor seemed to gain in the polls, he went on the attack: "This little man has flipped his lid. Yorty thinks everyone is against him. . . . [The] psychiatric term for this . . . [is] paranoia—and I think this is the best way to describe the Mayor of Los Angeles." But Brown never campaigned vigorously against Yorty; he dismissed him and saved his money for the general election.

When the primary returns came in on June 7, Brown was shaken. He had won, of course, but it was a near thing. Yorty had received almost a million votes, 38 percent of the Democratic total. One thing was immediately clear: If Yorty's supporters decided to vote for Ronald Reagan, the Republican nominee, in the general election, Brown would probably lose. Though a massive defection of voters from one party to another was unlikely, the governor was worried; he had to keep Yorty Democrats in the party fold.

The California Democratic party's leaders gathered less than a week after the primary to discuss their strategy for the general election, and they came away from the meeting confident that liberalism was alive and well. Reagan, who had walloped Christopher by more than seven hundred thousand votes, had "got a free ride" during the primaries, Robert L. Coate, the Democratic state chairman, announced. That would soon change, Eugene Wyman, California's Democratic National Committeeman, predicted, when the actor was exposed as a "staunch defender of the far right . . . a disgrace to the Republican Party and a threat to the politics of moderation which has given this state wise and able leadership in the past two decades."

In 1964 Lyndon Johnson and the Democratic party had succeeded in painting Barry Goldwater as an extremist who would jeopardize national security and gut popular federal programs. In 1966 Pat Brown and his Democratic supporters thought they could do the same thing to another fierce conservative who despised most government involvement in the marketplace and took strong law-and-order stands on crime, social unrest, and immorality.

But by the mid-1960s Ronald Reagan was not, nor did he appear to be, an extremist. Reagan spent much of the 1950s sharpening his conservative philosophy as a spokesman for General Electric; he travelled from plant to plant, promoted the company's image, and spoke to workers and businessmen about the evils of high taxes and big government. "The Speech," as his standard talk came to be called, interspersed lively and entertaining stories with political tidbits about the wonders of the free-enterprise system.

The year 1964 proved pivotal for both Ronald Reagan and the conservative movement. Having already become a well-known figure in California right-wing circles, he agreed to serve as state co-chairman of Citizens for Goldwater. His big moment came in the closing days of Goldwater's campaign. In a last-ditch effort to sway voters, Reagan went on national television to speak on behalf of Goldwater. The speech, "A Time for Choosing," did little to help the Republican presidential candidate, but conservatives found Reagan's performance so stirring that they immediately hailed him as one of the rising stars of the Republican right.

Holmes Tuttle and Henry Salvatori, two wealthy Southern California businessmen, liked what they saw so much that they asked Reagan to run for governor in 1966. Don't just say no, Tuttle pleaded; take some time to think about it. Reagan agreed, and the Friends of Reagan, the campaign's fund-raising arm, was organized. From the outset the candidate had the backing of many wealthy Angelenos. More important, he had shrewd political advisers who thought they knew how a conservative could win the governorship. Stu Spencer and Bill Roberts, California's top political consultants, advised Reagan to avoid ill-tempered remarks and to work with moderate Republicans; they designated him a "citizen-politician" and started calling his reform program the Creative Society, in hopes of blunting voters' fears of conservatives as out-of-touch nay-sayers; and they hired two behavioral psychologists, Kenneth Holden and Stanley Plog, to help Reagan with the issues. "He knew zero about California when we came in, I mean zero," Plog recalled, but Reagan was a quick study and knew how to convey his ideas in a clear and forceful manner.

He was also careful to avoid the more radical ideas and statements that had so harmed other conservatives. Goldwater, during his presidential campaign, had threatened to "lob [missiles] into the men's room at the Kremlin." During his race Reagan spoke of a better California. "Our problems are many," he said in the speech announcing his candidacy, "but our capacity for solving them is limitless." When pressed about his support from radical right-wingers, Reagan explained that *they* were buying *his* philosophy, not the other way around.

The only time he appeared to be a genuine fire-breathing radical came in March 1966, during a debate with George Christopher in front of the Negro Republican Assembly. Ben Peery, a black Los Angeles businessman, asked Reagan how he could solicit black votes after having opposed the 1964 Civil Rights Act. When Christopher expressed similar doubts, Reagan, who had been under attack all day, threw down his note cards. "I resent the implication that there is any bigotry in my nature," he shouted. "Don't anyone ever imply I lack integrity. I will not stand silent and let anyone imply that." Then he stormed out of the debate, muttering, "I'll get that S.O.B."

Holden, who was in the audience, watched appalled, then managed to reach Reagan at home and pleaded with him to return to the event: "Why don't you come back and have a drink with the delegates? It will ease a lot of hurt feelings." Reagan eventually did so, but his advisers were aghast. Nothing frightened them more than the charge of extremism. The issue had helped sink Goldwater in '64, and it could do the same to Reagan in '66. Another outburst, they warned, could doom his campaign and end his political career. Reagan promised that it would not happen again.

It didn't. In August 1966 California Democrats released a twenty-nine-page paper, "Ronald Reagan, Extremist Collaborator." Reagan was not a moderate Republican, it claimed, but actually a dangerous radical, his campaign was "riddled" with members of the John Birch Society, he accepted money from extremist groups, and he opposed government programs like Social Security and federal aid to education. Serious charges, but they didn't stick. When Democrats presented Reagan with a press release claiming that Spencer-Roberts—his own political consultants!—had once identified him as an "extremist," the candidate coolly called the move a "diversionary tactic to avoid campaigning on the issues." In the end Reagan just seemed too good-looking, too upbeat, and too witty to be a member of any lunatic fringe.

He had, in short, all the markings of a candidate with a finely tuned political campaign, something that conservatives, for all their ideological fervor, were unaccustomed to. He also represented a movement that, by the mid-sixties, was hell-bent on winning political power.

After the election was over, the Los Angeles *Times* reported: "Don Bradley, the governor's campaign chairman, said Brown was the victim of a national movement toward conservatives that resulted from voter resistance to Negro gains." Race, of course, has almost always played a central role in American politics. In the eighteenth

century the Constitutional Convention nearly dis-
banded over the issue of slavery; less than a century later the question re-emerged with such
force that it took six hundred thousand American
lives to settle the issue; in this century the great
black migrations from the rural South to the
urban North helped thrust civil rights to the center of national debate; and in the 1960s the growing disillusionment with the black struggle for
freedom gave conservatives a powerful issue with
which to pry lower-middle-class Americans from
the Democratic coalition.

Reagan's campaign was no exception. His
stances on fair housing, urban riots, crime, and
welfare all appealed to whites increasingly resentful (and fearful) of blacks and members of other
minorities who seemed to be getting "special privileges." Race was a central issue. But it was not, as
some have suggested, the only one. Rather it fitted
into a larger set of ideas about the iniquities of big
government. The two issues were so intertwined
that to understand Reagan's campaign—and the
rise of the right—we must understand how the
issue of race fitted in with and reinforced conservatives' broad antigovernment message.

Throughout the campaign Reagan repeatedly
charged that the bureaucratic welfare state coddled minorities, raised middle-class taxes to meet
the growing costs of welfare, threatened individual liberty, and failed to impose order on the
small but dangerous numbers of radicals, dissi-
dents, and criminals. In 1966 events helped reinforce Reagan's ideas.

No issue was bigger than public morality—law
and order—and Reagan rarely wasted an opportunity to expound on liberal shortcomings in this
area. Berkeley, much to his campaign's delight,
stayed in the news throughout 1966. In the first
week of May the state senate Sub-Committee on
Un-American Activities released a long-awaited report on the University of California. A few days
later Reagan appeared at the Cow Palace in San
Francisco and explained before a cheering throng
that he had not yet seen that report; then, suddenly, he whipped out a different one on Berkeley, from the Alameda County district attorney's

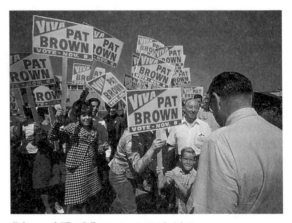

Edmund "Pat" Brown campaigning.

office (where the future Attorney General Ed
Meese worked), and said, "The incidents are so
bad, so contrary to our standards of decent
human behavior, that I cannot recite them to you
from this platform in detail." But he went right on
to describe—in detail—a dance at Berkeley sponsored by an antiwar group.

"The total crowd was in excess of 3,000, including a number of less-than-college-age juveniles," Reagan began. "Three rock 'n' roll bands
were in the center of the gymnasium playing simultaneously all during the dance, and all during
the dance movies were shown on two screens at
the opposite ends of the gymnasium. These
movies were the only lights in the gym proper.
They consisted of color sequences that gave the
appearance of different-colored liquid spreading
across the screen, followed by shots of men and
women[;] on occasion, shots were of the men's
and women's nude torsos, and persons twisted
and gyrated in provocative and sensual fashion.
The young people were seen standing against the
walls or lying on the floors and steps in a dazed
condition with glazed eyes consistent with the
condition of being under the influence of nar-
cotics. Sexual misconduct was blatant."

This moral decline, Reagan continued, had
begun in 1964, "when the so-called free-speech
advocates, who in truth have no appreciation for
freedom, were allowed to assault and humiliate

the symbol of law and order, a policeman, on the campus; and that was the moment when the ringleaders should have been taken by the scruff of the neck and thrown out of the university once and for all." The audience cheered.

Almost all the issues, in fact, fitted in with Reagan's promise to restore order. On Vietnam? Reagan proposed simply that we "go in there and do it." Antiwar demonstrators? Charge them with treason. Urban riots? Just invoke the law. Crime? Lock criminals in jail, and don't handicap the police.

Meanwhile Reagan used racial issues to draw attention to what he saw as the dangerous excesses of big government. His position on California's Fair Housing Act was typical. The law, he charged, embodied the dangers of an expansive and encroaching government. Yes, he said, he despised bigotry just as much as the next guy, but in the end the government had no right to tell people how to sell or rent their property. In 1966 welfare and taxes also became hot political issues. There were, Reagan said at one campaign stop after another, people moving to California not for the opportunity to work but for the chance to get on welfare: "You have to live in California for five years to be governor, but you can get on welfare in twenty-four hours."

Throughout the campaign Brown was on the defensive. Reagan called him "soft" on black rioters, campus degenerates, drug dealers, and hippies. As Berkeley imploded, Brown seemed indecisive. During the Free Speech Movement, for example, when students occupied Sproul Hall, he hesitated before calling in the cops to arrest them as trespassers. A local radio station interspersed its coverage of the arrests with a commencement address Brown had given at the University of Santa Clara a few years earlier. "Thank God," the governor had said that day, "for the spectacle of students picketing. . . . At last we're getting somewhere. The colleges have become boot camps for citizenship, and citizen-leaders are marching out of them. . . . Let us stand up for our students and be proud of them."

Pat Brown was a decent man. He cared about people, and he governed with the hope of im-proving their individual lives. But his sympathy for civil rights and student grievances and his concern for the growing urban poor gave voters the impression that he had encouraged many of the disruptive elements that had thrown California into its present turmoil. Even when he took decisive action—like calling out the National Guard to quell riots in San Francisco and Oakland—people wondered how he had let things get out of control in the first place. What, voters asked Reagan during the campaign, would he do "about those bastards at Berkeley"? More, he invariably replied, than Pat Brown ever would.

Nor could Brown count on the support of the more liberal members of his party. The Vietnam War and urban riots saw to that. As a staunch supporter of President Johnson's Vietnam policy, the governor had an unprecedented problem on his hands in 1966: Si Casady, the head of the California Democratic Council (CDC), the party's largest volunteer organization in the state, was encouraging young men to burn their draft cards. Under pressure from the White House, Brown forced Casady to resign. But the problem didn't go away. Students who in other times could have been counted on to hand out leaflets and knock on doors for the Democratic nominee continued to protest the war, and even its more moderate opponents had trouble getting excited about reelecting a man so strongly identified with the policy-makers in Washington.

The social upheavals of the early and midsixties had transformed the political climate. By 1966 Reagan's anti-government ideology had come to appear moderate, rational, and a force for order. Brown, by contrast, seemed allied to the radical left and the increasingly militant civil rights leadership. The governor admitted himself that he was caught in a "political vise" between a growing left-wing movement that attacked liberalism for not going far enough and a conservative revival promising, among other things, to restore order. It was not a good position to be in, because in 1966 the political center—which, as the historian Arthur Schlesinger, Jr. once put it, is "vital" to the preservation of freedom—collapsed.

During the desultory final days of the race, his lead gone, Pat Brown remained uncomprehending. "Why, oh, why, my friends," he pleaded, "would you turn this state over to a man who has never fought before a city council or a board of supervisors?" At a night rally in San Bernardino, when the electricity failed, Brown said, "They can cut off the electricity, but they can't shut up the greatest governor California has ever had."

On November 8, 1966, Reagan beat Brown by almost a million votes. Four years earlier, when Brown had defeated Nixon, the former Vice President, in a spasm of indignation and anger, had lit into the journalists arrayed before him. "You won't have Nixon to kick around anymore, because gentlemen, this is my last press conference." Brown was determined to avoid repeating that fiasco. When the votes were finally tabulated, he went before his deflated supporters and thanked California "for giving me eight wonderful, marvelous years." When he finished, his advisers suggested he leave through a rear exit. Instead the governor stepped down from the podium and plunged into the crowd of loyal supporters. Then he walked out to his limousine, climbed inside, and started to cry.

Sam Yorty had other plans that night. The maverick mayor had refused to endorse either candidate during the campaign, but as soon as Reagan's victory was assured, he left little doubt about where his sympathies lay; he hurried over to the hotel where the victory celebration was under way and congratulated the governor-elect.

Individual communities also told the story that day. Norwalk was one of the many Democratic working-class suburbs that had sprouted in recent years along the Pacific coast, and on Election Day 1966 Norwalk was one of many Southern California Democratic communities that voted overwhelmingly for Ronald Reagan.

Norwalk's rejection of Pat Brown is, on one level, strange. Three out of four voters were registered Democrats, and residents had traditionally favored liberal government programs like Social Security and workmen's compensation. And the government had done much to ensure the city's economic well-being; many residents worked at nearby defense and aerospace plants, and the Metropolitan State Hospital employed fourteen hundred men and women.

Yet on another level Norwalk's support for Reagan was not strange at all. The city had been conceived in a revolt against government. Like those of many nearby bedroom communities, Norwalk's residents resented the Los Angeles board of supervisors; simple street repairs sometimes required weeks of fighting with the county bureaucracy. The people of Norwalk wanted to control their own affairs, and in 1957 they won a charter from the county and incorporated. By the mid-sixties their grievances with government had reached the boiling point: Taxes were too high, the welfare state seemed out of control, the fair housing law was raising fears of lower property values and higher crime rates (in 1966 only three black families lived in the town), and the counterculture, the new left, minorities, and liberals seemed to have dedicated themselves to the common purpose of flouting the values that Norwalk residents held dear. Government had become a remote institution out of touch with the needs of ordinary citizens.

Why did Californians revolt against liberalism? Most studies of the sixties suggest that liberalism and conservatism were two separate, isolated political movements whose paths did not cross until the end of the decade, when liberals were already in retreat. Most books on the politics of this decade focus on some aspect of the American left: the civil rights movement, the counterculture, the antiwar movement. Studies of liberalism, of which there are surprisingly few, tend to explain the demise of the New Deal coalition as the result of internal weaknesses: failure in Vietnam and the limitations of the Great Society reforms. The few detailed studies of modern conservatism (which only recently has been recognized as a serious political movement worthy of scholarly attention) similarly emphasize changes within the movement—the growing number of right-wing organizations, the repudiation of extremists, and conservatives' use of social issues—to explain the right's success.

These accounts are important, but they don't explain—at least not entirely—how conservatism replaced liberalism as the dominant force in American political life. It is true that student protests, urban riots, pornography, and antipathy to civil rights did much to discredit liberalism. Liberal Democrats, after all, were the party in power, and on their watch things seemed to fall apart.

But liberalism failed for two other, lesser-known reasons. It collapsed first because the white working and middle classes, men and women in communities like Norwalk, had come to mistrust—and at times despise—what they had held in high regard since the 1930s: centralized government power. In the thirties liberals had used government to establish a lifeline for the millions of Americans left bewildered and impoverished by the Great Depression, but by the 1960s unprecedented prosperity, partly the product of liberal reforms, had given rise to a new middle class that was hostile to high taxes and to many of the social programs they financed. This newly minted middle class expected liberals to denounce immorality and social disorder, to speak out for traditional values, and to stop paying so much attention to the dispossessed—the poor, the minorities, the radicals. On all these counts this restive majority found liberals wanting. The white backlash was the most visible, and perhaps the most potent, issue feeding the new anti-government mood. But it was also part of a larger revolt, a much deeper disillusionment with liberal government and those who championed it.

Liberalism failed also because—and this is rarely acknowledged—conservatives had transformed themselves into powerful political contenders armed with a devastating critique of their opponents. In the mid-sixties the conservative movement emerged as a smoothly running political machine; it had repudiated extremism, developed a more positive political platform that stressed the efficacy of individual initiative, and found a middle class receptive to its message. By the mid-sixties the right was able successfully to portray liberals, the supposed champions of the common man, as elitists who had lost touch with the needs and aspirations of ordinary Americans.

The campaign between Pat Brown and Ronald Reagan shows that we can't understand the failure of liberalism without understanding the rise of the right. Brown's and Reagan's careers were not always linked, but their fates were. Brown became governor at a time when conservatives were just beginning to find a coherent political voice; his policies helped galvanize the movement, and his failure to resolve the social crises of the decade paved the way for Reagan's victory in 1966, a victory that came in part from years of conservative organizing.

Thirty years ago this November Pat Brown's political career—and the liberalism it epitomized—came to an abrupt end. As a politician Brown had his flaws: He wasn't terribly charismatic, he was not a man of powerful intelligence, he had been in office eight long years, and he looked bad on television. But in 1966 he possessed one crippling defect: He was a liberal. And when Pat Brown went down, so did the philosophy that he had clung to throughout his adult life. It has never really recovered.

Study Questions

1. For which values and policies did Pat Brown stand? Why did he think that he would have little trouble winning reelection in 1966?

2. Was California's history in the 66 years of the twentieth century one of liberalism or conservatism?

3. How did liberals and conservatives differ in terms of political philosophy and public policies?

4. What issues dominated the primaries and the gubernatorial race? What role did race play in the election?

5. How did Reagan's advisors shape his image to appeal to voters? How did Democratic politicians attempt to shape a negative image of Reagan as a wild-eyed radical?

6. What best explains the decline of liberalism and the rise of conservatism in the 1960s?

Bibliography

The rise of Reanald Reagan, and especially his role in the modern conservative movement and the California gubernatorial race of 1966, has received considerable attention in the last decade. Lou Cannon, *President Reagan: The Role of a Lifetime* (1991) is outstanding, as are Garry Wills, *Reagan's America* (1988) and Robert Dallek, *Ronald Reagan: The Politics of Symbolism* (1984). Robert Alan Goldberg, *Barry Goldwater* (1995), examines not only Goldwater but the movement he helped to launch. The decline of liberalism and the rise of conservatism are also detailed in Thomas Ferguson and Joel Rogers, *Turn Right: The Decline of the Democrats and the Future of American Politics* (1986); Steve Fraser and Gary Gerstle, *The Rise and Fall of the New Deal Order* (1990), and Lisa McGiss, *Suburban Warriors: The Origins of the New American Right* (2002).

READING 28

★ ★ ★

Perfect Bodies, Eternal Youth: The Obsession of Modern America

Randy Roberts and James S. Olson

The message comes at Americans from every direction, every hour of the day. The American obsession with body image has never been stronger. Diet books perennially occupy the top tier of bestseller book lists; plastic surgery "make-over" shows garner top Nielsen ratings on television; infommercials hawk a bewildering array of mechanical devices to shape the customers. Incidence rates of bulimia and anorexia nervosa among young women have never been higher. Yet, obesity is a national epidemic.

Sports programming dominates television, as if Americans have an insatiable need to watch football, baseball, basketball, bowling, bodybuilding, and a host of other competitions. Future linguists and anthropologists will study what have become the highlights of contemporary American popular culture—diet sodas, low-calorie beers, Lean Cuisine, sugarless gum, half-the-calories bread, Nautilus, jogging, Iron Man marathons, "fun runs," tennis, bicycling, 10 K races, Superbowls, play-offs, World Series, Grand Slams of golf and tennis, Little League, Pop Warner football, and championship after championship.

Modern America is not the first society to indulge in the emptiness of narcissism, but no other society has ever had such resources to spend on a fruitless crusade to prevent aging and deny death. In "Perfect Bodies, Eternal Youth: The Obsession of Modern America," Randy Roberts and James S. Olson examine the preoccupation with health, fitness, and youth in the United States, explaining how and why the members of an entire culture have become infatuated with their own bodies.

Fewer and fewer people these days argue that running shortens lives, while a lot of people say that it may strengthen them. If that's all we've got for the time being, it seems a good enough argument for running. Not airtight, but good enough.

—Jim Fixx

It was a perfect July day in Vermont—clear and cool. Jim Fixx, on the eve of a long-awaited vacation, put on his running togs and headed down a rural road for his daily run, expecting to do the usual twelve to fifteen miles. At fifty-two years of age, Fixx was a millionaire, the best-selling author of *The Complete Book of Running,* and the reigning guru of the American exercise cult. In 1968 he had weighed 214 pounds, smoked two packs of cigarettes a day, and worried about his family health history. Fixx's father had died of a heart attack at the age of forty-three. So Fixx started running and stopped smoking. He lost 60 pounds and introduced America to the virtues of strenuous exercise: longevity, freedom from depression, energy, and the "runner's high." He regularly ran 80 miles a week. When he hit the road on July 21, 1984, Fixx weighed 154 pounds and seemed the perfect image of fitness. Twenty minutes into the run he had a massive heart attack and died on the side of the road. A motorcyclist found his body later that afternoon.

Fixx's death shocked middle- and upper-class America. Of all people, how could Jim Fixx have died of a heart attack? Millions of joggers, runners, swimmers, cyclists, tri-athletes, walkers, weight-lifters, and aerobic dancers had convinced themselves that exercise preserved youth and post-

From Randy Roberts and James S. Olson, "Perfect Bodies, Eternal Youth: The Obsession of Modern America" in *Winning Is the Only Thing.* The Johns Hopkins University Press, Baltimore/London, 1989, pp. 213–34. Reprinted by permission.

poned death. It was the yuppie panacea; "working out" made them immune to the ravages of time.

The autopsy on Fixx was even more disturbing. In spite of all the running, his circulatory system was a shambles. Fixx's cholesterol levels had been dangerously high. One coronary artery was 98 percent blocked, a second one 85 percent blocked, and a third one 50 percent blocked. In the previous two to eight weeks, the wall of his left ventricle had badly deteriorated. On that clear Vermont day, Jim Fixx shouldn't have been running; he should have been undergoing triple-bypass surgery.

Even more puzzling, Fixx had been complaining for months of chest pains while running—clear signs of a deadly angina, the heart muscle protesting lack of oxygen. Friends had expressed concern and urged him to get a check-up. He resisted, attempting to will good health. In January 1984 he had agreed to a treadmill test, but he skipped the appointment that afternoon, running 16 miles instead. Why had someone so committed to health ignored such obvious warnings? How had sports, exercise, and fitness become such obsessions in the United States?

Modern society was the culprit. In an increasingly secular society, church membership no longer provided the discipline to bind people together into cohesive social groups. Well-integrated neighborhoods with long histories and strong identities had given way after World War II to faceless suburbs. Corporate and professional elites tended to be highly mobile, relocating whenever a pay raise was offered. The new American community had become fifty suburban homes and a 7-11 convenience store. New organizations, especially business and government bureaucracies, had assumed power in the United States, but those were hardly places where most Americans could feel comfortable and in control. Blessed with money but deprived of community in the 1970s and 1980s, Americans began to use sports to rebuild their sense of community and fitness and to define individual happiness and individual pleasure, creating a culture of competitive narcissism supported by a host of therapeutic panaceas, such as EST, psychotherapy, Scientology, and strenuous exercise.

For individuals, families, groups, and communities, sports had become a new cultural currency, a common ground upon which a diverse people could express their values and needs. Unlike European society, where such traditional institutions as the church, the aristocracy, and the monarchy had maintained order through established authority, America had been settled by lower-class working people and small farmers. The traditional institutions anchoring European society were absent. Without those same moorings, America had always confronted the centrifugal forces of individualism, capitalism, Protestantism, and ethnicity, using the culture of opportunity to stave off social disintegration. Social mobility, the westward movement, the abundance of land, and ruralism helped stabilize a highly complex society.

But in the twentieth century, when industrialization, urbanization, and the disappearance of the frontier changed the definitions of opportunity and progress, the values of individualism, community, and competition had to find new modes of expression, and sports became a prominent one. At the local, regional, and national levels, sports evolved into one of the most powerful expressions of identity. Outside observers marveled, for example, at the "religion" of high school football in the more than eleven hundred independent school districts of Texas. When viewed simply as sport, of course, the obsession with football seems absurd, but when viewed in terms of community identity, it becomes more understandable. In hundreds of rural areas, where scattered farms surround tiny county seats, the local high school, with its arbitrarily drawn district lines, was the central focus of community life. Rural Texans passionately opposed school district consolidations, even when it made good economic sense, because it threatened the high school, high school football, and community identity. For hundreds of small Texas towns—and rural areas throughout much of the rest of the country—high school athletics was literally the cement of community life.

It wasn't just high school sports which provided new identities in the United States. After World War II, social and economic pressures worked against the nuclear family. More and more women were working outside the home; more and more men were working at jobs that where long commutes from the suburbs; and divorce rates were way up. Childhood play became less spontaneous and more organized as schools, government, and communities assumed roles once played by the family. The most obvious consequence was the appearance of organized youth sports. Little League grew by leaps and bounds beginning in the 1950s; child's play, once the domain of the home and immediate neighborhood, became a spectator sport complete with uniforms, umpires, scoreboards, leagues, play-offs, drafts, and championships. By the 1980s, Little League was competing for time with Pop Warner football, Little Dribblers basketball, soccer, and swimming, with organized competition beginning in some sports at the age of three. In 1987 sports sociologists estimated that thirty million children under sixteen years of age were competing in organized sports.

Sports functioned as identity on the regional level as well. In an age when television, movies, and mass culture threatened regional distinctiveness, sports emerged as the single most powerful symbol of localism and community loyalty. That was obviously true of high school and college sports, but even in professional sports, when ownership shifted away from local businesses and entrepreneurs to conglomerates and national corporations, the regional identity of teams remained critically important to gate receipts and television revenues. The rivalries between the Chicago Bears and the Green Bay Packers, or the Boston Red Sox and the New York Yankees, or the Boston Celtics and the Los Angeles Lakers, filled stadiums, arenas, and living rooms with fans desperate for the home team to win. Five hundred years ago, European cities dedicated all their surplus capital over the course of 100 to 200 years to build elaborate cathedrals to God. In the United States during the 1970s and 1980s, the modern equivalent of the medieval cathedral was the domed stadium. For sports, not for God, American communities would sell bonds and mortgage themselves for the next generation.

Even on the national level, sports competition reflected and promoted American nationalism. Sports was a mirror of federalism, at once local in its community loyalties but national in its collective forms. The 1984 Olympic Games in Los Angeles did not just expose a rising tide of patriotism and national pride; they became a major force in stimulating a new American nationalism. Unlike the recent Olympic Games in Montreal, Moscow, and Seoul, the Los Angeles Games did not accumulate billion-dollar deficits and require the resources of national governments to prop them up. In 1984, "free enterprise capitalism" organized and conducted the Games, used existing facilities, and turned a profit. The Los Angeles Coliseum was filled with flag-waving Americans cheering every native athlete winning a medal. On television back home, Europeans watched the proceedings with astonishment and not a little fear, worrying about the burst of American patriotism, nationalism, and even chauvinism. Nearly a decade after the debacle in Vietnam, American pride and optimism were on the rebound, and the 1984 Olympic Games was center stage for the resurrection of the American sense of mission.

Modern sports in the United States also provided a sense of identity cutting across class, racial, and ethnic lines. In penitentiaries throughout the country, intense struggles were waged every evening over television and radio programming, black convicts wanting to watch soul stations and black sit-coms and whites demanding MTV or white sit-coms. But there was no trouble or debate on Sunday afternoon or Monday nights during the fall. It was football, only football, and blacks and whites watched the programs with equal enthusiasm. On Monday evenings in the fall, whether in the poorest ghetto tenement of the South Side of Chicago or the most tastefully appointed living room in the Lake Forest suburbs, televisions were tuned in to football, and discussions at work the next morning revolved around the game, who won and who lost, and why.

For ethnic minorities and immigrants, sports similarly became a way of identifying with the new society, a powerful form of acculturation. During the 1980s, for example, Los Angeles became the second largest Mexican city in the world, behind only Mexico City in Spanish-speaking population and larger now than Guadalajara in terms of Mexican residents. At Dodger Stadium in Los Angeles, Mexicans and Mexican Americans became an increasingly large part of the evening box office, helping to sustain Dodger attendance at its three million-plus levels each year. In September 1986, when Dodger pitcher Fernando Valenzuela won his twentieth game of the season, the Spanish cable network SIN broke into its regular programming nationwide for live interviews. The fact that sports was making its way to the headlines and front pages of major newspapers was no accident in the United States. It had become, indeed, a new cultural currency in modern America, a way to interpret change and express traditional values.

Women, too, used sports as a vehicle in their drive for equality and identity. The development of women's and men's sports in America has varied considerably. From the first, men's sports have emphasized fierce competition and the ruthless pursuit of expertise. Early male and female physical educators, however, believed women were uncompetitive and decided that women's sports should promote a woman's physical and mental qualities and thus make her more attractive to men. They also believed that sports and exercise should sublimate female sexual drives. As renowned nineteenth-century physical educator Dudley A. Sargent noted, "No one seems to realize that there is a time in the life of a girl when it is better for her and for the community to be something of a boy rather than too much of a girl."

But tomboyish behavior had to stop short of abrasive competition. Lucille Eaton Hill, director of physical training at Wellesley College, urged women to "avoid the evils which are so apparent . . . in the conduct of athletics for men." She and her fellow female physical educators encouraged widespread participation rather than narrow specialization. In short, women left spectator and professional sports to men. Indeed, not until 1924 were women allowed to compete in Olympic track and field events, and even then on a limited basis.

During the 1920s the tennis careers of Suzanne Langlen and Helen Wills were used to demonstrate the proper and improper pursuit of victory by athletic women. Tennis, for the great French champion Langlen, was not only a way of life: it was life. Her only object on a tennis court was to win, and between 1919 and 1926, when she turned professional, Langlen lost only two sets of singles and won 269 of 270 matches. But at what cost? Bulimic in her eating habits and subject to dramatic swings in emotions, she suffered several nervous breakdowns and lived in fear of losing. In addition, male critics noted that, far from keeping her looking young, tennis cruelly aged Langlen. Journalist Al Laney remarked that by the mid-1920s Langlen looked thirty years older than she actually was and that her complexion had turned dull and colorless. Her friend Ted Tinling agreed that before she turned twenty-five, "her face and expression had already the traces of deep emotional experiences far beyond the normal for her age."

In contrast, Helen Wills was a champion of great physical beauty. Before Wills, Americans tended to agree with journalist Paul Gallico that "pretty girls" did not excel in sports and that outstanding female athletes were simply compensating for their lack of beauty. Summarizing this school of thought, Larry Engelmann observed: "Athletics was their way of getting attention. If Suzanne Langlen were really beautiful, for instance, she wouldn't be running around like crazy on the tennis courts of Europe. She would have been quietly at home, happily married. Athletics proved a refuge and a last chance for the desperate female ugly duckling."

Yet Wills was beautiful, and she was great, winning every set of singles competition she played between 1927 and 1933. Journalists explained Wills's success and beauty by stressing the fact that tennis was only a game for her, not a way of life and certainly not life itself. Losses did not worry her. She always appeared composed. "My father, a doctor," she explained, "always told me not to wince or screw up my face while I was playing. He said it would put lines on my face." And no victory was worth a line.

Women were not fully emancipated from the older ideal until the 1970s, when they asserted their right to be as ruthless and competitive in athletics as men. Tennis champion Billy Jean King symbolized on the court as well as off this new attitude. Like Langlen, she single-mindedly pursued victory. And she was no more concerned with sweating and grimacing than Pete Rose. Unlike Wills, King was not interested in art or starting a family. When asked why she was not at home, she replied, "Why don't you ask Rod Laver why he isn't at home?" It was as eloquent a statement of athletic liberation as could be asked for.

To develop fully as an athlete, King had to earn money. Along with Gladys Heldman and Philip Morris Tobacco Company, King helped to organize the Virginia Slims women's tennis circuit in 1971. That year she became the first female athlete to earn $100,000 in a single year. More importantly, she labored to get women players a bigger share of the prize money at the major championships. In the early 1970s women's purses at Wimbledon and the U.S. Open were about 10 percent of the men's. By the mid-1980s the prize money split was equal. As if to punctuate the point that women's tennis had arrived, King defeated the former Wimbledon triple-crown champion (1939) Bobby Riggs 6–4, 6–3, 6–3, in a highly publicized match in the Houston Astrodome in 1973.

Even more important than King for the future of women's athletics was Title IX of the 1972 Educational Amendments Act. It outlawed sexual discrimination by school districts or colleges and universities which received federal aid. Certainly, athletic budgets in high schools and universities are not equally divided between male and female athletics. But women have made significant gains. Before Title IX less than 1 percent of athletic budgets went to women's sports. By the 1980s that figure had increased to over 10 percent. No longer is there a serious argument over the road women's sports should travel. Instead, the battle is over what portion of that pie they should receive.

But it wasn't just countries, cities, colleges, small towns, high schools, and ethnic groups which turned to sports in the 1980s as the most powerful way of defining their values. The most extraordinary development in contemporary popular culture was the extent to which individuals turned to athletics, exercise, and body image as a way of finding meaning in an increasingly dislocated society. In the mid-1980s, a Louis Harris poll indicated that 96 percent of all Americans found something about their bodies that they didn't like and would change if they could. Harris said that the "rampant obsessions of both men and women about their looks have produced an obvious boon for the cosmetics industry, plastic surgery, diet doctors, fitness and shape advisers, fat farms, and exercise clubs." The cult of fitness and the cult of individual happiness went hand in hand. Politicians used international sports at the Olympic level to confirm the superiority of various political systems or prove the equality of their Third World cultures; they mustered professional sports to project the quality of life in major American cities; collegiate sports touted the virtues of different universities; and in the 1970s and 1980s, millions of Americans embraced the cult of fitness to discover the meaning of life, retreating into the fantasy that they are how they look.

The cult of fitness and preoccupation with physical appearance first emerged in the United States during the John Kennedy administration. In the election of 1960, Kennedy used television as it had never been used before when he challenged Richard Nixon to a series of debates. Kennedy faced formidable odds. Young, handsome, and wealthy, he was considered perhaps too young, too handsome, and too wealthy to make an effective president. His Roman Catholicism seemed another albatross. Behind the polls, Kennedy needed a boost. The televised debates were perfect.

Nixon arrived in Chicago for the first debate looking tired and ill. He had injured his knee six weeks before, and a hospital stay had weakened

him. On the eve of the debate a chest cold left him hoarse. He looked like a nervous corpse—pale, twenty pounds underweight, and haggard. Make-up experts suggested covering his heavy beard with a thick powder, but Nixon accepted only a thin coat of Max Factor's "Lazy Shave," a pancake cosmetic.

Kennedy looked better, much better. He arrived at Chicago from California with a suntan. He didn't need make-up to look healthy, nor did he need special lighting to hide a weak profile. He did, however, change suits. He believed that a dark blue rather than a gray suit would look better under the bright lights. Kennedy was right, of course, as anyone who watches a nightly news program must realize. Once the debate started, Kennedy intentionally slowed down his delivery and watered down his ideas. His face was controlled and cool. He smiled with his eyes and perhaps the corners of his mouth, and his laugh was a mere suggestion of a laugh. Although Nixon marshalled a mountain of facts and closely reasoned arguments, he looked bad. Instead of hearing a knowledgeable candidate, viewers saw a nervous, uncertain man, one whose clothes didn't fit and whose face looked pasty and white. In contrast, Kennedy *looked* good, scored a victory in the polls, and went on to win the election by a razor-thin margin.

The first president born in the twentieth century, Kennedy had claimed in his inaugural address that "the torch had been passed to a new generation of Americans . . . tempered by war, disciplined by a hard and bitter peace, proud of our ancient heritage." Life around the White House soon reflected the instincts of a new generation. It wasn't just little Caroline and later John-John frolicking on the White House lawn. The Kennedys were fiercely competitive and obsessed with sports. At the family compound at Hyannisport or Robert Kennedy's "Hickory Hill" home in Virginia, the days were filled with tennis, golf, sailing, isometric exercise, swimming, horseback riding, badminton, and a brutal form of touch football, which overweight and overaged visitors dreaded, since the Kennedys expected everyone to give it a try. An atmosphere of youthful virility surrounded the Kennedy administration. To impress the Kennedys, one associate remembered, you had to "show raw guts, fall on your face now and then. Smash into the house once in a while going after a pass. Laugh off twisted ankles or a big hole torn in your best suit."

The whole country became infatuated with the sense of vitality, and the fifty-mile hike became the symbol of fitness. Marine Corps commandant General David M. Shoup, whom Kennedy especially admired, accepted Kennedy's challenge to see if his Marines could duplicate a feat of Theodore Roosevelt's 1908 Marines—march fifty miles in less than twenty hours. Shoup met the challenge, as did Attorney General Robert Kennedy, who walked his fifty miles along the path of the C & O canal. Kennedy's secretaries took up the challenge, and once the newspapers had picked up the story, tens of thousands of Americans tried it too. The spring of 1963 became the season of the fifty-mile hike.

These were also years of giddy infatuation with the Mercury astronauts, whose crew-cut fitness first came to public attention at their introductory press conference in 1959. All of them were military pilots, and John Glenn of Ohio emerged as their leader. Square-jawed with ramrod perfect posture, Glenn had a personality and value system to match. He was the ultimate "goody-goody," and America loved him. The country was also astounded at his daily fitness regimen—vigorous calisthenics followed by a two-mile jog along the beach. Two miles—every day! Even when it rained.

If John Glenn was the leading jogger of the 1960s, the scientific father of running was Kenneth Cooper, an Air Force physician. A high school track star in Oklahoma City, Cooper finished medical school and joined the Air Force as a physician at the School of Aerospace Medicine in San Antonio. He tested fitness levels in thousands of potential Air Force pilots and in the process developed new standards of conditioning. To really benefit from exercise, Americans had to get their heart rate above 130 beats a

minute for a sustained period. Jogging, running, racquetball, squash, cycling, walking, and swimming were the best exercises.

To please an increasingly technical, postindustrial clientele whose faith in science was unrivaled, Cooper even charted fitness, providing a quantified methodology to guarantee fitness. An aerobically fit person had to "earn 30 points a week." He or she could do this by walking three miles in no more than forty-one minutes five times a week; by swimming 700 yards in fifteen minutes five times a week; or by running a mile in eight minutes only twice a week. To measure fitness, Cooper recommended the "twelve minutes test." If a person can run or walk less than a mile in twelve minutes, he or she is in "very poor shape"; 1 to 1.25 miles is "poor"; 1.25 to 1.5 miles is "fair"; 1.5 to 1.75 miles is "good"; and more than 1.75 miles is "excellent." Cooper also warned people to watch out if their pulse rate exceeded 80 beats a minute. Fewer than 60 beats was "excellent." Vigorous exercise would reduce the heart rate. In Cooper's own words, "You might just save your heart some of those 20,000 to 30,000 extra beats you've forced on it every day."

The country was more than ready for Cooper's message. Early in the 1960s the first of the baby-boom generation hit college. The "don't trust anyone over thirty" culture had appeared, protesting war and inequality and proclaiming the virtues of brotherly love and sexual liberation. In 1961 half the American population was under thirty. By 1964 the median age had dropped to twenty-seven and in 1966 to twenty-five. America fell in love with youth, health, sex, and pleasure. Hippies, protests, "love-ins," "teach-ins," Woodstock, drugs, rebellion, and loud, self-righteous rejections of materialism emanated from college campuses.

But in 1967 the first baby-boom class graduated from college. The transformation of hippies into "yuppies" was underway. By 1971 those 1946 babies were twenty-five years old. The cruel tricks of gravity and heredity commenced. Bellies started to thicken, hairlines to recede. Women with babies looked despairingly at abdominal stretch marks and the faint beginnings of "crow's feet." The youth culture still survived, but individual youth was proving to be a temporary state. Middle age loomed as large as death.

Dr. Kenneth Cooper had the answer. Late in 1968, he coined a new word and wrote a book by the same name—*Aerobics.* By 1972 the book had sold nearly three million copies to anxious yuppies bent on postponing the inevitable. By the early 1970s, Cooper had an estimated eight million Americans, including astronaut John Glenn, adding up their weekly points, counting their pulse, testing their speed, taking their blood pressure, and weighing their bodies.

Throughout the 1970s and 1980s the cult of fitness reached extraordinary dimensions in the United States. More than twenty million Americans regularly exercised, and along with the running boom came a boom in racquetball, tennis, swimming, cycling, weightlifting, and "aerobic" dancing. In 1970 only 125 people entered the first New York City marathon, which took runners over a 26-mile course through all four boroughs; but in the 1986 marathon, 20,000 officially entered the race, and 19,412 finished it. The race was so popular that organizers had to reject thousands of applicants. Marathons became common events on every weekend all across the country.

The triathlon endurance was an even better gauge of the fitness cult. Known as the ultimate of the "ultrasports," the triathlon combined a 2-mile swim with a 112-mile cycle ride and a 26-mile run. In 1986 more than one million Americans competed in triathlon events around the country. And in what can only be considered the absurd limit of the fitness craze, Stu Mittleman won the "Sri Chinmoy 1,000 Mile Marathon" in New York City in 1986. His time of just under fifteen days "was my best ever."

The cult of fitness was rivaled only by the obsession with youth and body image which swept through American culture in the 1970s and 1980s. To be sure, this was nothing new. Americans had long been preoccupied with their bodies, and attempts to stay young had centered on staying thin, as if slenderness were in itself a foundation of youth. In the 1860s Harriet Beecher Stowe had written: "We in America have got so far out of the way of a womanhood that has any vigor of outline or opulence of physical proportion, that, when we see a woman made as a woman ought to be, she strikes us as a monster. Our willowy girls are afraid of nothing so much as growing stout."

To stay thin, nineteenth-century American women dieted and corseted their bodies. "It ain't stylish for young courting gals to let on like they have any appetite," admitted one female. And through tightlacing their corsets, women could maintain the proper girlish waistline of eighteen inches, with only such acceptable side effects as headaches, fainting spells, and uterine and spinal disorders.

If tightlacing and dieting led to serious health problems, illness was in itself admired. Consumptive women were romanticized and imbued with spiritual qualities. Little Eva in *Uncle Tom's Cabin,* Beth in *Little Women,* Mimi in *La Bohème*—all were thin, romantic consumptives who radiated spirituality and sensuality. Perhaps the ideal was the romantic ballerina—thin, ethereal, pale, pure, as certain to die young as poor broken-hearted Giselle.

Throughout the twentieth century, thinness has largely remained the feminine ideal, although sickliness generally declined as an attractive characteristic. The Gibson Girl of the turn of the century touted athletics, and during the 1920s the flapper exuded energy, vitality, and youth. And if the breast-bound flapper did not survive the 1929 stock market crash, an emphasis on thinness did. Indeed, only during the 1950s, when Marilyn Monroe was at her height, was there a serious challenge to the slender ideal.

Post–World War II culture has enshrined both thinness and youth for men as well as women. Advertisers have aided the process. Since photographers maintain that clothes look best on lean bodies, leading fashion models have always been thin and generally young. But since the 1960s, advertisers have used youth and thinness to sell other products as well. The evolution of Pepsi-Cola slogans illustrates this point:

1935: "Twice as Much."
1948: "Be Sociable—Have a Pepsi."
1960: "Now it's Pepsi for those who think young."
1965: "The Pepsi Generation."
1984: "Pepsi: The Choice of a New Generation."

Appeals to abundance ("twice as much") and social interaction ("be sociable") were replaced by the promise of eternal youth. As if to reinforce this appeal, Pepsi paid magnificent amounts to two thin, youthful Michaels as spokesmen: Michael Jackson and Michael J. Fox. Far from being sociable, Jackson is a virtual recluse, obsessed with personality change through plastic surgery. And Fox, as sure as Peter Pan, is the perpetual adolescent.

To fit the culture's procrustean mold, advertisers encourage Americans to binge and purge, consume and diet. Consume because "you are someone special" and "you can have it all." Diet because "you can never be too thin or too rich." In his perceptive book *Never Satisfied*, Hillel Schwartz argues that "dieting is an essentially nostalgic act, an attempt to return to a time when one *could* be satisfied, when one *was* thinner, when the range of choices in the world neither bewildered nor intimidated. To restrict one's range of choices, as all dieters must do, is not so much deficient as it is regressive. . . . Imagining a miraculous future, the dieter is always looking back."

In a secular, materialistic age, dieting has become an ascetic religion. Seventeenth-century poet and preacher John Donne wrote, "The flesh that God hath given us is affliction enough, but the flesh that the devil gives us, is affliction upon affliction and to that, there belongs a woe." To be fat in America has become a religious as well as a secular sin. Christian diet books emphasize John 3:30—"He must increase, but I must decrease."

In 1957 Charlie Shedd in his *Pray Your Weight Away* confessed, "We fatties are the only people on earth who can weigh our sin." His book inspired some Christians to lose weight and others to write diet books. Such works as Deborah Price's *I Prayed Myself Thin*, John Cavanaugh's *More of Jesus and Less of Me*, Reverend H. Victor Kane's *Devotion for Dieters,* and Francis Hunter's *God's Answer to Fat—Lose It!* emphasized that godliness is in league with thinness. Capturing the temper of her times, columnist Ellen Goodman wrote in 1975 that "eating has become the last bona fide sin left in America." And on this point, religion and secular humanism are in complete accord.

The fitness boom and body-image obsession financed a huge growth industry. To support their new interest in fitness, Americans needed equipment and clothes—shoes, shorts, shirts, racquets, bicycles, balls, paddles, bats, cleats, gloves, goggles, weights, scales, blood-pressure cuffs, timing watches, clubs, socks, headbands, wristbands, and leotards. Between 1975 and 1987 sporting goods sales in the United States increased from $8.9 billion to $27.5 billion. Americans spent $4 billion on athletic shoes alone in 1987. Health clubs, once the domain of the wealthy and a small clique of bodybuilders, multiplied in number from 350 in 1968 to more than 7,000 in 1986. Gross revenues in 1987 exceeded $650 million.

Exercise and fitness revenues were matched by those of the weight loss industry. Jean Nidetch founded Weight Watchers in 1962 and eventually franchised it, making sure that group leaders had been through the diet program and reached "maintenance" levels. Attendance doubled between 1983 and 1987, the gross revenues went past $200 million that year. Sybil Ferguson's Diet Center, Inc., founded in 1969, had two thousand franchises in 1987 and nearly $50 million in gross revenues. Americans spent $6 billion for diet soda in 1986, $5 billion for vitamins and health foods, and $350 million for diet capsules and liquid protein. The President's Council on Physical Fitness estimated that 65 million Americans were dieting in 1987. Diet Coke, Diet Pepsi, Diet Dr. Pepper, Lean Cuisine, Bud Light, Miller Lite, "lite" bread, sugarless gum, NutraSweet, Cambridge, and a host of other diet products entered American popular culture.

What dieting and exercise couldn't fix, plastic surgery could. Americans went on a plastic surgery binge in the 1980s—not to repair real damage to their bodies or birth defects, but to improve their appearance cosmetically and recapture the illusion of youth. In 1987 more than 500,000 Americans underwent cosmetic plastic surgery. The most popular procedures were abdominoplasty (tummy tucks), breast augmentation, liposuction (fat removal), blepharoplasty (eyes), and rhinoplasty (nose). Plastic surgeons were also beginning to perform "total body contour" procedures. To postpone middle age, yuppies made plastic surgery a $3 billion industry.

Americans also changed a number of their habits in the 1970s and 1980s. Cigarette consumption began to decline in 1982. In 1965, 52 percent of men and 34 percent of women smoked. By 1985 only 33 percent of men and 28 percent of women smoked, and at the end of 1987 the American Cancer Society estimated that only 27 percent of Americans were still smoking. Per capita whiskey consumption dropped nearly 20 percent between 1976 and 1986 as Americans turned to lower-alcohol-content beer and wine coolers. Beef and pork consumption dropped in favor of chicken and fish when cholesterol-conscious Americans turned away from "red meat." Caffeine was also suspect. Americans under twenty-five drank only a third of the coffee their parents did; sales of decaffeinated coffee and drinks like Pepsi Free and Pepper Free symbolized the new health consciousness.

The results were impressive, even though some of the gains had to be attributed to better drug therapy, the rise of heart bypass surgery, and improvement of cardiac care units in American hospitals. But the bottom line was that between 1950 and 1985, the death rate per 100,000 people from cardiovascular and cerebrovascular disease declined from 511 to 418, a dramatic improvement. The cult of fitness seemed to be paying dividends.

But there was an underside to the cult of fitness, an obsessive perfectionism which was the antithesis of good health. Jim Fixx and his daily runs in spite of chest pains were one example. Kathy Love Ormsby was another. The North Carolina State University junior, who held the U.S. collegiate women's record for 10,000 meters, had

difficulty dealing with failure. In the 1986 NCAA championships, after 6,400 meters, she was struggling along in fourth place, running a bad race. Then, as she approached a turn, she decided to keep going straight. She ducked under a railing and ran straight past Wisconsin team coach Peter Tegen. "It was eerie," he said. "Her eyes were focused straight ahead." She kept going—out of Indiana University's track stadium in Indianapolis, across a softball diamond, over a seven-foot fence, down New York Street, toward the bridge that spans the White River. Seventy-five feet onto the bridge she stopped, climbed over the railing, and jumped. After falling thirty-five feet, she landed on the soggy ground close to the river. She broke a rib, collapsed a lung, and fractured vertebrae. The doctor who attended her said that she would be permanently paralyzed from the waist down: "Given the distance that she fell, she's very lucky she's not a quadriplegic," Dr. Peter Hall noted. "She could have easily died."

Why? Ormsby was a high school valedictorian, a straight-A student, the record holder for the 800, 1,600, and 3,200 meters. At North Carolina State she was a track star and promising premed student. She was raised in a strong Christian family and was deeply religious herself. After her record-breaking 10,000-meter run, she told a reporter: "I just have to learn to do my best for myself and for God and to turn everything over to Him." Her leap had turned everything over to Him.

Some observers blamed Ormsby's consuming pursuit of perfection. Others blamed the pressure of world-class sport competition. Her father commented, "I believe . . . that it had something to do with the pressure that is put on young people to succeed." Certainly society's emphasis on the importance of sports places tremendous strains on young athletes. Often isolated from the world outside gyms and tracks and stadiums, they begin to think that their world has real, lasting meaning. Failure, then, becomes equated with death itself.

Such obsessive perfectionism also affected millions of other people, only a tiny fraction of whom were competitive athletes. For many people, exercise and weight loss became forms of psychological discipline, proof that the individual was in charge of his or her life. A 1986 Gallup Poll estimated that three million Americans, most of them women, suffered from eating disorders—anorexia nervosa and bulimia. In anorexia nervosa, victims virtually starve themselves to death, using laxatives, exercise, and absurdly low calorie intake to lose body weight. Most psychologists attribute the eating disorder to a sense of powerlessness in the victim. They strive for a sense of weightlessness, and in that weightlessness they find a sense of control missing from other areas of their lives. In 1984 the soft-rock vocalist Karen Carpenter brought the disease to national attention when she died of a heart attack induced by extreme weight loss. Even when their weight drops below 85 pounds and they resemble concentration camp victims, anorectics still look in the mirror and see themselves as fat, with round faces and flabby skin. Breasts disappear, menstruation stops, and their bodies return momentarily, just before death, to preadolescence.

Bulimia is a related disorder. The Gallup Poll concluded that nearly 10 percent of all American women between the ages of sixteen and twenty-five practice bulimia, an eating disorder characterized by huge calorie intake followed by self-induced vomiting. The Food and Drug Administration said that bulimic episodes may last up to eight hours, with an intake of 20,000 calories (an equivalent of 210 brownies, or 6 layer cakes, or 35 Big Macs), involve 25 to 30 vomiting episodes, and cost up to $75 a day for food purchases. If untreated, the disease causes irregular heartbeats, cramps, fatigue, and seizures by destroying the body's electrolyte balance. The gastric acid from vomiting will also erode teeth away.

In a country which historically has been keenly competitive and has periodically affirmed a belief in perfectionism, the idea of a better life through sports has been carried to obsessive lengths. Often the object of physical fitness has not been to produce health and well-being but to test or even to escape the limits of one's body. Ultra-distance runner Stu Mittleman, one of the leaders in his field during the 1980s, was the epitome of this tendency. For him a 26-mile marathon was unsatisfactory, a flat, almost meaningless endeavor. The 100-mile event was better, and in the early 1980s he established the American record with a 12:56:34 run. Better still was the six-day event, in which his 488 miles was also an American record.

In ultra-distance running Mittleman saw man rediscovering his lost past. "Our culture forces us to eliminate sensory input so that we can cope," he observed. "Sports re-sensitizes. I want to live life intensely. . . . Long slow running has a heritage in hunting and gathering. Sprinting is based on retreat, on flight." Life, then, is best experienced at the limits of endurance, well past what is good for one's health. Yet, sometimes even that does not seem enough. As Mittleman told an interviewer, "I plan to do a 12-hour run tomorrow. You know, it seems like so little now."

Among world-class athletes, performance is more important than health. During the nineteenth century athletes occasionally took drugs to enhance their performances. Cyclists, in particular, used drugs to extend their pain and endurance barriers. As early as 1869 some cyclists used "speed balls" of heroin and cocaine to increase endurance. Others used caffeine, alcohol, nitroglycerine, ethyl ether, strychnine, and opium to achieve the same effect.

Of course, not all athletes survived such experimentation. And in the twentieth century, as drug use became more frequent, the casualty rate climbed. In 1960 Danish cyclist Knut Jensen collapsed and died during the Rome Olympics. He had taken amphetamines and nicotinyl tartrate to improve his chances of victory. In 1967 Thomas Simpson died during the ascent of Mount Ventoux in the Tour de France. Amphetamines were discovered in his jersey pockets and luggage.

Since World War II, however, stimulants have done less damage than muscle-building drugs. During the 1920s American scientists isolated the male hormone testosterone. By the 1940s testosterone was being hailed as a potential fountain of youth. Science writer Paul de Kruif in *The Male*

Hormone (1945) noted that the newly developed synthetic testosterone "did more than give [the subjects] more energy and a gain in weight. . . . It changed them, and fundamentally . . . after many months on testosterone, their chest and shoulder muscles grew much heavier and stronger. . . . In some mysterious manner, testosterone caused the human body to synthesize protein, it caused the human body to be able to build the very stuff of its own life." There is evidence that during World War II testosterone was administered to German storm troopers to increase their strength and aggressiveness.

In 1945 de Kruif speculated, "It would be interesting to watch the productive power of [a] . . . professional group [of athletes] that would try a systematic supercharge with testosterone." By the 1952 Helsinki Olympics the Soviet Union had embarked on just such a campaign. That year Soviet weightlifters won seven Olympic medals, and U.S. Olympic weightlifting coach Bob Hoffman told reporters, "I know they're taking the hormone stuff to increase their strength."

At the 1954 World Weightlifting Championships in Vienna, a Soviet team physician confirmed Hoffman's belief. Upon returning home, Dr. John Ziegler, the U.S. team physician, acquired some testosterone and tested it on himself, Hoffman, and several American lifters. Concerned about the hormone's side effects—heightened aggression, increased libido, prostatic problems, and hirsutism—Ziegler approached the CIBA pharmaceutical company about producing a drug that would have testosterone's anabolic (muscle-building) effects without its androgenic (masculine characteristics) problems. The unsatisfactory result was the anabolic steroid Dianabol, a drug intended to aid burn victims and certain postoperative and geriatric patients.

Dianabol soon became the candy of the athletic world. By the 1960s nearly every world-class weightlifter was taking some form of anabolic steroid. In fact, steroids became the *sine qua non* of lifting. American superheavyweight weightlifting champion Ken Patera announced in 1971 that

he was anxious to meet his Russian counterpart Vasily Alexiev in the 1972 Olympics: "Last year, the only difference between me and him was that I couldn't afford his pharmacy bill. Now I can. When we hit Munich next year, I'll weigh in at about 340, maybe 350. Then we'll see which are better—his steroids or mine."

Track and field athletes, football players, and bodybuilders similarly improved their performances with the aid of drugs. Jay Sylvester, a member of the 1972 U.S. Olympic track and field team, polled his teammates and found that 68 percent had used steroids to prepare for the Games. They believed that without them they would be at a competitive disadvantage. The same was true in football. One San Diego Charger player told team psychiatrist Arnold J. Mandell, "Doc, I'm not about to go out one-on-one against a guy who's grunting and drooling and coming at me with big dilated pupils unless I'm in the same condition."

Testosterone and anabolic steroids have led to athletes' experimenting with other performance-enhancing drugs. One of the more popular recent additions to this drug array is human growth hormone (hGH), a hormone manufactured from the pituitary. As the authors of *The Underground Steroid Handbook* claimed, hGH could "overcome bad genetics. . . . We LOVE the stuff." Of course, it may also cause elongation of the chin, feet, and hands; thickening of the rib cage and wrists; and heart problems.

Risk is part of taking drugs. Anabolic steroids can cause a rare, fatal type of kidney tumor, high blood pressure, sterility, intestinal bleeding, hypoglycemia, heart problems, acne, a deepened voice, and a change in the distribution of body hair. Steroids and testosterone also make users more aggressive and irritable. One NFL player confessed that testosterone "definitely makes a person mean and aggressive. . . . On the field I've tried to hurt people in ways I never did before. . . . A lot of guys can't handle it. I'm not sure I can. I remember a while back five of the guys on our team went on the juice at the same time. A year later four of them were divorced and one was separated. I've lost a lot of hair from using it, but I have to admit it's great for football. . . . I lost my family, but I think I'm a better player now. Isn't that a hell of a trade-off?"

By the 1970s steroids had become part of America's drug culture, and athletes asserted the right to decide what could or could not go into their own bodies. Frederick C. Hatfield in *Anabolic Steroids: What Kind and How Many* (1982) wrote: "As pioneers, these athletes carefully weigh the risk-to-benefit ratio and proceed with caution and with open minds. Can there be much wrong with getting bigger and/or stronger?" Users, then, have been transformed into pioneers, "adventurers who think for themselves and who want to accomplish something noble before they are buried and become worm food."

Ironically, however, most of the users are not world-class athletes. In the 1980s use of steroids expanded out of the realm of world-class athletes to college and high school playing fields. An estimated one million young American men and women were consuming large amounts of anabolic steroids in 1987. The praise they received for "bulking up" was irresistible. When they reduced steroid use and lost muscle tissue, friends immediately commented on how "much smaller you are," and they would return to the pills. Like bulimia and anorexia nervosa, anabolic steroids were addictions linked inseparably with body image.

Steroid use was most pronounced in the subculture of body building. Most of these men and women are not competitive athletes trying to break a world record or win an Olympic gold metal—"to accomplish something noble"—but people who want to look "pumped." Like dieting and cosmetic surgery, steroid use has become a means to a better-looking body, and looks—not health—is the real objective.

The quest for the "ideal" body has been taken to its furthest pharmaceutical extremes by bodybuilders. Not only do they take steroids to build up muscle mass, but they also diet and take diuretics to achieve maximum muscular striation, or the "cut up" look. For weeks or even months before an important competition, bodybuilders eat as little as 1,000 calories a day and still work out eight or more hours a day. The result may be "the picture of health," but there is no reality behind the image. As one professional commented, "When we walk on stage we are closer to death than we are to life." And after a contest, in a bulimic binge, bodybuilders "pig out," often putting on fifteen pounds in one evening of eating.

Furthermore, to support their quest, many bodybuilders resort to homosexual "hustling." In theory, male bodybuilders have enshrined heterosexuality. Charles Atlas advertisements emphasized that the prize for the biggest biceps was the woman in the bathing suit. *Muscle and Fitness,* the leading bodybuilder magazine, reinforces this mythology by always picturing beautiful women hanging onto the biceps and thighs of "pumped," oiled men. "Ya know," said *Muscle and Fitness* editor Joe Weider, "in every age the women, they always go for the guy with the muscles, the bodybuilder. [The women] never go for the studious guy."

In fact, gay men have been a continual source of financial support for bodybuilders. Since serious bodybuilding is a full-time pursuit, the men involved need some source of income. Anthropologist Alan M. Kline estimated that 50 to 75 percent of southern California bodybuilders "hustle" the gay community for living expenses. Hustling ranges from posing for "beefcake" photographers and dancing nude at all-male events to pornography and sexual acts. Most bodybuilders, however, insist that they are not homosexual, that they have to hustle only to finance their bodybuilding habit. And besides, they insist, almost everyone does it. "People don't realize," noted one bodybuilder, "that in any given line-up of twenty competitors ten are hustling."

Many serious bodybuilders sacrifice heterosexual relationships as well as good health for their obsession. As one admitted, "On any given day I can go out with a woman, but it is not very satisfying. . . . Women demand time. I don't have that right now." Time, commitment, women, and even other men—all are obstacles to be mastered or avoided in the pursuit of a narcissistic ideal. To echo Michael

Jackson's popular 1988 song, life for these body-builders starts and ends with the man in the mirror.

By the end of the 1980s, sports had become the secular religion of America. The stadiums, tanning salons, health spas, and gymnasiums had become the new cathedrals; jogging, running, aerobic dancing, cycling, weightlifting, and dieting the new rituals; and televised events, newspapers, radio talk shows, and sports and health magazines the new liturgies. The most obsessive athletes have a disciplined devotion that even the most ascetic medieval saints would have envied. Alberto Salazar, the world-class marathoner, bragged about his willingness to run 105 miles a week on stress-fractured legs. In the heat of one marathon, he kept running even when his body temperature had reached 108 degrees, collapsed in heat prostration, and while

being packed in ice, received the last rites of the Roman Catholic Church.

Sports in the 1980s holds out secular salvation for nations, communities, and individuals. In competition and fitness, they locate the holy grail, the meaning of life in a world where God, church, and state no longer reign supreme. In *The Complete Book of Running,* Jim Fixx wrote: "It is here with my heart banging against my ribs that I discover how far beyond reason I can push myself. Furthermore, once a race has ended, I know what I am truly made of. Who can say how many of us have learned life's profoundest lessons while aching and gasping for breath?" On that Vermont road in 1986, with his body aching, his lungs gasping for breath, and his heart pounding against his ribs, Jim Fixx may have discovered the meaning of life.

Study Questions

1. Why did sports assume such an important dimension in American culture after World War II?

2. To what extent does sports in America reflect the aggressive, competitive spirit of the large culture?

3. What are the advantages and disadvantages to the new American obsession with sports?

4. In rural areas, why are high school sports so important to the community?

5. Why has plastic surgery become so popular in modern America?

6. How can anorexia nervosa and bulimia be seen as cultural, not merely physical, extremes?

7. What does the concept *cultural currency* mean? How do sports assist American society in transcending ethnic and religious divisions?

8. What is the connection between the cult of fitness and the post–World War II baby boom generation of yuppies?

Bibliography

For an extraordinary look at American values in the contemporary period, see Christopher Lasch, *The Culture of Narcissism: American Life in the Age of Dimin-*

ishing Expectations (1975); Bruce J. Schulman, *The Seventies: The Great Shift in American Culture, Society, and Politics* (2002); and David Frum, *How We Got Here: The 70's: The Decade That Brought You Modern Life—for Better or Worse* (2000). Also see Peter Clecak, *America's Quest for the Ideal Self* (1983). Randy Roberts and James S. Olson analyze the American obsession with sports in *Winning Is the Only Thing* (1989). Studs Terkel's *American Dreams: Lost and Found* (1980) is an oral history of how Americans coped with the social and economic changes of the 1970s and 1980s. Hillel Schwartz's *Never Satisfied: A Cultural History of Diets, Fantasies and Fat* (1986) is an outstanding examination of the American preoccupation with youth and body image. Also see Kim Chernin, *The Obsession: Reflections on the Tyranny of Slenderness* (1981). For the dangerous, pathologic dimension of weight consciousness in history, see Rudolph M. Bell, *Holy Anorexia* (1985).

READING 29

★ ★ ★

O.J. Simpson:
The Trial of the Century

Haynes Johnson

O.J. Simpson had spent his career in the national spotlight. In 1967 as a running back for the University of Southern California, he led the Trojans to a Rose Bowl. The following year, he became everybody's All-American, flashing across the nation's televisions with a combination of speed and moves unmatched in the history of football. He won the Heisman Trophy, the Maxwell Award, and the AP and UPI Player of the Year honors. As a professional he was equally spectacular. Not only did he become the first runner to rush for more than 2,000 yards in one season, he also set National Football League records for the most 100-yard games and the most yards in one game. But O.J. was always more than his statistics indicated. His charm, smile, and charisma made him an icon. He was the first African American athlete to become a major corporate spokesman, and after he retired, he became a film and television celebrity. Unlike previous black athletes, it seemed that every door in America was open to O.J.

All this changed on Friday, June 17, 1994. First, the Los Angeles County Police Department charged Simpson with the murder of his ex-wife, Nicole Brown Simpson, and her friend Ronald Goldman. Next, reporters tracked Simpson to a white Ford Bronco, driven by O.J.'s friend Al Cowlings. Followed by a flotilla of police cars and television helicopters, Cowlings drove Simpson along various Los Angeles freeways. Cheering spectators lined several stretches of highway, and all the major networks covered the entire drama. The trial that followed, which historian Haynes Johnson termed the trial of the century, became a media event that shed light on more than Simpson's innocence or guilt. It illuminated American culture in the late twentieth century.

Everyone thinks they know him: O.J., the good guy, always smiling, always charming, always nonthreatening, always ready to sign one more autograph for adoring fans; O.J., the all-American sports hero, the amiable athlete turned affable TV commentator; O.J., the entertaining pitchman who is constantly seen in American living rooms, courtesy of TV commercials, leaping over barricades and racing through airports as he promotes his sponsor's products; O.J., the loving father and family man; O.J., the black man, who plays so long and successful a role as an appealing, self-effacing American icon, that he's no longer seen as black. In fact, he doesn't see himself as black—he's often quoted as saying, "I'm not black, I'm O.J." In manner, language, lifestyle, and personal association he passes, seemingly effortlessly, into the upper echelons of the white world. Exposed to the good life, courted by the powerful, he belongs to the best country clubs, moves in the best social circles, golfs with the corporate elite, travels on private jets to fabulous resorts, rubs shoulders with influential deal makers.

So nonblack, so nonthreatening racially is O.J. that he becomes the first black athlete to be employed by corporate sponsors to endorse products not marketed solely to blacks. His marriage to a beautiful young blonde, a familiar golden girl of the Nineties type, draws none of the sneers and hatred and jealousies that mark other interracial celebrity marriages. In the American heart and mind, O.J. is colorless. His celebrity status is such that even some who resent him do not express their feelings publicly. That is particularly true, and particularly complicated, when it comes to blacks.

After O.J.'s arrest for the murders, some of these hidden emotions surface. "He forgot that he was black," one black woman says when she phones a Dallas talk-radio show devoted solely to the O.J. case. "He didn't show love to us that he should have showed. But deep in our hearts, all of

Never had an athlete risen and fallen as far as O.J. Simpson. From his days at USC to his trial for murder, he captured the attention of the nation.

us loved him. He left us years ago." Another black woman calls the same show to say: "Even though he was with a white woman, he was something for our race to be proud of. I feel hurt. I feel hurt."

O.J., the reality, is infinitely more complicated. His life story illuminates the continuing struggles of African Americans to escape the obstacles that keep them separated from the predominant white mainstream. O.J. Simpson, the gentle sports hero fans think they know, is, in fact, the product of a tough, violent upbringing in the slums of San Francisco.

His is a raw and painful childhood, but typical of blacks like him who live in the dismal public projects of the inner city. In the tough Potrero Hill district where he grows up, 70 percent of the blacks are on welfare, and, as in O.J.'s case, a majority of the children are raised without a father in the home. It's common for them to join a gang, as

Haynes Johnson, *The Best of Times: The Boom and Bust Years of America Before and After Everything Changed,* Harvest Books, Harcourt Inc., 2002.

O.J. does at the age of thirteen when he becomes a member of the Gladiators. A year later, at fourteen, he experiences his first arrest—for robbing a liquor store. In junior high he joins what he once described as his "first *fighting* gang," the Persian Warriors. With them, he participates in pitched battles, usually on weekends, with rival gangs. In their world, violence is commonplace; brawling and stoning cars are part of a normal weekend. Witnessing sudden death is also a common experience. Years later, O.J. remembers being in gang fights "where a couple of guys got croaked."

By the age of fifteen, he has earned a reputation as being especially good with his fists. "I only beat up dudes who deserved it," he once explained, "at least once a week, usually on Friday or Saturday night. If there wasn't no fight, it wasn't no weekend." It was then, barely into his teens, that he wins renown within the gang culture for the manner in which he beats an older, much feared, leader of a rival gang, the Roman Gents, the toughest gang in the city.

After he ends his pro-football career, O.J. recalls that fistfight in a 1976 *Playboy* interview that reveals much about him the public would later be forced to confront, but does not want to. His fight is with Winky, then a battle-hardened twenty-year-old. "One night I was at a dance in the Booker T. Washington Community Center," O.J. remembers, "when, all of a sudden, this *loud* little sucker—an older O.J.—comes up to me and says, 'What did you say about my sister?' I'd heard of Winky—just about everyone had—but I didn't know that was who this cat was, so I just said, 'Hey, man, I don't know your sister. I don't even know *you*.' It wasn't cool to fight in the community center, so the guy started walking away, but he was still talkin' crap to me and I yelled back, 'Fuck you, too, man!'

"Well, a few minutes later, I see a whole bunch of Roman Gents trying to get this cat to be cool, but nope, he's comin' over to me and he shouts, 'Motherfucker, I'm gonna kick your ass!!' And then—bingo!—the music stops and I hear everybody whisperin', 'Winky's gettin' ready to fight.' *Winky!* Damn, I didn't want to fight *him*. So as he

walks up to me, I say, 'Hey, man, I really didn't say *anything* about your sister.' But before I can say anything else, Winky's on me, and swingin'. Well, I beat his ass—I just cleaned up on the cat—and as I'm givin' it to him, I see this girl Paula, who I just loved, so *I* start getting loud. And as I'm punchin', I'm also shoutin': '*Muthafuckah! You gonna fuck with me??*'"

That's the O.J. his peers know. The public never does. Over the years, as he becomes enshrined among American sports heroes, O.J. adopts the style—and the speech—of the successful white world.

O.J. works hard at transforming his public persona from brawling street tough to smooth, confident member of the successful elite. Long before the brutal murders with which he's charged, Lee Strasberg, the acting coach who helped Marlon Brando, Marilyn Monroe, and other stars, and was then assisting O.J. in his Hollywood roles, says of O.J.: "He already is an actor, an excellent one." Strasberg adds, "A natural one." And once, while shooting a TV commercial with underprivileged black youths in Oakland, in the territory where he grew up, O.J.'s mask slips. Inadvertently, he begins employing the street language of his gang childhood. Furious, he announces he wants to redo the commercial. The second take goes perfectly. "That's what happens when I spend too much time with my boys," O.J. says afterward, in explaining his slip. "I forget how to talk white."

For O.J. and others like him, sports offers the surest path toward that road to success. It's not unusual for a black child from the slums with natural athletic ability to achieve an American Dream lifestyle and public fame. It is highly unusual, however, to become a superstar athlete in spite of suffering from a severe childhood physical handicap.

As a two-year-old, O.J. Simpson was afflicted with rickets. The disease, resulting from a lack of calcium in the bones, a commentary on his impoverished inner-city diet, withered his legs and left him bow-legged and pigeon-toed. To correct his disability, leg braces were required; his mother, however, couldn't afford them. So for the next three years, O.J. shuffled around his house with an improvised contraption that enabled him to walk, while strengthening his legs. For several hours every day he put on shoes connected to each other by an iron band and struggled to walk. Ultimately, his handicap was corrected. The tenacity and drive displayed by this bow-legged kid with rickets who couldn't walk unaided is as impressive as any of the subsequent stories in the Nineties that celebrate the determination to succeed of the new golden entrepreneurs of Technotimes.

From high school on, O.J.'s athletic prowess propels him up, and eventually out, of the world of his birth. His career ambitions are minimal. By his own account, he was "a lousy student" and "didn't exactly kill myself studying." He's so eager to leave the classroom that he thinks of enlisting in the Marines and fighting in Vietnam. By the time he graduates from junior college, he has smashed all existing football rushing records for that level of play and finds himself aggressively courted by recruiters of big-time collegiate athletics. They shower him with offers of full scholarships—and, typically, much more, most of it hidden.

Though ostensibly an amateur endeavor, guided by principles of good sportsmanship, American collegiate athletics, especially football, long since has passed into the realm of high-stakes, high-revenue professional sports. It's the biggest of businesses, awash in cash, commercialism, and corruption. It's all about money. A young potential superstar like O.J. finds himself at the center of a virtual bidding war. "A whole bunch of 'em were offering all kinds of under-the-table shit," he recalls of the college recruiters who besieged him. "In addition to a regular scholarship, most of the schools were talking about $400 or $500 a month and stuff like a car. One school was gonna arrange for my mother to clean up an office for $1,000 a month; another was gonna get my mother a house."

Whatever the offer, O.J. more than proves his worth; he richly rewards those who invest in him. Both in college at USC and then in the National Football League with the Buffalo Bills, his athletic

ability attracts legions of paying fans. They fill the stadiums. With them come the networks and the sponsors. They vie for the right to telecast his games, not only locally, but nationally. These generate still more revenue.

Through it all O.J. soars. As his earnings multiply, he acquires more of the taste for and the trappings of the affluent life. To an adoring public, he becomes a self-effacing, beloved superstar. It's an intoxicating role. O.J., like so many sports heroes who achieve celebrity at an early age, takes the fawning worship of starstruck fans and effusive praise of sports announcers as his due. So, too, he takes as his natural right the physical gratification that comes with quick fame and wealth—the easy and endless sexual conquests, the eager girls on their knees, the constant adulation of faithful camp followers. No wonder primal urges are unchecked. Stars believe they can always get away with outrageous behavior, and often do. In the Nineties, sports stars become involved in even more notorious cases, often resulting only in slaps on the wrist for the offenders, if that. Rules are made for lesser mortals.

But the idea that such a supposedly familiar public figure could be capable of the monstrous murders with which he's accused is simply inconceivable. Indeed, the public can be excused for being so misinformed about O.J. and the life he's led. The O.J. the public has grown to love is wholesome, charismatic, uncomplicated.

As with so many other celebrities, especially sports celebrities, O.J. has led a charmed life, protected by a cordon of publicists, agents, producers, sponsors, sportswriters, and commentators, and protected no less by the police who treat him as an untouchable. Even in prison, O.J. demonstrates the power of special privilege accorded the celebrated star. In the Los Angeles County Men's Central Jail, where he is incarcerated along with sixty-four hundred other inmates, O.J. lives alone in a row of seven cells. Most of the other inmates are housed two to six in a single cell. They wait in line to use pay phones. O.J. doesn't. They must bathe in communal showers. O.J. showers by himself. Other prisoners are limited to visits of only twenty minutes a day. O.J. sees his lawyers and forty specially designated visitors for up to ten hours a day.

When asked about this special treatment, a sheriff's deputy justifies it by saying: "O.J. Simpson was living in a Brentwood estate worth $5 million, now he's incarcerated in a 9-by-7-foot cell. . . . It's all relative."

Not until the aftermath of the murders do other aspects of his life become widely known.

Within days, former friends and associates tell reporters of his jealousies, his rages, his record of hitting on women, casually, repeatedly, his blatant sexism and possessiveness. Once, in a fine Santa Ana restaurant where O.J. was hosting a group of his friends and his wife for dinner, he grabbed Nicole's crotch and loudly proclaimed, "This belongs to me." On another occasion, as testimony later reveals, he boasted to an acquaintance how easy it would be to kill someone by slashing his neck with a knife—and demonstrated, with gestures, how he would do it. And once, according to information a former Hollywood associate of his tells prosecutors, when the subject of Nicole's boyfriends was raised O.J. angrily vowed to "cut their fucking heads off" if he ever finds them driving his cars.

The public knows nothing about this side of O.J. It certainly has no knowledge of the devastating record of desperate telephone calls Nicole Brown Simpson made to police emergency numbers over the years, both during her marriage and after her divorce, as she sought protection from a violent, battering O.J. Nicole's police emergency calls document not only O.J.'s explosive violent nature, but also the failure of both police and judicial authorities to take effective action to stop his abusive behavior. Not that such failure is unique in Nicole's case; police routinely fail the battered wife, as numerous court records show. That dreary kind of record was compounded by the circumstances of the O.J. case. O.J.'s a superstar; superstars receive different treatment.

All this changes after The Chase and the arrest. Police and prosecutors, or both, immediately slip tape recordings of many of Nicole's 911 police emergency calls to local TV stations and the networks. Along with the recordings are equally damaging leaked written reports of police investigations of those incidents.

One police report, on New Year's Day 1989, describes how Nicole, wearing only bra and sweatpants, runs from bushes where she's hiding after having called police from inside their Brentwood mansion. Badly beaten, her lip cut, one eye blackened, Nicole keeps telling officers, "He's going to kill me; he's going to kill me." Does he have any guns? police ask. "He's got lots of guns," she replies. Then she bitterly complains to the police: "You never do anything about him. You talk to him and then leave. I want him arrested."

At that point, according to the police account, O.J. appears in a bathrobe. "I don't want that woman in my bed anymore," he screams at police. "I got two other women, and I don't want that woman in my bed anymore." When warned he is going be arrested, O.J. yells: "The police have been out here eight times before and you're going to arrest me for this? This is a family matter. Why do you want to make a big deal out of it? We can handle it."

Ultimately, Nicole doesn't press charges, but a city attorney files misdemeanor charges of spousal abuse against O.J. He pleads no contest, is fined $970, ordered to perform 120 hours of community service, and attend counseling sessions twice a week for three months. He's also given two years' probation.

The incident attracts little news attention. It has no demonstrable effect on O.J.'s public popularity. "It was perplexing," a female former employee of NBC Sports remarks to *Sports Illustrated* immediately after the murders. "People at NBC Sports used to always remark about the beating, shaking their heads and saying, 'Here's a man who used to beat his wife, and none of America cares or remembers.' People refused to believe because they thought he was such a nice guy."

It isn't just the American people who don't believe or care about such behavior. Neither do O.J.'s corporate bosses. Three months after the 1989 incident, NBC signed O.J. to an annual $400,000 broadcast contract, and he got another contract for more than half a million dollars a year from Hertz rental car, the sponsor of his TV commercials.

Even more damaging are tapes leaked to CNN and then broadcast over that network in prime time days after O.J.'s arrest. These include a 911 call Nicole made to police from inside her home, after her 1992 divorce, on October 25, 1993. The transcript of that phone conversation frighteningly foreshadows her fate on the front steps of her townhouse less than a year later:

911 Operator: *911 emergency.*

Nicole: *Could you get someone over here now, to 325 Gretna Green. He's back. Please.*

911 Operator: *Okay. What does he look like?*

Nicole: *He's O.J. Simpson. I think you know his record. Could you just send somebody over here?*

911 Operator: *Okay, what is he doing there?*

Nicole: *He just drove up again. Can you just send somebody over?*

911 Operator: *He just drove up. Okay, wait a minute. What kind of car is he in?*

Nicole: *He's in a white Bronco. But first of all, he broke the back door down to get in.*

911 Operator: *Okay. Wait a minute. What's your name?*

Nicole: *Nicole Simpson.*

911 Operator: *Okay. Is he the sportscaster or whatever?*

Nicole: *Yeah.*

911 Operator: *Okay. What is—*

Nicole: *Thank you.*

911 Operator: *Wait a minute. We're sending the police. What is he doing? Is he threatening you?*

Nicole: *He's fuckin' going nuts.*

Her furious profane response doesn't stop the police operator from asking still more questions and still not responding swiftly.

In view of what happens later, Nicole's words as she tries to explain her fear of O.J. are espe-

cially chilling: "The kids are upstairs sleeping and I don't want anything to happen."

She explains to the police operator how O.J. came to her townhouse earlier, broke down her back door, went upstairs and pounded on her door until she fears it, too, will be broken. "Then he screamed and hollered," she says, "and I tried to get him out of the bedroom because the kids are sleeping in there."

The 911 Operator replies laconically, "Okay."

Nicole, her tone increasingly urgent, continues trying to describe the danger she feels. The operator interrupts, maddeningly, to say, "Okay. So basically you guys have just been arguing?"

At that point, the tape picks up the background sound of a male voice, roaring and shouting unintelligibly. The conversation continues:

911 Operator: *Is he inside right now?*

Nicole, desperately: *Yes, yes.*

911 Operator: *Okay, just a moment.*

O.J. Simpson: *[Unintelligible.]*

Through the sound of O.J.'s angry shouting, the tape clearly picks up a fragment of Nicole's plaintive voice: "—the kids. O.J.—O.J., the kids are sleeping."

The police operator interjects with yet another question: "He's still yelling at you? Just stay on the line, Okay?"

The conversation ends with a heartbreaking appeal from Nicole. "O.J. O.J. O.J. Could you please leave. Please leave."

After another frightening encounter with O.J., Nicole expressed the terror she felt in a tape recording. It's entered into the public record, along with a diary she kept in the years prior to her death. The diary details her fears of O.J.; it also describes the beatings and humiliations she suffers, including a vivid account of how O.J. once "beat me for hours." On the tape, she says that during O.J.'s rages he "gets a very animal look in him, his veins pop out and his eyes get black." Looking at him, she fears that "if it happened once more, it would be the last time." Eight months later, she's hacked to death.

In the aftermath of O.J.'s arrest, the revelations about Nicole's terror-stricken emergency calls and O.J.'s prior record for wife abuse initially focus great attention on the issue of domestic violence, particularly violence against women. For years, advocates and activists have been trying to place that issue squarely on the public agenda. Now O.J. gives them the perfect opportunity to get across their message about the prevalence of wife battering and spousal abuse. They appear on television to air the problem. They write op-ed pieces. Congress even holds hearings.

Black women are prominent among these advocates. Many speak out against O.J.'s violent behavior toward Nicole, as they have been doing repeatedly about violence committed against women by men, whether black men or white men. At this point in the O.J. story, they don't view the case along purely racial lines. As in the highly charged Supreme Court confirmation hearings for Clarence Thomas, women see abuse or harassment, while men see an "electronic lynching." Indeed, just a day after Nicole's body is discovered, the domestic violence issue appears to be creating further sharp divisions between African-American men and women.

On that Monday a female judge in Indiana refuses to free Mike Tyson, the former black heavyweight boxing champion then serving a six-year jail sentence for rape. Immediately, Indianapolis talk shows are besieged by angry callers. Women, many of whom identify themselves as black, praise her decision but add that Tyson should serve more, not less, prison time. Some believe he should have served the full sixty years to which he could have been sentenced after being convicted on two counts of criminal deviant sexual conduct and rape.

African-American male callers, by contrast, are outraged at the judge for not immediately freeing Tyson. The champ is "the greatest," they say. He never should have been imprisoned in the first place. He's the victim of a "scheming woman." The female judge's ruling proves how "the system" castrates and lynches black men. This becomes a theme that repeats itself ever more forcefully during the O.J. trial as the issue of domestic violence against women is overtaken by an even more combustible one—race.

The race card, as exemplified by the character of Mark Fuhrman, plays powerfully on deeply held African-American fears and resentments. It intensifies the already strong belief that blacks cannot expect fair treatment from the nation's criminal justice system. The O.J. case, in this reasoning, becomes an opportunity for racial payback to counter past wrongs extending back to the very beginnings of the American experiment—the wrongs of slavery, of murder, of rape, of castration, of lynching, of segregation, of discrimination, of injustice. Fanning racial flames even higher is the performance of the black press, where O.J. is portrayed as yet another "victim" of white racism perpetrated by the combined conspiratorial efforts of a white legal and police establishment and a "white media."

While O.J. becomes another example of a black hero being destroyed by the white conspiracy, Johnnie Cochran, O.J.'s lead attorney, is hailed as a new black hero. He's even called a new civil rights leader for his defense of O.J. In sharp contrast, one of the key prosecutors, Chris Darden, also black, is condemned in the same black press as being a contemptible "house Negro" for prosecuting O.J.

In the end, race, not domestic violence, not corruption at the core of professional athletics that inspires above-the-law attitudes among its pampered stars, not even murder, becomes the emotional touchstone of the O.J. case.

* * *

No thinking American in the Nineties could be surprised to learn that the United States still suffers from pervasive racial prejudice. Despite African-American advances in employment and income opportunities; despite the ending of legal segregation in housing, in schools, in the military; despite integration of previously all-white police departments enabling blacks to become chiefs of police in such former racial trouble spots as Birmingham, Alabama, and Charleston, South Carolina; despite anti-discrimination laws and affirmative action programs aimed at combating discrimination nationwide, racial suspicion and racial hostility still afflict the United States. The shock produced by the O.J. case comes not from the discovery that racial resentment and anger exist. The shock comes from the depth and virulence of them.

In the O.J. trial, everything is seen through the distorting prism of race. Blacks and whites examine the same evidence and draw starkly differing conclusions from it. One side sees a murderer; the other sees a victim. One sees clear and compelling evidence of guilt; the other sees a sinister conspiracy that seeks to convict the innocent.

Barely a month after O.J.'s arrest, 63 percent of whites answering a Time/CNN poll say they believe he will get a fair trial. Only 31 percent of blacks feel the same way. While 66 percent of whites believe he received a fair preliminary hearing, only 31 percent of blacks agree. Seventy-seven percent of whites believe the case against O.J. is either "very strong" or "fairly strong." Only 45 percent of blacks agree.

As the trial begins, the racial lines harden. Out of public view, the sequestered jury becomes riven with increasing racial tensions. Black and white jurors use separate gyms, watch movies in separate rooms. Black jurors complain that whites on their panel are given preferential treatment by sheriff's deputies. They suspect the deputies are secretly searching their housing quarters while they are on jury duty seeking evidence of bias against the prosecution or to discover they have been violating the judge's orders not to read news accounts about the case. One black juror, after being removed from the panel, goes on TV to accuse a white juror of kicking her. She says the same white stomped on the foot of another black juror in the jury box. Another black juror files a formal protest to Judge Ito about the racism perceived by black jury members.

Six months into the trial, a national survey by Lou Harris and Associates finds that 61 percent of whites believe Simpson is guilty. Sixty-eight percent of blacks think him innocent. Only 8 percent of all blacks surveyed believe that O.J. murdered Nicole and Ron. (Twenty-four percent of

blacks polled say they aren't sure about O.J.'s guilt or innocence.)

By trial's end, a state of near total racial polarization exists across America.

* * *

In the O.J. case, the public fascination with violent entertainment and courtroom drama mixes with the conjunction between capitalism and celebrity. The case becomes a prime example of how profit seekers can manufacture and exploit a mass audience and how television provides the perfect vehicle to promote that rush to profit. As Walter Lippmann observed in the wake of the TV quiz scandals that rocked the television world at the end of the Fifties, "While television is supposed to be 'free,' it has in fact become the creature, the servant, and indeed the prostitute, of merchandising." To that point, Lippmann thought television's major influence had been twofold: first, "to poison the innocent by the exhibition of violence, degeneracy, and crime, and second, to debase the public taste." He should have seen the Nineties.

In the O.J. case, everyone cashes in—the media, the lawyers, the judge, the jury, the publishers, the entertainment industry, the marketers of items bearing on the case. Even friends and foes of O.J. profit, eagerly, aggressively, shamelessly. Not least among them is O.J. himself, as well as supposedly bereaved relatives of the victims. The O.J. trial becomes not just "a rush to judgment," as his lawyer dramatically and repeatedly warns; it becomes a rush to capitalize, and capitalize in a way America has not witnessed before.

Not that the phenomenon of exploiting tragedy and sensation is new. . . .

In the O.J. case, the difference from the past lies not in the human instinct that lures crowds and hucksters to scenes of disaster. In the Nineties, the difference lies in the ability of everyone, everywhere, to participate vicariously in those scenes as they are occurring.

For this capacity, thank technology. Mobile TV minicams and earth-orbiting satellites provide the technical ability to go live, virtually instantly, from any scene of disaster or scandal. For the decision to bring more and more of these scenes into everyone's living room, credit a number of factors that converged in the Nineties. Intense competitive pressures among proliferating cable channels scrambling to wrest market share from the traditional networks created increasing demand to broadcast the latest, most sensational newsbreaks as they happen—and the more scandalous and lurid the better. As cable channels focused increasingly on the sensational and the scandalous, the old networks adapted by furnishing more of the same in an attempt to hold their declining audience.

The disgraceful attack talk-radio programs, with their growing audience and increasing influence, also affected the electronic and celebrity culture of the Nineties. With their daily airing of ideological conspiracies and preoccupation with scandals—proof never necessary and rarely even a consideration—the talk-radio shows demonstrated the impact, and the money, to be made by appealing to the worst in people. Television, especially cable, followed their lead; tabloid TV joined attack radio in filling more of the nation's airwaves. "Trash TV" was on the rise.

None of this readily explains the appeal of these offerings, however, or the paradox they present about American society in the Nineties. Americans, after all, were better educated, more sophisticated, more tolerant, more aware of subtlety and nuance and the imperfectability of public and private lives than ever before. They were, in the main, practical and realistic, generally hard-eyed, and not easily swayed by cheap appeals to emotion. So why were so many so captivated by such tawdry daily fare?

Part of the answer rests in the nature of the times. The best of times they may or may not have been, but they were certainly times blessed by an absence of crises—crises domestic or foreign, economic or social, environmental or medical. Freed from the kinds of concerns that compel public attention, Americans were also free to indulge in the titillation of gossip and scandal. They were free to be entertained by the spectacle of celebrities and public figures brought low. And with relentless, nonstop intensity, the electronic

media dished up scandal in helpings that enabled every citizen to share in every gory, sordid detail.

Nor was O.J. the first of the great scandalous spectacles Americans witnessed in the Nineties. By the time of O.J., Americans were conditioned to witnessing a succession of long-running scandalous episodes. No sooner did one end than another took its place. Each attracted an immense audience; each received frenzied media coverage; each was treated as if it said something significant about American society and thus deserved intense attention; each fueled an appetite for more of the same; each became a springboard for a successor, happily supplied by producers of Teletimes who sought and supplied the latest scandal for public consumption, all in a breakneck race to boost ratings.

So many were there, and so rapidly did they replace each other, that it seemed as if the single most defining characteristic of America in the Nineties was an all-consuming preoccupation with scandal—scandal that over time merged into one continuous serial production.

The names of the players and the particulars about the scandals changed, but the object was the same—scandal, always more scandal: Dr. Kevorkian and the first assisted suicide; Rodney King, beaten viciously by Los Angeles policemen; Jeffrey Dahmer, "the homosexual cannibal," and horrific acts of mass murder; Anita Hill, Clarence Thomas, sexual harassment, and pubic hairs; Mike Tyson and rape; Tailhook and sexual assault in the Air Force; the Packwood diaries and sex on Capitol Hill; Michael Jackson and that young boy; Nancy Kerrigan, Tonya Harding, and their violent skating rivalry; Lorena Bobbitt and her husband's severed penis.

All these occurred before O.J. Other episodes flitted across the TV screens during and after the long period when O.J. dominated the national stage: Susan Smith and her two drowned children; the Menendez brothers; JonBenet Ramsey, the pathetic six-year-old pushed by parents to compete in beauty pageants by tarting up and acting like a budding Lolita, found murdered in the basement of her home; Louise Woodward, the young British nanny, and the death of the child in her care; the murder of fashion designer Gianni Versace in a Palm Beach oceanfront mansion, perfectly providing a spectacle that combined synthetic glamour and glitz with salacious tales of gay sex; the clearly deeply troubled teacher, Mary Kay Letourneau, and her sad, sick affair—naturally labeled by the tabs "forbidden love"—with her thirteen-year-old student; Dick Morris, a president's Machiavellian pollster, sucking the toes of that prostitute on a Washington hotel balcony; Marv Albert, the loudmouth sportscaster, biting a woman in another hotel room near the capital, providing perfect fodder for the televised celebrity and scandal culture, and being returned to the air as a sports commentator, apparently no less popular, or perhaps more so, than when his scandalous behavior created yet another mass spectacle.

Drawing the most intense media focus and public attention were the trials that resulted from many of those episodes. They were the easiest to cover and offered a convenient running plot line of scandal and suspense.

The cumulative effect of these events was to divert attention from the really great episodes of the Nineties, and especially from two that came into play with tremendous force then. One, as we've seen, was the revolution in science, technology, and medicine rapidly changing life on the planet. The other was the growing concentration of great blocs of power through the greatest wave of mergers ever, creating new entities reshaping the basic economic and social structures of the nation.

As time passed, few Americans could recall specific details of the various episodes to which they were exposed or their outcomes. Nonetheless, stamped in the collective public memory was a hazy montage of sensationalized scandals. While people professed to be repelled by media excesses and obsessive attention to scandal, they also took guilty pleasure in watching, and wallowing in, the spectacle.

Two weeks after O.J.'s arrest, CNN dispatched its cameras, and a correspondent, to a popular Atlanta fast-food restaurant, aptly named The Varsity, for a daylong sounding of public attitudes about the O.J. case. The slice of vox populi aired was highly revealing. Virtually every person interviewed expressed the same kinds of underlying ambivalence. They hated what they were seeing, or so they said, but they were watching all of it.

* * *

Television provided much more than "updates." It offered a new form of public entertainment— a live, free theater of spectacle and sensation. O.J. had it all, the serious and the sordid. It was irresistible. In the process, old news barriers and taboos were broken; practices previously deemed unacceptable by mainstream news organizations became acceptable amid rapidly evolving standards of the electronic age. Even some talk-radio hosts expressed concern about the negative impact they were having on the public. Days after the murders, during a Los Angeles convention of national talk-show hosts, one of them acknowledged to a *CBS Evening News* interviewer that with the O.J. case talk radio had "gone totally over the line." Then the talk host quickly added: "With each case we say that—and the line gets pushed further." That didn't stop the lines separating accuracy from rumor, fairness from unfairness, good taste from bad, from being driven farther and farther apart.

Distinguished news executives from both print and television bemoaned the lowering of journalistic values, the cheapening of reportage, the omnipresent "gotcha" aspects, the circus atmosphere that typified the coverage. "I don't like the idea that a murder trial has been turned into an entertainment special," Don Hewitt, the executive producer of *60 Minutes,* wrote in a *New York Times* oped article. "There are certain moments in American life that have a certain dignity." Not an O.J. moment, though, especially an O.J. moment that increases ratings and one that shows the growing public appetite for more of the same—more of the spectacular, more of the sensational, more of the scandalous. Which, of course, is what the public got.

* * *

Long before the trial even began, virtually all hope had vanished that it would provide for a watching world an example of the American criminal justice system at its best, a serious civic proceeding that exemplified the most cherished judicial attributes: dignity, decorum, and fairness. It quickly degenerated into a spectacle that demonstrated some of the worst characteristics of Teletimes. No one escaped unscathed. The lawyers fought among themselves, played as much to the TV cameras as to the jury, argued their cases in impromptu press encounters at every opportunity, leaked damaging information to the press, and also exhibited a taste for cashing in on the instant celebrity television had conferred upon them. One attorney on the defense team was involved in a New York trial that conflicted with O.J.'s. He asked for and won a postponement from that engagement; then he asked for another postponement from his New York obligations, in effect arguing it would be unfair to him financially if he were denied the chance to participate in the O.J. show, never mind his East Coast client. This time, his request was denied.

The jurors squabbled among themselves. At times, they, too, acted petulantly. Once, they even acted mutinously. On that occasion, thirteen of the eighteen remaining members of the panel showed up in court dressed in black. They threatened to refuse to enter the jury box until Judge Ito heard their protests about his decision to dismiss three of their guards in the wake of charges the guards gave some jurors favorable treatment. Though it wasn't known until after the trial ended, many of the jurors already had sold their stories to tabloid TV shows, granting exclusive interviews immediately after the verdict. And the judge, despite early expressions of confidence that he would live up to his reputation for ensuring scrupulous courtroom discipline and decorum—Ito would exercise his usual "cool manner and firm hand," one puff piece had predicted before the trial—showed himself to be petty and temperamental, given to angry outbursts against media excesses and threatening often to ban cameras from his courtroom.

Yet Ito himself astounded lawyers and law professors across the country when he permitted himself to be interviewed extensively by a local Los Angeles TV correspondent in the midst of the O.J. proceedings taking place in his court. Portions of the interview, conducted at Ito's home, were then broadcast each night beginning at eleven o'clock Sunday, November 13, for an entire week over L.A.'s KCBS Channel 2. More astonishing yet, these nightly airings on the local "Action News" broadcast took place during one of four so-called sweeps periods each year. The sweeps are the critical times when TV audiences are measured to help set advertising rates—the bigger the audience, the more money stations can charge their advertisers. Nor was the timing of Ito's interview with the commercially crucial sweeps period accidental. The channel promoted those nightly segments of his interview in full-page newspaper ads and in on-air promos, all intended to entice more viewers.

Reaction in the legal community, and in some press circles, was swift and strongly critical. In San Diego, a defense lawyer expressed typical consternation. "It's out of control," Elisabeth Semel told the *San Francisco Chronicle's* legal affairs writer. "The side show is obscuring the heart of the case." In Los Angeles, another prominent defense attorney, Harland Braun, voiced astonishment at how "a garden variety murder involving a celebrity" now is "going off into all kinds of side shows. Ito has become a side show. It's unbelievable."

And in New York, a respected legal scholar on judicial ethics at the New York University School of Law, Stephen Gillers, reflected sadly that "There's something about the big publicity monster. It co-opts everybody."

It certainly did in the O.J. case, nor was that trial the first that raised serious questions about the "publicity monster" that accompanied sensationally televised court hearings. By the time of the O.J. case, forty-seven states permitted TV cameras in courtrooms, and with the advent of the around-the-clock cable telecasts of CNN and such popular programs as "Court TV," the televised trial had become a staple of the electronic media. "Court TV" alone had been televising them for several years before the O.J. trial.

As for the rhetoric about how televising the trial live from Los Angeles would provide a great national civics lesson, and all the pretrial arguments from freedom of the press advocates who urged that cameras be allowed in the courtroom not only as a constitutional right but as a check on abuses, in the end the O.J. Simpson trial produced more public cynicism and disgust.

When it works as it should, the American criminal justice system is a noble, indispensable defender of freedom and individual rights. That it often does not work as well amid the scandal culture of Teletimes is only one of many lessons emerging from the Nineties.

* * *

O.J.'s saga was over. After riveting the nation for a year and a half, after a trial lasting for nine months, after a jury was sequestered for 265 days facing a virtual ton of overwhelmingly incriminating evidence to assess, it took those O.J. Simpson jurors only three hours of deliberation before rendering their verdict on October 3, 1995—not guilty on all charges.

The same cameras and technology that brought O.J. live into people's homes and offices for all those months now captured America's reaction to the outcome.

Just as in the beginning, the cameras brought Americans together, and then sharply divided them.

In Los Angeles, a deathly silence settled over the courtroom when the clerk began reading the verdict beginning with the words, "In the matter of the people of the State of California versus Orenthal James Simpson, we the jury find the defendant. . . .

Screams of joy and cries of outrage rang out in the courtroom at the pronouncement "not guilty." Those same conflicting emotions were immediately displayed in televised scenes across the country.

Pandemonium swept black neighborhoods in Los Angeles. Worshipers in a black church there began jubilant celebrations. Others took to the streets amid wild cheering.

In Washington, D.C., in black neighborhoods along North Capitol Street in sight of the Capitol, young black men gleefully leaned out of passing cars and high-fived each other, some shouting, "The Juice is loose."

Outside public buildings where throngs gathered with people carrying portable TVs and radios, in public school classrooms where students listened over public address systems, in packed office conference rooms where workers watched the TV screen, news of the verdict showed blacks joyfully cheering and whites shocked into silence.

Of the many public-reaction scenes broadcast live that day and later repeated on evening network telecasts, two in particular showed the immensity of the racial divide the verdict exposed.

At Howard University, black law students, watching the verdict from the vantage of the school that more than any other has provided historic African-American leadership in the civil rights movement, spontaneously burst into prolonged cheers when they heard the words "not guilty." At the same moment, other cameras panning the faces of mostly white law students at Columbia University recorded stunned expressions and gasps of disbelief.

* * *

National reaction broke along the same racial fault lines. To an extraordinary degree, whites thought: O.J. literally got away with murder because of a racially biased jury. Blacks believed the verdict just because they thought sufficient evidence existed of a white police frame-up that more than raised reasonable doubts about his guilt, or because a not-guilty verdict symbolized payback by blacks against whites for past acts of injustice, or because of a combination of these and other factors. Out of the torrent of commentary the verdict unleashed, one remarkable example emerged, though it does not seem to have attracted much notice, certainly not the Pulitzer Prize for commentary it deserved.

Writing on deadline immediately after the verdict that day, Michael Wilbon, a *Washington Post* sports columnist who is black, memorably expressed the greater dimensions and significance of the case. Under the title "A Celebrity Goes Free," Wilbon described the uniformly jubilant reaction of blacks across America and commented:

All over urban America you could find these scenes yesterday. It was as if acquitting O.J.

Simpson made up for Rodney King and Emmit Till. For all the black fathers and uncles and grandfathers who'd been jailed unjustly, for every brother who has been framed or railroaded, beaten into a confession or placed at the scene of a crime when he was a million miles away. You know what? It doesn't make up for it. I'm a lot less concerned with O.J. Simpson's guilt or innocence than I am with this unqualified embrace of a man simply because he is a celebrity.

He addressed the greater implications of America's obsession with and glorification of celebrity, placing special emphasis on the effect on black Americans. "All of America has become mesmerized by celebrity in the past 20 years," he wrote.

But nobody buys into celebrity, nobody's suckered inescapably into it like black people, my people, the people who can least afford it. You know what happens every single day in urban court-rooms in this country? Black juries, or predominantly black juries, convict people of crimes with no more drama than necessary. Ordinary, everyday people. But not the chosen ones. You know who the chosen ones are in black America? People who dunk, tackle or sing. Can't touch them. A black delivery man on trial facing the same evidence Simpson faced is a black delivery man headed to prison for life. . . . I worry that the people who feel overjoyed at Simpson's acquittal don't get it. Simpson is free because he played football, because he turned that into a movie career and he's rich. Period. This doesn't symbolize anything or portend great changes in the judicial system to somehow ensure a better shake in the future for African-American citizens. . . . I worry that we, black people, are so desperate

for heroes we'll take the worst candidates on the face of the earth because they ran sweet or had a nice crossover dribble. In the last year we fawned over a drug user (Marion Barry), a convicted rapist (Mike Tyson), and a wife-beater (Simpson), as if those three somehow reflect the best of what we offer to society at-large or our own communities.

Wilbon wanted his readers to know he wasn't "naive about one of the primary emotions involved here: vengeance," adding:

A lot of black people could care less about Simpson and see him truly for what he is. They simply see this as payback, even if the score is still about 1 million to one. They feel the chickens might have come home to roost yesterday for all of our relatives and ancestors who've been beaten and raped and lynched and murdered by whites without any consequence whatsoever. . . . The bigger issue here, of course, is race. It's always race. What we've seen on television and heard on radio before and after the verdict only confirms that blacks and whites have a completely different reality when it comes to some things. You see evidence, I see a plant. I see a racist cop, you see a defense attorney's diversionary tactics. The lines aren't always that clear, but they were in this instance.

With disturbing eloquence, he posed the larger challenge arising from the Simpson case: "Until we as a nation begin to pay attention, those two separate realities will continue to exist. And in one of those worlds, a blind and undying love for anyone famous will continue to drain us of energy that ought to be channeled in another direction."

Study Questions

1. Why did O.J. Simpson become the first black athlete to be employed by corporate sponsors?

2. How did O.J.'s career as a celebrity differ from his childhood?

3. How did O.J.'s celebrity status shield the O.J. his friends knew from the public? Why did his previous actions with Nicole go unnoticed?

4. Why and how did race become the central issue in trials like the O.J. Simpson case?

5. What do trials like Mike Tyson's and O.J. Simpson's say about race relations in the United States?

6. The O.J. Simpson case illustrates the proliferation of the mass media in the 1990s. How has technology affected the way Americans in the 1990s receive and interpret news?

Bibliography

This piece first appeared in Haynes Johnson, *The Best of Times: The Boom and Bust Years of America Before and After Everything Changed* (2002). The debate over O.J. Simpson's guilt continues within the pages of several recent books. Jeffrey Toobin, *The Run of His Life: The People versus O.J. Simpson* (1997) argues that "overwhelming evidence" proves O.J. guilty, while Donald Freed, *Killing Time: The First Full Investigation into the Unsolved Murders of Nicole Brown Simpson and Ronald Goldman* (1996) offers several alternative scenarios for the murders. Janice E. Schuetz and Lin S. Lilley, eds., *The O.J. Simpson Trial: Rhetoric, Media, and the Law* (1999) discusses the connections between media representation and the Simpson trial. For a general introduction to the issue of race in the media, see Gail Dines and Jean Humez, *Gender, Race, and Class in Media: A Text-Reader* (2002). For an overview of the Mike Tyson trial, see Randy Roberts and J. Gregory Garrison, *Heavy Justice: The State of Indiana v. Michael G. Tyson* (1994).

Credits

★ ★ ★